The social history of Canada

MICHAEL BLISS, GENERAL EDITOR

Social planning for Canada

THE RESEARCH COMMITTEE OF THE LEAGUE
FOR SOCIAL RECONSTRUCTION

WITH AN INTRODUCTION BY F.R. SCOTT, LEONARD
MARSH, GRAHAM SPRY, J. KING GORDON,
EUGENE FORSEY, AND J.S. PARKINSON

UNIVERSITY OF TORONTO PRESS
Toronto and Buffalo

©University of Toronto Press 1975

Toronto and Buffalo

Printed in Canada

Library of Congress Cataloging in Publication Data

League for Social Reconstruction. Research Committee.
　Social planning for Canada.

　(The Social History of Canada; 26 ISSN 0085-6207)
　Reprint of the 1935 ed. published by T. Nelson, Toronto;
　with a new introd.
　Includes index.
　1. Socialism in Canada. 2. Canada — Economic conditions —
　1918-　3. Canada — Economic policy.
　I. Title. II. Series.
　HX106.L4 1975　　335'.00971　　72-94917
　ISBN 0-8020-1953-6
　ISBN 0-8020-6178-8 pbk

This book has been published with the help of a grant from the
Canada Council.

The original edition of this work was published in Toronto in 1935 by
Thomas Nelson & Sons Limited

An introduction

BY F.R. SCOTT, LEONARD MARSH,
GRAHAM SPRY, J. KING GORDON, EUGENE FORSEY,
AND J.S. PARKINSON

FORTY YEARS HAVE PASSED since J.S. Woodsworth wrote down the opening words of the foreword to the original edition of *Social Planning for Canada:* 'This volume is most timely. Never before have Canadians been forced to examine the very foundations of our present system.' If the book has a certain timeless quality about it which justifies its republication today it is because when it first appeared it was extremely relevant to the tragedy which hundreds of thousands of Canadians were experiencing during the years of the Great Depression.

The book was written, for the most part, by a group of university teachers who belonged to an organization known as The League for Social Reconstruction. It drew from many a respectable member of the establishment the comment that professors should stay in their classrooms and not interfere in politics or in the world of business. Its radical, critical analysis reflected the widespread discontent in Canadian society. It prescribed a program of action designed to bring about a more just and humane social order.

The Great Depression of the 1930s is passing out of living memory into the history books. Those who did not live through it find it difficult to understand the traumatic experiences of those who did. Before it was over, 25 to 30 per cent of the Canadian workforce suffered unemployment; the number of workers and farmers and their families dependent on 'relief' constituted 20 per cent of the total population. But statistics do not paint the picture of the prairies, where years of appallingly low prices, of drought, of blowing topsoil and plagues of grasshoppers had reduced farmers to desperate circumstances. They do not tell the story of the thousands of young men who 'rode the rods' across Canada in search of work, of the shelters and soup kitchens for the unemployed in the larger cities, of the humiliation of breadwinners who could no longer provide for their families. Nor do they afford a glimpse into the board rooms of the big companies in Montreal and Toronto where directors could still judge the 'state of business' by profit and loss accounts and echo the wistful optimism of Hoover, Ford, and the Rockefeller brothers assuring the public that prosperity was 'just around the corner.'

What was perhaps most shocking was the lack of public policy to cope with the tragic human consequences of the Depression and to reactivate an economic system that was in a state of collapse. Public welfare was not regarded as the responsibility of federal and provincial authorities, and for the most part relief was left to bankrupt municipalities and private organizations. The philosophy of free enterprise, shared alike by industry and government, excluded government from intervening in the nation's business to effect major repairs in the economic system. The cycle would run its course and prosperity would return. Meanwhile, authorities at all levels regarded public protests or demonstrations as acts of subversion. Their leaders were readily described as 'Communists' and against them the full force of the police and such notorious parts of the law as Section 98 of the Criminal Code could be directed. The RCMP were used to break up with violence a peaceful demonstration of the hunger marchers in Regina en route to Ottawa, while in Montreal the police employed savage repressive measures against alleged Communists merely because they were taking part in protest meetings for the unemployed. The first chapters of *Social Planning for Canada* portray the backdrop of tragedy against which the book was written.

While increasing public alarm and compassion were aroused by the devastation and human casualties resulting from the collapse of the economic system, there were those who were deeply concerned about the nature of the system itself. The plight of the jobless was evident; but what about the opportunities for a decent life for those still employed in profitable industries — the men and women in the garment trade in Montreal, the miners in Cape Breton, the women and girls in the textile mills of Quebec, the tobacco workers in southern Ontario? And could not the life of the western farmer be made more secure after the rains came and the dust settled and the wheat grew again? Was it not possible to devise plans that would level out the cyclical oscillations from boom to bust? Was it not even more necessary to reconstruct the economic system itself, if one wished to remove the social injustice and inequity that were so startingly evident?

It was to answer such questions and to meet these challenges that the League for Social Reconstruction was founded just two years after the Wall Street crash marked the beginning of the Depression. Its prime functions were to be those of research and education. It was largely modelled on the Fabian Society, which had been performing such a role in Britain for several decades. The belief that some such organization was needed in Canada originated in the fertile mind of F.H. Underhill, then professor of history at the University of Toronto. His analysis affords a good example of 'the uses of the past' – to quote the phrase of Herbert J. Muller, one of his favourite philosophers of history. It was the Depression which caused him to develop the idea, but it was his knowledge of history which enabled him to adapt it to Canadian experience and give it a specific Canadian purpose.

He suspected that the economic breakdown and consequent mass unemployment and hardship would stimulate new forms of political protest in Canada and, remembering how the Progressive Movement had eventually petered out in the 1920s, leaving only a small 'ginger group' under J.S. Woodsworth in the House of Commons, he concluded that an essential need for any new Canadian party with a radical approach to social problems would be a thorough analysis of the workings of the capitalist system, an analysis on which a lasting program of political action could be based. He wanted the new protest to result in something better than left-wing Liberalism, and to be protected against the enticements of Mackenzie King, which had so effectively dismembered the Progressives a decade before. It was to be the prime purpose of the LSR to provide such an analysis and to define the social goal toward which political action should be directed.

Underhill found colleagues with a like-minded concern in Toronto, among them Harry M. Cassidy of the Department of Social Science, J.F. Parkinson and Irene Biss of the Department of Political Science and Economics, G.M.A. Grube of Trinity, and Eric Havelock of Victoria. In August 1931, Underhill met F.R. Scott, professor of law at McGill, for the first time at a conference of the Williamstown Institute of Politics. They discussed the new idea and Scott agreed to organize a group of friends in Montreal to co-operate in the founding of the proposed society. He first brought together Eugene Forsey of the Department of Economics at McGill, J.K. Mergler, a labour lawyer, and David Lewis, a law student, head of the McGill Labour Club and about to be named Rhodes Scholar; to these four was soon added J. King Gordon, newly appointed professor of Christian ethics at the United Theological College.

The two groups entered into correspondence. A name for the society had first to be chosen. The 'League for Economic Democracy' was considered, suggested by the work of the 'League for

Industrial Democracy' then operating in American colleges. But finally it was decided to adopt as a name 'The League for Social Reconstruction.' More important was the formulation of a set of principles to indicate the philosophy and social objectives of the League. Looking back, it seems strange to some that the word 'socialist' was not at first used. But its omission was due less to fear of its unpopularity than to the fact that not many of the original supporters would have so labelled themselves at the time. There was also the obvious difficulty that the word 'socialist' — as some members contended at the 2nd Annual Convention of the LSR in 1933 — 'has such a variety of meanings as to have no meaning,' a condition from which succeeding years of world-wide usage have done little to free it. Nevertheless, the term began increasingly to be used, generally with the prefix 'democratic' to distinguish LSR beliefs from Marxian socialism on the one hand and 'national socialism' or Nazism on the other.

No single word being useful to describe the LSR program, it was necessary to spell it out at sufficient length to make clear its objectives. The first draft of a declaration of principles and plan of action was prepared in the autumn of 1931 by the Toronto group and sent to Montreal for comments and suggested revision. Discussion by correspondence and personal consultations continued to the end of the year. The Manifesto which emerged out of the inaugural convention of the LSR that was held in Toronto in January 1932 was a collective effort. While it bears the stamp of Underhill's drafting skill, it reveals the inter-disciplinary input from many members of the two founding groups. Because the Manifesto was not reproduced in *Social Planning for Canada,* and because of its obvious relationship to the Regina Manifesto of the Co-operative Commonwealth Federation approved in 1933, it is given here in its entirety:

LSR
THE LEAGUE FOR SOCIAL RECONSTRUCTION
The League for Social Reconstruction is an association of men and women who are working for the establishment in Canada of a social order in which the basic principle regulating production, distribution and service will be the common good rather than private profit.

The present capitalist system has shown itself unjust and inhuman, economically wasteful, and a standing threat to peace and democratic government. Over the whole world it has led to a struggle for raw materials and markets and to a consequent international competition in armaments which were among the main causes of the last great war and which constantly threaten to bring on new wars. In the advanced industrial countries it has led to the concentration of wealth in the hands of a small irresponsible minority of bankers and industrialists whose economic power constantly threatens to nullify our political democracy. The result in Canada is a society in which the interests of farmers and of wage and salaried workers — the great majority of the population — are habitually sacrificed to those of this small minority. Despite our abundant natural resources the mass of the people have not been freed from poverty and insecurity. Unregulated competitive production condemns them to alternate periods of feverish prosperity, in which the main benefits go to speculators and profiteers, and to catastrophic depression, in which the common man's normal state of insecurity and hardship is accentuated.

We are convinced that these evils are inherent in any system in which private profit is the main stimulus to economic effort. We therefore look to the establishment in Canada of a new social order which will substitute a planned and socialized economy for the existing chaotic individualism and which, by achieving an approximate economic equality among all men in place of the present glaring inequalities, will eliminate the domination of one class by another.

As essential first steps towards the realization of this new order we advocate:

1 Public ownership and operation of the public utilities connected with transportation, communications, and electric power, and of such other industries as are already approaching conditions of monopolistic control.
2 Nationalization of Banks and other financial institutions with a view to the regulation of all credit and investment operations.
3 The further development of agricultural co-operative institutions for the production and merchandising of agricultural products.
4 Social legislation to secure to the worker adequate income and leisure, freedom of association, insurance against illness, accident, old age, and unemployment, and an effective voice in the management of his industry.

5 Publicly organized health, hospital, and medical services.
6 A taxation policy emphasising steeply graduated income and inheritance taxes.
7 The creation of a National Planning Commission.
8 The vesting in Canada of the power to amend and interpret the Canadian constitution so as to give the federal government power to control the national economic development.
9 A foreign policy designed to secure internationaal co-operation in regulating trade, industry and finance, and to promote disarmament and world peace.

The League will work for the realization of its ideal by organizing groups to study and report on particular problems, and by issuing to the public in the form of pamphlets, articles, lectures, etc., the most accurate information obtainable about the nation's affairs in order to create an informed public opinion. It will support any political party in so far as its programme furthers the above principles; and will foster co-operation among all groups and individuals who desire in Canada the kind of social order at which the League aims.

After the adoption of the Manifesto, the League for Social Reconstruction was launched with J.S. Woodsworth, MP, as Honorary President and a national executive composed of F.H. Underhill, J.F. Parkinson, and E.A. Havelock from Toronto, and F.R. Scott and J. King Gordon from Montreal. It was decided to have three classes of membership – full, associate, and student: full and associate members paid $2 a year, students $.50. Full members were those who completely subscribed to the Manifesto. Associate members, who wished to express their general sympathy with the League's aims, were given full privileges of attending meetings and participating in discussions, but without voting rights.

Branches of the League were organized first in Toronto and Montreal. By the end of the first year Toronto was able to report a paid-up membership of 150, Montreal 100, and across Canada it was reported that there were seventeen LSR branches with a total membership of 500. At the second annual meeting of the LSR in February 1933 Mrs Angus MacInnis (Vancouver), Alexander Calhoun (Calgary), and Henry Spencer, MP (Battle River, Alberta) were added to the National Executive. It was also decided to establish a National Office in Toronto. Graham Spry, whose activities in the Canadian Radio League had led to the establishment of the CBC, was appointed National Secretary at the magnificent salary of $100 a month, and was assisted by Stuart Legge.

The League for Social Reconstruction took its educational role very seriously. Monthly meetings of branches usually dealt with some aspect of the crisis or with one of the 'essential first steps' in the Manifesto. Public meetings were held for visiting speakers such as Reinhold Niebuhr, Harry F. Ward, Fenner Brockway, Sir Stafford Cripps, and Walter Nash. Pamphleteering was carried out with missionary zeal: at the Montreal Branch meetings, Stanley Allen and Frank Aykroyd extolled the merits of the latest offerings from the Socialist League, the New Fabian Research Bureau, London, and the League for Industrial Democracy, New York. The first publication of the LSR was a bibliography of socialist literature: *What to Read.*

But the branch activities were just a beginning. The mood of the country was such that LSR members were in continual demand to address small — and sometimes not-so-small — meetings in churches, universities, trade unions, political organizations, and even service clubs. Many of these activities had an additional pay-off. The press, which at the editorial level generally regarded the LSR as mildly, or even virulently, subversive, insisted on reporting speeches. And so the word spread. The new CBC, concerned with its role in public education, sponsored series of talks by LSR spokesmen. The *Canadian Forum,* the *Farmers' Sun* (edited by Graham Spry), and the *Montreal Witness* carried articles by LSR members.

The LSR was but one manifestation of protest and intellectual ferment in Canadian society. The Protestant churches, already influenced by the earlier social gospel movement, erupted into a radical attack on the unchristian character of the economic system. In 1934 the Montreal Presbytery of the United Church adopted a report which urged 'that we pledge ourselves to work for a Christian Co-operative Commonwealth in which, in accordance with Christ's teachings, all social and economic arrangements shall be based on the service motive; and that we call upon the government of our country to undertake speedy, equitable and peaceful transition to a co-operative society in which the full Christian life can be realized.' The Toronto Conference of the United Church came out with a frank statement that capitalism was incompatible with Christianity.

The core of this discontent was to be found in an association founded a year after the LSR, known as 'The Fellowship for a

Christian Social Order.' In 1936 it was to put forward its Christian socialist thesis in the book *Towards a Christian Revolution.* Six of the authors – R.B.Y. Scott, Gregory Vlastos, J. King Gordon, Eugene Forsey, Eric Havelock, and J.W.A. Nicholson – were also LSR members.

While the strength of this social protest was to be found in the United Church, some members of other Protestant churches were outspoken. And in Cape Breton, centred in St Francis Xavier University, the Roman Catholic Church, led by such exceptional men as Father James Tompkins, Dr Moses Coady, and A.B. MacDonald, sponsored an adult education movement that resulted in the transformation of the lives of poor farmers and fishermen through producer co-operatives.

Meanwhile, on university campuses from coast to coast, student radicalism flourished. Labour clubs, socialist clubs, student branches of the LSR showed great activity. And the Student Christian Movement, increasingly regarded by boards of governors as a subversive manifestation, encouraged through public meetings, seminars, and conferences a searching examination of the ethical, economic, and political foundations of the contemporary social order.

On 1 August 1932 an event occurred that added a new dimension to the growing demand for social reconstruction in many sectors of Canadian society. Representatives of the Farmer and Labour parties of the four western provinces and the Canadian Brotherhood of Railway Employees – who had previously collaborated in Ottawa under the leadership of J.S. Woodsworth – met in Calgary to found the Co-operative Commonwealth Federation. For the first time there was a political movement – Woodsworth refused to call it a party – the goal of which was the 'establishment in Canada of a Co-operative Commonwealth in which the basic principles regulating production, distribution and exchange, will be the supplying of human needs instead of the making of profits.'

The launching of the CCF had an immediate effect on the LSR. Now there existed a political means of giving effective expression to the objectives set forth in its Manifesto. While it was decided that the LSR, being an educational organization, could not become affiliated with the CCF, its individual members were encouraged to – and did – play an active part. The new CCF clubs which mushroomed into existence, particularly in Ontario, drew heavily on the LSR for members, speakers, and literature. In the spring of 1933,

Underhill was asked by Woodsworth to prepare a statement of principles and program for the new movement. With the LSR Manifesto as model and in consultation with some of his LSR colleagues, Underhill prepared a draft which emerged from the first annual convention of the CCF in 1933 as the Regina Manifesto.

In the LSR there was an ongoing debate: was the League to be a broad-based membership organization devoted to enlarging the range of its educational activities, or a smaller, more select group of researchers, rather like the New Fabian Research Bureau in Britain? The issue was never resolved: some of its members were primarily researchers, some were educators, some were active politicians. Some were all three. The first Handbook of the LSR spelled out no less than ten functions its members should perform. Many of them related to group organizations.

By 1934, four pamphlets had been produced by the LSR under its Research Committee: *Dividends and the Depression* by Eugene Forsey; *Combines and the Consumer* by the Research Committee collectively; *Social Reconstruction and the BNA Act* by F.R. Scott; and *The Church and the Social Order* by Ernest Thomas. More were in preparation.

But the research work of LSR was by no means confined to the production of LSR pamphlets. H.M. Cassidy, in association with a few graduate students, was working on a comprehensive study: *Unemployment and Relief in Ontario, 1929-1932.* Cassidy and Scott carried out an enquiry into sweat-shop conditions in the garment shops in Montreal, *Labour Conditions in the Men's Clothing Industry.* At McGill, Leonard Marsh's researches focussed on unemployment, welfare services, medical care facilities, and housing.

Eugene Forsey, J. King Gordon, and J.A. Coote constituted a Social and Economic Research Committee for the Montreal Presbytery of the United Church. From 1932 to 1934 they published an *Information Bulletin,* one issue of which probed into the wage situation in Quebec's textile industry. As in the case of the Cassidy-Scott investigation of the garment industry, the findings anticipated the later work of H.H. Stevens' Royal Commission on Price Spreads.

Very early in the history of the League for Social Reconstruction, it was decided that what was needed was a comprehensive book that would bring together in a single volume important bits of individual research and spell out in some detail a plan of social and political action based on the LSR Manifesto. Cassidy, as head of the LSR Research Committee, mapped out the original proposal in consultation with Graham Spry and the Toronto group. By the end of 1932 the outline was complete and ready for discussion at the second annual conference.

The 'Note of Explanation' accompanying the outline contained some interesting suggestions as to procedure: 'The Members of the Committee recognize frankly that the general approach of the book may not be acceptable to a number of very competent people who would, nevertheless, be willing to assist in the preparation of particular sections. It is hoped, therefore, that such people, even if they cannot subscribe fully to the frankly socialist approach of the book, will be willing to render assistance and criticism on particular topics about which they are informed. The general feeling of the Committee is one of very keen desire to get every bit of assistance and advice possible in completing the ambitious project which they have initiated.'

Later, the 'Note' gives some practical advice: 'It is suggested to contributors that a real effort should be made to document suggestions and use cross-references so far as possible. For instance, the recent Papal Encyclical on Labour may be quoted at times in justification of some measures that are proposed: or reference may be made to war-time controls that were employed in Great Britain and Canada; or experiments in public ownership or precedents in taxation of incomes and inheritances, or instances of cooperative effort may be cited in justification of schemes that are outlined. The general idea is that we should attempt to show the Canadian public that we are not merely propounding theoretical proposals and that considerable precedent of a reputable nature can be found for many of our suggestions.' It was noted in conclusion that 'for the present' Mr Graham Spry and Mr H.M. Cassidy, Convenor of the LSR Research Committee, were to act as editors of the enterprise.

The sanguine optimism of the editors and their blissful innocence as to the ways of authors and publishers is revealed in the hope expressed that a good portion of the book would be in manuscript form by the latter part of April 1933 and ready for publication in June or July of the same year. 'It is particularly important that the work be done by this time so that the book may be available for the consideration of leaders of the CCF when the new political party meets in convention at Regina in mid-summer.'

To speed the work an important weekend meeting was held in April 1933 at the Burlington, Ontario, home of Mrs W.B. Somerset, a devoted LSR supporter. The conference brought together most of the prospective authors of the book, a number of CCF Members of Parliament from Ottawa, and other LSR members and friends – about forty in all. Even the sceptical Harold Innis attended briefly and gave his advice though not his adherence. It was a solid, slugging session going over semi-prepared drafts of chapters and re-examining structure and points of policy. The general tempo of the meeting is best described in a thank-you letter written by Underhill to our hostess: 'Having arrived home with my head still buzzing with four solid days of argument, I write to say how much indebted we all are to your kindness in entertaining us. We couldn't have met in more pleasant surroundings and, if the book comes off, it will have been mainly due to the days spent together in your house. I hope you will pardon me for my continuous neglect of my hostess and all of us for the ferocious way in which we devoted ourselves to business and only paid any attention to you when milk and eggs were on the table.' The signatures on the letter were: Frank H. Underhill, Elmore Philpott, Harry and Bea Cassidy, Howe Martyn, Edgar and Lorene McInnis, J.F. Parkinson, Wynne Plumptre, E.A. Havelock, Graham Spry, Irene Biss, J. King Gordon, D.C. MacGregor, F.R. Scott, G.C. Coote, Henry A. Holman, J.S. Woodsworth, E.J. Garland, Eugene Forsey, and Kenneth W. Taylor.

The work proceeded slowly. Academic duties, speaking engagements, increasing demands for direct political participation in the CCF, left few uninterrupted stretches of time for sustained writing. The task of final editing was horrendous, with the burden falling heavily on Cassidy and other members of the Research Committee, including Leonard Marsh, Stuart Legge, and Betty Ratz.

By February 1934, Cassidy could report progress on *Reconstruction – A Plan for Canada:* 'more than three-quarters of the manuscripts had already been received ... other manuscripts were in preparation, but so great was the editorial work that it was impossible at this time to give any definitive date of publication.' A year later in February 1935, at the Fourth Annual Meeting of the LSR, things looked brighter: 'Some ninety per cent of the manuscripts have been received, but several important gaps remain, and there is a large amount of editing and collating to be completed. It is therefore impossible to give any approximate date of publication.' It was about this time that the National Office of the LSR was moved to Montreal where Leonard Marsh and Eugene Forsey subjected the accumulated manuscripts to a thorough-going revision, filled any remaining gaps, and brought the materials up to date at points where new information had become available. So the book was completed. (In 1938 the Research Committee of the LSR produced a shortened and simpler version of *Social Planning* called *Democracy Needs Socialism,* intended to make the basic ideas of the book more readily available to the general public.)

Social Planning for Canada appeared in the autumn of 1935. It was variously received by reviewers. Advocating, as it did, a democratic form of socialism of the British and Scandinavian type, it was subject to criticism from the Left and Right. Enthusiastic praise came from Dr Salem Bland, who called it 'the most notable book that Canada has yet produced.' A reviewer in the *Toronto Star* felt it would do for Canada what the *Wealth of Nations* had done for England. Sir Stafford Cripps reviewed it favourably in the British *New Statesman.* On the other hand, theoretical Marxists like Wallis Lefeaux, an LSR member in Vancouver, wrote a scathing attack on the whole approach of the book, and of course Tim Buck, leader of the Communist party, could find no good in it. The severest criticism by a professional economist came from Professor H.A. Innis, for whom it was 'a pretentious political document' which demonstrated conclusively that social scientists had no business mixing themselves up in partisan politics.

The business community in Montreal shared this view. In 1936 a substantial pamphlet made its appearance in the city, which purported to answer the book, chapter by chapter, point by point. It bore the ponderous title: 'A Criticism of the Book / written by / (then came the authors' names) / and published by / the League for Social Reconstruction / under the title / Social Planning for Canada.' It was anonymous, and bore no name of publisher or date. It accused the authors of following 'the principles which Marx laid down with marked success' (sic) and stated that: 'As propaganda of hatred and envy the book undoubtedly deserves to be placed with such classics as the Report of the Price Spreads Commission and the

1935 speeches of the Hon. H.H. Stevens.' The writer proved to be Mr P.C. Armstrong, the 'economist' of the CPR, and a man well known to LSR members and others as delighting in attacking 'reds' and 'pink professors' at every opportunity. This pamphlet was distributed to leading businessmen in Canada – from the head office of the CPR! The resulting publicity caused so many extra copies of *Social Planning* to be sold that a second printing had to be ordered.

Social Planning for Canada is divided into two parts. In the first, the then-existing economic system is surveyed and analyzed, and the effects of its operations are exposed in all their unfairness and inefficiency. It is here that the reader will find the justification for the statement in the LSR Manifesto that: 'The present Capitalist system has shown itself unjust and inhuman, economically wasteful, and a standing threat to peace and democratic government.' The injustices disclosed in these pages lead on naturally to the principles and policies of social reconstruction which are designed to build a new and better social order. These take up the greater part of the book as Part II entitled: 'What Socialist Planning Really Means.'

There follow fifteen chapters describing the application of planning principles to various sectors of Canadian society, and suggesting how the instruments of planning can be fitted into the existing political system.

A re-reading of these chapters today indicates that the general approach was more pragmatic – not to say reformist – and less socialist, than we might have admitted at the time. On economic questions, for example, the conclusions were not always doctrinaire. They can be better described as a mixture of Fabian socialism, Keynesianism (a new thing in 1933-5), and the Welfare State (still unchristened as such). In short, while the book emphasized the need for public ownership of those large industries and financial institutions which occupy the commanding heights of the economy, it gave equal emphasis to such ideas as the stimulation of the economy by new fiscal and monetary measures, and to the ways in which greater equality could be brought about by tax reforms and an enlarged social assistance program.

This social planning required two approaches. On the one hand, to be effective it was necessary to bring into public ownership certain major capitalist institutions. On the other hand, it was also believed that the remaining private sector could be made to work humanely and effectively by the introduction of specific reforms. In the LSR philosophy, nationalization was an instrument but not a panacea.

What is difficult for us to grasp today is that the social planning which was prescribed by the LSR in the thirties was a major heresy for those in government and in the business community. Government had its role and business had its role and the two roles had to be kept separate. Government's 'interference' in business was restricted to the enactment and enforcement of safety and health standards in factories and mines, subsistence minimum wages, and regulations for the adjudication of industrial disputes – at best a guardian and umpire role. But for the government to intervene in the self-regulating economic system for the purpose of setting social goals that might inhibit the full play of the profit motive was regarded as a cardinal sin. To suggest further that government should plan the nation's economic life in the interests of the good of the majority of its people was to challenge the foundations of the faith.

All this has changed. While the free enterprise system continues to thrive at new levels of monopolies, conglomerates, and multinational corporations, the laissez-faire faith and philosophy of government is outmoded. Many of the prescriptions of change presented in the book have only historic interest for the simple reason that they have been put into effect. For example, we now have a central bank, wholly owned by the state; we now possess a fairly comprehensive system of provincially funded medical and hospital services; we now have a widely developed system of social insurance and social welfare to alleviate the burdens imposed on people by unemployment, old age, and the like.

To suggest that the book had any direct influence on bringing about these developments would be to exaggerate its importance, but there can be no question of the influence it exerted on the policies and platforms of the CCF and, indirectly, on those of the other parties. Beyond that, there can be little doubt that the events of the 1939-45 war, plus the increasing acceptance of the economic views of J.M. Keynes, did more than anything else to demonstrate to the Canadian people the merits of government planning, the better distribution of incomes, deficit financing, and so on. By means of initiatives and controls exerted by the federal government, the country was able to mobilize its resources so as to make an immense military effort while maintaining, and probably improving, the standard of living of the civilian population in the process. The mass unemployment of the 1930s was transformed into the full employment of the 1940s. This transformation involved the imposition of many forms of control and much higher levels of taxation of corporate enterprise and wealthy individuals than had been thought possible in the pre-war days. The lesson was not lost on the Canadian voter in the post-war years. It was no longer considered almost revolutionary – as it was in the thirties – to insist that governments have the obligation, and the ability, to see to it that the basic economic and social needs of their people are met.

Were *Social Planning* to be rewritten today, the problems, the priorities, and the remedies would obviously be stated differently, though the democratic socialist objectives would doubtless remain. The passage of forty years has wrought great changes in western society, resolving some of the issues discussed in *Social Planning* and creating many new ones. The evolution of new technology, new institutions – even new social classes – has created new situations and social tensions that seem to be more complex and to call for more complex analysis than that which seemed right in the thirties. For example, the owners of industry have themselves been largely divorced from or subordinated to the management. Such developments as the rise of multinational corporations, the growth of a semi-affluent society, the shift in emphasis from the production of goods to the production of services, have created new problems for governments aiming at political control of economic development.

A new *Social Planning* would have to grapple with the difficulties created by the growth of bureaucracies in government as well as in corporate business and trade unions, and their resistance to change and innovation, characteristics which seem to be common to capitalist and socialist countries alike. How right the book was, however, in pointing out the need for state regulation or control of the sources of energy: 'Shut off the sources of supply – hydro, coal, gas, oil – and you paralyze industry. Charge exorbitant prices and you cripple it. Demand a varied rate from different trades, you stimulate those you favour and force contraction upon the rest. The policy of the Association of Coal Merchants, the oil trust, or the dominant electric power producers has just these effects – effects of such moment to the whole community that it is essential that they should be directly in the control of a public authority' (pp 257-8).

Another *Social Planning* would also have to recognize that provincial governments and large metropolitan centres have – and should have – greater responsibilities than we assigned to them forty years ago in the fields of social and economic planning. Forty years ago many provinces and municipalities were close to financial bankruptcy and not too well supplied with skilled professional administrators and advisers. As a result, while the federal government of the time was not over-rich in management talent, it alone seemed capable of taking measures to mitigate the worst consequences of the Depression. One's approach today would be much less 'centralist.' In the same way, a new *Social Planning* would have to deal with the need of the ordinary citizen to participate more directly than he is able to do at present in the making of the decisions which impinge on his job, his neighbourhood, his housing, and his leisure time.

Today's reader will also be struck – as we were – by the complete omission of any mention of many of the problems which appear to dominate contemporary political thinking. The list would include, for example, the danger of environmental destruction, nuclear war, over-population, and the world shortage of energy. These omissions are understandable. On the other hand, the reader will observe that the question of the danger of foreign ownership was already being considered (cf. pp 53-9). The industries which were then largely foreign-owned or controlled were listed (in many cases British control was then more common than it is today). However, *foreign* control was not regarded in itself as necessarily evil: 'That foreigners control this or that particular industry will trouble none but those earnest patriots who, in defiance of all evidence, persist in believing that the Canadian capitalist is a different kind of being from the foreign, that one is a philanthropist, the other a robber and a cheat.'

For the authors of the book 'the most serious disadvantage of the large foreign investment in Canada is that even when we socialize industry it will be difficult to rid outselves of the annual tribute to the foreign investor. The domestic owner is easily disposed of: he can be compensated, and he is also more easily subject to taxation.

But this does not apply to the foreigner, who can retaliate by embargoes on our essential imports, by seizing our export credits to pay the indignant bondholder (which would be *pro tanto* an automatic embargo on our imports), or even by armed intervention.' However, on sober second thoughts, the authors felt that this danger may be exaggerated: 'A government making a forthright endeavour to eliminate the wastes of capitalism has no reason to fear its credit will be ruined.'

It will be noticed that problems concerning the place of Quebec in Confederation are not adequately reflected in the book. Indeed, little is said about Quebec per se largely because the *révolution tranquille* was still twenty-five years in the future. However, *Social Planning for Canada* did throw its spotlight on the industrial exploitation of the workers in the province – in the textile towns and in the sweat shops of Montreal. It described the weakness of the trade union movement in the province with half of its members in the Federation of Catholic Workers, completely controlled by the Roman Catholic hierarchy. 'Anti-militant, anti-class-conscious and anti-socialist, the Federation is dedicated to the proposition that "employees and employers must live agreeing with one another, helping and loving one another".'

In the section dealing with the need for constitutional change, it reaffirmed the minority rights of French-speaking Canadians in matters of race, language, religion, and education. Then, looking at Canada as a whole and taking into account the use of the nefarious Section 98, giving the provincial governments and police the power to suppress civil rights and to convert dissent and protest into subversion, the book states: 'An entrenched Bill of Rights in the BNA Act would do much to check the present drive against civil liberties – a drive which in Canada is promoted by men who pay lip service to liberty at the very moment they are legislating it out of existence.' In these as in other respects, the book was far ahead of its time.

Finally, were the authors writing the book today they would not write the same chapter on foreign policy. As it stands, it reflects the strong isolationism of Canada in the thirties, still fighting to eradicate the formal symbols of imperial dominance and seeking to stay clear of the cynical power politics of Europe, where the major states were debasing the League of Nations to serve their own purposes. It must be remembered that the book was written after the Great Powers had made a mockery of the collective security principles of the League of Nations Covenant, in the face of Japan's invasion of China and of Italy's threatened invasion of Ethiopia. The chapter also reflects the socialist view which was common enough in Britain and elsewhere in the thirties that war was an inevitable outcome of capitalist imperialism, and it ends on the note that only in a world of socialist states could a true system of collective security operate satisfactorily. Needless to say, the book was written before the Spanish Civil War, before Hitler's invasion of the Rhineland, and three years before Munich.

Even so, at the conclusion of the chapter there is a prophetic note: 'While the immediate urgency is to concentrate on keeping out of the wars that threaten, we must work for a world which is genuinely based on the collective organization of security. But security is not attainable without an equitable distribution of the opportunities for material well-being among all peoples of the world. The way to bring this about is to begin to build up in Geneva the institutions of world economic planning.'

These sentences could be taken as the beginning of a new book. The crisis which we faced in the 1930s seemed to us to be a crisis in Canada which could be dealt with by Canadians in Canada. We see now, with much more clarity, what we were beginning to see as we finished our work: that there is no guarantee of security for Canada except in a secure international order, there is no guarantee of social justice for Canadians unless, through the effective use of international institutions, there is justice for all peoples.

This new edition of the book reprints the original text in its entirety without change. To have attempted a revision bringing all the materials up to date would have been an impossible task. As it stands, we think it has its place in the history of Canadian political and economic thought. Indeed, it may even be claimed that as a contemporary description of the Canadian society of that time it has no rivals. Its social philosophy survives, however much the method of its application in Canadian society today would have to be modified. The belief in a planned and egalitarian society, attainable by democratic political methods, which the LSR steadfastly held before itself, embodies fundamental concepts of man and society

which are just as defensible today as they were in the 1930s. With
this in mind, we should like to think that *Social Planning for Canada*
stands as a contribution to the continuing worldwide struggle for
human emancipation from poverty, ignorance, insecurity, and
oppression.

NOTE

A full history of the League has at last been written, but in a doctor-
al thesis (University of Toronto) by Professor Michiel Horn, which
has not yet been published and so is virtually inaccessible to the
ordinary reader. The authors of this new introduction to the re-issue
of *Social Planning for Canada,* themselves all founding members of
the LSR and signers of SPC, wish to express their gratitude to Professor Horn for the fairness of his assessment, and for the great help
which his research has provided for their memory of things now long
past.

Social planning for Canada

THE RESEARCH COMMITTEE OF THE LEAGUE
FOR SOCIAL RECONSTRUCTION

FOREWORD

This volume is most timely. Never before have Canadians been forced to examine the very foundations of our present system. Canada is fortunate indeed to have among its "intellectuals" so many who are grappling seriously and fearlessly with our practical problems.

This L.S.R. book might be called, in commercial phrase, a "Pooled Product". To its preparation many specialists have contributed but throughout, there has been careful consultation and co-ordination. Facts gleaned from many sources, not readily accessible to the public, have been assembled within the compass of one volume so as to give a comprehensive survey of conditions in Canada.

The result is a rude jolt to the easy optimism which hitherto has characterized our youthful nation in this land of imagined unlimited opportunities. Further it is a telling indictment of the failures and contradictions of Capitalism. As such this book is surely a challenge alike to pioneer ideals and current business practices.

As we face the wide range of facts we cannot but realize the need, not of this or that particular "reform" but of a whole series of co-ordinated measures each forming part of a carefully worked-out plan. Socialism begins to emerge not as a dream—pleasant of bad—but as an urgent necessity.

Socialist literature has been scarce in Canada and for most people, unconvincing. The idealized pictures of Morris and Bellamy and Wells, while stimulating our imaginations carried with them a sense of unreality. The writings of the "Scientific Socialists" though keenly analytical were too abstract and left us cold. The devastating attacks on the evils of Capitalism by Upton Sinclair and Stuart Chase did not offer us any feasible way out. Information with regard to Soviet Russia was too heavily charged with propaganda and emotionalism to be of much service. The practical achievements of socialist efforts within a limited field in Great Britain, Vienna and the Scandinavian countries had been accomplished under conditions which differ widely from those existing in Canada. Even the excellent studies of the Fabian Society and the Socialist League do not altogether explain the Canadian situation or point out the next steps in the solution of our problems.

Now comes this first comprehensive treatise on Canadian economy from a socialist point of view. It is welcome to those of us who, through a new political organization, are seeking to establish a Co-operative Commonwealth in Canada.

While many subjects dealt with in this book have not been discussed either in the Conventions of the C.C.F. or by its National Council, and while confessedly there is room for considerable difference of opinion with regard to some of the proposals set forth, yet on the whole the book is undoubtedly in line with the Regina Manifesto. It should be of great service in the formulation of the future policies of the C.C.F.

We trust that every C.C.F. candidate and every Club will secure a copy. Every C.C.F. member ought to be able to give a reason for the faith that is in him.

J. S. Woodsworth

PREFACE

This book is the result of group discussion and co-operative writing on the part of a number of individuals over the past three years. Shortly after the League for Social Reconstruction was formed in 1931 some of its members felt that, before any constructive steps could be taken in the building of a new social order out of our present Canadian capitalism, there would have to be a careful analysis of our available resources and present inadequacies, a frank shedding of all current political beliefs not based on these realities, and a complete readiness to propose whatever changes in our political and economic framework seem necessary for the attainment of greater equality and social justice among the mass of our population.

The writers of this book desire to see these changes accomplished by democratic and orderly means; but they believe also that if democracy is to be *real* it implies two necessities—complete freedom to criticise existing institutions, provided that factual grounds are given for this criticism; and a much more widespread public knowledge than we have at present of the faults and deficiencies of our economic system, and of the constructive proposals to deal with them which spring from socialist ideals. Politically and economically, socialism simply represents the endeavour to put governments *by the people* and *for the people* into modern terms; but the socialist case will be ineffective so long as it continues to be dismissed as "radical agitation" or "Utopian idealism" on the one hand, and confused with communism on the other. If socialism means a definite system or body of proposals, however, it also crystallizes a protest— against gross inequality of income and economic power, against poverty and thwarted and repressed human lives, against waste and inefficiency, against the inhumanity and social stupidity of exploitation and war. Above all else, this protest has the right to be heard.

Our book is an attempt to set out this protest and these proposals in specifically Canadian terms. It is not a series of doctrinaire generalizations, but an attempt to analyze and prescribe by a group who have tried to visualize a real and richer "Canada for Canadians". We do not pretend, of course, that a single volume can contain all the thinking required in this process. Parts of this book deal all too summarily with deep problems; sheer limits of space have compelled us to omit such vital subjects as, for instance, education and the position of women in the new society. But we are hopeful that the material gathered here will be of assistance not only to those who are already acquainted with socialist thought, but to all those with sincere interest in the future of Canada who want to examine its problems realistically.

The book is a compilation from many contributions, so much so that no chapter has been the product of one hand alone. Inevitably, therefore, it lacks the uniformity of style which a single writer would have given it. Its production would not have been possible without assistance from many individuals besides those whose names appear at the end of this preface and who accept responsibility for the book as a whole. More than twenty men and women have offered memoranda, draft chapters, criticism and revision in the course of its preparation. Some of these, for personal reasons, do not wish their names to appear here but we take this opportunity of offering our thanks to them. Among those who have given valuable help and whom we include in our expression of thanks are: Miss Irene M. Biss, Prof. A. Brady, Mr. Humphrey Carver, Prof. G. M. A. Grube, Mr. Stuart Legge, Miss Betty Ratz, Prof. K. W. Taylor, and Prof. C. W. Topping. Of course no persons except the signers of this preface are to be held responsible for any opinions expressed in the book. We desire also to express our thanks to those members of the L.S.R. who have assisted in the work of proof-reading.

EUGENE FORSEY   J. F. PARKINSON

J. KING GORDON   F. R. SCOTT

LEONARD MARSH   GRAHAM SPRY

FRANK H. UNDERHILL

CONTENTS

ix

Contents

L.S.R.
LEAGUE FOR SOCIAL RECONSTRUCTION

Honorary President: Mr. J. S. Woodsworth, M.P., Ottawa.
President: Professor F. R. Scott, Montreal.
Vice-President: Professor G. M. A. Grube, Toronto.
General Secretary: Mr. Graham Spry, Toronto.

The League for Social Reconstruction was founded in 1932. It is an association of men and women who are convinced that the present economic order is unjust, cruel, wasteful and inefficient; who want to work for the establishment in Canada of a social order in which production, distribution and service will be organized for the common good rather than for private profit.

The L.S.R. is a national body, with headquarters in Toronto. It consists of a National Executive which exercises general control over the League's activities and is responsible for publications, and of local branches in different parts of the country. Such local branches may be organized wherever ten persons are prepared to accept the obligations of full membership. In addition, there are a number of individual members where no branch at present exists. Associate membership is open to all who are in general sympathy with the aims of the League but are not prepared to subscribe to the full platform as put down in the Manifesto: namely, the general principles of public ownership and control which are elaborated in this book.

The main aims of the L.S.R. are education and research: it strives to investigate our social and economic problems and to develop a body of well informed radical opinion in Canada by means of its own publications, by keeping its members informed of other books and pamphlets, by helping them to establish contacts with others working for the same goal, by lectures, broadcasts, meetings, discussions, study groups and other branch activities.

The L.S.R. is not affiliated with any political party, and has rejected the idea of such affiliation because it does not wish to make immediate political expediency its primary aim at any time. Many of its members, however, are engaged in active political work. Since the formation of the Co-operative Commonwealth Federation such members are usually found within its ranks, as the only party that aims at translating the objects of the League into political realities. Relations between the C.C.F. and the L.S.R. have therefore always been cordial and mutually helpful.

For further information apply to: L.S.R., 449 Walmer Road, Toronto.

PART I—THE PRESENT SYSTEM:
SURVEY AND ANALYSIS.

CHAPTER I.

THE END OF A CENTURY OF PROGRESS.

"Land of Limitless Opportunity".

THE Canadian people stand hesitant at the end of a century of progress. Until a few years ago our course seemed clearly marked. Now the path is uncertain. Canada believed in progress, her faith grounded firmly in the initiative and enterprise of her sons and in a guiding destiny which had marked her out for signal favour. Sturdy pioneers hewed their way into the primeval forest, founding homes for themselves and their families. Northward they pushed back the frontiers to mines and lumber camps. Westward until the great plains were reached. Westward to the foothills and wide ranges. Westward, tunnelling the mountains, to new mines, new forests, new fertile valleys. And from the labours of the pioneers sprang a new civilization, a new democracy free from the evils of the ageing empires of Europe.

The social philosophy of any generation rises out of the social and economic experience of the past generation. The faith and labours of Canadian pioneers in every field of industrial and commercial expansion responded to the demand of the 19th and early 20th centuries for new products and new markets. The achievements of the pioneers of yesterday determine the faith of to-day's generation. Mysteriously the onward march of progress has been interrupted, but the faith in progress remains.

Now, it is a characteristic of a faith in progress that it is uncritical both as to the nature of progress and the cause of progress. Economic progress may be confused with social and ethical progress; both may be confused with cultural progress. It is the purpose of this initial chapter to account for the contemporary popular social outlook of those who, one suspects, are the majority of Canadians and to analyze briefly the social and cultural aspects of our Canadian life in relation to the general economic development.

Our faith in progress is based upon the economic development of a new country and upon the technical and scientific advances of the last century and a half in which all industrialized nations have shared. We need only contemplate the life of the

3

majority of Canadians seventy-five years ago—without railways, without automobiles, without telephones or telegraphs, without electric light or electric power, without the thousand and one conveniences of the modern home, without aeroplanes, without radios, without Greta Garbo and without Gracie Allen—to appreciate how primitive was life before the rise of our modern era. Progress is essentially measured in terms of technical advances. A belief in progress is justified by the access to the means of a comfortable and secure life by a large group in society who formerly found life hazardous and uncongenial. The advance of medicine and surgery, the mastery of disease by science, the increased knowledge of the basis of public health and sanitation are characteristics of the modern age which mark it off from the primitive sordidness of the pre-scientific period. The advances in science have created a new attitude to the whole range of experience. For the first time man has begun to understand his world, and on the basis of that understanding he has become conscious of a sense of mastery. Age-old superstitions have been destroyed, and the human spirit set free. It is little wonder that in the past century, amid the manifold proofs of man's control over his environment, the evils which remained were thought of simply as a further challenge to man's growing intelligence but in no sense a challenge to the very basis of his social philosophy.

Nor was such a faith in progress merely a *zeitgeist* in which individuals shared vicariously. It was written deep into the thinking of each participant in the economic process, scientist, engineer, worker, employer alike. It was a faith in individual achievement. For those in the van of progress were the men of the new era who had risen from comparative obscurity to inconceivable positions of importance and affluence. Progress for the individual meant success. And success meant not only technical and scientific achievement but access to the new means of a fuller life in terms of the products of the new industries. It meant independence from the slave-like position of the property-less wage earner. It meant the power to command the services of others. So it was that in the new countries like Canada and the United States the belief became prevalent that their people had escaped from the economic and social abuses of the older lands, from slum and from factory town and from the sad and bitter history of class war. For in the new lands every man was free to succeed, every man was free to prosper.

It is natural that with such a prevailing optimism there was not to be found an accompanying clarity in social analysis. The appearance of the slum, the emergence of conditions in factory towns and mines similar to those in the older countries, the signs of deepening class lines were noted, but they roused little concern. These could be regarded merely as examples of a lag in social intelligence. They were problems for the educator, they were problems for the scientist, for the town planner, for the "social engineer". More enlightenment and they would miraculously disappear. Said Mr. Hoover, as he accepted nomination on August 11, 1928, "We in America are nearer to the final triumph over poverty than ever before in the history of any land. The poor-house is vanishing from among us. We have not yet reached the goal; but, given a chance to go forward with the policies of the last eight years, we shall soon with the help of God be in sight of the day when poverty shall be banished from this nation". From the disillusioned perspective of six years of catastrophic depression such a statement to-day appears fantastic, but at the heyday of the new era it represented but a modest estimate of the power of twentieth century man over controllable features of his environment. It is the persistence of the faith in progress to-day—when progress itself has been unaccountably interrupted—which enables us to comprehend how blindly the 19th and 20th centuries disregarded the obvious social consequences of an aggressively advancing industrialism, and at the same time renders us singularly unfit to cope intelligently with the critical stages of social disintegration.

It is fitting then to examine a little more closely what progress meant to the majority of people in a progressing industrial and commercial society. In the days of prosperity, success represented the achievement of economic security, possession of the means of participation in the material advantages of an advanced industrial society, freedom from the threat of poverty and economic subservience. Success expressed itself in terms of "standard of living", which was indicated by the annual income the individual received.

Standards of Living.

In the year 1929 Canada had reached the peak of prosperity. Never was industrial production greater—although agriculture had already entered upon its period of decline—never were profits higher, never was optimism and faith in Canada's future at a higher level. In the year 1929, the average wage in Canada in manufacturing was $1,045[1]. That this figure does not represent a typical figure for all industries is revealed by the fact that in the highly protected textile industry, employing 105,594 workers, the officially recorded average wage was $818[2]; in coal mining the average was $869.76[3]; in tobacco $644.11[4]. The agricultural labourer's wage, including an allowance for board is estimated at $627 on the average, while female wages for agricultural labour stood at $465[5].

The income statistics from the 1931 census covering the twelve months period prior to June, 1931, give a more detailed picture of the standard of living which most Canadians enjoyed when times were prosperous. (It may be noted in passing that during the first year of the depression—1930—wage reductions were not as drastic as in the subsequent years, nor did short time enter so importantly into a yearly computation). Of the individuals reporting under the census more than 96% filed returns on income, so that we may regard the census statistics as fairly comprehensive. From the census figures we ascertain that the yearly earnings of nearly two million Canadian male wage earners averaged $927, while the average yearly earnings of the five hundred and twenty-eight thousand female workers reporting was $560. A further classification under the census returns reveals the fact that more than 60% of male workers and more than 82% of female workers earned less than $1,000 in the census year. Nor can such figures be accounted for by beginners' wages and the earnings of young people. The classification by age groups shows that there are comparatively few workers under 18 years of age[6].

In the year 1930, before the depression began to wreak its most disastrous consequences upon Canadian life, 60% of the male workers and 82% of the female workers earned less than $1,000! What does that mean in terms of standard of living? According to the budget published by the Dominion Department of Labour a family needs between $800 and $1,000 to provide food and housing alone. If the minimum standard of decency is to be maintained this budget must be increased by

[1]*Wages and Hours of Labour in Canada.* Report 16, Department of Labour; *Report on Manufactures*, 1929. Dominion Bureau of Statistics.
[2]Census of Industry. *The Textile Industries of Canada*, 1929-30, D.B.S., p. 13.
[3]*Coal Statistics for Canada*, 1929. Dominion Bureau of Statistics.
[4]Census of Industry. *Tobacco Manufacturing*, 1929. D.B.S.
[5]*Wages and Hours of Labour in Canada.* Report 16, Department of Labour. App.B., p. 68.
[6]*Earnings Among Wage Earners for Canada and the Proviinces*, 1931. Dominion Bureau of Statistics.

50%, that is, to a figure between $1,200 and $1,500[7]. Allowing
for the fact that in a number of cases more than one member
of the family is contributing to the family budget, we are
driven to the conclusion that a majority of Canadian families
were, in the year 1930, and from all indications in the year 1929,
living below the bare standard of decent livelihood[8].

There are two fundamental fallacies involved in the blind
faith in progress which has characterized the social thinking of
this continent, the blind faith that affirms that the world moves
steadily onward and upward forever. The first fallacy is that
scientific and technical progress can be equated with social and
cultural progress. To a consideration of this fallacy we shall
return. The second major fallacy is that since technical advance
provides improved material conditions of living, therefore the
standard of material well-being of a society can be measured in
terms of technical advance.

Now this second fallacy can be exploded very simply and very
effectively by reference to the standard of living enjoyed by the
majority of Canadians as indicated by the statistical information above. An individual enjoys the material benefits of our
modern age precisely to the extent to which he can afford to buy
these benefits. If his income falls below that calculated to provide a decent living then even though he walk through streets
where shop windows proclaim to the world the refinements and
luxuries of the twentieth century, he will be living in the strin-
gency and insecurity of a pre-scientific age. Science may proclaim the conquest of disease, but his body enfeebled by the lack
of adequate diet or fatigued by over-work will be unprotected
against the ravages of illness. Moreover, unless he is prepared
to be placed in the category of a charity patient, he will have no
pecuniary reserves with which to pay for medical treatment for
himself and his family. Finally, after a lifetime of toil, desperately seeking an economic security which is denied him, he
will arrive at old age to find that society has no further use for
his labours and that he must face the prospect of becoming a

[7]Department of Labour Bulletins.

[8]A budget of minimum requirements for a family of five produced after a careful
survey by the Montreal Council of Social Agencies in 1926 placed the amount of the
necessary income at $1,102. Correcting this figure for variation in cost of living index
we have for the year 1930 the amount $1,059. An examination of the items included in
such a budget indicates a bare subsistence level, in no sense a level of comfort. The
best short publication on standards of living in Canada is "The Distribution of Personal
Income in Canada", by J. S. Woodsworth (1935). The figures used in it are mainly
census figures, supplemented by data from the Bureau of Statistics and the Department of
Labour.

charge upon the community or upon his ill-provided children[9].

Where Canadian Workers Live.

The housing problem which is beginning to cause concern to the Canadian public is probably fraught with graver social consequences than almost any other which Canada has to face at the present time. It illustrates not only the backwardness of our social intelligence but also the inseparable connection between the income of our people and the amenities of life which are open to them.

It is only recently that Canada would think of housing as constituting a problem. In the continental countries the slum and the ghetto were the natural outcome of the dark ages. The cities developed around and away from the sordid congestion and plague-ridden filth of the medieval town. The sudden development of industrialism demanded the rapid throwing up of hovels and the digging of warrens in which to house the industrial poor. Religious bigotry, social intolerance and economic incapacity combined to condemn the majority of the working population to surroundings which must inevitably result in lives dwarfed and distorted beyond hope of reclamation. Canada, a new country, was presumably free from this evil heritage. New cities would rise which, having learnt from the sad history of the cities of the old world, would provide an environment conducive to the healthy and happy life of their citizens. New knowledge of town planning, of sanitation, of the place of light and space in the construction of homes would be called upon to assist the builders of the new cities.

It comes as something of a shock to discover that in our new cities we have produced the same housing conditions which characterize the older European cities. The visitor to Canada, like the visitor to the old lands, may discover splendour in her cities, the giant department stores, the sky-scraping office buildings, the magnificent residences of Westmount, of Rosedale, of Shaughnessy Heights, the solid if aesthetically monstrous comfort of the homes of the middle class. But if he cares to investi-

---

[9]The *Labour Gazette* for February, 1935 (p. 142) gives the percentage of pensioners to the population over 70 years of age in those provinces which have old age pensions in force as at Dec. 31, 1934:

Alberta	41.80%	$17.69	Ontario	31.78%	$18.42
B. C.	36.43%	$19.29	P. E. I.	26.34%	$ 9.91
Manitoba	48.52%	$18.61	Saskatchewan	48.71%	$16.30
Nova Scotia	45.29%	$14.40			

The second columns of the table give the average monthly pension. The maximum pension is $20 per month. The amount of private income per month is equal to the difference between $20 and the actual amount paid in pension.

gate beyond the beaten thoroughfares of respectability he will find the same appalling slum conditions as have made notorious the cities of Europe. The new immigrant to Canada, with eyes dazzled by the glow of the western horizon, has too often awakened to discover that he has moved his abode from an old slum to a new slum of equal squalor.

What Canadians Think About Their Homes.

For nearly a quarter of a century, the attention of Canadians has been called to the state of the homes of our people.

1911 "There are few conditions found in the slums of Europe or in the greater American cities that have not been revealed in the city of Toronto, the difference being only of degree, and the conditions of lesser degree to-day will, if not corrected, become those of greater degree to-morrow."[10]

1916 "We are to-day reproducing some of the worst things that have characterized the old lands. We are getting slums in our cities. But we are doing worse than that. Apparently we are failing utterly to get to the root of the problem which makes slums".[11]

1919 "... this conference, recognizing that much industrial unrest, economic loss, and economic suffering has resulted from land speculation, poor and insufficient housing and high rents, heartily commends the action of the Dominion and Provincial Governments in their united effort to improve housing conditions and provide facilities for the proper and satisfactory housing of the people. . . ."[12]

1920 "The existing condition of the worker involves not only the absence of sufficient housing accommodation, but the inadequacy of those that are in existence. Poor sanitary conditions and insufficient rooms are the chief cause of complaint. The high price of building land and of building material have made it impossible for the worker to provide himself with a home and some means should be adopted, with as little delay as possible, to remedy the defect".[13]

10Dr. C. J. D. Hastings, in a Report of the Health Department for the City of Toronto.
11Sir Clifford Sifton, before the Civic Improvement League of Ottawa.
12The National Industrial Conference.
13Report of a Royal Commission set up as a result of the conference to report on social and industrial conditions in Canada.

1920 "With few exceptions, absolutely wretched". (Referring to the houses of the Cape Breton miners).[14]

1926 "Many families occupy houses that are much too small for their needs. The houses generally have no kitchen nor cellar, and in certain districts, in default of water works, water is either delivered by the operators in carts or has to be carried from a distance. Where water is piped into the houses, there is an almost total absence of bath rooms or water closets, due, we are informed, to a lack of sewers". (Referring to the homes of Cape Breton miners.)[15]

1934 "Our survey of Toronto housing conditions reveals that there are thousands of families living in houses which are insanitary, verminous and grossly overcrowded. The Committee confidently estimates that the number of dwellings which for these and other reasons constitute a definite menace to health and the decency of the occupants, is certainly not less than 2,000 and may be more than 3,000. In addition, there are probably half as many houses again which, while not in the same sense menacing, nevertheless lack the elementary amenities of life".[16]

1935 "The elements of the population of Montreal which are now compelled to find their abode in the slums or near-slum areas are not large in proportion to the whole population of Montreal, nor are the slums of Montreal as bad as those of many North American cities. However, they constitute a heavy burden, and the fact that they are widely spread to-day and rapidly extending, calls for serious effort towards what has been called 'the new day of housing' . . . The depression has brought the Montreal housing problem to an acute stage and has emphasized the unsoundness of our existing working class housing schemes".[17]

Now the significant truth emerges that, in spite of the continued concern of public-spirited Canadians over the housing conditions of our people, the problem has been continually growing more acute. The assumption that public enlightenment will

[14]Royal Commission investigating conditions in Nova Scotia mines.
[15]Royal Commission investigating conditions in Nova Scotia mines.
[16]Lieutenant-Governor's Committee on Housing Conditions in Toronto.
[17]*A Report on Housing and Slum Clearance for Montreal*, by a Joint Committee of the Montreal Board of Trade and the City Improvement League, March, 1935.

of itself eliminate the evils of congested and insanitary living conditions has not been justified.   One suspects that the slum is a more deeply rooted institution in our Canadian civilization than we care to acknowledge.   It is the latest report issued in Montreal which points out most clearly why bad housing conditions exist.   The report classifies 180,700 wage-earning households in Montreal on the basis of family income, giving the following table:[18]

Income	Percentage	Number of Households
$1,000—$1,500	32.1	58,000
$ 850—$1,000	19.4	35,100
$ 650—$ 850	29.0	52,100
Below $650	19.5	35,200
Total	100.0	180,700

The report estimates that no household belonging to either of the lowest income groupings can pay a rent exceeding $12.50 a month.   Furthermore, the report states: "To the number of low-wage earners striving to pay rents disproportionate to their incomes, have now been added 40,000 families on relief".[19]   Low rent areas are slum or potential slum areas since costs of maintenance, or ordinary requirements for reasonable living conditions cannot be provided out of the income the landlord receives.

Therefore, when we bring together, as we should bring together, our income analyses and our reports on housing conditions, we are driven to the arresting conclusion that gradually our towns and cities are being converted into slums, with protected areas of insular respectability.   Such a condition has dire consequences in terms of public health and social morality.   Well-housed citizens are healthy citizens; slum dwellers are subject to the ravages of disease and their expectancy of life is short. The infant mortality figures of the city of Montreal tell their own story.   In the period 1923-1932 the average number of infant deaths was 127 for 1,000 live births.   The figure of 98 for the year 1933 shows the progress which can be made through public health education and control, but it also shows the limitations to such control when the basic problems to contend with are poverty and slum.   In New Zealand, the infant mortality rate has been

18Cf. tables on pp. 9, 10, 13, of *A Report on Housing and Slum Clearance for Montreal.*
19*Ibid.,* p. 23.

reduced to 31! Tuberculosis is to a great extent a disease of poverty, undernourishment, poor housing conditions. A survey of Montreal by wards reveals a striking variation in tuberculosis mortality in relation to low rent and high rent areas, and the same may be said of Toronto.[20]   Even more serious are the wider social and moral effects of housing congestion combined with low income and insecurity.   Laurence Veiller writes: "When one's outlook on life is on some filthy alley, piled high with the cast-off refuse of humanity, noisome with odours, and when as far as the eye can reach, there is nothing but sordid stretches of drab, unpainted, dilapidated, uninteresting buildings, one vast waste space, it is not strange that one's mental outlook on life should be very much the same.   How one can expect either a healthy body or a healthy mind in people who have that kind of environment, day in and day out, is beyond understanding."[21]   Take the spot map of juvenile delinquency in any of our great cities; where housing is most congested, where incomes are lowest, where all the amenities of modern life are lacking, there you will find the fruitful training ground for our future criminals.[22]   The report of the Lieutenant-Governor's Committee on Housing Conditions in Toronto concludes with these statements: "In conclusion, it is abundantly clear that bad housing is opposed to the true welfare of the community.   It generates disease and increases mortality.   It leads the young into delinquency and the old into crime.   It throws increased financial burdens upon the taxpayer. And by the intensity of its attack upon such conditions may the social conscience of the community be judged".[23]

The Depression.

We have attempted to give some picture of the conditions of life for the majority of Canadian citizens whose standard of living and of security is determined by the income granted them under the present organization of our society.   We have attempted to describe "normal" conditions, unaggravated by economic depression.   We have been describing, for the most part, the "days of prosperity".

[20]"Tuberculosis, the disease of insanitation and under-nutrition, strikes hardest among the slum dwellers", p. 22, *Montreal Report on Housing*.   See also Ward Map p. 19.   One of the best summaries of the relation between mortality figures and housing is to be found in the Lieutenant-Governor's *Report on Housing Conditions in Toronto,*, pp. 41-4.

[21]Veiller, *Public Health and Hygiene*, p. 304.

[22]Cf.   Herman R. Ross, *Juvenile Delinquency in Montreal* (McGill University thesis, 1932).

[23]The Lieutenant-Governor's *Report* gives an excellent survey of the relationship between housing conditions and health and social problems.

It is now our duty to set forth just what the last five years of deepening economic chaos, which we still optimistically term "The Depression", has meant to the various groups in Canadian society.

Unemployment and Relief.

First, let us consider the number of those who are unemployed. A most valuable document concerning the direct relief situation in towns and cities throughout the Dominion has been prepared by the Department of Social Research of McGill University under the supervision of the Director, Leonard C. Marsh.[24] According to statistics included in this report, the number of wholly unemployed wage earners, *i.e.*, excluding those only temporarily "laid off", is about 400,000. If we were to include seasonally and temporarily unemployed we would probably have to add another 200,000, bringing the total up to 600,000 persons.[25] This figure represents about 23% of the wage earning population who are now without the means of securing gainful employment.

Coming now to a consideration of those who are on direct relief, *i.e.*, including the families of the unemployed, we are faced with the staggering figure of 1,054,821 as in February, 1935. The equivalent figure for February, 1934, was 1,154,822. To this figure we may legitimately add the numbers of the single men in provincial-federal relief camps, those who are on relief work on a wage basis, those who have been looked after by farm placements, those who are included in relief settlement schemes, and those on relief in the dried-out areas. The addition of these numbers, which do not include dependents, brings the total up to approximately 1,342,000 for February, 1935. The comparable figure for February, 1934, is 1,490,000. A further analysis by cities throughout Canada indicated that in the 90 largest towns of Canada, 16.7% of the population are on relief. In the city of Montreal, the figures for those on relief total 191,778, or 19.5%, while in Toronto the figures are 117,529, or 18.5%. The highest percentage is to be found in the little town of St. Michel on Montreal Island, where 47.2% of the population are on direct relief![26]

[24]*Comparative Statement of the Relief Situation in Canadian Municipalities*, prepared by the Department of Social Research, McGill University for the Organization Committee, Dominion Conference of Mayors, Hotel Mount Royal, Montreal, 25-26 March, 1935.

[25]These figures are based on Dominion Bureau of Statistics estimates. Professor Marsh's estimate for total number of unemployed in 1933 was 700,000, or 28 per cent. of wage earning population.

[26]*Comparative Statement of Relief Situation* as quoted above.

Now this new situation created by the collapse of our economic machinery presents a twofold problem. In the first place, it intensifies the insecurity and suffering of the lowest income group in the community. In the second place, it constitutes the major financial problem which all our governments, Federal, Provincial and Municipal, have to face. Let us touch upon the magnitude of the second problem. Since 1930, the Dominion Government alone has spent or appropriated for unemployment relief $175,794,000.[27] That this is only a fraction of the total relief bill in Canada may be seen from the fact that for the year ending February, 1935, the municipal relief expenditure of 90 Canadian cities was more than $19,000,000.[28] City after city throughout the Dominion is to-day faced with bankruptcy on account of the increased burden of relief costs. Mounting indebtedness, arrears in taxes, the resort to every conceivable means of raising new revenues or escaping from old obligations, is the picture of municipal finance from coast to coast.

But the financial aspect of the depression stated in terms of relief costs is as nothing when compared with its social aspect stated in terms of human life. One lesson the depression seems to have taught us is how difficult it is to starve people to death. The relief rates, varying a few cents or even a few dollars per month from city to city throughout Canada, provide a standard of living which a few years ago would have been considered a starvation level. To-day a family of five on relief in Montreal will receive $39.48 per month or $474.00 a year. They are, however, allowed to earn, if any casual work is available, up to $12 a month in addition. This would bring the yearly maximum up to $618. When we consider that the Department of Labour's standard of decency for the present year is somewhere between $900 and $1,025 we catch a glimpse of the lives of the families of the unemployed.

If the homes of our low-paid wage earners are a disgrace to a civilized community, we may imagine the nature of the homes of those on relief. The minimum is allowed in the way of rent and the majority of landlords refuse to take in tenants who are on relief. The Lieutenant-Governor's Commission on Housing in Toronto reports that "while many landlords refuse to accept tenants known to be on relief, the quality of accommodation offered by those who will accept the relief vouchers is in the

27*Ibid.*, p. 4.
28*Ibid.*, p. 17.

most cases the very meanest. The poorest families are therefore compelled to accept the meanest accommodation with little
chance of anything being done to improve it".[29] Unless that destination has already been arrived at, unemployment means a
march to the slums.

The immediate result or expression of economic collapse is
the creation of a large group of citizens to whom work is denied
and who become a permanent charge upon the community, to
be supported at the level of bare subsistence. Housed in the most
miserable of our dwellings, socially ostracized by the employed
section of the society, cowed into passive submission by the
official upholders of law and order, the older members knowing
they will not work again though at the peak of their mental and
physical powers, the younger members not knowing what it is
to work, the unemployed mutely challenge our society. Year by
year our juvenile crime figures mount; year by year our public
schools and high schools send out their thousands to waste away
their trained faculties in a hopeless search for work, year by
year grow the numbers of Canada's "wild children", beating
their way on our freights from coast to coast. How we are building a new land! "Canada, a young man's country!" For the depression is doing to the bodies and souls of one generation of
Canadians what the war did to the bodies and souls of another.
It will be the mocking irony of our economic system if it presents
as the ultimate, moral, "Christian", solution for unemployment—
another war.

But increased burdens of relief costs, the demoralization and
pauperization of our workless citizens, are but the beginnings of
the evils arising from the disintegration of our capitalist system.
All other social evils which were there in "the days of prosperity" are aggravated a thousandfold.

Distribution of Income.

If we are to understand the essential nature of the social
evils which we face in Canada to-day, it is necessary for us to
have some picture of the nature of our economy. Why is it
that in a period of alleged prosperity the majority of our citizens
were living on the subsistence level? Why is it that we have
allowed slums to grow up in our new cities? Why, even if for
the moment we do not question the inevitability of depressions,
must we treat our unemployed like paupers, slaves or criminals?

29Lieutenant-Governor's *Report*, p. 52.

Do we lack the technique and intelligence to produce sufficient for all? We know that such is not the case, but that paradoxically the creation of plenty has brought forth calamitous scarcity. Is it that there is not enough "wealth" to go round, and that we must share together our common sufferings? The easiest way to answer this last suggestion is to consult the available information on the distribution of Canada's national income.

The use of the adjective "easy" is perhaps not a happy one when we speak of gaining information about the distribution of Canadian income. There seems to be a concern on the part of our federal authorities to protect the humble and God-fearing members of our society against the vulgar display of the wealth of its privileged group. By reference, however, to the returns of the 1931 census, the annual income tax returns, and the compilations made in Mr. J. S. Woodsworth's pamphlet mentioned above,[30] we can gain some idea of how the wealth and national income of Canada is divided.

If we exclude from our calculations the group of farm labourers, for which there are no statistics available, we have approximately 2,713,000 wage earners and other income receivers. The following table indicates the distribution of income between various groups.

Size of Income	Number of Persons (Male and Female)	Per Cent. of Total	Income (Millions of Dollars)	Per Cent. of Total Income
Under $1,000.......	1,526,000	56.2	790.0	25.4
$1,000—$1,500......	643,000	23.7	805.0	25.9
$1,500—$3,000......	448,000	16.5	896.0	28.8
$3,000—$10,000.....	85,000	3.2	401.0	12.9
$10,000 and over....	11,000	0.4	219.0	7.0
Totals.........	2,713,000	100.0	3,111.0	100.0

From this table we can make the following striking discoveries.

(a)   56.2% of Canadian income receivers have incomes of less than $1,000 a year, and their total incomes constitute only one-fourth of the total.

(b)   23.7% of the workers receive between $1,000 and $1,500 and the aggregate of this group amounts to a little more than one quarter of the total.

30*The Distribution of Personal Income in Canada*, by J. S. Woodsworth, M.P., 1935.

(c)   The remaining 20% of the income receivers secure almost one-half of the total national income.

(d)   The group with the highest income, *i.e.*, those getting more than $10,000, receive an aggregate income equal to that of more than 400,000 of the lowest paid group.   (Actually if we were to divide the "$1,000 and under" group still further, we would find that it would take considerably more than 400,000 to make up the total of the wealthiest 20%).

In reply to a question from the floor of the House on May 9th, 1933, the Minister of National Revenue made a statement concerning the distribution of income of those paying income tax.   It will be noted on consulting the table presented that in the peak year of prosperity only 143,601 Canadians possessed sufficiently large incomes to make them liable to income tax, but that their incomes amounted to more than $815,000,000.

INCOMES OF INCOME TAX PAYERS, 1929

Size of Income	Number of Taxpayers	Per Cent. of Taxpayers	Amount of Income	Per Cent. of Income
$50,000 and over......	601	0.4	$ 52,128,425.30	6.4
$30,000—$50,000......	1,045	0.7	40,161,303.59	4.9
$25,000—$30,000......	784	0.5	20,413,111.67	2.5
$20,000—$25,000......	1,314	0.9	22,970,945.98	3.6
$15,000—$20,000......	2,878	2.0	51,844,021.21	6.4
$10,000—$15,000......	6,825	4.8	91,252,856.22	11.2
Under $10,000........	130,154	90.7	530,943,684.00	65.0
Totals...........	143,601	100.0	815,714,684.00	100.0

The large group of income tax payers with less than $10,000 a year is striking, as is the volume of income controlled by the 10% in the higher brackets.   By way of interesting comparison, it is worth noting that in 1929 the 1,646 individuals at the top of the Canadian economic ladder received as much as, or rather $6,000,000 more than, the entire combined income of the 105,504 workers in the protected textile industry![31]

The latest returns from the Department of National Revenue, announced April 19, 1935, show that 307 Canadians paid income tax on incomes of more than $50,000 a year.   Their tax amounted to $8,785,854, or an average of $28,618 apiece.   This amount con-

[31]*Textile Industries of Canada*, 1929-30.   D.B.S., p. 12.

stituted 30% of the total income tax for 1934. The report showed that the largest group of taxpayers were in the $2,000 and under class. They numbered 93,316 and contributed $989,083.[32] It is probably not necessary to remind ourselves that our concern here is not with the taxation policy of our government, but rather with the nature of the economy which permits the great majority of our working people to be without sufficient income to provide the bare necessities of life and at the same time rewards a comparatively small group in the highest economic level with an incredibly large share of the total national income.

Why Maldistribution of Income?

It must be apparent that while we are gradually gaining a picture of certain broad social aspects of our economic order which carry with them their own ethical implications, we are still dealing with symptoms and have not yet touched the root of social disease. It must be quite clear, however, that the symptoms all point in a single direction, i.e., towards the motivations and control of the economy. The Royal Commission on Price Spreads in its recently issued report makes the following statement in its introductory section:

"Owing to the variety of the subjects investigated and the interests concerned—producer, manufacturer, distributor, wage-earner, and consumer—it was not easy to compile a report which would be of reasonable length and possess both unity and clarity. At first sight, indeed, it appeared that the separate and distinct problems which emerged in the evidence called for separate treatment and almost separate reports. *On closer study, however, it became clear that many of the grievances complained of, and the problems disclosed, were manifestations of one fundamental and far-reaching social change, the concentration of economic power. This idea, therefore, runs through the whole of our report and gives it a certain unity which it might not otherwise possess.*"[33]

It is not a little significant that a report which deals with a social picture, in places as black as that which characterized England in the worst period of the Industrial Revolution, should begin with a long section on "Concentration and the Corporate System of Business". The opening sentences in that key chapter read as follows:

"The evidence before us has shown conclusively, and at

---

[32]Canadian Press dispatch, April 10, 1935.

[33]*Report of the Royal Commission on Price Spreads*, 1935, p. 3. (Italics ours). This is referred to hereafter as *Price Spreads Report.*

times graphically, the part played by the corporate form of business in Canada's economic life.

"It has shown that a few great corporations are prominent in the industries that have been investigated; also that this power, all the more dangerous because it is impersonal, can be wielded in such a way that competition within the industry is blocked, the welfare of the producer disregarded, and the interests of the investor ignored.

"As the hearings into the various forms of economic activity were carried on, it has been difficult not to be impressed by the fact that the corporate form of business, not only gives freedom from legal liability, but also facilitates the evasion of moral responsibility for inequitable and uneconomic practices. Therefore it is essential that any investigation into business practices should concern itself with the growth and significance to the national economy of a form of business activity which has harboured behind its imposing facade so much that needs cleansing."[34]

We are not interested here in a study of the corporate nature of Canadian industrial, financial, and commercial life; or in examining the degree to which ownership and control are concentrated in a few hands. Such matters are dealt with at length in Chapters III and IV. Nor, admitting the paramount importance of concentration, are we concerned here with a discussion of how it may be controlled. Certainly we are not interested in the insipid and insufficient conclusions arrived at by the Royal Commission, conclusions which seem to have little relationship to the evidence presented, or even to the premises upon which the Report is allegedly based. These questions will be examined in the chapter dealing with the possibilities of capitalist planning (Ch. VII.). What we are concerned with is the suggestion that there is an inseparable relation between concentration of power in our economic system and the exploitation of the least protected groups in the community. Even in times of perfect competition, in the economy described by Adam Smith and the classical economists, the weaker groups were exploited by the strong, the motive of profit operating to force down the wages of labour to the starvation level. The organization of workers acted in some slight measure to check this exploitation, and social legislation placed a restraining hand upon predatory entrepreneurs. But now, as the Report of the Royal Commission quite properly indicates, "concentration in production and distribution . . . has made the actual competitive

34*Ibid.*, p. 13.

scene progressively less like the simple competition of the laissez-faire economists".[35]   Before the power of the modern Frankenstein, the monster of big business, the individual, lesser groups within the community, the very state itself feels impotent and paralyzed. The story of the Canadian economy is the story of the predatory activities of the increasingly consolidated and compact "big business" group.

In times of prosperity, the operations of concentrated Canadian business were obscured by the inspired belief in progress. Big business prospered, and the newspapers of big business, the politicians of big business, the economists of big business, the court chaplains of big business, preached progress and prosperity. With the capitalist crisis, however, the illusion of progress was more difficult to maintain. In the first place, big business could not afford to subsidize social legislation and philanthropic ventures as in the days of prosperity, and in the second place big business, partly from necessity, and partly on account of the opportunities afforded, embarked upon a new career of candid and untrammelled exploitation. The Report suggests the situation in the mildest possible language when it states "An economic collapse may, like the rain, fall on both the just and the unjust, yet our evidence proves that there are some groups in our economic system who are able to escape the full force of the crash. Often the way of escape is at the expense of other groups less powerful and therefore less fortunate".[36]   Or again, "Faced with losses as the revenue from sales decreases and the expenses of the competitive struggle increase, powerful corporations naturally seek to shift the burden of losses on to others".[37]

Wages and Dividends.

The movements of dividends and wages during the depression tell their own story. We shall have occasion to study the record of a few of our greater industries, basing our conclusions largely upon the evidence which came out of the Price Spreads investigation. Just now let us look at the general movement of wages and dividends in those industries for which statistics are available. The following tables give some indication of the extent to which equality of sacrifice was practised by the "co-operating" groups in the Canadian industrial process.

35*Ibid.*, p. 5.
36*Ibid.*, p. 11.
37*Ibid.*, p. 8.

TABLE I

INDUSTRIES FOR WHICH DIVIDENDS, AND SALARIES AND WAGES (COMBINED) ARE AVAILABLE

	1929	1930	1931	1932
Dividends..........	$161,574,350	$163,753,330	$131,577,968	$ 84,633,984
Salaries and wages...	772,936,000	718,546,000	604,658,000	474,582,000
Index of dividends...	100	101.3	81.4	52.4
Index of wages and salaries.......	100	92.9	78.2	61.4

TABLE II

INDUSTRIES FOR WHICH DIVIDENDS, SALARIES, WAGES (SEPARATELY) ARE AVAILABLE

	1929	1930	1931	1932
Dividends..........	$123,554,295	$120,790,676	$ 97,983,957	$ 75,547,874
Salaries............	95,343,000	97,636,000	93,067,000	78,621,000
Wages.............	355,776,000	321,031,000	254,135,000	191,237,000
Index of dividends...	100	97.8	79.3	61.2
Index of salaries.....	100	102.4	97.6	82.5
Index of wages......	100	90.2	71.4	53.7

TABLE III

SHELTERED INDUSTRIES (INCLUDING GOLD MINING)

	1929	1930	1931	1932
Dividends..........	$ 74,222,243	$ 72,802,859	$ 74,703,939	$ 63,861,978
Salaries............	70,913,000	73,876,000	72,976,000	61,366,000
Wages.............	244,528,000	226,801,000	187,958,000	142,584,000
Index of dividends...	100	98.1	100.7	86.0
Index of salaries.....	100	104.2	102.9	86.6
Index of wages......	100	92.8	76.9	58.3

From the above tables certain conclusions are obvious. In the first Table, it is evident that the initial impact of the depression is felt by the wage earning and salaried group; that the dividend drawing group is protected, either by reserves or by the power to unload the burden of cost cutting upon the section of the industrial community in the least favourable position to protect itself. In the second place, by consulting Table II we learn that the salaried group suffers far less during a period of depression than does the wage earning group. The reason for this is obvious enough. In the third place, we gather from Table III that in the industries most protected against the cut-throat competitive practices which characterize a time of economic dislocation, and therefore best equipped to conserve their earning power, the greatest exploitation is practised against the wage earner, as the highest rate of dividends and salaries is maintained.

A further indication of the groups who bear the chief brunt of the depression is to be found in the average wages in manufacturing for the five years 1929-1933.

1929	$1,045
1930	1,001
1931	957
1932	852
1933	785[38]

Thus costs are cut not only by a reduction of staff and a shortening of hours, but by an actual reduction of wages.

What the Price Spreads Commission Unearthed: Textiles.

Let us now turn to certain concrete examples from the evidence of the Parliamentary Committee and Royal Commission. Examples of the exploitation of workers can be selected at random and *ad nauseam* from almost any of the industries or commercial establishments examined. Here is the protected textile industry. The average wage paid in all branches of the industry in 1933 was $674. Primary cottons, woollens, artificial silk and thread and cordage were the least affected by the depression, the decline in their annual earnings ranging only from 4% to 8%.[39] Nevertheless, average annual wages in cotton manufacturing decreased from $692 in 1930 to $660 in 1933. The table of average hours (Table 9, p. 2991, Royal Commission Evidence) shows that this appallingly low average cannot be accounted for by short time. Nor can the excuse be made that the percentage of female workers is high, since in cotton the proportion of males to females is almost the highest of any branch of the textile industry.

The following quotations from the Royal Commission's Report throw further light on the "golden rule" in operation in the textile industry.[40]

[38]*Report of Manufactures*, 1933. D.B.S.
[39]*Price Spreads Report*, p. 117.
[40]The inspired pamphlet issued by the Cotton Institute of Canada under the title "The Primary Cotton Textile Industry in Canada", contains these remarkable sentences in its conclusion: "The primary function of any industry is to render a service to the consumers of its products. In rendering that service, however, it must have regard to the interests of the workers engaged in the production of these products, and it must also provide a just and equitable return upon the capital of those who have

"In an industry with all the advantages that this one possesses (the silk industry) there should be no room for even a small factory such as M. E. Binz Co. Ltd., Montmagny, Que., where in February, 1934, the average wage rate for all male workers was 10 cents per hour; where 93% of all male workers in 1934 were paid less than the minimum rate for female workers; where on a 55-hour basis, the average full-time weekly earnings in 1934 for male and female employees was $5.72". (p. 118)

"Almost equally bad are the conditions in the Associated Textiles of Canada, Ltd., Louiseville, Que. . . increasingly profitable since it began operations in 1929; net profits amounting in 1933 to 11% on sales or 24% on invested capital. Nevertheless, average weekly rates in this company, based on a 55-hour week, in the two weeks ending February 25, 1934, were, male employees $13.43, female employees, $9.73. Ninety male and 130 female were paid at rates below $8 per week". (p. 118)

"In the hosiery and knit goods section, labour conditions, in view of the general economic situation, are probably not much worse than could be expected. . . . a more striking variation between mills. The record was as usual worse in Quebec than in Ontario. . . . In the case of the lowest paying mill, The Butterfly Hosiery Company, Ltd., annual earnings dropped from $668 in 1932 to $349 in 1933. *By a permission of the Minimum Wage Board of Quebec*, dated August 11, 1933, this company was enabled to classify most of its employees as inexperienced and pay them, with two exceptions, princely sums of $3 and $4 per week." (P. 119; italics ours.)

Clothing Trade.

In the clothing industry conditions are even more appalling. The evidence before the Parliamentary Committee based upon the investigation conducted by Prof. F. R. Scott and Prof. H. M. Cassidy would belong fittingly to the darkest ages of industrial-

---

invested in its securities. If in its operation an industry does not reasonably conform to these three requirements, it is not built upon a solid foundation".

Mr. A. O. Dawson, President of Canadian Cottons and President of the Canadian Chamber of Commerce is reported to have made the following statement at the annual meeting of the latter body in Winnipeg in September, 1934: "Relationships between employers and employees have vastly improved in recent years, and I believe it is not an extreme statement to say that the golden rule is destined to become the general rule in industry".

"The future course of the organization (i.e., The Canadian Chamber of Commerce) should be guided by the principle that progress is measured solely by the advancement in well-being socially and economically of the workers—those who work either for wages or salary or who are dependent upon their own individual effort."

"Industry was still opposed to national or international unions which asked the closed shop with its 'coercion, restraint and intimidation'. If there were any fighting to be done, then employer and employee should fight together as comrades, and not against each other as enemies". (*Montreal Gazette*, Sept. 12, 1934).

ism. In the Report of the Royal Commission, we find these summary contentions:

"(1) There are extreme variations in wage rates; ranging from less than 5 cents per hour in a Quebec home-work contract shop to 65 cents in a Toronto union factory. . .

(2) There are therefore extreme and unfair differences in cost, "unfair" because they do not result from differences in efficiency of management. For example, the making of boys' pants cost 25 cents per dozen in a Quebec country home-work-shop, $1.50 in a union shop. . . .

(3) Wage rates and earnings are often exceedingly low. Quebec country home-workers probably cannot average 50 cents per day. Male piece-workers in one large Montreal factory averaged 16 cents per hour, less than the minimum of 18 cents for inexperienced females. One man of ten years' experience worked 70 hours per week in a Montreal contract shop, to earn $7 at 10 cents per hour. . . .

It is bad enough to pay such wages as these. It is adding insult to injury to hand them to the workers, as is often done, in pay envelopes, which, thoughtfully provided by the banks, bear such encouraging advice as:

> Think of tomorrow,
> Divide your pay in two,
> Take what you need to live,
> Put the balance in safety. . . .

(4) Hours of employment are often oppressively long. Thirteen hours a day, 60 hours a week, are not uncommon in rush periods. . . .

(5) Frank exploitation of labour's weakness has been common. Evidence has followed evidence with monotonous regularity before the Commission to show that, in many cases, the welfare of the worker is almost the last consideration that enters into the minds of the employers in this industry.

(6) There are frequent and continuous violations of the laws about employment conditions, hours and wages. . . .

(7) Even where the physical working conditions were reasonably satisfactory, evidence was given to show that female operatives were sometimes forced to work at such high pressure for continuous hours that the result on health and morale was deplorable.

"With a full recognition of the problems which this industry has to meet . . . we cannot, in frankness, refrain from stating that the labour and wage conditions in this branch of Canada's industrial activity are such as to merit the most emphatic condemnation. They should not be tolerated in any state that claims to call itself civilized. . . "[41]

41*Price Spreads Report*, pp. 110, 111.

Chain and Department Stores.

The investigation into labour and wage conditions in the department stores and chain stores has received such full discussion in the press as not to require much comment. The statement of the Report on the wage policy of this new mercantile octopus is worth noting. "The labour policies of many chain store companies appear to have been characterized by close control in the matter of wage costs, but a lack of sympathetic direction in the application of these wage policies to the conditions of the workers involved. . .

"We have found that the position of the worker in the departmen and chain store fields is a particularly defenceless one".[42]

If one encounters the consolidation of the huge mercantile establishment or distributive agency in close juxtaposition with a group of defenceless and unorganized employees, one has the perfect conditions for exploitation. Average male weekly wages for eight of the largest food chains for which statistics were available were $11.72, $9.31, $9.53, $16.48, $9.78, $14.38 for Ontario, and $7.60, $7.65, $8.54, $14.55, $7.73 for Quebec. Average female wages for the same firms were $12.57, $10.64, $10.85, $15.38, $12.50, $11.92 for Ontario, and $9.33, $9.01, $9.59, $12.04, $9.40 for Quebec.[43]

In merchandizing establishments the employees are without the protection of minimum wage legislation (whatever that may mean!) In the Metropolitan Stores in Montreal, out of 1,234 female clerks, 937 are on part time and receive an average wage of 4.30 per week.[44] In the United 5c-$1.00 Stores the average wage for 200 employees in 1933 was $6.58.[45] In the Dominion Stores, 255 delivery boys averaged $3.99 per week, and in The Great Atlantic and Pacific Tea Company, 154 delivery boys averaged $3.61 per week.[46] One variety chain operating almost entirely in Quebec, paid more than 10 per cent of its female employees under $5, and 90 per cent under $10 per week.[47] The president of this company, in replying to comment from the Commission on such conditions, said: "The girls were content".

So we might continue the dismal tale through the other branches of industry investigated by the Commission. Or we might take the reports of earlier parliamentary committees and

42*Ibid.*, p. 123.
43*Ibid.*, p. 121.
44*Ibid.*, p 122; and Evidence before Commission.
45Evidence before Commission, p. 753.
46*Price Spreads Report*, p. 418.
47*Ibid.*, p. 122.

investigations under the Combines Act, concerning the distribution of the necessities of life, bread, and milk and coal, not to mention gasoline. But the tale repeats itself monotonously, and we are apt to forget that what is being recounted are the annals of this generation of Canadians in the grip of a predatory economic system which in its period of decline is yet able to wreak its most dire devastation.[48]

"The Smoke Gets in Your Eyes."

But a survey of the social consequences of Canadian monopolistic capitalism would not be complete without a brief tribute to the achievements of the tobacco moguls. In the field of tobacco, two companies stand alone, and actually one holds the effectual monopoly of the trade. Imperial Tobacco controls 70% of the business; W. C. Macdonald, Incorporated, the private preserve of Mr. Walter Stewart, controls about 12%. The Commission reports: "The most striking fact revealed by our evidence on the tobacco industry is the combination of low wages and high profits." (p. 115).

From the year 1929 to 1933 inclusive, bonuses to six executives of the Imperial Tobacco Co. amounted to $1,861,923. Dividends paid totalled $26,874,300. The undivided profits, represented by the surplus account, stand at the moment at $11,886,-573. During the period the company's net profits amounted to $36,225,253, after every form of taxation had been taken care of, and an amazingly liberal allowance made for depreciation of every conceivable kind. Concerning the profits end of the second company, W. C. MacDonald, Inc., we need merely quote the Report: "At the time of reorganization, the old company had undivided profits amounting to approximately $4,000,000, of which $2,500,000 was earmarked for withdrawal by the President and subsequently was drawn by him at the rate of $5,000 per week. At the end of 1933, the undivided profits of the new company amounted to nearly $600,000 and the capital account stood at $750,000". (p. 51)

We have been describing, it is quite apparent, a most profitable industry, one which has been able to prosper in a marked degree throughout the worst years of the depression. The other side of the picture may be very briefly sketched.[49]   Prices of

---

[48] Cf. *Combines and the Consumer*, by L.S.R. Research Committee.

[49] See the *Price Spreads Report*, pp. 147-153, on the tobacco grower. The Commission declares: "Possibly the clearest example of exploitation of the primary producer that came before us was that provided by the relationship between the tobacco manufacturers, especially the Imperial Tobacco Company of Canada, Limited, and the tobacco grower during the period preceding 1934".

products to consumers remained practically stationary, except for the drop in cigarette prices resulting from the lowering of the excise tax. Prices to the growers were cut in half during the period under consideration, by means of the unchallenged power of one dominant company in the buying market. Finally wages in the industry reached the lowest average of any manufacturing industry in Canada. The average wages for the tobacco industry follow:

1929	$644.11
1930	662.19
1931	597.48
1932	569.48
1933	555.35

Nor let it be forgotten that while the tobacco farmer was being ruined by the low prices dictated, while the workers were having to subsist on slave wages, depressed still further year by year, twenty-eight executives of Imperial Tobacco received in salary and bonuses $616,318 in 1931, $506,982 in 1932, and $421,388 in 1933. Mr. Walter Stewart of MacDonald's (or, more correctly, who is MacDonald's) denied himself the privilege of a salary but drew out of the company $260,000 per year, instead! Any further analysis of Canadian industrial policy and practice would be anti-climax. There is a quality of perfection about the tobacco picture. It may be taken as the ideal, as the goal, toward which Canadian industry and commerce should strive, are in fact striving. "The exorbitant profits that this company has been able to make, even in a period of general economic distress, are proof that a dominating position can be used to avoid the necessity of sharing in that distress".[50] Against such an achievement the weak may complain—the wage earner, the consumer, the primary producer. But from the standpoint of the ruling group in our industrial life there will come no protest. For big business exists for only one purpose, to serve the interests of big business; the interests of the rest of the community are an irrelevant consideration. It is doubtful if a more perfect set-up for serving the interests of our rulers can be devised than that of the tobacco industry. But the tobacco industry is but the summing up of the picture presented by a general study of the practices, policies and social philosophy of our economic system; in places the picture is incomplete, in places it is crudely sketched, in places it is distorted, but nowhere do we find evidence contradictory to the general trend.

[50]*Price Spreads Report*, p. 52.

The Farmer, The Fruit-Grower, and The Fisherman.

Before leaving the study of the conditions under which the majority of Canadians are compelled to live by reason of the nature of our economic system and the present disintegration which has seized hold of it, let us give some specific attention to that most important group—the primary producers. In many respects their problem is that of the weaker groups in the industrial and commercial constituency. But in addition they have peculiar problems of their own which make their lot particularly serious.

Let us consider the farmer in the first place. There has been a serious diminution in the value of the farmer's products. The net value of agricultural production in Canada, as estimated by the Dominion Bureau of Statistics, amounted to $758,791,743 in 1930, but had fallen to $538,192,000 in 1931 and only increased slightly to $565,400,000 in 1932.[51] A further analysis reveals an even more acute situation, for agricultural decline in Canada, as in the United States, began before the years 1929-30. Thus the total value of Canada's wheat crop had fallen from $442,221,000 in 1926 to $129,105,000 in 1932, in which period the price of wheat per bushel had dropped from $1.51 in 1926 to $0.60 in 1932.[52] A similar situation was true of livestock, and of vegetables, milk and dairy products, and of fruit.[53] We have already observed what happened to the prices of the producer of tobacco. The index figures show that the prices of farm products, on the base of 1929=100, fell to 50.6 in 1933, while wages fell to 75, retail prices to 77.7, manufactures to 75.5, iron and steel to 91.1. It is quite evident, then, both in relation to the producer of manufactured articles and even in relation to the recipient of industrial or commercial wages, the Canadian farmer has been the chief sufferer in the depression. (This is assuming that there was some equality during the twenties between the economic position of the farmer and of other economic groups).

While obviously it is difficult to estimate with any degree of exactitude the standard of living of the farm group, we can make some calculation by relating the total number of farms to the total net income from agricultural products. After deduction for depreciation, new equipment, wages, interest on mortgages and debt, this income in 1930 probably totalled $500,000,000. The

[51]*Canada*, 1935. D.B.S., p. 37. Farm profits show an even more spectacular decline stated in millions: 1927—$948.9; 1932—$273.3. See *Financial Post Business Year Book*, 1935.
[52]*Price Spreads Report*, p 10.
[53]*Canada Year Books*.

average per farm would then be slightly less than $700. The great reduction in farm income in the subsequent years would probably bring such a figure down to slightly more than $500. Since it has been estimated that about half of the six million farmers in the United States earn less than $350 a year, this average figure for Canada is probably not far astray.[54].

The plight of the farmer is reflected in the burden of debt which he is carrying and which he is unable to meet. The mortgage indebtedness of all farms in Canada, according to the 1931 census, amounted to $671,776,500. For the three prairie provinces the indebtedness is $324,400,000. In addition to this mortgage load, the farmers are carrying a tremendous burden in the form of loans from banks, and outstanding accounts to local merchants and farm machinery companies. What makes the situation particularly acute is that many of these debts were contracted in the days when prices of agricultural commodities were double or even treble what they are at this time. The full weight of this debt does not fall upon the farmer at present because of the Debt Adjustment Acts passed by the western provinces. It is questionable, however, how much protection will remain, should wheat farming, and incidentally foreclosure, once more become profitable. Already large financial houses are installing their own managers on groups of farms for which they hold the mortgages.

The western farmer faces disaster not only from the decline of wheat prices, not only by reason of the mounting volume of debt, but also because nature has dealt singularly harshly with him. Drought, laying waste thousands of square miles of central and south-eastern Saskatchewan, plagues of grasshoppers, dust storms turning arable land into desert—so nature assists men to redress the balance in a mad world where there is an over-abundance of wheat while millions are near starvation. The Canada Year Book of 1933 reports that, not including advances made for seed grain or for seeding operations, the Saskatchewan Relief Commission disbursed up to Dec. 31, 1933, $10,250,000. To this amount must be added the $5,000,000 mentioned in the Finance Minister's speech of March 22nd, 1935, having been expended in the year 1934-35. This indicates only in the barest outline the present suffering of the western farmer in the dry area.

Some further conception of the effect of economic crisis upon his social life may be gathered from the curtailment of

[54] J. S. Woodsworth, *The Distribution of Personal Income in Canada*, pp. 7-8.

already inadequate social services, educational facilities, and the ordinary amenities of civilized living. Between 1928 and 1933 the number of rural telephones in Manitoba decreased from 13,205 to 8,365—a decline of more than 36%. In Saskatchewan 30,000 rural telephones were taken out of service, more than 40% of the total, while in Alberta, the drop was from 21,269 to 10,162 or 52%. The most serious permanent effect of the crisis is probably to be found in the attenuation of school facilities and the decline in teachers' salaries.[55]

If we examine into causes, we find that the plight of our primary producers arises not only from the general depression of wheat prices in the world market, i.e., from a situation beyond the control of one country alone, but also from the same internal economic organization which we observed when studying the position of the Canadian worker. For, as the Price Spreads Commission's investigation clearly showed, the stock raiser is at the mercy of two great packing houses who exercise effective monopolistic control over the meat industry, and the fruit-grower is at the mercy of the canning combine. Further, as other investigations have shown, the milk producer is at the mercy of the great dairy companies. If we consider another primary productive industry, we discover that the total annual value of fish landed in the Maritimes fell from $19,823,557 in 1926 to $10,-266,474, in 1933. This condition is reflected in the earnings of fishermen, which, according to the evidence submitted, averaged from $75 to $400 per year according to the district. The mean rate was somewhere between $200 and $300. Here again there operates not only the condition of general depression but the superior position of the great buyer. Speaking of the low earnings of fishermen, the Royal Commission Report states: "They are the result of unfavourable economic conditions which have reflected themselves in the industry and which, for the fishermen, are intensified by the fact that on the side of the corporation buyer there is strong bargaining power and on his side, complete or almost complete absence of such power."[56] Thus quite apart from a condition of general economic disintegration, arising from inherent anomalies within the economic system itself, we find in our primary productive industries the same dire social and economic consequences arising from concentration of economic power wielded with the sole object of profit-making.

[55]See G. E. Britnell, *The Western Farmer* (Social Service Council of Canada); also Chapter V of this book: "Agriculture and the Farmer."
[56]*Price Spreads Report*, p. 185.

Professional Groups.

Our analysis of the economic and social disaster faced today by our wage earners and primary producers might lead one to suppose that our professional groups enjoyed an exemption which enabled them to rank with the privileged and independent classes. Such obviously is not the case. No group has suffered more in relation to its former security and achieved standard of living than the group of professional workers. No group would stand to gain more from an intelligently planned national economy.

Professional training will bring to an individual a superior standard of living precisely to the extent to which there is an effective economic demand for that training. A general contraction of the national economy is at once reflected in the slackening in the demand for engineers, architects, skilled superintendents and foremen, doctors, nurses, school teachers, business executives. The last six years in Canada have witnessed an increasing number of unemployed from the ranks of those who in the days of prosperity constituted the intelligentsia of our community. Nowhere is waste of talent more apparent. Medical men, crowded into our metropolitan areas to such an extent that only the oldest established are able to enjoy an adequate livelihood and carry on a practice in keeping with their years of training; rural districts left without proper medical services because they cannot support doctors or hospitals; engineers of years' experience overjoyed to find an odd job in some drafting office; teachers abandoning their overcrowded profession for uncertain commercial positions and those who remain in the school system enjoying incomes frequently less than those of inexperienced clerks—such is not an overdrawn picture of the economic position of our professional groups.

Even of greater social consequence is the plight of the graduates from our high schools and universities. For them the myth of the "land of opportunity" is exploded. Trained and fully equipped to make a valuable contribution to a society desperately in need of material and cultural amenities, a lost generation of Canadian youth searches aimlessly and hopelessly for mere employment. The land of rugged individualism, the land of the sturdy virtues of the pioneer, has become the land of the relief camp and the municipal refuge.

Political and Cultural Consequences of Canadian Capitalism.

We have dealt with the development of Canadian capitalism as reflected in the lives of Canadian citizens. We have seen how, given the concentration of economic power and the basic dynamic of the profit motive, the lines of industrial and commercial development are marked out and the resultant class divisions arise. We have seen how the social evils inherent in the capitalist system of industrial organization have been greatly accentuated during the period of capitalist decline, their effects reaching out into every economically dependent group in the community.

Peculiar to Canada as a new country is the slowness on the part of the majority of her citizens intelligently to diagnose the situation. The middle class optimism even of the disinherited groups, the lack of militancy in the trade union movement, the calm acceptance of the success psychology of individualism by the mass of the people, reveal the absence of a realistic analysis of our social structure. Less naive have been the attitudes and tactics of the privileged group. Behind a carefully controlled and manipulated press, our economic overlords have refurbished the fading illusions of individual independence and democratic freedom while they consolidated the control which completed the negation of these ideals.

Early in the industrial history of Canada, the Canadian Manufacturers' Association came to birth and provided a means for concerted action in the industrial and commercial fields. Even before the days when monopolistic control was accepted into the creed of business ethics, co-operative action in fields where the common interest (of manufacturers) was well defined, was not difficult to secure. The history of the tariff legislation presents a nice picture of the manner in which a group of enterprising citizens can set up exotic industries and reap vast fortunes from the exploitation of miserably paid wage earners and fleeced consumers. It is fairly obvious which group the tariff is designed to "protect". The history of our railway subsidies and land grants is rich in examples of business intervention in government, and incidentally (favourable) government intervention in business. There is no cause for surprise that a privileged and united group will utilize every conceivable institution in a country to maintain and improve its position. Nor is it surprising that, after the most startling revelations in the history of Canada in regard to the predatory nature of our industrial and commercial system, the President of the Canadian Chamber of Commerce should make the following statement: "While we are obliged to continue the campaign against disruptive economic forces, we have on our hands the additional campaign against the mastery of business by governments. Just when our whole

business world should be devoting itself to a concentrated fur-
therance of trade and commerce, our efforts must be divided lest
state interference and regulation by means of a general staff of
bureaucrats, impair business itself".[57]   What is surprising is
that our economic rulers can exercise their power and influence
so successfully, arouse such little public concern, and be classed
as public benefactors.

The merry-go-round of party politics in Canada is a fitting
sphere of influence for our economic leaders.   Minor issues may
confuse the Canadian elector as to which of the two major parties ought to be returned to power.   Seldom if ever is there any
doubt as to the "soundness" of the social philosophy of either.
Insofar as it affects the basic economic organization, and therefore the resultant social consequences, a general election is a flip
of a coin which has two heads.   Upon each side is engraved the
image and superscription of St. James Street.   This is an inevitable outcome of our political and social system as it is constituted.   For funds are required to equip a political party for
the fray and one must go to the source and giver of funds.   It
is a perfectly satisfactory arrangement on both sides, for tariff
privileges, the exclusive use of natural resources, personal
honour and advancement are the rewards given by a grateful
government in return for pecuniary election support.   Occasionally, the game gets out of hand, as in the case of the Beauharnois
"incident".   But this case is interesting in itself as illustrating
how unlikely it is that a political investigation into a colossal
steal of natural resources will be pushed to embarrassing lengths,
and how after a government steps in to save a great industrial
development from bankruptcy, the development itself will probably emerge in private hands.   The Prime Minister's statement
in the House, that he regretted that nothing could be done to
rescue Beauharnois from the Holt interests, presents the most
candid and at the same time most abject confession of impotence
on the part of the first representative of the people of Canada in
the face of Canada's greatest financial overlords.   But it is
unnecessary to single out one particular case of financial control
over our democratic institutions.   Our taxation schedules, and
the incidence of the various types of federal, provincial and
municipal taxes, illustrate all too clearly how effective is that
control.   The very secrecy which guards the incomes of the

[57]Mr. A. O. Dawson in a speech before the Chamber of Commerce of the United States
of America at Washington, April 30, 1935.   (Reported in Vancouver *Daily Province,*
May 1, 1935, from CP dispatch).

wealthy, and, until quite recently, the profits of many of our great corporations, is a proof of the inviolate position of wealth as well as of the lingering democratic predisposition in favour of equality. For a full revelation of the distribution of national wealth shatters at one blow the twin myths of democracy and of equality of opportunity.

Economic domination carries over in an interesting manner into the field of law despite the vaunted rights of individuals in a "British" nation. The legal and judicial system of the country is established to protect the civil rights and liberties of individuals. But more evidently it exists to protect the rights and privileges of property. Where the concentrated power of property tends to be the dominant interest in a country, the rights of individuals will be obscured. There is the practical inequality before the law of rich and poor, the expenses of counsel, of court and of appeal, placing a serious handicap in the way of the majority in the lower courts and making appeal a virtual impossibility. But there is a much more serious abuse of the processes of law in favour of the dominant class. The state sides with the class whose interest is in vested property rights in insisting that order is of higher social value than justice.[58] For order represents the maintenance of the *status quo* which, in rendering inviolate the accepted rights of property, perpetuates the injustice and inequality which concentrated economic power produces. When in a period of deepening distress and of growing insecurity the demand for a greater measure of social justice expresses itself in the rising protest of the disinherited groups and the awakening conscience of the middle class, it is met by repressive action on the part of the state. Troops are brought into the strike area of Cape Breton and more recently into Stratford. The Mayor of Vancouver reads the Riot Act when violence has been provoked by police brutality against relief camp strikers. Civil rights and freedom of speech and assembly are being ominously curtailed. The use of Section 98 of the Criminal Code to render illegal the Communist Party and to suppress 'agitation", the operation of the secret tribunal under the Immigration Act to deport without trial residents deemed undesirable, the conversion of the Royal Canadian Mounted Police into a government spy service, the rule of police law in our larger cities in the suppression of public assemblies, the justi-

[58]For other examples of repressive "class" legislation, see the David Bill and the Arcand Bill in the Province of Quebec, summarized by Prof. F. R. Scott in the May, 1935, issue of the *Canadian Journal of Economics and Political Science.*

fication of repression and police violence by high state officials and provincial attorneys-general, and the callously reactionary tone of the finance-dominated press, are but a few indications of the general trend.

Capitalist Culture.

The consideration of the economic life of our people has taken up much of this chapter. By implication, it might appear that we consider economic interests to be man's chief concern. On the contrary, we have merely paid greatest attention to that field of interest which in the present order occupies man's chief attention. Man does not live by bread alone, but at least he must have bread to live by. Until man's primitive needs are satisfied, it is clear that he will abandon any concern for other values than those of mere survival. It is the basic condemnation of our economic system that it dictates that man's chief concern shall be economic.

In such an economic system, "culture" will be thought of as a luxury to be acquired or indulged in by a privileged class. It will not be thought of as a quality of life, intrinsic in a society, of which all individuals will normally partake. In spite of our earlier democratic tradition, "education" has come to have a two-fold meaning. For the many is represents the *sine qua non* of an economically successful life. For the few who carry the passport of privilege, it represents the visa to "culture". The early democracy of our country called for a policy of universal education. The legislation of most provinces, with the significant exception of Quebec, calls for compulsory school attendance up to the age of fourteen. Even in the provinces where such compulsory attendance legislation is enforced, the number of children who continue to the end of high school is surprisingly small, while those who are able to complete a university course as well as high school are a small and privileged few compared with those who have to find work (if they can).[59] Now it is true that the cultural background of parents who have been themselves denied educational privileges may influence to some degree the numbers of educational casualties. But a far more important factor in deciding the number of children who leave school at an early age is the economic necessity of supplementing an inadequate family income at as early an age as possible. In the uni-

---

[59]In the whole of Canada in 1931, 16,800 out of 436,700 young men between the ages of 20 and 24 were in schools or colleges. The corresponding number of young women was only 9,000 out of 447,500. Cf. L. C. Marsh, *Employment Research*, Table 13, p. 307.

versities, the fees necessary to the maintenance of such institutions are an effective bar to all except those whose families can afford to finance them during the four to seven years' course, or whose families can do without the earnings they are able to accumulate in the summer months. This last source of income has been largely destroyed by the depression, so that many are now excluded from the universities who, on the basis of intelligence, are best fitted to proceed to higher studies.

Much might be written—in fact, has been written—about the cultural significance of our educational system, for those who can afford to share in its advantages. In spite of the protest of isolated educators, our school system remains the most satisfactory means of producing the standardized "Babbitt" type, the educational equivalent of the identical interchangeable parts which our mass industrial process turns out. It is not a little ironical that it is those carefully guarded institutions of "class education", the private schools, which are making the boldest experiments in the field of progressive education, aimed at calling forth self-expression and training in the skills of co-operative living.

Cultural development depends upon adequate leisure. Hence in vulgar parlance our "leisured classes" are our "cultured classes". The absence of leisure is an effective bar to cultural development. Those whose bodies and minds are rendered unfit by fatigue induced by a sixty or seventy hour working week are barred from participation in cultural activities. So are those whose curtailed education leaves them ill-equipped to make use of what leisure time they possess. So are those whose spiritual horizon is ever clouded by the haunting fear of economic necessity. For all of these the main concern of life is making a living. For most of them the dreams of economic security are unfulfilled. But through their thinking has seeped, like a poison, the philosophy of acquisition. They vacillate restlessly between the vision of riches and the dread of poverty. Barren of resources within themselves, what leisure time they possess is occupied for the most part in the vicarious excitement of commercialized sports and amusements. The quality of the average motion picture entertainment, the average radio programme, represents the approximate limits of intellectual criticism and cultural appreciation of the average member of our working and middle classes. These agencies which, in more civilized countries, are instruments of popular education, are in our country the agencies of profit-making concerns to minister to and perpetuate the peculiar quality of soul our economic society has created.

The cultural level of our privileged classes is perhaps an even greater condemnation of the ethical basis of our society. Amongst the privileged as amongst the underprivileged group, the predominant economic interest tends to colour the individual's entire outlook. The great condemnation of our system is that it makes an interest in "things" the major interest to the almost complete exclusion of an interest in values. The basis of privilege is wealth, the creed of privilege is a belief in the making of money, the measure of human achievement is a monetary yardstick. This philosophy of acquisition renders impotent the finer impulses. So are members of the privileged group known rather for a vulgar display of houses and lands, of yachts and automobiles, than for their contribution to the cultural life of our age.

Religion and Capitalism.

The cultural effects of capitalism are nowhere more clearly seen than in the field of religion. The development of the Canadian churches in the 19th century has clearly illustrated the general tendency of modern Christianity, and especially its Protestant branch, to succumb to the spirit of an acquisitive society. The religion which at its outset stood against "the world" has revised its charter to enable it at one and the same time to serve God and Mammon.

This is demonstrated both by the ethical attitudes which have characterized its thinking, and by the classes which have provided its chief support. While the Marxist epithet "opiate" is inadequate to describe the teaching of the churches for "the People", it is quite evident that there has been a singular absence of the social note, of a basic concern for social justice, and for the fulfilment of human personality which so characterized the teaching of the founder of the Christian religion. Instead, there has been a stress upon the individualistic virtues—which incidentally are the virtues lauded by an aggressive and successful capitalism—industry, thrift, honesty, temperance, combined with a pietistic personal religion. The "worldly asceticism" of the Calvinist has been demonstrated to no greater advantage than in the Canadian Protestant churches. Our churches have paid homage to St. James Street, and St. James Street has made lasting impressions on the padded pews of many a wealthy house of God. In fact, it is probable that Canadian Protestantism, with its earlier strict puritanical traditions, made a very significant contribution to the pioneer industrial expansion of this country. In the more primitive pioneer communities there appears to have been some attempt to realize a Christian social solidarity to the elimination of classes. As it became apparent, however, that a permanent and increasingly large group of the disinherited had become a feature of Canadian society, the social demands of the churches were emasculated into their customary expression in "Christian philanthropy". Thus by the churches was the existence and final status of "the poor" recognized and sanctioned.

The development of the Protestant churches has therefore been to a greater and greater extent within the middle class group, and subsidies for their work have been freely forthcoming from their members who have risen to be the financial overlords of the Dominion. "To the poor", however, the gospel has not been preached, and more and more have members of the working classes been alienated from the religion of the churches.

This is not the whole picture. Throughout the period of capitalism's development prophetic voices have been raised in the name of a high ethical religion against some of the more flagrant forms of social injustice. These have had from time to time the effect of mitigating the worst evils of the system. Since the beginning of the depression the revolt against the spirit and practices of a capitalist society has become widespread throughout all branches of the church. Even in the most conservative of the churches of Christendom, the Roman Catholic, the latest Papal Encyclical, and such enterprises as the aggressive programme of adult social education and co-operation carried on by the Extension Department of St. Francois Xavier University, (Antigonish, N.S.), shows a growing consciousness of the necessity for social change.

This rebirth of a social consciousness on the part of the churches is due probably to two causes. The imagination of the more liberal clergy has been awakened, as the inherent evils in the system have become accentuated by the crisis and the stark contrasts in the lives of our people thrown into high light. In the second place, the increasing insecurity among members of the middle class constituency of the churches has brought home to them a recognition of their identity of interest with the working classes. It is not an impossibility that radical Christian thought and action may play an important part in the coming period of social reconstruction.[60]

[60]See L.S.R. pamphlet, *The Church and Social Reconstruction*, by Ernest Thomas.

Conclusion.

In those memorable words of Calvin Coolidge, "The country is not in good condition"! Canada has not been exempt from those characteristics of modern industrialist development which pertain to the older lands whose civilization has been transformed by the machine. The same trends towards the greater and greater concentration of economic power are evident—the same maldistribution of wealth, the same shocking contrasts between luxury and indigence. Masses of official evidence point to the practice of exploitation and the futility of governments' efforts to control or to restrain. The firm establishment of western capitalism has resulted in the dissolution of the social bond which held together members of an earlier pioneer community. Antagonisms of class become more and more apparent, and the period of capitalist decline serves but to intensify the resentment of the dispossessed towards the owning and the ruling classes. This inevitable conflict permeates every sphere of life, corrupting politics and the press, warping the true course of social justice, distorting the law to serve the interests of the defenders of the *status quo,* debasing the religious and cultural expression of the people. The way before the Canadian people is plain. A return to a more primitive society is obviously impossible, nor would it be desirable were it within the realm of possibility. An intelligent reconstruction of our economic life is not beyond the capacity of Canadians to achieve, nor are the obstacles in the form of the economic interests and privileges of favoured groups insurmountable. The time is fast arriving when special privileges at the expense of the welfare of the community will be considered as a luxury which no civilized nation can afford.

CHAPTER II.

THE NATURE OF THE CANADIAN ECONOMY.

A. THE DEVELOPMENT OF THE ECONOMY.

THE present problems of the Canadian economy derive in large measure from the peculiar circumstances of its development. From the first it has been based on specialized production undertaken to satisfy a foreign demand. It is true that in the early days the *habitants* in Quebec and the pioneers in the Ontario backwoods were to a considerable extent self-sufficient through lack of transport facilities and the means of exchange, but these pockets of settlement grew up largely as adjuncts to commerce in trade products such as square timber and lumber; furs in Quebec; and potash and, later, wheat in Ontario.

This development of Canadian economic life as an off-shoot of the commercial revolution in Great Britain and Europe, combined with the geographic background (in particular the easy access to the heart of the northern part of the continent by the St. Lawrence and Hudson Bay), has given a dominant position to the production and export of staple raw materials. The commodities available for export have undergone great changes, with the result that Canada has suffered violent economic fluctuations "in response to such factors as improvements in the technique of transport, exhaustion of raw materials, and the advance of industrialism".[1] These demands for new products and new techniques in securing their production involved also a more effective financial mechanism and more plentiful capital.

The Exploitation of a New Country.

At first, fish and then furs were of primary importance. The decline of the Eastern fur trade, due to the effectiveness of the Hudson Bay route in penetrating to the more distant and less exhausted areas in Western Canada, was followed by the development of the timber trade in Eastern Canada.   White pine in the form of square timber was exported from the Ottawa and the Upper St. Lawrence during the period of the Napoleonic Wars and until it was exhausted.   The coming of iron and steam destroyed the lumbering and shipbuilding trades of the Mari-

1H. A. Innis, *Problems of Staple Production in Canada*, p. 82.

times. Meanwhile the increasing industrialism of Great Britain created demands for wheat and supplied capital and railroads for its production. The growing importance of wheat necessitated the construction of canals on the Upper St. Lawrence and the Welland, and in addition railroads as supplementary means of transportation. These developments called forth activity in coal mining and in the iron and steel trades. Meanwhile gold booms in the West and North contributed their share to the spasmodic nature of economic growth. The building of railroads has made possible the rapid expansion of mineral production, and of the pulp and paper industries, in connection with the exploitation of waterpower. The settlement of the West and the growth of towns have stimulated the Western lumber industry and given a start, with the help of protection, to domestic industrial growth.

The development of transport facilities has been unavoidably spasmodic. Such a project as the improvement of the St. Lawrence and Great Lakes system by a series of canals took time for completion. Once finished, the effect on the economy was immediate and revolutionary. The same thing was true of railroad development. This could not take place piecemeal in a new country like Canada. Gradual improvement was out of the question. New regions and resources could only be opened up by the building of lines where there had before been no transportation and no settlement. With the completion of an intercolonial or transcontinental railroad, a dominant new factor in the economic situation at once came into play, causing fundamental changes in economic relationships and possibilities, and consequent upheavals in the entire system.

Capital was at first supplied by English houses operating in Canada which financed commercial operations, or by small producers themselves. It became more plentiful with the emergence of the United Provinces and eventually of Confederation, which made possible the provision of government capital for improvements in transport. The recent development of corporation finance has in its turn assembled domestic capital and drawn in American investment to supplement government lending, British commercial capital, and the resources of family industries.

Under such circumstances economic development is inevitably intermittent, but the violence of the alternations between hectic expansion and abysmal depression has been greatly exaggerated by "boom-mania". Each new economic opportunity in turn has been the object of unbridled optimism and the pretext for speculative over-expansion, involving the building up at immense expense of elaborate capital equipment in railroads, waterways, docking facilities, highways, storage plants, power plants, mines, factories, public buildings and whole cities—equipment which would be sufficient to meet the needs of an expansion of world markets credible only to the incurable day-dreamer. The rapid development has meant a succession of periods of transient prosperity based on a rapid exhaustion of resources.

In some cases, the dissipation of a new material has been a necessary step in opening up the country, as with timber in Southern Ontario. There have been cases of the rate of exploitation being deliberately speeded up by such measures as the construction of the Temiskaming and Northern Ontario Railroad, which was designed to get the minerals out of the North country faster than would otherwise be possible. In still other cases there has been wanton and reckless waste—the squandering of gas in the Turner Valley development; the pointless slaughter of salmon in the Fraser River and elsewhere; the reckless destruction of oyster and lobster fisheries in the Maritime Provinces; logging operations in British Columbia which left behind from five to seven feet of what might have been good timber in useless stumps; the universal practice of discarding smaller logs, a debris of kindling wood for forest fires. Even yet it is necessary to urge that we have passed the pioneer stage of riches based on the lavish utilization of unbounded raw materials,—that sober and foresighted conservation of our natural resources is national common sense.

Government Aids.

Public authorities, Dominion, Provincial, and Municipal, have played an active part in forwarding economic development, especially in the provision or guarantee of funds and the compensation of losses, and in related fiscal operations. Political considerations have been responsible for some of this intervention. For example, Canada is probably the only country in the world with two railways written into its Constitution. The Intercolonial was built partly for defence, partly as a bait to tempt the Maritime Provinces into Confederation, partly as insurance against the threatened cancellation of the bonding privilege at United States ports by giving central Canada railway connection with the winter ports of Halifax and St. John. The C.P.R. was an essential part of the bargain which brought British Columbia into the Dominion. Nor is there much question that Sir John Macdonald adopted tariff protection less from reasoned economic conviction than from shrewd political intuition that it would win the election of 1878. Similarly our tariff-making ever since, almost without exception, has proceeded on the principle that "They should take who have the power, And they should keep who can". The Canadian tariff is the product not of the economist's study but of Red Parlours where contending lobbies have "arranged" matters with successive governments.

In addition, Canadian development has meant a constant struggle with the United States for business,—which is easily diverted from one side to the other of the boundary line by differences in tariffs, in the convenience and cost of transport, etc.,—and for settlers, who are considerably influenced by the prospects held out to them. Consequently, the development of transport facilities, power plants, municipal amenities and concessions of land and other natural resources has proceeded on the basis of competition with and as a defence against the United States rather than on the basis of an unprejudiced estimate of the needs and prospects of Canada's own economic life.[2] These circumstances also drew the Government into making economically unjustifiable expenditures, and encouraging the irresponsible exhaustion of natural resources, notably in the case of lumber.

The succession of booms and slumps has involved the state still further in economic responsibilities. In periods of prosperity enthusiastic private enterprise, often with state guarantees and subsidies undertakes large-scale investment, as, for instance, in the Abitibi power development and the Grand Trunk Pacific and the Canadian Northern Railways; or the government itself does so, in order to facilitate the opening up of supposedly rich resources as in the case of the National Transcontinental and T.N.O. Railroads. The cities have been caught in the same mistaken debt-engendering over-expansion of fixed equipment, as the street railways in South Vancouver and Edmonton bear witness. When the boom gives way to depression, or when realization falls short of the imagined prospects, the Dominion, province or municipality finds itself burdened with its own commitments, growing mountains of inflexible debt, and compelled to take over the losses of private undertakings at a good price as in the case of the C.N.R., either as guarantor of bonds or in order to save important interests from ruin. Meanwhile further capital ex-

2See L. C. A. Knowles, *The Economic Development of the British Overseas Empire*, Vol. II, especially Part II, Chapters 1, 7 and 8.

penditure is found necessary in a desperate effort to save depressed areas of the country from ruin by the development of improved transport facilities and the like, as with the opening of the Hudson Bay Railroad, at the behest of the Prairie Provinces.

Rigidities, Natural and Artificial.

The seasonal character of our production has been a further grave disadvantage. For we have to provide equipment to deal not with a given volume of business spread evenly over the whole year, but with that given volume concentrated in immense peak loads for short seasons and dwindling away to practically nothing for the rest of the year. Lake shipping, lake harbours, canals, the ports of Montreal and Quebec, developed to the pitch necessary for the huge summer traffic, must lie idle for the five months of winter and spring. The railway rolling stock needed for the short crop-moving period is grotesquely superabundant, though it brings in no returns, and piles up interest charges just as fast as if it were busy every hour of the day.

Nor is this the only handicap imposed by nature. Most of our resources lie in a very long but comparatively narrow strip along the United States border; and between Sudbury and Winnipeg stretch eight hundred miles of territory, appropriately known to railwaymen as "The Bridge", empty and barren. Ten million people scattered along the thin ribbons on either side of this gap, obviously need transport facilities on a scale that would be ridiculous for the ten millions of Pennsylvania; and though the traffic per mile is much less, the cost per mile is decidedly not proportionately smaller.

Further, there has been in recent years an increasing tendency to finance new equipment by bonds, the interest on which remains fixed regardless of returns, and by preferred stock whose dividends are less variable than those on common shares.

All these things mean exceptionally serious difficulties for a country like Canada, whose whole economy is based on a few staples (wheat, pulp, mineral products, paper, etc.) produced for export. In fact the essence of many of Canada's economic problems is simply this: our returns from export staples fluctuate sharply and swiftly while many of our costs remain rigid.

For example, during the present depression, bonded indebtedness (Dominion, provincial, municipal and corporation) has risen from $7,445,208,000 at January 1, in 1929, to $8,757,840,000 at

January 1, 1934.[3] Power rates, thanks to the industry's interest burden, and perhaps in some degree to public regulation which, though preventing increases in prosperous times hinders reductions during depression, have remained pretty much what they were. Railway freight rates have not changed at all; nor can they be expected to change quickly, again because of interest charges and public regulation, and further because the railway wage bill is necessarily a larger part of operating expenses than in most industries and harder to reduce because of the strength of the railway unions. Of course we do not for a moment suggest relaxation of control or a weakening of the unions, rather the contrary. But there is no doubt that both factors add to the rigidities of the situation. The banks have kept up their interest rates. Monopolistic industries, too, producing for the protected home market have in the main been able to keep up their prices, which are costs to the exporter. They have done so by drastic cuts in the number of their employees and in wage rates. We have solved the problem of fluctuating returns and rigid costs by squeezing the farmer, the working man and the civil servant, and to a less degree the shareholder in export industries.[4]

Some of these troubles as we have seen are of natural origin. But most of them are the legacy of an unplanned, haphazard expansion by and for private enterprise: waste and exploitation in the boom, debt and dislocation in the depression.

B. NATURAL RESOURCES.

If unplanned capitalism has brought us to this pass, the sensible thing to do is to substitute a plan. Equally clearly the first step is to see what resources we have at our disposal.

We have been brought up on the idea that our natural resources are fabulous. Actually our knowledge of them is limited and the estimates are often little more than guess-work. The difference between "potential" and immediately workable resources is not one to be glossed over, and the farther we get with careful and unimaginative surveys, the more the "vision splendid" of our after-dinner speeches "fades into the light of common day", a common day of relatively restricted horizons. Fully a third of the area of Canada is of no economic value whatever, and for the rest the golden age of swift and carefree exploitation is over, the urgent necessity for conservation is upon us.

3*Financial Post Business Year Book*, 1934, p. 131, quoting Dominion Bureau of Statistics for 1929 and A. E. Ames and Company for 1934.
4See below, "Prices and Production Under Monopoly," p. 118; also Forsey, *Dividends and the Depression.*

Farms, Forests and Minerals.

Of our 361,162,387 acres of agricultural land, 163,119,231 acres were already occupied in 1931, leaving 198,043,156 acres available for occupation, of which 90,121,398 acres were in the Prairie Provinces. Land under field crops in 1934 amounted to 56,042,420 acres; in pasture, 8,353,400.[5] Much of the unoccupied land is either inaccessible, or at least so far from markets or even railways as to be of only very slight practical importance. As to wheat land, Dr. D. A. MacGibbon, Dominion Grain Commissioner, in a careful study, states that "it is quite incorrect to assume that there are still vast areas of virgin soil to be taken up, just as good for wheat as those already occupied."[6] He estimates our maximum future production of wheat at 700,000,000 bushels.[7] Large areas of the prairies are too dry for mixed farming; but if markets can be found—a large proviso—this part of the country should be able to develop larger crops of other grains. Dairy farming and stock-raising may be expanded in certain sections. Fruit-growing may be further developed in British Columbia, Ontario, Quebec and Nova Scotia; market-gardening in British Columbia; vegetables and hay in the Maritimes; sheepraising and tobacco-growing in Ontario. Further developments in transportation and in agricultural science may make possible cultivation of areas now useless; but heavy transport costs, a short growing season, and danger of drought will put many of these at a permanent disadvantage.

Our *forest* resources, likewise, though large and valuable, are by no means "boundless". The official estimate of the accessible stand of timber is 165,846,000,000 cubic feet; 290,230,000,000 feet board measure of saw timber and 920,335,000 cords of pulpwood, cordwood, etc. Coniferous trees form over 80 per cent. of our forest resources and over 95 per cent. of our forest products as at present exploited, Canada being rivalled in her coniferous forests only by Asiatic Russia and the United States. During recent years, the annual drain on our forest resources, (estimated at 2,812,000,000 cubic feet in 1932) has generally exceeded the new growth. "During the years 1926-30, which were typical of

[5]*Canada Year Book*, 1934-35. p. 39. The National Development Bureau of the Department of the Interior in 1928 put the total extent of agricultural land at 290,200,000 acres. See the volumes on "Pioneer Problems", by Professors Mackintosh, Dawson and others. Other estimates of resources from *Canada Year Book*, 1933, unless otherwise stated.

[6]*The Future of the Canadian Grain Export Trade*, supplement to Volume XIX of *Transactions of the Royal Canadian Institute*, p. 27: also *Contributions to Canadian Economics*, V (Toronto University Studies), using *Report of Saskatchewan Royal Commisson on Immigration and Settlement*, 1930.

[7]Jenness, in *University of Toronto Quarterly*, July, 1932, p 396, gives a higher figure, 900,000,000. Peak production, 1928, 553,571,700. (*Canada Year Book*, 1929, p. 234).

pre-depression conditions, the average annual depletion due to use was approximately 2,000 million cubic feet of conifers and 970 million cubic feet of hardwoods. The average annual loss from fire was estimated at 185 million cubic feet of conifers and 45 million cubic feet of hardwoods. Though no widespread epidemics of insects or fungous diseases have occurred in recent years, local infestations which cause considerable loss develop practically every year. In Nova Scotia, in 1931, the balsam suffered severely from "gout". . . . In the Gaspé peninsula the spruce saw-fly became a serious menace. In the absence as yet of any basic data on which to estimate the annual depletion from these causes, it may be taken as 700 million cubic feet. The total annual depletion during the five-year period was therefore estimated to have been about 3,900 million cubic feet. To what extent this loss has been replaced by growth increment is not known, but, considering the preponderance of the younger age classes in the reproduction, it is believed there has been a considerable net depletion in the merchantable age classes. . . . It cannot be said that the measures so far taken by legislation and the application of scientific forestry . . . have been sufficient to assure us an adequate supply of timber for the future. Yet an annual increment of 10 cubic feet per acre, which is quite possible under forest management, would provide in perpetuity for a population of 26 millions at the present annual rate of use."[8]

In pulpwood, the basis of one of the staple industries on which we depend for existence, the situation is not less serious. A Royal Commission in 1924 estimated that Nova Scotia's supply would be exhausted in thirty to thirty-five years. New Brunswick's in twenty-four, Quebec's in forty-three or forty-four, Ontario's in about fifty-four. Only in British Columbia were growth and depletion approximately equal. In Nova Scotia the annual cut alone, apart altogether from losses by fire, insects, wind, and fungi, was almost twice the annual growth; in New Brunswick almost three times the growth; in Quebec appreciably more than the growth; in Ontario slightly less.[9] Conservation measures are now probably somewhat improved, and the depression has slowed the pace of pulpwood consumption. But between 1924 and 1929 Nova Scotian mills increased their capacity from 53 tons daily to 293, New Brunswick from 70 to

8*Canada Year Book*, 1934-35, pp. 40-42, 318.
9*Report* of the Royal Commission on Pulpwood, 1934, pp. 25, 26, 37, 38, 49, 50, 62, 79.

140, Quebec from 2,790 to 6,395, Ontario from 2,334 to 4,080, British Columbia from 546 to 786.[10]

In *minerals* our position is like Pepys' "crucifix",—"mighty fine, but not so fine as I expected". With the staples of modern industrialism we are in fact extraordinarily poorly supplied. Iron ore we have only in such low grades or small pockets as to be completely worthless. Our deposits of petroleum are meagre. Our *coal* resources are "the second largest in the world" and Alberta alone is said to have "more coal than France and Germany put together". But we have no real anthracite, and of the more than 400,000,000,000 tons of "actual" reserves in seams of one foot or more at depths of not more than four thousand feet, over ninety per cent. are lignite, while of the "probable" reserves over seventy per cent. are lignite. Moreover, our coal is all in the wrong places. The largest deposits of bituminous (industrial) coal are in British Columbia, and most of the rest in Alberta and Nova Scotia,[11] while the main centres of population and industry are in Ontario and Quebec which have no coal of any kind except a little lignite in a remote part of Ontario. The mines of Vancouver Island and Nova Scotia suffer from unavoidable high costs of operation. The strenuous efforts of Dominion and Provincial governments through the tariff, transportation subsidies, and propaganda, have utterly failed to secure any market for Alberta coal east of Port Arthur and Fort William or any appreciable market for Nova Scotia coal west of Montreal.[12] Between these points lies the acute fuel area, the main coal consuming region of the country, entirely dependent on imported fuels. Even in the Quebec market, Nova Scotia is seriously handicapped by the closing of the St. Lawrence during four months of the year. The upshot is that we must import almost all our domestic (anthracite) coal, 3,000,000 tons, and about half our industrial (bituminous) coal.[13]

Water Power.

To some degree these deficiencies are compensated by our immense wealth of *water power,* most of it providentially situ-

10*Evidence* before the Banking and Commerce Committee of the House of Commons, 1934, p. 890.

11*Canada Year Book,* 1933, pp. 372-373.

12For details as to high costs of operation and attempts to widen the markets for Canadian coal, see Forsey, *Economic and Social Aspects of the Nova Scotia Coal Industry,* pp. 43-44; and Draper, *The Alberta Coal Problem,* pp. 42-57 (both McGill University Economic Studies.)

13*Coal Statistics for Canada,* any year.

ated in or near the acute fuel area, in agreeable contrast to the United States, whose much larger resources are very distant from the main centres of industry. The 7,547,035 horse-power at present developed[14] are only about one-sixth of the total possible installation, but the production in central electric stations in the acute fuel area probably saves us, in a normal year, some 17,000,000 tons of coal which would have to be added to our imports.[15]

This is an important and valuable possession, but it would be foolish to make it the basis of extravagant hopes of industrial expansion. Power cost in most industries is, on the average, only about five per cent. of the total cost of production, rising to about forty per cent. for certain industries; the 3,500,000 horse-power still available to Canada from the St. Lawrence will be not "cheap", but "moderate-priced"; and power from the rich undeveloped sites in the north is likely to be decidedly expensive.[16] Moreover, there is the perennial problem that our domestic market for manufactures is small and foreign markets are hard to get and harder to keep. The most important industrial consumer of power at present is the pulp and paper industry, which takes about 40 per cent. of the total production of central electric stations, and produces for itself a considerable additional amount.[17] We certainly cannot look for any spectacular expansion here in the near future. The other principal consumers are flour milling, which is grotesquely over-developed,[18] non-ferrous metal mining, electro-metallurgy (note especially the aluminum refinery at Arvida), and electro-chemical plants. In 1932, when our total installation was 6,-528,533 horse-power, installations by industries were:[19]

Wood and paper	2,094,010
Iron and steel	623,888
Non-ferrous metals	450,271
Vegetable products	326,829
Non-metallic minerals	209,484
Chemicals	105,671
Pulp and paper	1,662,146
Flour milling	123,030
Primary iron and steel	237,063

[14]At January 1, 1935 (*Financial Post Business Year Book*, 1935, p. 125.)
[15]At 1.6 pounds of coal per K. W. H.
[16]Lesslie Thompson, *The St. Lawrence Waterway Problem*, pp. 83-84.
[17]Dominion Bureau of Statistics reports, 1933; *Financial Times*, April 20, 1934; *Financial Post*, March 30, 1935.
[18]See below, Chap. VII, "The Inefficiency of the System".
[19]*Report on Manufactures*, 1932, table 7.

Railway rolling stock	109,775
Non-ferrous metal smelting and refining	334,675
Cement	75,996
Electrical apparatus	87,634

To return to *minerals*: we produced in 1934 about 11½ per cent. of the world's gold, 9 per cent. of its silver, 9½ per cent. of its lead, and 8 per cent. of its zinc; and we normally produce almost half its cobalt, 60 per cent. of its asbestos, 9½ per cent. of its copper, and 86 per cent. of its nickel.[20] These minerals together in the calendar year 1934 made up about 23 per cent. of our total exports.[21] We have also considerable reserves of gypsum, salt, and construction material and chemicals.

Two natural products formerly of dominant importance, but now fallen into the background, are *furs* and *fish*. Both illustrate the problems of conservation and the change in staples of production. With the exhaustion of furs in accessible regions and the spread of settlement, the fur trade is turning from trapping to fur farming. Fisheries which have survived the reckless waste of pioneer days are now being fairly well conserved and developed and still play a large part in the life of the Maritimes and British Columbia.

Tourist Trade.

Not least among Canada's resources, especially in the balance of international indebtedness, are its attractions to tourists and sportsmen. Tourist trade, even in 1934, yielded us an income of $138,000,000,[22] our largest export except wheat. To a large degree, we pay for imports of goods by exports of scenery and recreation, just as Switzerland does,—this is one explanation of those "unfavourable" trade balances which cause periodical fits of hysterics among newspaper editors and Cabinet ministers, —and with proper conservation measures there is no reason why we should not continue to do so. If the markets for our export staples go on shrinking, our tourist trade may well become a mainstay. A socialist Canada, we may add, could "export" inspection of its social experiments by the tourist as the U.S.S.R. has done and so tap a new source of national income.

[20]*Canada Year Book*, 1933, pp. 358, 359, 366-369, 377; D.B.S. *Report on Mineral Production*, 1933, 1934; *Financial Post*, May 25, 1935.

[21]*Report on the Trade of Canada*, *March*, 1934. The figures include both merchandise and coin and bullion.

[22]Gross The net figure (after deducting Canadian tourists' expenditures abroad) was $84,000,000. *Canada Year Book*, 1934-35, p. 639.

Hordes of eager Americans coming over the border to see our socialized banking system, "the envy and admiration of the world", is a not unpleasing vision.

Geography, Climate and Exports.

In a rather equivocal place among our resources is our *geographical position.* It renders us immune from invasion, except by the United States. It gives us the world's finest hard wheat. The cold winters have, perhaps, an invigorating effect on us, physically and mentally. For the most part, however, our geography is a liability. Its contribution to the rigidities of the economy, especially in transportation, we have already noted. In addition, it inflicts on us a short growing season; a restricted range of agricultural products; heavy expenditures for warn, clothing, domestic fuel and railway fuel, for clearing railways, highways, and mine ventilators of snow and ice; serious obstacles to the movement of labour from one part of the country to another; formidable difficulties in the construction industries. It is responsible for the lack of raw cotton, raw silk, raw rubber, raw sugar, and other tropical products, which notably increases our dependence on foreign trade and our vulnerability to economic disturbances beyond our borders.

This last is one of the major limiting factors within which a Canadian planning authority will have to work.[23] Qualitative analysis of our imports in the fiscal year 1932[24] shows: first, raw materials which we cannot produce here at all (rubber, cotton, silk, sugar, aluminum, tin)—$48,397,000; second, raw materials which, in spite of prolonged fostering by the government, can apparently be produced here only at fantastic cost, or in inadequate amount, or in inferior quality (furs,[25] hides and skins, leather, wool, iron ore, coal, asphalt, petroleum, tobacco)—$92,-525,000; third, tropical products (fruits, nuts, vegetables, tea, coffee, cocoa, spices, oils, etc.)—$35,557,000; fourth, manufactured goods which come in free of duty or in spite of high duties—that is, goods which we do not even try to make or have never succeeded in making in sufficient quantity or at reasonable cost in spite of fifty-six years of tariff protection (certain textile products, fine paper, books, many iron and steel products and chemicals, certain distilled liquors, motion picture films,

---

23See below, "Foreign Trade", Ch. XIV.
24The proportions are about the same in any year.
25Note the modification of the "embargo" on imports from the U.S.S.R. to allow entry of Russian furs, which Canadian furriers declared indispensable.

china and glass)—$181,742,000. These four groups accounted for almost 70 per cent. of our merchandise imports in a year of depression and under a government which has done its best to make us as nearly self-sufficing as possible. They will probably continue in much the same proportion.

Our dependence on external markets is too well known to call for much comment. We export on an average about 30 per cent. of our total production: of our wheat 62 per cent., flour 34 per cent., fish 73 per cent., newsprint 92 per cent., pulp 20 per cent., gold 93 per cent., silver 72 per cent., nickel 90 per cent., copper 87 per cent., lead 68 per cent., zinc 84 per cent., asbestos practically 100 per cent., fertilizers 68 per cent., agricultural implements 27 per cent., distilled liquors 86 per cent., over a third of our motor cars and very nearly half our motor trucks.[26] These industries in 1933 gave employment directly to over 400,-000 persons.[27] The amount of employment for which they are indirectly responsible is not easy to estimate; but as we have pointed out elsewhere,[28] export staples are the basis of our whole economy. Hence anything which injures our export trade strikes at the livelihood not only of those actually employed in export industries, but in greater or less degree of every Canadian.

These large exports are a necessity to us. In the calendar year 1934 we had to find in foreign currencies about $230,000,-000 net to meet interest and dividend payments on Canadian securities held abroad; a further $21,000,000 net for freight payments; and about $358,000,000 for the essential raw materials, tropical and other products mentioned above: a total of $609,000,000.[29] The only means we have of getting the necessary foreign currencies are exports of goods or services, or

---

26For minerals, flour, newsprint, motor cars and motor trucks,—calendar year, 1934; for wheat—crop year, 1933-34; for other goods—1933. Figures of production from D.B.S. reports (*Census of Industry*) and trade returns and *Hansard*, 1935, p. 2455. Gold exports comprise gold ore, gold-bearing quartz and gold bullion.

27*Seventh Census of Canada*, Bulletin XXXI shows

	Farmers	Farm labourers	Total
Manitoba	93,431	43,533	136,964
Saskatchewan	204,473	80,988	285,461
Alberta	145,747	52,879	198,626
Total	443.651	177,400	621,051

Wheat acreage in those provinces was 60 per cent. of total field crop acreage. Assuming the same proportions for farmers and farm labourers, the gainfully employed dependent on wheat growing in the Prairie Provinces in 1931 must have numbered about 350,000 at least. Fishing, hunting and trapping, 47,917; logging, 43,983; other industries specified, 65,000. (*Census of Industry*).

28See p. 40.

29*Financial Post Business Year Book*, 1935, p. 61; and compilation from official trade returns.

foreign loans. Loans at the moment are not too easily obtainable, and at the best of times will be limited by the lender's opinion of our capacity to pay, which again ultimately involves our capacity to export. The tourist trade (our chief "service" export) netted us in 1934 a credit of about $84,000,000.[30] Most of the rest of our requirements we had to meet by exports of commodities. We can escape our dependence on foreign markets as little as our dependence on foreign sources of supply.

Sir Wilfrid Laurier in the early years of his rule fired the popular imagination with the slogan, "The twentieth century belongs to Canada". To-day we think in more modest terms. Few competent observers venture to suggest that we shall ever be able to support, at a decent standard of living, a population of more than 35,000,000,[31] and even that figure presupposes a return to relative sanity in international trade of which there is no immediate prospect. Our natural resources, despite serious gaps, are sufficient, if properly managed, to provide us all with a reasonably full life. They are not sufficient to allow us to go on with the catch-as-catch-can, devil-take-the-hindmost methods of private enterprise, unless we are prepared to face a continuous decline in our standard of living. Capitalism is a luxury we can no longer afford.

C. CAPITAL INVESTMENT.

Of most kinds of existing capital equipment, as we shall see,[32] we have more than enough even for the days of "prosperity". Its quality is probably surpassed only by that of the United States, Germany and perhaps Great Britain. Our "producers' equipment" is far superior to our "consumers' equipment", and deficiencies in "consumers' capital" (housing, for example) we discuss elsewhere.[33] But a specific Canadian problem is that of the amount of non-Canadian investment. Who besides Canadians have stakes in the country? How much control have they? How far must we depend on them for future supplies of capital?

At January 1, 1934, the ownership of capital in Canada was estimated to be (in millions of dollars) :[34]

---

[30]*Canada Year Book*, 1934-35, p. 639.

[31]See below, p. 59.

[32]For details of equipment see *Canada Year Book*; for excess capacity see below, Chap. VII, "The Inefficiency of the System".

[33]See Chap. XIX.

[34]*Financial Post Business Year Book*, 1934, p. 53. 1935 figures of total investment not available, but figures of foreign investment (*Financial Post Business Year Book*, 1935, p. 59) are much the same as for 1934.

	Total	Can-adian	British	U.S.	Other
Govt. and municipal securities..............	5,477	4,136	516	814	11
Railways.................	3,025	1,329	908	751	37
Public utilities.............	1,645	988	105	537	15
Pulp, paper and lumber....	1,025	513	69	440	3
Mining...................	825	529	56	230	10
Metallurgical industries	900	347	45	497	11
All other industries.........	1,550	1,067	175	293	15
Financial institutions.......	800	520	110	154	16
TOTALS.............	15,247	9,429	1,984	3,716	118
—Trading and service[35]			73	162	5
Land and mortgage........			192	90	51
TOTALS.............			2,249	3,968	174

Total external investment.... $6,391,410,000.00.

Nearly a third of this represents branch plants, some 1,500 in number, five-sixths of them American.[36]

With more than sixty per cent. of our business capital Canadian-owned, discussion of the degree of foreign control of our industries may seem a waste of time. But the thing is not quite as simple as it looks.

In the first place, some of the largest blocks of foreign investment are in key industries. Of our railway securities 56 per cent. are held abroad, of pulp and paper and lumber almost 50 per cent. of metallurgical industries over 61 per cent. of public utilities almost 40 per cent. The impression conveyed by these figures, however, is subject to some qualification, for they cover not only voting stocks but also bonds, debentures and non-voting stocks which have no direct voice in shaping policy. This might have been supposed to be of special importance in the case of the Canadian National Railways, whose securities are all bonds, debentures and non-voting stock. But the Prime Minister tells us[37] that the C.N.R. "is not the property of the people of Canada except to the extent to which the people own the securities which are in default. . . . This enterprise belongs to the investors", for whom the Dominion Government simply acts as trustee.

[35]*Financial Post Business Year Book*, 1934, p. 51.

[36]*Financial Post Business Year Book*, 1934, p. 48; 1935, pp. 62-63, gives elaborate figures from reports of the Dominion Bureau of Statistics and the U.S. Bureau of Foreign and Domestic Commerce.

[37]*House of Commons Debates*, 1933, p. 2859; also pp. 2853-2854.

Second, the structure of the modern corporation makes it perfectly easy for a small minority of shareholders to wield practically absolute control. This cuts both ways. On the one hand, Canadians holding only a small proportion of the shares may control a corporation mainly owned by foreigners. The overwhelming majority of C.P.R. stock, for example, is held abroad, but the control is unquestionably Canadian. But there certainly could be, and probably are, concerns of which the reverse is true.

Taking industry by industry, the situation is well illustrated by the list at the end of this section.

That foreigners control this or that *particular* industry will trouble none but those earnest patriots who, in defiance of all the evidence, persist in believing that the Canadian capitalist is a different kind of being from the foreign, that the one is a philanthropist, the other a robber and a cheat. For the rest of us, the real importance of foreign investment in Canada is something quite different.

The interest and dividends on foreign capital in Canada amounted in 1929 to $258,907,000; in 1934 to $290,000,000.[38] This is of course off-set to some extent by returns on Canadian investments abroad, which at January 1, 1935, amounted to $1,916,700,000;[39] but the net outflow was $171,021,000 in 1929 and $230,000,000 in 1934[40]. The necessity of exporting to meet these payments notably increases our dependence on the outside world. What is more, the necessity of making most of them in United States funds is apt to frighten the Canadian Government into desperate efforts to keep the dollar at par in New York, so that when the United States deflates, as it did disastrously from the end of 1929 till the spring of 1933, Canada is dragged at its heels. This is the policy known as "Canada First".

From the socialist point of view, however, the most serious disadvantage of the large foreign investment in Canada is that even when we socialize industry it will be difficult to rid ourselves of the annual tribute to the foreign investor. The domestic owner is easily disposed of: he can be compensated, and he is also more easily subject to taxation. But this does not

[38]*Canada Year Book*, 1933, p. 601; 1934-35, p. 639.
[39]*Financial Post Business Year Book*, 1935, p. 56, gives details.
[40]*Canada Year Books*.

apply to the foreigner, who could retaliate by embargoes on our essential imports, by seizing our export credits to pay the indignant bondholders (which would be *pro tanto* an automatic embargo on our imports), or even by armed intervention. If, of course, the foreign investor becomes so frightened by the advent of a socialist government that he flings huge blocks of his securities on the market to be sold for whatever they will bring, the Canadian government would be able to buy in at nominal prices.[41] Otherwise, unless the United States goes socialist when we do, or before, or has its hands very full with industrial and political unrest (likely enough eventualities all), even a socialist Canada will probably have to give preferential treatment to the foreign investor.

How far must we depend on the foreigner for future supplies of capital? A superficial reading of our "balance of indebtedness" figures is likely to suggest that we must always "behave" in case we should not be able to get any more money from Wall Street or the City of London. But it is easy to exaggerate this bogey. A government making a forthright endeavour to eliminate the wastes of capitalism has no reason to fear that its credit will be ruined. And for that matter our need of new industrial capital for some time in the future is not likely to be pressing, and we are likely to make better use of the supply available from our own sources.

NET BALANCES OF CAPITAL EXPORT AND IMPORT 1924-1933[42]

Year	Exports	Imports	Year	Exports	Imports
1924	$54,000,000	—	1929	—	$209,000,000
1925	160,000,000	—	1930	—	212,000,000
1926	4,000,000	—	1931	$61,000,000	—
1927	6,000,000	—	1932	23,000,000	—
1928	—	$16,000,000	1933	—	61,500,000
			1934	20,000,000	—

The main implication is that a Canadian socialist government must make a plain and honest statement of its foreign trade policy and include therein the extent to which it recognizes the obligation to the foreign investor.

41Cf. the German Government's buying of Dawes and Young bonds at reduced prices caused by fear of German inflation, during 1934.

42*Financial Post Business Year Book,* 1930, p. 30; 1932, p. 25; 1933, p. 45; 1934, p. 55; 1935. p. 61. Cf. *The Canadian Economy and Its Problems,* p. 225, which puts net imports of capital in 1921 and 1929 at more than $60,000,000, and net exports, 1920-1929 at $1,250,000,000.

THE DEGREE OF NON-CANADIAN OWNERSHIP IN CANADIAN INDUSTRY.

Power: Canadian Hydro-Electric, Duke-Price, and Aluminum Limited, all foreign-controlled, produce more than a quarter of the total output.[43]

Paper: Abitibi, International Power and Paper, Spruce Falls and Anglo-Canadian, all foreign-controlled, have 40 per cent. of our newsprint capacity.[44]

Railways: Canadians own 43 per cent., British 30 per cent., Americans 25 per cent.

Telephones: Bell Telephone is almost one-quarter owned by American Telephone and Telegraph, and British Columbia Telephone is controlled by Anglo-Canadian Telephone, controlled in turn by Associated Telephone and Telegraph.[45]

Steel: A good deal of American capital is understood to be invested in Algoma Steel, one of the three great primary producers.

Motor Cars: Practically no Canadian capital here.

Agricultural Implements: International Harvester, in the years 1929-1933, did 40.3 per cent. of the business done by twenty companies who together had 90 per cent. of the market.

Nickel: Practically a monopoly of the foreign-controlled International Nickel.

Aluminum: Monopoly of the Mellon interests.

Cans: American Can does 67.5 per cent. of the business.

Chemicals: Dominated by Canadian Industries Limited (controlled by Imperial Chemical Industries and E. I. du Pont de Nemours, Inc.)[46]

Paints: Sherwin-Williams, International Paints (Canada) and Canadian Industries Limited are all foreign-controlled.[47]

Oil Refining: Imperial Oil, controlled by Standard Oil of New Jersey, dominates overwhelmingly and

[43]*Dominion Bureau of Statistics Report*, 1933.
[44]*Evidence before the Banking Committee*, 1934, p. 890.
[45]*Poor's Manual of Public Utilities*, 1933, and *Financial Post*, April 27, 1935.
[46]See below, "Concentration of Control".
[47]*Financial Post Survey*, 1934.

	Canadian Oil Companies is an affiliate of National Refining Company of Cleveland, Ohio.[48]
Rubber:	Covered almost entirely by Dunlop (controlled by Dunlop of Great Britain and Canadian Industries Limited), Dominion (controlled by U.S. Rubber), Goodyear, and Goodrich (subsidiaries of the American companies of the same names).[48]
Thread:	Canadian Spool Cotton, subsidiary of the great English firm of Coats, does 70.4% of the business.[49]
Cordage:	Plymouth Cordage, an American company, does 40.2% of the business.
Retail trade:	Dominion Stores, largest retail food chain in Canada, is 71.1% American owned. Woolworth's, Kresge's, and the Great Atlantic and Pacific Tea Company are, of course, entirely American owned.
Fish:	Maritime National Fish Corporation, subsidiary of Atlantic Coast Fisheries of New York City, does 37% of the fresh fish business of the Maritime provinces.
Life insurance:	Metropolitan, of New York, does more business in Canada than any Canadian company except Sun Life, and British and foreign companies generally do about a third of the business.[50]
Electrical Apparatus:	Almost the whole field is occupied by the Canadian General Electric, (95% of whose common stock is held by General Electric (Schenectady, N.Y.), Canadian Westinghouse, English Electric, and Kelvinator of Canada, all subsidiaries or affiliates of foreign companies.[51]
Artificial Silk:	Almost completely controlled by Canadian Celanese and Courtauld's (Canada), subsidiaries of British firms.[51]
Dairies:	Borden's, subsidiary of the great American firm of the same name, occupies an important place.[52]

[48]*Financial Post Survey*, 1934; *Poor's Manual of Industrials*, 1933.
[49]Royal Commission on Price Spreads, 1934-1935, *Evidence*, pp. 4024, 3340, 3824, 284, 400, 2968, 791.
[50]*Financial Post Business Year Book*, 1934, p. 149.
[51]*Financial Post Survey*, 1934, and *Financial Post*, February 17 and August 18, 1934.
[52]House of Commons Committee on Agriculture and Colonization, 1933. *Inquiry into the Milk Trade, Evidence*, pp. 489, 490, 494, 505, 799.

| Motion pictures: | Almost completely controlled by Famous Players Canadian, subsidiary of Paramount Publix.[53] |
| Tobacco: | Dominated overwhelmingly by Imperial Tobacco, subsidiary of British American Tobacco of London, England.[46] |

D. HUMAN RESOURCES.

What of the human resources of the Dominion? This question, for practical purposes, must be put in three ways. Is our general labour supply sufficient in quantity? Have we enough human labour in all the forms—manual and directive, technical and clerical, skilled and semi-skilled, male and female —necessary to operate Canadian industry and utilize our resources to the greatest advantage? And can we expect, in a planned system in which government control plays a much greater part, and private or privileged competition and the spur of profits a much curtailed one, the same or a changed *will to work?*

Population Prospects.

The question of *quantity* is of course the general question of population. Here it is just as evident as in the matter of natural resources that a more sober and rational outlook must replace the easy talk of Canada as a country with a boundless future. A population of 80,000,000 to 100,000,000 is quite commonly and confidently predicted. Stephen Leacock, in one of his happiest sallies, has plumped for the good round figure of 250,000,000! If this has any basis, it can only be some quite unapparent, unpredictable, and practically unimaginable technical revolution. Plans for the future cannot be based on such idle speculations, and the trends which are at present discernible and calculable are of a very different order. Careful estimates agree in placing the probable population of Canada at the end of this century at about 20,000,000, and a probable ultimate maximum of from 25,000,000 to 35,000,000.[54]

That the rate of growth in the future will not be as great

---

[53]*Report of the Registrar under the Combines Investigation Act*, 1929.

[54]An estimate of the population at certain future dates, based on a careful fitting of a logistic curve to the 1891-1931 census figures, has been made by M. C. MacLean, of the Dominion Bureau of Statistics, as follows:

1940—11,700,000	1980—19,200,000
1950—13,500,000	2000—22,800,000
1960—15,400,000	2025—26,900,000
1970—17,300,000	2050—29,600,000

as in the past is very generally admitted. The percentage increases in past decades have been as follows, and still lower figures in the future are almost certain:

1871-81—17.2%	1901-11—34.2%
1881-91—11.8	1911-21—21.9
1891-1901—11.1	1921-31—18.0

The high rates from 1901 to 1921 were largely due to expansion in the West. The rate of growth in Eastern Canada has remained almost unchanged at 15 per cent per decade during the past thirty years. There is no area comparable to the Western prairies into which population is likely to expand in the future. Large parts of Eastern Canada show stationary or declining trends, and this tendency to stop increasing and to begin to decline is already appearing in the older parts of the West.[55]

This probability of a rate of growth much slower than is popularly anticipated is an advantage rather than cause for alarm.[56] The fact is that the balance of births over deaths will probably supply all the increase we shall need or effectively absorb, though this is not likely to be accepted by the protagonists of renewed large-scale immigration. But it is particularly appropriate at this time that our past mistakes in unplanned immigration policy should be placed in a clear light.

In the thirty years 1901-1931, Canada had an excess of births over deaths of approximately 3,350,000. In the same period we received 5,100,000 immigrants, or a total possible increase of about 8,500,000. The population of Canada in fact increased by barely 5,000,000 in these thirty years. In other words, nearly 3,500,000 persons, either immigrant or native-born, failed to find a permanent economic foothold. Probably rather less than 1,000,000 of these persons who left Canada were Canadian-born, and rather more than 2,500,000 were immigrants who returned home or went to the United States. In other words, we were unable to absorb about one-quarter of our natural increase of Canadian-born, and more than one-half of our immigrants. Or, in still other words, at very considerable public expense we cajoled or persuaded three times as many immigrants to come to Canada as we were actually able to absorb.[57] The cost of

---

[55]*Proceedings of the Canadian Political Science Association*, 1933, pp. 209-210.

[56]Anyone who is still terrified by the Malthusian bogey of a rising standard of living letting loose a flood of children will find that bogey very effectively demolished by Professor Robbins in *London Essays in Economics*.

[57]See *Canadian Historical Review*, June and December, 1932, articles by Professors Roland Wilson and A. R. M. Lower.

these huge mistakes is not to be measured merely by the misdirection of public funds, but also by the vast amount of human misery and suffering and personal maladjustment involved in all this unneccessary uprooting of human beings.

We have already shown that there is no longer any ground for assuming "inexhaustible natural resources". Resources are definitely exhaustible, if not in an absolute sense, at least in a relative sense. The Canadian frontier can be further extended to-day only to a distinctly limited extent. It is true that there is room for a very substantial increase through more intensive farming. But more intensive farming is roughly balanced by greater mechanization and efficiency, and it does not promise a large basis for the support of increased numbers. Of even greater significance, however, are the trends of world agricultural markets and particularly the population of Europe, to whom at present the bulk of our staple agricultural exports go. Our whole economy has grown up on the basis of rapidly increasing consumption, especially of wheat, in Europe. But the indications are clear that the population of Western and Northern Europe is rapidly approaching a stationary level and within a very few decades will begin to decline. Quite apart, therefore, from domestic agricultural policies in European countries—which are important enough—we shall shortly face a cessation in the increase of European demand for our foodstuffs, and may have to face an actual diminution in that demand. This may or may not be balanced by increased Oriental demand. What is clear is that in the past we have been geared to a programme of expansion based on rapidly increasing exports, and that in the future we must be prepared to face stability or even a permanent diminution of exports. This must affect our whole policy of wheat acreage, agricultural capital facilities and rural settlement.

The plain fact is that in every country in the world there are now more people on the land than can be provided with a decent living. Without a spectacular recovery—of which there is no present indication—in world markets for agricultural produce, or a fundamental economic change which would provide new home markets, there is no room for new farmers anywhere; least of all, perhaps, in Canada. Statistics of farm income show clearly that agriculture had already entered a depression of its own before 1929. The table of "facilities on farm homes" quoted in Chapter I is a sufficient commentary on the standard of living of our rural population; and to anyone who imagines that the problems of Canadian agriculture are few, small, temporary, or capable of quick and easy solution, we commend a study of the facts cited in Chapter V. In the face of this situation, "back to the land" schemes cannot possibly be regarded as a direct and all-sufficient remedy for unemployment. Even if the new settler grows no more than his own food, the net economic effect is to reduce the already insufficient market for farm products. If he grows a surplus over his needs, and begins to sell his produce, he makes a further contribution to his country's well-being by depressing a price level already too low. The political effect, of course, is to remove the unemployed from the influence of "agitators" who suggest the "subversive" notion of changing the economic system, and to make combined action among the dispossessed as difficult as possible.

The "back to the land" movement is fortunately not likely to get very far. Most of the unemployed, as even Sir Edward Beatty recognizes, are too thoroughly urban to achieve a pretence of success in farming. Sir Edward's own policy is agricultural immigration. "The time has come," he says, "for us to consider plans for the further expansion of our basic industry. The most urgent need in this country is a definite plan of land settlements. . . . All the unemployed who could conceivably become successful agriculturalists should be encouraged and aided to establish themselves on the soil. When we have done what we can in this way, we should proceed to seek abroad those who by race, by experience, and by the possession of a modest amount of capital, seem adapted to become successful settlers". He suggests the modest figure of "a hundred thousand more farmers".[58] All the factual evidence which is at present available, apart altogether from the history of Canadian immigration experiments since the War, makes this a proposal to be viewed with alarm.[59] It is one of the dangers of "national government" propaganda that it may help to give credence to the benefits of a new immigration boom. In a truly planned economy the time may come when new settlement will be necessary, in the interest of the whole community. That will be for the planning author-

58"Agriculture and Prosperity: The Farmer and His Wheat—The Basis of our National Life": a speech before the Toronto Canadian Club, May 20, 1935.

59Cf. the most recent study on this subject, *The British Immigrant*, Vol. 2 in the McGill University Social Research Series, (Oxford Press, 1935). "The supply of farm labourers at present appears definitely to exceed any visible demand. The relief bureaus of our cities are already crowded with surplus farm workers who have been unable to find satisfactory employment on the land, and fresh immigrants of the farm labouring class would inevitably be forced to turn in the same direction. Continued exclusion of immigrants of this class appears to be the only reasonable policy".

ity to determine. But if and when such a renewal of immigration takes place, it must be only as part of an integrated national plan, and along general lines laid down as far as possible in advance. And our immigration policy must be more carefully planned. On principle, we should not unnecessarily interfere with the free international movement of persons, but a definite policy of just but careful selection should be applied to new permanent settlers—taking account of mental and physical health, economic adaptability, cultural assimilability, and family connections already established in Canada. It should perhaps be added that, while previous occupational experience is an important criterion, it may be misinterpreted in more than one way: thus skilled immigrant labour does not necessarily displace Canadian workers, and it is also true that English agricultural labourers do not necessarily make good Canadian farmers.

The Supply of Skill.

If our labour supply is considered in the detail of occupational skills needed to work the country's resources, man its machines, and distribute its products—in terms of carpenters, clerks, machinists, engine drivers, telephone operators, barbers and so forth—there is, to say the least, no general evidence of a shortage. It is a matter of all too common knowledge that the ranks of the unemployed today contain representatives of every craft and calling, that white-collar workers and even professional men and specialized technicians as well as the rank and file of the manual wage-earners are unable to sell their services in the labour market. We have too many farmers or at least too much wheat. "Surplus" workers have been "drained off" into relief camps. Every year, boys and girls are leaving high school, and young men and women graduating from universities, with scant prospects of decently-paid or secure employment. Skilled men are being demoted to semi-skilled jobs, and skilled and semi-skilled alike are competing for low-grade work,—and being offered low-grade wages accordingly. The problem is not one of shortage, but of deterioration of skill and energy; of widespread failure to use our human resources to the best advantage.

Yet, potentially, census measurements of the occupations of the people show every type of worker required for the production of goods and services on a modern scale to be represented.[60]

60See Dominion Bureau of Statistics, *Census Bulletin XXXI*. For a detailed analysis of the Canadian working-force see L. C. Marsh, *Employment Research* (Oxford Press, 1935), Chap. IV. Appendix B of this book gives the estimate of the division of the working population into economic classes, quoted below.

It is true that more than a million of Canada's gainfully employed, (1,130,000 in 1931) are on farms either as operatives or labourers, and another 150,000 are in mining, quarrying, logging, fishing, etc. But the remaining number, equipped to work in all the various fields of manufacturing, trade, transportation, communication and services, total as many as 2,-650,000, or more than twice as many as those engaged in the primary or extractive industries. Undoubtedly a very large proportion of this 2,650,000 are directly dependent on agriculture, but if we are thinking of the skills and daily work of our employed population it is very far from true that we are a "land of farmers". Canada, no less than other countries throughout the world, is requiring less and less of its labour supply to be devoted to winning resources from the soil and, in spite of all the "back to the land" enthusiasts, an increasing proportion of us are living and working in urban centres.[61] According to the estimates of Professor Marsh in a recent publication,[62] the "skill and status" division of the Canadian working population of 3,239,000 persons (excluding extractive occupations) is as follows:

Economic Group	Totals			Percentages		
	Males	Females	Total	Males	Females	Total
I. Owners, employers, managers, etc.............	207,290	10,720	218,010	8.0	1.6	6.7
II. Professional (and quasi - professional) classes...	122,720	118,060	240,780	4.7	18.3	7.4
III. "White - collar" and responsible manual workers.	285,450	122,160	407,610	11.0	18.9	12.6
IV. Artisans and skilled wage earners.........	384,910	48,830	433,740	14.9	7.6	13.4
V. Semi-skilled and other intermediate wage earners	430,970	318,220	749,190	16.6	49.2	23.2
VI. Unskilled and low - wage group..........	1,160,890	28,510	1,189,400	44.8	4.4	36.7
TOTAL........	2,592,230	646,500	3,238,730	100	100	100

[61]The percentages of the population in urban areas as measured at census dates since 1891 are as follows: 31.8, 37.5, 45.4, 49.5, and 54.0 (1931).
[62]*Op. cit.*, p. 319.

These figures show over a million persons in the categories of professional and quasi-professional occupations (240,800), "white-collar" and responsible manual workers (407,600), and artisans and skilled wage-earners (433,700). In proportion to the total, and excluding as it does the bulk of machine-tending operatives and of the lower-paid service occupations, this can hardly be called inadequate.

It is striking to note, however, the marked increase in the size of the groups as one moves down the occupational scale. Canadian industry and trade uses—or rather has presumably used at some time or other in the past—just under 750,000 semi-skilled employees, in routine, light, or relatively low-paid white-collar jobs: while no less than 1,189,400 workers (1,160,890 of them men) fall into the group of unskilled workers, labourers and other low-wage earners. Undoubtedly modern industrial techniques are increasing the proportion of jobs involving fairly easily-learnt skills; electric power, mechanization and a rising level of general education may render the increase of semi-skilled employments quite compatible with higher wages and greater leisure.[63] The great extent of the unskilled group—if the table quoted above had included labourers in agriculture, mining and logging, the figures would be at least another 500,000 larger[64]—is a matter for much greater concern.

Although there are few statistics on the subject, it is well known that unskilled workers are by far the largest group among the unemployed. From the detailed results of the Census survey of unemployment for the year 1930-31 which are now available, it can be shown that out of a total of 432,600 wage earners (male and female) who lost some working time from unemployment or other causes, no less than 240,500 were in unskilled work.[65] It is abundantly clear that a drive to raise the occupational levels of this great section of our wage earners is a very necessary part of a policy for the improvement of workers' standards of living. There is no simple way of achieving this. The elimination of "blind-alley" jobs which prepare the way for unskilled employment in adult life, a determined attack on casual systems of hiring and firing, the extension and improvement of primary education, the overhauling of our facilities for technical education, a re-training programme as an integral part of a

---

[63]*The Report of the Royal Commission on Price Spreads* is sufficient indication that this happy state of affairs has not become established yet: the "semi-skilled" group is particularly the group of female workers in factories and in retail stores.
[64]571,390, according to Marsh, *op. cit.*, Table 21, p. 315.
[65]*Seventh Census of Canada*, Vol. VI, 1935.

comprehensive Employment Service, are all part of the task. But the thorough-going regulation of industry and extension of government services which this implies are essentially the characteristics of a planned economy.

Incentives: From Bottom to Top.

If there is any shortage at all in our human resources, it is only in a relatively few specialized fields of skill and training. The main problem is not one of supply, but of organization. What can be attempted through socialist planning is set out fully in the various sections of this book. It is of special relevance here to point out that the appeal of a planned economy is not confined to manual wage earners and their clerical and other "white-collar" co-workers. But it is well to put up, for all to view and answer for themselves, the old bogey that with government-regulated industry, and a wider sphere within which governments are the ultimate employers, incentives will be lost.

For the "rank and file" worker, this is equivalent to saying that he will be less willing to give his best in a plant in which he has guarantees of reasonable wages and working conditions than in one in which he has none; less willing in the factory where he has an opportunity through works committees or other devices of industrial democracy to make known his views to the management than in one where he is just a cog in the wheel; less energetic in a system which stresses production as a means of raising his standards of living than in one which puts his employers' profits first; less responsible given a properly organized and juster labour market, a network of social insurance to protect him from dependency or indigence, a system of education freed from the handicaps of income inequality, than if he is left to win a "successful career" out of the economic poker-game in which a few hold most of the chips. Between reconstruction and the present system there is little doubt which the mass of wage earners would choose.

What of the technical and the managerial groups?—relatively few in numbers, but of vital importance in modern industry; and in practice responsible for its smooth running from day to day, for the translation of science into the practical production of goods and services, for the satisfactory co-ordination of persons and processes which properly constitute efficiency. Plant superintendents, personnel managers, the engineers, statisticians, economists, chemists in industry, have the same functions to perform whether they are in the service of a government, socialized or government-regulated corporations or private capitalist concerns. In a planned economy they have nothing to lose and everything to gain: in prestige, in freedom from the necessity of measuring their work by its profit-making value, in better relations with the workers under their control or affected by their work. A planned economy which puts true efficiency and better standards before profit-making, must invite the allegiance of every individual of scientific training and systematic turn of mind who has, in addition, a sense of social justice and has not soured in his hopes of human nature.

Nobody in Canada can deny that we have the technicians. The bias of our university systems, even more than in Europe, has been towards the technical and vocational degrees. We have had an industrial Research Council, but no social Research Council, for years. We are proud of our engineers; we have always been sympathetic to the ideas of scientific management which have had such strong following in the United States. It is doubtful, however, if our technical and managerial economic classes yet feel free as a group to discuss and to decide on these major issues of social organization. But Canadian socialism in particular is certain to take cognizance of their views and to welcome their adherence. It is from the top ranks, from our business leaders, company promoters and directors, however, that we are most likely to hear the objection that "we haven't got the men". From the time when "radicals" first suggested a central bank for Canada until the Bank of Canada Act became law, almost every bank president and general manager in Canada told the public it was an impossible venture, because no one in Canada had the ability to run it. "Experience", they usually said; but an able man knows where to find experienced technical assistance. Similarly the Canadian business man is, on his own showing, fully able to plan and administer the affairs of a great corporation for his own profit or that of the shareholders; but, again on his own showing, quite incompetent to apply the same technique to industry as a whole for the benefit of the public. To paraphrase J. K. Stephen:

> "Two voices are there: one is of the deep
> And one is of an old half-witted sheep,
> And, Babbitt, both are thine."

We venture to think that the explanation lies in the difference between planning for oneself and planning for the public. The business man does not really mean that planning is impossible because he and all the rest of us are fools. He really means that we are all rascals, that a socialist community would fall to pieces because workers will not work unless goaded by fear, nor business men organize and direct except from greed. But we believe that the business man's estimate of himself is, in many instances, a libel. Doctors, artists, engineers, teachers, scientists, civil servants, do their work from a variety of motives: love of the job, pride in good work, desire to do better work than some rival, desire for public recognition and respect, love of country or of humanity. The desire for the "glittering prizes" of great wealth is only one motive, and not always the strongest, even in our capitalist civilization which exalts that desire above all others. We decline to believe that the business man is essentially different from other human beings, someone to whom only sordid motives make any appeal. His activity springs from the same varied sources as other people's, much of it from a love of power, a delight in the game, which are perfectly capable of being harnessed for the public good.

We shall be told, however, that governments and public enterprises are corrupt. Private business is of course stainless and beyond reproach in this respect: witness the evidence before the Stevens committee and in the numerous New Deal investigations in the United States, to which Sir Herbert Holt objects as embodying the "bad principle" of letting the public know how much money the leaders of finance and industry are getting out of it. Of course, capitalist governments are corrupt, more or less. That is the common fate of all institutions in capitalist society, and it would be very surprising if political institutions had escaped it. But what is the main source of the corruption? Read the official records of any of our major political scandals. Contracts, bounties, tariff increases, grants of land or water-powers, guarantees of bonds: these are the invariable themes. Public men and political parties are corrupted by private business for private business. The elimination of private enterprise and its abuses in the major industries is the surest way of destroying the foundations of all but the pettiest forms of political corruption. As Professor Scott asks, "Who would want to bribe whom for what? It would be as sensible to expect the chief inspector of hotels for the C.P.R. to bribe the superintendent for C.P.R. trains, or the Deputy Minister of Railways and Canals to bribe the officials of the Department of Trade and Commerce".[66]

The population of a socialist Canada will not be angels, but neither will they be demons. They will be ordinary men and women, rather above the general human average in physique and education. They will live and work in a society which will give them every encouragement to behave decently instead of offering premiums for "putting one over" their neighbours; a society which will no longer preach honesty to its children in church and schoolroom only to "send them out to be salesmen". There will be no great corporations, no Canadian Northern, no Beauharnois, to debauch governments and parliaments and public servants and loot the public treasury. Under these conditions our technicians and even our business men—especially those of both groups for whose services capitalism can find no place— should be able to endure the ignominy of serving their country not less faithfully than they would serve the great corporations.

To those who object that capitalism is "rooted in human nature", we answer: Possibly, but so was cannibalism. We no longer eat each other. A civilization is within our reach in which we shall no longer exploit each other. It calls for no more honesty and ability than are readily available in Canada. We *have* the men. The pioneer spirit is not dead, but the frontier which it must conquer has shifted from the physical to the intellectual and spiritual.

66*Queen's Quarterly*, Summer, 1935.

CHAPTER III.

THE STRUCTURE OF CANADIAN INDUSTRY.

A. Corporate Enterprise and the Business Unit.

In the early years of the Industrial Revolution, the characteristic form of business organization was individual proprietorship. The energetic capitalist personally launched, built up and ran his own business, using his own capital or what his personal credit could secure from the bank, and taking the whole risk on his own shoulders. If the business failed, its creditors could seize all his belongings down to his last shirt. In other words, ownership and control were in a single hand, and liability was unlimited.

Canadian farming is still organized in this way, and logging for the saw-mills of Eastern Canada is often carried on similarly by jobbers and sub-contractors. Individual proprietorships survive also to a significant extent in retail business, custom and repair work, boot and shoe manufacturing, the clothing trades, small-scale construction, and the professions. In many instances, notably in the practice of law and in investment banking, an unlimited liability partnership of several persons takes the place of individual enterprise.

The Joint Stock Company.

Both the "one-man" business and the partnership, however, have in most industries given way to a more complex type of business unit. Modern mechanized production calls for larger supplies of capital than any one man or small group is usually able to furnish; and even the richest capitalist may be unwilling to risk his whole fortune in a single enterprise. He prefers to "diversify his investments" and "spread his risk". But as long as his whole fortune is liable for his investment in each enterprise, he dare not extend his activities beyond the very few businesses of which he has personal knowledge and in whose management he can accordingly take an active and intelligent part. The small saver will be even more reluctant to expose his family to the hazards of unlimited liability. Skilled workmen, civil servants, many women, most professional men, and educational and charitable institutions, are obviously not in a position to take any effective part in the management of industry, and cannot take the risks of partnership. But they would like a higher return than they can get by leaving their money in the bank or lending it at a fixed rate of interest, and many of them are willing to risk *part* of what they own, especially if they can spread the risk. On the other hand, as the combined savings of these groups amount to a large sum, business men are eager to make use of them, but would prefer to do so without undertaking to pay a fixed rate of interest which in "bad times" would lay a heavy burden on the industry.

To these problems the modern joint-stock company, or corporation, provides the solution. For the shareholder in this type of concern is no longer subject to unlimited liability for its debts. If the C.P.R., for example, should go bankrupt, the man who had bought a $25.00 share of its stock might lose his $25.00 (or whatever he had paid for the share), but he could not lose more. The creditors of the company could not walk into his house and seize his dining-room table or his wife's hat or the baby's crib. The shareholder is liable only for the value of his share.

This "limited liability", the essential element of the modern corporation, is the basis on which there has grown up a very complex entity. In the eyes of the law, the corporation is a "person", and has most of the powers, rights and privileges of a "natural person", and some which no ordinary mortal can hope to achieve. It can hold and dispose of property, enter into contracts, sue and be sued in the courts, and merge its identity in others of its kind. It may even perform the functions of an executor of wills and a guardian to minors. It may grow practically without limit, but it cannot die, except by execution in the bankruptcy court or by its own hand through voluntary liquidation. Suicide, legally forbidden to the natural person, is not only permitted to the corporation but provided with legal facilities.[1]

This "juristic person" is the creation, in Canada, either of the Dominion Parliament or some provincial legislature, or of the Dominion or a provincial government acting under a general Companies Act. The "charter" constituting the corporation is usually issued at the instance of a group of "financiers" or "promoters", who "launch" or "float" the corporation by selling its "securities" to the public.

These securities are often of almost bewildering variety.

[1]Cf. *Price Spreads Report*, pp. 13-14.

First, *bonds*: bondholders are creditors of the corporation. They receive a fixed rate of interest, which is a first charge on the company's earnings, and if the interest is not paid they may step in and seize the property. Bonds, in fact, constitute a mortgage. Accordingly there may be first and second mortgage bonds, and sometimes still others so slightly secured as hardly to deserve the name of bonds at all. *Debentures,* like bonds, pay a fixed rate of interest but carry no right to foreclose. Neither bond- nor debenture-holders have any voice in the management of the business.

Next come various kinds of *preferred stock.* Usually the holder is entitled to a specified return, for example 8 per cent. "cumulative"; that is, if the company is able to pay him only 4 per cent. this year, the other 4 per cent. accumulates against future earnings as "arrears" which must be paid before common stockholders get anything. Sometimes the preferred stock is "participating preferred", that is, entitled not only to its specified "dividend", but to a share in the earnings which remain after this has been paid. Preferred stockholders may or may not have a voice in the management of the company, some preferred being "non-voting".

Finally, there is *common stock,* sometimes of "no par value", sometimes with a face value of $100, $25, or some other stipulated amount. In either case, each share represents a certain fraction of the earning capacity of the concern, and constitutes a *pro rata* claim on the earnings which remain after payment of interest and preferred dividends.

The voting stockholders, common and preferred, are the legal owners of the undertaking. Each share has one vote at the company's annual meeting, which elects, from among the shareholders, the board of directors, remunerated by fees and responsible for general policy: payment or "passing" of dividends, accumulation of reserves, and so forth. The active work of management is carried on by a salaried official responsible to the board.

This is the type of organization which has now in most Canadian industries superseded the individual enterprise or partnership.[2] The consequences of the change are revolutionary. In the individual enterprise, as we have seen, ownership, control and management are one. For the farm and for many small industrial or trading concerns, one might almost say ownership,

[2]*Price Spreads Report*, pp. 20-23.

control, management and labour are one; for the proprietor is himself one of the small group of manual or clerical workers in the enterprise, may get much the same income as his employees, and may even, as some impoverished farmers now do, think of himself rather as "worker" than as "employer". But "the development of the modern corporation has made it possible to own without controlling, and to control without owning."[3] Labour is far removed from ownership, control or management. Management is often in the hands of salaried technicians with little or no stake in ownership and slight influence upon the main lines of policy. Ownership is scattered across a continent or "dispersed through all the world".

65.99 per cent. of the stock of the C.P.R. is held in the United Kingdom, 17.35 per cent. in the United States, 4.43 per cent. in other foreign countries, 12.23 per cent. in Canada. Of 180,000 C.P.R. security-holders, 50,000 are Canadians. Holdings of ordinary shares by the directors amount to 34,024 shares, or 4.06 per cent. of the total; holdings by Canadian directors to 30,524; or 3.64 per cent. The largest holding of any director is less than 1.4 per cent., and this is almost three times as much as the next largest.[4]

The distribution of the shares of our four largest banks in 1933 was:[5]

Location	Mont-real	Royal	Com-merce	Nova Scotia	Total
Montreal..............	181,200	103,742	41,882	11,335	338,159
Montreal, non-resident..	25,023	—	—	—	25,023
Montreal, in U.S.A......	4,324	—	—	—	4,324
Toronto..............	41,925	50,949	132,435	31,166	256,475
Halifax..............	15,591	74,484	22,316	46,532	158,923
Calgary..............	2,635	3,432	1,523	395	7,985
Charlottetown.........	215	5,084	1,469	1,999	8,767
Regina..............	340	3,099	1,078	310	4,827
Saint John..........	2,661	4,172	1,933	7,345	16,111
Vancouver...........	6,729	5,428	4,770	1,221	18,148
Winnipeg............	3,965	9,169	3,885	1,948	18,967
New York...........	33,778	69,634	52,065	15,649	171,126
London..............	41,614	14,923	36,644	2,100	101,165
Georgetown, Br. Guiana.	—	5,884	—	—	—
TOTAL..........	360,000	350,000	300,000	120,000	1,130,000

3*Ibid.*, p. 14.
4C. P. R. annual report, 1934; speech by Sir E. W. Beatty to the Toronto Canadian Club, January 16, 1933; records of the United States Securities and Exchange Commission, quoted in *Financial Post*, June 29, 1935.
5*Financial Post*, May 12, May 19, June 2, August 18, 1934.

Shares of International Nickel, according to the president's report in the Montreal *Gazette* of March 28, 1934, were held 21.63% in Canada, 42.55% in the United States, 33.56% in Great Britain.

Minority Controls.

Clearly, in corporations like these, not more than a handful of shareholders can attend the annual meetings, and as everyone knows, not more than a handful ever does. Only rarely is there the faintest attempt even to question the directors' policy. Indeed, as the Royal Commission on Price Spreads points out in its *Report,* (p. 45), there is often no opportunity. The annual meetings, "as is well known, are more often concerned with securing the speedy performance of the statutory requirements, including the formal sanction of the company's annual statement, than with a serious examination by the shareholders into the company's activities and present position. The auditor of the company, who in theory represents the shareholders, need not be present and, indeed, is seldom available for questioning".

Rarely is any protest effective. For the board ordinarily holds enough "proxies" from the absent shareholders (power to vote on behalf of the absentees) to carry the day by a sweeping majority. An opposition group may of course circularize the shareholders, inviting them to send in proxies in its favour instead of the board's. But only a very wealthy group can do this; for while the board's proxy forms are printed and circulated at the expense of the company, the opposition must foot the bill out of its own pocket. The result is that it is no longer necessary to own a majority of shares in order to gain control. A tiny minority, even without special legal devices, may wield practically unchallenged power, and the directors nominally elected by and responsible to the whole body of shareholders, become in fact a self-perpetuating oligarchy.[6]

As we have seen, less than a sixth of C.P.R. stock is held in Canada. But almost all the directors are Canadians, and the control is unquestionably Canadian. In the Royal Bank, less than a third of the shares are held in Montreal, but control almost certainly rests there. In the Bank of Commerce, less than half the shares are held in Toronto, but Toronto controls. *The Canadian Macmillan Report*[7] shows that directors of our banks hold

[6]The debt of this whole chapter to A. A. Berle and G. C. Means, *The Modern Corporation and Private Property,* and to the *Report of the Royal Commission on Price Spreads,* Chapter III, is obvious.
[7]p. 101.

only 3.8 per cent. of the stock. *Financial Post* lists of shareholders with more than a hundred shares show directors and their families holding about 3¾ per cent. in the Bank of Montreal, a little over 3 per cent. in th Royal Bank, less than 3⅛ per cent. in the Bank of Commerce, and 4¾ per cent. in the Bank of Nova Scotia[8] But Sir Charles Gordon, president of the Bank of Montreal, admitted to the Banking and Commerce Committee of the House of Commons that the power of the mass of shareholders was a shadow. Mr. R. B. Hanson, chairman of the committee, and Mr. C. G. Power, M.P., had declared that they "did not believe directors were chosen by the shareholders" and suggested that vacancies were filled "by the remaining directors". Mr. Power then asked, "The shareholders have little or nothing to say in the choice of directors, is that fair?" Sir Charles Gordon: "How could they, Mr. Power? They come to an annual meeting and the shareholders are nearly all represented by proxy and those that are in the room are not going to make any objections at the last moment because they know those proxies are standing there and they are going to get voted down anyhow if they propose another slate."[9]

"Minority control", observes the Royal Commission on Price Spreads, "is most probable in a large concern where no one shareholder owns an appreciable proportion of the shares"—a sufficient comment on the theory that diffusion of ownership means economic democracy.

To gain "a general idea of the relative importance" of minority control in the Canadian corporate structure, the Commission sent out a questionnaire to the 145 largest non-financial corporations, asking for "the names and holdings of all shareholders who owned more than 1 per cent. of any class of stock issued, and for the total number of shareholders with less than 1 per cent. The information obtained . . . was analyzed to discover the relationship of ownership and control. . . . We classified as *privately owned* those companies with 80 per cent. or more of the voting stock owned by one person or group; as *majority controlled* those with 50 per cent. to 79.99 per cent.; as *minority controlled* those with 20 per cent. to 49.99 per cent. Companies with less than 6 per cent. of voting stock held by one group were classified as *management controlled,* on the assumption that with such a wide division of ownership the entrepreneurial group

---

[8]May 12, May 19, June 2, August 18, 1934.

[9]*Evidence before the Banking Committee*, April 19, 1934, pp. 510-511. Cf. *Price Spreads Report*, p 15.

could perpetuate itself in control; those with ownership ranging from 6 per cent. to 19.99 per cent. were regarded as *joint-minority-management controlled.*"[10] The table below shows the results.

	No. of companies	Assets	% of total assets
Management control............	26	$2,290,058,000	42.8
Joint-minority-management........	41	987,609,000	18.5
Minority control................	29	837,157,000	15.6
Majority control................	28	756,909,000	14.2
Private control................	21	476,941,000	8.9

Over 76 per cent. of the assets are controlled by groups owning less than half the voting stock, over 60 per cent. by management or joint-minority-management. If we leave out 40 subsidiary companies, the corresponding figures are 93.5 per cent. and 82.4 per cent.

"The significance of the results", adds the *Report,* "is further emphasized by the fact that very few directors owned more than 1 per cent. of the voting stock of the companies they directed. In 91 of the 145 companies, no directors owned more than 1 per cent. of the voting stock. Of the 101 directors of the other 54 companies (owning more than 1 per cent. of such stock) 60 held between 1 and 3 per cent., 25 between 3 and 10 per cent., 7 between 10 and 20 per cent., 5 between 20 and 30 per cent., and 4 above 30 per cent".[11]

As a further specific example we may note the flour milling companies.[12]

Company	Stocks		Directors' holdings
Lake of the Woods...	Preference:	$1,500,000	1.27%
	Common:	5,634,450	2.82%
Maple Leaf..........	A Preference:	2,930,000	.87% (7.87%)
	B Preference:	500,000	8.20% (24.20%)
	Common:	1,000,000	4.70% (24.50%)
Ogilvie.............	Preference:	2,000,000	3.06%
	Common:	2,500,000	5.41%
St. Lawrence........	Preference:	575,000	5.65%
	Common:	1,200,000	41.60%
Western Canada.....	Preference:	2,413,000	.11%
	Common:	2,205,000	10.28%

Figures in brackets indicate subsidiary Company holdings.

10*Report*, pp. 15-16.
11*Ibid.*, pp. 16-17, 325-427.
12*Ibid., Evidence*, pp. 3762-3774.

The scope of minority control has been enormously extended by the development of the "holding company" and "pyramiding". We have in Canada 276 industrial companies with gross assets of over $1,000,000, totalling $3,586,863,000. Of these, 29 are "pure" holding companies, owning nothing but the shares of other companies. These 29 control 19.5 per cent. of the total gross assets involved. A further 14 companies are "mixed", operating and holding, but primarily holding. They account for another 16.2 per cent. of the assets. "Pure" operating companies, 121 in number, control only 17.4 per cent. of the total assets.

As an example of "pyramiding", the Royal Commission on Price Spreads cites Drug Holding Company. G. Tamblyn Limited has a capitalization of $700,000 non-voting preferred and $20,000 voting no-par common, divided into 28,000 shares, of which Drug Holding Company has 14,100. Drug Holding Company itself has 200,000 shares, of which 122,978 are held by the Tamblyn estate. Mr. Tamblyn's executors are thus, without any considerable investment, "in effective control" of G. Tamblyn Limited.[13]

Standard Oil of New Jersey owns 65 per cent. of the stock of Imperial Oil, which owns almost all the preferred and 58 per cent. of the common of International Petroleum, 75 per cent. of Royalite Oil (which holds 51 per cent. of Dalhousie Oil), and 85.2 per cent. of Foothills Oil and Gas (which holds 58 per cent. of Southwest Petroleum). In other words, Standard Oil of New Jersey, though providing only 65 per cent. of 60 per cent., (that is, 39 per cent.) of the share capital, has complete control of International Petroleum. Similarly it controls Dalhousie Oil through what amounts to a 25 per cent. investment, Southwest Petroleum by 32. *British American Tobacco* of London, England, holds about 39½ per cent. of the stock of Imperial Tobacco Company of Canada, and the Tobacco Securities Trust Company of London (representing the same interests) has almost another 14½ per cent. Imperial in turn owns 50 per cent. of National Tobacco, 87 per cent. of B. Houde Company, 55½ per cent. of Tuckett's. This means that British-American controls National Tobacco by an investment of about 26 per cent., B. Houde Company by 45 per cent., Tuckett's by 28⅝ per cent. *C.P.R.* owned in 1932 51.6 per cent. of Consolidated Mining and Smelting, which in turn owned over 90 per cent. of West Kootenay Power, the majority of shares of Coast Copper, a "'controlling interest"

13*Ibid., Report,* pp. 18-19.

in Solar Development Company, Iva Fern Mines, Northern Lead-
Zinc and Pacific Coast Terminals, 53 per cent. of Buena Vista
Mining, 60 per cent. of Sunlock Mines, 93 per cent. of George
Gold Copper, and an option on 52 per cent. of the stock of Bridge
River Consolidated Mines. The controlling group in C.P.R.,
therefore, holding less than 20 per cent. of the stock, controls
"Smelters" by a 10 per cent. investment, West Kootenay and
George Gold Copper by 9 per cent., Coast Copper, Solar Develop-
ment, Iva Fern, Northern Lead-Zinc, Pacific Coast Terminals,
Buena Vista, Sunlock, and Bridge River by about 5 per cent.
American Telephone and Telegraph holds only 24.3 per cent. of
the stock of Bell Telephone Company of Canada, which in its
turn owns only minority interests in New Brunswick Telephone
and Maritime Telephone and Telegraph; but all of these are considered integral parts of the one A. T. & T. system. *Power
Corporation's* "substantial stock interest" gives it virtual control of Winnipeg Electric and subsidiaries and Southern Canada
Power, and it avowedly controls Canada Northern Power and
East Kootenay Power. For mill-controlled bakeries, the figures
show:

Company	Stocks		Holdings of Parent Company	Of Directors
Canada Bread.......	First preference	$1,250,000		.66%
	Second preference	2,500,000	21.8%	.22%
	Common	25,000	50.0%	.83%
Canadian Bakeries...	First preference	913,000		.15%
	Second preference	1,000,000	39.0%	12.50%
	Common	100,000	62.5%	1.48%
Consolidated Bakeries	Management	150	66.7%	33.33%
	Common	3,184,000	13.8%	9.12%
Eastern Bakeries	Preference	600,000	33.3%	3.75%
	Common	100	50.0%	14.04%
Inter-City Bakeries..		2,114,500	55.8%	3.87%
Inter-City Western ..	Preference	390,000	20.2%	—
	Common	1,300,000	88.5%	(negligible)

A very small investment in the parent or holding company
may secure control over millions of "other people's money"
invested in subsidiaries.[14]

14Information as to Imperial Tobacco from *Evidence before the House of Commons Committee on Price Spreads and Mass Buying,* 1934, pp. 1451, 1458, 1462, 1467, 1468, 1518.
Information on C.P.R. and Consolidated Mining and Smelting from *Evidence before the
Banking Committee,* 1934, p. 18, and from *Financial Post Surveys of Corporate Securities,*
1933 and 1934; on bakeries, Royal Commission on Price Spreads, 1934-1935, *Evidence,*
pp. 3767-3769. Information on other companies from *Financial Post Survey of Corporate
Securities,* 1934.

Alternative or supplementary mechanisms for securing the same ends are provided by the trust companies, life insurance companies and investment trusts (these last still in their infancy in Canada.) The shareholders' investment (capital and reserves) in our three largest trust companies in 1934 amounted to $16,500,000. The holdings of the controlling groups in these companies, to judge from the analogy of the banks and the C.P.R., were probably trifling. But the total assets controlled by the three companies reached the staggering sum of $1,849,683,732. Similarly our two largest Canadian life insurance companies, with a shareholders' investment (capital and shareholders' surplus) of $11,548,919, controlled assets of $907,741,241. The 876 shareholders of Sun Life, investing only $9,196,009, controlled assets of $665,378,716.[15] Of these makers of modern Canada the historian may write, "They risked a few hundred thousands and gained an empire".

A further means of securing control without venturing any appreciable quantity of one's own money is to issue enough bonds, debentures, and perhaps preferred stock to provide the necessary funds, reserving to an inner ring common stock, representing a negligible cash investment or none at all, but securing to this group absolute control. The classic example of this is the Canadian Northern Railway. Mackenzie and Mann got the funds (a) from cash subsidies by the Dominion, provinces and municipalities: $38,874,148, (b) from sales of land granted by the Dominion, provinces and municipalities: $16,603,295, (c) from mortgages on granted lands: $17,776,514, (d) from debentures guaranteed by the Dominion and provincial governments: $211,641,140, (e) from loans by the Dominion (never repaid). Mackenzie and Mann invested not one penny of their own money. But they held all the common stock, until they graciously agreed to part with 40 per cent. of it to the Dominion government in exchange for a loan, never repaid. The other 60 per cent. they later sold to the Dominion for $10,000,000 cash, after the Royal Commission had pronounced the shareholders' equity non-existent.[16] It was perhaps this feat which earned for Sir William Mackenzie at his death the pious tribute of the Montreal *Gazette* to "a great empire builder". The *Gazette* did not specify whose empire.

A contemporary example of an enterprise financed mainly

---

[15]*Financial Post Survey of Corporate Securities*, 1934; *Financial Post Business Year Book*, 1934; *Poor's Manual of Financial Corporations*, 1934; *Financial Post*, March 16 and 23, 1935.

[16]*Report of the Royal Commission on Transportation*, 1917. (Drayton-Acworth Report).

by bonds and non-voting stock is British Columbia Telephone, whose capital consists of $10,000,000 in bonds, $5,500,000 in non-voting preferred and preference stocks, and $4,500,000 in ordinary (voting) stock. The $4,500,000 have complete control, the $15,500,000 have none.[17]

Honeydew Company, Limited, has $1,500,000 of non-voting preferred and $108,500 of voting common. Analysis of the 145 largest non-financial corporations "showed that the non-voting stock method of control was not general"; but of $220,000,000 preferred, Class A and common sold to the public between 1926 and 1930 "only some 16 per cent. carried unrestricted voting rights".[18]

This kind of thing, of course, greatly increases the rigidity of our financial structure. A notable example is the pulp and paper industry. "Between 1925 and 1929", says a paper read to the Canadian Political Science Association in May, 1935, "total investment in pulp and paper rose $194,000,000. Of this, over $94,000,000 or 48½ per cent. came from bonds or debentures, and over $44,000,000 or 22½ per cent. from preferred stocks. Moreover, the Canada Power and Paper merger involved issue of $35,466,700 of new debentures for common stock of Laurentide and Wayagamack, and the Abitibi mergers increased preferred stocks by $16,012,300. The result was that while total investment rose 28½ per cent., interest in funded debt rose almost $7,000,000 or 82 per cent., and preferred dividend requirements almost $3,500,000, or 79 per cent. If this policy of rigid capital charges succeeds, it throws an undue share of the burden of depression on wage earners; the firm must cut wage bills to the bone to meet its bond interest. If . . . the policy breaks down, the result is bankruptcy, serious injury to the industry's credit, a violent shock to public confidence, dislocation of business generally, and ruin to investors beguiled by high-sounding phrases like 'first mortgage gold sinking fund bonds', into an illusion of security".

None of these developments touch the formal structure of the corporation. In legal theory, ultimate control is still vested in the shareholders. But our business leaders are apparently feeling less and less need of preserving this fiction. Senator Webster controlled the F. P. Weaver Companies without owning a single share, simply by lending the majority shareholder the

---

[17]*Poor's Manual of Public Utilities*, 1933; *Report of the Royal Commission on Price Spreads*, p. 20.

[18]*Price Spreads Report*, p. 20.

money to buy his share and holding the shares as security for the loan.[19] The auditors of the Stevens Committee were "informed" that Swift Canadian Company was controlled by Swift and Company of Chicago, but the stock is held in the names of individuals.[20] And in a number of recent instances the controlling group has boldly cast aside all pretence and placed control *de jure* as well as *de facto* in its own hands.

The two favourite legal devices for this purpose are the "voting trust" and "management preferred shares". In Asbestos Corporation the owners of the 113,586 shares placed effective control till 1941 in the hands of a voting trust of five persons. The capital structure of Consolidated Bakeries consists of 318,-440 ordinary shares carried in the books at $3,184,430, and 3 "management preferred" shares at $150. Control of the board of directors is legally vested in the "management preferred", a "majority" of which are held by Ogilvie Flour Mills: $100 controlling more than $3,000,000! Similarly Beauharnois Corporation, before it was reorganized, had 1,719,995 ordinary shares and 5 management preferred. Absolute control, till 1939, was to belong to the latter.[21]

What even legal theory is beginning to recognize and consecrate we may safely regard as established practice. Only an economic Rip van Winkle can now deny the divorce between ownership and control in the modern corporation.

Financial Manipulation.

The more realistic protagonists of big business, however, will probably reply boldly, "Well, what of it? What's wrong with it? Everyone knows the ordinary shareholder is far too ill-informed to take any intelligent part in running 'his' business. Why not admit it, and place control in the hands of 'men who know how', 'business leaders of proven capacity'?"

The defense is plausible. But it overlooks or evades two crucial facts: that the controlling group is utterly irresponsible, answerable to no one but itself; and that the interests of owners and controllers may clash. "Men who know how" to do what? "Proven capacity" to do what? In some instances, it seems clear, the answer must be "to do the shareholders". It is perfectly easy for the controllers, with only a trifling stake in the ownership of an industry, to profit not only at the expense of

---

[19]Montreal, *Gazette* report of proceedings in Superior Court at Quebec, October 14, 1934.
[20]House of Commons Committee on Price Spreads and Mass Buying. *Evidence*, p. 2376.
[21]*Financial Post Survey of Corporate Securities*, 1933

labour (this was often at least equally true of the "one-man" business), but also at the expense of the virtually helpless small investors, the "widows and orphans" in whose behalf capitalist propaganda is always so vociferous.

A board of directors may, for example, decide to withhold dividends: down goes the stock. The directors decide to resume dividends: up goes the stock. A director with advance knowledge of these manoeuvres can obviously make a very good thing out of them, though they do the company no good and may ruin a multitude of small investors.[22]   And this is only one of a number of ways of manipulating a company's affairs for stock exchange dealings which, though profitable to the "insiders", may be disastrous for the industry and its owners.

Or the controllers may shift profits from one class of stock to another, or from a subsidiary to a parent company (or vice versa), or from one subsidiary to another, in which they have a larger interest.   The provincial Royal Commission of 1925-1926 on the Nova Scotia coal industry found that for many years the Dominion Steel Corporation had been transferring coal from Dominion Coal Company, its mining subsidiary, to Dominion Iron and Steel Company, its steel mills, at prices which meant in effect that the coal mines were subsidizing the steel mills.   The Commission does not state the interest of the controlling group in either subsidiary; but clearly this sort of procedure *might* be used in a way that would mean profits for the controllers, losses for the owners.   Similarly a milling company which controlled, without owning, a chain of bakeries, could transfer flour to the bakeries at a price profitable to the mills but higher than the ordinary commercial price and correspondingly unprofitable to the bakeries.   This seems to be precisely what has at times happened in Canada.[23]

Or, again, the controllers may sell their private property to the corporation at an unduly high price, or buy part of the corporation's property at a bargain.   If the controlling group can make a gross profit of, for example, $2,000,000 on such transactions, and holds 55 per cent. of the corporation's stock, the net profit would be $1,100,000, at the expense of the remaining shareholders.

22Cf. an article by F. W. Wegenast, K.C., *Financial Post*, February 17, 1934, and *Price Spreads Report*, p. 43.

23L.S.R. pamphlet, *Combines and the Consumer*, p. 3.   For details, see *Report* by the Registrar under the Combines Investigation Act, on the Bread-Baking Industry, 1931, p. 41; also, Royal Commission on Price Spreads, 1934-1935. *Evidence*, pp. 3631-3634, 3694.

Then there is the chance to 'squeeze' both labour and investors (and sometimes the primary producer into the bargain) by
paying huge salaries and bonuses to the "great executives" in
the style of Mr. Wiggin and his friends of the Chase National
Bank, who "all sat in together". Something rather like this has
been uncovered in Canada in the milk trade and the Imperial
Tobacco Company, which, during one five-year period, distributed
200,000 shares to Sir Mortimer Davis and 220,000 to twenty-five
or thirty other executives at 40 per cent. below par value.[24]

Data on operations of these kinds in Canada are not very
plentiful, but it seems likely that as they have happened in the
United States, they may not infrequently have happened here
also.[25]

This sort of thing makes nonsense of the traditional arguments for the profit incentive. Adam Smith, who developed
those arguments, lived and died in a pre-Industrial Revolution
world, a world of individual proprietorships and partnerships.
The few joint stock companies of his own day he unhesitatingly
classed with government enterprises as inherently and hopelessly
inefficient. For such a world, the notion that the lure of profit
would stimulate the owner-controller-manager to bring the business to maximum efficiency had obviously a good deal of relevance. But in our world of great corporations that relevance is
fast disappearing. If the shareholder does not join the controlling group, "his title to ownership merely gives him the right to
share *pro rata* in the profits and losses of the enterprise. The
actual distribution of the proceeds depends upon the decision of
the directors who legally control the business. Thus more and
more the real position of the holder of ownership shares—common stock—becomes that of a security holder who is almost
divorced from the control of the property nominally owned, and
whose main interest is in the allocation of earnings made to him
by those in control.

" . . . Control over the instruments and physical assets of
production and distribution is passing from the property owner
to centralized managerial groups. Those who direct the modern
corporation are, more often than not, the owners of only a neg-

---

24On milk, see *Combines and the Consumer*, p. 11; on Imperial Tobacco, Committee on
Price Spreads, 1934. *Evidence*, p. 1567. Imperial Tobacco has a by-law under which
5% of the net profits go to the president, vice-presidents and directors, "as the president
and vice-presidents may determine", but as these bonuses vary with net profits, the shareholders will be "squeezed" only if unduly large amounts are set aside as reserves and
unduly small dividends paid out. Shareholders of Imperial Tobacco do not seem to have
suffered seriously in this respect! Labour is another matter.

25On the abuses of refinancing and reorganization, see *Price Spreads Report*, pp. 36-38,
349-363.

ligible proportion of the company's stock. It follows that the returns from profitable management of the corporation affect them directly only to a relatively minor degree, on the other hand, the stockholder to whom the profits accrue has less and less to do with the direction of the corporation".[26] Often the salaried technicians who carry on active management are concerned with profit scarcely at all. To the extent that they seek *long run* profit as an index or productive efficiency they may easily find themselves in conflict with the controllers, whose motto is "quick returns *for us*". The controllers, as we have seen, often stand to gain most not by promoting efficiency of production but by doing the opposite.

Corporate Reserves.

The owners have virtually ceased to play any part except the supplying of capital, and much even of this function is slipping away from them. Individual saving is giving way to saving by the corporations themselves, which reinvest large parts of their profits. In the 25 years 1908-1933, Imperial Tobacco and subsidiaries seem to have reinvested undivided profits of $21,961,523 (exclusive of the very large reserve of $3,954,617 against lands, buildings and equipment valued at $6,085,074).[27] Of the $100,-035,000 assets of the T. Eaton Company Limited, at least $42,-502,000 represents undivided profits.[28] Simpson's Limited (1929) assets of $35,137,602 include $4,513,632 of undivided profits.[29] Imperial Oil, from its incorporation in 1880 till 1930, had secured, according to its vice-president, $64,094,530 from stock issues and $75,163,998 from undivided profits reinvested.[30] Its 1934 balance sheet puts earned surplus at $95,400,000.[31]

The Steel Company of Canada, with assets of $61,956,705 shows earned surplus at $12,884,002.[32] The decision of how much shall be paid out as dividends, how much reinvested, rests of course with the small controlling group.

Even upon the supply of individual savings, the effects of changes in the rate of profit are not always easy to forecast. The millionaire saves, willy-nilly, a large and fairly constant proportion of his income simply because he can find nothing else to do

26*Ibid.*, p. 15.
27Committee on Price Spreads, 1934. *Evidence*, pp. 1443-1486.
28*Ibid.*, pp. 3056, 3066-67, 3072-3, 3085.
29*Ibid.*, pp. 2753, 2755.
30Banking and Commerce Committee, 1932. Inquiry into the Price of Gasoline. *Evidence*, p. 75.
31*Financial Post*, April 12, 1935.
32*Financial Post*, April 6, 1935.

with it. The rate of profit makes little difference in the amount of his savings. The middle-class saver, putting by enough for a fixed future income, may actually save more if the rate of return falls. The working-class saver has his eye on the total sum he can accumulate, not the current return; and most of his savings are likely to be deposits in banks at a fixed rate of interest. It is quite possible that individual savers as a whole would save more if there were not variable profit at all but only a fixed interest.[33] At all events the lure of profit, for the owners, is no longer what it was in the early years of our national existence, for the owner is a different being, economically.

B. CONCENTRATION OF CONTROL.

Not less catastrophic in its effect on traditional ideas is the expansion in the power of a few individuals which corporate enterprise has made possible. In the hey-day of laissez-faire the energetic capitalist-owner-controller-manager could hardly touch more than the one industry he could know thoroughly. Now a handful of business men, without even any considerable stake in the ownership of industry, can dominate enterprises covering almost every imaginable economic activity from cement to razor blades, from oil refining to brewing.

The revolutionary results of the supercession of individual enterprise by the corporation have been intensified and widened by the spectacular development of concentration of control within the realm of corporate enterprise. This has had two distinct aspects: on the one hand, concentration within a single industry or group of closely related industries; on the other, inter-industrial concentration, bringing the control of many different industries into a few hands.

Within each industry the tendency towards bigger and bigger units has been to a large extent the result of mergers between corporations. Since 1869, when the first merger of the modern type took place in Canada, there have been two hundred important consolidations. Between 1900 and 1933, there took place 374 consolidations, involving the absorption of 1,145 concerns. The two most active periods in the movement were 1909-1912, which witnessed 58 consolidations involving 244 companies, and 1923-1930, with 253 consolidations involving 709 companies. In 1910, there were 22 consolidations, absorbing 112 concerns; in

---

[33]See Gustav Cassel, *Nature and Necessity of Interest.*

1928, 68 absorbing 195; in 1929, 62 absorbing 149.[34] Some of these combines were "horizontal", uniting two or more companies producing the same product, as in power, cement, steel, asbestos, chemicals, nickel, textiles, canned goods, flour. bread, dairy products, and tobacco. Some were "vertical", taking in firms which dealt with different stages of a particular commodity or group of commodities, as the flour mills took over bakeries; the steel mills, coal mines; metal mines, refineries, and so forth. Some of the newer industries—automobiles, radios and artificial silk, for example—have from the outset been in the hands of a few great corporations.

Monopoly Capitalism.

Because of these tendencies, which have "marked the development of every industrial country in recent years",[35] we describe modern capitalism as "monopoly capitalism". Strictly speaking, monopoly means a single seller, with absolute and complete control of the supply in the market. Few industries in Canada, outside of certain public utilities, have reached this stage. "The more important", says the Royal Commission on Price Spreads, "are explosives, nickel and certain heavy chemical lines". It might have added cement.

"Monopoly, however, considered as any form of industrial organization with sufficient control over the supply of a commodity to enable the organization to modify the price to its own advantage, has made great headway. . . .

". . . In industries where there is monopolistic domination, a large measure of control may rest with a single concern, in spite of the fact that it is not alone in the field. Examples are cement, tobacco, meat packing, petroleum products, fruit and vegetable canning. In others, two or three concerns may dominate the market. In the latter case, agreements among a few producers may cause the public to suffer many of the disadvantages of monopoly with few of the potential economic advantages of centralized control or operation. At times, as in the electrical manufacturing and tin plate industries, these agreements are international, operating through control and exchange of patents and through agreements regarding markets. Under such international cartels, any control which the State might wish to exercise through reduction or removal of

[34]*Price Spreads Report*, p. 28. Cf. a series of special articles in the *Financial Post*, February-April, 1932.
[35]*Price Spreads Report*, p. 48.

customs duty, would be of little or no effect; foreign goods could be prevented from entering the market to any extent, duty or no duty.

"Another type of monopolistic control, usually comprising a larger number of producers or traders and representing all or nearly all the members of an industry, is exemplified by the combination of the eight manufacturers of rubber footwear in Canada. . . . The methods of such combinations vary; control of price is usually secured by a simple price-fixing agreement enforced by trade association supervision and . . . penalties. . . . The price agreement may be supplemented by a production or sales quota arrangement, by provisions for allocating customers and sales territories, or by eliminating competing plants by joint purchase or by a price war. . . . The establishment of a joint selling agency, such as has been attempted in the canning industry, can be of great benefit to its principals. . . .

" . . . Potential competition and the competition of substitute commodities are not always effective in protecting the public against monopoly. . . . Inter-industrial agreements can nullify the effect of the latter"—

with special ease in Canada, where inter-industrial concentration of control, as we shall see, is very advanced—

"and newcomers to an industry can be quickly assimilated".[36]

Nevertheless, there are those who insist that Canadian business as a whole is still competitive, that any considerable degree of concentration is altogether exceptional. Are they right?

Banking, Trust Companies, and Insurance.

Consider, first, finance. There were once more than forty banks in Canada. There are now ten. Of these, the three largest do 70 per cent. of the business, the four largest 80 per cent.; and though they compete strenuously in service, they present a united front on interest rates.[37]

Trust companies are much more numerous. *The Financial Post Business Year Book* for 1935 lists over forty, with total assets of $2,553,694,019. But the Montreal Trust Company alone accounts for almost a third of this, and the four largest

---

[36]Quotations from *Price Spreads Report*, pp. 48-49.

[37]*Financial Post Business Year Book*, 1935, p. 131. For sidelights on this, see *Evidence before the Banking and Commerce Committee of the House of Commons*, 1934, pp. 505 and 532; and A. H. Abramson, "Is Canadian Banking Competitive?" in the *Canadian Forum* for February, 1935.

companies (Montreal, Royal, National, Toronto General) for almost 78 per cent. Loan companies, though much less important, illustrate the same tendency. *The Business Year Book* lists over thirty, with combined assets of $205,791,934. Three of these, however, have 82½ per cent. of the total.

In life insurance, over sixty companies, Canadian, British, and foreign, have total assets (excluding foreign assets of outside companies) of $2,313,470,357. But Sun Life has almost 29 per cent. of this total; Sun, Metropolitan and Canada Life together have half, the six largest companies over two-thirds.[38]

In addition to this, the big trust companies, insurance companies, loan companies and investment trusts are closely linked with the banks, and, less closely, with each other. The President of the Bank of Montreal is president of the Royal Trust Company and sixteen of Royal Trust's twenty-five directors are directors of the Bank of Montreal,[39] of which Royal Trust is the largest single shareholder, controlling over 11,000 shares. Four of the fifteen directors of Sun Life are directors of the Bank of Montreal, in which Sun Life is the fourth largest shareholder (3,100 shares).[40] Similarly, the chairman of the Royal Bank is president of the Montreal Trust Company, eleven of whose twenty-four directors are directors of the Royal Bank.[41] Montreal Trust in turn holds 13,358 shares of Royal Bank Stock.[42] Montreal Trust Company stock is not for sale in the open market and cannot be sold except with the approval of the directors.[43]

The Canadian Bank of Commerce holds 4 per cent. of the stock of National Trust Company (1,200 shares).[44] National Trust returns the compliment by holding 1,404 shares of Canadian Bank of Commerce.[45] Ten of the thirty-four directors of the National Trust are also directors of the Canadian Bank of Commerce.[46]

Further interlocking between the banks and other financial institutions is shown by the following table:[47]

[38]*Financial Post*, March 16, 1935.
[39]*Evidence before the Banking Committee*, 1934, pp. 181, 495; *Financial Post*, March 23, 1935.
[40]*Financial Post*, May 12, 1934; March 16, 1935.
[41]*Evidence before the Banking Committee*, 1934, pp. 188, 529; *Financial Post*, March 23, 1935.
[42]*Financial Post*, August 18, 1934.
[43]*Evidence before the Banking Committee*, 1934, p. 528.
[44]*Evidence before the Banking Committee*, 1934, p. 545.
[45]*Financial Post*, June 2, 1934.
[46]*Evidence before the Banking Committee*, 1934, p. 185; *Financial Post*, March 23, 1935.
[47]*Evidence before the Banking Committee*, 1934, pp. 143-190; *Financial Post Survey of Corporate Securities*, 1934; *Financial Post*, March 16 and March 23, 1935.

Institution	Bank of Montreal	Royal Bank	Bank of Commerce	Bank of Nova Scotia	Bank of Toronto	Dominion Bank	Banque Canadienne Nationale	Imperial Bank	Barclay's Bank
	Number of directors from each bank								
Royal Trust	16	—	—	—	—	1	—	—	1
Montreal Trust	—	11	—	—	—	1	—	—	—
National Trust	—	3	10	3	—	—	—	—	—
Toronto General Trust	—	—	2	2	2	3	—	2	—
Eastern Trust	—	1	—	3	—	—	—	—	—
Crown Trust	1	—	—	—	1	1	—	—	—
Northern Trust	—	2	1	1	—	—	—	—	—
Canada Permanent Trust	—	—	1	—	3	1	—	—	—
Trust Général	—	—	1	—	—	—	5	—	—
Montreal C. & D. Savings Bank	1	1	—	—	—	—	—	—	—
Caisse d'Econ. N.D. de Quebec	—	—	—	—	—	—	3	—	1
Dominion Securities	—	—	1	—	—	—	—	—	—
Sun Life	4	3	—	1	—	—	—	—	1
Metropolitan Life	—	—	—	—	—	—	—	—	1
Canada Life	1	—	3	2	—	1	—	1	—
Mutual Life	2	1	—	—	—	—	—	1	—
Great West Life	—	2	3	—	—	—	—	—	—
Standard Life	2	—	—	—	—	—	—	—	—
Imperial Life	—	1	3	1	—	1	—	—	—
Confederation Life	—	—	2	—	3	1	—	—	1
Manufacturers' Life	—	—	—	—	2	1	—	—	—
Continental Life	—	—	—	—	—	—	1	1	—
North American Life	—	—	—	1	—	—	—	1	1
Huron & Erie Mortgage	1	—	—	—	—	—	—	—	—
Canada Permanent Mortgage	—	—	1	—	3	1	—	—	—
Northern Mortgage	—	3	1	—	—	—	—	—	—
Royal Exchange Assurance	2	—	1	—	—	—	—	—	—
Liverpool, London & Globe	2	—	—	—	—	—	—	—	2
Guarantee Co. of North America	2	—	1	—	—	—	—	—	—
Western Assurance	—	1	5	—	—	—	—	—	—
British America Assurance	—	1	5	—	—	—	—	—	—
Eastern Canada Savings	—	1	—	1	—	—	—	—	—
Central Canada Savings	—	—	2	1	—	—	—	—	—
Toronto Mortgage	—	—	3	—	—	—	—	—	—
Toronto Savings	—	—	4	2	—	—	—	—	—
Nova Scotia Savings	—	—	—	2	—	—	—	—	—
Halifax Fire	—	—	1	2	—	—	—	—	—
Canadian General Investments	—	—	4	—	—	—	—	—	—
Economic Investment Trust	1	—	—	—	—	—	—	—	—
Canadian Investment Trust	2	—	—	—	—	—	—	—	2
Hydro Electric Bond & Share	—	2	—	—	—	—	—	—	—
Montreal, London & General Investors	2	—	—	—	—	—	—	—	—
Securities Holding	—	—	—	1	—	—	—	2	—

Institution	Bank of Montreal	Royal Bank	Bank of Commerce	Bank of Nova Scotia	Bank of Toronto	Dominion Bank	Banque Canadienne Nationale	Imperial Bank	Barclay's Bank
Canadian International Investment Trust	1	—	—	1	—	—	—	—	—
Aldred Investment	—	2	—	—	1	—	—	—	—
Dominion & Anglo Investment	—	—	1	—	1	—	—	—	—
Debenture & Securities	—	—	1	—	1	—	—	—	—
General Accident Insurance	—	—	—	—	—	—	—	3	—
TOTAL	40	34	56	24	17	12	9	11	9

Life insurance companies control 12 per cent. of Canadian capital.[48] Reckoning on the same basis, the banks control 16 per cent., the trust companies 14 per cent., the loan companies just over 1 per cent., a total of 43 per cent. The four largest banks, four largest trust companies and three largest insurance companies control respectively 13½ per cent., 10½ per cent., and 6 per cent. of our capital, a total of 30 per cent. Even with the slight deduction necessary to allow for trust and insurance companies' holdings of bank stocks, and banks' foreign investments, these remain formidable figures.

Transportation, Communication, Fuel and Power.

Turn to industry, and take first transportation and communication. Railways, telegraphs, express, first class hotels to a large extent, and air transport are the preserves of the C.N.R. and the C.P.R., which jointly control Canadian Airways (five C.P.R. directors), are already pooling important passenger services and advertising, and have, unsuccessfully as yet, sought power to amalgamate their express and telegraph departments. Atlantic liner shipping is normally dominated by the North Atlantic Conference, of which the C.P.R. is an important member. A C.P.R. director is on the board of Canada Steamship Lines, which plays an important part in Canadian lake shipping. Telephones are publicly owned in the Prairie Provinces, but in Ontario and Quebec belong overwhelmingly to Bell Telephone, in New Brunswick and Nova Scotia to Bell affiliates, and in British Columbia to British Columbia Telephone Company.

[48] *Financial Post*, May 26, 1934.

In electric power, publicly owned enterprises produce about 23 per cent. of the output. The rest of the industry is one of the tightest and most powerful private monopolies in the world. The Holt interests control Shawinigan Water & Power and Montreal Light, Heat & Power Consolidated (through three directors in common, and a "substantial" Shawinigan stock interest in M.L.H.&P.) and are represented on the boards of British Columbia Power Corporation and of C.P.R. (which controls West Kootenay Power). Shawinigan also owns a 20 per cent. interest in Duke-Price Power. The Nesbitt Thomson interests control Power Corporation, which controls Canada Northern Power, Southern Canada Power, and East Kootenay Power, and has a "substantial" interest in British Columbia Power. The third main factor is Canadian Hydro-Electric, subsidiary of International Hydro-Electric, which interlocks with Duke-Price through Mr. Geoffrion, and holds stock in Shawinigan. These three groups— which are careful never to trespass on each other's territory— together control 80 per cent. of the output of the privately owned power industry.[49]

The larger power companies play an important part also in local transport. Shawinigan controls the street railway in Quebec city, and (jointly with M.L.H.&P.) the Montreal Tramways; also Provincial Transport and Frontier and Champlain Coach Lines, the main bus services in southern Quebec. British Columbia Power controls British Columbia Electric Railway; Winnipeg Electric controls the Winnipeg street railway.[50]

In oil refining, Imperial Oil in 1930 accounted for almost 90 per cent. of the production,[51] and the independents as a rule followed its lead in pricing. Imperial's share of production is said to have fallen to about 55 per cent. or 60 per cent., but its domination is still unchallenged.

In coal, Dominion Steel and Coal Corporation controls 85 per cent. of the Nova Scotia output.[52] Canadian Collieries holds a similar position for the main centres of population in British Columbia; and Senator Webster dominates the import trade in British anthracite.[53]

[49]Dominion Bureau of Statistics *Report,* 1934; *Financial Post Survey of Corporate Securities,* 1935; *Financial Post,* June 1, 1935.
[50]*Financial Post Survey of Corporate Securities,* 1934.
[51]*Combines and the Consumer,* pp. 23, 28. See also *Financial Post,* January 12, 1935.
[52]E. A. Forsey, *Economic and Social Aspects of the Nova Scotia Coal Industry,* p. 43.
[53]*Combines and the Consumer,* pp. 15-17.

Metals, Minerals and Other Staples.

The situation in the iron and steel group of industries is more complex but essentially not very different. There are three main primary producers (which produce many finished products as well) : Steel Company of Canada, Dominion Steel and Coal, and Algoma Steel. Steel of Canada and Dominion Steel and Coal share one powerful director in common. American Can Company in 1933 produced 67.5 per cent. of the output of cans for vegetables, meats and soups; Whittal Can, which follows the prices set by American Can, 17.5 per cent.[54] General Steel Wares, which dominates the rest of the sheet metal trade, interlocks with Algoma through Mr. J. C. Newman. Dominion Bridge, supreme in its field, has three directors from Steel of Canada and two from Dominion Steel. Hamilton Bridge interlocks with Steel of Canada through General Mewburn and with Sarnia Bridge through Mr. F. M. Ross. In agricultural implements, for the years 1929-1933, a survey by investigators for the Royal Commission on Price Spreads, covering fully 90 per cent. of the industry, showed International Harvester with 40.3 per cent. of the Canadian sales, Massey-Harris with 22.8 per cent., Cockshutt Plow with 12.3 per cent.[55] Massey-Harris interlocks with Dominion Steel through Mr. J. H. Gundy. Railway rolling stock is manufactured by C.N.R., C.P.R., Canadian Car and Foundry, National Steel Car, Canadian Locomotive and Eastern Car (subsidiary of Dominion Steel). But Senator Beaubien is a director of both Dominion Steel and Canadian Car and Foundry. So is Senator Webster. Mr. W. F. Angus is a director of Canadian Car and Foundry and Canadian Locomotive. Sir Charles Gordon and Sir Herbert Holt are directors of Dominion Steel and C.P.R. as well. Canadian Bronze, which enjoys an almost complete monopoly of bearings for railway cars, has three directors from C.P.R., two from Dominion Steel. In motor cars, General Motors of Canada, Ford of Canada and Chrysler of Canada are the main factors. In 1934, General Motors had 40 per cent. of the total sales, Ford 25.3 per cent., Chrysler 23.8 per cent. In automobile wheels, hubs and drums, Kelsey Wheel Company has a complete monopoly.[56]

Newsprint, our second largest manufacturing industry, has been grouped into a comparatively few large but ferociously com-

[54]Royal Commissison on Price Spreads, 1934-1935. *Evidence*, pp. 3340, 3823, 3824.
[55]*Ibid. Evidence*, pp. 4022, 4024; *Report*, p. 60.
[56]*Financial Post*, Feb. 16, 1935; and *Financial Post Survey of Corporate Securities*, 1934 and 1935.

peting units.[57] In heavy chemicals, Canadian Industries Limited is the dominant firm, though Dominion Tar and Chemical, Shawinigan Chemicals, (subsidiary of Shawinigan Water and Power), Consolidated Mining and Smelting (subsidiary of C.P.R.), and International Nickel (in which "Smelters" owns 10,000 shares), are important. Even among these few there is considerable interlocking of directors. And evidence before the Stevens Committee[58] showed the existence of a close network of agreements and associations among fertilizer companies all across Canada, resulting, for example, in a wide differential between prices east and west of Kingston.

Rubber is closely linked with chemicals. The three big firms are Dunlop, Dominion and Goodyear. The whole common stock of Dunlop is held by Dunlop Rubber of Great Britain (controlled by Imperial Chemical Industries), and Canadian Industries Limited (controlled by Imperial Chemical Industries and du Pont de Nemours jointly) whose president sits on the Dunlop board. Dominion Rubber is a subsidiary of U. S. Rubber (controlled by du Pont) and three directors of Canadian Industries Limited sit on its board.

The rubber footwear association, already referred to, has for its objects standardization, elimination of excess lines, withdrawal of numerous branch warehouse stocks, stabilization of prices, and regulation of discount differentials to various purchasers. The quotas of production are assigned as follows:

Dominion	38.92%	Northern	9.91%
Gutta Percha	11.29%	Canadian Goodrich	9.16%
Kaufman	10.58%	Woodstock	6.78%
Miner	10.62%	Acton	2.74%

The association holds bonds of members varying from $10,-000 to $75,000, on which it may levy penalties. A firm exceeding its quota must pay to the association penalties of from 25 to 40 per cent. of the excess.

Rubber tire manufacturers also have an association of which Dominion, Dunlop, Goodyear, Goodrich, Firestone, Seiberling, and Gutta Percha are members, and in 1933 did two-thirds of the total tire business.[59]

It is interesting to note also that, according to Dr. Harry Laidler's *Concentration in American Industry*, du Pont owns a

57E. A. Forsey in *Canadian Journal of Economics and Political Science*, August, 1935.
58Pp. 2029, 2032-7, 2064-2150. See also *Price Spreads Report*, pp. 76-78.
59*Committe on Price Spreads and Mass Buying*, 1934. Evidence, pp. 2151-53, 2160, 2209-2211; *Price Spreads Report*, pp. 72-74.

quarter of the shares in General Motors (in which C. I. L. also
is understood to have a substantial block) and a "large block" of
shares in Paramount Publix, parent company of Famous Players
Canadian, dominant in the Canadian motion picture theatre
field.[60]

In metals, the situation is shown by the following table:

Company	Gold	Silver	Copper	Nickel	Lead	Zinc
Lake Shore...............	15.9%	—	—	—	—	—
Hollinger.................	14.7	—	—	—	—	—
Noranda.................	8.3	—	19.2%	—	—	—
McIntyre-Porcupine.......	8.1	—	—	—	—	—
Wright-Hargreaves........	7.4	—	—	—	—	—
Dome...................	6.9	—	—	—	—	—
Teck-Hughes.............	5.6	—	—	—	—	—
Hudson Bay Mining and Smelting..............	3.3	8.1%	10.3	—	—	16.5%
International Nickel.......	2.5	6.1	53.4	71.0%	—	—
Consolidated Mining and Smelting..............	—	44.5	—	—	91.0%	74.0
Granby Consolidated Mining and Smelting........	—	—	10.1	—	—	—
TOTALS.............	72.7%	58.7%	93.0%	71.0%	91.0%	90.5%

Howe Sound produces much of the remainder of our silver
output. It should be noted also that Noranda and Hollinger
interlock through Mr. J. Y. Murdoch and Mr. N. A. Timmins,
and both with Wright-Hargreaves through Mr. Murdoch.[61] Proceedings before the Tariff Board have shown that Canadian copper and zinc are sometimes sold at a much higher price in Canada
than in London: copper at 9.05c and 8.13c respectively, zinc at
$4.25 and $3.85.[62] [63]

Electrical apparatus and supplies is one of the least competitive of our industries. Canadian General Electric interlocks
with Canadian Marconi through Mr. Dyment and with Rogers-
Majestic through Mr. Harrison Smith; Canadian Westinghouse
with Bell Telephone (controlling Northern Electric) through Mr.
Ahearn. Amalgamated Electric is controlled by Northern Electric. Canadian General Electric, Northern Electric, Canadian
Westinghouse, Canadian Marconi and Rogers-Majestic have an

[60]*Report of the Registrar under the Combines Investigation Act*, 1929.

[61]*Financial Post Survey of Corporate Securities*, 1935; *Financial Post*, January 5, 12, 26, March 9, April 6, 13, May 4, 11, 25, 1935.

[62]Montreal *Gazette*, April 17, 1934.

[63]Aluminum Limited, though a complete monopoly, is omitted here, as it does not handle Canadian ores.

agreement for interchange of patents.[64]   Mr. H. H. Stevens has recently drawn attention to the very considerable enhancement of the price of electric light bulbs which has resulted from the monopoly control of patents.[65]

Asbestos Corporation and Dominion Glass dominate their respective industries.   And cement is virtually the complete monopoly of Canada Cement: the Dominion Bureau of Statistics has to leave a blank opposite "Cement" in the 1933 Report on Manufactures.

Food and Drink and Clothing.

Five great companies rule the flour milling industry, with almost 73 per cent· of the capacity of all mills, and four of these control chains of bakeries which are an important factor in the bread trade, producing, in 1930 "over a third of the bread sold in the Dominion and over 90 per cent of the bread sold in the localities in which they operate".   For 1931, the latter percentage varied from 32 in Hamilton to 70 in Winnipeg.[66]

Canada Packers in 1933 has 59 per cent. of the total sales of the industry (a larger proportion than Swift and Armour together in the United States) ;[67] Swift Canadian 26 per cent.   Canada Packers' "leadership" seems to have been accepted by the lesser firms.[68]   In addition, Canada Packers owned 10 per cent. of the stock of Dominion Stores and 15 per cent. of Stop and Shop, two of the largest retail food chains.[69]

British Columbia Packers is a powerful factor in the fish curing and packing trade of the Pacific Coast.   In the Maritime Province, Maritime National Fish handles 15 per cent of the total catch (about 37 per cent. of the fresh fish trade), and admits sometimes arranging prices by telephone with the other three or four large firms.[70]

Canada and Dominion Sugar is "reported to sell about 50 per cent. of all the sugar used in Canada".   Acadia Sugar and Atlantic Sugar have about one-third of the capacity of the industry.   St. Lawrence Sugar and British Columbia Sugar account

[64]*Financial Post Survey of Corporate Securities*, 1935; *Financial Post*, February 17, August 18, 1934.

[65]*House of Commons Debates*, 1935, pp. 3362-3365.

[66]*Report of the Registrar under the Combines Investigation Act*, 1931, quoted in *Combines and the Consumer*, p. 2.   See also *Royal Commission on Price Spreads*, 1934-1935, pp. 3514-3515, 3541, 3663-3666; *Report*, pp. 86-104.

[67]Committee on Price Spreads, 1934.   *Evidence*, pp. 2240, 2269, 2293, 2363, 2389. *Price Spreads Report*, pp. 55-60.

[68]Committee on Price Spreads. 1934.   *Evidence*, pp. 1075-1082.

[69]Committee on Price Spreads. 1934.   *Evidence*, p. 2336.

[70]Royal Commission on Price Spreads, 1934-1935.   *Evidence*, pp. 357, 391, 400, 419. See also *Report*, p. 176.

for nearly all the rest. The degree of competition may be surmised from the plaintive observation of the *Financial Post* that Crosse and Blackwell sugar operations have "disorganized sugar marketing in Ontario to the detriment of the other companies."[71]

The Report of the House of Commons Committee of 1933 notes growing concentration of control in milk. The main firms are Borden's (nation-wide subsidiary of the great United States company of the same name), Eastern Dairies (which extends as far west as Winnipeg), Silverwood's (which covers Ontario), and Dairy Corporation.[72]

In some other food industries, the situation is similar. Canadian Canners, "the largest canners of fruits, vegetables, jams, jellies, catsups, meats, soups, etc., in the British Empire", have 67.2 per cent. of the total sales of this industry; Associated Quality Canners 16.2 per cent.; and Canadian Canners "pretty well" sets prices both to grower and consumer.[73] Canada Biscuit, George Weston, and Viau Biscuit, with the (American) National Biscuit Company, control that industry; and Catelli Macaroni, a merger of several smaller concerns, dominates its field.

In the grain trade, the 1934 report of the Board of Grain Commissioners shows 5,504 public country elevators in 1933-34; 45 public and semi-public terminal elevators. Of the country elevators, the Pools seem to have had about 1,655, the United Grain Growers 446. Ogilvie Flour Mills owned or controlled 154, and Reliance Grain, with which it interlocks, 192. Maple Leaf Milling had only two country elevators, but interlocks with Federal Grain (384), N. Bawlf Grain (116), and Alberta Pacific Grain (372). Lake of the Woods Milling had 125, Western Canada Flour Mills 83, Western Grain 279, Midland and Pacific 70. That is, farmers' organizations had over 2,100, the Maple Leaf group 874, the Ogilvie group 346, four other large concerns 557. Of the terminals at the head of the Lakes, the Pools had six, the United Grain Growers one, the Dominion Government one, the Grand Trunk Pacific Elevator Company one, Federal Grain three, N. Bawlf one, Reliance one, Canadian Consolidated Grain three, Western Grain one. On the Pacific Coast, the Alberta Pool has

---

71*Financial Post*, March 9, 1935. Acadia and Atlantic have daily capacities of 1,250,000 and 1,300,000 pounds. (*Financial Post Survey of Corporate Securities*, 1934). Total sugar production in 1929 when the industry was operating at 50% of capacity was 943,393,500 pounds. (*Financial Post Business Year Book*, 1932).

72*Financial Post*, April 21, July 7, July 14, 1934.

73*Financial Post Survey of Corporate Securities*, 1934. Royal Commission on Price Spreads, 1934-35. *Evidence*, pp. 3060, 3063, 3086, 3114, 3124-3130, 3157, 3310, 3403, 3422.

four, the United Grain Growers have one, Midland Pacific one.[74]

In brewing, National Breweries (with its subsidiary, Frontenac) does about 60 per cent. of the business in Quebec, and Molson's practically all the rest. Brewing Corporation has 55 per cent. of the capacity of all Ontario breweries and is now trying to secure control of one of the three considerable independents in Ontario, Canada Bud.[75] Hiram Walker-Gooderham and Worts, and Distillers' Corporation-Seagram's undoubtedly dominate distilling, in which their only serious rival (and that less than half the size of either) is Canadian Industrial Alcohol.

In tobacco manufacturing, Imperial Tobacco does 75 per cent. of the cigarette business, 66 per cent. of the cut tobacco, 49.8 per cent. of plug tobacco, 67 per cent. of cigars, 91 per cent. of snuff and little cigars. W. C. MacDonald, Inc., does another 17 per cent. of the cigarette business.[76] Mr. Spafford, Vice-President of Imperial Tobacco, admitted to the Stevens Committee that that Company controlled "the number of retailers who can buy direct" from it at a discount of 10 per cent., and the number of wholesalers of tobacco, and that a jobber who "failed to maintain prices" "cannot get his supply". Mr. Factor: "So you have the method of distribution pretty well controlled for yourselves, haven't you?" Mr. Spafford: "Yes, we have".[77] Further evidence of Mr. Spafford and of several other witnesses amply bears out this statement.[78]

Our basic textile industries present other beautiful examples of concentration. In cottons there are four main groups: Dominion Textiles-Montreal Cottons, Canadian Cottons, Wabasso, and Hamilton Cottons-Cosmos Imperial Mills. Dominion Textiles and Montreal Cottons in 1934 accounted for 54 per cent. of the total employment, Canadian Cottons 16.1 per cent., Wabasso 13.4 per cent., Hamilton 4 per cent., Cosmos 2 per cent. It is worth noting that Canadian Cottons interlocks with Dominion Textiles through Mr. W. A. Black; that there are several other personal links between the textile firms of which Mr. Dawson is president (Canadian Cottons, Dominion Woollens and Worsteds, Belding-Corticelli Silk) and those of which Sir Charles Gordon is president or

[74]Figures from *Report of Grain Commissioners, 1933; Overseas Trade Department Report on Canada, 1932-1933; Financial Post Survey of Corporate Securities, 1935*; D. A. Mac-Gibbon, *The Canadian Grain Trade,* p. 344. At p. 3606 of the *Evidence before the Royal Commission on Price Spreads,* it is stated that both Ogilvie and International Milling have subsidiary grain companies.

[75]*Fnancial Post,* May 5, May 26, June 2. June 23, 1934 .

[76]Committee on Price Spreads, 1934. *Evidence,* pp. 1577, 1724.

[77]Committee on Price Spreads, 1934. *Evidence,* p. 1811.

[78]Committee on Price Spreads, 1934. *Evidence,* pp. 1807-1821, 1823-1883, 1905-1923, 1925-1927. See also *Price Spreads Report,* pp. 52-54.

a director (Dominion Textiles, Montreal Cottons, Penman's,
Paton Manufacturing, Brinton-Peterboro Carpets, Canadian
Bag); that Sir Charles Gordon is president and Mr. Dawson a
director of the Bank of Montreal; and that Dominion Textiles
leaves the manufacture of denim to Canadian Cottons and Hamilton Cottons.[79]

Woollens, however, are competitive. Dominion Woollens and
Worsteds in 1934 had 18.26 per cent. of the total employment; no
other firm seems to have had anything approaching this figure.[80]

In real silk, Belding-Corticelli had (1933) 22.7 per cent. of the
employees, Associated Textiles 19.5 per cent., Bruck 18.8.[81] For
rayon (1933), Canadian Celanese and Courtauld's (Canada) together supplied 77½ per cent. of the demand. The rest was imported. Canadian Celanese, which monopolizes the manufacture
of cellulose acetate yarns (which it does not sell to the trade),
had 63.28 per cent. of the total employment, Courtauld's the rest.
The *Canadian Textile Journal* of December 29, 1933, estimated
1934 consumption of rayon yarns at 8,750,000 pounds: Courtauld's 5,500,000, Canadian Celanese 2,000,000, imports 1,250,-
000.[82]

Knitted goods, like woollens, are competitive. The only really large firm is Penman's, which in 1934 had 22.9 per cent. of the
employees. The next two, Mercury Mills and Eaton Knitting,
had only 6.4 each. Hosiery falls in the same category: Julius
Kayser and Company, Limited having in 1933 about 12 per cent.
of the total sales, Canadian Silk Products less than 7 per cent.,
the six largest together less than 36 per cent.[83]

Canadian Spool Cotton, subsidiary of the famous English firm
of Coats, in 1933 accounted for 70.4 per cent. of the employment
in the thread industry: Brantford Cordage for 43 per cent., and
Plymouth for 40.2 per cent. in cordage.[84] In carpets and rugs,
Toronto Carpets had 45.96 per cent. of employment, Brinton-
Peterboro 22.52, Harding 21.[85] In bags, Canadian Bag has over
40 per cent. of employment, none of its competitors more than
about 14 per cent.[86]

79Royal Commission on Price Spreads, 1934-1935. *Evidence*, pp. 2695-2696, 2997.
Report, p. 81.
80Royal Commission on Price Spreads. 1934-1935. *Evidence*, pp. 2824-2825.
81*Ibid., Evidence*, p. 2734.
82*Ibid., Evidence*, p. 2785, 2787, 2790. *Report*, p. 84.
83*Ibid., Evidence*, pp. 2859, 2934-2935.
84*Ibid., Evidence*, p. 2968.
85*Ibid., Evideice*, p. 2905.
86*Ibid., Evidence.* pp. 2980-2981. *Canadian Trade Index*, 1933.

The Movies, The Press, and Retail Trades.

A 1929 report, under the Combines Investigation Act, on the motion picture theatres, showed Famous Players Canadian Corporation in almost complete control there. In the daily newspaper field, the Southam chain reaches from Ottawa to the Pacific Coast, the Sifton chain from Winnipeg west, and the number of other papers is relatively small. The Canadian periodical press, such as it is, is the domain of a small number of publishers.

Even in retail trade, once the sanctuary of the "small man", a few large companies are becoming increasingly important. The 1931 census of merchandizing showed 31.1 per cent. of retail trade transacted by department and chain stores. Department stores had, in 1930, "roughly 12 per cent. of all the retail trade, 60 per cent. of the trade in home furnishings, 52 per cent. of dry goods and notions, 42 per cent. of women's clothing, 46 per cent. of furniture, 32 per cent. of shoes, and 27 per cent. of men's clothing." Three companies, Eaton's, Simpson's and Hudson's Bay, "accounted for slightly more than 80 per cent. of the total business" of all department stores. Eaton's alone did 58 per cent. of the department store business, or over 7 per cent. of all the retail trade (as compared with less than 1 per cent. for the largest department store in the United States). Simpson's and the Hudson's Bay Company do their European buying jointly. Chain stores in 1933 did 33.2 per cent. of the grocery and meat trade: 54.2 per cent. of the combined figures for Windsor, Toronto and Verdun, 16.8 per cent. for St. John, Halifax, Quebec, Victoria and Three Rivers.[87] Moreover, as the Stevens Committee has abundantly shown, the influence of the chain and department stores is out of all proportion to these percentages. More and more they set the pace, a pace which the small man finds it increasingly hard to stand.

Nor does even this exhaust the subject of concentration within particular industries. It leaves out the trade associations, and a host of more nebulous forms of agreement as to prices, sales territory, special lines of goods, and so forth, about which, naturally, information is very scanty. In R. H. Tawney's words, "The lords of the jungle do not hunt by day".

To sum up, industries "approaching a condition of monopoly" account for practically all our financial capital, most of our min-

---

[87]*Ibid., Report,* pp. 201, 203, 206, 207, 214, 232. Committee on Price Spreads, 1934. *Evidence,* p. 3815. *Financial Post Survey of Corporate Securities,* 1935.

ing capital, about three-quarters of the capital invested in manufacturing, and an appreciable proportion of the investment in
other types of business. If concentration is "exceptional", the
list of exceptions is impressive.

Agriculture, woollens, hosiery, knitted goods, the clothing
trades, boots and shoes, furniture, lumbering, and a few other
businesses are still carried on mainly by individual proprietors or
small competing companies. But as we shall see, this does not
mean that they are "independent" of Big Business, merely that
in these spheres Big Business exercises its control indirectly.

The Few Who Control.

Even more striking, however, than the march of concentration within industry is the close interrelation between industries
and the degree to which most of them are controlled by the same
relatively small group of men. Mr. Sanford Evans tells the
Canadian Chamber of Commerce that socialist planning of "the
infinitely complex and far-flung economic activities of the modern world" is not "within the capacity of human nature". "Each
of us knows", he explains, that "it takes a lifetime to acquire
familiarity with the details of a mere unit in business, and a
full day to keep in touch with each day's demands".[88] This particular argument largely ignores the fact that our big financiers
have activities far-flung beyond any socialist's dream.[89] For
example, Sir Charles Gordon in his "lifetime" has "acquired
familiarity" not with "a mere unit" but with twenty-four companies dealing in matters so diverse as banking, railways, power,
air transport, chemicals, rubber, steel, coal, glass, flour, cottons,
woollen underwear, milk, tobacco, carpets, locomotives, and a
hotel; and on no small scale either, for his directorships cover
financial institutions with gross assets of over $1,480,000,000
and non-financial corporations with $1,800,000,000.

> "We gaze and gaze and still the wonder grows,
> That one small head can carry all he knows."

Or consider his versatile compeer, Sir Herbert Holt, whose
range of twenty-eight companies includes banking, insurance,
railways, power, paper, air transport, steel, coal, bridges, electrical equipment, tar, cement, flour, cottons, woollens, tobacco,
furs, a department store, a hotel and safety razors: financial in-

[88]*Financial Post*, September 22, 1934.
[89]For full evidence on this point see pamphlet*Who Owns Canada*, by the C.C.F. Research
Bureau, 1935, with tables of directorates held by the "big shots".

stitutions with assets of over $2,200,000,000 and non-financial corporations with about the same figure. Both are also governors of McGill University, and Sir Charles of the Royal Victoria Hospital. Mr. Dawson, president of the Canadian Chamber of Commerce, goes in for banking, construction, three kinds of textiles, a theological college and a cemetery. So one might continue through the list of our great financiers. Ten of them, so far from finding their days as "full" as Mr. Evans would lead us to think, even manage to spare time to help shape their country's laws, in the Senate.

Our business leaders in fact spread their tentacles over the whole of human life. We are born in their hospitals, buried in their cemeteries. In the interval, it is they who decide what we shall eat, what we shall drink, wherewithal we shall be clothed, what we shall see, read, hear, and smoke, how we shall build our houses, till our land, invest our savings, get from place to place, amuse ourselves, or in fact do almost everything else imaginable. They do not find the direction of these "infinitely complex and far-flung activities" beyond the capacity of their human nature. Now that Mr. Evans has become a director of the Bank of Montreal, perhaps they will explain to him how it is done.

An irresponsible oligarchy, then, controls the individual corporations, the separate industries and the economy as a whole. It is no answer to protest that in any modern industrial society, capitalist, socialist, communist, fascist, what you please, the control of economic life will be and must be concentrated in a few hands; that we cannot turn over the management of the railways of Canada to the entire population of 10,500,000. Granted. But the question is: Shall those few be private individuals, answerable to no one but themselves, or public servants responsible to the people? The evil lies not in the inevitable concentration but in the irresponsibility. All history proves that irresponsible power is poisonous to those who wield it. At best they unconsciously identify the public interest with their own.

Nor is it a question of personalities. Replace our present industrial oligarchy with any other hundred and fifty men and the results will be substantially the same. The fault, dear Brutus, is not in themselves, but in their stars, alias the capitalist system. As long as the securing of profits is the test of their trusteeship, it is a sheer impossibility for them to behave very differently. In a pioneer agricultural community the idea of reforming society simply by changing individuals had some plausibility. Today it is nonsense.

The defenders of capitalism will protest here that "industry can exist only by supplying the needs of the people, by providing what the consumer wants. The capitalists who appear to control industry are in fact at the mercy of the plain man, the consumer whose whims they must satisfy". This is very pretty, but unfortunately not true. Capitalist industry does not exist to supply needs. It exists to make profits. As James Rorty puts it, "The logic of private business runs that an empty stomach is no customer unless the owner of the stomach can pay for what he eats, and pay enough to include profits all down the line from producer to retail dispenser".[90] "Service to the public" is purely incidental. If it "pays" we get it, if it doesn't we don't. "It's your money we want" is capitalism's grim slogan. If you have no money, capitalism is simply not interested.

Of course, capitalism must produce things the consumer will buy. But who decides how much income he shall have? Who controls the advertising which teaches him how he shall spend his income?[91] And if monopoly capitalism can make more money by selling him few goods at a high price rather than many at a low price, which will it do?

[90]New York *Nation*, August 22, 1934, p. 206.
[91]*Our Master's Voice*, by James Rorty, a study of advertising.

CHAPTER IV.

THE MECHANISM OF THE MARKET.

A. The Market in Theory and Practice.

It has become the fashion among radicals to say that "an economy of plenty is within our grasp". The statement is only relatively true. "Plenty" in comparison with what we have *is* within our grasp. Absolute plenty (the plenty of air and sunshine), is not. In spite of the enormous growth in productive power in the last century and a half, almost all our resources, human and material, are still limited in amount. There is not enough of them to satisfy without limit everybody's wants, nor is there likely to be in the near future.

Moreover, these limited resources have alternative uses. The community's supply of labour may, with suitable training, be used for laying bricks, mining coal, running locomotives, or any of a thousand other purposes. Our supply of steel may be used for rails, railway cars, ships, needles, cream separators, adding machines, the framework of office buildings. Our supply of capital may be used to produce houses or whiskey, bread or golf clubs, roads or munition factories, schools or flour mills, churches or ski-jumps, wheat or pumpkins.

Any economic system must decide somehow what goods and services are to be produced and how much of each, how much of its resources are to be assigned to which uses. That is the economic problem. At first sight it seems little short of miraculous that an unplanned system solves it at all. As business men are free to produce what they please, what prevents them from all throwing themselves and our resources into an orgy of pumpkin growing and leaving us breadless and houseless? The answer is, prices and markets.

Labour, capital, natural resources are to be had only at a price. Industries which can pay the price get the resources; industries which can't, don't. Industries which can pay for large quantites, get large quantities; industries which can only pay for small, get small. Each industry's ability to pay for resources depends on the demand for its products, and the demand for its products depends on their price. If the price is too high, demand is small, very little of the commodity is produced, and the industry concerned gets only a small part of the resources. If the price of the product is relatively low, demand is likely to be large, and the industry gets a large revenue, in other words, command over resources.

The Freedom of the Market.

Prices, whether of resources or of final products, are determined in markets. In a "freely competitive" market, each buyer tries to make sure of meeting his own requirements by offering a higher price than other buyers. Each seller similarly tries to make sure of disposing of his own supply by offering it at a lower price than other sellers. If the price rises, some buyers are eliminated, demand falls off; at the same time, further sellers are tempted to come forward, and supply increases. If the price falls, the reverse process takes place. Competition on both sides, accordingly, sets the price at a point where the amount offered by sellers is exactly the amount demanded by buyers.

Supply and demand are in equilibrium. Producers who can make a profit at this price survive, producers who cannot are, sooner or latter, eliminated. Abnormally high profits attract new producers to the industry, increase production, bring down prices, and reduce profits to the average. Losses, or very low profits, have the opposite effect.[1]

Hence the profit-seeking producer will make use of the most economical methods, the cheapest labour, capital and natural resources he can get. He will exert all his powers of ingenuity, inventiveness, initiative, shrewdness, and organizing ability. Competition among producers will pass on the benefits to consumers in the form of low prices. Thus the search for private profit automatically serves the social good: in Adam Smith's words, "Each, seeking only his own interest, is led as by an Invisible Hand to promote the interests of society".

The actual development of capitalism has belied Smith's cheerful expectations. And for a very simple reason. The markets of Smith's theory were free and competitive. Modern markets are neither.

The history of the emergence of the modern world from the mediaeval is essentially the story of the struggle for the free market. The enterprising business man had to sweep away the feudal restrictions upon his freedom to engage in any trade or industry he chose; and—not least in importance—to buy labour

[1]For a fuller account of the development and functions of markets and the pricing system, see Strachey, *Coming Struggle for Power;* and Wootton, *Plan or No Plan?*

as cheaply as he could get it and only for such periods as suited him, and to apply it as he saw fit.

This last point does not always receive the attention it deserves. It is almost impossible for most of us to imagine a condition where no worker would respond to the offer of money wages, so completely do we take for granted this fundamental characteristic of capitalism. The idea that industry could not be established merely for lack of a working class seems fantastic. Yet such was once the prevailing condition of society and such it remains in those places where capitalism has not yet developed, being, indeed, the chief obstacle to its development.

Two conditions must obtain before a labour market can develop. First, slavery and serfdom must be abolished. The slave-owner or the feudal lord has to feed, clothe and house his slaves or serfs even when it is unprofitable for him to do so. The employer must be free to let them starve. The workers then must be legally free to sell their labour if, as, and when they choose. Secondly, they must be *willing* to sell it, that is, unable to secure a livelihood in any other way. They must neither possess nor be able to secure the means of production for themselves. Otherwise, they will prefer to work for themselves and enjoy both the full product of their labour and the greater freedom involved. In short, the existence of capitalism depends on the existence of a "propertyless proletariat", a class of people who have no means of existence except by the sale of their ability to work.

Historically, the creation of a labour market has been accomplished in many ways, from the forcible dispossession of peasant proprietors[2] to the immigration propaganda of Canadian governments and railways. Once the process has started, however, it goes on automatically. The advancing technique of industrial production results in larger and more expensive capital equipment in each productive unit. At the same time, the new methods make possible more production at a low cost, thus rendering useless and obsolete the cheap, simple, productive equipment of the small producer and making it impossible for him to continue to produce and sell his product on the market. Thus an indirect economic compulsion is provided to force the individual to sell his labour. There is no legal compulsion: the worker is perfectly "free" to refuse to sell his labour if he pleases; he is "free" to starve if he "prefers".

2As, for example, the enclosures in England during the 16th and 17th centuries.

Capitalism made short work of the mediaeval restrictions on the freedom of the business man, and in Canada they have never troubled us. But their absence is not the only essential to a system of free markets. Buyers and sellers must not only be legally free. Buyer must compete against buyer, seller against seller, and all buyers and sellers must be fully informed of each others' bids and offers.

"Simple competition may be said to exist", says the *Report* of the Royal Commission on Price Spreads,[3] "where there are many small producers offering a commodity for sale, and many buyers offering to purchase relatively small quantities of that commodity without any preference for the product of any particular seller. Under such conditions . . . no seller can affect the price by withholding a part of his supply from the market, since he controls only an insignificant part of the whole. On the other hand, no seller has any difficulty in selling his whole supply at the market price. No buyer exercises any hold over any seller, for there are always plenty of buyers at the market price. . . . Price is very flexible and adjusts itself to conditions of supply and demand, and buyers and sellers adjust themselves to this prevailing price."

Canadian Markets.

In our complex modern society, markets of this kind do not arise by spontaneous generation. They must be elaborately organized. How far even such organized markets are really "free" and competitive, we shall see presently. For the moment we are concerned with a prior question: how far is the Canadian economy equipped with organized markets at all?

There is no *money market*, that is, no organized market for short-term loans and securities such as exists in London or New York. The banks are almost the sole source of short-term credit. The issue of long-term securities, bonds and shares, is handled by groups of investment dealers, who buy the issues *en bloc,* and sell to the public retail. For the sale of shares there is the highly organized stock exchange, but there is no organized bond market. In view of the tendency of corporations to raise an increasing proportion of their capital through bonds, this is a serious deficiency.

If the organization of the *capital markets* leaves much to be desired, *the labour market,* by comparison, hardly exists. There

3*Report*, p. 6.

are no places set aside for public competitive bidding, no news-paper reports of the trend of wages, no daily quotations for bricklayers and lumber-jacks and harvest hands. There is a Dominion-wide chain of free public employment offices, but these cover only a fraction of all employment transactions. Private employment offices, newspaper advertisement and appli-cation, contact with employers through friends and educational institutions, and the dreary and inefficient door-to-door search are the normal methods by which the worker finds a job. He moves in a fog of ignorance, within the narrow limits of his personal capacity to investigate employment possibilities. Dis-tance, the cost of education, class distinctions, differences of language and customs, impose even narrower limits. The coal-miner in Nova Scotia may be well aware that he could earn more as a teacher in Vancouver; but he has not money to get to Van-couver, to train himself for teaching, or to keep himself during the training, and he may lack the social polish expected of a teacher. The Jew, however able, will find many doors closed to him. Between Orange Toronto and French-Catholic Quebec, the mobility of labour is probably about the same as between either and China.

The markets for *natural resources* are if anything less or-ganized. Dealings in real estate, carried on through scattered offices, are peculiarly subject to the worst types of speculative frenzy, not untinged with fraud. The wreckage of the pre-war land booms, east and west, is still with us. Mineral rights, owned by the provinces, are rented to syndicates on a royalty basis, without competitive bidding. Timber lands, except in the Maritime Provinces, where most of them have been alienated to private owners,[4] are held by the provinces. Only cutting rights are sold: sometimes, as in British Columbia and Quebec, by public competition; sometimes by tender, as with saw timber in Ontario; sometimes by individual agreement.

The business unit obtains the necessary productive resources through the capital, the labour and the land markets. Markets also constitute the link between one stage of production and the next, and between the producer and the ultimate consumer. But these markets vary greatly both in structure and in degree of efficacy. The more highly standardized and widely used raw materials such as wheat or cotton are bought and sold on organ-

---

[4]Percentage of forest land in private hands: Prince Edward Island, 100%; Nova Scotia, 76%; New Brunswick, 50%; Quebec, 7%; Ontario, 3.3%; Manitoba, 11.3%; Saskatchewan, 10.4%; Alberta, 15.7%; B.C., 13%. (*Canada Year Book*, 1932, p. 92.)

ized exchanges by professional dealers, either on their own account or on behalf of clients. This opens the way to dealing in futures and speculative trading just as on the stock exchange. And it is difficult to check. The Wheat Pool aspired to substitute direct sales to such bodies as the British Co-operative Wholesale Society for sales through the elevator companies that hold seats on the exchange, but was forced to rescind this policy.

Some products, like wheat, just cited, are sold by the producers themselves through co-operative marketing agencies. Even in Canada, where this type of co-operative selling is rather highly developed, private jobbers still play a large part in the marketing of agricultural produce, purchasing supplies locally for resale to wholesalers in large centres. Middlemen who collect, select and distribute merchandise intervene at every further stage of production in the more individualistic trades. In some cases, however, the producers have met the problem by cutting out the buying and selling altogether and themselves obtaining control of sources of raw materials, each successive stage of production, and, in some cases, retail outlets for the finished goods. The grain, milling and baking trades are an excellent example of this type of integration of control. Equally the pulp and paper interests in Eastern Canada usually look after their logging operations or have them carried on for them by contractors, and in many cases make both the pulp and the newsprint within the same concern.

The *retail market* is the final link in the chain of production and consumption. It consists of a wide variety of institutions ranging all the way from the mail-order house to the door-to-door salesman. There is no central organization. There is no standardization. There is no co-ordinated information available. The general market is broken up into a multitude of small markets, sometimes created deliberately by brand advertising, otherwise by lack of shrewdness and care on the part of the consumers. A consumer who wants to purchase (say) a car, must make the rounds of endless different agencies, comparing prices and qualities, and evading high pressure salesmanship, before he can begin to make an intelligent decision as to what to buy. The housewife looking for laundry supplies must decide between buying them at a groceteria, a chain store, the corner grocer's or the basement of a department store. She must experiment with various brands and discover whether the inexpensive unbranded article is really inferior to the much-advertised products.

Being perhaps credulous, frightened, pressed for time, or careless, she succumbs in fact to one or other of the advertisers, and even the slender chance of effective competition which the market does offer is not realized.

B. "COMPETITIVE" LENDING.

For most of the Canadian economy there are not and never have been any organized markets at all. What has the growth of monopoly done to such markets as there are? Beginning with the capital market, the first thing to note is that a good deal both of the supply of capital and the demand for it no longer comes into the market at all. The great corporation provides for an increasing part of its requirements out of its own savings. In such circumstances the "market rate of interest" has very little meaning. Lender and borrower being one, the "price" at which the transaction takes places is a mere bookkeeping item, settled mainly by administrative convenience. The only competitive element is the possibility that the corporation could make more money by putting its surplus, or part of it, into the securities of other companies, as of course it often does. The fact remains, however, that the owner of the surplus has access to this supply of capital at any price he pleases, and, what is more, he can prevent a potential competitor from getting it at any price whatever.

Short-Term Borrowing.

One result of this is that Big Business is much more independent of the banks than many people suppose. The directorates of nearly all the great corporations, as we have seen, interlock with those of the banks, but Sir Charles Gordon has testified: "Most of the big companies with which I have anything to do are not borrowers at all from the banks. The biggest one, the Dominion Textile Company . . . does not owe the Bank of Montreal one cent. Once in a while we will borrow a little just to carry us over to the end of the month, as is the case with most of the companies with which I am concerned. All these companies with which I am connected are not dependent on the bank for their credits at all." On April 19, 1934, total borrowings from the Bank of Montreal by Bell Telephone, Northern Electric, Canada Steamships, Canadian Airways, Canadian Industries Limited, Canadian Bronze, Consolidated Paper, St. Lawrence Corporation, Consolidated Mining and Smelting, Dominion Bridge, Dominion Glass, Dominion Rubber, Dominion Textiles, Canadian

Cottons, Belding-Corticelli, International Nickel, Steel of Canada, Montreal Light, Heat and Power Consolidated, Borden's, The Tuckett Tobacco Company, Ogilvie Flour Mills, Canadian Bag, Royal Trust, two investment companies and six insurance companies (including Sun Life and Mutual Life) were only $17,280,-823. At December 31, 1933, all the companies (except C.P.R.) of which Sir Herbert Holt is a director together owed the Royal Bank only $2,090,255. Montreal Light, Heat and Power Consolidated is not a borrower at all. Of 143 firms with Canadian Bank of Commerce directors on their boards, only 28 are listed as "regular" and 9 more as "occasional" borrowers. The great corporations have become to a large extent their own bankers.[5]

On the other hand, small enterprise, notably agriculture, simply cannot exist without bank credits.

The result, broadly speaking, is a short-term market for industrial capital, beautifully competitive on the borrowers' side and almost completely non-competitive on the lenders': hundreds of thousands of farmers and small business men bargaining individually with a handful of powerful banks whose competition never, never takes the reprehensible, "unethical" form of price-cutting. In the traditional "free market", depression would have quickly brought down the rate of interest on bank loans. It has done so in Canada only slightly, and at long last, and as the result of strong governmental pressure upon a deeply reluctant banking community.[6] The *Financial Post* of August 11, 1934, quotes "a leading Canadian banker" who "believed he represented the great majority of Canadian bankers" as saying: "Ottawa and not the banks is behind the present move for still lower rates. . . He looked on the whole move as very largely political and was extremely doubtful of the wisdom of any further reduction . . . . Capital is entitled to a reward, and without a profit there can be no prosperity. Cheap money . . . spells business stagnation. . . . This authority stated emphatically that the first step towards better times was a rising interest rate. . . . Lower interest rates would discourage thrift. Very few people would leave their money in the bank if the rate was reduced to two per cent. . . . a plan will usually work in two opposite directions. . . . He could not reconcile the apparently divergent policies of the Government in seeking to raise commodity prices on the one hand and lower the wages of money on the other". It is

[5]*Evidence before the Banking Committee,* 1934, pp. 488, 506, 542, 851, 853.
[6]See Mr. Abramson's brilliant article, already referred to, in the *Canadian Forum,* February, 1935.

hardly surprising that this Solon preferred to remain anonymous.

Long-Term Borrowing.

In the long-term capital market the great corporation is much more dependent on the financial institutions. It is the banks and investment dealers who underwrite its new issues of securities, and though part of these may be sold to other industrial companies, a very large part must be bought by trust, loan and insurance companies and investment trusts.

This does not necessarily mean, however, that the long-term market is any freer than the other. The borrowing company is almost certain to be interlocked with a bank or an investment house or both, or even several of both. The lenders, whether industrial or financial corporations, likewise probably interlock with each other and with the borrowers. In such circumstances, how much competition is there among lenders, and how far are lender and borrower really distinct entities? Suppose the Lunar and Inter-Planetary Colonization Corporation (Amor de Muggins, president) floats a new issue of bonds secured by a first mortgage on the mountains of the moon and the rings of Saturn. The issue is underwritten by the Bank of Jupiter (Amor de Muggins, president), which has four directors on the Lunar Board, and the Arcturus Securities Corporation, whose president is a director of the Bank of Lunar. Large blocks of the issue are taken up by the Hades Trust Company (Amor de Muggins, president), and the Milky Way Life Insurance Company, on whose board sit Mr. de Muggins and several other Lunar directors. In these circumstances can we be perfectly sure that the mechanism of the market will work precisely as traditional theory tells us it should? What kind of bargain does Mr. de Muggins of the Lunar Corporation and two or three dozen other industrial companies drive with Mr. de Muggins of the Bank of Jupiter, Hades Trust, and Milky Way Life? If the capital markets are really free and competitive in this sense, it is a mystery how our financial leaders retain their sanity.

As an illustration of the lack of competition in the capital market, we need only cite the recent difficulties of the Province of Ontario in marketing its $15,000,000 bond issue. On the opening not one tender was received from the bond houses. The investment dealers of course denied collusion, but those interviewed by the press, "who asked that their names be withheld",

explained that they could not bid because they could not "expect
to re-sell to the big buyers, insurance companies, fraternal societies and similar groups" who ordinarily take "blocks totalling
70 to 75 per cent of the flotation".[7]

The controversy over whether "the banks" control "industry" is beating the air.   Finance and big industry are one, and
small industries are their playthings.

C.   THE LABOUR MARKET.

The Employers' Attitude.

In what is, by courtesy, termed the "labour market", Adam
Smith long ago remarked "everywhere a tacit combination among
masters to depress wages".   In present-day Canada this functions with an efficiency which would have made Adam Smith's
"masters" green with envy.   The great corporations which employ a large and increasing proportion of the country's wage-
earners are few and closely interlocked.   For them, joint action
on labour questions is simplicity, and if "tacit" combination
proves cumbersome, it can always be made explicit.   One of the
reasons for the pre-war steel mergers was the desire to "repress
labour unions".[8]   The smaller employers, seldom able to outbid
their powerful rivals, rarely show any wish to do so except on
wage-cutting, and any trade associations they form are on labour
questions faithful echoes of those rivals.   Serious competition
among the buyers of labour-power is negligible.

But perhaps Canadian employers are too "enlightened" to
use their power to depress wages?   Perhaps they realize that
"low wages don't pay"?   If so, to judge from wage statistics,
they have been remarkably successful in hiding this light under
a bushel.

Nor is it hard to see why.   The theory that high wages "pay"
the employer because of the increased efficiency they call forth
has only a very limited validity.   Of course it is worth an employer's while to pay $3 a day and get $5 worth of product rather
than $2 a day for $3 worth of product.   But it does not follow
that if he pays $4 he will get $7 worth of product.   He may get
only $5.50.   In these circumstances $3 is the wage that pays the
employer best.   But this need not be either a living wage or the
highest the employer can afford to pay.   A reasonable compromise might be left to the "working of the market" if the interests

7Montreal *Gazette*, June 13,1935.
8Donald, *Canadian Iron and Steel Industry*, p. 277.

of employers and workers were identical, but unfortunately they are not.

That, for their part, Canadian employers are enlightened enough to recognize this is clear from their almost unvarying hostility to trade unions, and their attitude toward social legislation, ranging from grudging acquiescence to frankly stated dislike. The general manager of the Canadian Bank of Commerce told the Banking Committee that his bank had "hundreds of married employees getting less than $2,500", that its minimum for married men, formerly $1,500, was now $1,200 or $1,000, and that for four years none of the employees had had increases. Asked whether he would "have any objection if the bank clerks, say *in your bank* (our italics) throughout Canada were to decide to organize a bank clerks' organization", he replied, with childlike candour, "I think we would much prefer to deal with our staff ourselves. We always have felt that we have treated our staff pretty well".[9]

> " 'I weep for you', the Walrus said, 'I deeply sympathize.'
> "With sobs and tears he sorted out those of the largest size,
> "Holding his pocket handkerchief before his streaming eyes."

This frank preference for individual bargaining as against even a "company union" is reminiscent of the Montreal *Gazette's* plaintive protest against the existence of a Department of Labour in Quebec: "It has introduced uncertainty where formerly there was perfect security". The *Gazette,* though perhaps not representative of all Canadian capitalists, undoubtedly speaks for a powerful group in its periodic snarls at the Dominion Department of Labour and the International Labour Office at Geneva, and its continued cavilling at every form of labour legislation. Its objection to a legal minimum wage of $7 a week for boys is typical. Such legislation, said the *Gazette,* was "socialistic", "a threat to Quebec's fine reputation for economic sanity", and an "interference with the boys' liberty to work for a reasonable wage."[10]

The president of the Whittall Can Company, confronted with the fact that practically all the 65 girls and 28 boys in his plant receive 15½c. an hour for an average week of 57 hours, replies calmly, "If you can buy eggs for 20c a dozen you don't pay 50c."[11]

Employers and their organs in other provinces usually speak

9*Evidence before the Banking Committee,* 1334, pp. 348-349.
10August 12, 1932.
11Royal Commission on Price Spreads, 1934-1935. *Evidence,* p. 3819.

in softer phrases but the substance of what they say (and do) is not very different. Certainly no one could fairly accuse, let us say, the Canadian Manufacturers' Association or the *Financial Post*, of enthusiasm for trade unionism or social legislation[12]; and the *Canadian Textile Journal* of September 21, 1934, had no hesitation in pronouncing "national recognition of any labour union absolutely contrary to the system of government in any capitalistic country". Mr. A. O. Dawson's speech to the 1934 meeting of the Canadian Chamber of Commerce we have already quoted.

Trade Union Organization.

The buyers of labour power, then, are pretty effectively organized and united. The workers, on the other hand, divided by language, creed, geographical barriers and differences of social standing are, for the most part, not organized at all. The total number of wage and salary earners in Canada in 1931, according to the census, was 2,570,000. If from this are excluded 25,000 priests, nuns, ministers, and other professional religious workers, 3,500 members of the defence forces, 55,000 civil servants (Dominion and provincial, other than postal workers), 200,000 agricultural labourers, and a generous allowance for salaried "executives" and technical staffs, there remain at least 2,000,000 whom an energetic trade union movement could hope to organize. Of this number, however, only 310,544 in 1931 belonged to unions of any kind, and the figure has since fallen to 286,220 (1933). This represents less than 15 per cent. of the total, and competent observers have put the figure as low as 12. The unskilled in all industries are largely unorganized. The only industries in which trade unions are really powerful are railways, printing, building, clothing, skilled metal-work, and musical entertainment.

The *Financial Post* of March 31, 1935, states that only 7 per cent. of factory workers are organized in unions (the needle trades, 33 per cent.; the printing trades, 23 per cent.; shoes and leather, 10 per cent.; and upholstery and furniture, 9 per cent.). In these and perhaps a few other trades, the existing unions have done what they could to carry on collective bargaining with employers; and some of them, prior to the depression, were quite successful in increasing wages and advancing their

---

12Cf. the C.M.A. protest against the new Workmen's Compensation Act in Quebec, Montreal *Star*, March 11, 1931.

members' interests in other ways. But even the strongest, the railway unions, have had to accept wage reductions and to make other substantial concessions during the depression; and when all the achievements of the unions have been noted, it cannot be said that they have been very effective to protect the great mass of Canadian workers.

Moreover, the unionists are divided among themselves. In Quebec, 26,894, more than half the total for that province, stand outside the "regular" trade union movement altogether, in the Federation of Catholic Workers, completely controlled by the Roman Catholic hierarchy. Anti-militant, anti-class-conscious, and anti-socialist, the Federation is dedicated to the proposition that "employees and employers must live agreeing with each other, helping and loving each other". Strikes are permitted only in undefined "extraordinary" circumstances, and never for public or utility employees. Affiliation "with any political party whatever" is explicitly forbidden. When we add that Archbishop Gauthier of Montreal, one of the most powerful ecclesiastical superiors of this organization, used his pastoral letter of January, 1932, to reproach the international unions for trying to keep up wages,[13] it is easy to imagine even the hardest-hearted employer "loving and helping" such a "union".

55,120 Canadian workers belong to "national" unions affiliated with the All-Canadian Congress of Labour. This body is the chief advocate of industrial unionism (one union for all the workers in each industry). At first glance, nothing could seem more desirable than this wider viewpoint in the realm of workers' associations. In practice, it must be frankly stated that a disproportionate amount of time and energy has been consumed in criticism and conflict between the All-Canadian and the American-affiliated Trades and Labour Congress groups.

The smallest but most active group of unionists is the Workers' Unity League (21,253 members in affiliated unions), no longer officially connected with the Red International of Labour Unions, but Communist in its sympathies. It was unions of this group which, against tremendous odds, fought with complete or partial success the furniture workers' strikes in Stratford and Toronto, and the poultry pluckers' strikes in Stratford in the summer of 1933. Less successful in the lumbermen's strikes in Ontario and Quebec in the winter of 1933, their action nevertheless undoubtedly helped to secure some

---

[13]Montreal *Star*, January 7, 1932.

legislative protection for the lumberjacks in Ontario, Quebec and New Brunswick. Their militancy at a time when most orthodox unions are in a state of coma has nearly doubled their membership in a single year.

The Federation of Catholic Workers, the All-Canadian Congress, and the Workers' Unity League are gaining an increasing number and proportion of the organized workers. In 1930, the peak of union membership since 1920, these groups had 78,477 members, or 24½ per cent of the total. In 1933 this had grown to 103,265, or over 36 per cent.

Most of the organized workers (167,720, or 58 per cent.), belong to the "international" unions, with headquarters in the United States and membership on both sides of the border. 103,550 (including some members of purely Canadian bodies like postal workers' organizations) are connected with the American Federation of Labour or its Canadian representative, the Trades and Labour Congress. 23,670 belong to railway organizations unaffiliated with the A. F. of L. Most of the internationals are organized on traditional "craft" lines, so that the total workers in a single industry are sometimes divided between half a dozen different unions. The obvious handicaps in the way of unified policy are mitigated to some extent by Building Trades Councils, Printing Trades Councils, the committee of general chairmen of the railway running trades, or other arrangements for co-operation; and at its last convention the A. F. of L. reluctantly began to take steps to form industrial unions in the new mass production industries.

The Trades and Labour Congress in its declared policy is less conservative than its parent body. It belongs to the International Federation of Trade Unions, advocates public ownership of public utilities, and is not officially opposed to the organization of political labour parties. In practice, however, its leaders have been, to say the least, exceedingly cautious, and its rank and file are not yet an effective political force, nor do they exert a unified influence on the labour market as a whole. Their primary concern with craft interests has by its nature confined their achievements to sectional fields.

Even with the most conservative trade union leaders, however, the average employer has usually been reluctant to have any dealings. The union official is in a stronger position than the ordinary worker. He usually knows more about the economic situation, and the employer cannot "fire" him. So the employer, who avails himself freely of the assistance of lawyers and other "outside" experts for his own business, protests indignantly if his employees try to do likewise by retaining independent professional negotiators to bargain for them. He will not negotiate with "outsiders". Hence the company union, darling of American employers under the N.R.A.: "collective bargaining" with the employer "on both sides of the table". The extent to which this device has been practised in Canada is suggested by figures in the *Financial Post* article of March 30, 1935, from which we have already quoted. "A survey made a few years ago in Ontario indicated that of some 300 firms employing 185,000 workers, 21 per cent of the firms, employing 48 per cent of the workers, had adopted this type of organization in their establishments. About one-fifth had well-organized works councils".

Peaceful Picketing.

If a group of workers succeeds in overcoming all these handicaps and tries to take action to better its standard of living, the path is still not clear. It may find itself in conflict with the state. Not for nothing do the province of Quebec and some of its municipalities officially advertise cheap and contented labour. Local police, sometimes under a local by-law, sometimes even without any legal right, have many times interfered with picketing, public meetings, and distribution of literature: rights recognized, explicitly or implicitly, by the law of the land.[14] In Ontario, Nova Scotia and Saskatchewan troops have been brought into industrial disputes on trivial provocation or none; provincial police have played a similar part in Nova Scotia in 1925 and in the lumber camps of northern Quebec as recently as the winter of 1933 and the fall of 1934.[15]. This is not, of course, a chronic and universal condition. The police of Toronto at least are in a somewhat more reasonable frame of mind than a year or so ago. No troops have been used in Nova Scotia since 1925. The Attorney-General of Ontario, to the pained surprise of some important persons, has announced that he will refuse requests for troops, and has asked the Dominion Government to remove its police from the northern Ontario

---

[14]Cf. the Quebec Act of 1934 respecting notices of public meetings (the David Act).

[15]Montreal *Gazette*, Dec. 5, 12, 21, 1933; Montreal *Star*, Dec. 7, 12, 1933, October 3, 1934.

lumbering district. But one can hardly be surprised if many workers feel some doubts of the permanence of this change of heart, or are sceptical of the perfect impartiality of the public authorities in future industrial disputes. Batons and revolvers are not supposed to be part of the equipment of a free market.

D. PRICE AND PRODUCTION POLICY UNDER MONOPOLY.

Under competition an impersonal automatic market mechanism (of sorts) settled simultaneously how much would be produced and at what prices it would be sold. No single producer was in a position to hold up prices or curtail production. If he tried, his rivals took away his business. But the monopolist *can* hold up prices or curtail production. Under monopoly, accordingly, pricing is no longer impersonal and automatic, but a matter of conscious decision and deliberate policy.

Prices in the Depression.

That this statement is no mere flight of the imagination the behaviour of Canadian finance and industry during the depression amply proves. The competitive industries, on the whole, met falling demand by lowering their prices and keeping up production. The monopolies or quasi-monopolies, on the contrary (apart from a few which produce mainly or largely for export) kept up prices and reduced production.[16]

Contrast, for example, agriculture and banking. Agricultural prices between 1929 and 1932 fell 52 per cent., agricultural production rose 13 per cent.; bank rate on commercial loans held absolutely steady, the volume of commercial loans in Canada fell over 31 per cent. Agricultural implement prices, between 1929 and 1932 fell 2.7 per cent. while production fell 91 per cent.[17] Nickel prices showed not even fractional change, while production fell almost 73 per cent.

Or compare woollens, hosiery and knitted goods, and boots and shoes, all competitive industries, with cottons. In woollens, prices fell 27 to 29 per cent., employment *rose* 7 per cent. In hosiery and knitted goods, prices fell 28 per cent., employment less than 3 per cent. In the boot and shoe industry, prices fell 15 per cent, employment less than 12 per cent. But in cottons, while prices fell 16 per cent. to 20 per cent., employment dropped

16Cf. *Price Spreads Report*, pp. 6-9.

17*Ibid.*, p. 9. For 1933, the fall in prices was 6.4 per cent., in production 86.4 per cent.

over 23 per cent. The operations of a tin cartel and the dominance of the American Can Company have resulted in practical stability in the price of cans during the depression. From 1929 to 1933 the value of tomatoes in a can of this product declined almost 30 per cent. but the cost of the can dropped only 5 per cent. Similar movements are reflectèd in the costs for other canned products and in a great many cases the canning companies pay more for the cans than for the products they contain.[18]

There are, of course, exceptions: furniture in the competitive group, meat packing, sugar refining and chemicals among the monopolies. In these and some other industries special factors help to account for the figures. But the general outlines are clear; a competitive economy, mainly agricultural, with *flexible* prices, exists side by side with a *monopoly* economy with *rigid* prices.

The results are little less than disastrous. The Canadian economy as a whole is burdened with further series of rigid costs which reduce its ability to adjust itself to fluctuating returns. Unemployment increases and with it expenditures on relief, financed to only a small degree by taxes on monopolists' incomes. The farmer and small business man must take drastic cuts in their standards of living and/or reduce the wages of their employees. The consequent[19] reduction in purchasing power of these groups might be thought to be offset by the increase in the purchasing power of shareholders in monopoly industries. But the purchasing power destroyed is mainly *consumer* purchasing power. The rich, unable to consume all their income, must, willy-nilly, save a considerable part. Therefore the compensating purchasing power created is largely *investor* purchasing power. During a depression, lack of confidence (engendered partly by the rigid price policy of the monopolies) makes industry reluctant to borrow and financial institutions reluctant to lend. The contraction in demand for consumers' goods is not in fact offset by expansion in demand for producers' goods. A rigid price policy, therefore, reduces not only consumer purchasing power but also total immediate purchasing power, and so intensifies the depression.[20]

18Royal Commission on Price Spreads, 1934. *Evidence*, p. 3124.

19We are dealing here only with the reduction in purchasing power which results from rigid prices in certain industries, not with the shrinkage in that purchasing power which results from dwindling export markets.

20See J. M. Keynes, *Treatise on Money*, and G. C. Means, *Industrial Prices and their Relative Inflexibility*, (U.S. Senate Document 13, 74th Congress, first session.)

Transfer Prices.

Less easily demonstrable, but probably not less serious, is the effect of inter-industrial concentration on the pricing mechanism. We have reason to be sceptical of the quality of the bargaining between inter-related financial and industrial concerns. For years the "transfer price" at which coal passed from the Dominion Steel Corporation's mines to its mills stood well below what the coal mines could have obtained in a free market.[21] Flour mills at various times have sold to subsidiary bakeries at more than the market price. "These companies", says the Registrar under the Combines Act, "are provided with an assured market . . . . one-eighth of the Canadian consumption in 1929. . . . There is no competition for this business, price competition or any other kind. There is no sales resistance to be overcome, and the subsidiary baking company is no longer in a position to bargain effectively as to price."[22]

That these cases are unique is conceivable, but unlikely. For Parliament has provided[23] for special duties on transactions of this kind between foreign companies and their Canadian subsidiaries; and the Lapointe Commission on Electric Rates in Quebec finds it impossible to compare Ontario and Quebec rates to large industrial consumers because in Ontario there are no "preferences" while in Quebec "the discretion of the management of the companies . . . has free play everywhere."[24]

At all events, there can be no question that the highly integrated industries (e.g., steel; grain, flour, and bread; telephones and telephone equipment) offer plenty of scope for such managed pricing.

Where buyer and seller have not been brought under unified control, but have one or more directors in common, the actual prices at which transactions take place are less likely to be affected. But the free working of the market may be no less effectively interfered with. When the Royal Bank heard that Lord Rothermere was "going to establish a pulp and paper mill down in your city of Quebec", the general manager of the Bank told Major Power of the Banking Committee of the House of Commons, "I distinctly remember ringing up Sir Herbert (Holt) and asking him whether he could see that we got that business.

[21]*Report of the Nova Scotia Royal Commission on the Coal Industry*, 1926.
[22]*Report of the Registrar under the Combines Investigation Act*, 1931, pp. 31, 41; see also, Commission on Price Spreads, 1934-1935, *Evidence*, pp. 3631-3634, 3694.
[23]Customs Tariff Act, 1930 (second session), section 6.
[24]Montreal *Star*, January 23, 1935.

He said, 'You know, I am going to be a director of that company; you have got it now'." In reply to a question by Mr. Coote, "Is it any advantage to an industrialist to be a bank director?" Sir Herbert himself said, "None that I know of, except to the bank." Mr. Coote: "You do attach considerable importance to that?" Sir Herbert: "Certainly I do." Mr. Wilson, general manager of the Royal Bank: "I do, the management does."[25] When the C. P. R. buys from any of the fifty-odd companies[26] with which it interlocks, is the bargain exactly the same as it would be in the absence of such a connection? In practice, it is impossible to answer, because there is no free market to serve as a standard of comparison. Do C. P. R. directors bring business to the companies on whose boards they sit, or the other way around, or are the relations precisely the same as between these companies and the C.N.R.? Is it for nothing that Canadian General Electric has three directors in common with Shawinigan, two in common with Montreal Light, Heat and Power Consolidated, and Duke-Price Power, one in common with British Columbia Power? Is it pure coincidence that Dominion Glass has three directors in common with Borden's, one with National Breweries; that Canadian Bag in 1933 shared two directors with Canada and Dominion Sugar, two with Ogilvie Flour Mills, one with British Columbia Sugar? Is there no significance in the interlocking of the large woollen and cotton firms with Canadian Converters, Woods Manufacturing, Brinton-Peterboro Carpets, and Tooke Brothers? It would seem that the characteristic form of the modern capitalist market tends to become more and more that of bargaining with oneself.

The Farmer and the Small Business.

Over the large sector of our economic life occupied by big business, competition has already largely disappeared. There remains, however, an important sector occupied by the competitive economy, exemplified by agriculture, the clothing trades, boots and shoes, and much retail trade. But are even these thoroughly competitive in the classic sense? The farmer, for example, must borrow from the banks, insurance companies and loan companies (all big business) at their non-competitive price. He must sell his wheat if not to the Pool, to the Canadian mil-

25Banking Committee, 1934. *Evidence,* pp. 860, 877.
26"Concentration in Canadian Industry", E. A. Forsey, *Canadian Forum,* October, 1933.

lers, or a combine of British millers,[27] (big business) at their price. If he grows tobacco, he was, until the Natural Products Marketing Act, at the mercy of Imperial Tobacco.[28] If his product is tomatoes, Canadian Canners dictates what he gets.[29] Similarly with livestock: Canada Packers dominates the situation.[30] As the Prime Minister sums it up, "Combines or monopolies or virtual monopolies (hold) a commanding position in their dealings with the producer of natural products. If the producer (has) only one buyer for his products, he (is) naturally not in a very good position to bargain".[31]

When Parliament, in the Marketing Act, seeks to redress the balance, the cries of injured monopolists ascend to heaven. "In the case of livestock," observes the *Financial Post* of March 16, 1935, "the application of the schemes would have vested complete control over production and sale of cattle, sheep and swine in one marketing agency. The packers, so far as their raw material is concerned, would have been in the hands of this monopoly. All free markets would have been suppressed and the price that packers would have had to pay would have been dictated not by the law of supply and demand but by executive order of the marketing agency". Satan rebuking sin!

Nor is the farmer in much better case when he buys. For whether it is agricultural implements,[32] motor cars, binder twine, wire fencing, fertilizer, or a good deal else, he must buy from the great corporation, again at *its* price.

The fate of other small enterprisers is similar. Of the fishermen of the Maritime Provinces the *Report* of the Royal Commission on Price Spreads remarks, "Limitation of domestic and foreign markets, concentration of distributors, the lessening of the number of buyers and agreement between the dealers in so far as purchases from the fishermen have been concerned, have inevitably led to an almost total loss to the fisherman of bargaining power without which he is reduced to the position of having to accept from the dealers for his fish whatever price they care to offer". A few large department stores, buying 42 per cent. of the output of women's clothing, confront an industry

27Commission on Price Spreads, 1934-1935. *Evidence*, p. 3917.
28Committee on Price Spreads, 1934. *Evidence*, pp. 1493-1497, 1501-1520, 1533-1563, 1753-1768.
29Commission on Price Spreads, 1934-1935. *Evidence*, pp. 3060, 3063, 3086, 3114, 3124-3130, 3310, 3422.
30Committee on Price Spreads, 1934. *Evidence;* a vast mass of information scattered throughout the first 1100 pages.
31Montreal *Star*, January 8, 1935.
32Commission on Price Spreads, 1934-1935. *Evidence*, pp. 4072, 4084.

in which 76 per cent. of the output comes from firms with less than $500,000 production. For boots and shoes the corresponding figures are 32 per cent. and 60 per cent., for men's clothing, 27 per cent. and 60 per cent.[33]

All these instances illustrate the truth of the *Report's* generalization that "if there is only one buyer for the product of many small producers, . . . the producers are at the buyer's mercy, just as the monopolistic producer has the buyers at his mercy when the situation is reversed".[34]

Over the competitive economy, monopoly rules by remote control.

As the small business man has lost his freedom and independence, so has the consumer. In a genuinely competitive economy the consumer counts for something. If he is not satisfied with what Jones offers, he can take his trade to Brown. But in the monopoly economy, there is no Brown to go to. If the consumer does not like what the monopolist offers, he can lump it. Usually, however, he *will* like it. He has to. The monopolist's advertising will see to that.[35] Big business therefore determines, directly or indirectly, not only the size of wage-earners' incomes, not only (through banks, trust and loan companies and insurance companies) how and where he shall invest whatever he can save, but also how he shall spend what remains. "Free consumers' choice" is as much a myth as "free competition". And sometimes monopoly may go so far—current revelations point out the tobacco industry as a perfect example—as to squeeze simultaneously primary producer, worker, consumer and retailer.

Interference with competition is not, of course, necessarily vicious in itself. It depends on the kind of interference. But when competition has disappeared, when (to quote the Prime Minister again), "the independent manufacturer [exists] only by the sufferance of the stranger," when "the open market place [has] ceased to be an open market place," when "the original checks and balances [have] failed in their essential functions,"[36] to go on relying on those checks and balances is to play the ostrich.

[33]*Price Spreads Report*, p 206
[34]*Ibid.*, p. 6.
[35]See James Rorty, *Our Master's Voice*. Note also the monopolist's control of retail outlets, exemplified by Imperial Tobacco, Canadian Canners and Canada Packers. See above, Chapter III (b).
[36]Montreal *Star*, January 8, 1935.

Is "Back to the Market" Feasible?

Some tell us that the remedy for this situation is to break up the mergers, "unscramble the egg", get back to the dear, dead days of small enterprise and free competition. "Back to the market" is, with variations, the common theme of Mr. Sanford Evans, ex-president of the Canadian Chamber of Commerce, Mr. Mackenzie King, Cardinal Villeneuve, the Montreal *Gazette* and the Winnipeg *Free Press*. That for most of the economy no effective free market ever existed does not trouble these bold theorists. Mr. Evans sighs for "a system . . . relying for the regulation of quantity and price mainly upon the test of an open market".[37] The Canadian Chamber of Commerce might be a little disconcerted if this were taken seriously, for it would involve among other things a veto on railway unification, abolition of the tariff and of course dissolution of most of the large companies. Mr. King is more modest: he would only modify the Natural Products Marketing Act and reduce the tariff to the level of 1930. (Or so one gathers. It takes an intrepid and persevering explorer to penetrate the verbal fog in which Mr. King shrouds his ideas.) The Cardinal[38] contents himself with "laying emphasis on the belief that there is not sufficient freedom of markets". In the *Gazette's* private heaven, the "law of supply and demand" is to be untrammelled save by monopolies, a high tariff and generous state subsidies and loans to a privileged few: income tax shall not corrupt nor social legislation break through and steal the fruits of the "honest toil" of St. James Street. The *Free Press* would doubtless abolish the tariff, what more we know not.

The most that is even faintly likely to emerge from any "back to the market campaign" is a slight reduction in the tariff, a further mild attempt at "trust-busting" through the Combines Act, and perhaps some whittling down of social legislation. No serious person expects to see Mr. King abolish the tariff or smash the monopolies; and not even a dictator dare take away any important part of our meagre social legislation. The social consequences of *laissez-faire* were too horrible for civilized communities to tolerate, and bred a working class discontent which had to be bought off.

Not even a Cardinal, an ex-premier, the Chamber of Com-

---

[37]Presidential address to the Canadian Chamber of Commerce, *Financial Post*, September 22, 1934.

[38]Montreal *Star*, January 5, 1934.

merce and two newspapers can "reverse the stream of history". Competition has destroyed itself. Modern industry is necessarily large-scale, and the wastes of competition between large units are often ruinous. Monopoly, it is true, is not always efficient: inefficiency sometimes "pays" better. Even when it is efficient, the consumer's share of the economies is often microscopic. In a socialized monopoly, these dangers disappear. But in one form or another, desirable or undesirable, monopoly is here to stay. The United States after forty years of uniformly unsuccessful attempts to destroy it, has abandoned the effort and is trying instead to encourage and "control". In German and Italy, Fascist propaganda bribed the small business man by promising to abolish Big Business, but Fascist governments have made Big Business bigger and more powerful than ever.

Superficially, Mr. Bennett's (and Mr. Roosevelt's) policy of "controlling" monopoly capitalism is more plausible. But it is doomed to equal futility, though of a different kind and for different reasons. It does not remove any of the fundamental reasons why modern capitalism fails to work. The proof of this statement demands a chapter to itself,[39] but the practical demonstration is plain for all to see. England has enjoyed all of Mr. Bennett's reforms for some years, most of them since before the War, many for half a century or more. They did not save her from unemployment and depression, though they mitigated the horrors of both and perhaps reduced slightly the amplitude of the swing. They did not abolish poverty nor touch the roots of the maldistribution of wealth. Much the same is true of Germany. Nothing in the brief experience of the United States under the New Deal in any way contradicts these conclusions. In fact, as every financial page testifies, the chief beneficiaries of Mr. Roosevelt's policies have been the profitmakers. Wages have barely kept pace with a rising cost of living, if indeed they have done so much; but dividends have risen nobly. The only distinctive lesson of the New Deal, in fact,—lost, apparently, on Mr. Bennett—is that in the modern world the great corporations are strong enough to bend or break any government which allows them to exist at all.[40] The only control of Big Business which can succeed is complete socialization.

[39]See below, Chap. VII, "Why the System Fails to Work," and "Why Capitaliism Cannot Plan".

[40]See Louis M. Hacker, *A Short History of the New Deal;* also Stolberg and Vinton, *Economic Consequences of the New Deal;* Methodist Federation for Social Service, *Social Questions Bulletin,* November, 1934.

In some sectors of the economy a real "open market" never existed; from the rest it has gone never to return. The choice between capitalism, "reformed" or unreformed, and socialism is not a choice between an automatic, impersonal, fool-proof system and one of new, untried, and cumbrous planning. Prices, the regulators of capitalism, are no longer self-adjusting. Capitalists already plan, after a fashion, but *piecemeal* (industry by industry, group by group), and *for themselves*. And the aim is scarcity, not abundance; the more effective their planning becomes the worse it will be for the rest of us.[41]   The choice before us is between anarchic planning for private profits, and unified and comprehensive planning for the common good.

[41]For fuller discussion of the possibility and nature of capitalist planning see below, Chapter VII, "Why the System Fails to Work", and "Why Capitalism Cannot Plan".   Both Engels and Lenin recognized the possibility of capitalist planning of sorts.   See Lenin, *State and Revolution*, p. 57 (Little Lenin Library, Vol. 14) and *Imperialism*, p. 155 (same series, Vol. 15), quoted below.

CHAPTER V.

AGRICULTURE AND THE FARMER.

A. THE IMPORTANCE OF AGRICULTURE.

AGRICULTURE is Canada's greatest primary industry. No lasting recovery and no fundamental reconstruction of the Canadian economy is possible except on the basis of a programme which gives to the farmer the share of attention which is his due.

The significance of agriculture to the economic life of Canada can be sketched in a few paragraphs. Take, first, the statistics of production. It will be seen from the table below that (taking a normal year) the net value of agricultural production in Canada in 1926 was roughly $1,400 millions. This figure comprised 38 per cent. of the grand total of production for all primary and secondary industries for Canada in that year. By 1930, it is true, agricultural output had fallen in value and the proportion had shrunk to 24 per cent., but the agricultural industry continued to make the largest contribution to the sum total of productive enterprises, excluding the manufactures group. The real importance of agriculture in the Canadian economy is, of course, much greater than these figures would indicate. Many of our important secondary industries are based upon agricultural production. In 1930, for example, the net value of the pro-

NET ANNUAL PRODUCTION OF CANADA.[1]

(Millions of $).

Year	Agriculture	Total
1926	1,400	3,640
1927	1,523	3,902
1928	1,501	4,123
1929	1,034	3,947
1930	759	3,217
1931	538	2,500
1932	565	2,105
1933	541	2,184
1934	623	2,585

[1]See *Canada Year Books, Financial Post Business Year Book,* 1935, 25.

ducts of all manufacturing industries concerned with commodities
of farm origin was roughly $400 millions over and above the
cost of the raw products produced in Canada themselves. That
is to say, Canadian industries, using some of the animal and
vegetable products of the farms of this country added another
$400 millions to their value. We may say, therefore, that agri-
culture was the origin of some $1,159 millions out of a total pro-
duction of $3,217 millions in 1930.

But statistical categories are deceptive. The importance of
agriculture in the Canadian economic scheme of things is not
brought out in production statistics. Population statistics are
rather more enlightening.[2] If, however, we examine the industrial, financial and transportation structure of Canada we find
that, historically, agricultural production has been the principal
support of our whole economic development; and the economic
fortune of Canada today is still bound up with the production
of the great export staples (farm products, forest products, minerals, etc.) more than anything else. Ordinarily (although the
greater relative decline in farm prices since the depression has
changed the present picture somewhat) farm products constitute
more than half of Canada's total exports.

CANADIAN EXPORTS: FISCAL YEARS 1928-35.

(Millions of $).

	1928	1929	1930	1931	1932	1933	1934	1935
Farm Products.....	628	712	428	309	224	222	236	259
Total Exports.......	1,228	1,364	1,120	800	576	474	579	667

The result is that a fall in the revenues of agriculture cannot, in the nature of things, rest only on the shoulders of the
farmer. A whole complex of interests has been established in
Canada to minister to the farmer, and depressed agriculture carries down these interests with it. The grain trade provides, perhaps, the most spectacular example of inter-connected industry.
The building of the trans-continental railways and branch lines,
the money expended on improving the St. Lawrence waterways
and the Great Lakes—deepening channels, digging canals, ex-

[2]The Census of 1931 revealed that 1,131,871 persons were "gainfully employed" in
agriculture. The total of "gainfully employed" persons in all occupations was 3,927,591
at the same period. Agriculture therefore provides for slightly under one-third of the total
"jobs" in Canada.

tending the harbours—were all pushed forward to carry the grain. The building of elevators and mills, the manufacture of agricultural implements, and other production goods were largely based on what was expected to be a profitable and continually expanding grain trade. Iron and steel industries grew up in the East to provide railway materials, and still depend to an important degree on this market. So too, with some coal mining in Canada. These latter industries are depressed because transportation is depressed—and railway losses are partly attributable to the decline in the grain trade. In this sense, then, every branch of Canadian economic activity is adversely affected by agricultural depression. The repercussions of falling prices have extended everywhere, reducing the incomes of governments, railroads, and Eastern industries, and diminishing urban employment as well as rural incomes. Regarded from another angle, it can be shown that the shrinkage in agricultural income derived from exports has made it difficult for Canadian governments and corporations to meet their foreign debt charges and maturities, except at the cost of some depreciation in the rate of the Canadian dollar on the foreign exchanges, a factor productive of additional budgetary difficulties to public authorities with large foreign debts.

The problem of depressed agriculture is not one, therefore, which Canadian governments can be content to ignore, even though the farming population fails to make its demand for reform felt. Actually, of course, there is in Canada widespread evidence of a growing discontent amongst rural people, springing from dissatisfaction with the present economic welfare of farmers. Coupled with this there is a growing belief that in some way their distress is due to the inadequacies of the present economic system.

Types of Agriculture.

Before examining the present conditions among farmers in general, it is as well to remind ourselves that "agriculture", of course, means many things. The generic title covers a variety of enterprises carried on under different climatic and economic conditions, and facing numerous but separate production and marketing problems. The 1,132,000 persons described as "gainfully employed" in agriculture (an ironic description to many of them today) cultivated 728,664 farms in 1931 with roughly sixty million acres under field crops and another eight million acres under pasture. They produced practically every type of agricultural product appropriate to the climatic and soil conditions. It is difficult, therefore, to speak of one agricultural problem. The Maritime has its fruit and vegetable crops, its oats and potatoes; Quebec and Ontario, whilst pre-eminently occupied with mixed farming, livestock and dairying, have their specialized cultivation of sheep, tobacco and, in the Niagara district, of small and large fruits; the Prairie Provinces, with their overwhelming specialization in the production of grains, have problems distinct from those of other rural areas, but are tending (in Manitoba areas, for example) towards mixed farming, or are changing back to stock-raising somewhat; in British Columbia a different type of agriculture is found in the form of fruit cultivation, and, along the coast, of market gardening.

These distinct types of agricultural producers are subject to different problems. Problems in the field of marketing, or of methods of sale, or of prices are not wholly uniform. The incidence of debt or of transportation costs is more burdensome in some regions than in others. One crop may be more subject to the "natural" visitations of drought and insect pests than another. Finally, in any one group of producers, the difficulties of the old established and possibly more efficient producers are less pressing than those facing the marginal producers.

Strictly speaking, therefore, we have not one agricultural problem, but a dozen varieties of agricultural problems. Nevertheless, certain factors in the general farming impoverishment of the last five years are common to the majority. All of them point to a great shrinkage in farm incomes and therefore in farm purchasing power and to a great decline of the standards of well-being of this large section of the Canadian economy.

B. The Plight of the Farmer.

To the farmer the income available for the purchases necessary to the maintenance of his standard of living depends upon the selling prices received for his products. What he can afford to buy for himself and his family will depend normally on what is left over after the deduction of cash payments for debt charges on his land, stock and implements, and the payments for seed, materials and depreciation of equipment. Any fall in farm incomes must result therefore in a reduction of the volume of farmers' purchases or in a cessation of debt payments, or a combination of both.

The Reduction in Farm Incomes.

The statistics of total agricultural revenue give some indication of the appalling nature of the shrinkage in farm incomes since the depression. The total dropped from a high of $1,523 millions in 1927 to $538 millions in 1931, the worst year. In 1931, in other words, farm incomes were roughly one-third of the incomes of 1927. The improvement since 1931 has, of course, been real—but slight.

A study of the more detailed statistics brings out the fact that every branch of agriculture has been affected—domestic products as well as those on an export basis. The explanation of this decline in net revenue lies, of course, partly in the fall in domestic and world prices, but partly also in a much smaller decline in sales volume.

PRICE INDEX NUMBERS, 1926-1934.

Year	All Commodities	Farm Products	Field Products	Animal Products	Retail Prices	Producers' Equipment
	(1)	(2)	(3)	(4)	(5)	(6)
1926.........	100.0	100.0	100.0	100.0	100.0	100.0
1927.........	97.7	102.1	99.9	105.7	98.4	101.1
1928.........	96.4	100.7	92.6	114.3	98.9	93.7
1929.........	95.6	100.8	93.8	112.5	99.9	94.6
1930.........	86.6	82.3	70.0	102.9	99.2	92.9
1931.........	72.2	56.3	43.6	77.6	89.6	90.0
1932.........	66.7	48.4	41.1	60.7	81.4	88.7
1933.........	67.1	51.0	45.8	59.7	77.7	86.0
1934.........	71.6	59.3	53.9	67.6	78.9	88.8

The fall in farm prices is shown in the above table. Contrasted with the index number of farm prices are those relating to retail prices and the cost of manufactured products and services. This table brings out the significant disparity (one which has widened in recent years) between the price received by farmers for their products, and the prices which must be paid for the things they are compelled to buy. It will be seen that the average price of farm products in 1934 was 59.3 per cent. of what it was in 1926, (53.9 per cent. for field products and 67.6 per cent. for animal products). Retail prices for the same year had only dropped to 78.9 per cent. of the 1926 figure, whilst producers' equipment was as high as 88.8 per cent. of the "prosperity" price.

In other words, there has been no great relief for farmers with diminished incomes in the cost of the things they purchase.

The explanation of the failure of manufactures to fall in price, is, broadly speaking, twofold. There is firstly the problem of overhead costs, enlarged by the investment ramp of prosperity days which rivetted an excessive, frequently watered, capital charge upon industry. The domination of heavy fixed charges finds additional support in the widespread tendency towards industrial monopoly in Canada, which operates so effectively under the protective shelter of the tariff. The effect of this trend is to make for the elimination of real competition and the adoption of price maintenance schemes for manufactured commodities. As one writer has put it,

"Canadian farmers must now buy sugar from one of the eight refineries operated by one or two concerns. If binders and mowers are needed, it is a case of interviewing the local representative of Massey-Harris or International Harvester Company. All cattle or hogs except the few sold to local butchers by specially located farmers must go to one of the 70 odd plants operated by Canada Packers, Burns & Company and one or two others. If cream is sold it has to go more and more to a creamery controlled by Eastern Dairies, Canada Dairy Corporation, Silverwood's, or Borden's. If a farmer wants a new barn he has to get his cement from the Canada Cement Company. If artificial fertilizer is wanted for the fall wheat or apple orchard, there are only a couple of possible sources of supply. Unless an understanding and more fortunate neighbour comes to the rescue, the farmer must have recourse to the local manager of one of our ten chartered banks, if he needs a short-term loan. Should he desire a radio or piano he must needs deal with one of about three firms regardless of the instrument he selects. Should he decide on a car it will be a case of buying from Ford, Chrysler or General Motors. If he wishes to read other than the local paper he must support one of a few national or international newspaper chains. His gasoline is almost certain to come from either British American or Imperial Oil Company, and even these are closely related. The wire for his fence, steel for his roof, twine for his grain, coal for his furnace, refrigerator for his kitchen, shirt for his back, salt for his cattle or himself, these and many more articles must each and all be procured from a very small number of extremely large organizations. In every case he must pay the price asked by one or two companies or do without. In short, the machine age has made the farmer dependent on the factories of the cities, while at the same time it has lowered his bargaining power in dealing with these factories".[3]

In the more primitive economic communities of earlier days a rough sort of justice would make those who do business with the producer or those to whom he is indebted share some portion of his losses. Our modern pecuniary and industrial society has changed all that. Farm sales and farm prices have fallen drastically, but the agricultural costs of production show no such proportionate decline in value. Implements, gasoline, freight rates, trucks, wire, steel, and the rest have not fallen greatly. In addition, the farmers' mortgage interest payments are absolutely fixed in terms of money, and are enforceable under penalty of the law. The various provincial systems of moratoria, or of debt adjustment legislation, and the Farmers' Creditors Arrangement Act adopted under pressure of the debtor classes, have done something, of course, to avoid foreclosures. They have done very little, however, to reduce the amount of debt outstanding. In addition to this factor, the increasing severity of the farming depression has driven an already debt-ridden community deeper into debt.

The Debt Burden of the Farmer.

The capital costs of farming, the costs incurred in purchasing land, implements, livestock and the rest obviously absorbed much more of the farm incomes in the spring of 1933, with wheat in the neighbourhood of 50c per bushel, than they did when wheat sold for three times as much money five years previously. In fact, at the level of prices ruling in the 1932-1933 crop year the debt burdens, whenever incurred, were quite incommensurate with existing farm incomes. Now the significant thing to observe is that at any level of farm prices likely to be achieved internationally, large sections of Canadian agriculture have become so permanently indebted, over the last decade or so, that the standard of living for farmers of the pre-slump days cannot, in the absence of any drastic change, be regained. Whilst it is true that the depression in agriculture makes it impossible for creditors to foreclose at present, it nevertheless remains a fact that any improvement in the farm situation is going to result in the surplus gains of farmers being transferred largely to creditors. It is also probable that the process of foreclosure will recommence just as soon as it becomes economically possible to re-sell

3W. M. Drummond: *The Canadian Farmer and the Machine Age,* Pamphlet No. 2 published by the Social Service Council of Canada.

the land. The increase in the number of tenant farmers in Canada is a partial indication of the manner by which impoverished cultivators are being gradually compelled to relinquish ownership.[4] The growth in the debt burden provides evidence of the extent to which an enormous number of Canadian farmers, particularly in the areas where farming is most commercial and capitalistic in character, are gradually losing all but the smallest amount of equity in their land. When mortgage payments absorb all but what is necessary to the maintenance of a minimum of subsistence, the farmer-owner may well come to envy the tenant farmer. In fact the transition to tenancy will be easy. The traditional Canadian class of independent owner-producer will have disappeared. Is this an exaggerated prophecy? Let us examine the statistics relating to farm debt and to farm values.

The Agricultural Census of 1931 brought out the facts that 242,850 farms in Canada, equal to 33 per cent. of the total number of fully-owned farms, had debts secured by mortgage or similar charge. The total of such debts amounted to $671,776,-500. The debt burden was also stated to be equal, roughly, to 41 per cent. of the value of the fully-owned farms to which the inquiry was addressed. Impressive as it is, this piece of information, unfortunately, is only part of the story. It greatly underestimates the debt burden, as the official returns point out, because all debts other than "mortgage" debts were excluded from the Census inquiry. No particulars were compiled, that is to say, of debts covered by crop liens, or by liens on implements, machinery or livestock. Nor do the official statistics cover the whole of Canadian agriculture; they relate only to "owned" farms, and exclude all reference to farms purchased under agreement for sale, and to tenant farmers or part-owned farms. Clearly in all such cases the proportion of debt would be considerably higher than the average. What then is the actual debt situation?

Unfortunately it has to be admitted that for our basic industry there exists no adequate official information on the subject. One is compelled, therefore, to make use of the method of sampling familiar to statisticians. Fortunately for our purpose, there is one excellent sample from which we can gain some idea of the colossal burden of agricultural debt in the Canadian West, where the probelm is most acute.[5]

4See below, Section c.

5Extensive material on this subject has been collected by the Pioneer Problems Research Committee. The table quoted above is from "The Economic Background of the Agricultural Situation in Saskatchewan"—an address delivered Jan. 25th, 1933, by Dr. Wm. Allen, of the Department of Farm Management, University of Saskatchewan.

Summary of Debts of 408 Saskatchewan Farm Owners.

(Summer, 1932)

Municipalities	Area No.	Owners Reporting Information	Owners Having Debts			
			No.	Acres Cropland Per Farm	Debt Per Farm	Debt per acre of Cropland
Rosemount (378)	1	218	202	401	$6,125	$15.27
Brokenshell (68).	2	48	47	341	2,938	8.62
Wellington (97).	3	59	58	457	6,174	13.52
Scott (98)......	4	83	83	623	14,770	23.69
Total......	—	408	390	449	$7,588	$16.88

This picture of the debt situation in four Saskatchewan muni-cipalities, representing four distinct types of farming conditions, is described as being quite representative of the areas from which they were obtained. If, as is probable, they are fairly typical of Western farming as a whole, then indeed the situation is a seri-ous one for the future well-being of Western farms themselves, and, by repercussion, for the rest of the Canadian economy. As the table indicates, of 408 farms considered, 390 reported debts averaging $7,588 per farm, which is a debt of $16.88 per acre of crop land. It will be observed that even in a region of this char-acter where a similar type of farming is pursued, there are very wide ranges of debt. A few farmers were able to keep out of debt, averaging perhaps five per cent. in all. Of the rest, the majority have incurred large debts. Incidentally it should be observed that the average debt for this area at $7,588 per owned farm is more than twice as great as the amount calculated from the official statistics as the average mortgage debt of the owned farms of Saskatchewan, namely $3,142, which is the figure most widely used in discussing this problem.

As indicated in this table, over sixty per cent. of the farms surveyed had debts in excess of $10.00 per acre of crop land, and over thirty per cent. had debts of over $20.00 per crop acre. As to the composition of these debts, the purchase of new farms or the expansion of old ones explains their nature. In the first area, the only one analyzed for the purpose, over 90 per cent. of all farm owners having debts owed large amounts on purchase of farm real estate, averaging roughly 80 per cent. of the total debt. The balance of debt was owing on the purchase of farm

implements, or to banks, on taxes, for lumber, gas, oil, feed, seed
and so forth.

DISTRIBUTION OF DEBTS OF 408 SASKATCHEWAN FARM OWNERS,
1932.[6]

Debt per acre of crop land	Per cent. of all farms				
	Area No. 1	Area No. 2	Area No. 3	Area No. 4	All Areas
Nil	7.3	4.3	1.7	—	4.7
Up to $10.00	29.8	62.4	35.6	22.9	33.0
$10.00 to $20.00	35.8	20.8	40.7	19.3	31.4
$20.00 to $30.00	16.5	10.4	13.5	22.9	16.7
$30.00 to $40.00	6.4	—	5.1	21.7	8.6
$40.00 to $50.00	3.7	2.1	3.4	6.0	3.9
$50.00 and over	0.5	—	—	7.2	1.7
Totals	100	100	100	100	100

But of course debts are relative: if prices of farm products
are low, they become crushing; if the prices of the things the
farmer must buy remain high, they spell impoverishment, want,
and despair of the future.

What, then, is the product or gross earning power of an acre
of crop land? Perhaps half the acreage is sown to wheat or to
other grains, bringing an average of (say) ten to twelve bushels
an acre at (say) 40 cents a bushel. Against this there is the
service of the debt to be met. The 408 farms surveyed in the
study already referred to carried debt averaging $16.31 per acre
of crop land, or about $33 per acre of wheat. As the author of
the survey remarks: "These farms have a burden of the most
depressing kind. Interest on this amount of debt at 8 per cent.
requires $1.30 per year for each acre of crop land. Even where
it is possible to secure amortization of the debt at 7 per cent., on
a 20 year basis, there would be needed an annual instalment of
$1.14 per acre of crop land". In all the debt service would re-
quire $2.44 per acre of crop land, or almost $5.00 per acre of
wheat, which is in excess of the gross return from wheat production at recent low prices, and far in excess of the net return after
all other production costs have been met.

Needless to say the position of farming in other parts of
Canada is by no means as desperate as this, and the degree of

[6]*Op. cit.*, p. 11.

subsistence provided by mixed farming in other areas mitigates the position somewhat. But the problem of low prices and relatively rigid costs is common to all branches of the industry.

Standards of Living in Western Canada.

For Western Canada at least the situation is desperate. Standards of living, never very high,[7] have been lowered to peasant levels in many cases. Food supplies are being increasingly drawn from the farm itself—when there is a crop—and not from the general store. New clothing in many cases comes only through the relief agencies. Farm homes are being permitted to fall into an acute state of disrepair. The rural telephone, a service of absolute necessity in semi-isolated districts, has been abandoned in thousands of farms along with the automobile. "Between 1928 and 1933 the number of rural telephones in Manitoba declined from 13,205 to 8,365, a loss of more than 36 per cent. Saskatchewan shows a loss of nearly 30,000, or more than 40 per cent. . . . Alberta . . . rural telephone subscribers declined from 21,269 to 10,162, a drop of 52 per cent.".[8]

The same condition is reflected in the breakdown of municipal governments and the bankruptcy of the educational and social services they administered. At the end of 1932 "828 rural school districts, 225 village school districts, and 48 town school districts were reported as in default to the debenture holders. At the same time the bank indebtedness of rural municipalities was $8,379,548.97; the amount due schools, rural co-operative telephone companies, etc., for the requisition of taxes amounted to $8,120,615.71; the uncollected arrears of taxes plus the tax sale holdings (which must be added to get a correct statement of total arrears) amounted to $30,368,345.82. Thus the total arrears at the end of 1932 were almost equal to two years' taxes

	Total coupons payable (principal and interest)	No. of companies in default	Default Principal	Default Interest	Default Per cent.
1929.....	$1,867,041.02	3	$ 420.37	$ 135.13	.003
1930.....	1,824,828.63	41	36,479.27	13,772.32	2.750
1931.....	1,768,519.50	278	299,416.78	105,386.15	22.889
1932.....	1,618,509.13	588	775,729.49	223,734.86	61.750

7Cf. Chapter I of this volume.
8G. E. Britnell. *The Western Farmer*, p. 8. (Pamphlet No. 6 of the Social Service Council of Canada.)

on every acre of farm land in Saskatchewan and this despite the adoption of coercive measures of tax collection in that year.

"The position of the rural telephone companies in Saskatchewan shows how the area of default has widened from year to year since 1929. (See table at foot of page 137).

" . . . It would appear that of the companies still carrying unretired debentures nearly 75 per cent. were in default at the end of 1932, and the general position can scarcely have improved since that time".[9]

The biggest problem of all has arisen over the maintenance of normal educational services in rural areas. "Although the permission of the Minister of Education (of Saskatchewan) is required when a rural school is operated for less than 200 teaching days a year, less than 40 per cent. of rural schools were open for the full year in 1932 as compared with 72.12 per cent. in 1931 and 73.22 per cent. in 1930. A considerable number of rural schools close for some months during the winter because (a) the school district cannot afford to buy coal; (b) the children have not sufficient warm clothes to go to school. The number of schools closed would, of course, be much greater if it were not for the activities of the government and private agencies in supplying clothes, and the energy of the Department of Education and the Relief Commission—not to mention the substantial generosity of the mine-owners—in providing coal for school districts in need of such assistance".[10]   Of course, it need hardly be added that a large part of the burden has fallen on the rural teachers. "A recent report of the Dominion Bureau of Statistics shows that rural teachers in Manitoba have taken a 33 per cent. cut in salary in the two-year period, 1931 to 1933. In Saskatchewan and Alberta, salary cuts have been fully as great, while in addition a great many teachers have had to teach for $100 and $200 a year, in cash, being forced to take the remainder . . . in school district notes. . . . Teachers affirm that there is generally no way of discounting these notes, even at 50 per cent".[11]   Many rural teachers have received no more than the minimum provincial grant of $1.00 per teaching day. This was the situation in the three prairie provinces in 1932 and 1933, and there has been no marked improvement since.

It is difficult, of course, to separate the problems incidental to

9G. E. Britnell. *The Western Farmer*, p. 8.

10G. E. Britnell. "Economic Conditions in Rural Saskatchewan", *Canadian Forum*, March, 1934.

11G. E. Britnell. *The Western Farmer*, pp. 8-9.

crop failure arising from drought and grasshoppers from those resulting from the depression in farm prices. The fact remains that a government delegation from Saskatchewan waiting upon the Prime Minister at Ottawa pointed out that more than one half the rural municipalities would need government assistance during the winter. "Feed for the distressed families, fodder for stock, and seed for next year would have to be provided in 140 municipalities, and 58 of these were absolutely bankrupt and unable to contribute any share of the cost". The fact is that the disastrous economic situation of the farmer during the last four years in this, as in other Western provinces, has so depleted the individual and community reserves that any partial crop failure means complete destitution. And all this in the same province which, according to the official estimate for 1931, ranked third amongst the provinces in aggregate wealth, and third in per capita wealth.

Agriculture in the East.

If this tragic picture is drawn with Prairie Provinces statistics only, there are no grounds for the inference that the Eastern farmer at least is well off. That (according to the 1931 census survey) only 10.4 per cent. of the farms in Ontario had water piped in the kitchen and only 6.3 per cent. water piped in the bathroom, is no indication of luxury. The province with the best showing in this respect—Quebec, 31.9 per cent. of whose farms have water laid on in the kitchen—has only 8.2 per cent of its farms with bathrooms supplied by piped water. If the latter facility is used as an index, the "prosperous" farms of the Maritime provinces do not appear to be very well equipped (Prince Edward Island 3.8 per cent., Nova Scotia 4.3 per cent., New Brunswick 4.0 per cent.). Only 16.8 per cent. of Ontario farms and 14.0 per cent. of Quebec farms are equipped with either gas or electric light, and the proportions are very much lower in the Maritimes (4.0, 9.5 and 7.4 per cent. in Prince Edward Island, Nova Scotia and New Brunswick respectively). The standards of ordinary living amenities would seem to be highest for farms in British Columbia, but even here only between 20 and 30 per cent. of the total have such equipment as telephone, radios, piped water, gas and electric light.

Moreover, a disproportionate fall in prices has characterized most farm products besides the staple grains. Home markets have failed as well as export markets, or—what in many cases is more to the point—the producer of meat, fruit, dairy products, tobacco, vegetables, etc., is faced with such terms by the large-scale buyers who constitute his market that his returns do not cover his costs. And serious as is the debt situation in the West, it is clear from the following figures (which incidentally do not represent all the farmers' obligations, besides covering only fully owned farms) that the problem is a Dominion-wide one.

MORTGAGE INDEBTEDNESS IN EASTERN AND WESTERN CANADA.

(as at 1931)

(Fully owned farms only)

Province	P. C. of Farms Reporting Mortgage Debts	Mortgage Debt as P. C. of Total Farm Value	Province	P. C. of Farms Reporting Mortgage Debts	Mortgage Debt as P. C. of Total Farm Value
Prince Edward Island........	33.5	33.7	Manitoba........	39.7	49.5
Nova Scotia	10.3	40.4	Saskatchewan...	46.0	38.1
New Brunswick.	17.6	38.3	Alberta.........	39.6	38.7
Quebec.........	31.7	38.3	British Columbia	25.9	34.8
Ontario........	40.8	44.8	Canada.........	35.6	40.9

As indicated below, loss of ownership and increasing resort to tenant-farming is making its mark on Eastern agriculture, even if it is as yet less obvious than in the West. Finally, it is a truth never to be forgotten in Canada that the East cannot prosper if the West declines. This is as true for Eastern agriculture as it is for manufacturing, to which the statement is more generally applied.

The fact is that throughout the length and breadth of Canada, with very few exceptions, farming is in a sorry plight. And the situation is not improving. The disappearance of working capital which is typical of every region places farmers under the stern necessity of adding to their debt, if production, the basis of livelihood, is to continue. The process of tightening the belt, appealing for public relief, and temporizing with the creditors, may create an illusion of stability, but it cannot be more than a temporary makeshift. Things will not improve by that method. As time goes on the debt burden mounts, and there takes place a steady depreciation of farm buildings, machinery and equipment which cannot fail to impair their productive efficiency for the future. These are the elements which are going to remain a depressing force in agriculture for decades, unless strenuous and radical efforts are made to remove them.

c. INDEPENDENT FARMER OR TIED TENANT?

One of the inevitable consequences of the conditions which have been outlined above is that tenant-farming is assuming considerable proportions in Canada. The whole picture of debt, insecurity and impoverishment is a significant commentary on that favourite delusion of many of our more complacent citizens that the farmer is a free and independent producer. It has always been a comforting thought to many of such people that the farmer in Canada stood on his own feet: any programme of co-operation or social control would founder on the rock of his rugged individualism. Capitalist politicians, for example, have taken great pains to keep the farmer safe for the Good Old Party by characterizing all intelligent proposals for agricultural reform as "confiscatory". They speak of the "loss of freedom" which would result from any plan of "regimentation" and of the confiscation of "the fruits of the farmers' honest toil".

But today the idea that the farmers of Canada own the land they work is a delusion. To a very substantial extent the mortgage companies and others own it. Not less characteristic of the present state of agriculture is the fact that the number of farmers who have no clear legal title to their land is large and rapidly increasing. Figures from agricultural census sources provide ample illustration of this point.

Measured against the year 1921, the only other year for which full statistics are available, the number of farmers who in 1931 possessed the nominal title to their farms had decreased by 28,842, despite soldiers settlement schemes (particularly in Alberta and British Columbia) and state-aided immigration and colonization schemes of various types on an unprecedented scale. On the other hand, the number of "full tenant farms" increased by practically 33 per cent. and the number of "part tenant and part owner" farms increased by over 70 per cent. The extent of landlordism is even more marked if the total acreage, rather than number of farms, be considered. On this basis we find that the acreage "partly owned, partly rented" has increased more than 100 per cent. and the acreage "wholly rented" by more than

50 per cent. The combined acreage of partly and fully rented land amounts to more than one third of the total acreage under cultivation.

But this, as we have suggested, does not tell the whole story. Of the 586,299 nominally "fully owned" farms in Canada, 208,-460 reported mortgage debts aggregating $566,016,900 equal to approximately 41 per cent. of the value of these farms.[12] But this total has reference only to debt secured by mortgage or an equivalent legal instrument, and takes no account of these other obligations which are a standing threat to the farmer's ownership in an unknown, but undoubtedly large, number of cases.

It will be seen, therefore, that the distinction between tenant and owner has become largely unreal. In fact a situation has been reached where the farmer who owns his land may find himself in worse position than the renter. With the drop in land values and the accumulation of interest charges on mortgage or bank loans, tax arrears, and special liens, a large number of farmers have no equity left in the land. After years of work, in the course of which farmers have in many cases paid more than the original purchase price, they find themselves still owing more than the present sale value of the land.[13] Being registered owner of the land means nothing except that if the land is worth less than the encumbrances, the farmer's personal assets may be seized for the difference. The freehold tenant who works his own farm is rapidly disappearing. The farmer's choice is merely between mortgage-hold and leasehold.

To claim that no large number of farmers have been dispossessed during the past few years, as disclosed by the number of foreclosures and mortgage sales, is beside the point. Under present conditions it does not pay the mortgage or land company to foreclose, as the sale value of the land is less than the company's claim against the farmer, and as it would be almost impossible to find a new tenant. But as soon as the prices of farm products improve it will become profitable to foreclose, and the farmer's reward for struggling through his present difficulties will be the loss of his land just when these difficulties are beginning to disappear.

It is not surprising that one result of the present situation has been the development of "chain" farming. A number of mortgage and loan companies have established a corporation to

[12]Agricultural Census, *Bulletin XIV*, p. 12.

[13]The average value per farm in Canada in 1931 was $7,202 as compared with $9,262 in 1921, the year of the last census. The drop from 1929 levels to the present has of course been much greater.

manage those farms on which the companies have any claim.[14]
The plan is not limited to purchasers and tenants and those who
have already lost their farms by foreclosure, but it also extends
to cover those farmers whose mortgages are in arrears. Such
farmers are forced "voluntarily" to accept the plan if they hope
to escape foreclosure. A zone manager is appointed to take
charge of all farms in a given district. He surveys the farm,
takes an inventory of buildings, stock and equipment, and draws
up a plan of farm operation. If the farmer will not accept the
plan voluntarily, the manager can force him to accept it under
threat of eviction. In short, the farmer's position is practically
the same as that of an industrial worker. The politicians and
press continue to assure us that the farmer is free and independent. But the bare statistics demonstrate that the number
of those who possess even legal title to their farms is steadily
diminishing. And many of these have to contribute a considerable
part of their income to the mortgage groups and to the interests
which support them.

CHANGES IN THE TENURE OF FARMS, 1921-1931.

Number and Acreage of Farms; Total for Canada.

Type of Tenure	1921	1931	P.C. Change
Owned Farms			%
No. of farms..................	615,180	586,299	−4.7
Total acreage (000's)..........	110,950	107,255	−3.4
Part Owned, Part Tenant			
No. of farms..................	39,932	67,942	+70.1
Total acreage (000's)..........	17,083	36,032	+110.9
Tenant or Rented Farms			
No. of farms..................	55,948	74,382	+33.0
Total acreage (000's)..........	13,041	20,039	+53.7

14E.g., the Colonization Finance Co.

CHAPTER VI.

GOVERNMENT INTERVENTION AND OWNERSHIP:

THE PRESENT SITUATION.

Canadian business men are fond of demanding that governments should "let business alone". They would be frightened nearly to death if governments took them at their word. For while it would be delightful to get rid of workmen's compensation, factory acts, minimum wage laws, public utility commissions and so forth, it would be anything but agreeable to be deprived of tariff protection, bounties, interest-free loans, guarantees of bonds and bank loans, and permission to value assets at fictitious prices to preserve solvency, or to be asked to repay the enormous gifts from public treasuries to private concerns. Any serious attempt to carry out such a programme would throw the whole economy into chaos.

In practice, of course, our business leaders put a good deal of government interference water into their *laissez-faire* wine. The Canadian Manufacturers' Association, for example, regards it as a "duty to co-operate with the Dominion Government, with the provinces, and the municipalities for the promotion of the national growth of Canada and the development of the country's resources". Nor is this "co-operation" a mere pious wish. No budget is framed without the kind assistance of the association and its members. Nowhere more freely than in Canada have business groups insisted on governmental aid in finding and keeping markets, in transporting goods to these markets, in financing business expansion. In few capitalist countries does the state play a larger part in the functioning of the economy.

The multiplicity of laws and regulations which have in fact grown up piecemeal in response to the pressure of various groups may be most conveniently described under three heads: (1) government regulation and control of industry, (2) government service and aid to industry, (3) government ownership and operation of industry. These sometimes overlap. For instance, the official grading of farm products is both a service to the farmer and a regulation of his business. Similarly government ownership and operation of canals is a service to shippers and shipowners, and many boards and commissions render technical service at the same time that they are exercising regulatory powers. The threefold classification, however, will help us to see just how far Canada has adhered to another theory beloved of business men, that the proper function of government is to "make the world safe for plutocracy": that is, to provide an atmosphere in which private business will thrive; to serve, not to control, and of course never, never to do anything that private enterprise can do itself.

A GOVERNMENT REGULATION.

We have already noted many reasons why the Canadian economy does not work as it is supposed to work. Individuals are *not* economically free and equal, business men do *not* always compete, public demand is *not* served in the cheapest and most efficient way. Sporadically public opinion has been roused to see these things, if only through a glass darkly, and to prod government into doing something about it. As a result, there has grown up a body of law which tells business men what they must and must not do.

The simplest form of regulation is the protection of the consumer against shoddy, impure, and harmful goods (food and drug laws), against short weight and fraud (standard weights and measures and government inspection of weighing and measuring devices), and against his own ignorance (grades and standards, compulsory description of contents of containers, standard sizes for cans, boxes, barrels). The revelations of Consumers' Research[1] provide an illuminating comment on the effectiveness of some of this legislation. Whether the "Commodity Standards" provisions of the new Trade and Industry Commission Act will have much effect remains to be seen; but as their enforcement is entrusted to the already over-burdened Tariff Board the prospects are not the brightest.

Regulation of public utility rates is largely the outcome of efforts by various business interests to get protection against one another. The Railway Commission controls railway, telegraph, telephone and express rates.[2] Public utility commissions or government departments in the province control, pretty effectively except in Quebec and British Columbia,[3] street railway, gas, light and power rates, and in Ontario, Quebec, Manitoba,

1100,000,000 *Guinea Pigs*, by F. J. Schlink. Several of the products named therein are freely sold in Canada.

2See S. J. McLean, *The Railway Commission.*

3See Hankin and MacDermot: *Recovery by Control,* on this and on the whole subject of existing government intervention.

Saskatchewan, and Alberta, milk prices. The Grain Commissioners control the services and rates of grain elevators, and, at least formally, inland water freight rates.

Some dawning realization of the wastes of capitalism is perhaps responsible for the Railway Commission's power over the location and construction of railways, for the "compulsory co-operation" clauses of the Canadian National-Canadian Pacific Act, 1933, and for some features of the Natural Products Marketing Act. The enterprising capitalist can no longer build a railway where and as he pleases, nor can the producers of fruits, vegetables, tobaccos, potatoes, jam, red cedar shingles, and some other commodities sell their products as they please.

Labour Legislation.

Another type of control has grown from the necessity of protecting workers, especially women and children, from the most flagrant abuses of unrestricted private enterprise, if only for efficiency's sake. All the provinces except Prince Edward Island have factory acts restricting child labour, limiting the hours of work for women and young persons, and prescribing certain rules for sanitation and safety. British Columbia is the one province which has seriously tried to limit the working day for men. The Dominion has just ratified the international convention providing for an eight-hour day (though whether the courts will sustain the validity of this action remains to be seen). Nova Scotia in the last few months seems to have passed a similar Act.[4] In most of the provinces there is also special provision for the health and welfare of workers in particular industries, such as coal mining, lumbering and highway transportation. The Dominion has adopted a minimum-wage law covering both men and women. Seven provinces have legal minimum wages for women; in Alberta men may not be paid less than women for work to which the Women's Minimum Wage Acts apply, and in Ontario and Quebec the Minimum Wage Boards may issue orders of a like kind. British Columbia and Manitoba have minimum wage laws for men, and Saskatchewan has a similar act, apparently inoperative. Quebec, Ontario and Alberta give legal force to collective labour agreements. New Brunswick has a minimum wage for forestry workers. Both Dominion and provinces provide machinery for conciliation in labour disputes.

Since 1918, there has been a national system of public employment offices, organized co-operatively by the Dominion and

[4] *Labour Gazette*, May, 1935.

provincial governments, which share the costs of administration. The Dominion has endeavoured, since 1921, to encourage technical education by paying subsidies to the provinces for this purpose. Prior to 1929 there was practically no other legislation dealing with employment and unemployment. But the depression has forced the Dominion, the provinces and the municipalities to come to the rescue of the unemployed by means of public works and "direct relief" (more properly, poor relief) on a huge scale.

Four types of state social insurance have emerged in Canada, workmen's compensation, old age pensions, mothers' allowances, and unemployment insurance. All the provinces except Prince Edward Island now have compensation acts, which provide for support of the accident-insurance funds by employers' contributions. Under the Dominion Old Age Pensions Act of 1927, and the legislation adopted since then by all the provinces except Quebec and New Brunswick (which has not brought its Act into operation), the Dominion and the provinces share the costs of pensions, not to exceed $20 monthly, to old persons of 70 years or more who are without the means of self-support. Six provinces[5] have similar state-supported, non-contributory schemes of mothers' pensions for the maintenance of widows, with children, who cannot keep themselves. The Dominion has just adopted a contributory unemployment insurance scheme on the British model, though this legislation, like the national eight-hour day and minimum wage law, has yet to run the gauntlet of the courts.[6] Alberta is experimenting with health insurance, and British Columbia has prepared a draft bill for introduction next year.

These measures represent a considerable breach in the wall of rugged individualism. A list of them reads very much like the sections devoted to the subject in official brochures designed to paint a rosy picture to the visitor from abroad; and taken by itself it might give the impression, to the uncritical reader, that Canada was a progressive commonwealth in this field. Actually, Canada is relatively backward in labour legislation, compared with European capitalist countries; and in the light of the standards which the authors of this book accept, positively reactionary.

Such legislation as we have may be criticized on four major

[5]The New Brunswick Act has not been brought into operation.

[6]See *Labour Gazette* and annual *Reports on Labour Legislation*, (Department of Labour). See also Chapter XV, "A Code for Labour".

grounds: (1) that it is incomplete and that it specifies only low standards; (2) that the principle of poor relief reigns in fields where the principles of insurance should prevail; (3) that there is no order nor uniformity about it from province to province; and (4) that it is administered ineffectively.

There are several great gaps in our legislation. Health insurance and unemployment insurance have only just reached the sphere of practical politics. We have hitherto limited the hours of labour of men scarcely at all, nor have we done anything of importance to protect men against sweated wages. Quebec and New Brunswick lack old age pension schemes, New Brunswick has no statutory minimum wages except for forestry workers, and Prince Edward Island has almost no labour legislation whatever. We have no national machinery to provide industrial retraining, to guide juveniles about to enter industry, to limit seasonal variations in employment, or to do the dozen and one things that are feasible, even in a capitalist economy, to lessen unemployment. Even the best of our protective items, workmen's compensation, provides protection against loss of wages from accident to only a portion of our wage-earners. Farm workers, for example, are not covered at all.

Moreover, the standards prescribed by statute are frequently very low. British Columbia has an eight-hour day, but in Ontario, for example, the existing law permits women to work 10 hours per day and 60 hours per week, or $12\frac{1}{2}$ hours per day and 72 hours per week, "as the exigencies of the trade require". It is interesting to note that in spite of this relic of the dark ages of industrialism remaining on the statute book, local politicians boast about Ontario's "advanced social legislation". The Quebec Act sets a limit of 55 hours per week, though there is an Act allowing the provincial government to set forty hours in industries which do not suffer from interprovincial competition. As may be imagined, the application of this has been very restricted.

Our "social insurance" measures which are actually in operation are, apart from workmen's compensation, not true forms of social insurance, but rather particularized forms of poor relief. Both the Old Age Pensions and Mothers' Pensions systems that prevail in Canada grant assistance only to those who are without the means of self-support—that is, to the destitute. Like all poor relief schemes, these are objectionable, because they discriminate against the thrifty and provident. Under social insurance proper, an insured person would obtain his old age pension at a specified age, whether he was destitute or not, and the fact that he owned his own house or that he had a small income from savings would not disqualify him, as it does at present.

The lack of uniformity in our labour legislation, from province to province, represents another serious defect. The British North America Act has, until this year, been generally construed as giving to the provinces major jurisdiction in this field, and they have exercised their powers unevenly. The Dominion has taken the lead with respect to several items, notably employment offices, old age pensions, and technical education, and has encouraged the provinces to adopt uniform laws by offering substantial subsidies. Success in this direction has been only partial, as might be expected from a method that is roundabout and cumbersome. Provincial autonomy in labour legislation represents a serious barrier to progressive measures. For it can always be argued, in Ontario, for example, that an advanced statute, say for sickness insurance, will impose a handicap on Ontario business from which Quebec business is free, and that Ontario dare not move on such a matter until Quebec does. Quebec and the Maritimes, as a matter of fact, have lagged behind Ontario and the western provinces in their legislation, and to some degree this operates to hold up further progressive action in the West. Clearly the existing constitutional procedure of provincial legislation is not favourable to uniformity nor to the enactment of advanced measures.

Still another criticism must be made of our labour legislation —that it has been weakly administered. The public employment offices, for example, have done much useful work, but they have not been built up to become a really efficient national placement service. Evidence before the House of Commons Committee on Price Spreads (the Stevens Committee) showed clearly that the enforcement of minimum wages for women in both Ontario and Quebec had become very imperfect by 1934. To quote the Royal Commission which followed,

"All the provinces together in 1933 spent for general factory inspection and minimum wage enforcement only $238,000. This was only slightly more than one-third of the amount spent for comparable purposes in the State of Illinois, which has approximately the same number of gainful workers, excluding agricultural, as Canada. While we spent only 8.5 cents per non-agriculture worker, in the United States they spent 14.9 cents. . . . New York, which ranks fourth among the states

in its relative expenditures for those purposes, spent 25.6 cents
. . . . and New Hampshire, which ranks thirty-fourth, 9.7 cents
. . . The Canadian figures include almost all phases of labour
regulation except workmen's compensation, while the American figures exclude not only workmen's compensation but also
the administration of minimum wage laws and other laws relating to the employment of women and children. In all Canada there are only seventy general factory or minimum wage
inspectors, of whom sixteen at least have had only an elementary school education or less, of whom none seems to have had
university training. . . . When provision is made for different
rates in six classes of communities and for six classes of
workers; when the hours for which these rates are payable
vary according to size of community and hours normally
worked by the firm; when the minimum wage may be averaged
over four weeks and is payable only to eighty per cent. of the
workers; when the major instrument of investigation consists
of the employers' own reports for sample weeks; then—
whether the A.B.C. firm violated the law by paying Miss Smith
15 cents an hour during a particular week—becomes a question
of law, custom, history, geography, accounting and arithmetic.
Probably the A.B.C. firm itself does not know. Certainly Miss
Smith will never know. Only the most expert and unhurried
inspector could ever find out".[7]

There is no space here to cite further examples, but they can
be found in practically every field of legislation and in all the
provinces. In general our governments, Dominion and provincial, have not shown much interest in their departments of labour, and too often they have appointed as administrators men
with no training or competence for the work or with no deep
interest in it. While there have been some honourable exceptions, e.g., in the field of workmen's compensation, the inevitable
result has been a good deal of ineffective administration.

Anti-Combine and Company Legislation.

While the state is trying to force co-operation on the railways and in some other industries, for most businesses it is still
rather half-heartedly doing just the opposite; trying, by means
of the Combines Investigation Act and Section 498 of the Criminal Code, to force business men to compete (a contradiction of
aims characteristic of legislation which results from unplanned,
piecemeal attempts to remedy specific ills). This legislation has
not prevented the growth of monopoly. On the contrary it has

[7]*Report*, pp. 129, 131.

perhaps facilitated it by frightening small businesses away from the co-operation which might have enabled them to survive. Nor has it protected the consumer from exploitation. There may be, as in the bread-making industry, a host of practices which keep prices unduly high; but as long as there is no actual conspiracy in restraint of trade, the state preserves an attitude of indifference.[8]

In addition to these direct government interventions, there are restrictions which arise from the fact that corporations are "creatures of the State". The Bank and Insurance Acts state what banks and insurance companies must do to obtain their charters or licenses, what account of their business they must make periodically to the government, and define the types of business which they may and may not undertake, and where they may conduct it. A government inspector visits the banks to see that the provisions of the Bank Act are not contravened. The various Companies Acts—Dominion and provincial—also state the conditions under which all corporations may come into being and issue stock, what statements as to their financial conditions must be made public, etc., but do not make provision for more direct governmental intervention into their business practices as in the case of banks, insurance companies and public utilities.

The defects of company law[9] in Canada are no less apparent. The most glaring is, of course, the lack of uniformity in Dominion and provincial Acts, with the inevitable results of a competition in laxity to obtain incorporation fees. But apart from this, and despite the recent improvements in the Dominion Act, none of the laws offer adequate protection to the public in the investment of its capital or subsequently as shareholders.

The provisions as to liability of the company issuing shares for statements made in the prospectus are practically a dead letter, since most issues are now made through financial houses which have, except in Manitoba, no legal responsibility for statements in the prospectus. The new Dominion Act, it is true, allows a purchaser to recover, within a certain period, what he has paid, if the seller's statements were untrue. The fact remains, however, that the prospective investor can obtain no authoritative information, no idea of the value of what he is

---

[8] See *Proceedings of the Canadian Political Science Association*, 1932.

[9] See "Corporation Finance and Company Law Reform", in *Proceedings of Canadian Political Science Association*, 1933; also "Securities and Security" by C. A. Ashley, in *Canadian Forum*, May 1933; also R. G. H. Smaills, "The Dominion Companies Act, 1934; An Appraisal", in *Canadian Journal of Economics and Political Science*, February, 1935; also the Companies Acts themselves.

buying. If it is a "no par value" share (a type of security which has become very common) he cannot tell how much of the capital he subscribes will go to the company and how much to the "investment dealer". Moreover, under the new Dominion Act, anything up to 25 per cent. of the proceeds of an issue of no par value shares, may if the contract of subscription so provides, and if the shareholder consent and the Secretary of State deems it expedient (inadequate safeguards both), be assigned to "distributable surplus" and paid out as dividends. In effect, the company can act as savings bank without being subject to the legislation governing savings banks; and the shareholders, unlike depositors in savings banks, cannot ask for their money back but must wait till the directors choose to return it. Dividends may thus be paid to preferred shareholders out of money contributed by common shareholders as capital: a proceeding which under other jurisdictions would be regarded as criminal. It is also apparently still legal, under the Dominion Act, to issue preferred shares redeemable at current market price, even though this be less than par: an open door to virtual swindling of preferred shareholders by directors.

Nor are shareholders assured of proper information about the operations of "their" companies. The new Dominion Act has tightened considerably the requirements regarding annual statements, but under some jurisdictions these can be met to the letter without disclosing the real state of assets, resources or income. The requirement that returns be made to the government (which files them without analysis) gives shareholders a sense of security which is quite illusory. The lack of publicity seriously limits directors' responsibility to shareholders and invites what amounts to fraudulent practices, for instance, buying and selling of securities by directors with inside information. (The new Dominion Act forbids this sort of thing). Action by shareholders against directors for actual fraud is expensive and difficult to start because of lack of full information.

It is instructive to observe the fate of the recommendation of the Price Spreads Report on this subject. The government paid no attention to the proposal that the use of any of the money received for no par value shares as distributable surplus should be prohibited. Most of the rest of the recommendations it embodied in a bill, which, though introduced by a minister who damned it with faint praise, passed the Commons. In the Senate, the investment dealers protested against the provision that no shares could be issued with exclusive rights of control, the clause compelling dealers to provide each buyer with a prospectus twenty-four hours before the stock was sold, and the provision to make dealers agents of the company whose securities they were selling and so make the prospectus clauses of the Act really operative.[10] The Senate obligingly deleted the last two provisions.

It may be added that the Royal Commission proposed to set up a Securities Board "to review the proposed capital structure of all companies incorporated under the Dominion Act and desiring to issue stock or bonds to the public. . . . The Board would pass on all issues after thorough investigation".[11] The only vestige of this recommendation which appeared in the Trade and Industry Commission bill was a provision that the Secretary of State "might request" the Commission to perform such functions. This also the Senate deleted.

Nearly always reluctantly undertaken, such social controls as we have devised have almost all been directed towards specific cases where uncontrolled private enterprise has become beyond question intolerable. Not until the establishment of the Bank of Canada in the present year (1935) was there the faintest attempt to control the economy as a whole. It is highly doubtful, however, whether central banking action alone can achieve this end, and perfectly certain that central banking on traditional lines cannot; and the development either of the necessary supplementary controls or of a new central banking policy is, under capitalism, remote and fraught with perils.

Of the confusion wrought by the Privy Council's perverse interpretation of the British North America Act, it is unnecessary to say anything here. "If you would see its monument, look about you".[12]

B. Government Aids to Industry.

Government services to industry cover a great variety of activities: everything from agricultural research to the tariff.

The farmer need no longer be an isolated producer working only with the knowledge handed down by his forefathers. The Dominion and provincial departments of Agriculture are busy providing him, at little or no cost, with all the results of modern

10Montreal Star, July 27, 1935.

11Report, p. 44.

12See also F. R. Scott, "Development of Canadian Federalism", in *Proceedings of the Canadian Political Science Association*, 1931, and H. C. Goldenberg, "Social and Economic Problems of Canadian Federalism", (*Canadian Bar Review*, September, 1934, pp. 422 ff.

research, made available through correspondence, a host of publications, lectures, fairs, demonstrations and permanent representatives throughout Canada; with information on markets, prices, size of crops; with legal facilities for watertight co-operative marketing schemes.

Producers of other primary products are similarly aided. Fishermen are benefitted directly and indirectly by the clearing of rivers, building of fishways, research into fish preserving, culture and conservation, distribution of weather, market and price information, maintenance of marine hospitals, lighthouses, wharves and a system of Government fish-collection boats, and by cash bonuses to sea-fishermen.

Services to the lumbering and forest-products industries include research by the Dominion Forest Products Laboratories into methods of preserving wood, making pulp and paper, etc., and maintenance of provincial fire-fighting and prevention corps.

Services available to the mining and mineral products industries include geological surveys and publication of results, issuing of maps, grants to mining and metallurgical research bodies, payment of bounties, and subsidizing shipments of coal to central Canadian markets. In addition, the Dominion Fuel Board, a body composed of technicians from the federal Departments of Mines and the Interior, make studies of Canadian fuel problems and publishes information aiming at increased and more efficient use of Canadian coal and coke.

Available to all are the myriad publications of the Dominion Bureau of Statistics and the provincial statistical bureaus giving information on prices, production and general business conditions in Canada. Producers and exporters are aided in finding overseas markets by the Commercial Intelligence Service which maintains trade commissioners all over the world. These commissioners make frequent reports upon opportunities for marketing of Canadian products and make connections between Canadian producers and foreign importers through the home office. On application to the Service, information on tariffs, transportation rates and market information is made available, and a weekly journal in both English and French is published.

If an employer wishes to hire a worker he may do so without cost through the Employment Service of Canada—a chain of employment offices across Canada, maintained by the provincial governments with federal aid in finance and direction. It is quite possible, too, that the worker will have been trained for him in some technical school operated by the province but subsidized by the Dominion.

Through the National Research Council, the Ontario Research Foundation, the Research Council of Alberta and the Saskatchewan Research Council, public funds (augmented to some extent by subscriptions from industries and private subscribers) and government administrative services are used to facilitate investigation into the technical problems of Canadian industry. A brief mention of some of the investigations will serve to illustrate the variety of assistance to industry which they represent: composition of wheat in relation to exposure to frost; methods of vulcanizing rubber; the utilization of waste apples; the heat conductivity of building materials; the welding of steel structures; the floatability of pulp-wood; the utilization of Canadian asbestos.

Government efforts at conservation have been spasmodic, ineffectual and generally undertaken too late. Positive action, as in the creation of national parks, forest and game preserves, reforestation work, fire-fighting, establishment of fish hatcheries and so on, has been most valuable as far as it goes. It is, however, but the smallest and newest of governmental functions. More negative efforts include the licensing or leasing of forest land and the charging of stumpage dues; the leasing of mineral lands and the charging of royalties; the leasing rather than outright sale of power resources; the game and fishing regulations; and the whole body of mining, fishing and forest laws. These regulations are in general so limited in value as conservation measures as to justify their inclusion here, under the heading "services and aid to industry", rather than in the previous section, "control and regulation".

In addition to all this aid to particular industries on particular problems of conservation, production and marketing, there are special cases in which the government has been called upon to remedy the economic disabilities of whole geographical areas. Under the Maritimes Freight Rates Act of 1927, for instance, freight rates within, and to and from the Maritimes are reduced 20 per cent., this loss being borne by the government. The Crows Nest Pass Agreement is another case in point, as are certain of the subsidies to the provinces.

Subsidies, Guarantees, and the Tariff.

Most of these activities are unexceptionable. But it is quite otherwise with the bounties, guarantees, tariff protection and other assistance granted to particular industries. The Drayton-Acworth Report of 1917 put public subsidies to private railways, to June 30, 1916, at $163,558,045, proceeds of sales of granted lands at $158,189,933, loans (never repaid) at $118,051,859, guarantees of securities at $268,542,992, and granted lands still in hand at 14,728,120 acres, valued by the companies at $139,-135,485. Public gifts to the C.P.R. alone were over $228,500,000 and 11,482,132 acres of land valued by the company at $119,250,-000, besides various tax exemptions and other privileges. Between 1916 and 1923 the "loans" to private railways increased by $12,509,454, and since the onset of the depression the Dominion Government has guaranteed a C.P.R. bank loan of $60,-000,000 and lent to the same company $2,447,223 interest-free and repayable only when the company resumes a 5 per cent. dividend on its common stock.[13] In addition much of the government's enormous investment in its "own" railways may be considered an indirect aid to business. Nor have railways been the sole beneficiaries. Between 1883 and 1912 steel companies received $17,396,434 in bounties;[14] bounties on crude petroleum (1917-1926) amounted to $858,669; on copper bars (1926-1932) $597,211; bounties and subventions on coal (1929-1935) $8,034,-000; on zinc (1919-1921) $395,183; on hemp (1926-1933) $26,-847; on linen yarn (1921-1923) $17,707; on lead (1919-1920) $4,869.[15] Subsidies to dry docks (1921-1935) totalled $8,345,972, and most of them have still many years to run.[16] Mail and steamship subventions since Confederation totalled $62,503,175—$2,220,661 in the last year alone.[17] The Beauharnois Corporation got a guarantee of its bank loan of over $15,000,000[18] and the government guarantee to Canadian Co-operative Wheat Producers (which really means to the banks) is over $11,500,000 net.[19] Any accurate estimate of the tariff "winnings" of protected industries since 1879 is completely impossible, but Professor Taylor's figures for woollen cloth in 1930 and Professor Rogers' for all industries for a single year,[20] indicate that the figure, if we could get it, would certainly be impressive. It is some of the

13*House of Commons Debates*, 1933, p. 3260.
14Donald, *The Canadian Iron and Steel Industry*, p. 335.
15*Public Accounts of Canada.*
16Port Arthur till October 5, 1937; Prince Rupert, March 10, 1943; Montreal, December 31, 1948; St. John, January 1, 1959; Burrard, April 1, 1960. (House of Commons Debates, 1935, pp. 2834-2835).
17*Public Accounts of Canada.*
18*House of Commons Debates*, 1933, p. 5130.
19At June 22, 1935, $11,621,000. Evidence before special committee of the House of Commons, reported in Montreal *Gazette*, June 28, 1935.
20See Chapter XIV.

representatives of these interests, fresh from enriching themselves at the public expense, who denounce unemployment insurance as a "dole", and demand, with unconscious humour, that
labour should "look after itself as business has done".

Many of these aids may have been wise and necessary; but
if so it can hardly be described as anything but a happy coincidence. For no one will pretend that these policies were made in
heaven, or worked out in the calm of the economist's study, or
devised by an impartial authority with a single eye to the public
interest. In the capitalist state there is no such impartial authority. Governments and parliaments, in Canada as elsewhere,
have merely registered the results of battles and bargains among
conflicting interests of unequal economic strength. In the jaunty
phrases of Sir John Macdonald, "Tell us what you want and we
will give you what you need. . . . The politician is the little boy
who climbs the tree to shake down acorns to the hogs below".
Nor is it necessary to assume that bribery and corruption play
major parts. On the contrary, in most instances bribery is probably superfluous. Thirty members of the Senate hold among
them directorships in 181 firms. One senator is on 19 boards, one
on 16, one on 12, nearly all on more than one. Power, pulp and
paper, the C.P.R., various manufacturing concerns (including,
inevitably, textiles), the banks, the insurance companies: all are
represented. The Prime Minister of Quebec cuts no mean figure
in the financial world.[21] That he is not unmindful of his responsibilities is evident from his reassuring words to power investors
rendered nervous by the Lapointe commission's investigation of
electric rates and municipalization in Quebec. Mr. Taschereau
appointed the commission. While it was still at work, he announced, "I receive appeals from widows, estate administrators,
religious orders, who ask for advice as to what to do with their
investments . . . in those companies, the savings of a lifetime,
which means the future of their families. I urge them not to be
frightened. . . . The Government will see that capital and savings will be protected. . . . Let investors keep their good stocks.
They are in no danger whatever."[22]

Even this fine performance does not quite reach the standard
set by Judge Laliberté who from the bench assured five coal
companies on trial for violation of Section 498 of the Criminal
Code, "that the sentences would not hurt the companies' trade,

[21]For a list of his directorates, see Banking Committee, 1934; *Evidence*, p. 178.
[22]Montreal *Star*, November 20, 1934.

should they be found guilty. He had given the same assurance to the five other companies in the first trial".[23]

Government *is* business. Sir Edward Beatty's words to the Canadian Chamber of Commerce, intended to refer probably to the citizenry as a whole, have the unhappy ring of being particularly applicable to his audience. "We have long ago passed the stage . . . where we feared the oppression of the State—for we long ago learned that we were the State".[24]

"Graft" is made much of by many critics, but in any wider analysis it is perhaps the least important of the methods by which government is induced to register the decisions of business. As Veblen puts it,[25] "Regulation of business has been in the nature of interference with trade and investment on behalf of the nation's mercantile community at large or particular favoured groups or classes. The common man comes into the case *only as the raw material of business traffic*: the consumer and the labourer".

One inevitable result of this state of affairs is that the economy is run on "short run" lines. Among the outstanding examples are the alienation of our forest resources and their rapid and wasteful depletion, the huge tracts of valuable land granted to the railways and private companies like the Hudson's Bay Company, and the rape of Beauharnois. But it is false economy. All the dominant interests who are trying to obtain the biggest immediate profit out of our natural resources are letting the devil take the hindmost and future generations.

"I believe", says the Prime Minister, "there is no government in Canada which does not regret that it has parted with some of these natural resources for considerations wholly inadequate and on terms that do not reflect the principle under which the Crown holds the natural resources in trust for all the people".[26] Admirable sentiment! But if we insist on preserving the economic system which has produced such results, can we expect the future to differ from the past?

C. PUBLIC OWNERSHIP AND OPERATION.

"Public ownership" in Canada covers a wide field: the post-office, all our roads, canals and harbours, more than half our railways, telegraph and express services, large electric power

---

[23]Montreal *Star*, November 13, 1934.
[24]Speech to the Canadian Chamber of Commerce, Winnipeg, September 11, 1934.
[25]Veblen, *On the Nature of Peace*, chapter 4.
[26]*House of Commons Debates*, 1932, p. 3036.

systems, most of the telephones in the prairie provinces, most of the merchandising of liquor, important terminal grain elevators, and a host of municipal services. The title to probably one-sixth of the wealth of the country rests with Dominion, provincial and municipal governments.

All this has taken place in a comparatively short time, for the most part without conscious intention, indeed rather in spite of deliberate public policy to the contrary. As a result, more than one observer has concluded that Canada is already socialized and that we have only to wait a few decades or generations for the process to complete itself. In this view, socialist propaganda is worse than useless, for it rouses the reactionary to what is going on under his unsuspecting nose. Let us rely, therefore, on economic evolution and the gradual progress of enlightenment to transform the capitalist tiger, painlessly and imperceptibly, into a gentle tabby purring contentedly on the communal hearth.

It is an attractive theory; but before we can accept it we must ask ourselves two questions. First, what are the forces which have brought about such "public ownership" as we have? Second, what kind of "public ownership" have they given us? In other words, will the process automatically complete itself, and if it should, will the result be socialism? With these questions in mind let us examine briefly our chief public enterprises.

Public Administration and Defence.

Even the most fanatical individualists now take it for granted that governments should collect their revenues themselves. "Farming" the taxes, as in pre-revolutionary France, proved itself so appallingly inefficient and corrupt, so menacing to public order, that not even the Canadian Chamber of Commerce has the temerity to suggest turning over the Department of National Revenue to a private corporation.

Rather similar considerations have prevailed to place the police and national defence in public hands. No single group of capitalists dare allow a rival group to control the police, the army, the navy, or the air force. The enterprising Chinese warlord, selling himself and his soldiers to the highest bidder, is an intolerable nuisance to "normal business".

The provision of war material, however, is still almost entirely in private hands, and likely to remain so as long as capitalism survives. The armament industry is a fruitful source of corruption (though by no means unique in this respect), and from the standpoint of "national defence" grotesquely inefficient, as British experience in the last war abundantly proved. But any attempt to extend the principle of "public ownership" from armies to armament manufacture is almost certain to come to grief. The Chinese war-lord is an excrescence on "normal business", but the armaments industry *is* "normal business". Almost any "heavy industry" can be turned overnight from the making of articles of peaceful commerce to the making of war materials; and the people who control the armament industry are the same people who control nearly everything else. To nationalize the manufacture of war materials, therefore, would mean nationalizing most of the basic industries; iron and steel, chemicals, motor cars and aircraft at the very least.

The Post Office.

Public ownership of the postal service is taken for granted almost, though not quite, as universally as public collection of government revenues. Monopoly is in both cases essential; but a private postal monopoly would mean a constant threat of extortion held over the head of every other business in the country. Moreover, postal service in many parts of Canada is unprofitable. A private corporation would have to charge more or abandon some services altogether. "Normal business" declines to contemplate either possibility. It prefers to leave the thing in the hands of the government and to see it financed out of taxation (customs duties, excise and sales taxes) collected in the main from the poorer classes. This at least is the conclusion it might be expected to reach if it thought about the matter at all; in this as in most questions of public policy conscious reflection probably plays only a slight part. But we may be sure that if the present organization of the postal service did not serve the purposes of "business" tolerably well, it would not last long.

Public Works.

Roads, bridges and canals, all now public enterprises, could be, and at times have been, privately owned. Toll roads, however, were grossly inefficient, and in a country so dependent on transportation as Canada, private control of these essential services would be almost as dangerous to other businesses as a private postal monopoly.

As with defence, however, we carry the principle only half way, (a clear indication, of course, that we are not acting from principle but from motives of immediate expediency). Public

works are financed by governments but almost always constructed by private contractors. The result is an excellent example of
the way in which public services in a capitalist economy are used
more as a means of enriching certain vested interests than of
serving the public. For the record of the private contractors,
as of the munition makers, has been thoroughly bad, especially
in the sinister influence they have exerted over governments. A
typical recent example of wholesale bribery and corruption of
public officials is the York Township Construction Contracts
case. *Saturday Night,* commenting editorially, on September
13, 1930, observed: "From the standpoint of the public interest
the shocking factor in the case is not that a few obscure individuals have been bribed, but that promotion of business by bribery
continues to be regarded as legitimate among the large class of
business men engaged in the construction and supply trades.
. . . The low ethical standards of the contracting class are a serious menace to the morale of the country. There are, of course,
some honest contractors. . . . but the moral atmosphere in which
they move is low, and there is a well-founded theory that as a
class they must be watched as carefully as department store de-
tectives watch suspected shoplifters." This judgment may be
unduly severe as applied to one particular group; *Saturday Night*
could have avoided invidious comparisons by substituting "capitalist class" for "contracting class."

But again, as with armaments, to push public enterprise back
a further stage would not solve the problem. If government
undertook the construction of public works it would still have to
buy raw materials and equipment from private business and the
same sinister influences would continue to operate, though in a
different sphere and perhaps on a smaller scale. The logical next
step would be government ownership and operation of the sources
of raw materials and the manufacture of equipment: all the
heavy industries and a number of others. Indeed if one starts
from the premise that public works construction should be a
public enterprise, one ends by advocating something very close to
public ownership all round.

Drainage, sewage disposal, water supply, fire protection, street
lighting and similar municipal services fall in much the same
category as public works.

Railways.

In the world as a whole, public ownership of railways is the
rule, private ownership the exception. Governments have tended

to look on railways in much the same light as defence services, in fact as essential parts of the defence services, and accordingly have seldom risked placing them in private hands. Often, too, the building of railways into remote districts has been too unprofitable to tempt private enterprise. For these and other reasons, therefore, most European and many overseas countries have made railways a government monopoly. Revenue has not usually been a main object, though the German State Railways were so lucrative that the Dawes Plan handed them over to a "mixed" company (in which, however, the German Government held a controlling interest) for the benefit of Germany's creditors.

In Great Britain, France and the United States, however, the countries with which Canada is most closely connected, private ownership has been the rule; and private ownership, with, as we have seen, generous government assistance, was the rule in Canada also down to 1917. But between 1917 and 1922 three large private systems came into the hands of the government, and the resulting Canadian National Railways now form one of the largest railway systems in the world. A knowledge of the facts of this development is so important in contemporary discussion that a separate section is devoted to it below.[27]

Besides the National Railways there are two small provincial railways, one in Ontario and one in British Columbia. Both were built to assist in the opening of new territory rather than as directly profit-making concerns.

With railways may be grouped publicly-owned municipal tramways. Of fifty-nine electric railways in the country, twenty-one, including a majority of the larger ones, are owned by public bodies. Comparison would indicate that the public systems have had a slightly better operating record than the private.[28] The publicly-owned Toronto system is considered the best in North America.

Telephones.

Twenty-five or thirty years ago, nationalization of telephones was part of the platform of the Conservative party. This proposal, however, was "sunk without a trace". Only in the Prairie Provinces are telephones actually publicly or co-operatively owned. In Manitoba the system is managed by a commission appointed by the Public Utilities Commission. This has largely obviated political interference and made possible fairly effective

[27]Section (c) of this chapter.
[28]Hankin and MacDermot. *Op. cit.*, p. 124.

control of expenditures, but from its inception in 1907 till the post-war boom, and again since 1929, the system has shown deficits. The experience of Alberta and Saskatchewan has been similar.

From the point of view of the balance sheet these public systems have been a burden. They have, however, supplied the prairie farmer with benefits which would not have been provided by private enterprise.

Electric Power.

Ontario is, outside of Russia, the *locus classicus* for public ownership of power. Rapid industrial development and lack of coal created a large market for hydro-electric power; concentration of supply at Niagara necessitated a heavier investment in transmission lines than private enterprise was always ready to undertake; and the absence of competing sources of energy (coal or oil) would have given a private power "trust" a stranglehold on Ontario industry. Quebec factories could secure Nova Scotia coal, Ontario could not.

The Hydro-Electric Power Commission of Ontario, set up in 1906, confined its activities at first to buying power wholesale from private generating stations, constructing transmission lines, and selling at cost to municipalities and large industrial consumers. Since 1917, however, the Commission has been generating power as well as distributing it, and now controls more than half the turbine installation of the province. The total investment is almost $400,000,000. Private companies for the most part now supply power only to certain mines and pulp and paper mills.

On the whole the system has been brilliantly successful. The provincial Commission has built up reserves of almost $70,000,-000, and, except in 1932 and 1933, has habitually shown a surplus, after providing for all charges, including interest, sinking fund and reserves. The municipal Commissions have reserves of nearly $60,000,000, have reduced their net debt to about half the value of their assets, and have usually shown a substantial surplus (in the years just before the depression, about $2,000,000 annually after all charges). In 1932 they broke about even, in 1933 they fell $627,011 short of providing the standard amount for depreciation. The Ontario government subsidises construction of rural lines by a 50 per cent. grant, but interest and sinking fund charges on such grants are normally only a small fraction of the annual surpluses shown by the system, and complete withdrawal of the subsidies would make only an infinitesimal difference in Hydro finances.

These results have been achieved, moreover, with rates almost always far below those charged for comparable services in Western New York State or in Montreal and Quebec.[29]

The administration has not been free from patronage and partisan interference, but there is nothing to show that these have been more serious than nepotism and divided loyalties in a private enterprise of the same size. The most serious form of political interference has been quite separate from administration: in contracts for purchases of power from private companies, and in the acquisition of private plants at inflated prices, as in the Abitibi deal. This sort of thing, we may again point ont, woud be impossible in a Socialist community.

In the other provinces (except Quebec and British Columbia, which remain the happy hunting grounds of private monopolies), public ownership has developed to a smaller extent and with interesting variations. In Nova Scotia the provincial government controls about three-quarters of the power generated (measured by capital investment), but private interests control about three-quarters of the distribution. In New Brunswick, private interests, producing mainly for export, have about four-fifths of the capital investment. Domestic demand is almost equally divided between public and private agencies. In the Prairie Provinces the field is approximately equally divided.[30]

The Sale of Liquor.

The various Liquor Control Boards are interesting as examples of the entrance of Government into distribution. The results of the free competition of rugged individuals in this field were so expensive to the taxpayer and so revolting to the most rudimentary sense of public order and decency, that by the end of the war the whole of Canada had outlawed the sale (though not the manufacture) of alcoholic beverages altogether. The results of prohibition, however, were disappointing, and rightly or wrongly the electors of every province except Prince Edward Island have now repealed their prohibitory legislation and substituted government monopoly or near-monopoly of the sale of some or all liquors.

[29]See very full and careful comparisons in *Electrical Utilities,* Mosher and others, summarised in Hankin and MacDermot, *Recovery by Control.*

[30]*Reports* of the Ontario Hydro-Electric Commission, and Hankin and MacDermot, *Recovery by Control.*

In Ontario, beer may be obtained in privately owned "beverage rooms". Otherwise, all sales are in the hands of a provincial board which keeps a fairly close check on individual purchases by a permit system. Advertising is prohibited. The board sets prices mainly with an eye to provincial revenue. In Quebec the control is much less strict. Sale of spirits is the monopoly of the provincial commission, but beer and wine may be purchased with meals, and beer is sold both by privately owned taverns and grocery stores. No records are kept of individual purchases, and advertising is unrestricted. The arrangements in other provinces, except of course Prince Edward Island, generally speaking fall somewhere between the Ontario and Quebec systems.

Unfortunately, no studies of comparative costs have been made in this field. But it seems clear that centralized buying, the restriction of retail outlets, and the elimination of much expensive advertising, must have produced substantial economies. As with armaments, however, only distribution has been brought under public control, and in this case incompletely. Manufacture remains in private hands.

C. THE SPECIAL CASE OF THE RAILWAYS.

The full story of the development of the Canadian government-owned railways would fill many volumes, but a brief resumé is necessary in view of much misunderstanding which is current, besides yielding valuable material for answering our original questions as to the sources and the real nature of "public ownership" in Canada.

The Intercolonial.

The Intercolonial Railway has been from its inception government-owned, partly perhaps for strategic reasons, (war with the United States was at that time far from "unthinkable"), partly because, serving a territory whose industries were based on water transport, it has never been more than a supplement to water transport and so has offered no "glittering prizes" to the capitalist. But whatever the risk of loss, the road had to be built. The Maritime Provinces insisted on it as part of the price of Confederation; everyone considered it essential for defence against American invasion, and Central Canada, fearful of the cancellation of bonding privileges at American ports, needed access to the winter ports of St. John and Halifax. This last cannot, of course, figure in the accounts of the Canadian National Railways, but it is worth remembering when we cast up their "moral" balance sheet.

Even the Fathers of Confederation, sanguine though they were about the future of interprovincial trade, hardly expected the Intercolonial to show a profit.[31]   Until the creation of the Canadian National, moreover, rates on the Intercolonial were deliberately kept below a commercial level, as a partial compensation to the Maritime Provinces for their losses from the protective tariff.   Nevertheless, the road need not have been as unprofitable as it usually was, and its history illustrates some of the dangers public ownership must guard against.   In the first place the route selected was partly the result of sectional political pressure; the line was twisted some miles out of its proper course to serve comparatively unimportant local interests.   Second, construction costs, almost $77,000 a mile, were higher than they need have been for the traffic, (though not nearly as high as on the privately built Grand Trunk).   The engineers had too free a hand.   And third, management by the Department of Railways and Canals left the road open to all the evils of political patronage at a time when patronage was far more widespread and shameless than it is now.   There was no independent board or commission to stand between the railway and the exigencies of party politics.   This affected not only appointments but also the possibilities of economy through curtailing services or reducing staffs.

The G.T.P. and the National Transcontinental.

The Grand Trunk, second chief constituent part of the Canadian National, was a private line, running from Chicago across southern Ontario and Quebec, to Portland, Maine.   Built by English contractors, for an English company, on a scale appropriate to English density of traffic, it suffered from the highest construction costs of any Canadian railway ($127,000 a mile), and from absentee ownership and control.   These factors, and the competition of water transport, prevented it from ever paying dividends on most of its stock; but had it not involved itself in the Grand Trunk Pacific scheme it could probably have survived.

At the turn of the century the C.P.R. was reaping from its virtual monopoly in the West profits fat enough to make the Grand Trunk shareholders' mouths water, and doing so by methods which had roused the prairie farmer to fury.   It was the

---

[31]Hon. George Brown, February 8, 1865: "As a commercial undertaking the Intercolonial Railway has not, I apprehend, any considerable merit."

golden age of "trust-busting" in the United States, and here as there, competition was looked upon as the solution to every economic problem. There had been those who prophesied utter ruin for the C.P.R. Its spectacular success had produced in the public mind, by reaction, the impression that we had room not merely for one transcontinental line but for two or three. Not only the politicians but sober business leaders fell victims to a fever of reckless optimism which could see no limits to Canadian expansion. A Royal Commission presided over by Sir William Van Horne of the C.P.R. actually recommended extending the Intercolonial from Montreal to Georgian Bay!

Into this scene step the railway promoters: the Grand Trunk, and Mackenzie and Mann, hats in hand. The Grand Trunk invited the government to subsidize an extension of Grand Trunk lines from North Bay to the Pacific Coast, with arrangements for routing ocean traffic over the Intercolonial. The government, however, was afraid that much of the ocean traffic would go to the Grand Trunk's own terminus, Portland. To secure "Canadian trade for Canadian ports" and to develop a (mythical) "clay belt" and other resources in Northern Ontario and Quebec, the government countered with a scheme of its own, which the Grand Trunk accepted. The Grand Trunk, through a subsidiary, the Grand Trunk Pacific, was to build a line from Winnipeg to Prince Rupert, to be financed by securities guaranteed in part by the government, and in larger part by the Grand Trunk. The eastern outlet, the National Transcontinental (Winnipeg to Moncton), was to be built by the government itself, and operated by the Grand Trunk Pacific, rent free for seven years, at 3 per cent. on cost for forty-three years. To protect the Grand Trunk Pacific against extravagantly high costs, Grand Trunk engineers were to supervise and inspect construction jointly with government engineers and were to have the right to refuse acceptance of work.

The territory traversed by the National Transcontinental is one of the most expensive in the world for railway construction. It is far from the industrial centres of Eastern Canada, and even today has very little local traffic. The outbreak of war, before the line was completed, sent the price of labour and materials soaring. As a result, instead of the estimated cost of $61,415,-000, the actual cost was almost $160,000,000, or over $88,000 per mile. The Grand Trunk Pacific therefore refused to take up its lease, in spite of the facts that its own engineers had been supervising, inspecting and accepting work and that its own construction costs averaged $98,000 per mile. The government was left "holding the bag".

Nor had the Grand Trunk Pacific itself fared much better. Completed earlier than the National Transcontinental it had been left for some time without any eastern outlet. By 1916 it was barely earning its operating expenses. The government had already been called upon to implement its guarantees of Grand Trunk Pacific securities, and the Grand Trunk (three weeks after paying a $2,500,000 dividend on its own guaranteed stock) had blandly announced that it could not implement its Grand Trunk Pacific guarantees and had invited the government to assume them!

The Canadian Northern.

Meanwhile, incredible as it may appear, the same government which was subsidizing and guaranteeing the bonds of one private transcontinental and building an eastern outlet for it, was also subsidizing and guaranteeing the securities of another, and for even larger sums! The Grand Trunk Pacific slew its thousands, but the Grand Trunk Pacific owners were far from the scene of action. The Canadian Northern slew its tens of thousands, for Mackenzie and Mann were on the spot. Beginning with a few small lines in Manitoba in 1896 they finally succeeded in building an entire transcontinental system without spending a cent of their own money. Almost the whole thing was financed by government subsidies, government "loans" on which no interest was ever paid, and government guaranteed bonds and debentures.

By 1916 the Canadian Northern and the Grand Trunk Pacific were bankrupt, the Grand Trunk if held to its G.T.P. obligations would have been bankrupt, and both the Canadian Northern and the Grand Trunk were insufficiently equipped to handle the traffic available to them. The Canadian Northern had been very cheaply built ($38,000 a mile, compared with $68,000 for the C.P.R.), the Grand Trunk had allowed its lines to deteriorate to an alarming degree. Both were in urgent need of additions, betterments, and new rolling stock. But neither could borrow on its own credit the huge sums necessary, some $100,000,000 over a five year period. In the midst of war, the government could not allow railway traffic to become congested. Clearly, further government assistance to these railways could not be avoided.

Nationalization.

But was the government to go on indefinitely assuming liabilities and leaving the assets in private hands? Was it to continue to subsidize two competing systems?

Ordinarily when an enterprise is unable to pay its debts, it goes into bankruptcy, and the investor bears the loss in the interest of "the proper working of the economic system." But to allow the Canadian Northern to go into receivership would not have relieved the Dominion government of its guarantees, would probably have bankrupted the prairie provinces by forcing them to implement their guarantees, and might have ruined the Canadian Bank of Commerce and various insurance companies which had invested heavily in the Canadian Northern. Similarly a large part of the Grand Trunk Pacific debt was guaranteed by the government and hence was, again, a burden *inescapable except by repudiation*. The Grand Trunk might more easily have been allowed to go into a receivership, but even this would have administered a severe shock to Canadian credit, which in the midst of the war might have been disastrous.

Faced with these difficulties the government fell back on the time-honoured device of a Royal Commission, made up of Sir Henry Drayton, then Chief Commissioner of the Railway Commission, afterwards Conservative Minister of Finance, Sir William Acworth, a distinguished English railway expert, and Mr. A. H. Smith of the New York Central. Sir William Acworth had written against public ownership of railways and Sir Henry Drayton was, to say the least, not enthusiastic about it. Nevertheless both signed a majority report recommending that the government take over the Grand Trunk, Grand Trunk Pacific and Canadian Northern, and operate them, with the Intercolonial and National Transcontinental, as a unified publicly owned system. To guard against partisan interferences in management the Drayton-Acworth report proposed to entrust the system to five trustees: two, professional railway men, to be appointed for terms of five and seven years respectively, three others to be appointed for two, four and six years respectively; all, like judges of the higher courts, to be removable only on address of both Houses of Parliament. Retiring trustees were to be eligible for reappointment, but vacancies were to be filled by the government only from a selected list of nominees drawn up by the trustees themselves. This would have secured public control of general policy, independence of management, continuity in the board of trustees, and frequent opportunity for the introduction of new blood.

The report went on to recommend (a) that the Intercolonial and National Transcontinental should be handed over to the trustees free of debt; (b) that Mackenzie and Mann should receive no cash compensation, but should be allowed to retain an amount of Canadian Northern common stock to be fixed by arbitration, such common stock to receive its due proportion of whatever part of the earnings of the unified system the arbitrators should decide to be assignable to the Canadian Northern properties; (c) that the Grand Trunk shareholders should be compensated by payment for seven years of an annuity equal to "a substantial proportion" of the average Grand Trunk dividends for the last few years before 1917 ($3,600,000), and after 1924 an increased annuity, details to be fixed by arbitration. Assuming immediate unification on this basis, it predicted total fixed charges of about $40,000,000, an initial net deficit of $12,500,000, and "at an early date", net operating revenues comparable to those of the C.P.R.

Had the government adopted the report, these cheerful prospects might well have been realized. But the government chose a different course. Instead of taking over all three private systems at once and unifying them with the existing government railways, it spread the process over five years. The Canadian Northern was indeed taken over in 1917 but the Grand Trunk Pacific, not until March 1919, and not placed under the Canadian National Railways board until October, 1920. Purchase of the Grand Trunk was deferred until October, 1919, and not till the end of the arbitration proceedings over compensation, in October, 1922, was it incorporated in the C.N.R. system. 1923 was the first year in which it was possible to see whether the Drayton-Acworth estimate of net earnings had any chance of realization. It is worth noting that by 1925, the third year of the consolidated system, net earnings were already well up towards the C.P.R. figure, and by 1926 were only $1,439,624 below it. But the delay in bringing about consolidation had prevented earlier achievement of the economies of consolidation and as a result had of course produced extra deficits and additions to the burden of debt.

Moreover, the government rejected the financial recommendations. The Intercolonial and National Transcontinental were *not* handed over free of debt, Mackenzie and Mann received $10,000,-000 cash, holders of Grand Trunk guaranteed 4 per cent. stock got a government guarantee of dividends in perpetuity, the remaining Grand Trunk shareholders got nothing. This last gave rise to expensive litigation and seriously injured Canadian credit in London.

Equally unhappy, and even more inauspicious for the success of the C.N.R., was the fate of the recommendations for the appointment of the trustees. This part of the report was jettisoned entirely. In its place the government put a board of directors holding office "at pleasure", and accordingly changing with every change of government. The directors, as it turned out, exercised little or no influence, and the financial control which a strong board of trustees might have exercised was absent.

The Canadian National System.

Between 1923 and 1929 Sir Henry Thornton succeeded in welding a heterogeneous mass of dilapidated roads into a unified, highly efficient system, known throughout the world for its enterprise in developing and adopting technical improvements and for the excellence of its relations with its employees. This process, however, involved heavy capital expenditures, $452,-000,000 in the years 1923-1931. Most of this was necessary to bring the system into first class condition.

The C.P.R. in the same nine years spent only $253,000,000 on capital account; but it must be remembered that the C.P.R. began the period in far better shape than its rival. In the matter of hotel building, for which the C.N.R. has been vociferously criticised, the comparison is really strongly in its favour. The C.P.R. started with a $25,000,000 investment in hotels and increased it by $46,000,000; the C.N.R. started with $10,000,000 and increased it by $22,000,000.

With the collapse of the boom, both railways found themselves in difficulties. In 1928 the C.N.R. operating surplus had been $51,335,569; by 1931 it had fallen to $1,192,167, and the total deficit was over $99,000,000. The C.P.R. in the same year earned not much more than its debenture interest, and 1932 seemed likely to be worse. Once more the government sought the aid of a Royal Commission. Its report, (the "Duff Report", December, 1932) recommended co-operation of the two railways

to eliminate duplication, and reform of the C.N.R. management
by replacing the board of seventeen directors by three trustees,
removable only on address of both Houses of Parliament, and re-
placeable only from a "panel" drawn up by the trustees themselves. This last suggestion the government rejected, the others
it embodied in legislation. Though both railways, especially the
C.N.R., are now doing much better than in 1932, the results of
"co-operation" have been disappointing.[32]

Capitalist propaganda delights to point to the C.N.R. as a
horrible example of the perils of socialism. In reality it is a
monument to the insanity of capitalism. The C.N.R. has been
reasonably well managed. Given favourable conditions, it has
shown its ability to produce operating surpluses quite comparable
with those of the C.P.R. The famous "deficits" are the consequence in the last few years partly of depression, otherwise almost wholly of events which took place *before* the government
took over the railways. The key to the history of the C.N.R. is
in the one word "guarantees". If governments before 1917 had
not guaranteed the securities of the Canadian Northern, Grand
Trunk and Grand Trunk Pacific we should probably have avoided
the triplication of lines which took place; and if the companies
had been unable to pay their interest they would have gone bankrupt in the ordinary way and started afresh with most of their
capital charges written off. The investors, not the taxpayers,
would have had to shoulder the loss. But the guarantees prevented this. Instead the original debt remains and each year
adds to it the difference between earnings and interest charges,
which of course means larger interest charges next year, and
so on, cumulatively.

But *who secured these guarantees* in the first place? Does
anyone in his senses believe that any government would have
embarked on such a policy of its own volition? *Capitalist promoters* secured the guarantees and the "loans" and the subsidies. They had a world to gain and nothing to lose but the
taxpayers' money. In a socialist society there would have been
no promoters. No one would have been in a position to profit by
foisting such schemes on the public. Accordingly railways would
have been built only when there was reasonable prospect of their
being needed. The stupidest planning authority could never

[32]This history of the C.N.R. is based on the Drayton-Acworth and Duff Reports. The
Duff Report frequently suggests inefficiency in the management of the C.N.R., but its
grounds for doing so have been thoroughly exploded by Professor J L. McDougall in the
February, 1935, issue of the *Canadian Journal of Economics and Political Science.*

have blundered on such a scale as the governments which the railway promoters controlled.

D. EXISTING STATE ENTERPRISES: CONCLUSIONS.

We have already developed in Canada a technique of "public ownership" which (including the post-war management of the railways) is quite reasonably enterprising and efficient, and which has had a restraining influence on capitalist exploitation. But what answer must we give to our original questions: "Why has this "public ownership" made its appearance at all?" and "Is it socialism?"

To the first question there seem to be at least five answers.

In the first place, private business has graciously allowed the government to undertake services essential to private business but in themselves unprofitable. This is one of the reasons for public ownership of the post-office, roads, canals, some railways, and telephones. As the bulk of government revenue in Canada comes from taxes on consumption, paid mainly by the poorer classes, this is a delightful arrangement for the rich to corner the profits while the poor bear the losses.

Second, to leave services like defence, the police, fire protection, the collection of revenue, the post-office, roads, harbours and canals in private hands, would be to present their owners with power to play the highwayman to every other enterprise in the country. Capitalist business in general, therefore, has used "public ownership" to protect itself against unlimited exploitation at the hands of particular interests. This is at least a partial explanation of the development of Ontario Hydro. It is also one reason, and a good one, for the widespread opposition to a C.P.R. railway monopoly. Sir Edward Beatty assures us that the competition of steamship, motor truck and aeroplane, and the control exercised by the Railway Commission, would safeguard us against extortion. But how much wheat moves from central Saskatchewan to Fort William or Vancouver by steamer, truck or aeroplane? Who appoints the Railway Commission and has *power to overrule its decisions?* The Cabinet, which of course would be quite beyond the influence of a private railway monopoly!

Third, the state has had to step in to *salvage bankrupt private enterprise for the benefit of the private investor.* The classic example is the C.N.R.

Liquor "control" presents a fourth and peculiar reason for

public ownership. The liquor interests in recent years have discovered by painful experience that the public will no longer tolerate unlimited private enterprise in this field. Faced with the alternative of complete suppression or cession of the sphere of distribution (or part of it) to the government, the brewers and distillers have naturally chosen the latter.

Fifth, there has been a genuine sentiment for "public ownership", particularly among the small business men and white collar workers who have everything to gain and nothing to lose from such public enterprises as the Ontario Hydro. In the case of the C.N.R. this sentiment was unquestionably exploited by the railway promoters who wanted the government to take their bankrupt businesses off their hands at a "satisfactory price". If a capitalist government takes over the C.P.R. or any other private business, the same thing will happen again. "Public ownership" sentiment could easily be massed behind a project to "take over" the C.P.R. with a guarantee of substantial dividends to its shareholders in perpetuity. Socialist opposition to anything of the sort would doubtless be regarded by many of the electorate as highly unreasonable!

In other words, what the "natural" forces of "gradual economic evolution" have given us is mainly "public ownership" for the benefit of private business; and if we trust to those forces for the future, that is what we shall continue to get, only more so. The great capitalists and their political mouthpieces are under no illusions about it, as two recent bursts of candour bear eloquent witness—"This property", says Mr. Bennett, of the C.N.R., "is not the property of the people of Canada . . This enterprise belongs to the investors."[33] The government operates the system as trustee for the bondholders. In the same vein, Mr. Beatty: "The publicly owned public utilities are not, in any economic sense, owned by the State at all. They are owned by private investors—and by a special class of private investors who are, by the State, and at the expense of the public, protected against the ordinary risk of investments."[34] As long as there is likelihood of large profits, capitalists will prefer to take the "risks". When that likelihood disappears, as in the present period of declining capitalism it more and more tends to do, they will prefer to sell out to the State in return for a guaranteed future income.

Isolated public enterprises in a capitalist society are in constant danger of being exploited by private concerns through ex-

[33]*House of Commons Debates*, 1933, pp. 2854, 2859. A most important speech.
[34]Speech to the Canadian Chamber of Commerce, Winnipeg, September 11, 1934.

travagant contracts and the like. To the extent that they succeed in defending themselves against this danger, they find themselves providing "cheap and efficient transport and power to a revivified system of profit-making enterprise",[35] a decisive objection to "gradualism" or piecemeal "socialization".

Even government ownership of *all* industry, however, would not necessarily be socialism. If the private owners of industry are compensated in full (which may be tactically necessary) and allowed to retain most of their compensation, the last state of the community may be worse than the first. *Unless the bulk of the compensation is promptly taken back from the rich former owners by drastic income and inheritance taxes,* the "publicly owned" industries would still be run on capitalist principles. To earn the bond interest would be the prime object of the management, and its labour policy would be indistinguishable from that of any private concern. The substitution of fixed-interest-bearing bonds for variable-dividend-bearing shares would add considerably to the rigidities of the economy, and when returns from our exports staples fell off, the *whole* loss would fall on the workers and farmers, instead of only most of it, as at present. This is not socialism but "state capitalism": the state operating industry on behalf of the capitalists. It would present all the worst features of the C.N.R. over again, but on a far larger scale; and the fundamental trouble with that enterprise, as we have seen, is not that it is publicly owned but that it isn't.

Finally, state capitalism is inevitably just as "scarcity-minded" as any other capitalism. Broadly speaking, the more abundant anything becomes the less bond interest it will produce. State capitalism therefore, will be under the same compulsion to restrict production as private capitalism. There is no half-way house between capitalism and the co-operative commonwealth.

35H. N. Brailsford, *C.C.F. Research Review*, December, 1934.

CHAPTER VII.

THE INEFFICIENCY OF THE SYSTEM.

A. The Consumer Pays.

The classic last-ditch defence of capitalism has always been, "Well, anyhow it works. It's efficient". At the very bottom of the depression we did not hear quite so much of this, but with the first signs of a slight upturn the saga of the bath-tub and the radio has burst forth again. It is therefore more than ever essential to insist that one of the main counts in our indictment of capitalism is that it is *not* efficient but on the contrary almost unbelievably wasteful.

Industrial Efficiency.

This may seem a hard saying. The ordinary citizen visiting a modern industrial plant comes away with an overwhelming impression of its efficiency. But the expert has a different story to tell. In 1921 a committee of the Federated American Engineering Societies surveyed in great detail 125 representative plants in six major industries of the United States. Taking 0 as "adherence to the best known or available practice", 20 as good technical efficiency", 40 as "fair", 60 "poor", 80 "thoroughly bad", it rated these industries as follows:

	Best	Average	Worst
Men's Clothing	27	64	84
Building	30	53	not given
Printing	30	58	67
Boots and Shoes	12	41	71
Metal trades	6	29	56
Textiles	28	49	72

In a world of change and experiment it is of course impossible to keep every plant up to maximum efficiency, but for the most efficient nation in the world these are nevertheless startling figures, and we know of no reason to believe that a similar survey to-day would give very different results. There has been no comparable survey of Canadian industry, but not even the boldest patriot is likely to suggest that Canadian industry in general is

176

more efficient than American.   To apply the United States figures to ourselves is probably excessively generous.

But why lay this waste at the door of capitalism? It might all have been the fault of labour. It might have been, but it wasn't. The committee assessed responsibility as follows:

	Management	Labour	The Public, etc.
Men's Clothing	75%	16%	9%
Building	65	21	14
Printing	63	28	9
Boots and Shoes	73	11	16
Metal Trades	81	9	10
Textiles	50	10	40

Much even of labour's share of responsibility can be traced to the injustice and stupidity of capitalism. Many workers get less than the wage necessary to maximum efficiency, and a growing number feel no obligation to put forth their best efforts to fill the employer's pocket. Dreading unemployment, too, they try to make the job last as long as possible.[1] Much also of the consumer's share of waste arises out of the nature of the economic system. Without the struggle for profits and the advertising it engenders, the changes of fashion which often make obsolete overnight expensive machinery and laboriously acquired skill would be far less swift and sweeping.

The connection between capitalism and inefficient management, if we recall the separation of ownership, control and management in modern business, is equally clear. Profit is the test of survival, and profit is by no means always an indication of efficiency, frequently the reverse. Even where capitalism does not foster positive inefficiency it is apt to breed inertia. Why trouble to eliminate waste when it is often so much easier to get the same profit by persuading the government to raise the tariff or competitors to enter a combine?

Inventions and Technical Improvements.

Waste of this kind in a particular concern, however, is only a minor by-product of capitalism. Much more serious is the loss to a whole industry which occurs because a competitive firm must keep to itself its technical discoveries instead of diffusing

---

[1]*The Economy of Abundance*, by Stuart Chase, p. 48, quoting S. B. Mathewson, *Restriction of Output Among Unorganized Workers.* See also Tawney, *The Acquisitive Society.*

the knowledge throughout the industry, or because a monopoly, for the sake of profit, suppresses new inventions altogether. This last becomes increasingly serious as capitalism moves out of its early phase of competition into its modern phase of monopoly.

In a recent decision of the United States Circuit Court of Appeals (Keystone Steel and Wire Company vs. Commissioner of Internal Revenue. No. 4514 C.C.A.) we read, "It is common knowledge that meritorious inventions are very often relegated to oblivion through machinations of well-entrenched and power-ful competitors". In the case of Blount Manufacturing Com-pany vs. Yale and Towne Company, in 1909, the judge observed, "it is a fact familiar in commercial history that patents have a commercial value for purposes of extinction, that many patents are purchased to prevent the competition of new inventions and new machines with the old machines already installed". Mr. Felix J. Fraser in *Common Sense*, October, 1934, quotes the Inventors' Guild to the same effect, and gives some specific in-stances: "The technical editor of a popular encyclopedia asked an engineer employed by one of the large manufacturers of Mazda Lamps to contribute the biography of Claude, the pat-entee of the Neon Lamp. His request was refused on the grounds that the $20,000,000 investment of the company was endangered by Claude's invention! Later he learned that this company had bought the American license and was quietly suppressing it!"

The Financial Post for March 2, 1935, draws attention to the furious lobbying of "Canadian business" against the pro-posed new Patents Act which would oblige holders of patents to put them to commercial use within three years instead of eighteen as prescribed by the present Act! "It was represented to the Senate committee that the enactment of this provision would hamper and retard industrial development, cause great loss and hardship, greatly increase the number of wholly or partially invalid patents, cause great discontent and apprehen-sion, deprive inventors of their just rewards, deprive Cana-dians of benefits they now enjoy under patent laws in other countries, perhaps necessitate Canada's withdrawal from the International Patent Convention, contribute to unemployment, encourage piracy of inventions, injure the revenues as well as the prestige of the country". (A catalogue of woes which seems to omit nothing but housemaid's knee!) "Rt. Hon. Arthur Meighen bore testimony to the many criticisms of the bill received from industrial companies"—industrial companies, be it noted, not inventors.

Price-Manipulation.

Even when these efforts fail and technical improvements somehow get made, the resources of capitalism against humanity are not exhausted. It can still prevent the consumer from reaping any more of the benefits of efficiency than suits the book of the profit-maker. One of the weapons forged for this purpose is the indiscriminate denunciation of price-cutting which is now all but universal. Almost any number of trade papers contain some reproof to "unethical" dealers who "demoralize" (superb example of unconscious irony) the markets by "unethical trade practices"; and the worst of all these is to reduce prices. We do not deny that price-cutting may in some circumstances be injurious to consumer, worker and employer alike. Low prices secured by sweating labour, cheating creditors through fraudulent bankruptcies or otherwise, reducing farmers to penury, or similar means, are of course utterly indefensible. The Cassidy-Scott report on the men's clothing industry, indeed, shows that price-cutting of this sort is often itself a major source of waste: the inefficient fly-by-night firms eliminate the efficient who pay their debts to wage-earners and other creditors—an industrial "Gresham's Law", bad firms driving out good. But that does not prove that prices must forever be kept at the level that best suits a particular trader. The mere fact that a factory sells cheaper than a handicraftsman or a chain or department store cheaper than a small retail merchant (or vice versa) is not necessarily the result of sweating. High prices to the consumer do not necessarily mean a living income for the farmer and worker. Improved methods of production or distribution *ought* to mean lower prices. Those who lose their livelihood as a result of the improvements would in a socialist society be trained for some other occupation, with decent maintenance during the process, but they would not be allowed to hold the rest of us to ransom indefinitely. Many of the retail merchants who appeared before the Stevens committee seem to labour under the delusion that they are a race apart, who must at all costs be preserved in that station of life to which they are accustomed. It is now their turn to hear capitalism say, as it has said to workers a thousand times, "You're scrapped. Overboard you go and get ashore if you can."

The profit-maker is always on the alert to exploit even the passion for social justice in order to fill his purse. There is real danger that the great corporations will use the grievances of the small merchant or manufacturer, and the outburst of public disgust at the revelations before the Stevens committee, to build up a popular psychology against any kind of price reduction for any reason whatever. Industrial sabotage, masquerading as "codes" or "control in the interests of the community" could then make Canada a monopolist's paradise.

Over-development and Surplus Capacity.

One of the major wastes of the economy has been the over-development of particular industries. In Canada the classic example is railways, but there are plenty of others, and it is not a problem created by the depression. The pulp and paper industry in 1929 had a surplus capacity of 20 per cent., and present capacity is 7.1 per cent. higher.[2] "Tonnage lost" in the coal mines in 1929 was 22 per cent. of capacity, 15 per cent. because of "lack of orders".[3] Oil refineries in 1930 were equipped to produce twice the consumption for that year.[4] Blast furnaces in 1929 operated at 72 per cent. of capacity, motor car plants at 79 per cent.,[5] sugar refineries at 50 per cent.,[6] flour mills in 1928 and 1929 at 53 per cent.

In 1919 Canada could have supplied the flour import requirements of the whole British Empire three times over, in 1932 the requirements of the whole world.[7] In the bread-baking industry in 1929, 72 of the 76 mill-controlled bakeries alone had a capacity of over 50,000,000 pounds more than the total sales of all bakeries. The mill-controlled bakeries themselves operated at only 35½ per cent. of capacity. Six mill-controlled bakeries in Montreal could have supplied four-fifths of the province of Quebec, six of the seven mill-controlled bakeries in Toronto more than half of Ontario, three in Winnipeg all of Manitoba, four in Vancouver more than all of British Columbia. By 1931 the number of mill-controlled bakeries had reached 92, with capacity of 21 per cent. greater than total production of all bakeries, and

---

[2]*Financial Post Business Year Book*, 1931, p. 10; *Evidence before the Banking Committee*, 1934, p. 890.

[3]*Coal Statistics for Canada*, 1929, (Dominion Bureau of Statistics).

[4]*House of Commons Debates*, special session of 1930, p. 535 (Mr. R. B. Bennett).

[5]*Iron and Steel Industry*, 1929 (Dominion Bureau of Statistics).

[6]*Financial Post Business Year Book*, 1932.

[7]*Financial Post Business Year Book*, 1931; Royal Commission on Price Spreads, 1934-1935, *Evidence*, pp. 3521, 3527-3529.

these 92 operating at only 27 per cent. of their capacity. Operating at only 40 per cent. of their "theoretical" capacity, the mill-controlled bakeries could have supplied 90 per cent. of the demand in Montreal, 122 per cent. in Toronto, 87 per cent. in Winnipeg.[8]

In railway rolling stock, National Steel Car and Eastern Car alone, without Canadian Car and Foundry, can produce 20,000 cars a year; in 1929 the total market was only 13,342. Canadian Locomotive can turn out 120 locomotives; in 1929 the total market for two companies was 98.[9]. Page-Hersey Tubes "entered the depression equipped for at least 30 per cent. more business than it had done in its record year".[10]

The capacity of all distilleries listed in the *Financial Post Survey* (except Canadian Industrial Alcohol and Brewers and Distillers of Vancouver) is 23,812,000 gallons. Total domestic consumption (of which Canadian distillers supplied only about half) plus exports in 1929 reached only 7,428,309 gallons, probably less than a quarter of total plant capacity. The total market, domestic and foreign, actually secured by Canadian distillers in 1929 was 4,901,872 gallons. Our largest distillery, with a capacity of 11,000,000 gallons, or our second largest, with 10,-000,000, could have supplied all of this with less than six months' operation.[11] For beer, figures of plant capacity for National Breweries (which is said to do 60 per cent. of the Quebec business), Molson's, Labatt's and Brewers and Distillers of Vancouver are not available. But the remaining breweries have capacity enough to supply the whole 1929 market.[12]

Three lead pencil factories can provide all we need with a few weeks of operation.[13] The number of gasoline filling stations is grotesquely beyond our requirements,[14]—three pumps in all the larger cities for every one necessary: two-thirds of the pumps in Nova Scotia doing less than ten gallons a day business. Under new legislation, Nova Scotia has been able to reduce the number of pumps 41 per cent.[15] Economical milk

8*Report of the Registrar under the Combines Investigation Act*, 1931, pp. 39-40; Royal Commission on Price Spreads, 1934-1935, *Evidence*, pp. 3663-3666.

9Plant capacity from *Financial Post Survey*, 1934; other figures from Dominion Bureau of Statistics *Report*.

10*Financial Post*, September 29, 1934.

11Plant capacity from *Financial Post Survey*, 1934; other figures from *Canada Year Book*, 1933, and *Report on the Trade of Canada for the Calendar Year* 1929, (Dominion Bureau of Statistics).

12Same sources as for distilleries.

13C. L. Burton, president of Simpson's, quoted in Ottawa *Journal*, September 12, 1934.

14*Combines and the Consumer*, p. 27; *Financial Post*, March 31 and July 28, 1934.

15*Financial Post*, January 12, 1935.

distribution calls for about 350 customers per wagon; the present average is about 150.[16]

The Ontario Hydro Chairman says (and his predecessors deny) that it has surpluses which may not be fully taken up for fifteen years.[17]   Private utilities have kept silence on the point. In 1933, of 80 plants of Canadian Canners, 18 were obsolete but 36 of the rest were idle; and even in 1929, besides the 18 obsolete, 15 had been idle.[18]   Cotton in 1929 had 14.01 per cent. of its spindles idle.[19]   Rubber tire plants in 1928 were producing at about 75 per cent. of capacity.[20]   Clearly, even if we get back to the 1929 level of activity we shall still have a formidable problem of idle capital.

Some of this over-development, of course, is more apparent than real, necessitated by our geographical position and climate. Some of it may represent obsolete or obsolescent plants.   But a good deal of it is the direct result of competitive capitalism, picturesquely described by M. Ilin in "New Russia's Primer" in the parable of Mr. Box, Mr. Cox, Mr. Fox and Mr. Knox and their hat factories.

The monopoly capitalist is under less temptation to overexpand productive equipment.[21]   He has a better idea of the size of at least the domestic market open to him, whereas under competition each of several firms may build plant enough to supply the whole market.   But this does not by any means wholly remove the danger of over-expansion.   There is always the possibility that another group of capitalists will try to "muscle in" on the monopolist's territory.   A really strong monopoly could probably use the government to prevent this.   Something of the sort showed signs of developing in the United States out of the N.R.A. and was suggested to the Banking Committee in this country by Sir Herbert Holt as a remedy for the ills of pulp and paper.[22] There is also the possibility that the monopolist may overestimate the share of total purchasing power his industry may capture: in rayon versus cotton, or beer versus whiskey.   And unless the monopoly is part of an international combine it may still over-expand on the strength of illusions about its possible

[16]*Financial Post*, October 6, 1934.

[17]*Financial Post*, August 18, 1934.

[18]Royal Commission on Price Spreads, 1934-1935, *Evidence*, p. 3049.

[19]*Census of Industry*.

[20]Committee on Price Spreads, 1934, *Evidence*, p. 2153.

[21]In cement, for example, there seems to be little or no excess capacity (given the 1929 market.)

[22]*Evidence before the Banking Committee*, 1934, p. 884.

share of foreign markets; and as the life of most international combines has been brief and precarious this is not much of a safeguard. The problem of surplus production capacity is likely to remain with us at least as long as capitalism.

Similarly with another of the enormous wastes of capitalism, competitive advertising and selling. Mr. Courtauld, one of the ablest of British business men, estimated Britain's 1930 advertising bill at £180,000,000, of which he said, four-fifths was from the standpoint of the community utterly useless, merely puffing one firm's goods against another's.[23] Nothing less than a single, all-embracing monopoly can eliminate this. A radio monopoly need no longer push one brand of radio as against another (though it sometimes does), but it still must push radio in general against food, movies, motor cars, travel.

The other wastes of distribution we discuss in detail elsewhere. Here it is enough to note that in most instances getting goods from factory to consumer costs more than all the rest of the productive process put together, and that costs of distribution are increasing. For very few goods is the cost of manufacture more than half of the retail price; it is often less than a fourth.[24] In the United States the "platform cost" (materials, parts, labour) of a $500 or $600 motor car has been authoritatively estimated at $105 to $125; dealer's profit and salesman's commission $150; advertising $25 to $30; the rest, 49 per cent. of the retail price, is overhead, zone supervision, profit, etc.[25]

Nepotism and "Pull".

Another by no means negligible source of inefficiency is inheritance. Business ability is not always hereditary, and great fortunes often fall into the hands of men and women not competent to put them to the economically (to say nothing of socially) best use. Anyone can supply illustrations from his own experience. Nor does the prospect of inheriting a fortune encourage initiative: see almost any Wodehouse novel.[26] More serious than these, however, is a less obvious aspect of the problem: nepotism and favouritism in industry. The propaganda of capitalism here again tries to cover one of its weakest spots by a bold excursion into the enemy's country. We are all familiar with the argument that socialism would collapse be-

---

23Quoted in A. L. Rowse, *Politics and the Younger Generation*, p. 126.
24D. M. Marvin, in *Proceedings of the Canadian Political Science Assoc.*, 1930, p. 16.
25*Steel*, April 17, 1933.
26For a serious, and very elaborate study, see Josiah Wedgwood, *Economics of Inheritance.*

cause "pull" would count more than ability. Under capitalism, we are given to understand "pull" does not count at all. But even the cautious British Liberal "Yellow Book" of 1928 expressed alarm at the prevalence of nepotism in British industry, and in Canada too, not infrequently, a young and inexperienced son succeeds to his father's directorship or rises rapidly to a vice-presidency. Everyone knows, also, that in applying for a job in any big capitalist concern, it "means something" to be the son of the president or a college friend of the general manager's brother. With the disappearance of the frontier, the crystallizing of class distinctions, the gross inequality of opportunity depicted in Chapter I of this volume, it is hardly too much to say that in the near future the leading positions in Canadian industry are likely to become the close hereditary preserve of a privileged social group.

If this group included all the ablest people in the country the situation might be, economically, tolerable. But in fact it is quite otherwise. The vast store of unused ability among the industrial rank and file is, as anyone who has taken part in workers' education can testify, one of the greatest, as it is one of the most tragic, wastes of capitalism. "An experienced history examiner at Oxford who went through a large number of Workers' Education Association essays, selected at haphazard, made the deliberate pronouncement that over a third reached the first class standards of the Oxford Modern History School."[27]

The Canadian Council of Social Hygiene estimates Canada's annual bill for ill-health at $311,000,000. "Two to three per cent. of the population are continuously on the sick-list. One person out of three dies ahead of his time from diseases that could be prevented. Over half of all disabling illness could be prevented".[28] To charge the whole of this to capitalism would be unfair, but beyond question much of it is the result of long hours, low wages, bad housing, overcrowding, inadequate education and similar by-products of the economic system. We "cannot afford" to conserve our human any more than our natural resources. There is often more profit to be made by doing the opposite, especially as the profit-makers can shift most of the cost on to the shoulders of others, contemporaries or posterity.

Losses to the community from monopoly restriction in var-

27London *Morning Post* (hardly a revolutionary journal!) quoted in Todd, *Theories of Social Progress*, p. 260.
28Quoted by Dr. Howden, M.P., in *House of Commons Debates*, 1932, p. 1328.

ious forms (including the tariff) are impossible to estimate. If the Canadian consumer were able to get everything he wants in as great quantity and as cheaply as modern technology makes possible, he would be better off than he is. How much better off, Professor Taylor's and Professor Rogers' tariff figures (already referred to) or a comparison of electricity rates in Ontario and Quebec[29] give some faint idea.

Booms and Depressions.

The precise causes of the trade cycle are still hotly disputed, but almost everyone agrees that recurrent depressions have been characteristic of capitalism hitherto, and that to eradicate them would at least call for very large changes in capitalist policy, and that there is no sign of governments or business men adopting any of the measures which their experts declare to be essential to stabilization. They cannot or will not control investment and company promotion. They will not "manage" their currencies in the "proper" ways. They cannot and will not go "back to the market". They will not or cannot banish the danger of war. All the factors which brought on previous depressions are still present, and nothing that we have done since 1929 lessens the chances of a repetition of the disasters of that year.

On the other hand, no competent thinker has been able to give any reason why a world socialist economy should suffer from industrial fluctuations at all; and even a single socialist community could lessen their sweep, and distribute the burdens equitably. For practical purposes then we may safely set down depressions as one of the major inefficiencies of capitalism.

The cost of depressions hardly needs illustration, but a few figures may not be amiss. Of unemployment we have no adequate statistics. But at the bottom of the depression, in the late winter of 1933, 1,500,000 Canadians (heads of families and dependents) were receiving public relief, all but about 100,000 of them because of unemployment. Almost one-third of the population of Montreal was on relief at this time. By June, 1934, the total had dropped to 1,000,000, of whom probably at least 850,000 were unemployed workers and their dependents, the rest drought victims.[30] The December, 1934, total was 1,182,-

29See Hankin and MacDermot *Recovery by Control,* and Mosher and Others, *Electrical Utilities.* On the general subject of monopoly restriction see Stuart Chase, *Economy of Abundance.*

30Montreal *Gazette,* August 13, 1934: Miss Charlotte Whitton to the Canadian Chamber of Commerce, quoted in *Financial Post,* Sept. 15, 1934; reports of the Dominion Commissioner of Unemployment Relief, etc.

123. 850,000 was probably the peak figure of unemployment of wage and salary earners. By October 1934 it had fallen to perhaps 650,000 or 700,000. The Prime Minister's recent estimate is 500,000. Our national income in goods and services (that is, *after allowing for the fall in prices*) dropped by more than a third between 1928 and 1932.[31] Farm profits dropped from $468,800,000 in 1929 to $272,312,000 in 1931. Agricultural wages fell from $89,000,000 in 1929 to $47,634,000 in 1932. Total wages and salaries fell from $2,722,100,000 in 1929 to $1,600,000,000 in 1933.[32] Total real wages in manufacturing and mining fell by almost 32 per cent. between 1929 and 1932.[33] Real agricultural income fell 45 per cent.[34] Here also, as with the cost of illness, the capitalist class shifts most of the burden. Unemployment imposes no direct charge on industry as such; the cost of relief is met largely by indirect taxes paid mainly by the poorer classes; and most of the reduction in income has fallen on farmers and wage-earners. Salaries, especially for the higher paid groups, have suffered relatively little, dividends in all but the export industries (an important exception) have fallen scarcely at all, interest payments are actually much larger now than before the depression.[35]

The Cost of War.

Finally there is war. That the activities of rival capitalists, especially armament makers, are at least one of the chief causes of war no serious student now questions. It is not so much that capitalists consciously plan wars (that is probably rare), but that they plan to get markets, concessions, preferred access to raw materials, and use for that purpose their national Foreign Offices, backed ultimately by their national armies, navies and air forces.[36].

The cost of the last war has been estimated by Nicholas Murray Butler (who is very far from being a radical agitator) at 30,000,000 lives and $400,000,000,000. "With that amount we could have built a $2,500 house with $1,000 worth of furniture, and placed it on five acres of land worth $100 an acre, for every family in the United States, Canada, Australia, England,

---

[31]Estimate by Professor Taylor of McMaster University.
[32]*Financial Post Business Year Book,* 1934, 1935.
[33]*Census of Industry Reports* (Dominion Bureau of Statistics): figures adjusted for 18 per cent. fall in retail prices.
[34]*Financial Post Business Year Book,* 1934: figures similarly adjusted.
[35]Forsey, *Dividends and the Depression,* and *Financial Post* records.
[36]See Hawtrey, *Economic Aspects of Sovereignty*; Charques and Ewen, *Profits and Politics*; Brailsford, *Property or Peace?*

Wales, Ireland, Scotland, France, Belgium, Germany and Russia. . . . There would have been enough left to give each city of 20,000 inhabitants and over in all the countries named a $5,-000,000 library and a $10,000,000 university. Out of the balance we could have set aside a sum at 5 per cent. interest which would pay for all time a $1,000 yearly salary each for 125,000 teachers and 125,000 nurses. After having done all this we could still have bought up all of France and Belgium, everything that France and Belgium possessed in 1914: every home, factory, church, railroad, street car".[37] Canada itself has a very small armament budget, but sixty cents of every dollar of Dominion taxes go to pay war pensions and interest on war debt.[38] Once more, of course, it is the masses who pay and, in the main, the capitalists who get paid.

Our bank and insurance companies "point with pride" to the fact that no Canadian depositor or policy-holder has lost a penny during the depression. It is an interesting sidelight on the ethics and the standards of efficiency of Canadian capitalism that its leaders actually make it a boast that they have behaved with common honesty and reasonable competence; feeling, apparently, that the most captious critic can ask no more. For some of us, however, it is not enough that Big Business plays the game more or less according to the rules (of its own making). The public is beginning to ask, "What is an economic system for?" and to supply the obvious answer, "To meet the needs of the people with the least possible expenditure of effort and resources". But to capitalism, as we have pointed out in an earlier chapter, "need" has no meaning. It is only the consumer's money which talks, and so the millionaire's slightest whim roars in a voice of thunder while the poor man's direst need barely whispers. Moreover capitalism is essentially and inescapably a scarcity economy: the nearer any commodity gets to being a "free good" like air or sunshine, the less profit there is in it for the capitalist. Capitalism, in short does not even try to do what an economic system should, rather the reverse; and what it does it does very badly. Its boasted efficiency is an imposition on public credulity. Not until we establish a socialist economy shall we begin to reap the fruits of the real efficiency which science has made possible.

[37]Quoted in *Canadian Business*, June, 1934.
[38]Brook Claxton, in *Canadian Business*, June, 1934.

B.   Why the System Fails to Work.

Trade Cycle or Chronic Depression?

Every depression before 1929 ended in a recovery which carried economic activity to a point above the pre-depression level.   The recovery which began in March, 1933, gives no such assurance.   Since July, 1934, there has been no appreciable gain in Canadian business as a whole.   This recovery movement, far from having brought us above the 1929 level, has not even reached it.   On the contrary the *Financial Post* business index now stands, and has stood for eleven months, more than 20 per cent. below the 1929 average.   Meanwhile the population has increased more than 8 per cent.   Monthly business index figures are higher than last year but decreasingly so.   In January the increase was 8.7 per cent., February 11.0, March 6.9, April 6.0, May 2.9.   The gap between 1934 and 1935 figures is narrowing. It is rather ominous that car loadings and railway gross revenues should be almost stationary at the 1934 level, and railway net earnings 24 per cent. below it.

In Great Britain, the United States, Germany and Italy[39] the situation is not substantially different.   Recovery is pro-

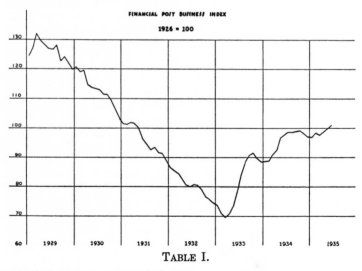

TABLE I.

[39]For details see below, Section c. of this chapter.

ceeding very slowly, if at all, and is certainly not firmly established. The apologists of capitalism will no doubt try to explain away these disagreeable facts by attributing them to temporary and special factors. They have their work cut out for them; and if they succeed, they will have to address themselves to a still more formidable task.

Down to the end of the War employment on the whole kept pace with a fairly rapid increase in population, and the standard of living rose. Large-scale unemployment was a feature of the periodic depressions, never a permanent chronic condition. In "prosperous" times at least, the system found no difficulty in absorbing not only the new recruits to industry from the schools and universities, but also large numbers displaced by technological changes. After the War, however, there appeared, even in the United States as well as in Great Britain and Germany, the novel and disquieting phenomenon of a growing volume of unemployment at the height of an unprecedented boom[40]. The system had ceased to absorb all the available labour.

We face not only the familiar problem of why capitalism suffers from recurrent breakdowns, but also the more harassing problem of why it apparently has lost, or is losing, its powers of recuperation and growth. For the first of these problems economists, professional and amateur, orthodox and unorthodox, have propounded a multitude of solutions, none perhaps completely satisfactory. To the second, few professional economists in the western world have devoted any attention at all.

Maladjustment of Savings and Investment.

There is no space nor is it necessary here to enter on an elaborate examination of the varied theories of the trade cycle. From a survey of monopoly capitalism in previous chapters, however, there emerge certain indisputable facts which provide at least the outlines of answers to both aspects of the problem "why the system fails to work".

We may rule out at once, as both irrelevant and fallacious, one popular theory, Major C. H. Douglas' "Social Credit". For if, as Major Douglas contends, the normal operation of industry, even without any saving or investment, necessarily produces a "deficiency of purchasing power", it is quite impossible to explain why we have ever had anything but depressions. The entire industrial era just has not happened!

40Prof. Wesley C. Mitchell puts the increase of unemployment in the United States between 1920 and 1927 at over 650,000. *Recent Economic Changes*, Vol. II, p. 878.

Perhaps even more popular, but with better reason, is Mr. J. A. Hobson's "underconsumption-oversaving" theory. This finds the underlying cause of the trade cycle in inequality of income. A few people get incomes so large that they cannot begin to consume them all. Willy-nilly, the very rich must save and invest a large part of their incomes. The result is a piling up of capital, which goes into factories and every other form of construction. While these are being built, purchasing power in the form of wages, etc., is distributed and everything goes well. But after they are finished, there comes a stage when the owners find that their capacity to produce is far beyond consumers' capacity to buy at existing prices. Prices therefore collapse and depression sets in. After a time, accumulated stocks of goods become exhausted, production equipment becomes obsolete, bankruptcies and moratoria relieve the pressure on debtors, a new invention or an armaments race provides new opportunities for profit, and the economy enters on a period of recovery. But the fundamental trouble remains and sooner or later must bring on another crash.

It is beautifully simple, and the idea of an economic nemesis for inequality of income is undeniably attractive. But there are two crucial questions which this theory wholly fails to answer.

In the first place, Mr. Hobson and his friends admit that there must be *some* saving. Society cannot spend all its income on immediate consumption. It must use some of its energies and resources to maintain its production equipment. It must keep up the flow of raw materials through industry. It must provide for the subsistence of workers engaged, for example, on construction jobs where the returns are long deferred. All these things involve saving. Raising the standard of living involves more saving. So far Mr. Hobson would agree; "but", he would add, "not too much". This is not very enlightening. How much is "too much"? The Soviet Union, since 1929, has been saving a larger proportion of its income than any other community in history. On Mr. Hobson's theory most of its population should now be unemployed. To reply that the Russian standard of living is low may be true, but is surely irrelevant. The theory says nothing about standards of living. It speaks only of proportion of income saved. If the Russians can save thirty or forty per cent. of their income without provoking a crisis, why should perhaps nineteen per cent.[41] bring Canada to the verge of ruin?

[41]Estimated from figures in *Canada Year Book*, 1932, p. 748; 1933, pp. 869, 879-880.

In the second place, why should piling up of savings necessarily produce a slump? If the supply of capital increases during prosperity at the terrifying pace Mr. Hobson suggests, why does not the price of the use of capital (i.e., the rate of interest) fall correspondingly? Why does not capital get nearer and nearer to the status of a "free good" like air or sunshine? There are always plenty of things we should like to do but can't because the necessary capital is too expensive.

Saving means a transfer of purchasing power from consumers to investors. *If the rate of interest falls fast enough and far enough* to induce industry to borrow all the capital available, then the shrinkage in consumers' purchasing power is offset by the expansion in investors' purchasing power. When the new factories come into operation, there will be no difficulty in disposing of their product *if the price is low enough;* and with a sufficient fall in the rate of interest, the factories will be able to make the price low enough without suffering a loss. To the unsophisticated, therefore, the logical result of the automatic saving of the very rich is abundance of cheap new capital available for undertakings which could not be afforded when capital was scarce and dear. Capitalists will have to be content with smaller and smaller profits. The expropriators will expropriate themselves! Capitalism will "wither away".

Mr. Stuart Chase[42] really seems to think it will. His faith, however, rests partly on the curious belief that there is a definite biological limit not merely to any particular want, but to human wants in general, and that therefore it is going to become increasingly hard to find anything for our capital to do. Even if he were right, the standard of living of the mass of mankind is still so low that the problem of what to do when we have satisfied all of everybody's wants is unlikely to trouble even our remote descendants.

We venture to think that earlier chapters of this volume provide several very cogent reasons why the expropriators will *not* expropriate themselves.

In the first place, broadly speaking, the nearer anything gets to being a "free good" the less there is in it for the capitalist. This is just as true for the competitive capitalist as for the monopolist; but the competitive capitalist cannot restrict production and hold up price, while the monopolist can and does.

42*The Economy of Abundance*, on which see John Strachey's review in *The Nation*, May 9, 1934.

This is why monopoly capitalism is essentially and inescapably a scarcity economy to a degree impossible to the competitive capitalism of earlier days.

Accordingly, the monopolists or semi-monopolists who control the supply of new capital lower the price only slowly and reluctantly and under strong pressure. They seem to doubt whether they can lend enough at lower rates to make up to them for the reduced percentage on each loan; and their doubts are probably well founded. Canadian bankers, reproached for the remarkable rigidity of interest rates in this country during the depression at a time when the surplus of savings justified lower rates, reply with much truth that in countries where rates have come down (unevenly and tardily), the increase in industrial activity has been disappointingly small. So the rate stays up or declines very slowly, savings lie idle, and the shrinkage in consumer purchasing power is *not* offset by expansion in investor purchasing power.

Even when the rate on new capital falls, there remains the rigidity of returns on previously invested capital. Modern business, as we have seen, gets more and more of its capital by issuing long-term bonds and debentures carrying a fixed rate of interest, or cumulative preferred stock which approximates more and more closely to the same type. Most of the flexibility of the small enterprise of earlier days is gone. The management is expected to make strenuous efforts to avoid default on the bonds. But factories cannot make the price low enough to call forth consumer demand sufficient to employ the whole production capacity. These rigidites go far to explain why the depression of 1929-1933 went deeper and lasted longer than its predecessors, and why recovery from it has been so restricted.

A second reason why the piling up of savings produces crises is that the planlessness of capitalism leads to overexpansion of production equipment. It is quite possible that capital invested in working-class housing in 1928 would have earned as high a return on the average as it has in pulp and paper or some other industries into which it flowed freely at that time. But investors thought otherwise. They saw "good things" elsewhere and flung themselves heedlessly into the process of making them "bad things". So our savings go into superfluous factories while large groups of our people go without proper housing because "capital is not available" to provide it at reasonable prices.[48]   In other words, the system breaks down periodically because "saving" outruns "investment" (the actual use of savings in productive undertakings) and this in its turn is the result of the rigidities and planlessness of monopoly capitalism.

The Final Stage of Capitalist Development.

But why can the system no longer recover and expand as it once did?   Why is the general trend now, apparently, unevenly downward instead of unevenly upward as it used to be?   The real explanation lies in the process of capitalist development.

The first captains of industry, in nineteenth century England, had the world for their oyster.   Labour was cheap and plentiful, rich and virgin natural resources were waiting to be tapped, foreign tariffs were ridiculously inadequate to stem the flood of cheap machine-made English goods.   Moreover, as capitalism developed the new cheap mechanical transport, it became possible to exploit not only the natural resources and labour of Britain, but also of Europe, and then the even richer resources of the Americas, Asia, and Africa, and the incredibly cheap labour of the Orient.   No wonder profits were easy!

This process could not go on forever.   British capitalism in its search for profit exported not only finished consumers' goods but also machines, skilled mechanics, enterprising business men, and above all, money.   The inevitable result, of course, was the growth of "native" capitalisms in what had been almost exclusively British markets.   Britain is no longer the "workshop of the world".   Germany, the United States, and Japan especially, other countries to a lesser degree, compete with Britain and with each other, in each others' home markets and in neutral markets: compete not only for the consumer's dollar but also for supplies of raw materials and for outlets for capital investment.   Each national group of capitalists, its profits threatened by foreign competition, naturally appeals to its government to shut out the foreigner by tariffs, quotas and other restrictions, to subsidize exports, and to bend every effort to secure colonies or concessions or privileges of some kind or other in "backward" countries.   The governments obligingly comply, and of course in so doing intensify the process whose effects they are seeking to remedy.   As the appeals become more urgent, and the protective measures more drastic, the export markets

---

43On this whole subject, cf. Barbara Wootton, *Plan or No Plan*; E. F. M. Durbin, *Purchasing Power and Trade Depression*; John Strachey, *The Nature of Capitalist Crisis.*

of the great industrial nations no longer expand at their old pace, some stop expanding at all, and some even begin to decline; and the export market of the raw material producing countries suffers correspondingly.

Nor is this the whole story. As industry spreads, there comes a time when the natural resources already developed are no longer quite so cheap to work, and remaining land, forests and mines no longer quite so rich nor so accessible. Labour, first in Europe, then in America, in recent years even in the Orient, begins to learn how to organize and so force from its employers higher wages, shorter hours, "expensive" health and safety legislation and social services. These costs are undoubtedly offset to some extent by increased productivity per worker, but once they are instituted any attempt to reduce them can only be carried through in the face of great resistance.[44] Even more rigid, however, are the rights of the bond and stock holders which come to be built in the system of production for private profit.

With costs rising and foreign markets tending to shrink, industry might be expected to turn to the home market. But here too nemesis awaits it. A very large number of industries in all industrialized countries are now either monopolized or tending towards monopoly, and the competitive industries, as we have seen, are largely at the mercy of the monopolies. It is true that it may sometimes pay the monopolist better to sell many articles at a low price than a few at a high price. But it is at least equally true that it may often pay him to restrict his market; and it is highly unlikely that the price which gives him maximum profit will be the lowest price at which he could afford to sell without loss. The home market also, therefore, tends to shrink, or at best fails to keep pace with the expansion of productive capacity.[45]

In short, the opportunities for profit by *expansion* are, to say the least of it, no longer what they once were. Capitalism is driven, inexorably, to secure its profits by *restriction*, (impossible under competition, but easy under monopoly). Hence the characteristic feature of all recent capitalist "recovery" measures is restriction of production. The "recovery" in view is

[44]There has, of course, been an impressive increase in productivity per worker; but much of this is probably the result of improved machinery and "speeding up", rather than of greater vigour and willingness to work.

[45]On this whole matter, cf. the pamphlet, *Unemployment in the Machine Age*, by E. A. Forsey, published by the Social Service Council of Canada; and John Strachey, *The Nature of Capitalist Crisis*.

recovery of profit, and for that purpose the measures taken are, at least for the time being, very effective. The one unquestioned achievement, alike of the Nazis in Germany, of the N.R.A. in the United States, and of the National Government in England, is a spectacular restoration of profits, a restoration in which Canada has shared. It begins to look as if henceforth the best we can expect under capitalism, is successive temporary stabilizations on progressively lower levels, for everything but profits.

As John Strachey writes, "The most responsible capitalist economists themselves recognize the permanent character of the present crisis. 'We live', writes Professor Robbins, 'not in the fourth but in the nineteenth year of the world crisis'. (1933) The League of Nations World Economic Survey tells us that from 1860 to 1913 production increased 'with remarkable regularity of trend. . . . If the line of trend from 1860 to 1913 is extended to 1932 the rather startling conclusion is reached that the index of world production, on the hypothesis that nothing had occurred to alter its regular upward trend for the fifty preceding years, would to-day be twice as great as it actually is'."[46]

The Contradictions of Capitalism.

In this period of declining capitalism the contradictions of the system become glaringly clear.

(1) It needs peace. Another great war may easily be fatal. But the struggle for profit, for foreign markets and concessions, drives it towards war whether it will or no.

(2) It needs international trade. But it breeds the economic nationalism which destroys international trade. All our statesmen recognize that "the barriers must come down"; but "Que messieurs les assassins commencent". Others must do what we won't.

(3) Capital inevitably seeks foreign outlets for investment. This export of capital creates rival national capitalisms and ruins its own foreign market.

(4) Capitalism can work smoothly and automatically only in the "open market place" which inevitably it destroys.

(5) Planlessness, rigidities and above all the restriction of markets enforced by pursuit of profit produce a situation in which consumption chronically lags behind capacity to produce.

(6) Capitalism, by its inequality of incomes, inevitably

46Strachey, *op. cit.*, p. 20.

produces an enormous accumulation of capital. By monopoly, which it produces with the same inevitability, it effectively delays or prevents altogether the fall in interest rates which is essential if much of the accumulated savings is not to lie idle.

(7)　Capitalism has made possible an economy of plenty; but by its waste, by the destruction wrought by wars, and by deliberate restriction of production, it enforces scarcity.

(8)　Capitalism has fostered the development of science, but its planlessness is forcing restriction here as elsewhere. At Aberdeen last year, Sir Josiah Stamp pleaded with the British Association for the Advancement (!) of Science "to put a brake on the rush of new inventions before it wrecked the whole economic order. 'I tremble with dread,' he said, 'as to what is going to happen to any kind of economic organism which is trying to keep in balance, particularly under an individualistic form of society'."[47] This is typical of hundreds of recent utterances from similar quarters. Capitalism, which once gloried in science, is becoming anti-scientific and anti-intellectual. It is becoming clear that science and capitalism cannot both continue to exist; so of course science must go.

These contradictions are inherent in capitalism and inseparable from it. They are independent of the volition of any individual capitalist. The great industrialists and financiers do not consciously plot their own destruction. But to reverse Adam Smith's phrase, "Each, seeking only his own interest, is led as by an Invisible Hand to promote the ruin of society."

C.　Why Capitalists Cannot Plan.

It is not surprising that many, even in capitalist circles, are now willing to admit that unplanned capitalism can no longer work. Planning, they agree, is essential. But, they add consolingly, we can have planning without socialism, "the palm without the dust". We can plan, yet lay no profane hand on profits, the ark of the covenant. But is a planned capitalism possible? The argument that it is takes two forms.

The Prospects of Monopoly.

First, just as there are those who rely on "gradual evolution" to transform capitalism into socialism, so there are those who believe that it will change unplanned capitalism into planned.

[47]*New York Times,* September 7, 1934.

Already, they point out, business is moving rapidly towards monopoly. Each existing monopoly plans within its own industry or group of industries, often with scant regard for the traditional pricing process: one department subsidizes others. Surely the ultimate logical result is a single vast super-monopoly, national or international, embracing all industries, and planning its activities in the same way?

There is perhaps a remote chance of a national super-monopoly developing in this way. But we have had experience, in Canada, of the difficulty of securing "voluntary co-operation" among even the few great corporations in the pulp and paper industry, let alone the multitude of small enterprises in the furniture industry or the clothing trades. The relative strength of rival groups of capitalists is constantly changing. If they succeed in composing their differences, the agreement lasts only until the group whose strength is increasing feels that it can gain more by breaking the agreement than by keeping it. Of the three cartels in the Canadian newsprint industry since 1927, only one, the most recent—and the weakest—has been all-inclusive, none has lasted more than about two years, and none has been successful.[48] For permanent agreement (unless government steps in, a possibility we shall consider presently) we shall have to wait until one group has succeeded in bankrupting or buying up all its rivals: a long, painful and costly process. In fact, no one seriously believes that we shall allow the "robber barons" to fight it out to the bitter end.

Of the emergence of a world super-monopoly, there seems to be no prospect at all, except as the outcome of a struggle which will leave one of the national monopolies enthroned upon a heap of skulls. There have been, and are, plenty of international combines. But, with perhaps the ominous exception of the armament and related industries, they have seldom achieved a world monopoly even of a single trade, and never for long.[49] For the relative strength of national capitalisms, like that of rival capitalist groups within the nation, is never constant, and as it changes, the spoils must be re-divided. This involves not only the economic strength of each nation but also its diplomatic and military strength. Each national capitalism has at its disposal the national Foreign Office and the national armed

48 See a speech by Charles Vining, president of "Nemac", to the Empire Club, Toronto, March 28, 1935; also a paper read to the Canadian Political Science Association, 1935, by Eugene Forsey (*Canadian Journal of Economics and Political Science*, August, 1935).

49 See A Plummer, *International Combines in Modern Industry*.

forces, and in the last resort differences over markets, concessions, colonies, are settled by war.[50] If national super-monopo-
lies develop, the danger of war will increase. A world in which
U.S.A., Inc., confronts Great Britain Sons and Company, Japan
Incorporated, Deutschland G.m.b.H., France Société Anonyme,
and so forth, will have even less hope of peace than our own;
and the chance of capitalism in any form surviving the battle is
small.

Most capitalist planners, however, would protest that this
sort of development is not what they have in mind at all. For
one thing, it would take too long; for another, to paraphrase
Gilbert:

> "The prospect of a lot
> Of business men in close proximity
> All planning for themselves is what
> No man can face with equanimity."

We cannot wait until some group of monopolists has succeeded
in liquidating all its rivals. The state must enforce "co-operation" among business men, and on terms which will safeguard
"the public interest".

State-Capitalist Planning.

This is the second form of the argument that planned capitalism is possible. "State-capitalist planning," though as yet
nowhere fully developed, is the type to which the economic systems of all capitalist countries are now approximating. Its
chief characteristics are (a) state organized combines, enforcing their decrees through the state's legal machinery ("self-
government in industry") ; (b) state regulation of the relations
between monopolies; (c) state subsidies, loans, guarantees and
so forth, to private industry on an unprecedented scale; (d) a
growing volume of social legislation, paid for, as far as possible,
by the workers; (e) ownership and operation of certain important industries or services by the state for the benefit of the
investors. The avowed aim of the whole thing is the preserva-
tion of profit and as far as possible of private ownership of
industry. On this point Mr. Roosevelt, Mr. Bennett and Mr.
Stevens are as clear and emphatic as Signor Mussolini. They
believe it can be done without destroying political democracy.
He does not. The economic policies of the "democratic" and the

---

[50]See Lenin, *Imperialism*, and R. D. Charques and A. H. Ewen, *Profits and Politics*.

fascist countries differ only in degree. As a witty American journalist puts it, "Fascism is just capitalism gone nudist".

The similarity in the economic framework of Fascist and non-Fascist countries becomes obvious the moment we examine them in the light of the five characteristics of state-capitalist planning just cited.

(a) "Self-government in industry", meaning "government of industry by big business for big business", was already highly developed in Germany before the Nazi revolution, but hampered by the existence of strong trade unions. Herr Hitler has obligingly removed this impediment, and under his benevolent eye Herr Thyssen has been able to carry self-government in the steel industry to its logical conclusion by ejecting his Roman Catholic and Jewish rivals and absorbing their enterprises. Mussolini likewise has destroyed the free trade unions, and organized the business men into Fascist confederations. Successive British governments have grouped the railways into four great regional systems, forced a measure of combination on the coal industry, fostered the tin pool and rubber restriction schemes, and are "rationalizing" agriculture by the Marketing Act. Mr. Roosevelt is "co-ordinating" the railways, and has tried to free American business from the trammels of anti-trust laws, organizing most of it into pretty effective cartels (regulated by "code authorities" made up almost exclusively of representatives of the large firms). The A.A.A. has striven to bring the blessings of monopoly to the farmers.[51] Mr. Bennett's Marketing Act has armed the producers "with a weapon whereby they can create their monopolies and so join in the merry game of raising prices".[52] Sir Herbert Holt has urged the provincial governments to force "co-operation" upon the newsprint manufacturers,[53] and the Quebec government is taking his advice.[54] The Mass Buying Committee and Commission heard proposals for "self-government" or "codes" for rubber tire manufacturing,[55] furniture,[56] garments,[57] various branches of retail trade,[58] and other industries. The Commission's Report recommends "more complete organization of in-

[51]Louis Hacker, *Short History of the New Deal*; and Stolberg and Vinton, *Economic Consequences of the New Deal*.
[52]F. R. Scott, "Mr Bennett's Reforms", *McGill News*. 1935.
[53]*Evidence before the Banking Committee*, 1934. Pp. 882-884.
[54]Montreal *Gazette*, April 11, 12, 1935.
[55]*Committee on Price Spreads*, 1934, *Evidence*, p. 2178-2180.
[56]*Ibid.*, p. 4305.
[57]*Ibid.*, pp. 293-294.
[58]*Ibid.*, pp. 353, 2611, 2842-2843.

dustry into employers' and trade associations", "the recognition and regulation of monopoly in special situations where competition cannot be restored", and "the granting of powers of self-government in special situations where competition seems undesirable"[59]—phrases which, read in conjunction with the Marketing Act and the Canadian National-Canadian Pacific Act, are almost enough to consign competition to the museums.

(b) "State regulation of the monopolies to safeguard the public interest" is a fine phrase and it is a pity that it means nothing, or almost nothing. For, as we have pointed out in discussing government intervention in the Canadian economy, "Government is business". In Germany, "government" means, for economic purposes, the eminent banker Dr. Schacht, assisted by an advisory council of great industrialists. (The Nazis came into power on a wave of denunciation of bankers and big business). In Italy, government has displayed its impartiality by wiping out the trade unions and enforcing savage wage cuts.[60] In the New Deal, the controls have from the first been mainly in the hands of big business. Of the code authorities, only "a very few" included representatives of labour or consumers, or any appreciable representation even of small business men.[61] "The regulation of exchanges and the suppression of pools was turned over to the chairmanship of Mr. Joseph P. Kennedy, who had been shown up as one of the most notorious pool manipulators in the very investigation which led to his appointment"; and the chairman of the National Industrial Recovery Board for a time was Mr. Clay Williams, president of Reynolds Tobacco, the man who more than any other prevented codification of the tobacco industry! (This industry took advantage of a $10,000,000 processing tax to raise its prices $60,000,000).[62]

(c) State subsidies, loans and guarantees are an old story, in Canada and elsewhere, but since the depression they have been scattered with a more lavish hand than before. Canadian history in this respect we have already outlined.[63] Italian experience far outshines it. When the depression struck Italy, the government ordered the banks to "support" bank and industrial securities on the stock exchanges. When this policy had loaded the banks with high-priced securities of embarrassed enterprises,

[59]Pp. xx, xxv, 125, 126, 267, 274. The Trade and Industry Commission Act provides for this "self-government".
[60]*Report of the Commercial Counsellor to the British Embassy in Rome*, 1933, p. 175.
[61]Hacker, *Short History of the New Deal*, pp. 46, 112-113.
[62]Stolberg and Vinton, *Economic Consequences of the New Deal*, pp. 18-19, 42.
[63]See Chapter VI.

the government bought out one large bank and created two state agencies to take over, at something like pre-depression prices, the worthless holdings of others. "The whole process", says an admiring chronicler,[64] "amounts to relieving investors of their holdings—either directly or through the intermediary of banks—by government securities which at a time of crisis command more confidence". Italian workers and consumers, whose pre-depression standard of living was almost the lowest in Europe,[65] foot the bill by wage cuts and stiff duties and sales taxes on the necessities of life. The Reconstruction Finance Corporation in the United States lent to private industry and finance almost $2,000,000,000 under Mr. Hoover, and a further $1,800,000,000 under the New Deal.[66] Germany, the classic land of subsidies, has since Herr Hitler's accession to power, spent some 15,000,000,000 or 16,000,000,000 marks for this purpose,[67] and Britain under her "National" government has indulged in an orgy of subsidies.

(d) To include social legislation among expedients for pre-serving profit may seem paradoxical. In its lusty youth, capitalism could afford to get along without minimum wage laws, limitation of hours, expensive systems of public education, and social insurance. Indeed, it would not have tolerated such deductions from profit. But unhappily for capitalists, the development of their system inevitably creates a large working class, makes it more and more difficult for members of that class to rise into the employing class, and so breeds class-consciousness and a discontent which must be bought off. The price is disagreeable, but revolution would be more so. A frequent defence of the British unemployment insurance scheme is that it has "saved England from revolution".

Moreover, it is always possible to arrange for the workers to pay a large part of the price. Limitation of hours can be used to spread a given amount of work (and wages) over a larger number of people and by so much place the cost of unemployment on the shoulders of the worker. In the absence of strong trade unions, the introduction of a legal minimum wage may simply mean that employers will recoup themselves by cutting the wages of the more highly paid workers.

[64]Paul Einzig, *Economic Foundations of Fascism.*
[65]*International Labour Review*, July, October, November, 1928, January, 1929.
[66]Stolberg and Vinton, *op. cit.*, pp. 24, 28; Hacker, *op. cit.*, p. 61.
[67]O. D. Tolischus, special correspondent New York *Times*—Mont·eal *Gazette*, May 7, 1935. Official figures not published.

Public education, skilfully managed, may do much to inoculate young minds against "subversive" doctrines. Financed largely by taxes on consumption and real estate, its cost is to that extent borne mainly by the poor.

Social insurance, of course, is almost always contributory. The worker pays his own contribution directly. If he has no strong trade union, he will probably pay the employer's contribution too: the employer will cut wages or fail to increase them when he might have done so. Monopolistic industries are likely to pass on the employer's contribution to the consumer by higher prices. The government's contribution comes to a great extent from taxes on consumption.

In Canada we have almost no strong unions and the rich have been peculiarly adroit in keeping taxation of incomes and inheritances at a minimum. Even with the new Dominion surtax on unearned income, not more than 18 per cent. of Dominion and provincial revenues combined will come from income and inheritance taxes. The corresponding figure for Great Britain in 1932-33 was 50 per cent.[68] It is noteworthy, too, that one of Mr. Bennett's "reforms" is apparently to be the replacement of non-contributory old-age pensions by contributory, "which will serve you (whom?) better". Canadian capitalists, therefore, are in a position to buy off working class discontent almost wholly at the expense of the working class!

Capitalist social insurance (and social legislation generally) may be described as insurance of the capitalists by the workers against social revolution. No wonder it has made converts in high places!

The only recent social legislation that seems to be an exception to this rule is the widespread attempt to give legal force to collective labour agreements: the Italian "Labour Charter"; the British Cotton Industry (Temporary Provisions) Act, 1934; section 7(a) of the N.I.R.A.; the Quebec Labour Agreements Extension Act; the Ontario and Alberta Industrial Standards Acts; and the recommendations along the same line in the Report of the Price Spreads Commission. Graded scales of wages for different groups of labourers meet the main working-class objection to minimum wage laws. Have we, then, discovered at last an example of capitalist disinterestedness? Hardly.

True, the British Cotton Industry Act applies only to

---

[68]Dominion and provincial public accounts: Budget speech of Hon. E. N. Rhodes, Minister of Finance, March 22, 1935. *House of Commons Debates*, pp. 2135-2136, 2155; *Economist*, April 13, 1935.

agreements made by unions representing a majority of the workers concerned, and in England trade unions are free. The Ontario and Alberta Acts are intended to exclude from their provisions agreements made with company unions, the rates set are apparently to be only minimum, variable upwards, and no agreement becomes binding on a whole industry unless the Minister considers that it has been made by a "proper and sufficient representative" of both sides.[69] On the other hand, Italy professes to enforce agreements arrived at between Fascist unions and employers, but strikes are illegal, the Fascist unions are thoroughly emasculated, and "unauthorized" reductions of wages had in 1932 reached proportions that, in the opinion of the government commissioner for syndicated labour, "called for drastic action". Section 7(a) of the N.I.R.A., except in a few highly unionized industries, proved worse than a dead letter. It positively encouraged a host of "company unions" completely under the thumb of the employers.[70] The Quebec Labour Agreements Extension Act establishes not minima but rates variable in *either* direction; the "association of employees" need not represent a majority of the workers concerned; and for the term of the agreement strikes are probably (and almost certainly were intended to be) illegal. It is perfectly possible for the government to force on a whole industry a scale of low wages agreed on by a half a dozen employees and so hamstring the genuine unions; or, alternatively, to undermine the genuine unions by enforcing at the beginning rates favourable enough to make their members feel it superfluous to pay dues. In fact, most of the agreements approved have been concluded by the "tame" Catholic unions: the only notable exception is in the clothing industry.[71] The characteristic attitude of the Quebec authorities towards strikes does not inspire confidence in the future of the Act.

The point of such criticism has evidently not been lost on the Price Spreads Commission. For its *Report* insists that Dominion legislation for collective labour agreements extension must not impair the right to strike, must enforce only agreements "genuinely representative of the recognized interests of a majority of the workers in the industry concerned", must

[69]*Labour Gazette*, June, 1935.
[70]On Italian legislation, see *Report of Commercial Counsellor to the British Embassy at Rome, 1923*, p. 175; on American, see Stolberg and Vinton, *Economic Consequences of the New Deal*, p. 58.
[71]See F. R. Scott's note on this legislation in *Canadian Journal of Economics and Political Science*, May, 1935. The Ontario Act is similar.

"not be used as a method of crystallizing low wage rates", and "must protect the public interest against monopolistic combination of employers and workers."[72] This is all admirable, but the fate of section 7(a) of the N.I.R.A. warns us that the most explicit language in an Act of Parliament is not enough if administration remains in capitalist hands.

(e) State-capitalist public ownership we have analyzed in a previous chapter.[73] The phenomena there described are by no means peculiar to Canada. In Italy, the railways have long been publicly owned, and the process of guaranteeing private industry has brought into the hands of the state Institute for Industrial Reconstruction (I.R.I.) large blocks of industrial shares and ownership of the "big four" banks. But I.R.I. is selling its industrial shares to private interests. "In a year this process of transfer from public to private ownership will perhaps be complete. The big four banks may then again become private concerns."[74] In Britain, the most recent examples of public ownership are the Central Electricity Commission and the London Passenger Transport Board.

Accomplishments of State-Capitalist Planning:Profits, Wages and Employment.

Such is the framework of state-capitalist planning as far as it has yet developed. What has it accomplished?

In view of Mr. Bennett's "reform" proposals, it might perhaps be more to the point to ask, What has it *not* accomplished? Canada hitherto has lacked a good deal of the machinery for state-capitalist planning. Mr. Bennett is now filling up the gaps, and assures us that when he has finished he will have removed the causes of depression and ushered in a new, bigger, better, and brighter prosperity. Comparison of his proposals with our explanation of why capitalism fails to work is enough to cast some doubt on these claims: and unluckily for Mr. Bennett they can be submitted not only to theoretical scrutiny, but to the test of experience, with discouraging results. For none of the "reforms" are new. All have been tried, most of them in several countries and over long periods. Germany, Britain and Italy had nearly all of them for years before 1929.[75] The United

---

72P. 135.
73See above, "Government Intervention and Ownership", Chapter VI.
74*Economist*, March 30, 1935.
75The idea cherished by many Canadian business men that Great Britain has "recovered" without "government interference" of the kind proposed by Mr. Bennett, is a delusion. There has been no "New Deal" in Britain because it has been part of the "Old Deal" for twenty years.

States since 1933 has been rapidly acquiring such of them as it lacked. Measures of this sort did not prevent the crash of 1929, nor have they restored prosperity in any country, except to the favoured few.

In the United States the business indices show a condition of arrested recovery, which in view of the increase in population and industrial efficiency since 1929 is alarming. American unemployment throughout 1934 averaged over 10,500,000 as against 3,947,000 in 1929.[76] In the spring of 1935 the federal government reported 20,500,000 on relief; and in New York city the mayor's committee estimated in April, 1935, that there were 666,000 families with unemployed wage-earners (37 per cent of the population), though only 341,451 families and single persons were on relief. Of every three persons in New York employed even in 1930, one is now unemployed; and 2,500,000 of the city's 7,000,000 people are "intimately affected by the resultant loss of family income."[77] Weekly real wages in December, 1934, stood at 90 per cent. of the 1929 level, in March, 1935, at 93 per cent. But March showed less improvement over December than in the previous year.[78]

By contrast, 1,435 manufacturing and trading companies increased their net profits from $640,000,000 in 1933 to $1,051,-000,000 in 1934, or 64 per cent.: an achievement the news of which appeared in the press, very suitably, on All Fools' Day.[79]

CORPORATION PROFITS, U.S.A., 1932-1934.

Industry	In millions of dollars		
	1932	1933	1934
Industrial and mercantile, total..........	10.8	250.0	436.4
Automobiles, parts, and accessories........	26.8*	128.8	130.8
Foods.................................	87.2	93.2	92.4
Metals and mining.....................	6.0*	10.8	32.0
Machinery............................	4.0*	0.0	16.1
Oil...................................	24.8	10.0	24.0
Steel and railroad equipment.............	129.2*	64.4*	16.8
Miscellaneous.........................	54.8	106.8	158.8
Railroads, class 1.....................	287.6	452.1	455.6
Public utilities........................	247.6	224.0	214.4

*Deficit.

[76]American Federation of Labour estimates, *International Labour Review*, March, 1934, and 1935.
[77]*Economist*, April 13, 1935.
[78]National Industrial Conference Board, *International Labour Review*, May, 1935.
[79]Montreal *Star*, April 1, 1935.

During the first nine months of 1934, the chemical companies reported a 45 per cent. increase in profits, mines and metals 360 per cent., office equipment 157 per cent., tobacco 166 per cent. The United States Department of Commerce has recently published remarkable figures of corporation profits: (see table, p. 205)[80]

For most industries the upward trend in profits has continued through the early months of 1935 with no signs of any sharp curbing.

In 1933, income taxpayers with less than $10,000 a year had seen their incomes fall 5 per cent. in comparison with 1932, but the top 8,000, with incomes of over $50,000 had increased their incomes 10 per cent., the top 2,000, 16 per cent. The number of persons with incomes of over $1,000,000 had increased from 20 to 46![81] There seems little doubt that 1934 income tax figures when they become available will show a further redistribution of wealth upwards.

Great Britain has balanced its budget—by defaulting on 80 per cent. of its debt to the United States—and restored business activity to the 1929 level. But 1929 in Britain was far from being a boom year: there were, on the average, 994,091 wholly and 268,400 temporarily unemployed. In April, 1935, the corresponding figures were 1,764,127 and 280,333, and the May total of both was 292 higher. This represents a considerable recovery from the 2,422,808 and 532,640 of January, 1933, but the pace of recovery has slowed down to almost nothing as far as unemployment is concerned. The Labour opposition in a recent debate in the Commons (July, 1935), pointed out that in the period from the beginning of the "National" government's term of office to Dec., 1934, the figures of those on the Poor Law rose from 953,000 to 1,620,000. But again, as in the United States, profits have notably improved. The *Economist's* figures, after dropping for eleven quarters in succession, remained almost steady for two-quarters and then increased by no less than 30 per cent. in the fourth quarter of 1933, 5 per cent. in the first, 18.2 per cent. in the second, 27 per cent. in the third, and 32.9 per cent. in the fourth, quarters of 1934.[82]

So much for the legend of British prosperity, sedulously propagated in recent months by the kept press of capitalism and by prominent Canadian business men and ecclesiastics re-

80*New Commonwealth*, May 4, 1935
81Stolberg and Vinton, *op. cit.*, pp. 35, 36, 85.
82*Economist*, April 13, 20, 1935.

turning from Cook's tours. The same authorities are fond of assuring us that heavy taxes and social legistlation have already practically equalized wealth and abolished poverty in "the Old Land", and that social reconstruction is therefore superfluous. To anyone who knows England beyond the confines of the West End of London and a few tourist resorts, statements of this kind are simply childish. It is true that British taxation of incomes and inheritances is heavy enough to make our most valiant efforts in that direction seem trifling by comparison. It is true also that Great Britain relieves destitution more efficiently, more cheaply, and probably more adequately, than we do. But far from solving "the riddle of social justice", all the taxes and social legislation put together have barely touched the fringe of the problems of inequality and poverty.

Germany's official figures of unemployment have fallen from 6,014,000 in January 1933 to 2,233,721 in April, 1935. But since July, 1933, the statistics no longer include workers in labour camps; and large numbers of women have been unceremoniously bundled out of German industry and industrial statistics altogether. It is significant that Hitler himself, in March 1934, when the official statistics showed 2,798,000 unemployed, spoke of "5,000,000"! What improvement there is, is largely the result of wage reductions and lavish subsidies to employers; and, as in England, the pace of recovery is falling off. In January, 1934, unemployment was 286,263 *below* December, 1933; in January, 1935, it was 368,844 *above* December, 1934. Unemployment in January 1935 was 21.2 per cent. below January, 1934; for February, March and April the corresponding figures were 18, 14.2, and 14.4.[83]

But, again, profits have recovered magnificently. The *Economist* of April 20, 1935, notes that "the number of dividend increases or resumption of dividends is very large", and that "some companies which have earned enough to pay very high dividends have recently used their surplus profits to strengthen their reserves, reduce debt, or write down assets. . . . I. G. Farbenindustrie has written off on plant the largest sum in its history ".

In none of these countries, however, is state-capitalist planning so fully developed or so long established as in Italy. The blessings it has brought to Italian big business we have already

83Ministry of Labour *Gazette*, Jan.-June, 1935; *International Labour Review*, Jan.-May, 1934 and 1935; *Economist*, April 13, 1935.

noted. What has it done for the mass of the Italian people? As we have said, Italian real wages before the depression were already almost the lowest in Europe.[84] Between 1927 and 1932 the cost of living fell 15.73 per cent. The legal reductions in wages in the same period were:[85]

Industry	Reduction	Industry	Reduction
Cottons	40%	Metallurgical trades(a)	23%
Silk weaving	38%	Gas, water, electricity	22%
Glass	30 - 40%	Chemicals	20 - 25%
Jute, hemp and linen	30%	Rayon(b)	20%
Building trades	30%	Garment trades	20%
Mining	30%	Woodworking	18%
Woollens	27%	Printing trades	16%

(a)Besides special reductions in individual firms, accorded on a vast scale
(b)Besides a further 18% in the two largest mills.

There were also widespread "arbitrary reductions, without negotiation, by re-grading of staff and systematic reduction of piece-work rates".[85]

In April, 1934, the government proclaimed further extensive all-round cuts.[86] The number of wholly unemployed in March 1935 was 853,189, a formidable figure for a country relatively little industrialized, and these figures are officially described as "incomplete". The only favourable feature of the situation is that, thanks to the preparations for war against Ethiopia, the number of unemployed is falling off at an increasingly rapid pace.[87] Comparison with earlier years is difficult because the basis of the statistics has been changed, but the present level of unemployment, on the Italian government's own showing, is still almost three times as high as in 1929.[88] This is the more remarkable in view of the drastic wage reductions, which have, of course, made it worth employers' while to take on more men than they otherwise would have done.

Canada's apparatus for state-capitalist planning is as yet less complete than that of the United States, Britain, Germany or Italy, but the course of events in Canada, as we saw in the last chapter, has been much the same. Recovery is slowing down

[84]*International Labour Review*, July, October, November, 1928, January, 1929.
[85]*Report on Economic Conditions in Italy*, 1933, by the Commercial Advisor to the British Embassy at Rome, (Department of Overseas Trade), p. 175. Based on an article by the President of the National Confederation of Syndicated Labour.
[86]Palme Dutt, *Fascism and Social Revolution*.
[87]The percentage change compared with 1934 was 4.0 in January, 13.4 in February, and 19.3 in March.
[88]*International Labour Review*, March, April, May, 1934 and 1935.

to a snail's pace, *in everything but profits.* Dividends in 1934 amounted to \$185,759,716, an increase of 37.9 per cent. from 1933. Net earnings of 154 companies increased 73.7 per cent. Dividends for the first seven months of 1935 have been 8.5 per cent. above the same period of 1934.[89].

Moreover, we must bear in mind that even the restoration of the 1929 level of employment—something not even in sight in any capitalist country—would still leave the world with 'millions of unemployed: six years' increase of population to find jobs for!

The theorists of state-capitalist planning may protest that no country has yet adopted the one indispensable element in their system: complete state control of banking and investment, and that therefore the system has never had a fair trial. This argument has a certain plausibility. Most capitalist and other economists now agree that if we are to escape the cycle of booms and depressions, we must maintain equilibrium between saving and investment and among different types of investment.[90] If capitalism is to survive at all it can no longer allow savings periodically to outrun the use of savings, nor permit people to invest what they please where they please. It must see to it that new capital gets used, that the purchasing power diverted from consumption gets diverted into production, not down the gutter; and that expansion of production takes place in industries not already equipped to meet all the demand in sight. This probably means nationalizing the financial system.

Pretty clearly our business men are in no mood for such heroic remedies at present. They are putting up a strenuous, and on the whole successful, fight against even the very mild social controls of the New Deals (American and Canadian), which hardly touch the frontiers of their power. Are they likely to surrender the citadel at the blast of some academic trumpet, even though the surrender be ultimately for their own benefit?

But suppose they did. State-capitalist planning, complete or incomplete, is essentially and inescapably planning for scarcity. "Self-government for industry", says a reviewer in the *Economist* of March 30, 1935, "would inevitably produce a gigantic restriction of production", or, in the wise and witty

[89]*Financial Post Business Year Book,* 1935; *Financial Times,* March 29, 1935; *Financial Post* monthly summaries of dividend payments

[90]See J. M. Keynes, *Treatise on Money;* Barbara Wootton, *Plan or No Plan;* E. F. M. Durkin, *Purchasing Power and Trade Depression,* and *A Socialist Credit Policy;* John Strachey, *The Coming Struggle for Power,* and *Nature of Capitalist Crisis;* F. A. von Hayek, *Prices and Production.*

phrase of Mrs. Wootton, "a world more planned against than planning". This has been most clearly evident in the N.R.A. and A.A.A.; and the comment of Clarence Darrow and W. O. Thompson of the National Recovery Review Board is decisive: "To give the sanction of government to sustain profits is not a planned economy but a regimented organization for exploitation.[91]

In other words, state-capitalist planning also is "a lot of business men in close proximity, all planning for themselves" and using the state for the purpose.   Under capitalism the "public interest" is served only so far as it happens to be identical with the interest of the dominant capitalist group. When capitalism was competitive and expanding, there was room for the liberal ideal (shared by Mr. Roosevelt, Mr. Bennett and their school) of increased welfare all round: rising profits and rising wages. But declining monopoly capitalism thrusts on us the grim choice of profits *or* plenty. That is why state-capitalist planning is bound to develop towards Fascism.

The Outlook: The Demands of Worker and Consumer.

Modern capitalism works on too narrow a margin to be able to buy off working-class discontent as the older capitalism did.   Its efforts to cut costs (wages and social services); its deliberate restriction of production, imposing on the masses a standard of living obviously far below what is technologically within reach; its growing inequality of wealth: these things, sooner or later, will breed revolt, and revolt, repression.

In the initial stages the capitalists and their hangers-on try to gain their ends by "advice".   Dr. Ira S. Wile, of New York City, tells Montreal social workers that "the average income to-day is sufficient to maintain the 1913 standard of living, but unfortunately (!) people have been educated to a standard two or three times as high. . . Much of the mental suffering in the world is due to the fact that people do not adjust themselves easily and quickly to a lowered income".[92]   To the capitalist mind, of course, it is self-evident that man must be cut to fit the income capitalism sees fit to provide for him.   In the same vein, Sir Michael Sadler, of Oxford, hints that Britain has too many educated men (i.e., more than capitalism can find jobs for).   "An over-supply of education", he sapiently observes,

[91]Hacker, *Short History of the New Deal*, p. 113.
[92]Montreal *Star*, March 12, 1935.

"breeds student-agitators like mosquitoes". The Montreal *Star* draws the logical (capitalist) conclusion that we must cut down on education.[93] General Johnson assures the American Federation of Labour that "Labour does not need to strike under the Roosevelt plan. . . . From beginning to end of this process (code-making and the adjustment of labour disputes) you are given a complete and highly effective protection of your rights. . . You cannot tolerate the strike. . . If . . . you permit or countenance this economic sabotage·. . . public opinion will turn against you". It was no long step from this to the General's Phi Beta Kappa oration at Berkeley, California, less than a year later, when he denounced the San Francisco general strike as "civil war" and "bloody insurrection", and said that if the government did not act, "the people would . . . to wipe out this subversive element as you clean a chalk mark on a blackboard with a wet sponge".[94] When "advice" is not taken, there are other means of persuasion.

Repression may succeed for a time. The poor have from time immemorial been unbelievably patient. But since 1917 there is a new element in the situation. If the U.S.S.R. succeeds, as it seems to be doing, in building a new society in which "the whole produce of labour belongs to the workers", how long can the world continue economically "half slave and half free"?

The final threat to the stability of state-capitalist planning is war. The more thoroughly government becomes identified with big business, the greater is the danger of war; and if academic freedom, free speech, and free association are suppressed, almost the last thin shields against war are taken from us. After war, what? Certainly not capitalism as we know it. Perhaps communism, perhaps barbarism.

Capitalism has made planning *possible*. As Engels wrote in 1891, "When we pass from joint stock companies to trusts which control and monopolize whole branches of industry, not only private production comes to an end, but also planlessness".[95] Lenin in 1916 made the same point, "When a big enterprise becomes a gigantic one and, working on the basis of exactly computed mass data, systematically organizes the supply of primary raw materials to the extent of two-thirds or three-fourths of what is necessary for tens of millions of people; when these raw

93Montreal *Star*, March 13, 1935.
94Hacker, *Short History of the New Deal*, pp. 117, 127.
95Quoted in Lenin, *State and Revolution*, p. 57.

materials are transported to the most suitable places of production, sometimes hundreds or thousands of miles from each other in a systematic and organized manner; when one centre controls all the successive stages of working up the raw materials right up to the manufacture of numerous varieties of finished articles; when these articles are distributed according to a single plan among tens and hundreds of millions of consumers, . . . then it becomes evident that we have socialization of production going on right before our eyes".[96] "Socialization of production" *only,* however, be it noted, not socialization of the economic system. Lenin is careful to add to Engels' words the comment, "The trusts, of course, have not created, do not create now, and cannot create full and complete planning"; and to complete his own description with, "It becomes evident that private business relations, and private property relations constitute a shell which is no longer suitable to its contents". "However much of a plan (the trusts) may create, however closely business magnates may estimate in advance the extent of production, . . . however systematically they may regulate it, we still remain under *capitalism*—capitalism, it is true, in its new stage, but still, unquestionably, capitalism".[97] And if "still unquestionably capitalism", subject to all the consequences of its inherent contradictions, planning for the few cannot meet the mass of our people's demands. Capitalist industry in this as in much else has provided the technique for socialism, but the effective use of the technique is impossible as long as the inequality of capitalist control survives.

[96]Lenin, *Imperialism, the Highest Stage of Capitalism,* p. 115.
[97]Lenin, *State and Revolution,* p. 57.

PART II.   WHAT SOCIALIST PLANNING REALLY
MEANS.

CHAPTER VIII.

THE LOGIC OF PLANNING.

A. THE BACKGROUND.

THE logic of planning is familiar enough. Every competent housewife, every business man, plans in some way, i.e., arranges in some ordered manner how the household resources, or the personnel, the materials and the capital of the business, are to be disposed of. Where more than one business man or housewife are concerned, the significance of working to a plan may be made clear by a trivial example. Two picnic parties set out. The members of one have been told to bring "anything they like". When they open their lunch they find that there is a plethora of salmon sandwiches and an acute shortage of pie. The members of the other appoint a secretary who, after consulting their wishes, tells everyone what to bring, with the result that they enjoy a well-balanced meal.

An illustration of greater practical importance is provided by city planning. With each individual left free to build what and where he likes, with few or poorly enforced regulations, the result has been the familiar haphazard town with its internal discords in purpose and in style, its speculative development, its slums and "second-hand" housing. Negative planning is provided by regulations imposed upon personal liberty in the interests of health or of property-owners to eliminate at least the most striking discords in objectives. Positive planning, however, applied to the development of the city as a whole, comes into being only if architects, health officers, public utility engineers and other experts work out a scheme to arrange streets and buildings in such a way as to secure the most healthy and pleasant living conditions possible, combined with the most economical provision of local improvements and the most complete harmony of design and style. There are plenty of examples of older cities which have been improved, and of parts of new cities which have been entirely built on the basis of such plans.

In industry, planning is well recognized in the form of "scientific management", first built up by F. W. Taylor from his studies of the inefficiencies prevalent in engineering plants towards the end of the last century. The Taylor system involves, essentially, the planning of operations within an industrial plant on the basis of detailed observations and records of experience. A central planning department is set up to direct and co-ordinate successive operations instead of leaving them to the discretion of individual foremen. Duplication, idle capacity and waste effort are eliminated; harmonious integration of the entire plant is made possible. In the chaos of post-war depression, this idea of deliberate, systematic control has been extended from the plant to the firm, and finally as "rationalization"—a pretext for industrial combination—from the firm to whole industries.

Such experiments in business planning provide interesting suggestions as to what may be done under "normal" conditions, but they are thrown into the shade by spectacular emergency experiments in planning on a national scale. Wartime experience showed what can be done in a crisis. The war created sudden and violent demands upon an economy geared to meet the requirements of peace. Private enterprise proved incapable of making the violent readjustments called for. The governments of the belligerent countries were compelled to take deliberate action. They instituted comprehensive systems of national planning to secure the necessary realignment of economic activities and to mobilize the resources of the nation to meet the crisis with the greatest possible efficiency. With more effective co-ordination of services such as transportation, with the elimination of waste and systematic search for better methods, efficiency was maintained and even increased. The acute shortage of food supplies, raw materials and freight accommodation was met by the application of the common-sense notion of priorities and a comprehensive system of rationing to allot these resources to their most urgent uses.[1] Responsibility was not left to the automatic adjustment of the pricing process: the prices of essential materials and foodstuffs were rigorously controlled; a deliberate allocation of supplies was instituted in place of the free play of supply and demand. The conditions under which the experiment was carried out were, of course, politically, economically and psychologically exceptional. None the less, the achievements of such organizations as the Ministry of Munitions, of Shipping, and of Food, the Railway Executive Committee and the Coal Committee in Great Britain; the War Industries and War Labour Boards, the Railroad, Food and Fuel Administra-

---

[1]See Sir L. Chiozza Money: *The Triumph of Nationalisation*; and Alvin Johnson: *What Priorities Mean*, in the New Republic, June 30, 1917.

tions, the Capital Issues Committee and the Housing Corporation in the U.S.A., to say nothing of the Food Control Board in Canada, provide a remarkable illustration of what human organization can accomplish when the will to do so is sufficiently strong, even in the face of grave difficulties and the opposition of vested interests. Moreover, the war-time organization extended in some instances beyond national boundaries. Inter-Allied Shipping Control[2] was an immensely encouraging experiment in effective international co-operation.

With the return of peace, *laissez-faire* reasserted itself in most countries, though the idea of planning survived to a slight extent in certain "reconstruction" institutions such as the Whitley Councils in Great Britain, and the National Economic Council in Germany. Two countries, Russia and Italy, emerged from the war with dictatorships pledged to undertake the task of economic organization. After various experiments with different methods of control, Russia has led the way in economic planning; the development of a remarkable administrative machinery made possible the formulation and amazingly successful execution of the first Five Year Plan, and the inception of a second Five Year Plan. Instead of leaving the trend of economic development to the cumulative discretion of individual producers, the National Planning authority made a full survey of the nation's needs and resources and of the technique at its disposal. The results of this survey and the recommendations of local producers enabled it to formulate a programme of economic development, allotting to each group of producers its part in the productive process, checking results and making the necessary adjustments at each stage of advance.

Under the stress of prolonged depression the idea of planning has become increasingly popular, and more or less comprehensive plans have been applied by widely diverse governments. Thus, the *Planwirtschaft* has been popular in Germany in many forms since the War, but, after the advent of Hitler, it has followed the Italian form of the "corporative state" in which economic development schemes are only part of a general policy for refashioning German life in accordance with Nazi ideas. In Great Britain the idea of planning is finding expression in far less spectacular but more specific fashion, in such new co-ordinating organizations as the London Passenger Transport Board,

---

2See Sir Arthur Salter: *Inter-Allied Shipping Control During the War* (Carnegie Foundation for International Peace Studies).

the Electricity Commission and Central Electricity Board. The most influential for Canada of all the depression-born excursions into national planning is the series of plans for agriculture, for industry, for finance and for other branches of economic activity which constitute the "New Deal" in the United States. President Roosevelt has undertaken the direction of a very considerable sector of the nation's economic affairs, though the controls which he exercised are for the most part regulatory in character rather than positive. Canada itself has not escaped the general movement. Indeed, we have been accustomed to a considerable amount of half-hearted economic planning ever since the formation of the Dominion. The "National Policy" and Government participation in transport development, for instance, were real though partial experiments in this direction. The pre-election activities of the Dominion Government foreshadow a drastic extension of the principle through such measures as the Natural Products Marketing Act, the Grain Board, and some of the legislation suggested by the Royal Commission on Price Spreads; while the activities of the provincial governments of British Columbia and Alberta also indicate how far the idea has seized the public imagination.

But the logic of planning does not leave us here, for our analysis up to this point has demonstrated certain other things as well: that negative regulation is not enough, that a hybrid system of *laissez-faire* and piecemeal state control is too defective to remove the major inequalities of present economic society, that capitalist planning must by its nature be largely planning *for* the capitalist. How can we secure true social planning which shall put the interests of the mass of the population first?

It must be done by grafting the organs of expert direction on to our present democratic machinery (which must itself be made more democratic in effect). It may be said at once that what is essential is not so much a fixed *plan*, as continuous *planning*. Planning in a socialized economy means, not an omnipotent blueprint set out once and for all, but that technicians of every type required in the modern economic system are brought into organized relation both with the *organs* and the *aims* of government. This deliberate control over economic development is represented centrally by a National Planning Commission: it is undertaken because only thus can industry be organized to serve the interests of the many, as both producers and consumers, rather than the interests of the few.

The Planning Commission must have a staff of experts at its command, and also a comprehensive statistical department (developed from the Dominion Bureau of Statistics). These will collect information from all the available and required sources, and co-ordinate the returns and recommendations of local managements, trade unions, consumers' councils, and similar agencies. In the light of such data the Commission is able to view the direction and control of economic activities as a whole: and to make specific proposals for the adjustment of taxes and tariffs, freight rates, wage policies, social insurance, farm relief, financial and investment regulations, and all the other items of economic policy in their relation to each other, thus securing concerted action. This planned policy, once approved, is put into effect through the appropriate organs of government and business administration. Planning is therefore threefold; it involves: (1) a technique of survey, (2) the formulation of a co-ordinated programme, and (3) the execution and administration of that programme in both the political and the economic field.

B. WHY IS PLANNING NECESSARY?

The first argument in favour of planning is that it is unavoidable. The evolution of machine production and minute specialization has made it absolutely essential to secure smooth co-ordination in the work of multifarious human and mechanical specialists. As this need becomes more urgent, the efficiency of automatic economic adjustment, through the market relationships of entirely independent firms, dwindles. Intricate mechanical equipment means heavy overhead costs. Heavy overhead costs mean that competition works imperfectly and spasmodically; that "cost of production" ceases to have much meaning as the basis of price adjustment,[3] and that high pressure salesmanship becomes violent. Mass production means the organization of operations by immense corporations, whose strength increases the disparities of bargaining power between these enterprises and their employees, their customers, as well as the small-scale producers of their materials. The economy inevitably falls into a chaos of cut-throat bargaining and competitive struggle; salvation from this can be found only in the comprehensive substitution of deliberate human decision. For in an attempt to find relief, enterprises combine, thus widening the

[3]See J. M. Clark: *The Economics of Overhead Costs.*

sphere of control ever further. The giant corporation dominant
today has substituted administrative control of output and price
(in other words, planning) for ruinous competition.[4] Producers
of raw materials combine in co-operatives (as did the wheat-
growers) in an attempt to secure better terms, to hold prices
steady, and to introduce order into a chaotic market. Employees organize to obtain better wages and conditions and
greater security of life. In every land frantic appeals are made
to the State to relieve intolerable conditions, to compel the performance of essential economic functions when the ordinary
methods of securing efficiency have failed, and to arbitrate in
the distribution of costs and returns when market methods no
longer provide effective regulation. And every step taken to
meet the defects of automatic adjustment introduces greater
rigidities; the machinery becomes still less effective, and the
choice between central control and planning or complete collapse
and chaos becomes inescapable.

Such economic planning as has been undertaken so far has,
except in Russia, been piecemeal and spasmodic in character.
But piecemeal planning is a contradiction in terms. The necessity for planning arises fundamentally from the need, which
machine industry has created, of co-ordination both as between
specialists and as over a period of time. The urgency of such
close co-ordination and balance can be fully illustrated from the
situation of many industries, but our railway development perhaps best illustrates the disastrous effects of planlessness.[5] The
only way to secure harmonious unity in the railroad system as a
whole—a way rejected as carrying with it a danger of monopoly
—would have been to develop it under a single management,
which could plan extensions with a full knowledge of the possibilities and requirements of existing equipment, so that the whole
territory might be served with the maximum efficiency and
economy. Since its re-organization under a single management
the C.N.R. has "won approval by its success in welding together
the various working forces of the separate companies". The
measure of co-operation between the C.P.R. and the C.N.R. imposed by the C.N.-C.P. Act of 1933 has led to an estimated
annual joint saving of $1\frac{1}{4}$ million dollars. Sir Edward Beatty

---

[4] See Berle and Means: *The Modern Corporation and Private Property.*
[5] See *Report of the Royal Commission to Enquire into Railways and Transportation,*
1931, p. 2.

claims that a further 75 million dollars a year could be saved if the two railways were put under one management.[6]

If co-ordination between the different parts of a railway system is vital, it is at least as necessary between the different methods of transportation. Unregulated competition between waterways, motor traffic, and railroads may have equally disastrous effects by creating extravagant duplications and by neglect of complementary services. These considerations apply not only to transportation but to every branch of economic activity. The wastefulness of unplanned distributive services, such as the distribution of milk and gasoline, is notorious.[7] There are equally striking wastes in manufacturing; for example the competitive over-expansion of the pulp and paper industry in Canada before the depression.

Co-ordination is needed, therefore, not only within each industry but between the different industries and aspects of the economy as a whole. With this degree of planning, each industry would have the benefit of the experience of every other; no one trade would be permitted to interfere with general prosperity by needless competition, over-production or inefficiency. The central authority could establish and insist upon the maintenance of standards in each industry.

In the widest sense of all, the Canadian economy is an integral unit, built up on the basis of the production and export of certain staple products. In an industrial plant, any serious disproportion in the capacity of complementary departments means serious waste and inefficiency; any severe change in conditions which introduces such a disproportion calls for immediate re-adjustment to prevent disastrous dislocation. Exactly the same principle applies in the organization of the economy as a whole. If the balance is disturbed, the dislocation brings depression. Left to work out its own adjustment, recovery proceeds slowly and inefficiently, especially in a country like Canada which is particularly subject to inflexibilities of organization. A national planning authority is essential therefore, if the task of deliberately effecting the necessary re-adjustments is to be taken up as efficiently as possible, in order to reduce the severity and length of the depressions unavoidably thrust upon us by conditions beyond our borders. The requisite flexibility

6E. W. Beatty: *The Case for Railway Unification, Proceedings of the Canadian Political Science Association, 1934.*

7See L.S.R. pamphlet No. 2: *Combines and the Consumer;* and Chap. XVIII of this volume.

of organization in the face of violent economic change can be secured only through the deliberate action of a competent national authority, with power and discretion to revise the terms of contracts in which economic relationships are embodied. Otherwise the burden of adjustment is unequally shared, while the rigidities which remain prevent other adjustments from bearing fruit.

A planning authority would be invaluable, not only in carrying out re-adjustments on a national scale, but, further, in guarding against dislocation by eradicating such sources of economic disruption as are subject to human control. In particular it would take steps to organize two specific counterbalances to economic fluctuation, a programme of public works and a technique of credit control.

Undoubtedly some dislocations and consequent shrinkages of the national income cannot be altogether prevented, even by planning. But at present such disturbances fall most unequally upon different groups in the community, depending on such arbitrary circumstances as whether their incomes are sheltered by tariff barriers or are exposed to the fluctuations of demand in a foreign market, whether they enjoy the protection of the rigidities and vested interests of our economy or are squeezed by its arbitrary fluctuations. If some fluctuations must be endured, this only makes the appointment of a national planning authority the more urgent. For it could be entrusted with the responsibility of using the social machinery of taxes, railroad rate control and the like, to secure an even distribution of the effects of depression, making not only for greater justice and economy in the application of a restricted national income, but helping to cut short the period of dislocation.

The basic logic of central planning is the need for some authority with the responsibility and the competence to see the economic problems of the entire nation as an integral whole. The rationalization not merely of one firm, or of one trade, but of our whole economic life demands that all the units in the economy should work together under leadership toward a common goal. The sectionalism which is the curse of the Canadian economy must be overcome.

As yet we lack much necessary information as to Canada's economic processes and their place in the world economy. One of the first tasks of the national planning authority would be to collect and co-ordinate all the requisite information. Only on the basis of such comprehensive study can we ever hope to understand' and thus control economic processes.[8] Only so can we ever aspire to forecast, and therefore prepare for, disruptive changes in conditions. Only a unified authority, at first national, and finally, when this becomes possible, international, can bring together and apply the available information with a sufficiently general view.

C. PROBLEMS AND DIFFICULTIES IN CANADA.

The urgency of the need for planning does not mean that it is a simple thing to carry out. It is, in fact, a most formidable undertaking. "While it is generally accepted that the larger the enterprise the greater the planning function, yet we expect the greatest enterprise of all, industry as a whole, to get along without a definite plan",[9] simply because it is appalling to think of entrusting to any fallible and corruptible human authority a task of such immensity and delicacy as the direction of the whole of the nation's economic activities. But the failure of natural laws to perform the task effectively compels us to face the difficulties involved in deliberately assuming responsibility for it.

In Canada these difficulties are especially great. Economic development in this country has involved building up specialized capital equipment in the form of waterways, railroads, power plants, elevators, pulp and paper mills and the like.   This equipment is by its very nature inflexible in character, and cannot be contracted or diverted to new uses rapidly or at will. Once built it stays built, and the decision to build it must be taken on the basis of an estimate of future probabilities.

Unhappily these probabilities depend upon a number of factors which even the best informed planning authority could not predict with certainty. The vagaries of harvests, the discovery of new resources or the exhaustion of the old ones, changes in technique and the fluctuations of foreign demands, are all fundamental in the functioning of the Canadian economy.

---

[8] An interesting example of such study preparatory to planning is the work of the Canadian Pioneer Problems Committee, which is being published in "The Canadian Frontiers of Settlement" Series. In Volume I, *Prairie Settlement*, pp. xiv and xv, Professor W. K. Mackintosh writes of pioneering experiments, "So much human welfare is at stake, so much government expenditure is involved, so much private capital is risked in the settlement of a new area, that here if anywhere is a case for social planning. . . . It is hoped . . . to show the need, scope and direction of such planning. . . . The need for the systematic planning and control of settlements, if heavy financial and human costs are to be avoided, is likely to be greater in the future than it has been in the past".

[9] H. S. Person, Managing Director, Taylor Society, quoted by F. George Frederick, *Readings in Planning*, p. 337.

Besides being unpredictable elements in the situation, these are not directly subject to human control. Nobody, for instance, can plan where, when and how new gold discoveries are to be made. A drought in the West or a *Putsch* in Germany may upset the best laid plans and disrupt the whole balance of the economy. Dependent as we are in Canada upon international economic relations through the export of staple products, foreign investment, and the trends of technique in more advanced centres, we are peculiarly vulnerable.

But if such difficulties make planning harder, they also make it a thousand times more urgent. Since plans for the future must involve estimates, those estimates should be worked out on the basis of exhaustive study, so that prediction may be as accurate as is humanly possible. It is sometimes argued that the mistakes of one individual will offset those of another in an unco-ordinated economy, while the mistakes of a central planning authority are universally disastrous. To-day, however, the mistakes of independent business men seem to be cumulative in character, due to the alternations of over-optimism and over-pessimism which sweep the business world, and to the frantic outbursts of imitation of new ideas successfully floated in the first instance. Canada has been especially subject to such "boom mania". There is no guarantee that a planning authority will be free from miscalculations, but, working in the light of the most comprehensive information humanly obtainable, not only as to past developments, prevailing prices and business conditions, but as to the future plans of all the businesses concerned, such an authority is likely to make estimates that are soberer and safer than those of unco-ordinated firms necessarily working in the dark as to many important factors.

A planning authority would be able to bring down the unpredictables in the economic equation to their irreducible minimum. In time it could do the same with what are at present uncontrollable elements. Many forces which, *from the individual firm's point of view*, are arbitrary and intractable, could be brought under control by general social action; for example, the movement of foreign exchange rates, or the total production for a competitive market. It is true that there still remains to be faced the problem of forces which are subject only to international control. But the only hope of effective international action surely depends upon the growth of prerequisite national machinery. In the absence of national planning, i.e., organizations with the power to effect the necessary reconciliation of conflicting sectional interests *within* the country, how can we ever hope to provide the machinery for international co-operation and control? National planning is also important as a very real step towards the realization of that international control.

It is well to stress once again the urgent necessity of establishing machinery for securing deliberate readjustments to such changing conditions as cannot themselves be controlled. Even though it may be impossible to regulate the discovery of new methods of production, or new resources, it would be perfectly possible to control more rationally the time and rate of their use. Even though crops may fluctuate unpreventably and foreign markets lapse into a chaos of uncontrollable nationalism, the impact of these disturbances on the economy can be minimized by immediate and vigorous measures. These, however, can only be expected from a permanent, well-informed authority which is fully acquainted with the character of the nation's processes. The only alternative is the mass of inflexible contractual relationships and price systems which today intensify depression and throttle recovery.

Wide powers placed in the hands of a central planning board undoubtedly involve the possibility of interference with personal initiative and freedom. There is always and inevitably a conflict between the demands of personal liberty and the necessities of order and organization. Yet the conflict is in a sense superficial. Order is itself a necessary condition for the full realisation of personal freedom; willing co-operation in concerted social action is a prerequisite of the enlargement of individual liberty in the fullest sense. To the extent that we are each individually dependent for an income upon selling a specialized crop or securing a particular form of employment we are unavoidably subject to the control of outside forces over which we have no personal power. An unemployed man, a wheat farmer whose crop has failed, or a store-keeper who has lost his business through the unemployment of his customers, may be legally "free", but not in any real sense. True freedom— opportunities for unfettered personal development—can only be enjoyed by people whose work and incomes are secure against arbitrary disaster and afford them a reasonable chance of a decent living and leisure. In the age of machinery and minute specialization this basic economic welfare depends entirely on the healthy operation of the economic organization as a whole. This can only be realized through such deliberate centralized organization as we have termed national economic planning. The control which is needed to secure economic efficiency is therefore the essential prelude to a truer personal liberty than we have as yet achieved.

The price which we must pay for this organization is naturally the surrender of some measure of independence of action. This sacrifice may be unavoidable, but the resulting gain will make it well worth while. With the development of nineteenth century capitalism and the exaltation of unfettered private enterprise, industrial and social disorder reached such proportions that governments and industries themselves were forced, reluctantly enough, to apply controls. Today, disaster threatens unless these are made more complete and effective. The contemporary reaction from liberty to control is a natural reflection of the situation. The exuberant outburst of private initiative which characterized the heyday of individualistic capitalism brought incalculable improvements in industrial techique, but it is necessary to consolidate and apply these advances through more effective organization. Exuberant individual initiative is invaluable in the frontier stages of economic development, whether in pioneering new techniques or in exploring virgin resources. It is a most desirable element in any society. But it can be highly dangerous if it is exercised without restraint or direction in an economy which is past the frontier stage and in which effective co-ordination has become urgently necessary. The problem of securing order without imposing a deadening tyranny, of maintaining freedom without suffering chaos, is indeed difficult of solution. But of late chaos seems to have predominated. Control is primarily needed to redress the balance.

None the less it should not be impossible to reconcile planning with freedom of action and personal initiative. The absolute independence of the man who takes a chance on his own responsibility, without a by-your-leave to anyone, and personally bears the brunt of the outcome, cannot perhaps be preserved in its entirety. It is disappearing already with the advance of mergers, the financial integration of private business, and the rapid assumption by giant corporations of a dominant position in the economic life of the country.[10] Only a very few can any

10See Berle and Means: *The Modern Corporation and Private Property*, especially Book I. Conditions are strictly comparable in Canada. Many of the two hundred dominant corporations, discussed there have Canadian subsidiaries. In addition we have our own "giants".

longer enjoy the exercise of such unlimited initiative. But there is, under a planning authority, still plenty of room for original and independent people, if they co-operate with others. Bureaucratic systems of hierarchical boards and committees would certainly cramp their freedom. Stagnation and inertia, which would be fatal to an authority vitally concerned with the maintenance of economic balance, must be guarded against in every possible way. Planning does not mean a deadening of initiative. The type of planning authority which we visualize would be alert to maintain flexibility and freedom of individual and local action to the fullest possible extent,[11] and to stimulate enterprise and experiment wherever the conditions and resources of the economy permitted. Planning does imply, however, that personal initiative must be directed, not to the fulfilment of such individual objects as are disruptive to the community at large, but to the more effective realisation of social ends.

The problem of how these social ends are to be defined raises yet another deep-seated difficulty. We advocate planning because it appears to be the only way of bringing economic forces under human control, of making the economic system the servant rather than the master of the people. Yet there is a real danger that in this way we should only jump out of the frying pan into the fire by "enslaving the people to a state". One reads that "we" should plan "our" economic activities. Actually that is nonsense. If we want planning, then "we", that is, the generality of Canadians, have to delegate the task of formulating and administering a plan to some particular group or groups of men. These men will have great power over the lives and fortunes of their fellow citizens. How are they to be selected, directed, and controlled?

In facing this question we must realize that we are compelled to choose between alternatives. Firstly, as the present tendency to industrial concentration continues, a small group of financial and business magnates are undertaking the responsibility of planning whether we like it or not. This power is a power of economic government in which we have little or no share. Secondly, there are not wanting those who urge as the remedy a Fascist type of dictatorship, which will effectively centralize economic and political control together. They despair of the possibility of social planning under a democracy or with a representative Parliament. They hold that its methods and machinery must be by their nature utterly inefficient, since they are

[11]See below, Chapter IX, (d).

designed rather to make sure that nothing is done than to provide the organization for administering effectively a complex economy.

These are strong arguments; but we are convinced that democratic planning is not only feasible, but the only type of planning which can have permanent stability. It should be frankly recognized that it may be far harder, both to institute in the first place and to maintain thereafter, than planning under a dictatorship. But democracy so far has been inefficient partly because it has been called upon to do things for which it was never designed. Democratic decision on such highly technical points as whether tariffs should be low or high, or what the percentage of bank reserves should be, is naturally absurd. The value of a true democracy (and it is perhaps unnecessary to add that the forms of democracy which exist today are illusory) largely lies in the fact that it provides potential machinery through which the people may put on record their fundamental aspirations and select men who express those aspirations. No more should be expected of it. How to do this effectively is the chief problem: and unless we succeed in solving it, democracy is doomed.

But it is not impossible to reconcile the functions of a parliamentary system with those of a planning authority. The legislature would initially define ends and select the final administrative authority. The technical task of working out the means for securing those ends, however, would be left to the planning commission. Parliament thus acts in the capacity of a householder choosing an architect and instructing him as to the type of house he desires, then leaving the architect to find out how best and most effectively such a house can be built with the resources at the disposal of his client. None of this is possible, however, if Parliament itself is not to be freed from the autocracy of business to which it is today largely subject. Neither Parliament nor Planning Authority would be able to dominate the giant corporations of today, if the objectives of those corporations remained the accumulation of private property and private power. The development of effective machinery of economic control by the state must therefore be supplemented by state ownership of the industries most essential in the nation's economic life, and by the prevention of the private accumulation of great fortunes. Only so can we hope to secure economic democracy without which political democracy is a vain aspiration.

CHAPTER IX.

NATIONAL PLANNING IN PRACTICE.

THE proposed machinery for the formulation and execution of a national plan presented in this chapter, is not a final and irrevocable blue-print of the necessary organization. In practice, administrative forms are constantly changing. When planning is actually put into effect in Canada, it will seek to adapt its technique to such new political and economic forms as provide useful organs of control or channels of information. The probable politico-economic machinery is outlined here in order to put the proposal in specific and concrete terms, but its flexibility in points of detail should go without saying.

A. THE ASSUMPTIONS OF A PLANNED STATE.

At the outset, the following fundamental conditions are assumed:

1. The ultimate responsibility of a modified but democratic parliamentary system to public opinion.
2. The conferring of adequate powers upon the federal government to render its control of economic policy full and effective.
3. The development of organs of economic planning for the formulation of economic policy, and the necessary modification of the procedure and structure of parliament to ensure that full advantage is taken of expert knowledge.
4. The reorganization of finance, commerce and industry to ensure the effective administration of national economic planning.

In the planned state, the final authority of government is to rest, as it does theoretically today, in Parliament. More specifically, this means that the nation's primary executive is the Cabinet, subject only to the established democratic convention that it shall have the confidence of the House of Commons.

Also, though important and far-reaching changes are required in the functioning of departments, executive and legislature, the ultimate responsibility of Parliament to public opinion is not questioned or denied. Indeed, the prime assumption upon which this book is based is that it is possible for a democracy to control economic policy intelligently: not the abolition, but the improvement, of the functioning of democratic government, is the purpose of the reforms proposed.

The first and pivotal organ to be added to existing machinery is the National Planning Commission, an expert thinking body, directly and intimately in touch with the political ministers of state but completely free to the extent its important functions demand—those of formulating a comprehensive national economic policy and keeping under continuous survey the changes and development of economic and social conditions. A Bureau of Statistics, a Bureau of National Research, and other cognate organs are to be given a wide extension of scope and personnel to equip them as the auxiliaries in this task.

Second, the major economic activities of the country are co-ordinated in various appropriate types of organization. Key industries are developed into state enterprises and administered as semi-autonomous corporations. Some of these will be responsible to regulatory commissions created by Parliament to supervise particular fields of activity much as are our present Board of Railway Commissioners and the Board of Grain Commissioners today. Canada is familiar with "commission government", and its general principles are clear. The state-owned corporation is responsible for *operation* and its officials are business executives; the Commission is an independent, quasi-judicial, *regulatory* body, with members appointed for a fixed term to give them security of tenure, whose function is to ensure that the industry shall work within the general lines laid down by statutes and regulations of Parliament.

Private enterprises which still remain are to be subject to such controls as are necessary to maintain their labour standards and to keep their demands on the country's resources, their realized surpluses, etc., consistent with the aims of a democratic economy. The Trade and Industry Commission whose supervision will provide for this will be a stronger form of the Commission of this name which has recently been recommended in the Report of the Price Spreads Commission.

Clearly, fundamental changes both in industry and in the present functioning of Parliament are here envisaged. The chief financial, commercial and industrial activities of the nation cease to be owned and controlled by private capitalist investors and either become direct governmental enterprises, or are subordinated to appropriate administrative organs of the State. The power to formulate economic policy is transferred from competitive private enterprise to the government; for the play of haphazard forces is substituted an ordered public policy.

While the provinces, and for that matter, all the organs of regional government can play their part in economic planning, it is essential that the Dominion government, in the final analysis, should have full control. Within the provisions of the British North America Act a large measure of power to secure and exercise such control is now possible, but it is apparent that a redistribution of powers between the Dominion and Provincial Governments will be required. While the cultural and racial rights of minorities must be preserved, recognition of the need for a broad national policy must mean the amendment of the B.N.A. Act to ensure that the Dominion Government has the powers essential to make economic planning effective.[1] Without such control, the planning authority would be continually subject to delays arising from negotiations with the provinces, or from submission to the courts of legal and constitutional points. In the final power to authorize economic policy, the Dominion Parliament must be supreme.

B. THE CABINET AS POLITICAL EXECUTIVE.

No amendment is proposed to the constitutional theory that the executive authority of the Dominion is vested in the Cabinet. But it is apparent that in Canada the ministers constituting the Cabinet, on whose advice the Crown acts, provide both as to their responsibilities and their selection, an ineffective and obsolete executive, inadequate to the task imposed by the economic problems of the time.

The Canadian Cabinet is both executive and representative. Chosen by the leader of the party in power, after he has been summoned by the Governor-General to form a government, the ministers are required to direct the various departments of government, to formulate national policy, as well as to provide representation to the different sections and groups in Canada.

Thus, the Cabinet itself, as at present constituted, is federal rather than unitary in character. Each Canadian Cabinet must provide representation for the Maritimes, Quebec, Ontario, the Prairies and British Columbia. Quebec is invariably given a quota of French ministers and, equally invariably, the English Protestant minority must be represented. It is also necessary that the Irish Catholic element in the nation be given a minister.

1See Chapter XXI(b).

Similarly, eastern, central and western Ontario must contribute members. The element of representation, indeed, is given more importance in the selection of ministers than quality and capacity. If a minority in a section happens to have returned representatives of mediocre ability, it is still necessary for the Prime Minister to select one or more of that minority for cabinet office. This partly explains the weakness of Canadian Cabinets and the growth in the power of the Prime Minister. It is apparent, when such importance is attached to representing the various elements within the Canadian nation, that it is only by the readiness of the Prime Minister to compromise or to dominate that a coherent national policy may be sought.

It is, of course, in the interest of Canadian nationality, at least in the present stage of its development, that adequate and just recognition be given to the various elements composing it. Obviously, French Canada must be given equitable representation; obviously, lesser minorities are similarly entitled to representatives. And with so scattered a population, divided into sections with different traditions, economic opportunities, and racial characteristics, as well as geographical separateness, the different sections of Canada present a serious problem of sectionalism which must be met.

But a Cabinet primarily selected with a view to representing sections of the Canadian people must inevitably produce a less able personnel and, in consequence, a less intelligent national policy. Upon no other thesis can the appointment of most recent ministers be explained. The contrary assumption that the cabinets represent the most able members of Parliament is too pathetic a commentary upon the ability of the Canadian people to be accepted. Undoubtedly a Prime Minister unhampered by sectional considerations would select a Cabinet of higher order.

It is proposed, therefore, to make the choice of the Prime Minister more free, to free the ministers appointed from some of the burdens of routine in the House and in their departments, and to divide the Cabinet into senior and departmental ministers. The senior ministers, consisting of the Prime Minister and four others, would not be charged with the detailed administration of departments, but only with broad questions of national policy; they would, in effect, constitute an inner cabinet, or committee of the Cabinet. The members of this inner cabinet, with the exception of the Prime Minister, might be appointed as Secretaries of State without specific departments to administer. The inner cabinet would probably meet more frequently than the full Cabinet council and would, in effect, constitute a co-ordinating group, bringing to bear a full range of considerations, economic, political, and external, on national policy. Legal responsibility, however, such as the passing of orders-in-council, would remain with the full Cabinet council as at present.

Obviously, the selection of the senior secretaries of state would be primarily based upon the capacity of the members of Parliament under consideration, and as little as possible upon the plan of giving representation to sections of the country. It is probably too great a hope that in such a nation as Canada these considerations would be entirely dismissed; but the division between senior and departmental ministers should both help to widen the Prime Minister's range of choice, and release some at least of the Cabinet from the routine of departmental work. The analogy is that of the War Cabinet of Great Britain under Mr. Lloyd George, and it is specifically intended that the inner cabinet under the reformed state in Canada should be selected from the regular representatives of the electorate in Parliament.

It may be argued, in criticism of this proposal, that ministers of the capacity required will not be nominated and elected by democratic procedure. But it must be emphasized that these ministers do not have to be technicians, economists, or statisticians. Their responsibility is simply to see that the plans which the Planning Commission presents are in line with the general wishes of the country, and in harmony with other aspects of national policy. In other words, they are political leaders, not economic experts. Under a democratic system there is always the serious danger that such leaders may be mere demagogues. But there is at least an equal danger of this—perhaps greater— under a dictatorship, as the experience of Germany has amply shown. We cannot do better in political leadership than the intelligence and ability of the general population will permit. If it is not possible to elect a House of Commons from which men of high and sincere capacity can be selected for the great responsibilities of a planned economy, then democracy will fail. But we believe that the chances of securing sound leadership are as high under democracy as under any other system yet discovered. The chances are definitely higher, if the electoral system is improved, if the subversive and corrupting influences of private interests are largely or totally removed, and if the party forming the government represents an electorate of which a strong majority will be firm in their support of the reforms to be undertaken.

The power and influence not only of cabinets but of prime ministers have tended to grow in Canada, either through the adroitness of such a Prime Minister as Mr. Mackenzie King, or the "blasting" temperament of such as Mr. R. B. Bennett; but the secretariat through which the prime ministers have worked has shown no corresponding development. It is necessary, therefore, both to ease the burden resting upon the leader of the government and to improve the secretariat aiding him.

The Prime Minister will, as at present, be the leader of the House of Commons, and, as well, president of the Council, but it is undesirable that he should bear, as recent prime ministers have borne, the additional burdens of the Department of External Affairs or other departments such as Finance. He should, indeed, be as completely free as possible from detailed departmental affairs and routine administration.

Moreover, in place of a few secretaries (one of whom may act in practice as Cabinet Secretary though without formal status), there should be an adequate and properly constituted cabinet secretariat. A Secretary to the Cabinet exists in Great Britain, and it has been suggested before (by Mr. Mackenzie King) that one should be appointed in Canada. A similar proposal is here made. Such a secretary will, in effect, be the principal secretary of the Prime Minister and will be present, where necessary, at Cabinet meetings. He will keep an abstract of the discussions of the Cabinet, and will act as a connecting link between the Prime Minister and the various departments. His main functions, however, will derive from his position as the senior member of a cabinet secretariat.

c. The National Planning Commission and Its Auxiliaries.

The National Planning Commission, charged with the formulation of national economic policy in its detailed and technical aspects, should be a body of from three to five members. Its policies will be arrived at in consultation with the various industrial corporations established by the State, and with parliamentary committees on specific subjects set up by Parliament from its own members. The policies and programmes thus formulated will be given the force of law after approval by the Cabinet and House of Commons.

The Planning Commission is primarily a thinking body. It is not a representative body, seeking to give representation to different parts of Canada or to specific interests. It seeks primarily, if not solely, to provide an economic general staff to investigate and hammer out a concerted economic policy. It is not a legislative body: the function of giving legal force to the plans worked out by the committee remains as heretofore with Parliament. Nor is it an executive body: administration rests with the departments of government or with autonomous bodies to be set up under the socialized industrial system. The Commission is specifically a body for investigating, for studying, and for proposing a continuing plan of economic development. When its policy and proposals are formulated after consultation with its auxiliary organs, they are submitted to the Cabinet for consideration, to Parliament for enactment, and finally to departments, state corporations, or government commissions, for execution.

The National Planning Commission will be established by Act of Parliament. The Act will set forth its powers and responsibilities. Its membership should embrace men with adequate knowledge of economics, of finance, and business administration. There should be on the Commission men with knowledge of agriculture, of departments of the government, and of the commercial structure and character of Canada. But "youth" (which is liable in government to mean any age under forty-five) should not be a barrier to appointment, and "experience" should not be the sole criterion of qualification.

The salaries of the Commissioners must be adequate and, in addition, they must be given security by the provision of an adequate retiring pension. We suggest that the Commissioners should be appointed for a period of seven years, but should be eligible for reappointment. During their period of office they would have a tenure similar to that of a judge, so that they will be able to offer frank, impartial, and scientific advice, even if it may appear to offend the cabinet of the day. At the outset, it might perhaps be desirable to appoint one Commissioner for three years, one for four, one for five, etc., so as to provide after three years that at least one Commissioner will be retiring annually.

The Planning Commission will be responsible to Parliament through the Prime Minister and the inner cabinet. It will have an adequate secretariat. A number of supporting branches or bureaus should be subordinate to it, with full powers of securing information. The Bureau of Statistics, Costings and Accounting in particular, must have full charge of all national statistics, and be able to secure, through powers conferred on it, any statistics or similar essential information, from any department of government, state trust or commission, provincial or municipal authority, and such private industries as may be continued.

The National Research Council, which will have responsibility for industrial research and for establishing engineering and other technical standards, will continue to function under the powers conferred on it by the present Act. In addition, a Consumers' Research Institute might usefully be established, to act partly as an expert and partly as a representative body, on the model of the existing National Research Council; with the (full-time, salaried) president a technically trained man, and the members of the council representing the consumers on a geographical basis. The purpose of the Institute would be to study the wants of consumers, investigate the quality of goods sold, and do other related work. It would use the laboratory facilities of the National Research Council and co-operate with the health branch of the Department of Public Welfare.

Related to all of these, a Bureau of Public Information would probably have to be created to maintain a constant stream of information on economic problems and methods of dealing with them, and to present adequate information to the public, through bulletins, the press and the radio, etc., of the details of the economic plans being undertaken.

The Planning Commission will invite the attendance for consultation of any senior officer of the Central Bank, the Investment Board, the Insurance Corporation, the railway and other boards dealing with transportation and communication, any Deputy Minister, any officer of an industrial corporation, and any senior officer of the distributive services, as well as representatives of persisting private enterprises whenever any of the fields with which they are concerned are under consideration.

D. MAKING THE PLAN.

It is immensely important that the plan should not be simply a neat artificial system created *in vacuo* by a small group of bureaucrats and imposed by them from above on an unco-operative public. Such a plan would be out of touch with eco-nomic realities. It must enlist the sympathy and the whole-hearted co-operation of those who must actually put it into practice. The plan must spring from the needs and capacities of the farms and factories, the mines and lumber camps, the banks, the railroads, the stores, and workers in them, the house-wives who buy their products, who are the people *planned for*. In Russia, they boast that "millions make the Plan". No plan can in fact succeed otherwise. Every man, woman, and child in the country must play a part so that it is everybody's plan, and enthusiastic participation of the whole community is essen-tial if it is to work well.

The Planning Commission, therefore, is not the be-all and end-all of planning. It acts merely as the thinking and co-ordinating centre. The plan itself must grow up to begin with from the local units of economic organization. Before the plan is drawn up each year, the organizations actually concerned with producing goods and rendering services—state trusts, co-operatives, industrial councils—would draw up plans for the year, advise on alternative possibilities, and submit estimates and proposals. These would be collated by the various Indus-trial Commissions and forwarded to the Planning Commission, which would work out its general programme accordingly. In this way the danger of the plan being imposed arbitrarily by an artificial authority would be avoided. Its original source would be the local plants, which would thus take an active initiative in the direction of industry, instead of merely submitting to orders from above.

By such means the plan will come, not merely from the wisdom of five commissioners, but from the collective advice, co-ordinated by the Commission, of the numerous bodies which are directing the economic life of the state. In particu-lar, the managers of the state trusts will be concerned with planning within their respective financial and industrial spheres. Their advice will be of special importance, although the Com-mission alone will be directly responsible for the co-ordinated plans submitted to Parliament.

The various organs of public economic policy—the Central Bank, the Investment Board, the state trusts, the domestic and overseas trade bodies, and the various commissions of the sub-ordinate producing units—will also be given the opportunity to

assist in working up the plan. When the co-ordinated programme is outlined as a whole, they will receive it in order to
examine and develop those aspects of its final form which concern them, and will return the detailed development of their
sector of the plan to the Commission.

The Planning Commission will then, with such further consultation as may be necessary, formulate the complete plan.
On the basis of this, a National Planning Bill will be drafted
and submitted to the Prime Minister and Cabinet. In effect,
the Planning Bill will replace the present budget, and will constitute the most important item of annual Parliamentary business.

It is worth emphasizing that the Planning Bill would em-
body only general lines of policy. It would not prescribe the
complete details to which, for example, a public corporation
would have to conform. For, as has been pointed out elsewhere,
the greatest possible measure of industrial autonomy is essential. Nothing else would secure efficiency. If the Cabinet feels
that it could not persuade the country to accept it, it will ask
the Planning Commission to prepare an alternative plan on general lines laid down by the Cabinet. *Both* plans will then be laid
before Parliament. Parliament is, of course, most likely to
accept the plan recommended by the Cabinet, unless it is prepared to defeat the Cabinet! But the country will have some
evidence whereby to judge the reigning government's policy.
The work of the Planning Commission is not simply to initiate
the most desirable legislation from a purely economic point of
view, but to initiate legislation that will command the support
of public opinion and will play a part in educating public opinion. These things it cannot do, however, *unless its reports, and
especially its annual plan, are made public in the form in which
they were submitted to the Cabinet.*

On the presentation of the Planning Bill to Parliament, the
House of Commons will deal with it in the ordinary manner.[2]

2Possibly it would be useful for the bill to be referred to parliamentary committees.
That portion of it which dealt, for example, with agriculture, and similarly portions
dealing with other matters, would receive examination before committees, which would
be empowered to call witnesses and have present, as required, members of the Planning
Commission, government departments, and state corporations. Some most valuable work
might be performed by members of Parliament on these Committees, and the combination
of expert and amateur—of administrators and the public—would be wholesome to all
concerned. Such special parliamentary committees should be small in number and broadly
representative, firstly, of the economic interest under examination, and secondly, of the
particular regions of Canada most concerned with the proposed plan. The Committees
should then report to the House and the Planning Bill would then proceed through second
reading with a limited debate. Such a system would only be possible, however, if definite
provision were made to expedite business and eliminate delay.

There need not be a new plan every year. The planning period must necessarily be considerable, five years or more, but the plan will be subject to annual revision.

The question may be asked: what will occur if Parliament rejects the plan? This is a possibility to be recognized, but it is minimized by the considerations, first, that there will be frequent and progressive consultation between the Planning Commission and subordinate state organs of industry and finance; and secondly, that the Planning Commission, through its bureaus of information, will have full opportunity to keep public opinion acquainted with its views and policies.

The eventuality, however, may be considered. As a tentative proposal for dealing with a conflict between the economic organs of government and the political representative organs, it is suggested that, should Parliament reject the Planning Bill, it be referred back to the Planning Commission for amendment. On amendment (which may be performed after the Commission has conducted reconsultations with such agencies as it wishes) it must return by way of the Cabinet to the final stages of enactment, namely, the third reading. The Cabinet may be opposed to the bill, but must submit it without delay or alteration. Then, if, as well as the Cabinet, Parliament again rejects the bill, the rejection is final, and a new plan must be submitted.

In the unlikely possibility of the ensuing new Planning Bill (now revised twice) being rejected by the majority in the House of Commons, the resulting deadlock would require for its solution an immediate general election, the country dividing mainly on the issue of the plan proposed. If the electorate endorsed the plan, then the next government, formed from the majority so returned, would be in a position to proceed promptly with the Planning Bill, without the necessity of prolonged delay.

All of these processes are easier, however, if the electoral system is made more truly responsible and more democratic. The existing party machines, a public opinion at the mercy of special interests and fed by a press dependent for its existence primarily upon advertisement-revenue from capitalist private industries, mean that the House of Commons cannot constitute either a fair expression of the will of the nation or an efficient instrument of government. Cluttered with detail, obscured by partisan warfare, engaging in useless and unnecessary debate on unimportant and petty detail, the present House of Com-

mons is incapable of satisfactory national government. With
the procedure and party organization of today, it would be a
menace rather than an aid. Reform of the Parliamentary system and changes in Parliamentary procedure are necessary, to
speed up and make more rational the process by which legislation
is enacted.

CHAPTER X.

THE SOCIALIZATION OF INDUSTRY.

A. THE NECESSITY FOR POSITIVE CONTROL.

CANADA has already experimented with a wide diversity of types of public administration and control. In the regulations imposed upon private economic activity which already exist we have some degree of "negative planning". But more coherent system and more efficient administration are essential to make them effective. More comprehensive labour legislation, more adequate company laws, regulation of speculation and a more intelligent use of tariffs, for instance, would go far to remove some of the outstanding deficiencies of the present situation, but such negative controls, although they constitute an important ingredient in planning, cannot, by themselves, secure unity of purpose and the maximum of concerted action in our economic life. Nor can they overcome the basic factors in our economic collapse: inefficiency, waste, duplication, and violent fluctuations in business activity; monopoly exploitation of consumers, farmers, and workers; disruptive financial manipulation and speculative profit making; extreme inequality of wealth; the concentration of industrial and social control in the hands of a few. These can only be met by central directive planning.

It is essential that the vital functions in the economy should be carried out with the active object, not of obtaining profit, but of securing the good of the whole. This means a socially effective allocation of productive resources, stable production and consumption as far as possible, as harmless and as fair a distribution as may be of those fluctuations in the national income which cannot be eliminated. It means that other socially detrimental profits, such as those derived from the wasteful exploitation of natural resources, should be eliminated. It means that economies due to amalgamation among, for example, milling companies and among dairies should be passed on to the community in the form of lower prices, instead of serving simply as the basis for a large issue of shares to the public, whose purchase money contributes a high reward to the "re-organizing" investment bankers. But so long as our productive equipment is controlled with a view to securing private profits and not with a view to rendering the most efficient service possible, no amount

241

of regulation of the ways in which profits can be made will overcome the possibilities of financial manipulation and distortion of values, or prevent economies due to rationalization being used as a pretext for promoters' profits; so that the permanent social benefits of planning are lost in the rush for private speculative profit, or accrue exclusively to certain astute financiers.[1] So long as the possibility of private profits offers its temptation, there will always be ambitious and able men in the community, who will find a way round government regulations, if indeed they cannot break through them, or have them designed to their own advantage. The attempt to reconstruct society, therefore, only through the restrictive regulation of anti-social ways of making profits is bound to fail. At least a substantial part of productive activity must be socialized if planning is to have any fundamental and durable effects.

The conclusive argument against socialism used to be "not that it would divide badly what is produced, but that there would be so much less to divide". To-day the immediate urgency of the socialization of industry arises chiefly from the fact that we are producing so little when we are equipped to produce so much. But, even now, it is most urgent to abolish the extreme inequalities in the distribution of wealth, both on social and on purely economic grounds. So long as we depend on private profit for the motivation of the business system, great fortunes are bound to accumulate in the hands of a few. The successful competitor, or the man who succeeds in avoiding competition—whether his success is due to ability, to particular pull and privilege, or to luck,—collects a large profit. The possession of resources permits further ventures, or fortunes may even swell of their own momentum through the cumulative effect of compound interest and inheritance.

Inequality inevitably brings discontent and envy. It nourishes socially unhealthy phenomena such as property-crimes and gangsterism. It stimulates competitive ostentation in expenditure[2] and permeates society with purely materialistic values, even in spheres of activity, such as religion and art, where objectives and criteria should be non-economic. It has at least some share in bringing about industrial crises.

Most of all, however, the concentration of property in the hands of a small group of wealthy men produces a one-sided

[1] Consider, for example, the history of combinations in Canada in the pre-war decade: H. G. Stapells, *Combinations in Canada*.
[2] See Thorstein Veblen, *Theory of the Leisure Class*.

control of the economic machine; wielded generally without full consciousness of its social effects, this power extends to the whole political and social system. Real democracy, not merely in economic affairs, but in most of the other spheres of life, is impossible without a reduction of the extremes of economic inequality.

The first element, therefore, in the sort of planning which alone can be effective in creating a more democratic economic order, is the socialization of certain key functions and basic industries which are of strategic importance in the operations of the economy as a whole. With the key functions within its control, a socialist government can achieve a sufficient socialization of economic life even though a number of individual industries still remain in private hands, as may be, in some cases, highly desirable.

B. FORMS OF SOCIALIZED ENTERPRISE.

The complete socialization of all industry at once is, of course, not possible. Some period of transition must be expected, during which a socialist government would endeavour to make the best possible use of private business, extending its control step by step, consolidating each advance as it is made, and learning by experience to avoid mistakes and to apply improved methods in each new industry as it is taken over. This, at least, would be the probable course of events unless the crisis which brings socialism into power is so serious as to compel it to undertake the comprehensive reorganization of all industry at emergency speed.

The Criteria for Action.

Assuming that socialization is to be undertaken step by step, therefore, the question as to which industries should be taken over first can be answered by reference to four tests. (1) Is it a key industry? (2) Is it operated under conditions of monopoly? (3) Is it seriously inefficient? (4) Does it control important natural resources?

The "key functions", with their power over the economic system as a whole, must be dealt with first. Other industries, which have reached a state of complete or practical monopoly, with their obvious threat to primary producers, workers, and consumers, come next in importance. Once controlled in the public interest, monopolies are far easier to administer than an unco-ordinated or competitive industry. Given that they are to be fitted into the general industrial plan, therefore, they may be welcomed and encouraged as a means to the stabilization and co-ordination of production. To compel them to dissolve would be unnecessary and quite possibly destructive of efficiency. But negative attempts to control monopoly, such as the Combines Investigation Act, have been singularly ineffective in Canada and elsewhere. So long as the danger of exploitation persists, the only way out is to run the monopoly in the public interest. Thirdly, where private enterprise has shown itself to be inefficient, either through chaotic competition, over-expansion and duplication of productive capacity, or in any other way, there is again a clear necessity for the industry to be taken over and reorganized by the State. Waste of productive power cannot be tolerated, not only in itself but because of its reactions on the prosperity and smooth functioning of the economy as a whole. Finally, any industry which handles vital natural resources is "affected with a public interest"; this may be so urgent in some cases as to call for socialization, although control by the State of the disposal of these natural resources to the trade is likely to be sufficient, in most cases, for the time being.

The existence of any one or more of these four situations in a particular industry would probably necessitate its socialization at an early date in order to permit really effective planning. It is further possible that sabotage by those in control of other industries might compel the State to take them over as well.

Under these conditions, the State becomes the owner of a considerable part of the country's productive property, besides undertaking the responsibility for operating a number of industries. It must be emphasized at the outset that this can be done in a number of different ways. The idea, which still persists, that socialization means the attempt to run every industry on a stereotyped and bureaucratic model like the Post Office is very far indeed from the modern concept of reconstructive economic planning. The character and technique of the industrial transition which is actually to be envisaged, including the special cases of industries so important as banking and transportation, are outlined below. But it will be well to indicate here some of the forms which socialized enterprize can readily take.

State Holding Companies and State Trusts.

In the simplest case, control by the state authority can be established through the existing financial mechanism of the joint stock company.[3] By purchasing, for example, 51 per cent. of the voting shares it would be able to dictate policy, just as effectively as privately-owned parent concerns to-day can dictate policy to their subsidiaries. The financial mechanism is just as much open to the public interest as to private interests if we wish to make it so. Holding companies could be set up by the State to bring whole industries under unified direction, without any undue interference with the autonomy of constituent units.

If a more complete form of socialization is necessary, however, the whole ownership of the enterprise could be transferred to the State, which would simply take the place of private shareholders, and control policy through the appointment of its executives. These would be responsible to the appropriate supervisory commission, and ultimately to a Cabinet minister, for the running of their industry in accordance with the national plan. Such a State Trust would be run by a small group of, say, from three to five, expert trustees, selected by the Appointments Commissioner on the recommendation of the existing board of trustees, or, in the beginning, of a council of the existing managing directors (always provided that these were willing to co-operate). Trustees would take the place of present directors. They would pursue "efficiency" as much as a private firm— with the vital difference that workers' standards and the social objectives of the National Plan would be a prior consideration. The difficulty of large-scale management would be no greater than that which exists in any great private trust, and no more than is made inevitable by the advance of mass production and industrial integration. Local plants would retain their identity and internal autonomy, subject to general supervision, co-ordination with other units, and constant competitive comparison to maintain efficiency.

Other Forms of Organization.

Alongside of these state trusts there would be room for a number of other types of business organization both socialized, semi-socialized, and private.

Naturally, those activities which are already satisfactorily

[3] See Chapter III(a).

operated by provincial or Dominion governments, such as the post-office or forest services, would not be touched, though the probability is that such departmental organization would not be much extended.

Municipal enterprise, however, is a field which should be much further developed. A considerable number of economic activities are already carried on by municipalities and their specialized subsidiaries, notably those commonly known as "public utilities", such as the provision for drainage and water supply, of street paving and cleaning, and of street railway services, for example those provided by the Toronto Transportation Commission. In Ontario and other provinces, electrical power is distributed and even generated by a commission operating on behalf of a union of municipalities. These fields are already more or less socialized, and this technique could be extended with but few alterations.

Producers' Co-operatives such as are now in existence provide yet another type of machinery for socialized industry. Their object is already not profit-making but the efficient performance of some definite service such as marketing milk. There would be little difficulty in absorbing them much as they stand into a general scheme of production for use, and in extending this type of organization to spheres at present occupied by private enterprise. The distribution of milk in large cities is an important case: the principle has already been utilized, under the Public Utilities Board of Manitoba, in the distribution of milk in Winnipeg. With such organization it is of course conceivable that what might be efficient from the producers' point of view might be undesirable from the point of view of the consumer, or equally the interests of one group of producers might diverge from the general social interest. The means of reconciling these differences and of bringing individual enterprises into line with the national plan would be provided by the commission system discussed below.

Non-profit-making trusts or corporations. Similar in principle to the co-operatives are those undertakings which exist not primarily for profit, but to perform some function of social importance, often financed through charitable endowment or at least self-denying investment. Examples are perhaps more common in England,[4] though in the United States research institutes

[4]Such garden cities as Letchworth have been built on this principle and the older universities are semi-public institutions of this type.

such as the Carnegie and Rockefeller Foundations, and in Canada such universities as McMaster and many hospitals provide examples. There are also endowments in which a part of the funds is provided by public authorities, but a great deal of freedom is left to the supported organization: the University of Toronto is a case in point. There are many types of neglected productive activity for which semi-public institutions of this type would provide a suitable mechanism. Thus limited-profit housing corporations could be established to clear slum areas and provide adequate working class accommodation, and certain types of medical services could be organized on a similar plan.[5]

In those fields of manufacturing, mining, farming, trade, etc., which require decentralization or are best carried on on a small scale, a large part of the necessary co-ordination could be secured through the formation or reconstitution of *Trade Associations*. A strong association covering most of the concerns in the trade could easily constitute a council for the industry without disturbing the autonomy of member-firms. Their major executives or other appointees would sit as representatives on this council, pool their information and thresh out the problems of the trade, carrying back recommendations to their own firms. In some cases the industrial council might become an administrative authority competent to issue orders to the member businesses, either on such matters as were declared major points of policy, or perhaps when a two-thirds majority of the council agreed that it was necessary to enforce some decision, to secure either the interests of the industry or conformity with the National Plan. In highly localized trades, such as some retail services, councils would be organized on a local basis, and regional and provincial councils might in any case be a desirable supplement to a Dominion council. Besides representing the constituent firms the councils would offer an opportunity for representation of the various interests involved in the trade: the farmers from whom it buys its supplies, the trade unions whose members are employed in the industry, and the consumers of its products. It would also be necessary for the State to appoint one or more members of the council to secure co-ordination with other parts of the economic machine. In other words, the Council built up from the industry or trade association would become a well-equipped advisory body or

[5]See Chapter XIX and Chapter XVI

equivalent to a super-board of directors for the trade as a whole, according to circumstances.

The Rôle of Commissions.

The next problem to be faced is the co-ordination of the activities of the councils and of the various socialized, semi-socialized and private undertakings, to bring them into harmony with the National Plan. It is here that effective adaptation can be made of the Commission system of controlling industry which has already been widely applied in Canada.[6]   Commissions similar to the existing Board of Railway Commissioners, the Board of Grain Commissioners, the Ontario Hydro-Electric Commission, or the Public Utilities Commissions of the Prairie Provinces, will be established for each industry or group of industries.[7]   The powers of the commissions must naturally vary, but each will act as a central clearing-house of information for the undertakings within its jurisdiction, exercise a general supervision over such activities within the plant as are of more than domestic concern, see that the National Plan is carried out, and possibly render some centralized service for the industry on the model of the electric power "grid" in England.   All matters affecting the trade, such as market information, will be communicated to the secretariat of the commission, and each firm will keep it informed as to its policy, methods and programme.   Since each subsidiary of the commission will have access to such information, each will be able to work with full knowledge of the state of production in relation to demand, and with the latest information as to methods and experiments available to it.   Just as the Board of Railway Commissioners is responsible for fixing freight rates, a matter too important to be left to the discretion of the private industry, so the Commission for, say, the staple food industries, might be, made responsible for seeing that the prices charged for flour are reasonable and that the contract policy with bakeries is not detrimental to consumers' interests.   Similarly, the Commission for mineral development (or the Department of Mines) might have to intervene to prevent expansion of a wasteful or unduly speculative character in mining enterprise.

6See H. A. Innis, *Problems of Staple Production in Canadian Industry*, Part II, "Government in Industry", and Hankin & MacDermot, *Recovery by Control*.

7In some cases where a government department already provides machinery equal to this work, it may at least for the time being save confusion and waste to hand over to it the functions of a commission, as well as of a government department.   The independence which a separate commission enjoys is to be desired however.

Again, Commissions must have sufficient authority to prevent overlapping and waste among the firms responsible to them. If in the lumber industry, for instance, Company A applies to be allowed to develop certain timber limits, the Forestry Commission would be able to refuse such permission if it would mean duplication of railroad facilities, while a simple extension at a later date of the line already used by Company B. would provide for adequate lumbering development.   Generally, the Commission would exercise arbitrary power only in the last resort. By promoting conference within the industry (such as is secured by the existing conferences of Superintendents of Insurance), it would seek to secure co-ordination by spontaneous co-operation rather than by regulations.   The Commissions, however, are the obvious bodies to which the Cabinet's ultimate administrative authority, in terms of the detailed work of supervision, should be delegated.   Being in constant touch with every concern, socialized and private, within their specific spheres, and exercising surveillance over local industrial matters directly, they are clearly in the best position to guide the carrying out of the agreed plan.   While this essential control is secured, at the same time each firm is left free to make its own decisions in individual matters, just as the railways direct their own technical operations without reference to the Board of Railway Commissioners.

In the case of private enterprises, the supervisory function of the Commissions in seeing that the necessary regulations were carried out and the provisions of the Plan not infringed, would loom the largest.   In both private and socialized industries, however, one of their most important functions would be that of providing a link between the National Planning Commission and actual operation in particular fields.

Commissions whose fields were represented by socialized industries would have the responsibility of seeing that the Boards of Trustees operate their state corporations efficiently and in accordance with the Plan.   The Commissions here would act as a new form of Board of Directors, exercising general control over the policy and activities of the Executives of the Corporation, but on behalf of the general public instead of on behalf of private shareholders.   The Trustees would report to the Commissions and not directly to the Cabinet Ministers who head the government departments concerned with them.   This would insure as far as possible, that the operation of industry is "kept out of politics", and run as a business, not as a government enterprise. The Commission would act as an insulator between the politics of the Cabinet and the operation of the Board of Trustees, maintaining for the latter the freedom to carry on their work in accordance with the Plan undistorted by partisan considerations.

Obviously, much depends upon the personnel of these Commissions.[8] Normally they would consist of a small group (say three) of administrative experts. In some rare circumstances it might be found desirable to employ representative or elective principles in the formation of Commissions. But the particulars of the mode of establishment, the allocation of duties, and delimitation of Commissioners' spheres, cannot be dogmatically laid down in advance. The Planning Commission together with preliminary Committees of Reorganization established in each industry in order to effect the necessary changes, would be charged with the recommendation of these details on the basis of specific study of each industry.

C. KEY FUNCTIONS AND MAJOR INDUSTRIES.

Banking and Investment.

It is beyond question that, of all the key functions in the modern economy, the control of monetary and credit policy and of investment is the most fundamental. The first necessity of a socialist programme is the deliberate control of our financial machinery. In order to achieve this, state ownership must be substituted for the present private ownership of the chartered banks as well as the new Central Bank, and the management of investment in a co-ordinated fashion must be placed in the hands of a National Investment Board.[9] When this is done, the State will be in a position to ensure efficiency in industrial operation, to discipline non-co-operative industries, and if necessary dictate major lines of policy, just as the banks could, if they so desired, and, in some cases, do dictate to the firms who borrow from them to-day.[10] The National Investment Board will be in a position to enforce the decisions of the National Planning Commission as to which trades should be developed

---

8 See below, Chapter XI(b).

9 See Chapter XII(d).

10 The Bank of Commerce has on its own account established a sort of hospital for the sick businesses which it finds upon its hands, keeping a staff of experts to diagnose their troubles and possible remedies.

and which cut down, by granting or withholding the necessary supplies of capital. To a lesser extent, at first at least, the State will be able to accelerate or retard general economic activity by credit expansion or contraction: though these powers should grow only as the work of the Planning Commission gradually achieves a more integrated economic structure. These financial powers, taken together, will provide the necessary means of elasticity in the economic structure and equip the State with an instrument for distributing economic losses among the different sections and groups in the country. These are not new powers. They exist already. The essential thing is that they should be vested in a disinterested authority capable of seeing the interests of the community as a whole, and that they should be wielded deliberately and with an intelligent consciousness of their effects.

Transportation.

Next to the control of finance, the control of transportation services and rates ranks the highest in importance. Freight rates and railway developments dominate productive activity in Canada as perhaps in no other country. Rescind the Crow's Nest Pass agreement and you ruin whole sections in the West.[11] Open a Hudson Bay route with low charges and you awaken dormant districts to economic activity. Build and subsidize a Temiskaming and Northern Ontario Railroad to provide cheap transportation for the north country and you launch a host of mining prospects. Transport is the key to the development of our resources. If the State controls this, it can control the tempo and direction of economic development. If it controls the rate structure (and supports it by means of tariffs or other taxation) it can dictate the incidence of economic benefits and losses among the different parts of the country. Once again, if it may be noticed that such control is already exercised, through such agencies as the Crow's Nest Pass Agreement, through the Board of Railway Commissioners, and through state subsidies and land grants to railroads, apart altogether from outright state or provincial operation of such lines as the C.N.R. and the T.N.O. What is required is the consolidation of these controls, and then a deliberate use of them to forward a conscious and consistent social policy, instead of moving haphazardly from one line of action to another.

11On the whole subject, see H. A. Innis, *Problem of Staple Production in Canada,* Part II.

Amalgamation of the Railways.

It is hardly necessary to add that the railways demand attention on another count: the impossibility of any ordered attack on the present problems of duplication, inefficiencies, and debt without a unified administration of the two main systems as a whole. But important as it looms in contemporary political controversy, "the railway problem" in a planned State is only a particular case of a general principle. The railways should be state-administered not because one of them does not make profits, but because they are a vital industry in the Canadian community.

The way has been prepared in fact, far more than in most other comparable industries.[12] We recommend that the C.P.R. should be nationalized without further ado, in accordance with the following plan. Instead of a Board of Arbitration and two separate executives, the combined railways would be put under the control of a single Board of Trustees upon which the chairmen of both systems will be asked to serve. These trustees will run the railroad system as a single unit (apart from provincial lines) subject to the supervision of the Board of Railway Commissioners whose powers will, however, be extended, so that they become the Commissioners for Transport and Communications, having under their control all forms of transport by rail, water, road and air. This reconstituted Commission will be responsible for seeing that these different types of transport are effectively integrated, securing adequate service and eliminating duplication and cut-throat competition.

But, it will be said, what of other proposals for unification? In practice there are only those advocated by the C.P.R. to consider. For the government's stand, for reasons best known to themselves, has been "competition ever, amalgamation never"; and the "proposals" of the "National Government"-ers have been pathetically vague.

Undoubtedly the chief attraction of the C.P.R. plan has been the economies promised. Sir Edward Beatty tells us that unification under private management would save $75,000,000 a year. But how far does this bear examination? In the first place, Sir Edward himself is careful to add the qualifying words "on a normal traffic volume, taking 1930 as a normal traffic

---

12Cf. the terms of the Drayton-Acworth Report, the Report of the Duff Commission, the C.N.R.-C.P.R. Bill, etc. See also Chapter VI(d) in this volume, and H. A. Innis, "Economic Planning by Arbitration", in the *Canadian Forum*, December, 1932.

base".[13] Combined gross earnings in 1934 were almost a third lower than in 1930[14] and in the first six months of 1935 not quite up to the 1934 level; and, under capitalism, the prospects of further recovery in general business activity are not good. It seems rash, therefore, to count on a volume of traffic much above last year's. This at once cuts the $75,000,000 to $50,-000,000. In the second place, nothing like the whole $50,000,000 could be made available immediately without wholesale dismissals of railway labour. Sir Edward recognizes this when he remarks that "normal turnover by withdrawals due to ill health, death, retirements, and voluntary changes run from five to six per cent per annum of the total number of employees. Therefore, from natural causes, in the event vacancies were not filled, the personnel of Canadian railways would be reduced in five years from 25 to 30 per cent., and it would not be possible to administer the unified properties with a staff reduced below 75 or 70 per cent. of normal".[15]

If the plan is followed, the immediate saving is correspondingly reduced; and, though there is no problem of finding employment for displaced railway men, there remains the problem of finding employment for young men who would otherwise have been absorbed by the railways. If, on the other hand, wholesale dismissals do take place, the full saving can be secured much sooner, but only at the cost of railway labour and the taxpayer, who will have to supply relief to some of the displaced, at least temporarily. Sir Edward counts on "the improvement in the general economic condition of the country as the result of unification, to provide employment for actual or potential railwaymen no longer required", and in the long run he may be right. But the admission that "if necessary some of the savings of unified management could be devoted to compensation for labour displaced"[16] shows misgivings about the short run. For maintaining the men during the period of readjustment, training them for whatever new work is available, and placing them in new jobs, Canada has at present no adequate machinery and under capitalism is unlikely to develop any. Compensation or relief for the railwaymen would constitute a further deduction, of unknown amount, from the hypothetical $50,000,000.

13Speech to the Toronto Canadian Club, May 20, 1935.
14*Railway Statistics for Canada.*
15Speech to the Toronto Canadian Club, January 16, 1933.
16Speech to the Toronto Canadian Club, May 20, 1935.

The alternative is to save more money for the capitalist at the expense of labour.

Thirdly, to get the full saving the C.N.R. would have to abandon 3,200 miles of line and the C.P.R. 1,800. As the Minister of Railways pertinently asks, "What would you do with 200,000 people who are on these abandoned lines? Are the settlers and industries and towns to be compensated? If so, how much will it cost? Are they to be moved? If so, where?"[17] Sir Edward's answer is that ".care will be used to avoid any grave hardship. Abandonments would not be considered which would deprive communities of reasonable access to transportation service". As for the "loss to those who have located at railway terminals, shops or towns", the answer is: "After time has permitted us to assess the true loss, compensation should be made in individual cases on their merits".[18] This again is vague, but in any case presents the same dilemma as the previous question of railway labour. If anything is done for the 200,000 people it will be another formidable reduction from that fast-shrinking $50,000,000. If nothing is done, it is another case of exploitation of the defenceless.

Probably no one can say precisely what net saving the Beatty plan would produce. We can only be sure that it would be far less than the $75,000,000 glibly quoted (out of its context) by advocates of a "national" government.

We can also be sure that the taxpayer will not get the whole of whatever saving there is. Sir Edward Beatty says, "at least one half".[19] As Canadian National gross earnings amount to only 56 or 57 per cent of combined gross earnings, it is most unlikely that the government's share of economies would be more than 60 per cent. Of the C.P.R.'s part of the savings, the bulk would go to shareholders outside the country.

When, therefore, the ordinary citizen hears that "we" could save this, that or the other enticing sum by unifying the railways under C.P.R. management, he would do well to ask not only how the figures are arrived at, but also who "we" are.

The dangers of a privately-owned monopoly, according to Sir Edward, "are now mythical", first, because of the competition of "lakes and rivers, the motor vehicle, and the aero-

17Speech to the Toronto Canadian Club, May 1, 1935, reported in *Financial Post*, May 11, 1935. Sir Edward in his reply did not challenge these figures, so they are presumably correct.

18Speech to the Toronto Canadian Club, May 20, 1935.

19Speech to the Toronto Canadian Club, May 20, 1935.

plane",[20] second, because "the public interest can be fully protected by public control through the Board of Railway Commissioners and the Government".[21] But this is far from convincing. The Minister of Railways recently put to Sir Edward twelve pointed questions. He might have added three more. (1) How much wheat moves from central Saskatchewan to Fort William or Vancouver by "lakes and rivers, the motor vehicle, and the aeroplane"? (2) Is it or is it not true that the railways already control the dominant air transport company? (3) What is to stop the railway monopoly from buying up the competing forms of transportation? As for the Railway Commission, it is true that under present conditions it safeguards the interests of shippers and the travelling public pretty effectively. But that is no proof that it would do so under the shadow of a C.P.R. monopoly. Its members are appointed by the Cabinet and its decisions may, on appeal, be overruled by the Cabinet. A private railway monopoly would be able to exert enormous pressure to see that only "sound" men were appointed in the first place and to have "unsound" decisions reversed or referred back for reconsideration.

Some may object that this argument allows nothing for the known integrity and public spirit of the C.P.R.'s present head. But Sir Edward Beatty is not all-powerful in the affairs of the C.P.R. His board of directors is not composed of nonentities; and whatever confidence the public may feel in Sir Edward himself does not extend to all his colleagues. In any event, it is never safe to entrust irresponsible power even to the best of men. On the prairies, the memory of a previous C.P.R. monopoly is still green and fragrant.[22]

The final criticism of the capitalist unification scheme is that it can be carried into effect only by sabotaging our political democracy. Everyone agrees that it would be political suicide for either the Conservatives or the Liberals to touch it. It can be put through only by a coalition or "national" government. Formed after the present election, this could present the people four years hence with a *fait accompli;* formed before the next election, it could, after the manner of its British prototype, ask for a "doctor's mandate". It would carefully refrain from committing itself to any definite plan. On the contrary, the strat-

---

20Speech to the Toronto Canadian Club, January 16, 1933.
21Speech before the Canadian Political Science Association, Montreal, May 22, 1934.
22For reasons, see Patton, *Grain Growers' Co-Operation in Western Canada.*

egy would be to profess an "open mind", promise "the fullest consideration of all points of view", "justice for all", perhaps another inquiry by an "impartial" Royal Commission, and "a business solution" of the problem.[23] These tactics might delude genuine supporters of public ownership as tactics of the same kind hoaxed Lord Snowden. But, "once aboard the lugger and the girl is mine!"

The capitalist solution of the railway problem is in fact no solution at all. In an unplanned capitalist economy, unification is bound to be just one more repetition of the old story: benefits for the few at the expense of the many. But in a planned, socialized economy the objections disappear. The railway problem is no longer viewed in isolation, but as part of a general plan. Reduction of railway personnel or abandonment of lines can be carried out as fast as may be necessary because the government is prepared to take full responsibility for the maintenance, training and placement of displaced workers or settlers, and because under socialism it can afford to accept this responsibility and can be sure of fulfilling the task. A socialist economy can do what a declining capitalism dare not even attempt. Improvements in the mechanism of production are no longer fraught with menace to the livelihood of the worker.

Under socialism, too, the whole saving of unification (less the compensation to C.P.R. security holders which we propose below) goes to the public. The dangers of monopoly disappear when the monopoly is controlled by responsible public servants. Above all, the whole process is carried through *in the open*, by democratic means, as the result of a definite mandate from an electorate consulted beforehand and told precisely what it is voting for.

A Socialized Transport and Communication System.

Co-ordination should not stop short at the railways alone. It is essential that our whole system of transport and communication should be considered as a unit, each type of service being an integral part of the whole. The powers of the Commission should be adjusted accordingly but would generally be

---

[23]When these words were written, we had not read "Address No. 2" of the League for National Government pamphlets. On page 8, it contains these words: "To those who persistently endeavour to create the impression that our movement has as its objective the amalgamation of the railways we wish to say again that this is not the case. We believe that a Government of truly National representation—a government prepared to approach its deliberations upon business-like lines—a government freed from partizan entanglements, will know best how to deal with the matter. Such a government will be in a position to give consideration to the views of those for and against this and that solution".

similar in character to those exercised at present over the railroads, i.e., mainly of a supervisory nature. There would be no attempt to take control of provincial highway construction out of the hands of the Provinces, nor to socialize every bus and trucking service in the country. An appropriate Board, as a branch of the Department of Communications and Transport, should, however, be put in charge of the licensing of motor vehicles, with instructions to use the system to effect what control is necessary. Air transport does not yet present the same urgency as the railroads, but the prospects of future development are such that it is immensely important that this should be effectively controlled. State ownership and operation of the projected transcontinental and transatlantic services (as well as State construction of the route) are highly desirable. The transference of Canadian Airways from control by a private to a public board of directors charged with the development of aerial services in co-ordination with other forms of transport, could be effected with little difficulty at the same time as the reorganization of the railways.

The waterways of this country, being already under public control, can be assimilated to the scheme as a whole without drastic changes of machinery. It might be necessary to control more narrowly the shipping which uses the canal and river systems, but this, again, could be done through licensing.

The important telegraph systems could be brought into public hands at the same time as the railways. In the Prairie Provinces and elsewhere telephone service is already provided by the municipalities and provinces. The private telephone companies operating in Ontario and Quebec, which exercise practical monopoly power in their respective fields by the control of patents and by the nature of the service which they render, should be re-constituted as public concerns. As for radio, the mercantile radio services remain in the care of the Department of Mercantile Marine; while the powers and activities of the existing Radio Commission could be readily extended, following the model of the British Broadcasting Corporation.

Power and Fuel.

Everywhere in the Machine Age the control of *power* gives control of production. Shut off the sources of supply—hydro, coal, gas, oil—and you paralyze industry. Charge exorbitant prices and you cripple it. Demand a varied rate from different trades, you stimulate those you favour and force contraction upon the rest.[24]   The policy of the Association of Coal Merchants, the oil trust, or the dominant electrical power producers, has just these effects—effects of such moment to the whole community that it is essential that they should be directly in the control of a public authority.   This is, of course, already true of electrical power in Ontario and most of the other provinces, Quebec being the outstanding exception.

The industries which supply power, fuel and light conform in fact to all four of the tests outlined above and stand in urgent need of control.   A Dominion Power Commission should therefore be established to supervise the supply and the prices of these important services, and to provide for the co-ordination of the different sources of each.   Under the aegis of this Commission an Electrical Power Board would be established to control electrical development.   The Ontario Hydro and other publicly owned systems would not be touched, since they are already organized on a social basis and would fit straight into the general scheme.   The Electrical Power Board would be responsible for controlling the activities of such private power companies as remain in the Province of Quebec, and elsewhere, and for supervising their transference to public control when this becomes feasible.[25]   The Board would also be empowered to exercise a general control on the activities of mining or pulp and paper companies which develop power in connection with their operations, and by co-operation with the provincial governments would be able to promote the regional co-ordination of power development.   The difficulties of the coal industry and the plight of the mining populations are such that coal production would probably have to be socialized at an early date.   In any case, the import of coal would come under the control of the Import Board,[26] and its distribution under the Commission for Internal Trade, which last would also be responsible for the control of gasoline distribution.   Should large supplies of oil be discovered in Canada, the fortunate province concerned would be required to secure co-ordinated and economical development, as seems appropriate.   The gas industry can be left to the

[24]The matter is especially important in the electrical industry, as there the heavy overhead costs and problems of peak loads inevitably imply a somewhat arbitrary allotment of charges and price fixing, which may lead to an undesirable policy of price discrimination.
[25]The present agitation for the municipalization of power services in Quebec suggests that the time is ripe for their transfer to public ownership and operation.
[26]See below, Chapter XIV: "Foreign Trade".

supervision of the central Commission, without any attempt to socialize every small source in the regions of natural gas.

Other Industries.

In so far as duplication and monopoly are detrimental to both the primary producers and consumers in the supplying of flour and bread, meat, stock canned goods, and milk and dairy produce, it seems essential to extend a large measure of government control to the flour-milling, baking, meat-packing, and dairy industries. Detailed proposals are discussed below;[27] but in general it is proposed that the production of these foods should be co-ordinated under a central Food Commission, which will also be responsible for the supervision of prices and quality in other food trades, through tests undertaken by the Research Bureau, through enforced publicity, or, wherever necessary, through direct regulation. Among other industries which must undoubtedly be considered at appropriate stages in the programme of socialization are pulp and paper, mineral development, iron and steel; all of these are intimately concerned with the development of the economy, are dominated by heavy overhead costs with resultant cut-throat competition, and are particularly subject to over-capitalization and speculative "boom mania". Probably also some part of the construction industry may have to be socialized for the more effective promotion of a rehousing programme.

With control of finance, of transport, and of power, the State holds the reins of economic authority. Ownership of the country's *natural resources* would transfer yet another strategic field to its charge. Farming land has, of course, mostly been alienated. There is no suggestion of wholesale expropriation of present farmers, but no more land would be handed over to private owners in the future. In the Maritime Provinces most of the timber lands have already been alienated, but in the rest of the Provinces this is true of only a small proportion of such land. Future grants of cutting rights would be made only in accordance with the National Plan. Mining licences would be issued in the same way. All development of still unexploited resources would be carried out on the basis of careful survey and systematic planning.[28]

27See Chapter XVIII; also "The Staff of Life Supports the Millers", *Canadian Forum*, June, 1933; the *Report of the Milling Enquiry*; and H G. Stapells, *The Recent Consolidation Movement in Canadian Industry*, (Unpublished thesis, University of Toronto, 1922).

28For instance, timber limits in British Columbia would be thoroughly "cruised" before they are handed over for development.

Research—very definitely a key industry to-day—which is already semi-socialized, must be fully promoted by the State and given every opportunity to contribute to the planned development of the community. One of the most important subsidiaries of the National Planning Commission would be the Bureau of Research, an extension of the existing National Research Council. While this would be responsible for the development of vital research in the fields of State-controlled industry, no less important a function would be its co-operation in encouraging local and individual research elsewhere.

One further power already in the hands of the State, to wit, *taxation,* provides an invaluable set of tools for shaping the nation's economic destiny. Fiscal policy is discussed in detail later. Here it is sufficient to point out that it can be used not merely to collect revenue but also to redistribute the national income if necessary, to stimulate or to penalize particular industries by such time-honoured Canadian institutions as tariffs and subsidies or by taxation of profits, and, if necessary, to discipline recalcitrant enterprises.

If the exercise of these powers is supplemented by organized economic activities and socialized projects, it would clearly be possible for the State to secure a very fair degree of co-ordination in economic undertakings, and of adherence to socially desirable policies. Even so, it is clear that certain other industries will have to be socialized. Property which must of technical necessity be used communally, and which is vital to the welfare of the whole community,[29] cannot be left at the disposal of private owners. Industries which, while not absolutely of "key" rank, are producers of basic means of industrial production, must be brought under such systems of control as will insure administration in the interests of the people as a whole. There will always be a few exceptions, of which farming is an important one, since efficient production can be secured on the basis of family operation, while the owners are so numerous and their holdings on so small a scale that there is no danger of their exploiting the community. For the rest, however, it is clear that socialization will extend in scope, once the first elements of planning are established.

---

[29]This refers only to the *instruments of production* and not to consumers' goods such as clothes, automobiles, furniture, houses, etc.

D. THE TECHNIQUE OF TRANSFERENCE.

How is the transition from private ownership to social control to be effected? In considering the methods which appear best suited to Canadian conditions, we reject that of confiscation or transference without compensation. Expert appraisal, the issue of compensation bonds, and progressive taxation thereafter are the main elements of the technique proposed.

A Court of Appraisal.

As a first step, a Court of Appraisal must be established, subordinate to the National Planning Commission and in close touch with the Reconstruction Committees in the trades concerned. Its personnel would draw on economists, statisticians, investment managers and engineers, and it should include representatives of the private owners and the executive officers or managers of the plant. As the Planning Commission decides upon the socialization of an industry, its physical equipment (e.g., steam engines, tracks, bridges, stations and so forth, in the case of railroads) will be placed under State ownership (Dominion, provincial or municipal) forthwith, and put under the control of the appropriate Commission and Board of Trustees. Meanwhile, the question of the value of the plant will be put before the Court of Appraisal, which will examine past earnings and future prospects closely as a basis for establishing a valuation. Such relevant matters as costs of production, market price of shares, book capitalization and the like will be taken into account only so far as they throw light on the real problem of future earning power. It is essential that the value of the socialized concerns should be established in this way by a semi-expert, semi-arbitral authority; otherwise there is always the danger that the rumour of projected socialization may rush market prices of securities and other assets up to unwarranted heights, imposing an impossible burden of debt upon the community.

Compensation Bonds.

The value of a business being settled, its former owners will receive compensation to its full amount, in proportion to their security holdings. Compensation will take the form of government-guaranteed bonds, similar to the ordinary market bond except in two respects. First, they will be redeemable at their face value on demand, in order to facilitate the rapid extinction of the public debt. Secondly, their rate of interest will vary with the contraction and expansion of the national income, and with the general (internal) price level, in order to secure flexibility of the financial structure and so avoid future penalization of the community at large for the benefit of the bond holders, such as takes place at present.

The present owners of industry would, by this means, receive fair, but not extravagant, compensation for relinquishing (or, if necessary, being compelled to abandon) their claims. The change to Compensation Bonds by itself would not bring any substantial reduction in the inequality in wealth, though it provides a necessary foundation for a permanent policy. Eradication of the extreme inequalities of property holdings can only be brought about by steeply graded direct taxation. With the proceeds of taxation, some part at least of the bonds outstanding could be bought up and cancelled; and bonds could also be accepted at par in payment of taxes by the Revenue Department. Taxation is an integral element in a programme of socialization because it can be used to affect the distribution, not only of industrial control and ownership, but also the right to benefit from the income which industry yields.

This method may seem roundabout, underhand and pusillanimous to some, but it has decisive advantages in the conditions we contemplate, and in a country such as Canada. It provides a flexible mode of socialization, which permits the speed of assumption of state control to be varied as circumstances warrant. Secondly, the conditions of equity can be more easily preserved. The owners of bonds or stock in those industries which are first socialized will not necessarily be the most wealthy people in Canada. It is both unfair and inexpedient that they should suffer from the arbitrary discrimination which would be involved in appropriation without compensation—in effect, an uneven and disruptive tax. Discrepancies in wealth can be much more effectively and consistently eliminated by the application of steeply progressive taxes whose incidence is in proportion to wealth.

Further, Canada is burdened with heavy foreign obligations.[30] Our industries, and particularly our transport system, are owned to a considerable extent by shareholders abroad or

[30]See Chapter II, section c. It will be noticed that the weight of this burden is not so great as it is sometimes believed to be.

financed by bonds payable in the United States or in Great Britain. Simple repudiation of foreign debts is not to be recommended; while discrimination against Canadian and in favour of foreign security holders is unfair and inexpedient. The system of compensation, plus taxation, avoids these difficulties. It would not be such a shock to confidence in the foreign investment market, yet at the same time it would not preclude the possibility of taxing at the source interest on bonds held abroad —a practice commonly adopted elsewhere, as in Britain.

Finally, while providing for reasonable fairness in the process of socialization, this method avoids the opposite danger, that of subsidizing bond holders at the public expense. The expert appraisal of capital values safeguards the State from the danger of buying up concerns which are bound for the Bankruptcy Court through exhaustion of raw material supplies, inappropriateness, or inefficiency, at a price calculated only to save the owners from ruin.

Recommendation of this particular method of socialization does not, of course, exclude the adoption of other methods as circumstances dictate. If depression has reduced the prices of securities even below the level justified by future prospects, the State might well be able to transfer an industry to public hands simply by purchasing its shares and bonds on the market at bargain prices. Widespread bankruptcies and reorganizations of industry similarly might provide opportunities for the purchase of concerns through the ordinary financial mechanism. Such procedure would, of course, be peculiarly subject to the danger that the public would become burdened with "dead horse" trades which would otherwise disappear of their own accord. Great discretion would need to be exercised in such cases, purchases being made only with the full concurrence of the National Planning Commission.

Confiscation, tempered by the payment of "compassionate allowances" to widows and orphans and others for whom this would mean destitution or the loss of life savings, is an alternative which would not need to be considered if the above plan were given a fair chance. Confiscation tempered by the payment of annuities for a stated period, or during the lifetime of the expropriated person, is also often urged. But neither of these schemes completely meets the fundamental objection to compensation—that it perpetuates private ownership unnecessarily—while both are subject to the difficulties of unfair discrimination and international complications.

However, should circumstances arise which make gradual socialization impossible, and compel wholesale transference of ownership of control to public authorities—or should the whole existing financial machinery collapse—the much simpler method of direct transference of all private property in productive resources and equipment[31] to public hands might have to be adopted. It would be blinking realities not to add that drastic steps through orders-in-council might be necessary to prevent the financial powers-that-be from wrecking the whole scheme. Foreign pressure will certainly be brought to bear on any government bent on making fundamental socialist changes in industrial control, though some of such pressure will equally certainly be inspired from within Canada. Cries of alarm from abroad, however, should be ignored, more particularly if they are raised against socialization based on our preferred technique above. So also can the inevitable panic forecasts of doom, which Canadian financiers will issue. Socialization *will* be fatal, but in only one sense—fatal to the profit-making interests vested in the present system, which must give way before the needs of the community at large.

What Socialization Does Not Mean.

It may be just as well to indicate also some of the things which socialization does *not* mean. In a period of transition some dislocation is unavoidable. There is a danger that among those whose prospects appear to be threatened many who do not realize the necessity of some sacrifice will give way to panic: and they will naturally try to inspire the public with their own fears. But if the public opinion behind the government is a fully informed one, there is no need for these fears to get out of hand and cause disruption.

In the first place, socialization does not mean a complete transformation of the industrial order overnight. It is impossible to lay down rigid rules in advance as to the speed with which public control will be extended. If conditions are favourable, a gradual extension of social control is to be preferred as this will give opportunity for experiment in methods, and for profiting from experience. On the other hand, the mere prom-

[31]To be clearly distinguished, as before, from private property in personal and consumers' goods.

ise of socialization may so alarm some sections of industry, or so dangerously stimulate sabotage, or the chance to introduce the new system may come under conditions so critical, that bold and comprehensive steps will have to be taken at once by any socialist government coming into power.

The precise rate of socialization must therefore be decided by, and adjusted to, the conditions prevailing. We propose that public responsibility for economic activities should be undertaken on the basis of careful examination of conditions and possibilities by Reorganizing Committees formed for each industry concerned, to work under the National Planning Commission. These committees would be composed of business men actively engaged in the trade as well as of economic experts and representatives of the banks and the government, somewhat on the lines of the representative committee to further reorganization which was appointed for the iron and steel trades in Great Britain, when reorganization of this industry was begun there. They would be responsible for drawing up the first plans for the organization of the industry as a socialized concern as well as plans for the actual process of socialization. These would be submitted to the National Planning Commission for approval. On this basis, attention would first be directed to finance and investment, and to the basic industries, particularly transportation. The further extension of public ownership and operation would be undertaken as the time became ripe, or as the reactions of private enterprise made it necessary in the view of the Planning Commission and of Parliament. There would certainly be room, and need, for private enterprise for considerable time to come.

Secondly, the distinction between *financial* and *industrial* transformation should be clearly kept in mind. There is a great deal of difference between the view to be taken by the director or shareholder and the manager or rank-and-file employee. Financial values and the stock market might quite possibly react violently. There might a scramble to sell, a fall in security prices, a check to the flow of investment, but steps can be taken to counteract these effects. But the actual physical processes of production, transportation, wholesale and retail sales, and consumption, need not be in the least disturbed. The transfer of share ownership and the reconstruction of the board of directors into a public agency need not affect the routine of the factory. The employee of the socialized concern will come to work as usual each morning, and the housewife will go down to do her shopping in the same stores as before. Only gradually will the effects of socialization become apparent in steadier work, shorter hours, and better pay, more efficient organization, lower prices, and better quality.

Even in methods of control, there need be no wholesale scrapping of the old machinery in favour of new and untried systems, if the government is afforded reasonable co-operation. Executive arrangements could probably be maintained intact in each business. The ingenious device of interlocking director- ates and majority shareholders could be fully utilized—this time to give public control in the organization of the industries taken over. Associations of business men either for specific or for general purposes would be used to secure necessary co-ordina- tion. Existing commissions such as the Board of Railway Com- missioners, the Grain Commissioners and the Tariff Board would be readily developed into instruments for the control of socialized industry. In other words, if the concept of control in the public interest is accepted at the outset, the new order can be built up out of the material provided by the old, upon the basis provided by the existing system. Where there is ineffi- ciency, or a lack of machinery, there must of course be modifi- cation of structure and new agencies. But this does not mean a dramatic sweeping away of present industrial forms and the erection in their place of some fantastic paper scheme.[32]

It should be pointed out once more also, that there is room in a socialist economy, just as there has been room in a capitalist economy, for many different types of industrial structure. Some of these will survive in the unsocialized fringe of economic activity, but many will persist among the socialized trades them- selves. Socialism is not an inelastic method of running busi- ness through government departments administered from Ot- tawa by politicians and hidebound civil servants. It implies simply public ownership, production for the general good in- stead of for a private profit, and the placing of ultimate auth- ority in the hands of the State instead of in the hands of pri- vate shareholders. This is all compatible with local and indi- vidual initiative in industry, and a considerable amount of in- dependence in operation. It is also compatible with varied

---

[32]All this, of course, presupposes that the new system is introduced in an orderly man- ner by constitutional means. In the case of a violent breakdown of society, more sweeping changes in industrial structure would undoubtedly be necessary.

types of organization according to the needs of particular trades, ranging from farmers' co-operatives to joint stock companies as we have already shown.

Fourthly, socialization does not mean that all executives would be dismissed. Existing managerial and technical ability and experience can be used just as effectively in a public-controlled as in a private-controlled business, and probably more so. There would be no change in the administrative and technical personnel of an industry taken over by the State, unless of course the executives refused to co-operate or proved inefficient. In such cases it would be necessary to appoint new members to the general staff of a concern, to replace its displaced members, or to supplement the work of those who remain. Socialism can only be effected through the active co-operation of the working force of industry. This does not, of course, include the pure financier, who, while he controls in the ultimate sense, takes no direct part in the organization and management of productive processes. The function of the pure financier must be taken over by public agencies. Even here, however, it should be noted, there are posts for the financial specialists provided they are prepared to render their services henceforth to the State, and not for their private gain.

One of the "dangers" of socialization which will certainly be raised, is the assertion that it will open wide the doors to political corruption and jobbery. That there is a germ of truth in this is a reflection not on socialism but on our present political and economic systems. There is no gainsaying that the possibility will continue for some time; but corruption is usually connected with the securing of privileges which are a source of private profits. If the possibilities of large-scale profit-making are removed, the incentive to corruption will be greatly diminished.[33] In addition, however, the technique of socialized administration which has been proposed here is deliberately designed to keep industrial management as far from unwarranted political influence as possible, by the provision of "cushions" between Parliament and the actual conduct of industry, in the form of non-political appointments and the independent supervisory commissions outlined above.[34]

An equal danger, which is not likely to receive the same de-

[33]See Lincoln Steffens' *Autobiography* for an interesting exposition of this point.
[34]See H. A. Innis, *Problems of Staple Production in Canada*, for a discussion of actual experience in Commission control in Canada.

gree of publicity, is that the State is likely to be offered bankrupt concerns for socialization. In Canada we have had plenty of experience of governments having taken over collapsing concerns, such as the Abitibi Canyon, in order to save their owners from ruin. Once it became known that the State was acquiring businesses on a large scale, there would be a rush of near-bankrupts to Ottawa trying to dispose of their undertakings at a profitable price. It is essential that the State beware of taking over "dead-horse" industries, with which it may easily be swamped. Some may of course have to be accepted in order to save the distressed working population until it has been re-absorbed into productive industry, or on some other ground of social importance of which the cost is clearly˙ and explicitly recognized, but there is no room for national acquisition simply in order to save investments for influential people.

Finally, we must not forget the most common of all the objections raised against a socializing plan—that enterprise will disappear from the land when the profit-motive is abandoned. But to this submission the whole of the present book is the proper answer. We have surveyed not only the "achievements" of the profit-motive, but also the ineffectiveness of negative regulation to curb its anti-social results. The stabler but more equitable development of a socialized economy is the only logical solution.

CHAPTER XI.

ADMINISTRATION IN A SOCIALIZED STATE.

A. THE REORGANIZATION OF DEPARTMENTAL ADMINISTRATION.

OBVIOUSLY, the establishment of planning machinery and the socialization of a large part of industry would necessitate considerable changes in the organs of government administration. But much of this reórganization could be built up from the existing framework. Certain important functions of administration which are already carried out by government departments such as the Department of Labour, the Department of the Interior, and the Department of Trade and Commerce, could undoubtedly be handed over to the relevant commissions. This would make possible a simpler and more effective distribution of duties, especially of those which apply to one branch of economic activity but are now divided between a commission and a government department. A case in point is the Board of Railway Commissioners, the Department of Railways and Canals, and the various departments dealing with modes of transport and communication. A comprehensive Department of Transport and Communications is needed to replace the latter, with a National Transportation Commission and a National Communications Commission, taking over the supervisory work of these particular fields of industry.

Certain other functions of government departments apply in common to many industries. The various provincial Departments of Labour, for instance, are concerned with the maintenance of standards of working conditions. Their work therefore covers a multitude of industries. Such specialized yet universal functions can be most effectively carried out directly by one co-ordinating department with, of course, the co-operation of Commissions concerned.

General surveillance over the various commissions rests with the government departments. The Cabinet, acting as the administrative organ of Parliament, is of course finally responsible for the approval and enforcement of the National Plan and must, therefore, be in a position to intervene if necessary. But the regulations applicable to particular industries which are necessary for the realization or maintenance of the Plan will normally be the province of the commissioners. The trustees in their turn will direct the actual operations of their plants, offices and factories.

The reconstruction of the economic system calls for considerable reorganization of government departments and corresponding changes in their spheres of operation. The present departments are the product of a growth which has not always been consistent: they were called into being by the need for further administration and, in part, as concessions to political necessity. From time to time, they or their branches have been changed, withdrawn or enlarged. A National Plan involves a fundamental realignment to meet the administrative neccessities of a planned economy and an economic system from which private enterprise and the profit-motive are largely eliminated.

An outline of the probable framework of government departments, with a brief suggestion of their responsibilities and spheres of operation is given below. It is not possible in practice to separate departments concerned with economic policy completely from those concerned with other aspects of government. For example, the Departments of External Affairs and of Trade and Commerce may both be concerned with trade treaties, or the Department of Communications and Transport and the Department of Justice may both be interested in a legal issue. But a broad separation is suggested here as a convenient indication of the division of responsibilities among ministers.

General Departments.

The Minister of External Affairs, responsible for foreign and imperial affairs, and all relations of Canada with other states and international bodies such as the League of Nations, the International Labour Office and the Permanent Court of International Justice.

The Minister of Justice, combining with his present responsibilities those of the present Secretary of State.

The Minister of Public Welfare, responsible for the general supervision of health service in all branches, including education in standards of health, state medicine, investigation and control of foods and patent medicines, housing standards, child welfare, and the health aspects generally of industrial working conditions and a national minimum standard of living.

The Minister of National Defence, (to be a much less important portfolio than at present), with his present responsibilities.

Economic Departments.

The Minister of Finance, with his present responsibilities and, in addition, responsibility for (but not detailed administration of) the Central Bank, the Investment Board, the National Insurance Corporation, the Department of the Auditor-General, the Department of the Controller of the Treasury, Customs and Excise, and all Internal Revenue Departments.

The Minister of Communications and Transport, administering the present branches of the Minister of Marine, of Railways and Canals, and, in addition, telegraphs, telephones, and all forms of radio-broadcasting. Thus, the national transportation system under a public commission, the Canadian Radio Broadcasting Commission controlling every kind of radio communication, and similar independent, semi-autonomous corporations, would be publicly controlled as to major policy, but not as to detailed administration, by the Minister of Communications and Transport. It is through this Minister that these bodies would secure their appropriations for capital expenditure; it is to this Minister that they report; and it is this Minister who would be responsible in Parliament for any legislation affecting independent corporations providing transportation or communication services.

The Minister of Industry and Power would be the head of the department concerned with manufacturing, and would also administer national power and fuel resources so far as they were under federal jurisdiction. His control would be primarily concerned with production. He would license new industries, or deprive obsolete industries of their licenses. He would also control most of those matters which now come under the Department of Public Works. *The Minister of Agriculture* would have the same responsibilities as at present, but with such changes as would follow a reallotment of power between the Dominion and the provinces, and the *Minister of Primary Production* would be concerned with the development of the mineral, forest, fishing, and fur resources of the Dominion, so far as these matters came within the federal power. These departments similarly would be primarily concerned with production.

The Minister of Trade and Commerce, whose department would include the responsibilities, divided between domestic and overseas trade, of the present Department of this name, would administer in addition all legislation affecting trading establishments and companies in the distributing field which were still under private enterprise. State distributive services and the Internal Trade Commission would also be responsible through the Minister to Parliament.

The Minister of Labour and Immigration would combine the present responsibilities of the Departments of Labour and of Immigration, and would be concerned generally with all questions affecting labour in the Dominion, including national minimum wages and conditions of labour, industrial representation, social insurance, and negotiations and arbitration between workers and the state management.

Clearly, departmental Ministers under this reorganization will have extensive responsibilities, since their jurisdiction will extend over a wider range of matters than is the case with Ministers today. But their burden will in practice be greatly lightened through the delegation of responsibility to the various regulatory Commissions, and by the appointment of Parliamentary Secretaries, drawn from the House of Commons. In such circumstances, a Minister will be able to devote himself to a general supervision of his department, without squandering time on routine or details. Greater co-ordination and a clearer direction can be achieved in administration than is the case today.

This is further assisted by the "division of labour" in the Cabinet which has previously been outlined. The *inner cabinet,* concerned with major policy and the plans for economic development, will be in touch with the work of all the departments of government, but not as specific Ministers. The *departmental Ministers* will be concerned, as at present, with particular fields of supervision, and it is through their departments that ultimate responsibility to the Cabinet and to Parliament for the formulation and administration of the National Plan will be maintained.

B. The Recruitment of Personnel.

In a sense the problem of planning is the problem of personnel.

> "For forms of government, let fools contest,
> Whate'er is best administered is best".

Administration in any modern government, or in any large corporation, is already complicated and difficult. In a government administering a planned and socialized economy, the problem of administration, especially in the transition stages, is necessarily still greater. Officials of the highest capacity and experience will be required if the increased burden which will rest upon government departments, the commissions, the state corporations, and all the other machinery of directing not only the present services but the essential economic functions of the country is to be efficiently carried.[1]

Types of Public Servants.

Under the present as well as under future forms of government, there are three broad classes of public servants to be considered, whose appointments must be made to ensure that the quality of administration is high. There is (a) the large class of civil servants employed in government departments. The total number of "enumerated" Dominion Civil Service employees is about 44,000 if all grades from that of deputy minister to janitor are included. In addition, there is a large group in the non-enumerated classes of employees, including rural postmasters, casual labour and minor office positions.[2]

There is (b) the group of chairmen and commissioners, trustees, and other directors of public commissions or corporations, such as the trustees of the Canadian National Railways, the Board of Railway Commissioners, the Board of Grain Commissioners, the Tariff Commission, the Farm Loan Board, the Radio Broadcasting Commission, the Board of Pension Commissioners, the various Harbour Commissions, and the numerous other similar operating or regulating bodies vested with large powers by legislation.

In the provinces and, indeed, in the municipalities, there is a large number of similar officials. Under a planned economy, with a gradual supersession of private enterprise, the number of public servants of this grade will necessarily increase.

(c) A third class already exists, and has grown rapidly in numbers since the war. That class is composed of employees of public corporations, who are responsible to but not administered by departments of the government. Of this group at the present

---

[1]"The quality of public administration cannot be better than the quality of the public administrators." Alexander Brady, *Canadian Problems*, p. 43.

[2]See *Proceedings of the Select Special Committee of the House of Commons on Civil Service and Civil Service Act.* 1932.

time, the largest section is the employees of the government-owned Canadian National Railways.

Each of these groups of public servants presents particular problems of appointment, remuneration, discipline, promotion, dismissal, and superannuation. But owing to the melon-cutting conception of government held by Canadians, and particularly by Canadian politicians, one common problem runs through all these groups: the problem of patronage. Job-seeking has long been a game played by politicians, and it is all too common for Canadians, particularly in the eastern provinces, to look to their elected representatives to use their influence in the government to secure remunerative positions for themselves, their sons, daughters or friends.

The Problem of Patronage.

From time to time there have been public outbursts against political patronage, both in appointments and in government contracts; and, especially in the federal government, through the establishment of a Civil Service Commission in 1918 by the Union Government, there has been some improvement. But the evil still persists and is the most serious problem affecting administration in some services of the federal government (e.g., postmasterships), and in most of the provinces and city governments. Indeed, it may be said of some provincial governments that public positions are primarily rewards for party services. In some city governments, the offices are subject to the influence of fraternal organizations with a political character, and efficiency and merit are subordinate to quite extraneous considerations. Even in securing employment with a contractor completing a government work, political patronage creeps in. Applicants for pick-and-shovel jobs have been compelled in more than one city to pay a subscription and join the local organization of the party in power.

It is no exaggeration, therefore, to say that there is not a province in the Dominion which could not save thousands, and perhaps millions of dollars a year, if the civil services were staffed and administered purely on a merit and efficiency basis. This is, in some measure, also true of both federal and municipal administrations.

The evils of patronage are too clear to need much discussion. Political appointments, in the first place, restrict the area of selection from the whole people to one party. They subordinate experience, ability and character to party considerations. They threaten the integrity of the service and weaken the sense of security and fair dealing of those already in the employment of the state. They tend to enlarge departments and services beyond neccessity, thereby reducing the efficiency of the personnel and increasing the cost to the community. They create within the service a privileged class, deriving their privileges not from loyal service or even capacity, but from the irrelevant fact of friendship with some politician or service to the party.

Under no system of government can political patronage lead to the highest efficiency in administration and it is clear that throughout all public services, whether under the existing or a reconstructed society, the problem of personnel must be faced and solved. Throughout municipal, provincial, federal or corporate public services the principles should be, in the words of Dr. W. J. Roche, former chairman of the Civil Service Commission, "first, that every citizen shall have the right to compete for positions in the service of his country; and second, that the 'best shall serve the state'."[3]

The problem of securing the right men—or women—is patently of crucial importance. Without the most competent officials, adequately trained, thoroughly experienced, and imbued with a sense of service to the new state, a planned economy can hardly succeed. The test of planning lies in its administration, and effective administration depends upon administrators. More particularly, however, this relates to senior executive and administrative positions. These appointments include deputy heads of government departments, commissioners, trustees, chairmen or directors of state trusts, members of the Planning Commission, the Import and Export Boards, the Central Bank, the National Investment Board, and all other similar boards.

Have we in Canada men and women capable of undertaking these responsibilities? In the early days, Canada had to borrow many of her skilled administrators from other more advanced countries such as Great Britain and the United States, where they had received the requisite training.[4] Such borrowing may still be necessary in some cases, but today we have already at our disposal many able men experienced in the type of work required as a result of their activities upon existing commissions or in government departments. A great many more

---

[3]*Evidence before Select Special Committee of the House of Commons on Civil Service and Civil Service Act*, 1932, p. 4.
[4]For example, Van Horne of the C.P.R.

are at present in private business of all kinds. Some are also on university and college staffs. Ready to be trained for responsible posts, there are undoubtedly also the best of our university graduates of post-war years, some of them in unsatisfactory work, some in the United States, some without employment at all.

Today our problem is not to conjure a whole new administrative personnel out of the air, but to build better with what we have. It will be necessary to use some of those who are already engaged in public administration in new roles and to pick the rest from elsewhere. The main problem is how these administrators are to be found and appointed.

Methods of Appointment: an Appointments Commissioner.

At the present time, although the legal procedure for the appointment of deputy ministers, members of commissions, and other senior public servants is that of an order-in-council, appointments are in practice largely made by the Prime Minister. But the Prime Minister is not in the happiest position for making the wisest appointments. He is subject to pressure of every kind, both from within and from without his cabinet; he is compelled of necessity to consider the sectional and racial antipathies and prejudices of the Canadian people, and burdened at the same time with an infinity of other and perhaps more compelling questions; and he knows, for the most part, only those in Canada with whom his professional or party associations have given him contact.

The responsibility for major appointments must, of course, continue to rest with the Cabinet and in a large measure with the Prime Minister. But some assistance in the forms of impartial and skilled investigation and advice from an independent and competent authority is also necessary.

There should be appointed by the Cabinet, therefore, a permanent official with the status and independence of a justice of the Supreme Court who will be charged with the responsibility for advising, on the basis of investigation and personal contact, the appointment of senior officials. The present legal procedure and responsibility will rest, as at present, with the Cabinet, but there will be, at the service of the Prime Minister and the Cabinet, the advice of a Commissioner of Appointments concerned only with finding the best man. Being in effect a Civil

Service Commissioner for senior appointments, he would work in close relation with the existing Civil Service Commission, but without being bound in any way to give preference to an applicant already in the Service if the qualifications he sought were not met.

In drawing up these qualifications, two kinds of knowledge would be necessary: knowledge of the responsibilities involved in the office to be filled, and knowledge of the capacities and experience of the persons under consideration for the appointment. To provide himself with this essential knowledge, the Commissioner of Appointments would consult the department or state corporation or commission concerned, and fully acquaint himself with the duties to be performed in the vacant office. In seeking men to perform those duties, he would, if it were desirable, consult professional or other bodies from which candidates could be drawn, such as, for example, the Canadian Mining and Metallurgical Institute, or the Association of Chartered Accountants, or such other associations as might tender useful advice in relation to the vacant office.

The Commissioner of Appointments must have the power to make recommendations to the Cabinet in all senior appointments. Such recommendations would be made public, but it would not be obligatory upon the cabinet to accept them. Both from the point of view of the Cabinet and of the Commissioner, what is desired is the widest canvass of possible appointees and the most useful advice.

It is also important that such appointments should be kept as independent of political considerations as possible. It is fatal to the efficient maintenance of administrative services to have them arbitrarily disrupted as the result of an irrelevant election "swing-over". The history of public services in almost any province, to say nothing of recent events in Ontario, makes it very clear that everything possible should be done to keep the administrative personnel independent of the succession of parties in power. Complete insulation is not necessarily the ideal, as in the last resort political action, carrying as it does a threat of house-cleaning, may be a necessary stimulus to efficiency, or an essential way of meeting sabotage. This will only be true, however, as long as the tests applied are those of efficiency in the application of accepted policy, and not party patriotism, spite, or demagogic advertising.

In addition to the safeguard provided by the existence of a Commissioner of Appointments, a further safeguard might be applied in the case of such semi-independent organizations as commissions. These bodies would be themselves required to co-operate with the Commissioner of Appointments in making out a panel of names[5] from which the Prime Minister could make his selection. If he were not prepared to appoint anyone whose name appeared in the panel this would be referred back to the commission and the Appointments Commissioner (at each reference the reasons for the action being made public) until agreement is reached.

An example will illustrate the method of securing, and recommending to the cabinet, candidates for senior public office: a chairman or manager of the Bureau of Costing and Accounting would be recommended and appointed by the following procedure. First, the post would be publicly advertised, secondly, the Commissioner of Appointments would consult an *ad hoc* committee consisting of the Minister of Industry, an officer of the Association of Chartered Accountants, and perhaps the Minister of Finance or his Deputy. The senior executives of the Bureau would co-operate with the Commissioner in making out a panel of names. This would then come before the Cabinet through the Prime Minister, and the appointment would be made by order-in-council.

The appointment, when finally made, would thus be recommended by an *ad hoc* body, changing with the type of appointment to be made, understanding in much larger measure than under the present procedure both the duties of the office to be filled and the personnel available to fill it.

In the selection of the operating personnel of State Trusts, the responsibility for the appointment of the rank and file would devolve entirely upon the trustees, just as the power of appointment of subordinates lies in the hands of the executive in any private business. Skilled personnel departments would be built up to assist in this work, however, and the co-operation of the relevant trade unions enlisted. The trustees themselves would be selected by the supervising commission in co-operation with the Commissioner of Appointments. In this way appointments, would be kept as clear as possible of political entanglements,

---

[5]Compare the proposals in the *Report* of the Royal Commission to Inquire into Railways and Transportation in Canada, 1931-32, p. 64: "Vacancies among the Trustees shall be filled from a panel of eight named by the remaining trustees."

C. THE WORKING OF THE PRICE SYSTEM.

We have now outlined the kind of planning which we believe to be required. In this chapter we have concerned ourselves hitherto with the question of political administration. It may help to make the general position clearer if, before proceeding to the specific topics of the later chapters, we indicate generally the place of the price system in a socialized economy.

Prices as an Index to Action.

The price system in its widest sense—the determination of profits, prices and costs—is in practice a vital element in economic administration. What would happen in a socialized economy? The answer is that the price mechanism would be maintained intact but the framework within which prices and the play of "demand and supply" operated would be different. The regulation of production and consumption in accordance with price-levels is valuable and desirable, firstly, as a simple accounting device and, secondly, because it leaves freedom of choice to the consumer.

The alternative to the system of buying and selling for a price would be some system of rationing, by which every consumer was alloted so much of each possible kind of commodity or service, and each industry alloted so many machines, so many raw materials, and specific quantities of labour, capital, and land. The relationship of one industry to another, and of industry to the consumer, would in this case necessarily become the subject of dictation by some central authority. Individual freedom of action would be endangered, while a useful accounting method would be jettisoned. Rationing is necessary in an emergency, but as a day-to-day method of administration it would render the task of planning cumbersome to the point of impossibility.

In the socialized system, therefore, individual concerns, whether public or private, will continue to buy the productive resources they use at a market price settled as far as possible by the play of supply and demand.[6] They will purchase machinery, buildings and raw materials from the industries at the

---

[6] See G Cassel, *A Theory of Social Economy,* and two articles by H. D Dickinson: *Economic Journal,* (June, 1933) "Price Formation in a Socialist Community" and (March, 1934) "Problems of a Socialist Economy: a Rejoinder". The increasingly important cases in which ordinary supply and demand fail to establish a determinate price are dealt with above.

market price, and in turn sell their products to the highest bidder. Subject to the necessities of the national plan and the supervision of the commissions, they will be left free to make their own transactions as they see fit, buying when the prospects of production justify the expenditure; accepting offers that cover costs of production, or, in cases of excessive demand, those that promise the highest return; and rejecting those that do not seem worth while.

In ensuring freedom of choice for the consumer the price system is especially valuable. Consumers, of course, are not always good judges of their own interests, and they are often gullible, but it is also true that the modern market gives them little chance. When social essentials, such as sanitation and education, are more generally available, when deliberate attempts to mislead and bully the buyer are abandoned and, most important of all, when incomes are approximately equal, consumers will probably get the greatest satisfaction if they are allowed to give free rein to their own tastes and preferences, purchasing what they please. In the socialist state, Mr. Brown and Miss Jones will go downtown to spend the salaries they receive for their work in the National Railroad System or the Hydro-Electric Commission on such products of the Co-operative Bakers, or the Dominion Textile Trust, as they wish. The National Plan will be worked out with detailed reference to consumption trends (as expressed in purchases) and the prices at which sales can be effected. Consumers' demand price will remain the final arbiter of industrial activity, but industry will far more than today be concerned to study our desires and respond to them.[7]

All this assumes the possibility of prices being determined on the basis of some clear objective standard. This standard, so far as it at present exists, is that of "competitive equilibrium". When a multitude of small sellers are dealing with a multitude of small buyers, all in effective competition with each other, the price of the goods with which they are concerned tends to settle at a level at which the amount offered for sale on the market is just equal to the amount which people are ready to buy. The productive resources of the community are so distributed that no one could benefit himself by altering their application. This is the ideal economic balance of "perfect competition".

---

[7]Advertising could then be used to educate tastes, not to switch or buldgeon them for private profit.

Price Determination in Practice.

Such market conditions, as we have abundantly seen, are in practice never even approximately realized: and the trend of industrial technique and business structure is carrying us ever farther from them. Prices become less and less effective as an objective guide to the appropriate organization of the country's resources. Few goods to-day are uniform and standardized, few are sold in free and open competition: variations in quality or specification, advertising or other methods of high pressure salesmanship, are as important as price changes in establishing such balance as there is. The present inequality of incomes means that prices register not needs but money demands. And even the rich consumer is not always the first consideration. The individual business man in his decision as to prices, quality and sales expenditure, has to consider the effects not only on the consumer but also upon his rival's policies. Under such circumstances, economic balance can hardly be expected. When the price of goods or services is the subject of bargaining between monopolies or semi-monopolies—an employers' association and a trade union, or a chain store and a milling company—there is likely to be no price which will secure balance of demand and supply but merely an upper and a lower limit beyond which it cannot go. If there is monopoly on one side and competition on the other, a price which will "adjust" supply and demand can be fixed but the balance will be so onesided as to be intolerable and useless as a test of economic welfare. When successive products are handled by a single firm, it is very difficult to set a price on them at each stage, unless indeed there are other firms working under comparable conditions and selling their goods on an open market which can be used to set a standard. Where two or more products are derived from the same source (as in the meat packing industry) or where there are heavy overhead costs, it becomes impossible to distinguish the exact cost of each separate product: if production in this case is at all monopolistic, discrimination in charges can be and commonly is practiced.

There is, then, nothing absolute or "natural" about present market prices. They represent in a high proportion of cases a balance of bargaining power,[8] the upshot of a strike or lockout, the power of monopoly, the forced acceptance of a weak economic position, not a balance of social cost and gain. They

[8] See Zeuthen: *Economic Warfare.*

become the subject of administrative decision (as in the case of the price attributed by a large steel trust to the coal which it produced and uses in its smelters, or the case of the traffic of a railway company) or else the subject of conscious and deliberate agreement. The idea of an automatic market adjustment free from bungling human intervention is very far from reality. Prices are necessarily "artificial", and registers of the economic system as a whole.

Here therefore is another reason why economic control should be in the hands of a national authority responsible to the public and aware of the effects of its decisions on different sections of the economy. The control of prices amounts to deliberate arbitration between different groups in the community as to how much of the national income they are to receive. Such power cannot be left to the hazards of unequal bargaining or to the discretion of private sectional interests.[9]

It is important, however, that the scarce productive resources of the community should be "economized", i.e., distributed to the best advantage. They must not be applied in trivial uses at the expense of more urgent needs. A uniform price on similar goods just sufficient to limit demand to the amount available will prevent this.[10] Price then becomes the measure of scarcity and the measure of the social cost involved in applying resources in one particular use, at the expense of possible alternative uses. Sale "at cost" will mean sale at a price which just measures the sacrifice of alternative opportunities of applying resources productively.

Prices and National Accounting.

On such bases prices can be assessed in the social accounts for all productive resources—land, labour, capital, organizing ability. These can be distributed to their appropriate uses, demand can be fitted to supply, and economic order secured with comparatively little cumbersome intervention.

The reduction of profit-incomes is quite consistent with the retention of "profits" in the sense of surpluses over expenses of costs. For sheer mechanical convenience in accountancy profit reckoning and the allotment of resources according to comparative returns will be maintained in socialized industry, ex-

9See an article touching on this by V. W. Bladen in *Commerce Club Journal*, (Univ. of Toronto), 1934.

10Providing that the price charged for a commodity or service must not be less than that for which it could be obtained elsewhere.

cept that there will be no watered stock, no hidden reserves, etc., and more equitable wage rates. The efficiency of a concern and the need for its service will be tested on a profit and loss basis. Generally speaking, enterprises which yield a large profit will be pushed, and those which involve a loss will be eliminated. Labour and investment will be applied where earnings are highest. Industry will be carried on in accordance with a rigorous examination of returns.

Of course, this mechanical profit and loss accounting will have to be severely checked by the application of other tests which reflect considerations that cannot adequately be expressed in monetary terms.[11] Social or "non-economic" considerations, besides certain inherent defects in profit-accounting, will make it necessary in some cases to promote "non-paying" but socially desirable undertakings. It is important that decisions to adopt such measures should be made in full recognition of the economic costs involved, which must be weighed against the expected benefit. The use of social profit and loss accounting will ensure this.

The "Nationalization" of Profits.

This proposal to maintain the price-profit system as an instrument of economic organization must be distinguished sharply from the present practice of leaving the determination of personal incomes to the play of the same forces. Interest on capital and rent on land should be maintained in socialized production as a necessary accounting device,[12] but they will no longer accrue to private individuals as income. And the same applies to the profits of state corporations and co-operative concerns. The grosser aspects of personal profit-making and of inequalities of unearned income from interest and rent must and will disappear with the disappearance of large-scale private ownership of productive plants. Again there will be exceptions. In some cases the earnings of small operators will accrue to them in the form of a margin between the price realized from the

---

11See J. M. Keynes, "National Self-Sufficiency", in *New Statesman and Nation*, July 15, 1933: "The Nineteenth Century carried to extravagant lengths the criterion of what one can call for short the financial results, as a test of the advisability of any course of action sponsored by private or collective action. The whole conduct of life was made into a sort of parody of an accountant's nightmare. . . . The minds of this generation are still so beclouded by bogus calculation that they distrust conclusions which should be obvious, out of a reliance on a system of financial accounting which casts doubts on whether such an operation (slum clearance for example) will "pay". We have to remain poor because it will not "pay" to be rich. We have to live in hovels, not because we cannot build palaces, but because we cannot "afford" them. . . . The same rule of destructive financial calculation governs every walk in life."

12The land and capital and businesses which still remain in private hands during the period of transition and (in some quantity) thereafter, will, of course, yield a private income.

sale of produce and outlay in production: farmers and small retailers are the most important examples. In such cases, however, the productive property is being directly used by the owner: profits, rent and interest of this type are on a very different footing from the profits, rents and dividends of large concerns employing thousands of hands.

Apart from such exceptions, all the personnel of industry will work for salaries, up to and including the Trustees and the Commissioners. All the profits derived from the completely socialized concerns, over and above the cost of production,[13] become automatically a part of the revenue of the State (whether represented by the Dominion, provincial or municipal authorities) as owner of the property. This revenue will be subject to a special tax for the support of the non-productive government departments, as is the case with the returns to industry to-day. The remainder will be the source of social savings, either being "ploughed back" directly into the business or applied to new lines of investment, according to the decision of the National Investment Board. If there is still a surplus, after the capital needs of industry have been adequately met and government requirements satisfied, this will be available to reduce personal taxation and to augment the incomes paid out to all Canadians in the form of salaries, insurance benefits, and greater leisure. The general standard of living will be raised accordingly. In co-operative concerns, and those still in private hands, but subject to the control of a Commission, the surplus profits of the industry will be pooled and applied in transfers to the National Exchequer, capital extensions or increased salaries, as the National Plan demands.

The broad result is clear. There will be an end to the accumulation of property in individual hands and to great personal profits whether derived from productive operations, or from mere shrewdness, bargaining power, or luck in buying and selling. With the progressive disappearance of large-scale private property and private profits as more and more industries are socialized,[14] the chief sources of unequal wealth will disappear, and the foundations of economic equality will be solidly laid as personal incomes become simply a matter of earnings, plus social insurance benefits.

---

[13]Including agreed salaries and social insurance contributions.
[14]Together with the operation of inheritance taxation.

This does not mean a rigid uniformity in salaries. The fantastic extremes of divergence between the income of the manual worker or farmer, and the big business executive will be done away with, but a limited differentiation may quite equitably be retained whether as a stimulus or a recognition of efficiency and contribution. Since the income of every Canadian will depend on the size of the national dividend, and therefore to some extent on the efficiency of each, the whole system implies a sort of national bonus scheme. A more direct and individual type of bonus payment (or a modified piece-wage system) might also be applied if it were regarded as useful and acceptable in particular industries.

Whatever the minor modifications, the two main fundamental objectives would be attained. Income would be obtainable only by productive effort (except in the case of children, the aged or infirm) and not by ownership alone, or speculation, or financial manipulation. Further, economic power would be vested not in the hands of a small group of wealthy property owners, exerting willy-nilly an ulterior control over our economic and political activities, distorting social habits and values, and making democratic government a fiction; but in the hands of the agents of the public endowed with recognized functional authority and, in the last analysis, subject to democratic control.

Chapter XII.

MONEY, BANKING AND INVESTMENT.

A. Money and the Banks.

In the modern economy those who control and direct to-day's financial system can dictate the type, the volume and the methods of to-morrow's production. This power is far too great to be left in the hands of private interests, not only because in the past it has operated in such a manner as to aggravate the instabilities of the present economic order, but also because the greatest degree of socialization of ordinary industry would be ineffective unless accompanied by the socialization of finance. "Finance" of course must be interpreted not merely as meaning the monetary system of Canada: it involves the entire field of capital investment as well. The inter-dependence between industry on the one hand and credit institutions on the other is patent. This will be as true of a planned and socialized economic order as of capitalist society. The co-ordination of industrial activities to be brought about through the direction of short-term and long-term credit in accordance with the National Plan would be a vital feature of the socialist state; and this necessitates the extension of state control to all financial agencies—the Central Bank, the chartered banks, insurance companies, agricultural credit, and other mortgage institutions.

There is no connection, however, between the proposals put forward in this chapter, and the suggestions with which a bewildered world is bombarded by the advocates of "social credit" and even more esoteric monetary schemes. The subject of money is necessarily complex, and it can be made mysterious. As such, it lends itself to the treatment of cranks and demagogues. The unfortunate result of this has been the emergence of numerous doctrines designed to show that all the pathological results of capitalism—unemployment, business depressions, shrinking trade, war, etc.—would disappear, if only more money were available. It has been a comparatively easy task for such crusaders to divert the search for economic sanity into these byways of "easy money". Anxious to provide the victims of the depression with a scapegoat, the monetary cranks have nominated the banker for the position. By means of over-simplification or fallacious analysis of the nature of our economic system, they assert that the cause of our difficulties lies in the contraction of credit, or in the debt-creating system, or in the "gold racket" or whatnot—with all of which it is easy to identify the banker. But it is even easier to ignore the other faults in the economy of which financial maladministration is only part.

The continued currency of these vaguenesses and misunderstandings, however, makes it necessary to undertake some explanation of the actual working of the monetary system before outlining proposals for its socialized reorganization.

The Functions of Money.

The modern economic system, whether based on socialist or capitalist principles, is essentially one of wide subdivision of labour. This makes possible a greater volume of production, but it means that production is carried on for sale in a market, instead of for personal consumption. The primary use of money is as a medium of exchange, making possible instead of barter the buying and selling which goes on in an exchange economy. It is with money that producers purchase goods, buy capital equipment, hire labour and so forth; and it is in the form of money that the various recipients of income derive their command over consumable goods and services.

Society made a great leap forward when, in the course of centuries of growth and evolution, it came to use gold and silver and other metals as money. But in the course of the last two centuries still further advantages were derived from the use of paper currency and other credit instruments in substitution for metallic money.

Now whether money is issued in the form of coins or of credit, it has come to be recognized from experience that any increase in the volume of money which is out of all proportion to the available stream of purchasable goods and services causes prices to rise and dislocates business. Governments have accordingly sought in various ways to place limits on the supplies of money. The power of issuing money gradually came to be considered too important a matter to be left to private institutions. In the course of the 19th century the right to issue paper currency reverted to governments, or to the central banks which were the creatures of government. (Canada was until only recently one of the rare examples of a country which permitted private banks to issues banknotes.) The issue of legal tender currency was made dependent upon a reserve of gold. The most intelligent justification for the "gold standard" system lay in the fact that, while it was in operation, the values of the currencies in all countries were linked together. This was, of course, an essential requirement in a free international system of trade and finance in which the obstructive effects of political boundaries were largely minimized. It may be observed, in passing, that the breakdown of the international gold standard in the last five or six years is largely symptomatic of the disappearance of those remnants of economic internationalism which survived the rise of economic imperialism and the Great War.

Just as gold coins have long since ceased to circulate in national trade, so has paper currency ceased to act as the principal medium of exchange. Bank-deposits drawn on by cheques and bills of exchange have taken their place. Perhaps 95 per cent. of the monetary transactions which take place daily in Canada are completed by the transfer of bank deposits. The figure of "bank deposits withdrawable on demand" represents therefore a sort of reservoir of money which is used to circulate goods from producer to consumer, and to pay for the use of labour and resources of all kinds.

To-day it is the changes in the size of this reservoir, rather than changes in the amount of coins and notes, which have the most important consequences on the state of business activity and on the economic welfare of society. Alterations in the volume of purchasing power in a country, in the absence of compensatory influences, give rise to a change in the general level of commodity prices, or in the rate of interest and the amount of borrowing and new capital expenditure, or in the external value of the country's currency—or a combination of all of them. In particular, a contraction in the quantity of money may, by deflating commodity prices, produce a state of economic dislocation; and a sharp increase in the volume of purchasing power will produce the equally drastic state of economic dislocation of somewhat different character, which we associate with "inflation". Between these two extremes there are a number of intermediate positions, varying with the monetary policy pursued at the time. This does not mean that changes in the state of business depend *only* upon monetary policy. All that we are saying is that given any particular set of economic conditions (some of them beyond immediate control, such as depressed export markets) there is, in theory, a monetary policy appropriate to that particular case. The question arises, therefore, what guarantee have we that that monetary policy will be pursued?

Banks and the Creation of Credit.

As we have seen already the quantity of money in Canada corresponds, to all intents and purposes, to the volume of bank deposits withdrawable or transferable on demand. Whatever monetary policy is appropriate to a given set of economic conditions, it must operate by controlling the size of this reservoir of bank deposits. This raises the vexed question as to the genesis of bank deposits. As is often the case in controversies of this kind, the reactionary tendency is to deny outright that banks ever create deposits. The monetary crank, on the other hand, presses the argument too far in the other direction, by asserting that banks alone can, and do, determine the volume of deposit-currency.

By and large, our Canadian bankers display what might be called a branch-bank mentality. As branch bankers they learned that whatever money came into their branch came in from the outside. Thus they concluded that the Great Outside was the Source of Money. The idea that what came in from outside was almost entirely determined by how liberal their fellow bankers were in their loaning and investing policies has apparently been too great a leap of the imagination for them.

A typical statement by a Canadian banker may be enlightening. Speaking before the Winnipeg Board of Trade in March, 1933, the General Manager of the Bank of Montreal said: "It is a matter of importance to the banks and to the country at large that deposits should be maintained, for it is upon notice or savings deposits that banks depend for funds to lend to borrowers for the legitimate additional requirements of their business. This obvious relationship would not be admitted by those whose minds work in reverse only and who contend that instead of growing out of deposits, loans really create deposits".

Not only do Canadian bankers claim that they have little or no control over the volume of deposits and loans; they further disclaim any responsibility for using whatever general influence they may possess. In his prepared evidence before the House of Commons Committee on Banking and Commerce in 1928, the president of the Canadian Bankers Association explained: "The banker is primarily and mainly concerned about the safety of his advances. . . . He is not thinking about the volume of credit in the country nor the effect which the granting or withholding of credit in the particular instance will have upon the price level of commodities in the country". The same view was put forward by the banks in the briefs presented by them to the Macmillan Commission in 1933.

In general, we feel inclined to believe that these admissions of ignorance, incapacity or irresponsibility are made in good faith, although there is a large and growing section of opinion which believes that they are pure bluff. The confusion arises simply from a historical change in the way in which the public chooses to carry on its business.

In the old days, when the majority of transactions were made with metal coins issued by the government, it was clearly true to say that the banks of a country could only lend out the coins which members of the public happened to be able to spare and to deposit with them. That is, the total volume of deposits determined the ability of the banks to lend and invest. Since this used to be true some half century ago it is still, of course, the accepted conservative theory. But today the facts have changed. Very nearly all "money" is in the form of a credit "on deposit" at the bank, and only a small proportion of money remains out in circulation as notes and coins. Very nearly all business is carried on by means of cheques, transferring "money" by book entry from one deposit to another.

In view of this it is obviously true to say that the changing, variable factors are in the volume of loans and investments made by the banks; and the volume of deposits is the result of banking policy in these spheres. This argument runs counter to the conservative theory which envisages banks as passive intermediaries between savers (depositors) and borrowers. It is admitted by practically no leading Canadian banker. But fortunately for the validity of our analysis, this relationship is now recognized by every modern monetary expert, and was attested by the *Canadian Macmillan Report* of 1933. It follows logically that if the volume of money depends mainly on the lending policies of the banks, great responsibility for the economic welfare of society is thrust upon them. It was because it was felt that private institutions were not equal to such responsibilities that the Macmillan Commission proposed the introduction of new monetary controls.

Acting upon the suggestions made in this *Report*, the Dominion Government established the Bank of Canada in 1934, endowing it with all the customary powers of a central bank. It will therefore be useful at this point to indicate what can be expected of a central bank. This will be, in effect, to point out the extent to which this new piece of economic machinery, (essential to a socialist as well as to a capitalist society), must inevitably fail, by itself, to cope with the major causes of economic instability.

B. THE POWERS AND LIMITS OF CENTRAL BANK CONTROL.

A central bank is an instrument for increasing or contracting the cash base of the country. Within limits it may lend currency (or central bank deposits) to the chartered banks directly, or it may increase their cash reserves indirectly by the purchase of securities. By either of these devices,—"rediscounting" or "open market policy",—it may put the banks in a position to lend larger sums to the public, at lower rates of interest. Alternately it may reverse these processes and produce a contraction of credit and a raising of interest rates. Ideally the policy of the central bank at any given time will be determined by its judgment as to the existence of economic maladjustment, always assuming that such troubles are of the type which can be corrected by monetary policy.

Naturally, if the monetary and banking system is itself defective—which it will be if it is not sufficiently independent of political pressure—far less that this ideal can be hoped from it. In Canada it is not hard to find examples of operations which have in fact worsened rather than remedied the economic situation. The *Macmillan Report* itself points out that during the prosperity period the "re-discount" rate charged by the Treasury Board in making advances to the banks was not used as a device for controlling credit. The rates were "mainly varied to meet the exigencies of the Dominion Government's finances". That is, they were held at too low a level. The *Report* also pointed out that these loans made by the Treasury Board to the banks "were not subject to the restriction of a gold reserve. The Treasury Board did not assume the responsibility of ensuring that the uses made of the Finance Act were consistent with the requirements of a convertible currency. The banks, on the other hand, which could take the initiative of expanding the credit base through advances of Dominion notes under the Finance Act, were under no obligation to use this initiative in maintaining the gold standard". There is, in these and other paragraphs of the *Report,* a strong suggestion of the kind frequently entertained these days that there was an organic connection between the expansion of bank loans and the development of unsound "boom" conditions, a situation which, so we are assured, might have been prevented by central bank policy. The *Macmillan Report* seems to infer that, despite the appearance of storm signals (deterioration in Canada's balance of international payments, gold outflow, exchange depreciation, excessive "re-discounting" on the part of the banks, etc.) neither the Treasury Board nor the banks attempted to make for harbour.

Undoubtedly an all-wise, strong, and independent central bank might at that time (1928-9) have so restricted the size of the cash basis as to induce the banks to lend less and thereby contract prices somewhat. Such a development, especially if coupled with an increase in interest rates in the early period *might* have prevented certain of those examples of business expansion (e.g. in transportation or the newsprint industry) which proved subsequently to be extravagant and wasteful. It is possible, too, that such a policy *might* have checked the speculative fever of the stock markets which gave rise to the investment excesses of the period. Had these restricting influences been brought to bear, the depression would not have been prevented, since Canada is necessarily affected by the existence of grave economic crises in her chief markets for commodities and capital. But if the economic expansion had been reasonably well-balanced, and based upon cautious anticipations of world markets, the slump would have been to that extent less severe. We can admit, therefore, the possibility of such action by a central bank. Whether it would happen in practice, however, depends on certain conditions which we shall examine.

Two examples may be cited to demonstrate how essential it is for some impartial authority (that is, one which is independent of the chartered banks and of any other minority-interest) to exercise control over the behaviour of money in Canada. Both of them are factors which have obstructed the forces of "recovery" during the last five or six years.

The Control of Exchange Rates.

The first of these defects concerns the instability of the Canadian dollar on the foreign exchanges. During 1926-28 Canada was formally on the gold standard. Unfortunately for the argument of those who would have us return to that state of blessedness, the monetary foundations of that system were (as the *Macmillan Report* agreed) somewhat precarious. The first whiff of economic grapeshot sent the Canadian currency toppling from its perch.

The legal provisions making for the convertibility of the currency into gold (which convertibility would have maintained the dollar at par) became a dead letter as early as 1929, although their formal burial was not completed until 1932. Since early in 1929, then, the foreign value of the Canadian dollar has been subject to a series of uncontrolled fluctuations both in terms of sterling and the U.S. dollar, and has depreciated from its gold-standard rate. Now the real question at issue is not whether that depreciation was preventable or not. In the circumstances it was an unavoidable accompaniment of the decline in exports and the diminution in the flow of foreign capital on which the economy had tended to lean. In addition, a depreciated dollar was probably the most satisfactory method of insulating the depressed areas of Canada from the worst effects of a world price deflation. The real question was the absence of any adequate mechanism for considered control. For depreciation of the gold rate of the dollar is not inconsistent with the maintenance of a stable dollar on the foreign exchanges, i.e., in terms of other important currencies. But until quite recently there was no authority in Canada capable of exerting its influence to depress the foreign exchange rate to whatever level was most consistent with internal stability of commodity prices, and likewise no authority capable of stabilizing the dollar at that position. The banks were themselves unwilling to assume such responsibility, and hostile to the proposals for setting up a Central Bank which could. The result was that the foreign value of the dollar fluctuated with the changing winds of economic and political speculation, to the disadvantage of Canada's many-sided international economic relations. Canada enjoyed neither the relief which would have been provided by a deliberately depressed exchange rate,[1] nor the advantages of comparative currency stability.

---

[1] Australia, situated in a like position, profited considerably from the operations of a system of exchange-control in the earlier years of the depression. See *D. B. Copland, Australia in the World Crisis* 1929-1933, Chap. 5. Depreciation of the exchange value of the Canadian dollar means that a larger amount of Canadian currency would be obtained in exchange for a given amount of foreign currency. If, therefore, a fall in the Liverpool price of wheat happened to be accompanied by a rise in the value of the pound sterling the reduction in the English price would be compensated, so far as the Canadian shipper is concerned, by the fact that the English pound would be converted into a larger amount of Canadian currency. The net effect would be to maintain the price of wheat in *Canada*. See Innis & Plumptre, *The Canadian Economy and its Problems*, p. 165, ff.

Now it is sometimes argued that the establishment of the Bank of Canada has removed the possibility of any repetition of this situation of economic impotence. Nothing could be farther from the truth. However adequate the machinery for controlling the exchange rate, the essential question is: will it be used in the best interests of the country? The apostles of the doctrine of a "controlled capitalism" labour under the delusion that decisions calling for the intervention of the State (or the Central Bank) can and will be made by experts independently of government pressure. In answer to this it must be said that there is nothing in the history of the exchange problem of the last six years to show that any policy can be discovered *which will not be prejudicial to some interests.* The idea of depressing the exchange rate in order to help maintain the domestic price of export commodities is perfectly feasible. The purpose of such a policy is, in effect, to shift a small part of the burden of shrinking markets on to other classes in the community. It happens, however, that other classes have not shown any anxiety to carry part of the load. Financial groups have consistently deprecated any proposals to depreciate the Canadian dollar. They have felt (rightly or wrongly) that their interests would ultimately be jeopardized by such measures. The government itself has been unfavourable to the idea mainly because it would mean an increase in the cost of servicing the debt which is held abroad. Exchange depreciation, of course, would mean that the government would be forced to increase its tax-collections, an unattractive prospect for its supporters. We can see, therefore, that whether the Central Bank in the future adopts a foreign exchange policy which is favourable to the primary producers or otherwise, will depend on the government in power, and upon the particular economic interests most prominent in its counsels. There is no guarantee that the decisions of such a government will always coincide with the views of an "impartial" Governor of the Bank of Canada as to the national interests.

Banking Practices in Boom and Depression.

The second defect which results from leaving the regulation of the monetary mechanism largely in the hands of the private banks is a more general one. More often than not, the practices of the banking system, as long as it remains a group of private unco-ordinated and non-responsible institutions, operate in direct opposition to the proper objective, which should be to maintain a relatively stable level of prices, and a relatively balanced state of economic development. When prices are rising and business is temporarily booming the chartered banks, infected with the same heady optimism which pervades the business world generally, extend credit freely. The effect is to aggravate the basic mal-adjustments which are being produced. Conversely, after the bubble is pricked and prices are falling, the commercial banks tend to call in their loans with unwarrantable speed. The effect of this is to decrease the volume of purchasing power and in-crease the trend towards deflation and industrial stagnation. From the commercial banking point of view, governed as it is by the criteria of profits, liquidity, and the avoidance of risk, this is the natural reaction. But it may go so far as to produce a secondary recession of business.

The tendency is amply illustrated by the operations of the commercial banks over the last four or five years. The most conspicuous feature of these operations has been a marked shrinkage in assets, particularly marked in the case of commer-cial loans and discounts.[2] It is undeniable that the openly pro-fessed desire on the part of the banks for increased liquidity has been achieved by calling in commercial loans or by refraining from new lending or discounting. No doubt the banks could de-fend this policy on the ground that every such action has been justified by the subsequent fall in wholesale prices, business profits and collateral values, and therefore especially prudent from a commercial banking point of view. What the banks do not recognize is that each was being forced to contract its lend-ing operations because each of the others was doing likewise, and that the subsequent fall in wholesale prices, business profits and collateral values was partly the result of the banks' own action. This is part of the explanation of the severe deflation of the last four years, for which the fault lies in the banking sys-tem as a whole.[3] Canada has paid too high a price for the liquidity of its banking system.

This is not to argue that the prime causes of the deflation and depression are to be found in the banking system alone. The principal cause is, of course, the shrinkage of export markets. It remains true, however, that the banking system is responsible for giving a secondary impetus to the initial deflation, thereby increasing the severity of depression and unemployment.

[2] In direct contrast to the situation in Great Britain, where an "expansionist" monetary policy has been pursued since 1931.
[3] The liquid assets of the banks, in proportion to their total public liabilities, rose from 32 to 41 per cent. during the period.

But this question of the shrinkage in the volume of bank loans cannot be considered separately from the question of interest rates. Short-term interest rates have been maintained by the commercial banks until very recently at pre-depression levels. The effect of this policy has been to aggravate the existing situation. Borrowers, who had found no difficulty in paying six or seven per cent. when prices and profits were higher, found that interest charges could not be met out of their lowered earnings, and were forced to reduce their borrowings and curtail their business operations, thereby contributing to further depression and unemployment. And since bank rates in Canada dominate the whole interest rate structure to an unusual degree, the maintenance of high interest rates on the part of the banks has tended to keep all other rates high. This has effectively smothered any prospect of a revival of investment or expansion of industrial activity, and maintained the burden of debtor groups to an intolerable degree.

These examples are enough to suggest that a central bank might have prevented some at least of the extreme consequences of the deflation and depression in Canada. By a policy of credit restriction in the pre-depression period, it might have prevented some of the excesses of the boom. By freely exercising its powers of re-discounting during the depression it might have supplied the commercial banks with sufficient cash to satisfy their desire for liquidity without any unnecessary and rapid reduction of loans. By a policy of exchange rate control it might have mitigated the severity of the price-deflation of 1930-33 in a manner which gave assistance where it could be most fruitful, i.e., in the export industries. Lastly, an aggressive policy designed to reduce interest rates might have eased the burden of the debtor classes (particularly farmers), made possible a reduction in the cost of government debt, and stimulated some measure of activity in the construction industries,—possibly in housing.

However, we should be careful not to exaggerate the powers of monetary control, nor should we underestimate the obstacles that have to be surmounted before a central bank can choose the most appropriate policy. Certain conditions must first be fulfilled.

In the first place, the mechanism at the disposal of the central bank must be appropriate to its tasks. It is to be doubted (though there is no space to develop the point here) whether its present resources are adequate for the purpose under the existing constitution of the Bank of Canada, and whether the type of control effective in (say) England is going to be of much use in a debtor country.[4] More important still it is necessary for the Bank to be independent of government pressure. In a capitalist society, in which the government is the instrument through which group pressures are exerted, it is highly unlikely that this condition will be fulfilled. The lesson of Canadian history is that government-appointed commissions are apt to be influenced by the governments which appoint them. Where sectional or group interests conflict, that policy is followed which is favourable to the interests served by the government in power. And those interests in the past have been often very far from the interests of the country as a whole. There is therefore every reason to be dubious as to the power of a central bank *alone*, to prevent or mitigate economic slumps.

Let us assume that we had such a bank in Canada in 1928-29. What would it have felt called upon to do? Export prices were high, capital—domestic and foreign—was plentiful. Business was prosperous. What was there to tell the Bank that the price of wheat was unreal and impermanent, that the influx of capital which was accelerating the speed of our economic development was about to cease, that the stock market boom was speculative and unsound, that new capital was going into equipment to make more pulp and paper, more automobiles, more electric power, more textiles than our economic system could distribute profitably? We have not yet attempted to develop either our statistical resources or the idea of economic equilibrium to the point where they are used as actual guides to policy. And it takes a very special brand of credulity to believe that a Central Bank, unsupported by other institutions of national planning, could have successfully backed its opinion against that of the whole capitalist world. A Central Bank by itself is no panacea for the mistakes of capitalism or for the resolution of its conflicting interests into one common effective policy.

A Central Bank and a Planned Economy.

If the principles of social planning are applied to the rest of the economy (including the chartered banks), however, the key position of the central bank in regard to credit and currency would be greatly enhanced. Its function would be to determine

---

4The Commonwealth Bank of Australia has pursued a policy of monetary control with reasonable success. Relatively, however, its powers are stronger, and certain other economic conditions are more favourable.

precisely what volume of credit and currency was needed in the country and also to exercise control over the foreign exchange rate. Perhaps the term "Central Bank" is misleading; for the institution which we have in mind does not closely resemble the central banks at present operating in other countries. It would not be an advisory or persuasive body which, through certain manipulations of interest and discount rates and of the volume of its security purchases, tried to influence the more or less irresponsible policies of competing, profit-seeking and often recalcitrant commercial banks. Rather it would simply be the "head office" of the unified Canadian banking system.

Several important changes in the constitution of the present Central Bank would be required before this could be possible. In the first place, the entire control of the Bank would have to be vested in the government, represented by the governor of the Bank. It would be necessary, therefore, to replace the existing privately-owned capital by public funds, or in some other way to deprive private individuals and interests of their power to appoint directors, etc.[5] It would also be necessary to revoke those clauses of the Bank of Canada Act which subordinate the monetary policy of the country to the exigencies of the defunct international gold standard. The principal of national autonomy in currency matters must be preserved by Canada. If, as we propose elsewhere, industrial and monetary policies are to be determined in accordance with the requirements of a national plan, we should not surrender ourselves in advance to the possible adverse influences of British or American monetary policy. An attempt to maintain the present gold-reserve and gold-convertibility requirements of the currency at all times, would have precisely this effect. These requirements, (while not operative at the moment) must be removed. They are out of line with intelligent monetary policy even in a capitalist world.

This change would mean, in effect, that while the Bank of Canada would keep currency reserves available to meet any temporarily adverse balances in Canada's international accounts, it could keep them, in part, in the form of U.S. or sterling funds, without any intention of declaring (by implication) that the standard for Canada is either gold, sterling, or U.S. funds. The

---

[5]The capital of the Bank of Canada, standing at 5 millions, is at present all privately held. The present directors were elected entirely from a slate put forward by the Canadian Chamber of Commerce, essentially a private minority group. It is an ironical reflection on this system of appointment to a public authority that the Chamber of Commerce saw fit— at a time when public interest demanded lower interest rates—to propose as its first choice a man who represents largely the insurance and financial interests of Canada.

maintenance of any one of these standards might, in certain unexpected circumstances, prove too onerous a task.

C. MONETARY POLICY IN THE PLANNED STATE.

Stability in the Purchasing Power of Money.

It is now possible to indicate, in broad outline, what should be the objectives of monetary policy in a socially-planned state, bearing in mind that the success of such a policy will depend equally upon the efficiency of the planning agencies in the industrial, agricultural, foreign trade and other sectors of the economy.

First of all, monetary policy should be directed toward the maintenance of an approximately stable level of prices, or in other words, an approximately stable purchasing power of the dollar, so far as monetary policy can attain this end. It is impossible to achieve either an economically just or an economically stable society unless there is an assurance that the purchasing power of money is not subject to great changes, whether over short or long periods. We do not claim that the achievement of a stable price level alone will eliminate depressions. It is nevertheless true that economic instability and waste will never be eliminated as long as price levels show violent fluctuations. It is worth emphasizing that stability in the purchasing power of money is absolutely essential to the achievement of economic justice or stability in any society, socialist or capitalist. As long as people receive incomes measured in money they must be certain that their money will be worth as much when they spend it as when they earn it. While individuals and businesses contract to make payments covering interest and rent payments, as at present, or old age and sickness allowances and payments from one public body to another, as in a socialist state—there is the same need for a stable or "honest" dollar.

If this objective be accepted, it follows that the banking system should seek to maintain a stable proportion between the purchasing power of the community and the volume of goods produced and services rendered within the community. This implies that the volume of bank loans should be expanded or contracted in accord with the following principles.

First: If a part of the income of the community has been set aside as savings and is not being invested (i.e., spent by a borrower) the result will be a decrease in the volume of purchasing power, which will depress prices unless it is balanced by an in-

crease elsewhere, and vice versa. It will be the business of the
monetary and banking system to correct this deficiency.

Second: If there is an unused capacity for production in the
form of idle equipment, stocks of material or labour, the effect
of an increase in purchasing power, providing it is confined to
these outlets, will be to stimulate production rather than to raise
prices. The volume of bank credit would therefore be expanded
in such directions whenever such a condition of widespread excess capacity and unemployment existed, as at present.[6] Such a
qualitative control of purchasing power can only be operated, of
course, under a planned and socialized economy. It is incapable
of any effective use in a privately operated and competitive one.

Third: If the total volume of goods and services is increasing
it will be necessary to increase the volume of purchasing power,
and vice versa. The volume of bank loans would therefore be increased or decreased according to increases or decreases in the
volume of goods produced and services rendered.

The regulation of bank loans in accord with these principles
would be a necessary feature of a sound monetary policy in any
economic order.[7] But the institutions involved in the process
would be different in the socialized state. Short-term savings
would come chiefly from the temporary surpluses of socialized or
co-operative industries rather than from individuals, and loans
would be made to other socialized industries, co-operatives, or
social service agencies. But the same balance would have to be
maintained in order to achieve stability.

Exchanges and Internal Prices.

An equally desirable objective of currency policy is the maintenance of the Canadian dollar at a stable value in terms of foreign currencies. It is obvious that these two objectives, stable
prices and a stable dollar, may at times be incompatible. If the
general level of prices in other countries were rapidly rising or
falling, it would be impossible to maintain both a stable purchasing power of the Canadian dollar and a stable rate of exchange
with other currencies of unstable purchasing power.

There is room for an honest difference of opinion as to which
is the better policy in any particular instance; whether it is pre-
ferable to keep the level of prices stable and let exchange rates
fluctuate, or to keep exchange rates stable and let the price level

[6]See Chapter XIII, "Taxation and Fiscal Policy".

[7]With this difference, that the attainment of this objective is possible and reasonably
probable in a socialist economy, but largely impossible within the framework of capitalism.

fluctuate. We favour the view that the balance of advantage will usually be on the side of a stable internal price level. Especially is this true on occasions of violent deflation abroad such as has occurred during the last six years. In such circumstances, a conscious policy of controlled exchange depreciation would be a desirable method of minimizing the effects in Canada of this deflation elsewhere. But such a policy is not inconsistent with the avoidance of wide fluctuations in exchange rates over short periods. Frequent fluctuations from day to day should be avoided and long period changes introduced in an orderly way.

This policy of foreign exchange control would, of course, be exercised by the Central Bank. In this Bank all foreign exchange transactions would be centralized and co-ordinated. This would clearly bring the Central Bank into close relationship with the Import and Export Boards. To facilitate unity of action, there would be interlocking between the directorates of these Boards and the Central Bank.[8] The results would be that the Bank would have a very full measure of control over the Canadian exchange rate; for it would be both the chief buyer and the chief seller of Canadian money in exchange for foreign currency. To it would be sold all the foreign exchange which was obtained by the Export Board in return for Canadian exports, and also all foreign money which came into the banks from tourists and other sources. From it the Import Board would have to get its supplies of foreign money to pay for Canadian imports; and from it, too, the banks would have to obtain foreign money for their customers. The Central Bank would, of course, be in continuous and direct communication with the money markets of New York and London.

On the other hand, the general problem of controlling the volume of credit in existence would bring the Central Bank directly into contact with the Board of National Investment, with the Dominion Department of Finance and with the National Planning Commission. In this whole field the Bank should be able to exercise a strong measure of influence. For it would have the final voice in restricting the ever-present demands of individuals and public corporations, all of them competing for as large a share as possible of what, relative to needs, are the scarce physical and human resources of society.[9]

8Also, of course, between the Central Bank, the Board of the nationalized banking system, and the Board of National Investment (see below).
9At any particular time, only a part of the funds of these bodies—and when the Central Bank feared that inflationary tendencies were developing, none of them—would come from credit newly created by the banking system under the guidance of the Central Bank, as is suggested below.

The Chartered Banks and Social Planning.

One of the limitations of the Central Bank under present arrangements, is that it deals almost entirely with the chartered banks. It does not lend directly to industry, agriculture or commerce. Its methods of control are more remote; it attempts to influence the lending policies of banks by varying the quantity of cash reserves at their disposal. Whether it is successful or not in its objectives depends upon what the banks (and their clients) choose to do with such cash.

It is the business of chartered banks to advance money for working-capital purposes to industry and commerce. To a considerable extent, these banks can be considered as the custodians of a revolving fund of purchasing power which is continually being lent out to business men, and repaid. The total volume of bank loans depends upon the bankers' decisions as to the probability of speedy repayment, the value of the collateral offered, and other such considerations, as well as on the cash reserves in their possession.

We are now in a position to explain why the best intentions of a state-controlled central bank may be defeated by circumstances over which it exercises no control. In the first place, it often happens that the banks find themselves unable to increase their loans, although capable of doing so, because of the unwillingness of producers to borrow. If economic conditions generally are so dislocated that the opportunities for profitable enterprise are narrowed, the volume of loans (and therefore of deposits) may fall off. The Central Bank, in other words, may fill the chartered banks with cash but it cannot always cause them to increase their loans. The "reflationist" policies of President Roosevelt have foundered on this rock. To create the necessary condition of economic harmony requires a recasting of economic resources, incomes, etc., which capitalist society cannot do. A socialized banking system, however, could promote the ends of a national economic plan by virtue of its power to grant, restrict or withhold working capital. The banks occupy such a strategic position for control purposes that no planning authority could neglect to use them for that purpose.

In the second place, monetary control of the kind exercised by a central bank does not extend to the *types* of investment. The Bank of Canada may (within the limits referred to above) influence the volume of loans but it cannot determine the direction which lending takes. But it is important to the balanced development of an economy to see that new purchasing power flows into the correct channels. Is there any likelihood that it will, so long as we continue to leave the provision of most of the short-period credit (and a good deal of the long-term investment besides) to private institutions?

Before answering this question, it is as well to make clear how the chartered banks operate today. Their operations are regulated, of course, by a Bank Act enacted by the federal government, from whom they derive their charters. Perhaps because of this regulation the Canadian banks have been free from the sort of defect which plunged the whole American banking system into panic in 1933. Canadian banks have kept clear of the worst type of speculative loan (e.g., real estate). No bank failure has taken place in Canada since the Home Bank closed in 1924. Nothing comparable to the disclosures made with respect to the investment activities of the big banks in the United States has emerged in Canada. At the same time, the competition between the banks would seem to guarantee reasonably fair and competitive treatment to all comers.

In general, then,—and certainly from any superficial point of view—the chartered banks present a picture of a stable, well ordered set of institutions; a tower of strength in time of trouble, as they not infrequently remind us. There is no doubt that a defective banking system enormously aggravates the inherent instability of the capitalist system; and Canada has been spared that complication. (It is impossible to say the same of our investment institutions and syndicates).

Most of the current criticism of the chartered banks is picayune stuff. It might equally be applied to any large scale corporation. There is no reason why we should expect one private institution more than another to subordinate its interests to those of the public at large. Thus, if the provision of agricultural credit is inadequate (as it clearly is) it is senseless to expect the banks to remedy it. If they do not lend already, the reason is that such loans are not liquid, or not profitable. The duty of the banker to his shareholders is to avoid endangering the liquidity of his assets and to make profits. If no institution can be found willing to grant credit of the type and on the terms suitable to farmers or fishermen or any other group, the simple reason is that it doesn't pay. There are plenty of services which do not get done under capitalism (health, housing, etc.) because they "don't pay". Credit facilities will be provided for them only if separate state-assisted arrangements are made to subsidize such services, or if the state takes over responsibility for the banking system and grants credit in those directions which are desirable but not "paying", at the expense of those functions which, however well they pay, are less desirable from a social point of view. Under a public banking system it is perfectly possible to finance depressed regions or industries or re-housing plans, etc., by curtailing the financing of luxury trades, stock market speculation and the rest. But it will not be done voluntarily by private profit-making institutions—nor is there any reason why we should expect it.

The public frequently objects to the high cost of banking facilities (interest rates, commissions, etc.) but, clearly, banks are not the sole target of public criticism on this account. As in other fields, however, banking costs could be reduced—and the economies passed on to their clients—if certain forms of competition were avoided. There has, of course, been a great competitive duplication of branch banks, even though hundreds of them have been closed since the depression. This represents a form of waste for which the public ultimately pays. There is also a good deal of duplication in the ten head-office staffs. Though in itself this is not a primary reason for the socialization of banking, there is room for considerable economy of operation in a nationalized and unified system.

What of the question of bank profits? The profits of Canadian banks are obtained largely out of the difference between what the banks earn from their loans and investments and what they pay to their depositors in interest, plus expenses for salaries, buildings, etc. The profits from bank stock, while ample, are not excessive if we compare them with other industries,—say tobacco. The great profits received by bank directors are not made from investments in bank stock, nor from directors' fees. They are derived rather from industrial undertakings, and are frequently enhanced by the fact that such directors may be able to use their influence to get the banks to support business "deals" and to lend to projects which they hope to be profitable to themselves.

The Macmillian Commission recognized the possibility of this situation when it recommended that "directors should not vote or be present at meetings of their boards, when credits to themselves or any firm or corporation of which they are partners or directors are under consideration." If this recommendation were carried out it might often be hard to get a quorum. It is interesting to know that there are people in the world who still have such faith in capitalist integrity as to imagine, for example, that the directorate of the Royal Bank of Canada would more easily refuse to lend money to the Montreal Light, Heat and Power Consolidated provided Sir Herbert Holt (who is the chairman of both institutions) stayed away from the meeting. Less simple minds will not be so reassured.

Now at this point we have discovered the signal weakness in the banking system. In Canada, as elsewhere, there has been consummated what we might call,—after its chief American exponent,—a morganatic marriage between industry and finance. The directors of banks are, in the majority of cases, closely identified with the control of the dominant industrial, commercial, and financial institutions of Canada, all of which necessarily look to the banks for accommodation.[10] To expect any "impartial" and competitive distribution of bank credit in these circumstances would be altogether too naive. A few Canadian banks are believed to be relatively free from this type of influence. In the majority of cases, however, this combination of financial and industrial control has meant that very frequently bank credit has been made available to private interests for uses which did not warrant it. In other words, the Canadian banking system has been deprived of the supposed safeguards and self-adjusting mechanisms of a genuinely competitive economy. The result may be seen in the frequency with which unsound and unbalanced economic developments take place, and in the unnecessary instability of Canadian industrial development. To conform to the requirements of a competitive economy it would be necessary for bank directors to sever all their connections with other companies (trust, mortgage, insurance companies, and all transportation, utility, and industrial corporations, etc.) or be replaced by a group of independent economic advisors who could quite easily perform the relatively light "advisory" functions of the existing directorates. There is, of course, no likelihood of the directors making this act of self-abnegation. Nor can we expect the Central Bank to restrict or control the detailed operations of chartered banks.

A Socialized Banking System.

To apply the method of economic planning to Canada, there is nothing for it, therefore, but to socialize the banking system—

10See Chapter III, section b.

to make it publicly owned and operated. The Canadian chartered banks, when so nationalized, would in many respects stay remarkably unchanged. In general, the same executive staff would
perform the same sort of jobs for the same sort of salaries—
except insofar as they felt called upon to resign their position
rather than to attempt to serve their country instead of their
present employers. But nationalization does not mean that the
direction of banks shall pass into the hands of elected politicians:
this must be emphasized because the propagandists of reaction
in Canada have done their level best to becloud this issue.

Nationalization of the banking system would be achieved, as
in other cases of the kind, by the purchase of the existing stock
at a fair valuation by the Dominion Government or (what
amounts to practically the same thing) by the exchange of bonds,
bearing a rate of return varying with the profits of the system
and the national income of the country, for the existing stock.
The next step would be the appointment of a single board of
directors to take the place of the ten boards which now exist.[11]

The work of the unified system built from the chartered
banks would be quite similar to the work they now carry on.
The branches would make loans and accept deposits. The cheque
system would be maintained to facilitate transfers of money. As
at present, care and judgment would have to be exercised not
to make extravagant loans in one direction, at the expense of
more worthy activities. And in these matters the experience of
the existing personnel of the banking system would be essential
and invaluable.

The difference between the present and the nationalized system is that the power of the banks to lend or to withhold credit
will be consciously used as an instrument of national policy.
While the local managers and district inspectors might, as at
present, discriminate between individual concerns (public or
private) the banking system as a whole will discriminate between
areas and industries in conformity with the national plan. Thus,
if it were felt that mixed farming should be encouraged in certain localities—possibly at the expense of the newsprint industry—the banking system would act accordingly.

It would continue, of course, to make an interest charge to all
borrowing concerns so as to ration the competing demands for
credits. It is fairly certain, however, that existing rates of in-

---

[11]Should this system of "compensation" perpetuate any existing gross inequality of
income it would be left to the taxing authorities to provde for it. The power which such
ownership would yield would not, as now, be out of all proportion to the amount of capital-
stock involved.

terest are unnecessarily high. There seems no reason, for example, why interest should be paid upon deposits at present. There is considerable scope for economy of operation in a nationalized and unified banking system which does not labour under the hallucination that its deposits would all disappear, presumably into thin air, if the payment of interest on them were reduced or abolished. It is certainly undesirable in times of depression to encourage people or institutions to accumulate large idle balances in the form of saving deposits. Nor can we foresee much likelihood of circumstances arising under a socially planned economy in which it would be desirable to pay interest upon deposits. The abolition of deposit-interest might cause some people to keep more money in the form of cash and less on deposit. But the great convenience and safety of deposits subject to cheque would militate strongly against such a movement.[12]

On the other hand, there is no reason to view with alarm the possibility that depositors might demand currency in exchange for deposits. There seems no reason, once the banking system were unified and nationalized, why the public should not hold its money in the form of Bank of Canada notes rather than deposits if it preferred to do so. This would merely involve the exchange of a "deposit" liability for a "note" liability on the part of the banking system. But the freedom of individuals to buy foreign exchange, especially for speculative purposes, or to "transfer" their deposits abroad, would have to be severely curtailed.

Notwithstanding the possibilities of economies of operation and greater independence of direction, however, it is worthy of final emphasis that a unified and socialized banking system would be useless taken by itself. Unless they are part of a general scheme of economic planning the banks might as well be left alone. So long as the means of production generally remain in private hands a government-owned banking system would merely provide one more battleground for the struggles of private, acquisitive interests. One group of borrowers might, through governmental pressure, gain accommodation at the expense of another; and there is every reason to suppose that such privileges would go, as now, to those minority groups who need them least. The essential reason for expecting social advantage from a nationalized banking system lies in the uses to which it could be turned in the field of economic planning.

[12]None of the above paragraph need apply to small depositors with balances of, say, under $1,000. A specific scheme for small savers, on something like the same lines as the British Post Office Savings Accounts, could easily be maintained by a nationalized banking system.

D. THE CONTROL OF INVESTMENT.

The commonest defence of the rich is that they invest their money instead of spending it, and so make the world still richer in capital equipment, and provide employment for the poor. The facts are, however, that a good deal of investment under present arrangements is entirely wasted or misapplied, so that the country is not necessarily enriched. Meanwhile, we may agree that investment is necessary. No society can afford to spend the whole of its income on consumable goods. If it is growing in population, or if it wishes to raise the general standard of living, it must divert part of its resources into the provision of new capital goods, and maintain or replace those instruments of production which wear out or become obsolete. There is need, therefore, for "investment" in this sense. The question is how this business can best be managed in the general interest.

The legitimate function of investment institutions is the mobilization of the savings of individuals and corporate bodies so as to make them available for permanent investment. The progress of the national economy depends on an adequate flow of investment for the development of new industries and the expansion of plant and equipment already established in industries, including agriculture.

Present Institutions for the Mobilization of Savings.

The most usual form of business organization today is the joint stock company or corporation. The development of new industries and expansion of capital equipment is accomplished by the formation of these companies and the sale of their securities to the public. The stock exchange and bond dealers throughout the country are the channels through which these securities are sold. The purchasers consist of banks, insurance companies, corporations and the general public. There are at present about a dozen stock exchanges throughout Canada, but those in Montreal and Toronto predominate. There is no open market for the sale of bonds. The bond dealers, of whom there are over one hundred in Canada, buy on their own account and sell directly to the public. They are thus interested parties in every transaction.[13] It is through the bond market that Canadian governments, federal, provincial and municipal, have borrowed money in the past, although one provincial government (Ontario) has recently found

[13]In general, it is true to say that there has been infinitely more "racketeering" in bonds than in stocks,—although this may come as a surprise to some readers.

itself compelled to sell bonds direct to the public (and, incidentally has been able to do so,—although how directly we are not sure.)

By and large, the most important institutions concerned with new investment are the life insurance companies. The regular collection of premiums from a large number of policyholders results in a steady flow of funds and these savings are placed into investment on a large scale. Other institutions instrumental in the raising of money for investment are the mortgage, trust, and loan companies. These companies are inclined to specialize in loans on real estate, although investing smaller amounts in other types of securities. They secure their funds from the sale of debentures to the public, the management of estates, and by receiving savings deposits.

In addition to investment in or through such corporations, there is a large amount of individual investment in private enterprises. And, finally, an even more significant volume of saving is undertaken through the re-investment of corporation profits.

It is of importance to note in passing that perhaps the greater part of current investment is already undertaken by public bodies or by corporations which by the proposals in this book will become publicly-owned. For the inference is that there need be no fear that any drive towards a greater equality of incomes will materially reduce the amount of investment.

The Objectives of an Investment Policy.

As in the case of monetary and banking policy, it is possible to outline the social principles which should guide investment. It is desirable that there should be adequate guarantees that the savings to be invested are not unduly diverted to the pockets of promoters. It is also desirable that the transfer of funds be accomplished at the lowest possible cost. Furthermore, it is of utmost importance that there should be no prepondance of influence of any industrial or financial group such as would result in the undue diversion of capital into particular channels of investment. The institutions which collect and distribute the savings of the community should be completely free from such pressure so as to enable an impartial and independent selection among alternative opportunities for investment. Only in this way can there be any guarantee that the self-regulating mechanism of competitive pricing is free to operate.[14]

14Cf. Chapter XI, section c.

Looking at the problem from the production side, it is necessary to preserve a balance between the output of consumption goods, and the portion of income which is spent on consumption on the one hand, and between the production of capital goods (buildings, plant, machinery, etc.) and the amount of income which is saved, on the other.   Any distortion in these balances will produce business depression and economic waste.

The Deficiencies of the Present System.

If we examine the actual operation of present investment institutions, we reach the conclusion that none of these conditions are adequately fulfilled.   The financing of new capital construction through the medium of stock and bond issues, assisted by an army of socially useless functionaries, has been a most fruitful source of instability, speculation and waste in Canadian economic life.   The raising of capital in boom periods has been far too easy and profitable for any careful selection of investments, and too one-sided a process for the adequate protection of the investor.[15]   Many of the stock and bond dealers nominally in existence to serve the investing public, are themselves concerned with promoting the enterprises whose securities they sell.   High pressure sales of worthless securities are only one product of this system.   The formation of "investment trusts", a delightful method of selling otherwise unsaleable securities to the public, is another.   It is no exaggeration to say that at present the small investor is certain to get less than a square deal.   In the conflict of interest arising between the many different and powerful financial institutions of the country, "the investor is certain to be the butt of their saw-off agreements."[16]

There is no need, however, to develop this theme.   It is difficult to speak of it in stronger terms than are used in the Report of the Royal Commission on Price Spreads in the section which deals with corporate practices and abuses.

We may also observe that during the last few decades there has been a steady drift toward a common control of industrial, financial and investment institutions.   This concentration of economic power has gone far to nullify our political democracy. Unfortunately for the stability of capitalism, this control is

[15]See papers by J. L. McDougall, H. R. Jackman, and I. M. Biss in *Proceedings of the Canadian Political Science Association*, 1933.   For a recent (English) account of the abuses of company promotion and "high finance", see Thomas Johnson, *Finances and the Nation*.

[16]*Financial Post*, April 5, 1933.

divided between separate groups of powerful individuals—between competing Montreal and Toronto interests for example, as illustrated in the earlier struggles over railways and to-day over hydro-electric power as in the case of Beauharnois.

Partial and divided control of our modern industrial society through finance is worse than no control at all. On the one hand, it deprives the economy of the resiliency and automatic adjustments of a really competitive society. On the other hand, it makes no provision for either quantitative or qualitative control of investment in the interest of a proper functioning of the whole economy. The result is an intensification of the tendency toward excessive and unbalanced capital expansion in boom periods coupled with an inability to make the necessary readjustments when the collapse occurs.[17]

Such violent fluctuations are inevitable as long as this vital function is left to be decided by the varying hopes and fears of individual investors and promoters whose policies are governed by their expectation of private profit. An absolute prerequisite to the full and stable utilization of our resources is the control of the volume and direction of savings and investment, to ensure a balanced expansion of production in relation to the needs and purchasing power of the community. A sound policy must therefore include a qualitative control of investment to avoid, in prosperous periods, feverish competition and the building of duplicate and unnecessary machinery of production and transportation. It must also include a quantitative control of investment to avoid the alternating periods of rapid capital development and absolute slump in construction, typical of the so-called business cycle.

Such an investment policy would imply a large measure of economic planning in place of the present method of uncoordinated industrial development. A sound financial policy cannot be pursued except within the wider framework of a planned economic order, and the most effective method of planning will be through the co-ordination and control of investment.

A National Investment Board.

For the partial and divided control over finance now exercised by private interests there must be substituted a unified control covering the whole field of finance; controlling authorities must be made responsible to the people as a whole. Only thus

---

[17]Thus the practice of overcapitalization and excessive bond issues has burdened industry with a high percentage of fixed charges which cannot be met in a period of decreased income.

can the operations of finance be harnessed to the aims of a planned economy.

The first step to be taken in the reorganization of finance should be the establishment of a National Investment Board, with powers to bring under unified public control the existing institutions which compete for the public's earnings. Ultimately this Board would operate the entire machinery of investment in co-operation with the socialized banking system and the Planning Commission. In the course of arriving at this stage it would be possible to effect great economies in cutting down the excessive duplication of bond, insurance and real estate selling which at present exists. The abilities of the present host of agents could readily be put to other productive uses in a society which was reconstructing its financial and industrial controls.

In the transition period, the Board would be given power to license or veto all new issues of securities and all the forms of borrowing for capital purposes. The Federal government has recently applied this practice to certain provincial governments in Canada, obtaining the right by virtue of its control of the purse-strings. This principle should be extended to cover all private borrowing, including that undertaken for conversion purposes. The remedial measures proposed in the Price Spreads Report involving the establishment of a Dominion Securities Board for the purpose of preventing "stock watering" are, of course, very laudable but quite inadequate for the type of constructive control which is proposed here.

It would be folly to propose the immediate abolition of stock and bond sales as a means of raising capital. But it would be necessary for these methods to be brought under rigid control. All speculation on margin would be stopped[18] and no sale of securities would be permitted except through properly regulated security exchanges, which would come under the control of the Investment Board. In the licensing of all investments the Board would consider the following:

1. The probable effect on employment and prices.

2. The relative merits, from a national viewpoint, of different uses for the available supply of capital, taking particular care to avoid any wastefully competitive duplication of capital equipment.

---

[18]Speculation is of course essential under capitalism if a continuous and competitive market is to exist, in the interests of security-holders themselves.

3. Whether agricultural financing was being jeopardized by too great a flow of capital into industry, or vice versa.

4. Whether promotion costs were excessive.

5. If external borrowings were involved, whether the repayment would be likely to put undue strain on foreign exchange reserves.

It is not likely, however, that existing channels of investment would be greatly used under a socialist regime. The very existence of a socialist State would be inevitably lead to a contraction of private investment. Thus one of the earliest tasks of the Board would be to offset the deflationary tendency which would follow such a move. In co-operation with the central bank it would have to assume responsibility for the financing of an immediate programme of capital development to provide work for the unemployed on socially necessary projects. It would also, of course, be called upon to assist in financing the transfer of key industries from private to social ownership. Additional functions of the Investment Board may be summarized as follows:

1. The Board would formulate a plan for the compulsory conversion of the national debt to a lower rate of interest. Similarly it would engineer a reduction of the heavy burden of debt which at present overwhelms the farmer and many small home owners. The methods followed by Australia (where the constitutional obstacles were just as formidable as in Canada) might provide an excellent model.

2. The Board should extend and co-ordinate the present inadequate machinery for the supplying of intermediate credit to agriculture. The *Macmillan Report* deplored the lack of such facilities but little has been done to repair the omission.

3. The Board would formulate and assist in plans for the nationalization of provincial and (through the provinces) municipal finances. Such plans should include provision for co-operation among the smaller governmental units for the purpose of borrowing through a single agency, to ensure greater stability and lower cost, and a standardization of municipal taxation.

4. Finally, the Board would exercise a strict control over all foreign borrowing of public and private agencies, to keep such borrowings within the limits imposed by Canada's ability to meet the cost of repayment without endangering the stability of the exchanges. Canadian governmental and corporate bodies

have been far too prone in the past to take the short view in borrowing abroad. The present burden of foreign debt is too heavy for a country whose export income (out of which it must be met) is so unstable. In addition to this, the anticipated increase in debt costs arising from any depreciation of the exchange has already cramped our monetary policy and would continue to do so. There would be far greater freedom of action in the sphere of exchange control if only our foreign debts were less burdensome and less inflexible. The Board would attempt to correct both these deficiencies.

The functions of the Board in the transition period would therefore be partly positive and partly regulatory. It is to be expected that private investment would ultimately decline in importance as it is superseded by collective investment, and collective provision for personal security (ill-health, accident, old age, unemployment, etc.) which individual savings provide— or fail to provide—to-day.

The National Investment Board would begin by absorbing a small part of the present investment machinery, sufficient to provide for the collection and disbursement of the savings of the economy. But it should not be too much to hope that the rest of the whole unsavoury structure of modern finance, including stock exchanges, board rooms, stock brokers, investment bankers, promoters, bond salesmen and inflated directorates would eventually disappear forever.

The Board should become the agency for the collection and distribution of all new savings for the development of socialized industries and services. New capital would be obtained from the surplus profits of socialized industries, from taxation, and from such credit expansion as the Central Bank considered desirable to promote stable prices and the full utilization of resources. We could then rest assured that the occasion would never arise for the Investment Board to say, after the habit of capitalist finance. "We have unemployed men, idle machinery, surplus stocks of materials, and unused natural resources, but, stretch our imaginations as we will, we cannot for the life of us think what to do about it!"

It is easy to exaggerate the extent to which we have the resources in Canada for a higher standard of living. It is not to be forgotten that at present much of our capital equipment and natural resources are highly specialized in those industries producing for export. But with the resources we have, funds can be made available to bring about certain highly desirable extensions of production. Not least among the powers of an Investment Board would be the possibility of ensuring that capital was available for the undertaking of all these socially desirable but "non-paying" enterprises,—slum clearance, re-housing, social services, conservation of natural resources and the like—which are so sadly, but inevitably, neglected under the present system.

E. The Futility of "Social Credit".

OUR discussion of the financial system up to this point will have made it clear that we consider financial and monetary reform an essential part of any attempt at socialization, but that we differ from monetary cranks in that we do not regard monetary reform *alone* as a panacea for all our ills. To look upon it as such indicates a narrow concentration of attention upon one single aspect of the present system and a total failure to understand the workings of that system as a whole.

"Social credit" theories, however, have acquired a great popularity in certain parts of Canada. They originate, of course, with Major C. H. Douglas, some of them being even more erroneous simplifications of his opinions; and they appeal strongly to communities in which the burden of debt is so heavy as to make men look hopefully to any system that promises quick alleviation of their sufferings, however unsound and impossible the system may be. In view of this it is advisable to examine more closely the fundamental assumptions of the partisans of "social credit" and the remedies they propose.

The "social credit" diagnosis begins, quite properly, by pointing out that society has already gone a long way towards solving the problem of how to produce an abundance of material goods. It is manifestly absurd that Canada should allow people to remain in idleness year after year, supported by meagre doles drawn from taxation or loans, while so much of our resources and equipment is lying idle. No one will disagree on this point. We can further agree that to attempt to solve the paradox of poverty in the midst of plenty by destroying the plenty—precisely what capitalism is compelled to do—is the height of economic insanity.

People cannot buy the goods produced because they have not sufficient money. Let the government, says the "social credit" catechism, create the money (credit) and—by a series of complicated devices—distribute it to the people as consumers, or as common heirs to the "national heritage". The creation of credit is essentially a social activity. It has become the monopoly of the bankers whose interests may conflict with those of the community at large. Let the people take over the job and "monetize the real wealth of the country" so that enough money is made available to circulate all the goods that the community is capable of producing.

This diagnosis is a mixture of half-truth and over-simplification. We agree that bankers create credit, and that this function should be in the hands of the state. As we have already explained, the contraction of credit at the wrong time may aggravate a depression, but so may the creation of credit at the wrong time (in a boom period) increase our difficulties. This the "social credit" exponents ignore, as also the fact that it is essential that the new credit be directed into the proper channels. They merely impute ulterior motives to the banker, shift the onus of depression entirely upon his shoulders, and readily find in him the personification of evil. Is he not the man who causes money to breed money?

While this sort of argument is common to all monetary prophets, it would be doing Major Douglas an injustice to class him among such crude sectarians as Mr. Aberhart, Mayor McGeer and Father Coughlin. The Douglas scheme puts it all in a more sophisticated and quasi-mathematical fashion, and his proposals are more subtle. That is why they have been favourably received by intelligent people who are impressed by the use of simple algebraical equations in the elucidation of economic theories (such as Professors of English Literature and Deans of the Church of England), while any mass support which the movement may receive is due to the fact that it crystallizes and gives direction to the anti-banker complex common among debtor groups. The latter will care little for Major Douglas' subtleties. Let us, however, turn to the specific details of the theory that require analysis.

The A plus B Theorem.

The fundamental trouble with the present system then, according to Major Douglas, is that the purchasing power available is less than the collective prices of the goods for sale; that there is not enough money to buy what we produce. When baiting the banker, he attributes this to the fact that bankers call in their loans or refuse to make new loans when they should, thus preventing business from "getting ahead". But this is not his only explanation of the shortage. He also maintains that "(1) Wages, salaries and dividends will not purchase the total production. This difficulty is cumulative. (2) The only sources of the purchasing power necessary to make up the difference are loans and export credits."

The supposed proof of these statements is incorporated in the well-known "A plus B Theorem". The following is the most familiar statement of it:

A factory or other productive organization has, besides its economic function as a producer of goods, a financial aspect: it may be regarded on the one hand as a device for the distribution of purchasing-power to individuals through the media of wages, salaries and dividends; and on the other hand as a manufactory of prices, i.e., financial values. From this standpoint its payments may be divided into two groups:

Group A—All payments made to individuals (wages, salaries and dividends).

Group B—All payments made to other organizations (raw materials, bank charges and other external costs).

Now the rate of flow of purchasing power to individuals is represented by A, but since all payments go into prices, the rate of flow of prices cannot be less than A plus B. The product of any factory may be considered as something which the public ought to be able to buy, although in many cases it is an intermediate product of no use to individuals but only to a subsequent manufacture; but since A will not purchase A + B, a proportion of the product at least equivalent to B must be distributed by a form of purchasing-power which is not comprised in the descriptions grouped under A.

Where then does the purchasing-power come from? Major Douglas' reply is that additional purchasing-power is provided by loan credit (bank overdrafts) or export credit, and, he quotes with approval the remarks of a fellow Social Creditor:

"The explanation of this is that in highly developed countries such as ours, practically all purchasing-power commences life as a credit by the banks. These credits are created at the instance of manufacturers and dealers; are distributed by them in the shape of wages, salaries, and profits, and spent. Trade is thus almost entirely carried on with borrowed money or credit although the fact may be hidden at various points. The goods we buy are produced on borrowed money; the money we buy them with goes to extinguish the debt; but money itself is derived from credits that have been borrowed from the banks, and consequently its value must reappear in selling prices somewhere, and be recovered again from the consumer if the banks are to be repaid their advances. It is clear, therefore, that one credit is only cancelled by the creation of another and larger credit."

This is roughly the problem of the "double circuit of money," often described as the "flaw in the price system". In addition, to make confusion worse confounded, Major Douglas has the theory that the re-investment of savings further complicates the situation, by aggravating the deficiency of purchasing power. The idea is that money distributed in the course of production has gone into the prices of these goods. If the money is then saved the goods cannot be sold "within the credit area in which they are produced, and are therefore, in the economic sense, wasted. The investment of the fund so saved means the reappearance of the same sum of money in a fresh set of prices, so that on each occasion that a given sum of money is re-invested, a fresh set of values is created without the creation of fresh purchasing power." And so we must put an end to the present system of saving.

As will be observed, Major Douglas has three different explanations of why a deficiency of purchasing power results. Those who disagree with his diagnosis are compelled to refute all three. Just as one is getting to grips with the problem involved in the "A plus B Theorem" one is apt to find that one's Social Credit opponent has shifted his ground so as to rest his case on the problem of savings; or on the tendency of bankers to contract credit.

This discussion will confine itself to the "A plus B Theorem". Roughly speaking, this asserts that goods cannot ordinarily be sold profitably because part of the money expended in producing them is not available to consumers. The economists have always pointed out that the incomes of people, whatever their form (i.e., wages, salaries, dividends, profits, etc.) all originate in production. That is to say, purchasing power follows a circular route, going out as costs of production and returning to the producer as a result of consumers' purchases.

Major Douglas, however, argues that there is a "double circuit" of money, the second circuit being made up of the movement of bank-money, which is lent to producers to finance production and subsequently repaid to the banks—and cancelled. This is what he means when he says that part of the costs of production (the "B payments") do not get into the income circuit. Notice the distinction he draws between the two kinds of expenditure which are incurred in a factory. The "A payments" (costs of production) distribute purchasing power to individuals — wages, salaries, dividends. The "B payments" are those paid to "other organizations"—for raw materials, bank charges, and other external costs. The cost of the goods will therefore be A plus B. The "rate of flow of purchasing power" (incomes) is A. But A is obviously insufficient to buy A plus B; hence the break down of this pricing system.

Obviously this statement is full of ambiguity. Why omit interest from the A payments? Even if we admit that some interest goes to the banks, the mass of interest payments made by Canadian producers is paid in respect of bonds and mortgages which accrue to individuals in the same way as dividends (which Major Douglas includes among the A payments). This surely is a serious omission—unless the intention is to confuse such payments with bank interest, in which case it is smart play, but not evidence.

Now observe the definition Major Douglas gives of the "B payments",—"payments made to other organizations." These represent presumably, if we take a Canadian farmer as typical, payments for seed, feed, implements, taxes, mortgage interest, binder-twine, gasoline, etc. These monies are not apparently available as consumers' income. Why not? The answer given by Major Douglas is ambiguous and unsatisfactory. "They may be considered in the light of the repayment of a bank loan by all the concerns to whom they are made." This surely is stating as a fact what has to be proved. If it could be shown that a large part of all business receipts were used to pay off bank loans Major Douglas would have proved something—though not as much as he thinks. But he does not attempt to prove it. He merely asserts that "they may be considered, etc." and leaves it at that.

What are the facts? Let us trace what happens to the money spent by the farmer on "B payments" in order to discover whether it is available to buy the farmer's potatoes or not (leaving foreign trade complications out of account, as Major Douglas is apt to do). The mortgage interest paid by a farmer goes to an individual or to a trust, mortgage or insurance company.

If the latter, then the depositor, shareholder, or policy-holder gets the money. We need not stop to consider whether they get more than they deserve or not; Major Douglas is above such petty considerations. The point is that individuals get it. The money is then available as purchasing power. Or take implements. The purchase-money goes to the manufacturer who allocates it between his A and B payments—sending us off on a wild chase in search of the ultimate destination of his B payments. Anyone with enough patience and endurance can discover that somewhere or other, sooner or later, these B payments become payments made to individuals (i.e., incomes)— in other words, A payments. Indeed all costs of production can be finally resolved into A payments, provided you trace them far enough. That is to say all costs of production are, ultimately, incomes.

This is not to say that wages and salaries are the only costs. On the contrary, some costs of production are payments for the use of capital or land or property or business acumen. But they all go to individuals at some stage, even though they may seem to disappear into the maw of some financial institution or other corporation.

Before leaving the "A plus B Theorem" attention should be drawn to a passage in Major Douglas' writings where he says:

> "Let not the reader allow himself to be confused by the fact that B has at some previous time been represented by payments of wages, salaries, and dividends. While this is true, it is irrelevant—it is the rate of flow which is vital. The whole economic system is in ceaseless motion—purchasing power is constantly flowing back from the individuals into the credit system whence it came, and if the outflow is less than the inflow, someone has to lose purchasing power."

This, it will be seen, brushes aside all the objections to the argument raised above. But it cannot be allowed to pass. In the first place the idea of a "rate of flow" is one which ought to suggest to Major Douglas the possibilitiy that the "velocity of circulation" of money is just as important as the quantity of money. A given volume of purchasing power may suffice to turn over a large quantity of goods if the money circulates more rapidly. Now the familiar feature of depression is the manner in which the turn-over of bank deposits—an equivalent concept—has declined since 1929. May not this be the form which the deficiency of purchasing power takes? Major Douglas neglects this possibility. It is a serious omission, because in this fact may lie the explanation of how a deficiency of purchasing power might develop irrespective of banking policy.

Indeed this is precisely the rock on which the Rooseveltian monetary policy has foundered. The Federal Reserve System has practised since 1933 a consistent policy of pumping money into the banks by its "open market" operations. Some expansion of bank loans has resulted. But the results have been more than counterbalanced by the declining velocity of circulation of such bank money. Business men who come into possession of money do not turn it over as rapidly as in prosperity days. Something other than a "shortage of money" is therefore at fault.

A slightly different and more plausible explanation of the "A plus B Theorem" is sometimes offered by its advocates. This variant recognizes the fact that there is a lapse of time between the distribution of incomes involved in the earlier stages of the production of (say) coal and iron and the offer for sale of the finished automobile. For this reason, they say, consumers' incomes will not be sufficient to buy all the commodities currently offered for sale at prices which cover their costs of production. Money has been paid out in the past in producing such goods, but it has been spent long since. The selling price of the automobile must, however, include the cost of the labour which went to mine the coal or the iron ore possibly six months ago—but these incomes have been spent.

Quite obviously this argument omits to take into account the simple fact that, taking economic activity all round, the production of goods at all stages is roughly continuous. This is to say, incomes are always being earned in the course of producing raw materials and intermediate goods which will not be ready for final sale to consumers for some time. Such incomes, however, are likely to be spent partly on goods produced in an earlier cycle of production, and will tend to counterbalance the deficiency of purchasing power to which the theory refers. There may be a lack of balance at certain times, but to point out that, in fact, production in general is discontinuous is to beg the question. What we have to discover is the reason for the ups and downs of capitalist production. There is a futile circularity about any thesis which suggests that, after the depression (discontinuous production) has occurred, certain deficiencies of purchasing power develop, which cause the depression. Nevertheless, many otherwise intelligent people continue to be bewitched by the fantastic logic displayed in the variants of the "A plus B Theorem".

"Social Credit" and Canada.

Major Douglas' Canadian disciples do not, in their writings, recognize any peculiarly Canadian problems of economic organization. But, while Canadian capitalism is in many respects like modern capitalism elsewhere, the economic structure of Canada is not the same as that of Great Britain or the United States. And the attempt to apply the Douglas analysis to Canada, fortunately for our case, brings out very clearly the inadequacy of the "social credit" diagnosis and programme.

The typical "social credit" explanation of the depression in Canada traces everything to a shortage of money. All the concrete proposals involve increasing the quantity of money, and nothing else. The more traditional proposal is that consumers should be subsidized (or compensated) for the supposed deficiency of money by the distribution of state-created money. In Major Douglas' original plan, all consumers were to receive a discount from the government on every purchase they happened to make. (Evidence presented before the House of Commons Committee on Banking and Currency, Ottawa, 1923). Latterly he proposes that the subsidy take the form of a compulsory reduction of all prices, and the producer be compensated by the issue of newly created money. (Evidence presented to the Macmillan Commission in England, 1931.) Both methods of subsidy have the same end in view. The degree of subsidy is usually quoted by Major Douglas, for purposes of illustration, as 25 per cent. This, presumably, represents the deficiency of purchasing power arising from the application of the "A plus B Theorem". But there is nowhere any explanation of how the figure is computed, either for Canada or any other country.

In addition to this type of bounty, "the consumer is to receive a national dividend representing his share of the increment from the common heritage which has accumulated to mankind from mechanical inventions to facilitate and cheapen production". The purpose of the "national dividend" is to enable consumption to keep pace with technical development. But (though we cannot here elucidate the reason why) the first subsidy cannot be used for this purpose. The fact is important in view of developments in Alberta, where the idea of the "national dividend" has been taken up and embodied in the platform of a new political party led by Mr. Aberhart. Mr. Aberhart has gone one better than his English master. While Major Douglas has offered the people a share in the "national dividend" he has remained vague as to the amount likely to be distributed. Worse that that, the method by which it was to be done has always been so ambiguous and complicated as to discourage even its exponents. Mr. Aberhart has changed all that. He is more specific, or seemed to be before August 22, 1935. He proposes to pay every adult citizen in Alberta $25 per month. The money is to be obtained by a tax on production—a sort of sales tax—which will cost the people nothing. He has proved to his own satisfaction that this will come from the "unearned increment". Mr. Aberhart was satisfied that ten million dollars would be sufficient for the purpose, having regard to the rapidity of turn-over of money. More cautious people calculate that one hundred and twenty million dollars would be nearer the mark. At all events, more money is to be made available by the use of the national (and possibily, provincial) power to create credit.

Leaving aside the differences of analysis and plan which distinguish the more exuberant outgrowths of the Douglas Theory, what relation have these general theses to the economic problems of Canada? Was the depression the result of a shortage of money? Will more money produce recovery? Will a re-vamped monetary system drive depression from Canada for evermore? The "social credit" answer to these questions is always a convinced affirmative. What follows is a quotation from a speech made by Mr. Charles Bowman, editor of the Ottawa *Citizen*, one of the leading exponents of the theory.

> "The foundations of real credit are as substantial in Canada as they are in any country. With such natural resources, with no shortage of intelligent and willing labour, with adequate industrial equipment—certainly with no lack of transportation services and distributive machinery, from banks to retail stores—it would surely be possible to relate the national credit of Canada to the national productive capacity, so that the Canadian people could supply themselves from Canadian resources without being devastated by recurring periods of industrial depression and artificial scarcity. No revolutionary interference with capitalism or the control of industry is proposed in the Douglas Plan. It does not involve the nationalization of industry or bureaucratic interference with business in any form. It is a scientific plan to make more purchasing

power available to consumers without adding to the community burden of debt, without increasing taxation, and without the dangerous consequences of inflation."

We have already argued elsewhere in this chapter that the banks cannot be acquitted of all responsibility: their credit policies encouraged many of the excesses of the boom; the later reduction in loans went far beyond what was necessary, and in this they shared the panic mentality of the business community as a whole; most important of all, their failure to reduce interest rates and their attitude to depreciation of the foreign exchange value of the dollar helped to prevent an amelioration. But this is far from saying that the credit policy of the banks caused the depression. The reduction of bank loans was the result, not the cause, of the crisis. People borrowed less because they saw no prospect of using the borrowed capital profitably. The economic problem of the time was one which no scheme for manipulating money could begin to solve, and it is the analysis of this problem which enables one to find the true answer to the question: Why is there less money available now than six years ago?

Such an analysis would emphasize two factors. The first of these is that the Canadian economic structure is built upon a shifting foundation provided by relatively few but large exporting industries. The second is that the interdependence of the parts of that economy is secured by a system of prices and markets which works very imperfectly: competition is relied on to preserve balance and harmony, but competition is imperfect or lacking altogether so that the smooth working of the economic machine is destroyed. The business dislocation was the inevitable result of the world economic crisis which narrowed the opportunities for selling Canadian goods abroad; declining profits and unemployment naturally followed. Prices became lower, requiring a smaller amount of working capital for any given volume of business, opportunities for profitable business diminished; and the demand for loans diminished also. Bank loans were repaid and not renewed and the volume of money (bank deposits) was rapidly reduced in consequence. But the initiative came from business as much as from the banks.

The business man's problem under these circumstances is either to discover methods of making business profitable or to turn economic activity into new channels. In both cases, granting the slow-moving character of adjustment under a system of private enterprise, the change is bound to be slow. Needless to say, the characteristically capitalist device of trying to keep up prices (a procedure confined to the quasi-monopolistic, domestic or sheltered industries) by reducing output only prolongs the dislocation. But the granting of bank credits (directly or indirectly) to unprofitable industries would have the same effect.

What do the "social credit" advocates propose to do either to correct or to prevent a repetition of this? There appears to be nothing in the entire writings of Major Douglas, or in those of his followers, to indicate that they are aware of the nature of the situation. This defect is illustrated by the remarks of Mr. Bowman quoted above. Like his fellow "social creditors" he fails completely to grasp the problem. He does not see it in terms of misapplied (and therefore wasted) natural resources, materials and labour. For, whatever the volume of purchasing power, resources can still be misused and misdirected; the eggs may all go into the wrong baskets. "Social credit" would do nothing to prevent this. To do anything constructive involves social control and social ownership, both of which the "social credit" advocates dislike.

So much for the nature of the depression. But the "social credit" proposals for making the best of the present situation are even more fallacious. Let the reader go back to the first two sentences quoted from Mr. Bowman where he conveys the idea that we have the natural resources, the industrial equipment, the labour and materials, all in large enough quantities to supply Canadians with all they want, *from Canadian sources*. Then contrast this with the true position of affairs. As a result of economic influences exerted in the past a great deal—the greater part—of the Canadian economic structure is specialized in the production of export goods (or of goods used by the export industries). If we are not able to sell these goods abroad, importing in return goods which we cannot make so effectively or which we cannot produce at all, then so much of our resources, capital, equipment and labour, has been wasted. And we are the poorer to-day to that extent.

The task of adjusting the organization of the economy to the changed conditions is bound to be enormous in a purely physical and technical sense. But it will be doubly difficult (a) if the position is disguised and distorted by price changes resulting from the issuance of more money—the "social credit" solution; (b) if we have to rely only on the price and profit

mechanism which is the principal instrument of change in a
capitalist economy.

The secret of the "social credit" appeal lies in its promise
to bring forth a new economic order by painless methods—a
twilight-sleep form of social change. It threatens no existing
interest or privilege, with the possible exception of the bankers.
No recasting of the social and economic structure is called for.
The existing stratification of classes can remain unchanged.
Differences of wealth and income can be perpetuated. Private
enterprise in business does not run the risk of encountering
any extension of government intervention. The poorer classes
are promised a minimum of subsistence through the medium of
"basic dividends", so that their present discontents will presumably disappear. The middle class shares these "dividends" and
is further promised the ultimate disappearance of taxes and
debt. The business man is to benefit from the increased markets
following upon the distribution of extra purchasing power to
consumers. We are still to rely upon private enterprise, with
its price-and-profit mechanism, to bring about a proper allocation of resources between the various alternative uses to which
they may be put. "Social credit" has no proposals for preventing
any misdirection of effort in the future, and none to provide a
reorganization of industry which would meet more domestic
needs out of domestic resources—tasks which are bound to be
difficult because so much of our physical and human resources
is highly specialized in a few directions. A *laissez-faire* economy is quite unequal to the problem. Nothing short of a planned and socialized economy could even begin to tackle it. But
"social credit" is no help here. It only provides a mental haven
to distressed debtors who will not face the necessity for genuine
social reconstruction. That haven will be found to be a mirage
over the waters of despair.[19]

19For further refutations of the Douglas theories see H N Gaitskill's chapter on
Monetary Heretics in *What Everybody Wants to know about Money* (edited by G D H.
Cole). Also John Lewis, *Douglas Fallacies*; E. F. Durbin, *Purchasing Power and Trade
Depression;* the *Monthly Review* of the Bank of Nova Scotia for May and June 1935; and
John Strachey, *The Nature of Capitalist Crisis.*

CHAPTER XIII.

TAXATION AND FISCAL POLICY.

A. Finance and the The Transition Period.

THE QUERY "Where will the money come from?" shares with "You can't change human nature" the doubtful honour of first place among popular objections to socialism. This widespread belief that public finance will be an insuperable barrier to the success of a socialist government results from a misconception of the problem and a misreading of European experience.

It is quite true that several nominally socialist governments, the British Labour cabinet of 1929-1931 among them, have come to grief over questions of public finance. In every case, however, it was not their socialism which destroyed them, but their lack of it. Only a socialist economic system can support a decent standard of living and adequate social services for the masses. Monopoly capitalism in decline cannot "afford" even the most half-hearted and gradual approach to such objectives. The attempt to make it do so is foredoomed to failure. Yet it was precisely this attempt which the Labour party made in 1929-1931. Instead of reconstruction, it contented itself with "reform". It left capitalism in being, but tried to squeeze out of it a few extra pounds. Any Canadian government which makes the same attempt will suffer the same fate, but no genuinely socialist government would be foolish enough to try.

So much for the misreading of experience. The misconception of the nature of the problem calls for more extended treatment.

The first thing to note is that in the fully socialized economy there will be no problem of public finance as such. Taxes will disappear. When the State owns or controls all the main sources of income, it can get the money for capital investment, social insurance, administrative expenses and so forth, from the profits of state industries and services. The simplicity and economy of this procedure, as against the present method of allowing all the proceeds of industry to go to individuals and then taking back part for public uses, are obvious.

The real problems of socialist public finance are those of

the transition from capitalism to socialism: the financing of (1) the socialization of industry, (2) emergency public works, (3) the national debt, and (4) social insurance.

Socialization of industry involves no actual "money" at all. The private owners simply exchange one set of securities for another on the lines already set forth.[1] As the amount of compensation will depend on the earning capacity of each industry concerned, the annual payment on these securities represents no budgetary problem. It will come from the proceeds of the socialized industries themselves. The function of taxation will be to recover from wealthy former owners all their compensation except the modest sum necessary to give them reasonable economic security and moderate inducement to refrain from sabotage. The net annual payments to former owners, therefore, will be small. The bulk of the profits earned by the industries before socialization, plus the savings resulting from eliminating the wastes of capitalism, will be available for social use: applicable to increased wages, social services, or development of productive equipment, as the planning authority thinks fit.

The money for emergency public works can be obtained by credits from the socialized banking system,[2] even without departing from traditional lines. Parliament has already given the Cabinet power to revalue gold, and revaluation at the present commercial price of $35 an ounce has increased the gold reserve almost 75 per cent.[3] Each $100 in the reserve provides a basis for $400 of Bank of Canada notes, and each dollar of notes a basis for ten dollars of credit. There are ample funds here which can be used without adding to the national debt; for whatever interest the government paid the banking system for public works loans, it would receive back as owner of the system. Nor would such action be inflationary; the creation of credit would be balanced by creation of goods and services.

B.   The Problem of the Debt.

Interest on the national debt in 1933-34 absorbed 43 per cent. of the Dominion's revenue; in 1934-35 it was 38 per cent. and it will take at least 35 per cent. of the estimated revenue for the fiscal year 1935-36. This situation, not unnaturally, is

---

1See Chapter X, "The Socialization of Industry".
2See Chapter XII, section c.
3i.e., its dollar value.

DOMINION GOVERNMENT BUDGETS, 1930-35.

(In thousands of dollars)

(1) REVENUE.

Item	1930-31	1931-32	1932-33	1933-34	1934-35	Average
a. *Taxation*						
Customs	131,209	104,133	70,073	66,305	77,300	89,804
Excise	57,747	48,655	37,834	35,494	44,640	44,874
Banks	1,429	1,390	1,328	1,336	1,386	1,374
Insurance Cos.	74	12	826	742	740	479
Income Tax	71,048	61,255	62,067	61,399	65,600	64,274
Delayed business profits tax	34	3	—	—	—	7
Sales tax	20,784	41,734	56,814	61,392	72,600	50,665
Manufacturers, stamp, transport, etc.	13,951	17,872	25,377	45,184	39,800	28,437
Tax on gold	—	—	—	—	3,984	797
Total	296,276	275,054	254,319	271,852	306,050	280,711
b. *Non-tax Revenue*						
Post Office	30,212	32,235	30,928	30,893	31,184	31,090
Total	53,291	51,757	52,318	52,210	53,324	52,580
c. *Special Revenue*	6,622	7,028	4,493	418	3,000	4,312
Grand Total	356,189	333,839	311,130	324,480	362,374	337,603

DOMINION GOVERNMENT BUDGETS, 1930-35

(In thousands of dollars)

(2) EXPENDITURE (Principal Items).

Item	1930-31	1931-32	1932-33	1933-34	1934-35	Average
a. *Ordinary Expenditure*						
Interest	121,290	121,151	134,999	139,725	138,529	131,139
Provincial subsidies	19,036	15,295	15,277	15,328	15,369	16,061
Old age pensions	5,658	10,032	11,513	12,314	14,900	10,883
Militia	10,953	9,700	8,719	8,774	9,335	9,496
Naval service	3,598	3,043	2,167	2,171	2,222	2,640
National revenue	13,972	13,920	10,846	10,354	10,264	11,871
Treatment of returned soldiers	9,774	11,154	10,066	9,124	9,687	9,961
War pensions	45,541	48,249	45,079	43,883	43,638	45,278
Post office	37,892	36,052	31,607	30,554	30,528	33,327
Public works	25,453	17,648	13,108	10,827	10,106	15,428
Maritime Freight Rates Account	3,615	2,555	1,921	1,989	2,573	2,531
R.C.M.P.	3,192	3,488	5,626	5,315	6,000	4,724
Total	382,827	365,873	349,811	346,649	356,638	360,360
b. *Special Expenditure*						
Relief	4,432	38,296	36,721	35,898	51,948	33,459
Total	16,789	55,476	43,365	42,787	66,157	44,915
c. *C.N.R. Deficits*	35,137	58,888	62,140	58,955	48,408	52,706
Grand Total	468,463	459,208	531,764	457,977	480,074	479,497

Source. Based on figures given in the Budget speech, Hansard 1935. pp. 2135-2146.

causing some perturbation, especially among business men. Advocates of a "national government" go so far as to describe debt as "one of the great problems" which that instrument is designed to solve. But they are conveniently vague as to the precise methods. Indeed, we have yet to hear from capitalist sources any definite proposals to this end which will bear serious examination.

Some Economy Proposals.

The one great cure-all, railway unification under C.P.R. management, we have considered elsewhere[4]. Suffice it to say here that, under capitalism, the saving to the Treasury could hardly reach more than $6,000,000 in the first year and a maximum of $30,000,000 in the fifth and subsequent years[5], and the promised relief to the taxpayer, it would seem, would be bought at heavy social cost. A socialist government, on the other hand, should be able without injury to any legitimate interest, to save some $10,000,000 immediately on this head.

A second economy programme comes from the Montreal *Gazette*. Its formula, if of doubtful social value, has at least the merit of simplicity: withdraw from the League of Nations and the International Labour Organization, abolish the National Research Council and the departments of Labour, Interior, and Railways and Canals. That sounds as if it should save unnumbered millions. But when we look at the public accounts we find that the expenditure on the League, the I.L.O., and the Research Council is trifling, and that most of the expenditure of the Departments of Labour, Interior and Railways and Canals would have to go on whether there is a department or not. Unless we are prepared to repeal the Old Age Pensions Act, the Technical Education Act, and the Employment Offices Co-ordination Act, abolish the Railway Commission, and let our canals go to rack and ruin, the savings from abolishing the departments would be negligible. The following table, allowing for the fantastic assumption that all the officials of the Departments of Labour, Interior, and Railways and Canals could be dismissed and their duties performed by officials already employed in other departments, tells its own story:

---

[4] See Chapter X, (c).

[5] Sir Edward Beatty proposes to spread the process of economizing over a period of five years.

COST OF ENUMERATED CANADIAN GOVERNMENT OBLIGATIONS
AND DEPARTMENTS: FISCAL YEAR 1933-34.

League of Nations and International Labour Organization (dues paid, cost of delegations, publications, grant to League of Nations Society in Canada, etc.) ....$	258,246.82
Disarmament Conference (non-recurring)	4,264.36
World Economic Conference (do.)	14,924.33
National Research Council	379,499.93
Department of Labour (civil government and contingencies, etc.)	222,293.36
Department of the Interior (do.)	605,171.16
Department of Railways and Canals (do.)...........	204,166.02
Total..........$	1,688,565.98

"The mountain has been long in labour and has brought forth a mouse".

By contrast, abolition of our superfluous militia and naval service would save $11,000,000, and the reduction of the R.C.M.P. to its pre-depression level another $3,000,000. These two items alone would meet practically the whole cost of cash benefits of $12 a week under a Dominion health insurance scheme.[6]

A third economy proposal concerns mainly provincial expenditures. It would eliminate duplication by Dominion and Provincial Departments of Agriculture, and amalgamate the three Prairie Provinces and the three Maritime Provinces. How much duplication is occurring in Departments of Agriculture is problematical, but as the total cost of all provincial Departments of Agriculture together is only about $6,000,000, any saving here would not be impressive. Amalgamation of the three Prairie Provinces might save perhaps $2,000,000, of the Maritime Provinces $1,000,000; quite probably much less in both instances. The new mergers would have to carry the present provincial debts and presumably the present social services. In a total Dominion-provincial revenue (allowing for Dominion subsidies to the provinces) of about $487,000,000, the amounts which might be realized by these means are small.

But as every practical person knows, it is in the highest degree unlikely that any such provincial mergers will ever take place, especially in the Maritimes. Historic political units can-

6See Chapter XVI.

not be amalgamated as if they were so many cement companies, and the attempt would stir up far more trouble than it is worth.

Of the suggestion that we should abolish *all* the provinces, it is only necessary to say three things. First, it is politically impossible under any government, Conservative, Liberal, C.C.F., "National", Communist or "Reconstruction". Second, to administer half a continent direct from Ottawa would certainly be more expensive than decentralized administration. Third, comparisons of legislators and civil servants per capita in Canada and other countries are worthless. A wide-spread, sparsely populated country needs proportionately more of both than a compact, densely populated area; and a great deal depends on how far each country leaves certain services to be performed by private enterprise or entrusts them to government. Canada, with far more public ownership than the United States, for example, would inevitably have a relatively larger number of public employees—and, by the same token, a relatively smaller number of private employees. The superstition that services performed by private enterprise cost the public nothing is so silly that it carries its own refutation; the comparative efficiency of public and private enterprise we discuss elsewhere.[7]

In fact, the only major economies, apart from the railways, available to a "national" or any other capitalist government are our social services; and then the total abolition of all these would reduce present Dominion expenditure by little more than the $15,000,000 for old age pensions, and future expenditure by the extra $14,000,000 or so necessary for the government's share of unemployment insurance.[8]

Annual Dominion expenditure on relief, indeed, from $35,000,000 to $52,000,000 a year.[9] Only a "national government", we are daily assured, can solve this problem. But how? According to the Montreal *Star*, it will balance the budget by drastic economies, and then float a loan to provide work for all

---

[7]For a skilful and devastating analysis of Canadian Chamber of Commerce economy propaganda, see H. F. Angus, "The Economy Campaign on the Western Front," *Canadian Forum*, April, 1934.

[8]"If the total government expenses could be reduced in proportion to the fall in the national income, without at the same time reducing bond interest, there would not be enough left over to provide even the essential services of federal and provincial governments, neglecting altogether the services rendered by municipalities which would require another hundred and fifty millions. These statements are made advisedly, on the assumption that drastic new economies are effected . . . . and that no capital expenditures whatever are undertaken." D. C. MacGregor, in *Canadian Forum*, July, 1934.

[9]Even for the provincial treasuries, savings from social services would not be very considerable unless there were slashing reductions on education and hospitals. Mothers' allowances and old age pensions together cost all the provinces less than $10,000,000. Relief costs the provinces about $35,700,000, the municipalities $27,300,000: *Financial Post*, June 1, 1935

the unemployed. But even at the subsistence wages of Mr. Roosevelt's work-relief projects, it takes $2,000 to re-employ one man. We have at present about 500,000 unemployed. We should therefore have to borrow at least $1,000,000,000, on which the annual interest charges would be $30,000,000 to $35,000,000. The net saving to the Dominion treasury would be small. To be sure, we should have something to show for the money. But a socialist government could secure the same end, pay the men decent wages, and add nothing to the national debt.

There is one sure way to reduce the debt which the Chambers of Commerce, great executives, and capitalist newspapers or politicians never mention. The single real achievement of the British "national" government has been its brilliant default on the American debt. But much as our financial community seems to admire this "tried and true" British method of balancing the budget when practised at a distance and at someone else's expense, we may safely assume that it will continue to look on our own debt charges as an "uncontrollable" expenditure.

On the basis of its own principles it can do nothing else. No capitalist will suggest cutting down his own investment, and no capitalist government dare attempt it unless at the point of financial death, and even then usually only in a disguised form. Only a socialist government can tackle the problem openly and effectively.

A Debt-Redemption Levy.

The way to reduce debt is to reduce it. We are not suggesting repudiation, which, as Professor K. W. Taylor pointed out to the Liberal Summer School in 1933, "is grossly unfair when applied to a single type of creditor (the owner of government bonds)". "Inflation, and a rapid rise in prices," he adds, "have the same effect as highly regressive taxation, bearing unfairly on wage-earner and bond-holder, and giving large unearned increments to manufacturers and owners of equities". The fairest and most satisfactory measure is the debt-redemption levy, imposed once only and for this specific purpose. Of this Professor Taylor observes that it is "practicable, fair and theoretically sound. Detailed specifications have been worked out in England, both officially and unofficially. No such calculations have been made in Canada, but probably at least $2,000,000,000 could be wiped out in this way without any serious disturbing effects on the foundations of our economic life."[10]

Since 1929 the wholesale price index has fallen from 96 to 72. That is, the purchasing power of the dollar, and with it much of the burden of debt, has risen by about a third. It is surely not unreasonable to ask the wealthier members of society to surrender, at long last, the windfall gift of the depression.

Professor Taylor's estimate of the proceeds of such a levy is conservative. Foreign investment in Canada at January 1, 1935, was about $6,406,000,000.[11] This is generally reckoned as about 35 per cent. of our total business capital, which would therefore stand at about $18,500,000,000. Exempting foreign holdings[12] leaves $12,000,000,000. From this we could afford to grant generous exemptions to holders of small amounts of capital, and still have a sum large enough to yield the $2,000-000,000 at even less than the suggested 33 per cent. average rate.

Payment would be made in cash, or preferably in approved securities which would be accepted at a fair valuation based on earning capacity, to be determined by the Court of Appraisal. Dominion bonds paid in would, of course, be cancelled. Other securities would give the State just that much share in the ownership and revenues of industry. The levy would therefore serve a double purpose: debt reduction and socialization. The present net debt of the Dominion is about $2,850,000,000: in concrete terms, the levy could relieve the Treasury of more than $90,000,000 a year in interest charges.

A measure of this sort is bound to work some hardship upon those who may have recently bought securities at relatively high prices. But for practical purposes, the exemption of the small investor and the very dubious ethical basis of all large fortunes, rob this objection of most of its weight. Moreover, as the alternative is probably inflation, whether in the grand manner of Major Douglas or otherwise, the rich might be well advised to choose a single levy of known proportions.

Attempts by Canadians to take their securities out of the country or transfer them to foreign "dummies" could be fairly adequately controlled once the State had taken over the key institutions of the banking system. The flight of securities

[10]*The Liberal Way*, pp. 45-46, with Professor Taylor's correction of a misprint of the amount.
[11]*Financial Post Business Year Book*, 1935.
[12]To avoid international complications.

could not be prevented, but the payment of returns on them could be stopped. It should be clearly announced beforehand that if the flight took place in anticipation of a socialist victory at the polls, the government would decline to recognize transfers made within the preceding three or six months (or some other specified period), and would seize the culprits' physical assets to an amount equivalent to the levy he would have paid. Some flight or evasion would no doubt succeed, but growing economic difficulties and social unrest in other countries will make it increasingly hard for frightened Canadian magnates to find a safe refuge. It will be better left in a new "Canada for the Canadians".

C. ORDINARY REVENUE AND ITS ALLOCATION.

Inheritance Taxes.

The proceeds of a second instrument of socialization and debt reduction, a Dominion inheritance tax, it is unfortunately impossible to estimate with any exactness. All the provinces levy succession duties (to the amount of $13,105,000 in 1933), but it is reasonable to expect that federal rates might be as much as twice as high as those collectable by the provinces. The figures for Great Britain are given below.

ESTATES AND DEATH DUTIES, 1933-34: GREAT BRITAIN.

—	Numbers		Net capital value		Receipts	
	Number	Per cent.	000£	Per cent.	000£	Per cent.
Small.............	52,077	38.8	14,350	2.74	99	.13
100 - 5,000.........	66,491	49.52	105,473	20.15	2,879	3.82
5,000 - 10,000......	7,291	5.44	56,452	10.77	2,238	2.96
10,000 - 25,000.....	5,388	4.03	87,039	16.60	5,980	7.92
25,000 - 50,000.....	1,758	1.31	63,804	12.17	7,369	9.76
50,000 - 100,000....	738	.56	53,233	10.15	9,043	11.98
100,000 - 200,000...	287	.21	41,512	7.93	9,102	12.06
200,000 - 500,000...	128	.10	37,850	7.22	10,746	14.24
500,000 - 1,000,000..	31	.02	18,636	3.56	6,471	8.57
1,000,000 - 3,000,000	11	.01	19,779	3.78	8,576	11.36
3,000,000 and over..	1	—	25,858	4.93	12,991	17.21
(Settlement)......	—	—	—	—	(−6)	(−.01)
Totals...........	134,193	100	523,987	100	75,488	100

Source: *Economist,* April 13, 1935. Total receipts for all types of "Death Duties" in 1933-34 were £85,270,000; in 1934-35 were £81,360,000.

In the absence of Canadian federal figures, we rely on estimates based on Australian and New Zealand experience. In Australia in 1931-32, estates falling under tax amounted to £48,459,192. From these the Commonwealth collected £1,385,811, the states £3,163,775; a total, at present rates of exchange, equivalent to about $18,000,000.[13] This shows an average of just over 9 per cent. of the value of the estates. Canada's population is about 60 per cent. larger than Australia's, our total national wealth probably almost twice as large as Australia's[14] and certainly more unequally distributed. New Zealand in the year ending March 31, 1934, collected death duties of £1,390,742 (about $5,500,000) on estates of £14,728,384. Of the total value of these estates almost 37 per cent. was in fortunes of £20,000 and over, over 50 per cent. in fortunes of £10,000 and over.[15] Our population is over seven times as large as New Zealand's. New Zealand's per capita wealth and income are certainly not greater and probably less than ours, and her income tax statistics show less inequality of distribution.[16] A capitalist government in Canada taxing inheritances on the Australian scale should be able to raise $18,000,000 to $23,000,000 (after deducting present provincial duties of $13,000,000). On the New Zealand scale the net yield should be about $25,000,000.

A Canadian socialist government would, of course, have to allow for a reduction of nearly a third on account of property taken over under the debt-redemption levy. On the other hand, there are at least three reasons why it should be able to collect more than any capitalist government. In the first place, the latter is always timid about taxing estates too heavily for fear of discouraging "thrift", "enterprise", "initiative" and so forth, and so stalling the economic machinery. The fear is probably groundless: there is reason to believe that the inheriting of large fortunes offers no appreciable encouragement to enterprise.[17] But even if heavy death duties would stall the capitalist economic machine, the prospect has no terrors for a socialist government. For the socialist government is not proposing to go on with the old machinery but to supplant it with new,

13*Australian Year Book*, 1933.

14The *Australian Year Book* gives an estimate of *private* wealth, but no estimate of national wealth strictly comparable with those in the *Canada Year Book*.

15*New Zealand Year Book*, 1935.

16New Zealand's national wealth, 1933, was £820,000,000. The *New Zealand Year Book* estimates *private* income, but not national income, so that again exact comparison with Canada is not easy.

17For an elaborate analysis, see *The Economics of Inheritance*, by Rt. Hon. Josiah Wedgwood, M.P.; also Hugh Dalton, *The Inequality of Incomes in Modern Communities*.

which will not depend on the motive power of private profit.

In the second place, the socialist government through owner-ship of the banks, trust companies and life insurance compan-ies, would enjoy unrivalled facilities for efficient collection of this and other taxes.   Evasion would be much less possible than it is to-day.

Thirdly, the initial receipts could be increased, and the pro-cesses of socialization and debt redemption speeded up, if neces-sary, by having the state life insurance trusts hand over forth-with the present value of taxes on large policies falling due in the future.

Taking these factors into consideration, it seems not un-reasonable to count on an initial net yield of $20,000,000, applic-able to the interest on the public debt.   The death duties, like the debt-redemption levy, could be payable in securities. As socializa-tion proceeded, inherited wealth and the revenue from death duties with it would, of course, diminish, but as the profits of state industry would increase at the same rate, this raises no fiscal difficulty.

Possibilities of Conversion.

A third means of reducing debt is a compulsory conversion, Australian style, of that part of the debt (at least 75 per cent.) held by Canadians. Professor Taylor in 1931, in the speech to the Liberal Summer School already quoted, said that "skilful conversion operations" might reduce the burden of debt "10 or 15 per cent."[18]   He was speaking of voluntary conversions, some of which have since been carried out.   After applying the special levy and the death duties, there would still remain some $35,000,000 of interest charges.   Compulsory conversion from the present 4.15 per cent. average[19] to 3.5 per cent., on bonds held by Canadians, would save another $4,000,000.   The new securi-ties should be of the varying-return type used in compensating the private owners of industry.[20]

It would be most inadvisable to apply any of these drastic fiscal measures to foreign holdings. If, however, foreigners take fright and rush off to sell, that will merely afford an op-portunity for the socialist government to follow the example of that eminent capitalist financier, Dr. Schacht, and buy in at "fire sale" prices. This might considerably reduce the foreign

18*The Liberal Way,* p. 45.
19*House of Commons Debates,* 1935, p. 2347. (Government answer to a question).
20See above, Chapter IX, "Socialization of Industry".

commitments of both government and industry, and again speed up debt redemption and socialization.[21]

Income Tax.

For the financing of social insurance, the economies and new taxes already proposed (debt-levy, death-duties, conversion, savings on railways), with about $20,000,000 from the abolition of interest on savings deposits in the socialized banks,[22] should make available about $145,000,000. This would obviously have to be supplemented by greatly increased receipts from income tax. How much can be obtained from this source?

Canadian income tax statistics are unfortunately very incomplete compared with British, Australian, New Zealand or United States figures. "In countries where income tax is a normal feature of the revenue system", says the Dominion Bureau of Statistics,[23] "the statistics of incomes that come to the knowledge of the income tax officials have long been regarded as furnishing a guide both to the aggregate amount of the national income and more particularly to its distribution by income classes. . . , Thus most estimates of the amount and distribution of income in the United Kingdom and the United States take as their starting point the statistics of incomes coming under review". This is, significantly, not the Canadian practice, and a brief comparison of the totals of incomes assessed with total national income estimated by other means will show why. (In New Zealand, incomes assessed for income tax constitute about 60 per cent of total "private income". Canada does not publish strictly comparable figures of "private income".)

The total national income in 1930, however, was $5,150,000,-000[24]; income assessed in the fiscal year 1931-32 (which means, according to the Bureau of Statistics, "for the most part income earned in the calendar year 1930") amounted to $660,107,257 for individuals, and $332,498,963 for corporations, a total of $992,606,220. Even if we deduct from the total national income the agricultural income, which pays practically nothing, the net figure is $4,391,000,000. The discrepancy between this and the income tax statistics remains so wide as to

---

[21]The problem of tax-free bonds (interest on which now amounts to $17,529,544—*House of Commons Debates*, 1935, p. 2701) and of payments to Canadians on bonds whose interest is payable in foreign currency, can be dealt with by legislation.

[22]At 2 per cent. on the volume of savings deposits (including only accounts above $1,000. See p. 307.) shown in the return of April 30, 1935, *Financial Post*, June 8, 1935.

[23]*Incomes Assessed for Income War Tax in Canada*, 1932: D. B. S. Bulletin.

[24]*Financial Post Business Year Book*, 1935, p. 25.

make these latter of very slight value for our purposes. And their value is further reduced by the government's solicitude for the privacy of the rich. Nothing short of a question in Parliament will elicit figures of total incomes assessed by income groups, and even that furnishes no information about the higher groups beyond a cryptic "$50,000 and over". For Canada, the figures are available even in this limited form only for the fiscal year 1931-1932. For New Zealand, they are given much more fully and given every year as a matter of course. The defect in the New Zealand figures is that they do not separate companies and individuals, (though they give figures for "earned" incomes of individuals) so that the official statistics in the accompanying table are not strictly comparable. To facilitate some comparison, therefore, we have added an estimate of Canadian corporation incomes secured by multiplying the tax receipts at 10 per cent—the rate applicable in 1931-32—and reducing the totals by 9.71 per cent. to reach the actual grand total.[25]

INCOME TAX STATISTICS: CANADA AND NEW ZEALAND, 1931-32.

Canada: Individuals.

Income Group	Estimated Total Income	Number of Taxpayers
Under $2,000	$ 62,154,736	37,002
2,000 – 3,000	45,696,004	19,595
3,000 – 4,000	73,336,841	21,160
4,000 – 5,000	73,904,744	16,555
5,000 – 6,000	58,151,504	10,410
6,000 – 7,000	44,795,795	6,839
7,000 – 8,000	33,523,798	4,573
8,000 – 9,000	26,748,889	3,238
9,000 – 10,000	22,770,081	2,462
10,000 – 15,000	69,317,807	5,901
15,000 – 20,000	36,528,039	2,405
20,000 – 25,000	20,949,618	1,123
25,000 – 30,000	14,839,274	646
30,000 – 35,000	11,215,103	491
35,000 – 40,000	6,994,814	267
40,000 – 45,000	6,466,932	197
45,000 – 50,000	4,106,543	143
50,000 and over	48,606,735	614
Total	$660,107,257	133,621

25New Zealand figures in the table from *New Zealand Year Book*, 1935, pp. 565-567. For Canada, figures of individuals' income by income groups from *House of Commons Debates*, 1934, p. 340; other figures from *Incomes Assessed for Income War Tax in Canada*, 1932.

Canada: *Corporations*

Income Group	Estimated Total Income	Number of Taxpayers
Under $2,000............................	—	—
2,000 – 3,000........................	$ 490,248	1,123
3,000 – 4,000........................	823,571	555
4,000 – 5,000........................	1,105,339	431
5,000 – 6,000........................	1,308,812	343
6,000 – 7,000........................	1,329,096	294
7,000 – 8,000........................	1,225,615	222
8,000 – 9,000........................	1,293,576	197
9,000 – 10,000........................	1,126,850	140
10,000 – 15,000........................	4,972,451	495
15,000 – 20,000........................	4,452,873	354
20,000 – 25,000........................	4,486,763	229
25,000 – 30,000........................	3,947,497	176
30,000 – 35,000........................	5,014,716	175
35,000 – 40,000........................	4,132,194	119
40,000 – 45,000........................	4,027,440	100
45,000 – 50,000........................	3,658,921	80
50,000 and over....................	287,737,192	971
Total.........................	$331,133,154(a)	6,483

(a)Estimates total: Actual total, $332,498,963.

Canada: *Combined Figures.*

Income Group	Estimated Total Income	Number of Taxpayers
Under $2,000........................	$ 62,154,736	37,002
2,000 – 3,000........................	46,186,252	20,178
3,000 – 4,000........................	74,160,412	21,715
4,000 – 5,000........................	75,010,083	16,986
5,000 – 6,000........................	59,460,316	10,753
6,000 – 7,000........................	46,124,891	7,133
7,000 – 8,000........................	34,749,413	4,795
8,000 – 9,000........................	28,042,465	3,435
9,000 – 10,000........................	23,896,931	2,602
10,000 – 15,000........................	74,290,258	6,396
15,000 – 20,000........................	40,980,912	2,759
20,000 – 25,000........................	25,436,381	1,352
25,000 – 30,000........................	18,786,771	822
30,000 – 35,000........................	16,229,819	666
35,000 – 40,000........................	11,127,018	386
40,000 – 45,000........................	10,494,372	297
45,000 – 50,000........................	7,765,464	223
50,000 and over....................	336,343,927	1,585
Total.........................	$991,240,421(b)	139,625(c)

(b)Estimates total: Actual total, $992,606,220.
(c)6 unclassified corporations not included.

New Zealand.

Income Group	Total Incomes	Number of Taxpayers
Under £ 300.	£ 11,452,875	15,663
300 – 399.	12,547,945	26,881
400 – 499.	6,765,759	14,497
500 – 599.	4,040,112	7,356
600 – 699.	2,856,481	4,397
700 – 799.	1,972,599	2,616
800 – 899.	1,472,656	1,727
900 – 999.	1,219,078	1,273
1,000 – 1,999.	5,651,150	4,226
2,000 – 4,999.	3,603,457	1,271
5,000 – 9,999.	1,221,530	185
10,000 – 19,999.	944,970	67
20,000 – 49,999.	1,617,445	52
50,000 – 99,999.	1,739,810	23
100,000 and over.	3,062,525	11
Total.	£ 60,168,392	80,245
Corporations.	£ 9,960,799	3,287

In proportion to population and wealth, New Zealand's receipts from income tax are about the same as the estimated yield of Dominion and provincial income taxes in Canada for 1935-36. Australian income taxes, Commonwealth and state, in 1931-32 produced $90,000,000. Allowing for differences in population, wealth and distribution of income, a similar rate applied here should have produced at least $145,000,000. Thf actual return was $61,255,000 to the Dominion and $7,710,000 to the provinces, a total of about $69,000,000. The Dominion Minister of Finance expects to get $76,000,000 from income tax and his new surtax in 1935-36, which with provincial income taxes might mean a total of perhaps $82,500,000 for the whole country (provincial income tax receipts in 1933 having fallen to $6,642,307). National income being about 20 per cent. lower than in 1930, the Australian rates should now produce here about $114,000,000, or an extra $30,000,000 for the Dominion.

British income tax in 1932-33 absorbed 9 or 10 per cent. of the national income[26], Canadian about 2 per cent. (excluding agriculture). Yet a comparison of British and Canadian rates,

[26]Estimate of British national income, 1931, from Colin Clark: *The National Income, 1924-1931.*

as in the accompanying table, shows that at least on large incomes our rates are not as far below the British as might have been supposed. Clearly, the major cause for the relatively small yield in Canada lies in the relative inefficiency of our system of collection. At present, a large amount of income escapes the taxing authority altogether. In Britain, the tax is collected at the source, and anyone overtaxed must prove his right to a rebate. The same system in Canada, rigorously applied, would work wonders.

A COMPARISON OF INCOME TAX AND SURTAX RATES (*for Married Couple with Three Children*) :GREAT BRITAIN AND CANADA.

(*a*) *Great Britain* (1933-34[a]).

Income	All Earned		All Investment	
	Amount	%	Amount	%
	£. s. d.		£. s. d.	
£ 300		—	2.10. 0	.83
400	5. 0. 0	1.25	15. 0. 0	3.75
500	15. 0. 0	3.0	33. 2. 6	6.6
1,000	108. 2. 6	10.8	158. 2. 6	15.8
2,000	333. 2. 6	16.7	408. 2. 6	20.4
5,000	1,420. 0. 0	28.4	1,495. 0. 0	29.9
10,000	3,852.10. 0	38.5	3,927. 10 0	39.3
50,000	28,290. 0. 0	56.6	28,365. 0. 0	56.7

(*b*) *Canada* (1935-36[b]).

Income	All Earned		All Investment	
	Amount	%	Amount	%
$ 5,000	$ 65.10	1.3	$ 65.10	1.3
10,000	422.10	4.2	527.10	5.3
25,000	3,458.70	13.8	3,689.70	14.8
50,000	11,375.70	22.75	11,606.70	23.2
250,000	113,742.30	45.5	113,973.30	45.6

(a)*Economist*, April 13, 1935.
   (b)Statutes of Canada; Budget speech, Mar. 22, 1935; *Financial Post*. Mar. 30 and Apr. 13, 1935
   On a $500,000 income the Canadian tax is about 55 per cent., on a $1,000,000 income a little over 60 per cent.

"From the narrow fiscal viewpoint", says Professor Mac-Gregor, in the *Canadian Forum* of July, 1934, "the principal defect of Canadian public finance is this: the tax-collecting capacity of governments is less than the tax-paying capacity of the people. This is chiefly due to the incompetence of both the federal and provincial civil service, almost none of whom are properly qualified for administering finance in the post-war world. But the present legislative framework must bear its share of the blame, while the weakness and rustic ignorance of many politicians necessarily hinders the introduction of common-sense reforms, especially in the law and administration of the income tax. . . . In Ontario and Quebec, where four-fifths of the taxable income exists, the moderately well-to-do are virtually untaxed".

"The minimum rates of income tax", says the same authority in the *Canadian Forum* of March, 1933, "could be raised to four or five times the present ones . . . and the maximum rates raised to perhaps 75 per cent."

A Canadian socialist government would have to deduct from any current estimate of taxable income the annual revenue from assets taken over under the debt-redemption levy and death duties, and from debt conversion and the abolition of interest on savings deposits in the socialized banks. But for reasons already indicated in discussing inheritance taxes, it should be able to secure far more of what remains than any government which is trying to maintain capitalism. By setting a maximum income of $10,000 and collecting the tax at the source, it should be able to get in some $50,000,000 more than the 1935-36 estimate. If this seems an extravagant claim, it must be remembered that we do not propose to go on maintaining one-eighth of the population in idleness. We take seriously the Prime Minister's dictum, "If we cannot abolish the dole, we should abolish the system." This is exactly what socialization means. It would set the unemployed to work at decent wages, and the national income would be correspondingly increased.

Such a programme will no doubt be very displeasing to our business leaders. But it is time they were reminded of a few plain facts. In the first place, Canada is not a heavily taxed country. Dominion and provincial taxation in 1931 took only 9.4 per cent. of the total national income, or 11 per cent. of the non-agricultural income. British taxes in the same year took 20.9 per cent. of national income. This does not include municipal taxes, but no one familiar with both countries will have the hardihood to assert that municipal taxation is heavier here than in Britain. Second, as we have already seen, the rich in

Canada pay very little of what taxation there is, their perpetual lamentations to the contrary notwithstanding. Third, they have incessantly exhorted us to "follow the British way", declaring that Britain's methods have brought that country out of the depression faster and farther than any other in the world. One of the most characteristic of British methods is heavy taxation of incomes and inheritance. Our millionaires should therefore derive much spiritual consolation from the fact that we are taking their advice.

It is also worth emphasizing that the taxation policy here proposed is avowedly a means to, and part of, a fundamental social change, and must be judged as such.

The Application of the Revenue.

The most damaging criticism of our proposals is that the total amount they would provide for social insurance is so inadequate. $195,000,000 would certainly not cover the financing of the schemes outlined in Chapter XV (A Code for Labour) in their fullest form. We must repeat, however, that only a fully socialized economy can provide a proper standard of living and adequate social services, and that this chapter is dealing with public finance *at the beginning of the transition from capitalism to socialism.* To demand from the transitional economy what can only be secured when the transition has been completed is to ask the impossible.

Nor is it safe to count heavily, at least at the outset, on huge revenues from socialized industry or from elimination of the inefficiencies of capitalism. Political difficulties may delay socialization, and there is bound to be a certain amount of economic dislocation. In the very early stages of the transition we shall be fortunate if the profits of socialized industry, other than the banks and the railways, cover the costs of new administrative services.

The funds available, however, would suffice to do a good deal. To extend the present unemployment insurance scheme to all workers, put it on a non-contributory basis, and raise the benefits 50 per cent., would take about $150,000,000.[27] Health insurance cash benefits of $8 a week for British Columbia workers, about one-tenth of the Dominion total, are estimated in the

---

[27]The retention of certain contributory features in the scheme during the transition period would, of course, reduce this sum (as a charge to be met in the Dominion budget) very considerably. See Chapter XV, section c.

British Columbia draft scheme at $1,000,000. A Dominion scheme with $12 benefits should, therefore, allowing for administration expenses of 15 per cent., cost about $17,250,000. To extend old age pensions to Quebec and New Brunswick would mean taking in about 25,500 persons from the former and 7,200 from the latter, and would cost about $8,000,000.[28] The present cost for seven provinces is about $15,000,000 to the Dominion and $5,000,000 to the provinces. Bringing in the two extra provinces, transferring the whole cost to the Dominion and raising the benefits by 50 per cent., with extra administration costs would necessitate new Dominion expenditure of about $29,750,000. This makes a total additional expenditure of $197,-000,000 as against extra estimated revenue of $195,000,000. Even a slight reduction in unemployment would soon allow the Dominion to take over mothers' allowances and extend them to Quebec, New Brunswick, and Prince Edward Island.

The Finance Minister is budgeting for an estimated deficit cf $95,900,000 in 1935-36, on account of relief and railways. A socialist government could scarcely hope to extinguish this immediately. But its re-employment policy should soon cut relief expenditures drastically, and its railway policy, by getting rid of wasteful duplication, should stop the drain from that quarter. Provided socialization is not obstructed, balancing the budget should be a matter of two or three years at the outside.

It has been pointed out more than once that at present far too much of our revenue comes from taxes on consumption. The nearer we get to equality of income, however, the less burdensome these become, and as socialization proceeds, a planned pricing policy, as suggested above, will do away with the necessity for them altogether.

The problem of financial relations between the Dominion and the provinces is too complex to be dealt with fully here. It should be the subject of a careful survey by the Planning Commission and conferences between the governments. But in a socialist Canada, the problem would be much less acute than it is now. The assumption by the Dominion of full responsibility for social insurance would at once relieve the provinces of $10,-000,000 of their present expenditure and of the possibility of indefinite future demands on them for such purposes. Getting the unemployed back to work would save provincial treasuries

---

28The trend of population will make this a much heavier expense as time goes on; probably almost three times as heavy by 1971.

at least a considerable part of the present $35,000,000 or so (and municipal treasuries a good part of $25,000,000), and the resulting increase in business activity would raise their revenues. If these measures together did not eliminate the current provincial deficits of $60,000,000, they should at least reduce the amount to manageable proportions.

This outline of a socialist public finance policy obviously leaves much unsaid. But it is only an outline. It deals largely with a programme for the transition period, and assumes immediate socialization of financial institutions and railways. It can be fully understood only if it is read in conjunction with the rest of the book, especially the chapters on planning, banking and investment, the distributive services, and foreign trade.

Chapter XIV.

FOREIGN TRADE.

A SECTOR of our economy so large and important as our foreign trade obviously cannot be left unplanned, if only because of our dependence on external supplies of certain goods and on external markets for our products, and because of the impossibility of leaving socialized industries at the mercy of foreign capitalist sabotage.

There are of course those who will say that national planning in this sphere is useless; that we must wait for international agreement or world planning. The argument is plausible. There is no question that international agreements to reduce tariffs, for example, would be of great value. There is equally no question that planning, to be thoroughly satisfactory, must ultimately be on a world scale. But the complete failure of two world economic conferences, one held in a period of "prosperity" and relative stability (1927), the other at a time of unexampled depression (1933), is not impressive evidence of capitalism's ability to achieve even the most rudimentary international planning. Nor do we believe that this failure is accidental. Its causes, we have suggested in earlier chapters, are inherent in the system. Even if capitalism could plan, however, we are not prepared to hand over to a board of capitalist international planners control of Canada's raw materials, foreign trade and immigration. We look forward to a planned world economy; but for the world, as for the nation, only socialist planning is in the last analysis safe, stable or even tolerable. The day of a socialist world plan is not yet. But unless we first set our own house in order that day will never arrive. When it does come, the work to be done should be made infinitely easier by the existence of national plans designed to fit into the whole.

A. SELF-SUFFICIENCY AND THE TARIFF.

There is a widespread impression that planning necessarily involves a policy of self-sufficiency. In reality, there is no logical connection whatever. On the contrary, the more we plan our economy,—the more integrated and unified our society becomes—the more clearly we shall see how wasteful it is to try to make expensively at home what we can buy cheaply elsewhere.

Some Tariff Arguments.

No reader of this book would dream of trying to make himself self-sufficing. To do so would indeed "keep his money at home", i.e., in his own pocket, and provide him with plenty of "employment". But unfortunately it would provide him with very little else. Nor would any citizen of Ontario or Quebec dream of supporting a tariff on coal high enough to give the whole market of central Canada to the Nova Scotia coal industry. Yet the logic of protectionism leads straight to these conclusions.

For fifty-six years we have followed that logic. It has built up for us a number of important secondary industries, notably in the iron and steel and textile groups. But it has done so at the cost of unnecessarily high prices to the consumer and at the expense of the non-protected and especially the export industries.

For in the first place, the very fact that an industry needs protection is normally proof that it cannot, at least for the time being, produce as cheaply as its foreign competitors. Protection, therefore, means as a rule that we have to pay more for the protected domestic goods than we should pay for the same goods freely imported. In the woollen cloth industry, for example, salaries and wages of 3,900 employees in 1930 amounted to $3,400,000. Professor Taylor of McMaster University estimates that "the total excess cost to Canadian consumers (calculated at manufacturers' or import prices) of their supply of woollen cloth was at least $7,000,000 or more than double the amount of all salaries and wages".

Again, no one will question that in the absence of the tariff, more especially in the absence of tariff increases, the prices of textiles and iron and steel products in Canada would in the last three years have fallen much faster and farther than in fact they have. A comparison of the fall in prices in textile raw materials and textile manufactures certainly lends support to this view. Between 1929 and November, 1932, raw cotton fell 63 per cent.; cotton yarn, 19.4 per cent.; cotton fabrics, 15.8 per cent.; cotton knitted goods, 15.2 per cent. Raw wool fell 65 per cent.; woollen yarn, 29 per cent.; woollen hosiery and knitted goods, 28.4 per cent.; woollen blankets, 26.6 per cent.; woollen clot, 28 per cent. Raw silk fell 62 per cent.; silk yarn and thread, 18 per cent.; silk hosiery, 27 per cent.; silk fabrics, 34 per cent.[1]

[1]*Financial Post Business Year Book*, 1933, pp. 141-143. By February, 1933 (the low point of the wholesale price index) woollen blankets had fallen 36.1%; raw silk, 71.5%; silk yarn and thread, 26%; silk hosiery, 30.6%. The other figures were practically unchanged.

Protected goods, then, cost more than they otherwise would have cost; (though not necessarily more than they *had* cost at some previous time before duties were imposed or raised; for an increase in tariffs may coincide with a catastrophic fall in the general price level more than sufficient to outweigh the price-raising tendency of the higher duties, as has happened in the years 1930-1933). There is no reason why non-protected goods should cost less than they otherwise would have cost. Indeed if the tariff covers a wide range of goods and all stages of production, as it does in Canada, the non-protected goods will also probably cost more. If the farmer, fisherman, lumberman, miner, paper-manufacturer, have to pay more for their machinery or their clothing, for example, the price of their products will certainly not be lower than it would have been in the absence of the tariff, and is likely to be higher. Goods in general will be scarcer, the purchasing power of the dollar will be less. This is what is meant by "unnecessarily high prices to the consumer".

At this point someone is sure to ask "What about infant industries? Is there not a case for protecting new industries of a kind which, once established, could produce at least as cheaply as their foreign competitors, but which cannot get started without protection because powerful foreign firms are ready to kill them by reckless price-cutting?". There is. But experience suggest that it is not easy to decide beforehand which "infants" are likely, within a reasonable time, to be able to dispense with protection; nor to take away protection once granted, however debilitated the "infant" may prove to be. Sir Charles Tupper, before the "National Policy" of 1878 was adopted, prophesied that in fifteen years we should be able to do away with protection. Sir Josiah Stamp is forced to admit, even in the act of pleading for the adoption of protection in Britain, "the universal experience that a tariff cannot be properly devised by our political machine in the single economic interest of the country and kept politically undebauched."[2]

There is also the "guaranteed market" argument. Given a protective duty which guarantees the whole domestic market, cannot an industry sometimes plan its output to secure the maximum economies of mass production and so sell to the consumer at a price as low as he could find anywhere? Yes, provided the industry is a monopoly. With a number of competing firms, no single establishment would have any guarantee at all.

[2]*Papers on Gold and the Price Level*, p. 61.

What is more important, the public would have no guarantee that a monopolist would not take advantage of the tariff. In practice, therefore, the application of this argument also is likely to be very limited.

The direct results of the tariff for the consumer, however, are by no means the only ill effects which flow from it. The primary aim of a protective tariff is to restrict imports. What does this mean to the exporter?

The Technique of Trade.

To answer this question we must ask what happens when we import. The usual practice of course is for the Canadian importer to give his foreign creditor a bill of exchange. This bill may be drawn in terms of Canadian money or of some foreign money. If it is in terms of foreign money, the Canadian will have to obtain foreign money to pay it. This he can do only by (a) selling something (goods or services) to foreigners and so securing a claim to foreign money, or (b) by buying such a claim to foreign money from some other Canadian who has sold something to foreigners, or (c) by borrowing foreign money from foreigners. The first two methods obviously involve exports of goods or services by Canada; and as foreign loans must ultimately be paid the third method also involves Canadian exports sooner or later.

If the bill of exchange is in terms of Canadian money, the foreign creditor may do one of several things with it:

1. As long as we were on the gold standard, he could claim Canadian currency, exchange it for gold at the rate of 23.22 grains to the dollar, and take the gold out of the country. Since Canada is a gold-producing and gold-exporting country, the foreigner ordinarily did this with part of his claims to our money, to the mutual satisfaction of himself and the Canadian gold mining companies. But the foreigner's actual demand for our gold is normally very limited. From 1926 to 1931 our net exports of gold were never more than $85,000,000 a year while total annual exports averaged over $1,000,000,000. In 1934, net exports of gold were $94,215,736; total exports $751,649,391. Moreover, our monetary gold reserve is always relatively small ($90,000,000 to $140,000,000) and our annual gold production smaller still ($40,000,000 to $102,453,960), while our imports of goods for the years 1928 to 1931 averaged over $1,000,000,000 a year, and in 1934 $513,469,497. Clearly the foreigner who sells

goods to us simply cannot begin to convert all his claims to Canadian money into gold for shipment abroad. If he tried he would soon find us forbidding the free export of gold, as indeed we have done.

2. But what is to prevent him from claiming Canadian money other than gold and taking that out of the country? Nothing, except common sense. Canadian bronze or silver coins, dollar bills, bank notes or cheques on Canadian banks are of practically no use outside Canada. A German who sells goods to Canadians and gets Canadian money for them cannot proffer that Canadian money to his grocer to pay for the week's supply of sauerkraut.

3. The foreigner may of course exchange his claim to Canadian money for foreign money. But this involves finding someone who has foreign money and wants Canadian. This someone can only be a Canadian who has sold something abroad and so got possession of foreign money which he cannot use at home, or a foreigner who has bought something from Canadians and needs Canadian money to pay for it. In other words, this process also sooner or later involves Canadian exports of goods or services.

4. The foreigner may use his claim to Canadian money to pay debts to Canadians or interest on such debts. Selling us goods or services is in fact ultimately the only way he can get our money to pay what he owes us.

5. He may invest his Canadian money in Canada, either by leaving it on deposit in Canadian banks or by buying Canadian securities or setting up new industries in Canada.

6. He may use it to buy Canadian services: for example, to travel in Canada, buying Canadian food, drink, hotel accommodation, transportation, scenery, amusements, hair-cuts, shoe-shines. He does this in normal times to the tune of $175,000,000 a year, ($84,000,000 net in 1934).

7. He may use it to buy Canadian goods: wheat, flour, paper, minerals, etc. This, as our trade returns show, is what he does with most of it.

When we restrict imports by our tariff we prevent the foreigner from getting as much Canadian money as he otherwise would have got. We make it hard for him to pay his debts to us. We force him to cut down either his annual investment in Canada or his purchases of Canadian goods and services, or both.

To use a familiar metaphor, the "tariff wall" keeps foreign goods out, but it also keeps our own goods in .

This disposes of the famous arguments that the tariff increases since 1930 have been necessary (1) to secure a "favourable" balance (surplus of exports, visible and invisible) to pay the interest and dividends on Canadian securities held abroad, and (2) to "defend the dollar", that is, presumably, to keep it at a high level in terms of gold. It should also be clear that a protective tariff can increase employment and wages in the protected industries only at the expense of employment and/or the standard of living in non-protected industries, especially the export trades.

The Fallacy of Self-Sufficiency.

But even if there is no necessary logical connection between planning and self-sufficiency, will not the prevailing tendency of most nations towards self-sufficiency force us in the same direction? If other countries refuse to take our goods or services, what can we do but shut our door against theirs? The answer is that in the conditions supposed no action on our part will be necessary. Circumstances will have shut the door for us. If our exports of goods and services cease, our foreign credits disappear. Without foreign credits we cannot buy from the outside world. Whether we had a high tariff or none at all, we should be as completely isolated as the most benighted protectionist could wish, as self-sufficient as a tribe of Eskimos before the coming of the white man,—and probably with a rather similar standard of living.

No one, of course, really expects the madness of economic nationalism to go quite as far as this. Long before it did the catastrophic fall in standards of living would have provoked revolution in every important trading country. But it may easily go far enough to impose on Canada a very considerable reduction in exports and hence in the foreign credits necessary to procure imports. The briefest examination of our list of imports[3] is enough to show how serious would be the effect on our standard of living. Under any system a decline in our foreign trade means national impoverishment. The increased efficiency due to planning might offset even a large drop in exports. But if other countries persist, even in face of such inducements to trade as we propose below, in excluding our goods more and more completely, we shall utimately have no

[3]See also Chapter II.

choice but to adjust ourselves to a lower *average* level of incomes, and the function of the planning authority will be simply to make the adjustment as quickly and equitably as possible, instead of allowing certain groups to suffer a prolonged agony while others are protected.[4] To meet the difficulties caused by higher foreign tariffs by raising our own tariff is simply to speed up the process of national semi-starvation. It will, of course, maintain or develop the protected industries. But the purchasing-power necessary for this does not fall as the gentle rain from heaven. It comes from the pockets of consumers and exporters already impoverished by higher foreign tariffs. The prairie farmer, deprived of markets by the Hawley-Smoot tariff, finds cold comfort in a policy which keeps up or increases the cost of his implements and clothing and makes it harder for his remaining customers to buy. Because the policy of other countries may eventually thrust poverty upon us, need we, seeing it afar off, run to embrace it?

B. A POLICY OF NON-DISCRIMINATION.

Protectionisim, in fact, is the antithesis of socialist planning. For protection fosters home industries more or less regardless of cost. A socialist community, on the other hand, seeking the highest possible standard of living for its members, tries to meet its wants with the minimum expenditure of its resources, human and material. In the words of Mr. H. D. Dickinson of Leeds University,[5] "The principle of comparative costs applies to a socialist economy as to a capitalist one. If a good can be obtained from abroad in return for the export of goods whose cost is less than the cost of producing the first-mentioned good at home, then a net gain of economic welfare results from importing the good instead of producing it at home. This is subject to qualifications. For example, it is only true of costs reckoned in the long run, and not of short-period prices, which may diverge considerably from cost. It is not worth while importing goods that are temporarily cheap owing to a price-cutting policy, if their introduction necessitates changes in the allocation of capital and labour at home that have quickly to be reversed again. Even if the imports are permanently cheap, the adjustments in home production may cost more than the savings

---

[4]See L.S.R. pamphlet No. 1. *Dividends and the Depression.* Also Innis and Plumptre, *The Canadian Economy and Its Problems.*
[5]*Economic Journal*, June, 1933, "Price Formation in a Socialist Community". A most valuable article.

effected by importation. Now a socialist community can make allowance in its estimates for *all* the relevant costs (abandonment of specialized plant, retraining of skilled labour, etc.) and can spread the charge over that period of time during which equipment and labour would naturally be renewed".

Mr. Dickinson goes on to suggest that "there may be political reasons for not being dependent on foreign countries for particular products". This argument, Adam Smith's "Defence is better than opulence" in modern dress, is, we think, irrelevant to the Canadian situation. Canada's geographical position makes her practically invulnerable to attack except by the United States, against whom no conceivable preparedness would be of any use. For Canada to sacrifice "opulence" to "defence" would be to give the substance for the shadow.

There may be, also, to quote Mr. Dickinson once more, "social reasons for developing certain branches of domestic production beyond the point indicated by the principle of non-discrimination. In all these cases definite subsidies should be paid to the industries concerned. In this way it will be possible to see clearly the real social cost of a policy of exclusion. . . . But these exceptions apart, the policy of a socialist community with regard to foreign trade should be . . . . non-discrimination between domestic and foreign sources of supply".

It should be noted that this implies also non-discrimination between imperial and foreign sources of supply. There is no economic reason why we should extend to any part of the empire any concessions which we are not ready to extend equally to every foreign country. An agreement with Britain which would cheapen British goods for us and give us a larger share of the British market would of course be very welcome. But so would a similar agreement with China, Abyssinia, the United States, or Soviet Russia. If Britain will give us particularly good terms for our exports, it may pay us to buy British goods even if they are more expensive than some others. Exactly the same is true, however, of our dealings with any other country, and especially with the United States, our nearest and largest potential market.

The chief non-economic argument for a "soft-boiled" policy is the one that we must protect our national culture against the inroads of Americanism.   How far we have a national culture distinguishable from that of the United States is a point on which Englishmen and Canadians, for example, may differ.

The directorates of Canadian industry certainly do not reveal any great gulf fixed between American and Canadian business men, nor any profound repugnance in the latter to have "truck or trade with the Yankees". However this may be, if the chief bulwark of Canadian nationality is a tariff, one of whose main and most belauded results is the widespread establishment of American branch factories in Canada, then Canadian nationality is in a sorry plight. For our part, we do not believe that Canadians will love their country only if they are kept poor.

Acceptance of the policy of non-discrimination would mean a revolution in our fiscal policy: the striking off of the shackles from our export trade—one of the first and most urgent tasks of reconstruction—and the eventual disappearance of a number of protected secondary industries. We do not, of course, propose to abolish these over-night. The planning authority will have quite enough problems on its hands without gratuitously adding to them by reckless action. But industries which habitually depend on the tariff for their existence are living on a dole which our export staples cannot much longer afford to pay. These parasites must be got rid of just as fast as the planning authority can provide new employment for the displaced workers.

The relief to the exporter and consumer resulting from the abolition of protection will set free purchasing power. Some of this can go to expand the market of, and employment in, existing non-protected industries. The rest will be available for providing new opportunities of employment, the training necessary to take advantage of them and adequate maintenance during the period of reorganization. It is worth recalling here that in the woollen cloth industry, as Professor Taylor's computation shows, we could afford to pension off the whole working force at much more than its present low wages and still show a modest net gain to the nation; and what is true of this industry may easily be true of others. Professor Norman Rogers, in a brief submitted to a Nova Scotia Royal Commission on behalf of the Nova Scotia Government, estimates the cost of the tariff to Canadian consumers in 1931 at $425,448,000.[6]

The Effects on Particular Industries.

The popular notion that abolition of protection would make us a nation of hewers of wood and drawers of water is, of course,

---

[6]*A Submission on Dominion-Provincial Relations and the Fiscal Disabilities of Nova Scotia,* 1934, p. 96. For a criticism of his method in reaching this estimate see D. C. MacGregor, "The Provincial Incidence of the Canadian Tariff," in the *Canadian Journal of Economics and Political Science,* Aug., 1935.

fantastic. But just how many of our industries would disappear in such a fiscal revolution is not easy to say. An industry's own plea that it would collapse without protection cannot always be taken at its face value. When the protection is not more than about 20 per cent.[7] (and sometimes perhaps even where it is much higher) it is possible that reorganization,[8] or the general expansion and greater stability to be expected of a planned economy, or the relief afforded by the new fiscal policy in the form of cheaper raw materials or machinery, might enable a protected industry to survive.

We cannot insist too often that we do not propose simply to remove protection but rather to substitute for it *effective control* in the interests of the community. In chemicals, for example, the fertilizer section is on an export basis, while the rest of the industry is rather highly protected. But whether replacement of protection by a guaranteed market for such products as the industry could deliver at not more than the long-term price offered by its foreign competitors would mean serious contraction is not easy to say, especially as many chemical products are by-products of other industries, such as electric power and non-ferrous metal smelting and refining, which are certain to persist under any policy.

In the iron and steel group, the agricultural implement industry could almost certainly carry on. In 1930,[9] 45 per cent. of its production was for export, another 10 per cent. was custom and repair work, and a large part of the rest enjoyed protection of not more than about 14 per cent. In 1931 production was little more than a quarter of the 1929 figure. The main hope of revival or even survival here lies in the return of prosperity to the farmer. If this can be assured, the agricultural implement industry could afford to view removal of its protection with stoic calm (though it might be very far from actually doing so).

It is probable also that most of the primary iron and steel section would survive. Rolling mill products, which in 1931 made up 70 per cent. of its production, had protection of about 8 per cent. to 19 per cent.; ferro-alloys and direct castings were on the free list or only slightly protected, and imports of these were

[7]Duties calculated throughout on basis of January, 1933, rates plus sales tax, plus special "excise" on imported goods, less sales and/or excise on domestic products.

[8]For example, in sugar refining, which, even in 1929, was operating at only about 50% of capacity: *Financial Post Business Year Book*, 1933, p. 53.

[9]These and similar figures, except where otherwise stated, are from D.B.S. reports, usually the *Census of Industry*, 1931. As the trend of business in 1935 seems to be carrying us back to about the 1931 level, we have used 1931 figures in preference to 1932 or 1933. 1934 figures are not yet available.

negligible. Pig-iron alone in this section is substantially protected, but as production in 1932 was only 144,000 tons as against 1,090,000 in 1929, this problem is no longer formidable.

Motor cars are highly protected. But Mr. Ford in 1926 declared that his plant could do without protection;[10] and the abolition of duties on motor car parts, coupled with the maintenance of preferential rates on "Canadian" cars in other parts of the empire might make it worth while for General Motors to continue at least partial operation of its plant.

Railway rolling stock enjoys protection of 14 per cent. to 36 per cent., but 40 per cent. of its production in 1931 was custom and repair work which would continue anyhow.

From the iron and steel group, therefore, there might disappear pig-iron, castings and forgings, boilers, tanks and engines, machinery (other than agricultural), perhaps two-thirds of the motor car section, motor car parts, perhaps 60 per cent. of railway rolling stock production, some wire goods, sheet metal products (except custom and repair work), hardware and tools: fixed capital of $260,000,000; 67,000 employees and $82,000,000 in salaries and wages. It is highly improbable that all of this would go, but it is well not to underestimate the problem.

Distilling, though highly protected, is on an export basis. Brewing, also highly protected, is controlled by six or seven strong companies,[11] with almost no funded debt. To both of these, protection is probably superfluous.

In tobacco manufacturing, cigars and cigarettes have substantial protection. The industry is dominated by one company of great financial strength (a subsidiary of British-American),[12] which even during the depression has kept its dividends at a steady $5,000,000 or so. Fixed capital is about $12,500,000, employees number about 9,000, salaries and wages are over $8,000,-000. It seems possible that at least the moderately protected chewing and smoking tobacco sections—about one-third of the whole—might continue.

The textile industry is among our most heavily protected, and it is likely that a good deal of it would vanish, unless the raising of the present low wages were accompanied by a more than proportional increase in efficiency. Many specialty companies, however, would probably remain, and much of the knitted goods industry. Even the fate of the basic textiles is perhaps proble-

10Aikman, *The Automobile Industry of Canada*, p. 41. (McGill Economic Studies, 1926).
11*Financial Post Survey of Corporate Securities*, 1932, pp. 112-120; 1933, pp. 137-143.
12*Ibid.*, 1932, p. 258; 1933, p. 266.

matical. The silk industry has expanded considerably even during the depression, and the financial statements of its leading companies[13] show that they have been doing very nicely for themselves. The cotton industry is dominated by three financial groups, the two largest interlocking with each other and with two of the three important woollen concerns. The six cotton and woollen concerns controlled by these interests were before the depression in a fairly strong financial position, and even in 1932 paid dividends almost as large as in 1929.[14] At worst, total disappearance of basic textiles and two-thirds of the knitted goods would involve fixed capital of about $98,000,000; 44,000 employees; and $36,500,000 in salaries and wages.

The boot and shoe industry, highly protected, seems to be also highly competitive. With unification, therefore, it might survive the loss of protection. Fixed capital is $11,266,000; employees number 14,000; salaries and wages amount to $12,340,000.

In the coal industry, withdrawal of protection would probably drive Nova Scotia out of the St. Lawrence market. Even with a return of prosperity, it is doubtful whether the Maritime Provinces and Newfoundland could absorb more than about half the capacity output of Nova Scotia mines. The probable contraction in coal would be: fixed capital $24,000,000; employees 6,000; salaries and wages $7,000,000.

Petroleum products have rather more than moderate protection (19 per cent. to 28 per cent.) but the very strong financial position of the dominant company (a subsidiary of Standard Oil of New Jersey) suggests that a socialized oil-refining industry could hold its own comfortably against foreign competition. In 1932, the industry paid dividends of $7,566,894, approximately the same as in 1929 (despite a falling off in capital invested). Its payroll was $6,142,000.[15]

The total possible contraction in industry, taking together the specified sections of iron and steel, textiles, boots and shoes, tobacco and coal, would be: fixed capital $400,000,000; employees 137,000; salaries and wages $144,000,000.

These are formidable figures. They are the measure of the exploitation of the consumer, the exporter and the non-protected industries and trades generally. The total contraction in employ-

13*Ibid.*, 1932, pp. 149-150; 1933, p. 124 and elsewhere. See also L.S.R. pamphlet No. 1, *Dividends and the Depression; Price Spreads Report*, p. 83.

14*Financial Post Survey of Corporate Securities*, 1932; pp. 147-155, pp. 122-131. On the profits of the primary cotton and woollen manufacturers, see *Report of the Royal Commission on Price Spreads*, pp. 81-82.

15Dividend figures from *Financial Post Survey of Corporate Securities*, 1934, deducting Imperial Oil's foreign earnings.

ment, for example, large as it is, must be set against the much larger number of persons (well over 500,000) engaged in the export industries which for half a century have been bled by the "National Policy".

Removal of protection, even if spread over a number of years, as it would have to be, would certainly mean a considerable industrial dislocation. But it must mean, also, a great increase in exports (which alone can pay for increased imports), and a large saving to consumers on purchases running into hundreds of millions. The Canadian people would be able to supply themselves with more of the goods concerned, at lower prices, and so have a large amount of "new" purchasing power available for industrial expansion of the kind which the plan contemplates.

Moreover: (1) it is possible that rationalization measures might effect a sufficient reduction in cost to make it worth while to retain some of these industries, at least as long as the present capital equipment is up-to-date and in working order.

(2) State monopoly by a socialized industry might effect such a reduction in marketing expenses as to put some of these industries in a position to produce at a reasonable cost.

(3) As population and standards of living increase, and as industrialization advances, many industries which are at present uneconomic will become well suited to Canada. The question of import policy will then become a part of the general problem of planning the development of industries.

It is worth remembering, too, that the problem of dislocation is far less formidable now than it would have been in 1929. The depression has already done a large part of the job. Between 1929 and 1931, in the sections of iron and steel likely to disappear under the new policy, employment declined by 26,000, salaries and wages by $50,000,000. 1932 witnessed a further shrinkage of 13,000 and $23,000,000. Two of the largest iron and steel companies are virtually or even formally bankrupt. In basic textiles and knitted goods, the decline (1929-1931) was 4,700 and $4,998,000; in boots and shoes 1,400 and $2,690,000; in coal 1,700 and $13,250,000; in tobacco (cigars and cigarettes) 240 and $258,000; grand totals, taking 1931 figures, of 34,000 and $71,-000,000. Why try to re-absorb these displaced workers into parasitic industries? The attempt is contrary to the whole idea of planning. Now is the time to begin to cut our losses and start afresh on a sound basis.

The principle of non-discrimination is, of course, very far

from being the whole socialist policy for foreign trade. Indeed it is no more essentially a socialist principle than is cleanliness. An intelligent socialist community will practise both as a matter of course, as indispensable conditions of progress. But just as capitalism may make cleanliness practically unattainable for many people, so it may lead to the adoption of foreign trade policies which, from the point of view of the community, are foolish to the verge of incredibility.

For though protection is demonstrably injurious to the economic welfare of the community, it can unquestionably net a handsome profit to the protected industries; and under capitalism it is the private, not the public, interest which is decisive. When, as in Britain from 1860 to 1930, non-discrimination suits the book of the most powerful economic groups, even a capitalist state will practise it. When, as in most capitalist countries most of the time, and flagrantly in Canada since 1878, it is precisely those who profit by protection who control the political machinery, the principle of non-discrimination is relegated to the universities.

Tariff-making is only an unusually obvious illustration of how the state is used as the instrument of capitalist exploitation, protection only one form of that exploitation. Nothing is more pathetic than the idea that we can get rid of this particular kind of "legalized robbery" and leave the capitalist framework intact. To expect a capitalist Canada to practise non-discrimination is to expect that mud shall cease to be dirty.

C. A Socialist Policy for Foreign Trade.

If non-discrimination is no more than a basic assumption of socialist foreign trade policy, what are to be the aims of that policy?

The first is not, as one might perhaps expect, imports as cheap as possible, but the best obtainable combination of cheap imports and good export markets. If the United States, for example, were ready to offer us preferential entry to her market in return for special terms for her goods here, it might pay us to accept, even if it meant buying a certain proportion of our textiles or steel at higher prices than we should pay for similar British, French or German products. The widening of our export markets might be worth the sacrifice (if it were not, we ought not to make it), and in a socialist Canada it should be easy to arrange an equitable division of the net gain to the community.

Here again is nothing essentially socialist, except the practicability of such arrangements under socialism and their almost complete impracticability under capitalism. Of the latter, the very meagre results of the Ottawa Conference are illustration enough. The political strength of the protected industries imposed a veto on serious concessions.

Foreign Trade and Socialist Planning.

The second aim is in a different category. If we could socialize everything over-night, any special foreign trade policy or organization would probably be superfluous. Within the limits laid down by the national plan and commercial treaties, and under the control of the national bank, the various socialized industries and services might be left to manage their own importing and exporting. But socialism in the twinkling of an eye is out of the question. Large sections of industry will inevitably remain for a time in private hands. It is in this transition period that the battle for socialism will be won or lost. In that battle, control of the foreign exchanges is an essential weapon. But effective control of the exchanges would be difficult if private firms were free to deal directly with their foreign customers. The advent of a socialist government in Canada would be a strong inducement to the exporter to leave the proceeds of his sales on deposit in foreign banks instead of selling his foreign exchange for Canadian funds and so making it available for Canadian import purchases. The result might be a famine in foreign exchange, a collapse of the Canadian dollar, which would make the price of all but the most essential imports absolutely prohibitive and would seriously curtail our purchases even of them. The consequent scarcity of consumers' goods might easily bring about the fall of the government; nor would the prospect of such an event act as a deterrent to firms which contemplated building up balances abroad.

Even if the private exporters neglected this dazzling opportunity for sabotage there would still remain a danger hardly less serious from the side of the importers. If importing is left in private hands, what is to prevent certain importers from buying raw materials cheap abroad and selling finished products dear at home? Foreign competition? But the importer may be a member of an international combine. New domestic competition? That would probably be prohibited under the plan as wasteful duplication. British war-time experience showed clearly that in such circumstances the most valiant attempts at price control are, in the absence of import control, largely futile.[16]   And a socialist government which failed to control profiteering would enjoy an existence "poor, nasty, brutish and short".

To leave foreign trade in private hands, therefore, is to invite disaster. The policy of non-discrimination, and trade treaties on that basis, require no more than adjustments of the tariff, revolutionary in their consequences but not novel in kind. But the mobilization of export credits for the purposes of the plan, and the control of prices charged by private industry during the transition period, call for a completely new method of control. Foreign trade, like finance, is one of the key functions of the economy which must be socialized at once.

Import and Export Boards.

The new machinery fortunately need not be very elaborate. Foreign trade would be under the general supervision of the Department of Trade and Commerce, whose chief function on its external trade side would be to assist and advise the Department of External Affairs in the negotiation of commercial treaties. Responsibility for the actual conduct of foreign trade would be entrusted to two boards, import and export. The Import Board should consist of ten members, one appointed by the central bank, one by the railway management, one by the Commission of Internal Trade, and seven by the government, with the advice of the Commissioner of Appointments, to represent the chief importing interests. The Export Board similarly would have ten members: one appointed by the bank, one by the railway, and eight by the government to represent the chief export interests and shipping. When any major industry had been socialized or organized on a co-operative basis, it would take over from the government the appointment of its representative on the Import or Export Board. In this way, the boards would be intimately related not only with the industries directly concerned, but with banking, transport and internal trade, and would be kept from becoming instruments of capitalist vested interests.

The two boards would have complete control of the whole of our foreign trade. This does not of course mean that the Export Board would itself engage in exporting everything from newsprint to rubber goods, nor that the Import Board would be the sole importer of everything from raw cotton to Viennese finger-bowls. On the contrary, the main function of each board

---

[16]E. M. H Lloyd, *Experiments in State Control*, is a most valuable reference on this subject.

would be to set up as fast as possible subordinate organizations to deal in particular commodities or groups of commodities.[17] These organizations would inevitably make very wide use of the methods, mechanism and technical personnel of existing private concerns. With many specialty imports, indeed, the Import Board need not trouble itself at all: *de minimis non curat lex*. It would be quite sufficient to grant, for example, to department stores, a block of foreign exchange to be spent as the importer saw fit. (His buying would of course be governed by the demand at home.) Similarly, with small tourist purchases. Decentralization and the avoidance of bureaucracy should be the key-notes of the whole process. In this, as in many other aspects of a socialist system, much the same people would continue to do much the same work as now. The difference would lie in the change from private to public control and in the very different end in view.

As each industry became socialized or organized on a co-operative basis, it would gain complete freedom to conduct its own foreign business as it pleased, subject only, of course, in this as in all else, to the plan and the responsibility to the public which that involved. Wheat exporting, for example, has already been turned over to a reconstituted Wheat Board. As socialization advances, the Import and Export Boards will "wither away".

Meanwhile, within the limits of the plan and of commercial treaties, the boards and their subordinate organizations would do business on ordinary commercial lines. The Export Board would deposit its foreign bills and drafts with the bank in exchange for Canadian money which it would pay to the organizations on whose behalf it had been dealing. The bank would have at its disposal foreign exchange from this source and from tourist trade and other "invisible" exports. From its total foreign exchange holdings it would deduct what it thought necessary for its own reserves, the service of foreign loans, and in years of high export prices a further sum for a stabilization fund to be used to help keep up the national income in times of low export prices. The rest it would hand over to the Import Board which would use it to buy foreign goods or services for re-sale to import-consuming industries. If desired, the board could serve as an instrument of public finance by selling at a profit. The Canadian money received would be deposited in the bank where it would be available for the Export Board's payment to exporters.

As we may continue to sell to Britain more than we buy from her, and buy from the United States more than we sell to her,

17Cf. the machinery of the Natural Products Marketing Board.

the Import Board may find itself with a surplus of sterling and a deficiency of United States dollars. This, however, need cause the board no more anxiety than it causes private traders at present. Through the bank the board may sell sterling for United States dollars precisely as private traders, viewed collectively, do now.

The two boards would co-operate in the establishment of foreign agencies (which could absorb the Commercial Intelligence Service) and in advising the government, through the Department of Trade and Commerce, in the negotiation of commercial treaties. In these negotiations the government would, as now, ask other countries for quotas or lower duties for Canadian exports, and would be able to offer in exchange, as it can hardly do now, to take a specified quantity, or proportion of our requirements, of given commodities from this or that nation. The Import Board ought, however, to be free to buy *within* the nation concerned at the best prices it can get.

The disappearance of parasitic vested interests would enable us to offer concessions of real value, to insinuate and reciprocate rather than "blast" our way into world markets. Socialism would, in fact, give us a bargaining strength of which free trade and protection alike would deprive us: free trade because it would oblige us to deny special concessions to any *one* country, protection because it prevents substantial concessions to *any* country. Only a socialist government is free to bargain with a single eye to the interests of the whole nation. Particular socialized industries no doubt might sometimes try to gain special advantages at the expense of the whole. But the atmosphere of a socialist community is unfavourable to such attempts, and the searchlight of publicity too bright and penetrating to give them much chance of success. In general, the only pressure would be from importers to buy cheap and from exporters to sell dear, which, within proper limits, is highly desirable.

The whole complexion of international trading is changing, and has now reached a point where it is absurd to think that we can go on trying to sell or buy abroad on the old individualist lines or even by the favourite Canadian method of tariff bargaining. In the past, trade between nations was carried on between hundreds or thousands of individuals. The Canadian farmer sold wheat in Britain in a genuinely competitive market, competitive as between seller and seller and as between buyer and buyer. Today he sells not to competing buyers but to a combine of British millers, who agree among themselves what the price shall be.[18] Similarly, when we buy anthracite coal we do not buy from numerous independent producers in a free market, but from an air-tight combine of British coal exporters or from its counterpart in the United States. Whether we are buying abroad or selling abroad, we have to deal with huge combines of tremendous bargaining power. No wonder we have to sell more of our own products to get the imports we need! No wonder the major part of the burden of falling world prices has been shifted to our shoulders! The unorganized producer and consumer will always be exploited; only by organizing can they hope to bargain on equal terms with the great corporations.[19]

A single Canadian export organization should be able, especially when dealing with several competing buyers, to get a better price than several Canadian exporters competing among themselves. Similarly, a single import organization should be able to get lower quotations than a number of small importers bidding against each other.

Objections Answered.

The objections to the policy outlined fall under four heads. As far as Canada is concerned, they can all be disposed of very briefly.

There is, first, the complexity of the technical problems. But, as already pointed out, the existing mechanism can be adapted to new purposes, comparatively simply. The amount of new machinery to be set up is very small. Moreover, most of our trade is with Britain and the United States, which greatly lessens the complexity of the technical problem; and we can draw on a considerable fund of war-time experience of such controls both here, and even more in Britain[20]—to say nothing of the U.S.S.R.

Second, it is urged, a system of Import and Export Boards may be used as a cloak for protectionist exploitation. This is true enough, but an intelligent socialist government would avoid the danger by operating the system on a basis of non-discrimination.

Third, state control of foreign trade may be a danger to world peace. But since our trade is mainly with Britain and the United

[18]Cf. *Evidence before the Banking Committee*, 1934, p. 120; Royal Commission on Price Spreads, 1934-1935, *Evidence*, p. 3917.

[19]This is avowedly the motive behind the Natural Products Marketing Act, 1934. See Mr. Bennett's speech, *House of Commons Debates*, June 7, 1934.

[20]E. M. H. Lloyd, *op. cit.*, and A. Berriedale Keith, *War Government of the British Dominions.*

States, with either of whom a war is hardly conceivable, this objection need not detain us, especially as any tariff we are likely to adopt will certainly be fraught with at least equal perils.

Fourth, disappearance of the tariff would mean a serious loss of government revenue. We have already pointed out that the Import Board could be used as an instrument of public finance, but much more than this can be said in countering this argument. First, this objection applies equally to free trade. Second, under a protective regime the greater the protection the less the revenue (as even Canadian protectionists are beginning to realize). Third, customs revenue has already shrunk so much that it is no longer nearly as important absolutely or relatively as it once was:[21] (here again the depression has smoothed the way to reconstruction). Fourth, the complete abolition of customs duties would be a stimulus to much needed reform in our taxation. Socialists will shed no tears over the disappearance of a tax of which Sir John Simon in his early days once said that "It taxes a man according to the size of his stomach, not of his pocket".

The policy here presented provides a tried and proven means of controlling many prices in the transition period by fixing a percentage of profit on the price at which the Import Board sells to the manufacturer or wholesaler. It substitutes a simple control for a cumbersome, uncertain tariff mechanism which is at present one of the chief obstacles to our foreign trade. It ends protectionist exploitation of the consumer, sets free our export trade, and eliminates the tariff lobby which has poisoned Canadian politics for half a century. It gives us new bargaining power in a world drifting more and more towards extreme economic nationalism. It has above all the supreme merit of depriving the enemies of socialism of two means of sabotage which might otherwise prove fatal.

[21]*Canada Year Book*, 1933, pp. 826-827; *H. of C. Debates*, 1935, pp. 2135-2136.

	1929	1932	1933
Customs Revenue	$187,206,332	$104,132,677	$ 70,073,000
Total Revenue	460,151,481	336,721,305	311,130,000

CHAPTER XV

A CODE FOR LABOUR.

A. THE NEED FOR A LABOUR CODE.

ONE OF the basic convictions which has motivated the writing of this book is that two great classes of Canadian citizens—workers and farmers—seem condemned to live in poverty and economic insecurity, or with the threat of these twin evils hanging constantly over their heads. Even before the depression, the majority of the wage-earners, with whom we are particularly concerned in this chapter, did not earn wages high enough to live in any kind of comfort, or to give their children a healthy and a wholesome start in life. Against the ever-present risks that their wage incomes would cease on account of unemployment, sickness, accident, death or old age, they had no protection at all, or at best very inadequate protection. Their hours of work were often long and their conditions of work unsanitary and unfair. These were the outward, physical manifestations of the fact that Canadian workers, like those in other capitalist countries, were a subordinate class whose well-being was not a primary concern of the rulers of business and industry. The depression, of course, has sharpened the workers' problems immensely. But the problems of the present are essentially the same in kind, if not in degree, as those of 1929. The lot of the Canadian worker then, as well as now, was utterly unsatisfactory and unjust.

It is these basic problems of the worker, along with those of a similar nature which beset the farmer, which our programme of reconstruction is designed to solve. Its aim, so far as labour is concerned, is to provide for working people (1) an adequate and secure scale of living, (2) healthy and decent conditions of work, and (3) genuine democracy in the conduct of industry.

Since the achievement of these objectives is the central concern of the plans outlined in this book, it may be asked why the problems of labour have not been approached more directly, rather than dealing at such length with economic planning, the socialization of finance, and other broad economic issues. The reason is simply that a solution of the ills of the common man in Canada takes us far afield from his low wage, from his lack of a job, from the low price of his farm produce, from his cramped household, from the health of his children, and from his other immediate worries. For the ills of labour spring from a capitalist economic order, and only as that order is overthrown and replaced by a socialist commonwealth, will emancipation from poverty and economic insecurity be achieved. The attention of the planner therefore must first be devoted to the economic system in general and to proposals for its socialist reconstruction.

Reconstruction is needed to provide a solid foundation for the well-being of the mass of the population. But in addition there will be necessary a super-structure of social measures to harness the great basic reforms of economic planning, socialized finance and nationalized industry, to human welfare. In a planned, socialized economy there will still be problems of wages to be solved; there will still remain some risk of unemployment; sickness and old age will interfere with the individual's capacity to work and earn; flesh and blood and spirit will still be in conflict with the demands of machine industry; and problems of democracy in the conduct of industry will remain to be worked out. To meet with these problems, therefore, there must be a variety of social measures—a labour code.

The code outlined in this chapter represents, in large part, the extension and amplification of measures already present in Canada. It was recognized early in the period of the Industrial Revolution that the twin combination of machine industry and *laissez-faire* had but little regard for the human claims of the wage-earners. Trade unionism has emerged, in Canada, as elsewhere, as an instrument of protection for the workers. To some extent employers themselves have introduced "welfare plans" to mitigate some of the grosser hardships of the undiluted wage system. Governments also have intervened to protect the worker. But it is clear that Canada has no genuine national labour code. Nor has any province a logical coherent system of legislation. In each one the existing scheme has been built up piece by piece, without careful planning and co-ordination of one measure with another.

Trade unionism, which ought to be a major element in any system of labour protection, is relatively undeveloped and ineffective in Canada. The unions, few as well as divided among themselves, have so far not been able to make any strong appeal to Canadian workmen to desert the dominant national faith in individualism.

Employers' welfare work as an element in a labour code may be dismissed with a sentence of two. While some Canadian industrialists have followed those of the United States in providing for employees pension schemes, health services, recreation facilities and the like, these plans have done no more than touch the fringe of the great basic problems of labour.

Thus it appears that our existing methods of protecting the workers against the evils of capitalist industrialism are very limited. Even if labour legislation, collective bargaining and company welfare work were much further developed than they are in Canada, they would still fail to solve the problems of labour. Measures of this sort can have but a limited effectiveness in a capitalist economy. For that matter, they are largely incompatible with the capitalist scheme of things; for in general they undertake to protect the worker through a process of comprehensive interference with that free play of competitive forces which is the driving force of the system. If pressed very far, this is intolerable to capitalism, a regime of private enterprise. Whatever lip-service they may pay to it, business interests are generally opposed to social legislation and trade unionism, and no business man will undertake welfare services so expensive as to handicap him in competition with his rivals. Moreover, such protective schemes as do exist are constantly limited in what they can do by the conditions of business. Minimum Wage Boards dare not set wage rates too high for fear of creating unemployment. Trade unions must accept wage reductions when the labour market is glutted. Governments cannot "afford" to make appropriations for social insurance or for proper administration of labour measures when business is poor and taxes are not coming in. The mounting cost of government, particularly of education and the social services, is a favourite lament of business men. If the pressure of government interference in the interests of labour becomes too severe, they will marshal their political forces in a frontal assault on the social services, using the war cries of "economy and retrenchment" and "relief from an insufferable burden of taxation". And, as the real controllers of political power, they will generally be successful.

It is only in a socialist economy, where the wastes of business competition, speculation and financial irresponsibility are eliminated, where it is economically possible to pay good wages, where the risk of unemployment has been minimized, and where schemes to protect the individual against the evils of industrialism do not run counter to the very nature of the economic order, that social legislation, collective bargaining and welfare plans can function adequately. The proposals for a labour code that follow are therefore based upon the assumption that a proper socialist setting is created, within which the detailed measures of the code can work effectively and harmoniously.

A labour code that will meet the objectives outlined above must clearly be organized on a national scale. While there are some sections that might differ from province to province and that might be administered by the provinces without serious consequences, such as technical education, vocational guidance, health and safety provisions, that is not true of such major items as wage regulation, protection against unemployment, social insurance, and the regulation of working hours. With respect to these there must be substantial uniformity across the country, so as to provide for the workman in Halifax the same measure of social justice as for the workman in Vancouver, and so as to put upon industry in all sections of the country an equal burden. It is essential, therefore, that the labour code be worked out under the direction of the national government.

A reformed and expanded Dominion Department of Labour would be the logical agency to undertake this great task. Its work would fall into five great sections: wage regulation, protection against unemployment, social insurance, regulation of working conditions, and industrial democracy. There might be separate divisions of the Department to deal with each major branch of work. The direct administration of a great part of the labour code would be in the hands of the Department. But we do not suggest stripping the provinces completely of authority to legislate in behalf of labour, and we look forward to trade unionism exercising important functions of control. In those spheres of activity reserved to the provinces and the trade unions the Dominion Department would naturally be relatively inactive. Its function, with respect to such fields, would be to encourage uniformity of practice, to stimulate high standards of administration, and to give such guidance and assistance as only the co-ordinating agency of the labour code could provide. Thus even in these fields, it would have a real— and essentially final—responsibility to see that the protection of labour was adequate.

The proposal that the Dominion should take over from the

provinces so much responsibility brings up immediately the problem of administration. How can a national labour code be administered from Ottawa, in view of the great area of Canada? Clearly, the task could only become manageable with a distinct system of administrative decentralization. It would be desirable, no doubt, to establish branches of the Department of Labour for the five main areas of Canada: the Maritimes, Quebec, Ontario, the Prairies and British Columbia. Regional officers for each major service would have their headquarters at these branch offices, so that each branch might function as a miniature Department of Labour for its particular area, in somewhat the way that the provincial departments have operated in the past. It should not be impossible to work out a system for the branch offices whereby they were given a good deal of autonomy with respect to administrative detail, while at the same time they pursued uniform policies in general.

B. Wages and Employment.

Raising and protecting the standard of living of the worker calls for action on a threefold front—wage regulation, the provision of employment, and social insurance. But the importance of the latter requires a section by itself.

Wage Regulation.

The labour code must aim to protect all workers against having to work for "unfair" wages. In the socialist state to which we look forward, industry is to be operated for the benefit of the workers,[1] and arrangements must be made to return to them in wages just as much of the value of their production as is not required for the great social purposes of capital investment, education, government administration and the like, and to divide the wages fund fairly among individuals. In the socialist state we can depend upon this being done "automatically", by the free play of economic forces, even less than in the capitalist state; and it is necessary that we establish a comprehensive system of state wage regulation to achieve this purpose.

Four principles of wage regulation may be suggested to guide the state wage boards—the basic needs of the workers,

---

[1] It should not be necessary to point out that this means "workers by hand and brain"—all those who contribute to the production of useful goods and services, whether by swinging a pick, wielding a pen, managing a factory, treating the sick, or educating the young—but as protection against uninformed criticism, we stress the point.

industry's capacity to pay, the maintenance of fair differentials, and family allowances.

In the first place, wages that are too low to maintain a minimum standard of health and decency should not be permitted. In enforcing such a rule, the wage boards would carry on the work which the present provincial minimum wage boards profess to do for women, and would extend protection to male workers as well. Attempts have been made for years in capitalist countries to apply this principle, that no one should work for less than a "living wage", but only with very partial success. The conditions under which it can work properly are essentially those of the socialist commonwealth.

Secondly, wages should be set as high as industry—the productivity of the country—can afford to pay. It will not be sufficient for workers to have merely a minimum-subsistence wage. They must also be paid as much more than this as is consistent with industrial production and other social claims on that production. The wage boards, therefore, should follow a clear-cut policy of progressively advancing wages as the productivity and efficiency of industry increase. This is required not only in justice to the workers, but also as a means of guaranteeing that consumers' purchasing power is increased to take off the market the expanding production of industry and to forestall "overproduction", or more accurately, "underconsumption", and the unemployment that follows. In applying this principle, the wage boards would have to work closely with the National Planning Commission. The Commission would have to exercise a general control over the amount and the proportion of national income going to wages, to see that too much did not go in this direction when funds were urgently needed for social services or capital investment. The wage boards, concerned to get as much as possible "here and now" for the workers, would naturally press the claims of wages strongly before the Planning Commission. When the Commission's decision was made finally, this would constitute for the boards a general policy which they would administer in detail.

Fair differentials between different classes of workers would also be established and maintained. The achievement of socialist economic "equality" does not preclude the payment of wages and salaries of differing amounts, within reasonable limits. It is both necessary and desirable that the more skilled and able workers should receive higher wage rates than those who are not so valuable to industry and therefore to the community. But a differential system of wages and salaries, sufficient to reward and to encourage initiative and ability adequately, can be worked out without having salaries and fees mount to the ridiculous figures that are often paid at present. Merely to illustrate the point, it may be suggested that differentials might be such that no annual salary or wage, even for the highest official, would exceed $10,000, while the lowest, for an adult, would be at least $1,200. Within these limits there is ample room for a system of differential payments for all classes of workers.

Family Allowances.

A most important principle which should be followed is that of family allowances. Our existing wage system, based theoretically upon payment for results, discriminates against the large family. The unskilled worker who has no one but himself to support may live relatively comfortably on a wage of $3.00 to $4.00 a day. But his fellow workman with a wife and three children to support is mired in poverty. At present the children in large families inevitably suffer. Moreover, it is difficult or impossible under the existing system to fix by law minimum wages high enough to provide for the needs of the large or moderate family. If the minimum cost of living for a family of five is accepted as the basis of wage payments for unskilled labour, the wage burden thrust upon industry becomes impossible under present conditions of productivity and industrial earnings.

These difficulties can be overcome if the wage system is reconstructed by varying earnings in accordance with family responsibilities. There is no space here to do more than suggest how this principle could be applied. To begin with, it would be necessary to decide upon a "basic wage", adequate for a single man, or for a man and wife, to be paid to men without children. Then additional allowances, possibly calculated as percentages of the basic wages, would be paid to those with dependent children. The common labourer, for instance, might receive a basic wage of $4.00 per day if he were single or married without children. But for one dependent child, he might receive an additional allowance of 10 per cent. of his basic wage, for two children an allowance of 18 per cent. and so on. The semi-skilled factory worker might receive a basic wage of $6.00 per day and the skilled printer $8.00 per day, with a similar percentage allowances for dependents. On such a basis the allowance system is not incompatible with wage differentials based on skill, length of service, and responsibility.

Administration of the family allowance principle would require the formation of funds (somewhat akin to social insurance funds) for groups of industrial enterprises, into which each would pay, weekly or monthly, determined portions of its wage bill, so much for each employee, whether he had dependent children or not, and out of which the allowances would be paid. This "clearing fund" system has long been in operation in France and other countries; and it is noteworthy that it effectively prevents discrimination in employment against workers with families, which might otherwise result.

The family allowance system, like most of the other detailed proposals of this chapter, is not new or untried. France and Belgium have had long experience with it, and Australia and New Zealand have tried it out. During the War the dependents of Canadian soldiers received "separation allowances". And unemployment insurance schemes—not to mention relief disbursements—have always recognized the principle. Dependents' allowances have proved to be thoroughly practicable, even under economic conditions much more difficult than those to be anticipated in the planned economy of the future. Some of the worst fears of the opponents of the system have not been realized in practice. For instance, it has not led to the breeding of large families by the weakest elements of the population. Other social factors are at work which increasingly make for low birth rates. Nor has it proved impossibly expensive. It does not involve of necessity an increase in industry's wage bill. The essential idea of the system is rather to redistribute a given wage bill fairly to protect family interests. But, of course, it may and should be employed in connection with a much larger total wage bill than has yet been available.

Wage Boards.

To make these principles of wage regulation effective over the broad field of Canadian industry there would be required a series of wage boards, with a Dominion Wage Board (one of the major divisions of the Department of Labour) at the top. This senior body would give the lead in policy to the various subordinate boards, it would ratify their decisions, it would pass on appeals from their decisions, and it would supervise the enforcement of wage awards.

The subsidiary boards would be directly responsible for setting actual wage rates for different classes of workers. So far as possible, there should probably be "trade boards" established for particular industries, made up of equal numbers of workers and managerial members, with some additional members nominated by the Dominion Board. Where trade unions were in existence they would naturally nominate the workers' representatives; and where there were no unions workers would be encouraged to organize themselves sufficiently to nominate members. Thus procedure in the industrial wage boards would partake considerably of the nature of collective bargaining between organized workers and management, with the friendly assistance of officials or representatives of the Dominion Wage Board. The awards of the trade boards, when ratified by the Dominion Board, would be legally enforceable minimum wage rates. Certain penalties for violation of the regulations would be necessary, and the wage boards would have to have some means of enforcing their decisions. If trade unions were well-developed, they would provide quite effective unofficial machinery of enforcement.

Provision of Employment.

The right to work or the correlative right to maintenance has long been demanded by labour. Full acceptance of this principle must be one of the corner-stones of a labour code. But this does not imply reliance mainly upon relief and insurance schemes, as at present, to give effect to it. A prior principle should be the opportunity of useful work for everyone, with measures of insurance and relief in the background as reserves to meet unavoidable individual cases of unemployment or occasional emergencies. The purpose of the programme of economic planning and reform of economic policy is to stabilize the economy and to curtail unemployment. In this sense, the whole plan is a labour code.

In a more limited sense, however, measures to provide and protect employment should be incorporated in the labour code. Besides the large-scale schemes of economic stabilization to be carried out under the direction of the Planning Commission, there should be many detailed provisions to guarantee security of employment. This work should properly be undertaken by a branch of the Department of Labour, which might be called the Employment Division; but the Division would naturally work very closely with the Planning Commission. To it the Commission would look for information about the state of the labour market and the availability or non-availability of labour for programmes of development. Its statistical reports would reflect the effectiveness of the various policies of planning and control with respect to employment, and it would send back critical reports and suggestions to the Planning Commission.

One of the important sub-departments of the Division of Employment would be an expanded and improved Employment Service of Canada, to be operated entirely as a Dominion service. It is absolutely essential to have an efficient national system of public employment offices that will bring together men and jobs with a minimum of difficulty and expense. Such a system would seem to be meditated by the recent Social Insurance Bill, if the letter of the law is to be taken for its spirit. But it is not merely cavilling to say that whether a really comprehensive employment service is its actual result or not depends on the sincerity with which the need for this reorganization and expansion is regarded. There is no field in which public money can be more justifiably spent, if it is spent scientifically and on proper principles. Firstly, the personnel of the Service should be improved by increasing the educational requirements for officers, providing them with special training and offering salaries which are consistent with the importance of their work. Secondly, the Service should set up specialized departments to deal with the placement of various classes of skilled, clerical, and professional workers for whom it has failed to cater adequately in the past. Thirdly, it should develop the highly important and hitherto neglected work of juvenile placement, co-operating with the schools for this purpose. Finally, it should perform much more of an individual rather than a mass or routine placement job, taking real pains to see that individuals are carefully chosen for new jobs, that the square pegs are put in the square holes.

If policies of this kind are followed and the prestige of the Service raised, the system should become so useful to both workers and employers that they will use the public employment offices as a matter of course and the great bulk of placements will be made through them. This is as it should be. There is scarcely any field in which monopoly of a service is more desirable than that of placement. To make this objective sure of attainment, it may be desirable to inaugurate the compulsory notification of vacancies, such as has been proposed from various quarters in Great Britain. In this event, it would be compulsory for employers to notify the employment offices of all permanent vacancies in their establishments, so that they would have complete information about all job opportunities. The employer would still retain the right to reject the applicant sent from the employment office and to fill the position by other means if he wished to do so.

Another service to be carried on under the direction of the Employment Division would be that of technical education and vocational guidance for young persons. The main responsibility for technical education might remain, as at present, in the hands of the provinces. But the system should be revised and improved in the light of the probable needs for labour in the future, and there should be associated with it a well-ordered plan of vocational guidance. A sub-department of the Division would be required to deal with these problems, meeting some of them directly, laying down standards and policies for the whole country, co-ordinating the work of the provinces and of various private groups, and offering a general service of leadership.

The displacement of workers by technological change would be still another of the problems requiring the attention of the Employment Division. To reduce this difficulty it might seek, in some cases, to slow up the rate of technological change. It might meet the situation by calling a halt to recruiting for the affected trades. Or it might find it necessary to transfer substantial numbers of workers from one locality to another. Again, it might find it expedient to organize special retraining schemes to fit workers to enter another industry. Or it might arrange for the retirement of older workers on pension or for the shortening of working hours. A variety of ways of meeting problems of the kind exist, and different methods may be appropriate in different circumstances. What is needed to make them practical is their integration in a national plan.

The problem of stabilizing the operations of particular enterprises and industries which vary seasonally is so important in Canada that it might be made the work of another specialized sub-department. For while a good deal of seasonal variation in productive industry is probably inevitable in this country, much might be done to lessen it, as the records of progressively managed firms in Canada and the United States prove. A great deal of building could be done in the winter months if the construction business were properly organized for all-year operations, the garment trades could be regularized considerably if cut-throat "style" competition were curtailed, and in almost every branch of industry good management can find ways and means of lessening seasonal fluctuations. This is a field in which the technical staffs of industries could even today do a great deal if they were not hampered by the exigencies of profit-making. A sub-division of the Employment Division, with the co-operation and goodwill of such staffs, could be charged with the task of making a particular study of methods of lessening seasonal variations; and it could be equipped to offer an expert planning and engineering service to productive enterprises, both those that are publicly and those that are privately owned.

Still another of the important tasks of the Division would be to set up permanent machinery, through one of its sub-departments, for the provision of special employment in case of emergency. This department would be concerned particularly with the long-range planning of public works, by the Dominion, provincial and municipal branches of government. Supported by appropriate legislation, it would offer an expert service to the governments with respect to the planning of public construction, and would help them organize their plans so that, in case of need, they might increase construction sharply. Whatever is done to free us from the worst excesses of the business cycle, we shall be affected by the swings of prosperity and depression in other countries so long as we export and import goods in large quantities; and we should be prepared with special measures, such as plans of public construction, to counteract the forces of depression whenever they appear.

It is clear from the foregoing suggestions that the work of the Employment Division would be of the greatest importance. More than any other agency in the system of planning and control outlined in this book, it would be concerned to give real meaning to the "right to work". It would supplement the general work of stabilization to be carried on by the central planning machinery with much detailed work on particular factors that now make for unemployment and contribute heavily to the present total, although they do not always stand out clearly from the general business depression.

C. SOCIAL INSURANCE.

Social insurance which is to measure up to the standards of a socialized economy will be formulated on two principles. First it must be really comprehensive. The major hazards against which the worker and his family need protection are unemployment, sickness, industrial accidents, death and old age. A piecemeal attack which deals partly with one and not at all with another, which covers some workers or some areas and leaves others exposed, is unsatisfactory, whether as a matter of social justice or of administrative efficiency. In addition to such measures as we already have, therefore,—workmen's compensation, old age pensions, mothers' allowances—there must be full-scale unemployment insurance and health insurance. The weaknesses and inadequacies of the existing schemes must be remedied and the whole system co-ordinated, with a major share of the functions of organization and administration falling upon the federal government.

Secondly, social provision of this type must be insurance and not relief: insurance not in the strict actuarial sense, but in the sense of a pooled reserve of money or services or both, to a share in which the worker or his family has a claim if the breadwinner's ability to work is impaired. The right to that claim rests in the fact that the worker is normally a contributor to the wealth of the country. A "dole" which can only be secured if the applicant is destitute or after he has exhausted his own resources is obviously unjust to the thrifty. Our present mothers' pensions and old age pensions are not free from this criticism, and the whole scheme of insurance should be recast so as to make benefits available as of right, instead of being based on a "means" principle.

Little need be said here in defence of social insurance. Its various types are generally accepted now, not only by the public, but by all serious students of the problem, as the best way of providing wage-earners with economic security. The work which requires to be done is to extend them as far as the conditions of Canada demand.

The system should have broad coverings, including all sections of the country, all industries, and all workers requiring protection. Even the best of our existing schemes, workmen's compensation, provides only partial coverings. It does not touch, for example, domestic servants, agricultural workers and the bulk of commercial employees. While it is essential that this principle be accepted in justice to the workers, it must be recognized that its application may not prove easy. Agricultural workers, domestic servants, independent artisans, workers in highly seasonal trades, and workers in frontier industries such as fishing, lumbering and trapping, are notoriously difficult to bring within the scope of social insurance plans, and a good deal of ingenuity may be required to work out a comprehensive programme that will fit all these, and other, particular cases. But with an Employment Service deliberately organized to offer special facilities for special categories of workers, a great deal can be done.

Contributions and Benefits.

Next, we suggest that contributions for all forms of insurance except workmen's compensation, should be made jointly by employers (whether state or private enterprise) and workers, with the Dominion government providing the costs of administration. Industry has an obvious responsibility towards workers who are unable to work and earn, and it is generally conceded that industry should contribute to social insurance. It is not so generally agreed, in socialist circles, that workers should contribute, and there has been much talk, of late, about "noncontributory" social insurance. But we think workers should contribute from their wages towards protection against economic hazards, mainly because of the very real value of an active sense of participation in an enterprise. When workers contribute they realize much more keenly that the total wage bill of the community is being spread over their periods of work and idleness, and they are much more likely to take personal interest in the wise and economical management of the insurance funds. Moreover, direct contributions from the workers will give their representatives an unquestioned right to active participation in management. While we think these are good reasons for favouring workers' contributions, we should add that the issue is much less important than it is usually considered in labour circles. For in a socialist state, if workers do not contribute to the funds, employers will have to give more, and there will be less money available for wages. In the end, therefore, it comes pretty much to the same thing, so far as workers' standards of living are concerned.

The foregoing argument, it should be emphasized, applies to social insurance in the socialist state. With socialist objectives achieved, there will be no huge personal incomes, as at present, and no unappropriated "economic surpluses", such as huge profits on speculative gains. Under these circumstances workers will have no cause to complain if deductions are made from their nominal wages (which should be far higher than they are at present) to provide for them protection against the hazards of unemployment, accident or sickness. For they will see that social insurance is essentially a device for spreading wages over periods of work and of enforced idleness, which is of great value to them; and that in a truly socialist state social insurance revenues, no matter how they are raised, must represent very largely a tax upon wages. The amount of this tax will be substantial, for really adequate social insurance payments, such as are proposed here, may be annually as much as 12 or 15 per cent. of the total wages bill.

With social insurance in the capitalist state and in the transition to socialism, it is different. The wages of most workers are now so low that deductions for social insurance represent an intolerable burden. Moreover, and even more important, there are now large incomes, pockets of profit, and pools of speculative gain, which are held privately at the expense, and as a result of the exploitation of, the workers. These economic surpluses should be taxed to provide funds for social insurance before the workers are asked to contribute; and to the extent that these sources of funds exist, "non-contributory" insurance is thoroughly justified. But it is fair to suggest that these facilities should be extended, not to workers at present in employment, but to those now unemployed or in precarious or underpaid employments. It would not be hard, through co-operative administrative arrangements between the Employment Service and the Wage Board, to organize the necessary transition as workers were placed into more adequate jobs and raised to higher wage-scales.

Insurance benefits should be so adjusted as to protect, so far as possible, differential standards of living. To achieve this objective, it is suggested that they be worked out in proportion to the ordinary wage (plus the family allowance) of the insured person. Thus a labourer with dependent children receiving ordinarily, in wages and allowances, $5.00 per day, might receive as unemployment or sick benefit 80 per cent. of this amount, or $4.00; a printer receiving $8.00 per day, $6,40; and so on. This would mean that a worker who had built up a good standard of living would have that standard protected, rather than receiving, when he was unable to work, only the bare means of subsistence. An upper limit would of course have to be set so that benefits would not be so attractive as to encourage imposition upon the funds.

Every effort must be made to ensure that administration of the social insurance funds is intelligent, efficient, and economical. A unified national system would represent a huge enterprise, with many difficult problems to face, and it would require a large administrative staff. Only as the staff administered the system intelligently and efficiently would it prove satisfactory. The directors of the scheme should be the best men available who are acquainted with the principles and the practice of social insurance; and they would have to train, as rapidly as possible, capable subordinates to carry on the detailed work. Effective administration would be advanced by making the fullest use of the provisions for the democratic participation of insured persons, by means of representatives on boards of appeal, advisory committees, and other administrative bodies.

Types of Social Insurance.

Unemployment insurance will be necessary in socialist Canada, for we are not so optimistic as to prophesy that planning and control will eliminate unemployment altogether. We do contend, however, that it can be reduced to moderate proportions by wise policies of control. Unemployment insurance can then fulfil its proper function of protecting those who suffer such unemployment as cannot be prevented. With relatively light unemployment, benefits can be generous and long periods of eligibility for benefits can be permitted without fear of the scheme going off a sound actuarial basis, as has happened in so many capitalist countries during the depression. While there is no need for a supplementary system of extended benefits with a means test, there should be established a decently ordered system of relief and unemployment assistance to provide for those individuals who fall through the net of protection provided by the labour code, or are still unable to find their way into the ranks of the regularly employed.

Health insurance should provide only cash benefits. Medical benefits would be unnecessary because a medical service for the whole population should be provided, separately from health insurance, through a system of state medicine which will be outlined in the next chapter.

Workmen's compensation is a type of social insurance which, in many ways, stands by itself. Industrial accidents are now generally recognized as particularly the responsibility of industry, and under even the existing schemes industrial enterprises bear the full costs of compensation payments. This principle could be continued. The reforms that we advocate in this field are the extension of the existing systems to all workers, making benefits more generous, and transferring administration from the provinces to the Dominion. And of course, with state medicine in operation, existing workmen's compensation medical services would be transferred to the new schemes of socialized medicine.

The present provincial systems of mothers' pensions should be superseded by a national scheme of widows' and orphans' insurance, under which the widow or dependent child of an insured worker would be entitled to pensions irrespective of their means. This would be the equivalent of compulsory life insurance, in many ways. It would have the double advantage of protecting mothers and children against the death of the wage-earner husband, and of making unnecessary the pitiful attempts to buy small amounts of expensive life insurance from private companies which wage-earners make at present.

Finally, the present inadequate system of old age pensions should be superseded by a national scheme of old age insurance, under which a worker would be entitled to a fair pension at a specified age, irrespective of his means at that time. A retirement age of 65 might be suggested for men, and one of 60 for women. However, there is no reason why a scheme could not be worked out which would permit people to retire from industry earlier, if they wished, at lower-than-standard rates of pension.

The administrative machine to work this great system of social insurance would be a section of the Dominion Department of Labour: the Social Insurance Division. Subsections would be required for each type of insurance in operation, but to a considerable extent there could probably be unified administration. For example, it would no doubt prove possible to have employers pay weekly to a central office lump sums to cover all contributions towards social insurance by them and by their workers. And in small towns one social insurance officer might do administrative work for all types of insurance. Perhaps record-keeping and statistics for all branches could be unified in large measure. But unification should not go too far. The different types of social insurance deal with different problems, and each would have administrative work peculiar to it alone.

D. Working Conditions and Industrial Democracy.

In the plant or the factory the code for labour must be concerned with two particular matters: physical working conditions, and the means to democracy in industry.

Regulation of Working Conditions.

A comprehensive system must be built up and enforced to protect wage earners against long hours of work and against bad working conditions, with special measures for the protection of particular groups, notably women and children.

The regulation of working hours is so important an economic measure that it demands uniformity throughout the country. Therefore it must be a national system. As a minimum standard of general application we should anticipate the eight-hour day and the 44-hour week; and the seven-hour day and the 40-hour week should be achieved as rapidly as possible.

There are many other detailed provisions for industrial health, safety and convenience which are required, too numerous to be specified here. Suffice it to say that the most up-to-date findings of industrial hygiene should be incorporated in these measures, which would go far beyond the provisions of our present factory acts. Inspection and enforcement must be made much more effective. In addition, there should be special legislation for women and young persons in industry, limiting night work, prohibiting their employment in trades unsuitable for them, forbidding entirely the employment of boys and girls under 16, and so forth. For other classes, also, such as seamen and miners, special protective legislation would be required.

A separate section of the Dominion Department of Labour should direct this work. Regulation of working hours it might undertake directly. However, the other items in this part of the labour code might be left to provincial administration. The Division of Labour Protection of the Federal Department would exercise a general supervision over the work of the provinces on these matters and would endeavour to obtain uniformity in legislation and in quality of administration throughout the country.

Industrial Democracy.

The final section of our labour code should aim to introduce and establish genuine democracy in the conduct of industry. It should give positive encouragement to trade unionism, collective bargaining, machinery for the settlement of industrial disputes, works councils and other means of giving an opportunity to labour, both of hand and brain, to make its voice heard. Another branch of the Department of Labour, which might be called the Division of Labour Organization, should undertake this work.

The first means of making this programme effective is to relieve trade unionism from all legal interferences. While unions are legal in Canada, unfriendly courts and police have found various ways and means of interfering with their work. While this danger would be very much less if a socialist government were in office at Ottawa, it would no doubt be wise to do away with it entirely by adopting new trade union legislation to specify clearly the rights of organization and of collective bargaining—something similar to but more effective than the famous section 7A of the American National Recovery Act. The Division of Labour Organization would endeavour to make this legislation effective by upholding the rights of unions in disputes with employers, whether state or private enterprises, by collecting information on problems of organization, by giving publicity to the major issues in departmental reports, and by other means.

However, it is not legislation by the state nor the work of a state department that will build up trade unions. This the workers must do by and for themselves. They must overcome the factionalism which has thus far prevented the emergence of a unified labour movement, they must extend organization to the great manufacturing and distributive industries and they must interest the mass of the workers in the organization. Indeed, they must do a great deal in this direction before the socialist labour code proposed in this chapter can be gained at all.

With widespread trade unionism as a basis, joint industrial councils and works councils, representative of workers and management, can be organized throughout industry to consider matters of interest and importance to labour. It should not be necessary to have them established by law. It would be better to have them develop more spontaneously, from the pressure of trade unions, the promotion of the Division of Labour Organization, and the friendly policy of socialized enterprises.

Through these councils the trade union representatives of the workers would have an opportunity of presenting the views of labour on the hundred and one workshop and industrial problems that concern employees urgently. They would report to the councils infringements of the labour code established by law and would endeavour to have these violations adjusted by the management, without setting in motion the state machinery of enforcement. Thus the councils would become themselves the real agencies of enforcement of the state code, and in the measure of their success would make unnecessary the detailed work of inspection and enforcement which state labour departments must carry on at present if they are to be effective. The workers themselves may substitute democracy for bureaucracy if they wish.

Besides exercising this "police" function, to see that the state labour code was fairly interpreted and obeyed, the councils would have numerous other functions. They would work out for their own plants or industries, by joint agreement, certain schemes of protection of labour on matters of detail not covered by the state code. They would concern themselves with apprenticeship and training inside the plant or the industry, with schemes of employment stabilization and sharing of work, with the joint management of welfare services and with other matters of importance. They might also consider production problems, operating as the agencies through which workers would assist management in solving problems of production, as has been done with some degree of success already in the repair shops of the Canadian National Railways.

Besides having their representatives on these councils, it is to be strongly urged that organized workers should be represented on other agencies concerned with the administration of the labour code. We have proposed already that they should have members on the wage boards. To administer the code successfully there would have to be numerous other committees or boards, for particular purposes, notably in connection with social insurance, whose active interest would be of the greatest importance. The principle of direct representation of the workers on these bodies should be generally followed.

By this means, the principle of collective bargaining can be carried over into our socialist state. But it would be a type of collective bargaining much more developed, more widely employed, and more recognized by law than that which prevails to-day. In effect, it would be part and parcel of the national labour code; and thus labour would take a large place in its administration.

While trade unions and other workers' associations would therefore perform functions that are now carried on almost exclusively by state officials, we do not propose that the unions themselves should be in any way subordinate to the Department of Labour. They must be entirely free of formal connection with the state, having their own freely elected officers, their own funds, and autonomy to reach their own decisions. Moreover, they must be free to call strikes should they desire to do so. The right to strike has always been the final great weapon of labour, and we do not propose that it should be taken away.

However, it is reasonable to believe that a plan of labour participation in determining the conditions of employment and administering the labour code, such as we have proposed, will go very far to prevent strikes. Disputes between representatives of labour and management are bound to occur. But under the conditions outlined they can be settled by direct negotiation in most cases. To deal with those disputes that are more serious, a conciliation service should be provided by the Labour Organization Division.

These various provisions would make for real democracy in the conduct of industry. Labour would participate fully in the making of all decisions affecting conditions of work and employment, from the smallest to the highest. Labour organizations would assume positive and constructive functions in the management of industry, at the same time that technical control and management lay in the hands of managerial experts. These would be conditions under which wage-earners could feel truly that they were part owners and operators of industry, not merely its hired wage-slaves.

Summary.

So much detailed proposal has preceded that it is desirable to summarize briefly what has been said. A national labour code is proposed, to be worked out under the Dominion Government. An expanded and reformed Department of Labour would be the senior agency of the code. Under it would be five main divisions, those of Wage Regulation, Employment, Social Insurance, Regulation of Working Conditions, and Labour Organization, to administer the statutes falling under each of these heads. Five regional bureaus of the Department would be established for the main economic divisions of Canada to make for administrative decentralization. The various divisions of the Department, particularly those of Wage Regulation and Employment, would work closely with the National Planning Commission, to see that labour policy was closely integrated with the general economic policy of the state. The code would aim to protect workers and their families as completely as possible against loss of wage income through unemployment, sickness, accident, death or old age. It would determine "fair" basic wages for all classes of workers, with additional allowances for those with children. It would endeavour to reduce the risk of unemployment to a minimum. It would regulate working conditions in the interest of the workers. Finally, it would provide for workers' representation in setting the conditions of employment, through trade unions, collective bargaining and works and industrial councils.

The freedom and the responsibilities offered to workers' associations, besides making for industrial democracy, would also safeguard political democracy in the socialist state. The unions would represent a powerful force to counteract any tendency to dictatorial methods which might develop in the state "bureaucracy".

The great part of the legislative and administrative responsibility for this large programme would be assumed by the Dominion Government, rather than by the provincial governments, as at present. Whether this is possible under the British North America Act as it stands, is still controversial. Our proposals, therefore, call for important amendments to the Canadian constitution to make the position clear. The necessary amendments, we think, should be such as to make the Dominion absolutely supreme in the field of labour legislation. This would not preclude the possibility of certain realms of regulations remaining in provincial hands, subject to Dominion approval: thus it has been suggested that the control of working conditions, in particular, might continue to be a provincial function. Nevertheless, our sweeping proposals for a labour code lead us to the threshold of the constitutional problem, which is discussed in detail in another chapter.[2]

2Chapter XXI.

CHAPTER XVI.

HEALTH AND WELFARE SERVICES.

A. PRESENT HEALTH AND MEDICAL SERVICES.

ECONOMIC security for the mass of the population has been a main objective of the programme presented in this book. But economic security alone is not enough. There must also be social provision to protect and improve the health, physical and mental, of every citizen; and there must be "social services" to care for the destitute, the defective and the delinquent. Apart from the obvious point that good health is a most important item in well-being which the socialist state should aim at providing for its citizens, it is economically desirable that ill-health should be kept to a minimum to reduce the costs of medical care and the burden of cash benefits to be assumed by the social insurance funds, and to increase the productive power of the community. Similar considerations, both ethical and economic, point to the desirability of providing special services to assist, reclaim and re-establish those who are too weak to solve by themselves the problem of living at a reasonable economic, moral and cultural level. It need hardly be said that health service is a matter of concern for wage earners, farmers, and their families alike.

At present, in Canada, private enterprise dominates in the field of health as in most other fields of industry or service. In general, doctors, dentists and nurses practice "curative medicine"[1] by selling services privately, on a fee basis, while drugs and medicines are distributed through the private wholesale and retail drug trade. But there are important exceptions to this rule: the Workmen's Compensation medical services, the "municipal doctors" on salary in Saskatchewan and Alberta, hospital out-patient departments (which give treatment to the indigent and the near-indigent), such public clinics as deal with venereal disease, tuberculosis and child welfare, the Dominion Government medical service for war veteran pensioners, and the health service plans which are operated in numerous industries. And, perhaps most important of all, the provinces and municipalities are increasingly granting rudimentary medical services free to those in receipt of unemployment relief.

Hospitals are generally operated throughout Canada either

---

[1] As distinguished from "preventive medicine". (See below).

as public institutions or as non-profit-making philanthropic or religious institutions.   But few hospitals derive revenues from patients' fees sufficient to meet their costs and their deficits are made up by heavy provincial and municipal contributions and grants from private philanthropy.   Special hospitals, e.g. for tuberculous and mental patients, are operated by a number of the provincial governments and receive only a small proportion of their revenues from patients' fees.

In the field of preventive medicine public effort is supreme. Most of the provinces have departments or bureaus of health which administer various public health acts and supervise the public health work performed by the municipal authorities. Their work includes the collection of vital statistics, sanitary inspection and supervision of water, milk, food supplies, disposal of sewage and garbage, the control of infectious disease, pre-natal and post-natal care of mothers and babies, medical inspection of school children, public health nursing, and various types of health education.

The Costs of Medical Care.

But health authorities are practically unanimous in the conclusion that the existing health services are inadequate.   The American Committee on the Costs of Medical Care, after the most exhaustive research, has shown conclusively that the great majority of the American people did not obtain adequate medical service, even before the depression, and there is no reason to believe that conditions are any better in Canada.   The Committee's studies showed that for every 1,000 persons in the population, 1,385 days of hospital care per year were required in the interests of maintaining good health, while only 746 days of hospital care were actually given; that of every 5,650 home, office and clinical calls by physicians required, only 2,391 calls were actually made; that of 1,000 persons requiring dental care in each year only 244 received any; and that 942 health examinations were required but only 82 were made.[2]   These figures are bad enough.   But they represent *averages* for the whole population, rich and poor together.   Figures for the poorer members of the population were very much worse; it was found that they received much less medical care than the well-to-do, in spite of the fact that there was far more sickness among them, and that their needs for medical service were much greater.

2Committee on the Costs of Medical Care, *The Costs of Medical Care*, p. 73.

The depression has, of course, made the situation vastly worse. Thousands upon thousands of people have become quite unable to pay anything for medical care, and have been forced to do without it, to obtain free service from the health practitioner, or to rely upon such rudimentary public service as might be granted to the indigent. In the face of this situation the state has had to extend its medical services to deal with the most urgent cases of need. Clearly private enterprise in the field of medicine, which was operating inadequately enough before the depression, has broken down completely during these tragic years. The medical profession, to a large degree because of its ideals of service, has made great sacrifices. Had it not been for the granting of free service by physicians on a huge scale (contrary to all the rules of capitalist enterprise) the bankruptcy of the existing system would have been generally recognized long since.

The major reason for the inadequacy of medical care is, of course, that most people can't afford it. This is true not only of the unemployed, the poorer wage earners and a great many farmers, but also of those in the middle income groups who are comparatively well-off. The great difficulty with medical bills is that they come suddenly, without warning, and that a person cannot budget in advance for them. Many families which might be able to pay on a monthly basis the average costs of medical care, are quite unable to meet the exceedingly heavy medical charges with which they are faced at particular moments.

But the problem is by no means entirely one of the inability of the mass of the population to buy medical care when it is most needed. There are many other objections to the existing situation. For one thing, there is serious maldistribution of medical facilities. Doctors, dentists, nurses, laboratories, etc., are concentrated in the main centres of population to the disadvantage of country districts. There is much avoidable waste and inefficiency in the practice of all aspects of medicine. Many doctors and dentists who practice individually cannot afford expensive modern equipment and, in consequence, have to get along without it. Individual practice also leads to excessive overhead charges for office rent, service of nurses, equipment, and collection of accounts. Hospitals operate independently of other hospitals, and there is a surplus of beds in one while another is overcrowded. Drug stores carry on their shelves unnecessary stock because competing manufacturers force upon them and upon the community the same drugs and medicines under different brand names. Associated with this is the prevalence of self-medication by patients, inspired partly by patent-medicine and other "health" advertising and partly by the hope of patients that they can substitute a small drug-store bill for a large physician's fee. The physician's fee thus discourages consultation in the early stages of illness. Frequently when the patient does consult a doctor in the late stages of illness, the best time for treatment has passed. This, of course, is quite contrary to the precepts of preventive medicine, which call for prompt treatment when there is the greatest hope of cure. Indeed, there is little of true preventive medicine in the present organization of medical practice. For most health practitioners outside the public health field there is no financial incentive to do more than the curative work that comes their way and they have only a limited interest in the preventive approach.

In spite of all these inadequacies, our existing medical facilities are very much under-employed. Doctors and dentists complain about their lack of patients; the extent of unemployment and under-employment among nurses is notorious; and hospital beds, in many places, are empty. Naturally this is reflected in low incomes for the medical practitioners, who complain that they are underpaid. Here again is the familiar paradox of capitalism in a less publicized field—men, women and children urgently needing services while the industry that is equipped to provide them cannot sell its goods.

Present Government Services and Public Health Organization.

The public health services offered by our provinces and municipalities are good, bad, or indifferent, differing in quality and extent from place to place. But in no Canadian community is there a really adequate public health service. Toronto, perhaps, has as adequate a public health service as any Canadian city, and yet Toronto in the year 1930, before depression curtailments in expenditure, spent only $1.55 per capita of the population upon public health, about a dollar less than the $2.50 per capita which Dr. Louis Dublin of the Metropolitan Life Company and other authorities consider reasonably sufficient. With such an expenditure, Dr. Dublin argues in his book *Health and Wealth*, infant mortality rates could be cut in American and Canadian cities to the low levels prevailing in New Zealand, the safest country in the world for new-born babies; the average expectation of life could be increased by from five to seven years; and the extent of sickness could be greatly reduced. Dr. Dublin's argument is conceded to be correct in essentials by the leaders of public health in Canada, and they are generally impatient with the small provision made by governments for their work.

A fundamental criticism of the existing system of public health organization is that it is based very largely upon existing municipal units. The municipality is large enough for efficient work when it is a city such as Montreal, Toronto or Vancouver, although even in the case of the larger cities it would be much better if the unit of public health administration were the metropolitan area (Toronto plus some ten adjoining urban municipalities, for example) rather than the cities alone. But the smaller units, particularly the rural municipalities, are much too small to sustain full-time health officers and nurses, and the other elements of an efficient organization. In Ontario alone there are nearly a thousand separate municipalities, and it is quite impossible to expect efficient public health service from each and every one of them. To meet this problem there has been some quite successful experimentation in Quebec and in the Western provinces, with public health units organized on a county or district basis, covering areas much larger than those generally embraced within the boundaries of the rural municipalities. But there is no Dominion co-ordination of these services.

Most of the provinces have special agencies to deal with mental disorders and venereal disease and tuberculosis. Good work has been done in combating tuberculosis, particularly in the province of Saskatchewan, where the death rate from "the great white plague" has been progressively reduced until it is much the lowest of all the provinces. But to a large degree the emphasis has been upon giving care to those who are afflicted with the disease, without much stress upon preventive work. In the field of mental disease, there has been even less concern with preventive measures. On the other hand, the different provinces have built more and more mental hospitals to give expensive institutional care to the growing number of mental patients. Ontario with its travelling mental clinics and its psychiatric hospital in Toronto has done a good deal in recent years to protect mental health and to effect earlier cures, but in general Canada has no really adequate programme of mental hygiene. For venereal disease, free clinics are operated by most of the provinces. For some years after the War, they were assisted by grants from the Dominion Government, but these were withdrawn in 1932 for reasons of "economy". The provincial clinics fulfil a useful function, but their work has not been extensive enough to stamp out or control very effectively this great social disease.

In practically every branch of the public health field the same thing holds true—that there are great possibilities of cutting down sickness rates and death rates, but that there is not enough of men, money or organization to do the job properly. Governments have not been willing to provide the money or the opportunity for the experts in public health who could, if they were adequately supported and organized, protect human life and advance our health standards on a tremendous scale. Within a few years money spent wisely on extended public health services would be saved many times over, to governments and to the community at large, in lessened costs of sickness and premature death, and in increased economic efficiency.

B. STATE MEDICINE AND PUBLIC HEALTH REORGANIZATION.

From this brief review of our existing health services the conclusion emerges that they are quite insufficient to meet the health needs of the population. Private enterprise in medical practice has failed so lamentably that the State has already been forced to appropriate the public health field almost entirely and to render a great deal of service also in the field of curative medicine.

Recognition of the breakdown of private practice in the field which has been traditionally its own, has become so general that the need for some form of health insurance is now widely conceded, and two provinces, Alberta and British Columbia, have taken definite steps to establish health insurance plans.

A socialist policy on health calls for much more than the conventional forms of health insurance imported from Europe and for even more than the distinctively Canadian plans already worked out in Alberta and British Columbia. It must demand that adequate health service, curative and preventive, shall be made freely available to every citizen, just as educational service is now available. To achieve this objective it is necessary to establish, in every province of Canada, completely socialized health services under the control and the direction of the provincial governments.

Such a state health service would have two main divisions. Broadly, the first would be concerned with curative medicine and the second with preventive medicine. But this distinction should not be stressed unduly, because there should be no hard and fast division between the two types of practice; and, indeed, the preventive point of view should dominate the practitioners in both. The term "state medicine" may be used to describe the first division and the term "public health" the second.

A Comprehensive State Medical Service.

The state medicine plan should make available for every member of the community in need, a complete medical service, to consist of the services of the general medical practitioner and of the medical specialist, necessary hospital service, nursing service, dental service, laboratory and diagnostic service and medicines, drugs and surgical supplies. The general practitioner or "family doctor" would be the central figure in the scheme, and it would be on his certification that patients would be granted the other services mentioned. Every qualified physician would be entitled to practice under the plan, and, within reasonable limits, each patient would be entitled to choose the doctor he preferred. To a large degree medical practice would be carried on as it is at present, except that there would be no bills for the patient to pay directly, and therefore no economic barrier between him and his physician.

Doctors and dentists might be paid for their services in several different ways. Probably the capitation plan, which prevails under the British scheme of health insurance, would be the most satisfactory. According to this method a doctor has a certain number of persons attached to his "panel" and he is paid a fixed amount per person per year, irrespective of the amount of work he is required to do. Payments to doctors and dentists, of course, should be fair and reasonable—sufficient to guarantee them generous standards of living and to compensate them fairly for their long and arduous professional training, their special skill and highly responsible work. They should not be confined to practise under the plan of state medicine, but should be allowed to do "private practice" outside of it, for those persons who demand more attention than the state scheme authorizes.

It is probable that a good deal might be done to effect economies and improvements in medical care by extending "group practice" as compared with individual practice. Already there has been considerable development in this direction, for example through the organization of hospital out-patient clinics and the collaboration of individual specialists for certain purposes. The idea of the hospital as the medical centre of the future, giving service to ambulatory patients even more than to the bed-ridden, has been suggested by a number of eminent medical men. It should be a major duty of the state medical administration to explore thoroughly the possibilities of group practice and to organize clinics, medical centres, collaboration between specialists, the pooling of equipment and other methods of group practice by doctors and dentists so far as this proves feasible and desirable. Since the problem of such reorganization is intimately tied up with the quality of medical practice (and also the question of personal relation between doctor and patient) it would be essential to consult medical opinion very carefully in laying plans for reorganization.

In the case of nursing service it seems quite clear that the state medical administration would have to work out quite different methods from those that now prevail. The scheme might have its own nurses, some of whom would be engaged on salary to provide a visiting nurse service in the home for a short time each day (as the Victorian Order of Nurses does at present) with some also available to take on steady-duty cases. These latter should not have to depend upon fees from irregular employment, as private duty nurses do at present, but should be given some basic payment, at least while they are on call. For example, they might be paid a flat salary of $50 per month, plus daily fees for their periods of duty. If this were done the number of nurses engaged could be kept down to a reasonable figure, they would be under the general control of the administration whether they were on or off duty, and reasonably steady work could be provided for all.

As for other types of medical service, the state medicine authority might either provide service directly or buy it from other health agencies. For example, there is no reason why existing municipal or philanthropic hospitals should not continue to operate under their present boards of management, so long as they fit into the general scheme of medical service for the community which is established. However, in many cases it would probably be desirable for medical administration to take over hospitals from their present proprietors (public or private), paying them fairly for the property and equipment acquired, and to operate them as state institutions. In any event, there would have to be co-ordination of hospital facilities, to bring about effective and economical use of hospital beds and other facilities that are now in existence. The distribution of drugs and medicines might be carried on by dispensaries established directly by the state medicine authority, which would be paid for sales. Only certain specified drugs would be handled in any case, and there would be no place for patent medicines or trade-marked drugs which serve no useful function.

The administration of this plan could be undertaken by the provincial department of health or by a provincial commission appointed especially for the purpose. Whether the one method or the other is followed there should be a highly qualified medical man directly in charge of the whole scheme of medical service. Moreover, the administration should be assisted by representatives of the organized medical professions, at least in an advisory way. It is most important for the successful operation of such a plan that the medical professions accord it a large measure of support; and there is no better way of gaining their co-operation than by giving to their elected representatives full opportunity of presenting their views on all medical questions of importance. There should also be a' general advisory committee, and possibly a number of local committees, to represent the consumers of medical service, to be formed by having labour, farmer, professional and other organizations nominate their respective representatives.

A further word should be said about some questions which frequently agitate medical men when state medicine is discussed. Many of them fear, quite honestly, that state medicine, or even health insurance, will lead to serious abuses of their privileges by patients, will debase the quality of medical practice and will bring about an intolerable regimentation of the medical professions. Provided that the plan is organized soundly and wisely, these fears, we believe, are groundless. The plan here proposed incorporates most of the principles for health insurance proposed by the Committee on Economics of the Canadian Medical Association, in an extensive report presented to the annual meeting of the Association at Calgary in 1934. With free choice of doctor by the patient, medical control of medical questions, fair remuneration for the health practitioner, a competent administration assisted by medical advisory committees to lay down detailed rules and regulations, and reasonable co-operation from the medical profession, there is no reason to fear that state medicine will not work well. If some abuses do develop, such as excessive prescribing of drugs by some doctors or unnecessary calls on physicians by patients, they can be dealt with by making small charges for drugs or for unecessary calls or by other administrative devices. The danger of such difficulties is small in comparison with the immense advantages to be expected from a really adequate medical service for the community.

The finances of state medicine could be raised by general taxation, or by special contributions for the purpose. While the first method is simpler, the second has the advantage that it would represent a specific assignment by the individual for a specific purpose. Under the contributory method, wage earners would contribute weekly or monthly from their wages, their contributions being matched by contributions from their employers (who would in many cases come to be the State) and collections being made through the regular Dominion social insurance machinery; farmers and the self-employed would be covered by an appropriate contribution paid either to the State Medicine Authority, or through the tax machinery; those receiving incomes over a certain amount, say $3,000 annually, who wished to be covered, could make their payments with their income tax returns; while workers who were unemployed or earning wages less than a given minimum, would have their contributions paid for them by the province. A complete medical service, such as the one proposed, could be provided in Canada for $20 or less per head per year, according to various estimates that have been made in this country and in the United States. Since there are, on the average, about one and one-half dependents for every wage-earner, this would mean that the fund to be budgetted for would have to represent about $50 per year for each worker. Perhaps two-thirds of this would be provided by the provinces. With wages depressed as they are at present, the average worker's contribution would be less than two per cent. of his wages. But with a generally increased level of wages, the percentage would be distinctly smaller than this. Moreover, the charge would not represent an entirely new and additional payment, but rather a substitution for payments that are already being made, at least in some degree, by those workers who are self-supporting.

A Reconstituted Public Health System.

The second division of the state medical service which we advocate would be an improved and extended public health scheme. This should be carried on by the provincial departments of health and by local health boards, as at present. The provincial departments should continue with their supervision of local effort and should also conduct special services, such as vital statistics, tuberculosis control, mental hygiene, venereal disease and cancer research. In all of these fields there is room for great improvement. In particular, far more attention should be paid to work that is definitely preventive. With really adequate preventive programmes tuberculosis could be made almost as uncommon as diphtheria or typhoid; the venereal diseases and their consequences, such as general paresis of the insane, could be reduced to small proportions; mental breakdowns could be materially lessened in number; cancer could be rendered far less a fatal disease. We do not need more tuberculosis sanatoria (although in some provinces more beds are definitely required) so much as extended free clinic facilities, provisions for early case-finding, more social service work among patients and their families, education of the general public and the medical profession regarding the dangers of these diseases, and effective co-operation on the part of all health practitioners with the venereal disease services. In the field of mental hygiene there should be less concern to keep patients indefinitely in expensive mental hospitals and more effort in the direction of preventive work through psychiatric clinics, mental hygiene programmes in the schools, and early treatment in psychopathic hospitals. In these important fields a number of the provinces have no specialized, unified services, and it is highly desirable that these should be established.

The work of municipal boards of health should be continued and extended along the lines already worked out in cities such as Toronto. But it is essential that standards of public health work in all local communities be brought up to and even beyond those now prevailing in the most progressive communities. It is necessary also that the local unit for public health purposes be much larger than the small rural municipality. The same thing might be said, of course, about education and other services usually conducted by the local authorities: the problem of a unit of proper size for purposes of public health organization is closely connected with the general problem of the reorganization of local government in Canada. Health units sufficiently large must be established so that every community may have a public health service with a full-time salaried health officer, and with full-time salaried public health nurses and other workers. It is essential that the provincial departments of health supervise closely the work of the local units, and that they take the initiative in organizing them on a proper basis. Amongst other things, they should exercise effective control over the appointment of health officers and nurses, to see that properly trained men and women are chosen for he work. Local councils cannot always be trusted to make satisfactory technical appointments, and a greater measure of standard prescription in such matters is necessary.

The cost of this programme is surprisingly small, when the advantages in health and well-being that would flow from it are taken into account. A doubling or trebling of the present small expenditures would permit great achievements. Of course, it would be difficult or impossible for many municipalities to increase their expenditures under present conditions. As a matter of principle, also, municipalities should not be asked to raise, by means of property taxes, very large amounts for public health. It would therefore be reasonable for the provincial governments to bear most of the expense of public health work, paying entirely for the general work and for the special services they would conduct and making substantial grants-in-aid to the municipalities or other local health units to assist them in their part of the programme.

As already suggested, there should be no sharp line of distinction between state medicine and public health. It is absolutely necessary that these two divisions of public medical service work harmoniously together. The doctor, the dentist and the nurse serving under the state medicine administration should all work in co-operation with the public health agencies. The doctors in general practice, for example, should give their patients periodical physical examinations to detect conditions requiring treatment, they should refer tuberculous patients or tuberculosis contacts to the provincial T.B. service, they should report venereal cases to the venereal disease service, and they should refer patients in whom they observe incipient mental disorder to the mental hygiene service. Moreover, they should assist in carrying on among their patients a programme of health education. Their object should be to ward off illness and to keep their patients well, rather than merely to treat them when they are sick, as is the ordinary practice today.

The integration and co-ordination of the two divisions of medical service can be accomplished by unified or joint control at the top. If the provincial department of health administers both services, unified control will be automatic. If there is a provincial commission to administer state medicine, however, the senior provincial health officer should be a member of the commission, as is proposed in the plan of health insurance which has been sponsored recently by the Government of British Columbia.

A word should be said about the functions of the Dominion in connection with health. We think that, in general, the provinces should continue to assume major responsibility in this field, since it is one in which the separate provinces can operate successfully by themselves, largely without reference to what is being done in other provinces. But this does not absolve the Dominion from complete responsibility. In every field of governmental effort the Dominion must exercise a general and supervisory authority even if it does not carry on service directly. There ought to be reasonable uniformity in the health services as between the various provinces, and the Dominion should exercise its power and authority to achieve this result. This it may do by conducting research work in health problems, by collecting statistical materials, by offering a technical service of advice to the provinces and the local health units, and, perhaps, by offering modest grants of money to provinces or communities that measure up to good standards. In addition, of course, the Dominion must continue its health work in connection with immigrants, with sailors, with war veterans, with Indians and with others who are its special responsibilities. The new services of expert assistance and leadership for the provinces which we propose could be given by a Dominion Bureau of Health staffed by a small group of health experts.

C. SOCIAL WELFARE SERVICES.

When we turn to consider the existing "social services" in Canada, we find that they consist of a diffuse and largely uncoordinated mass of endeavours, public and private. At present the great bulk of public effort and money in this field is going into relief—unemployment relief, poor relief to families where there is no employable member, mothers' pensions, old age pensions. In addition, there are provincial and municipal provisions for child welfare, adult and juvenile delinquency and recreation, which are very uneven both in extent and in quality. Public effort is supplemented, at least in the larger communities, by organized private philanthropy of one type or another and in practically every community there are representatives of the varied types of elementary private effort which come under the heading of "social service".

Relief.

There is little to be said for unemployment relief as it exists today in Canada, except that in general it has kept our people from starvation and from serious physical deterioration during the depression. But it offers them nothing but a dole of the barest necessities of life, it is essentially pauperizing and degrading, it is generally administered on a drab plane of uniformity, and it has still, even in the sixth year of the depression, many gaps, inconsistencies, anomalies and inequalities.

Incredible as it may seem to the historian of the future, relief is still inadequate in many places (in spite of appreciable improvements during the period of the depression) ; there is lack of uniformity from municipality to municipality; there are no definite rules as between the provinces or even as between the municipalities of some of the provinces for dealing with transient individuals or families; there is little occupational provision for relief recipients except on municipal pick and shovel work projects; and relief is generally given by vouchers (food orders, rent orders, etc.) instead of in cash. In relief administration alone—apart altogether from the re-employment of those now on relief—enormous improvements could be made in the lot of the unemployed if more reasonable and intelligent methods were to prevail.

A major share of responsibility for this condition must be placed upon the Dominion Government. Since 1930 the Dominion has been pouring out millions of dollars yearly upon relief. But the view has been taken that this was an "emergency" action, that at any time Dominion grants might be stopped, even more, that since relief was essentially a local affair, it was not necessary for the Dominion to advise the provinces and municipalities as to how they should administer it. While the provinces have been unwilling to accept the federal attitude, they have not been inclined, until recently, to adopt a very different policy towards the municipalities. The municipalities have been compelled, therefore, to carry on as best they could. Inevitably, under these circumstances, relief policies have differed from place to place; and in general the standard of relief administration has been low. The Dominion, the senior authority in this country, has continued to maintain the stupid attitude of assuming only partial financial responsibility during the "emergency", without making any serious attempt to bring order or good standards of administration into the situation.

The ineptitude of Domonion policy has been exemplified by the annual statements of the Minister of Labour each spring that the Dominion would shortly cut off relief grants to the provinces, a policy which everybody in the country who has been even slightly informed about the situation has known to be impossible.

Other existing public social services, in general, minister only to the more urgent needs of those who cannot care for themselves. The best developed are those concerned with child welfare. Some of the provinces do good work in protecting neglected and dependent children, either directly through provincial machinery or through semi-public children's aid societies. Juvenile delinquency is dealt with through juvenile courts and industrial schools or reformatories, with a certain amount of probation work in some places. Municipal authorities in large centres have made a beginning upon recreation programmes with public playground systems. Private charitable effort, in the larger cities, has contributed notably to good standards in the social services, with emphasis upon constructive work to reclaim and rehabilitate those unable to stand upon their own feet in the struggle of life, but they have succeeded in touching only a small portion of the total problem. While there are good pieces of work being done in particular communities, the quality of service differs enormously from place to place. Moreover, the organization of the social services is generally very poor. Even the strictly provincial services are not properly co-ordinated, in most provinces, and there is no adequate integration of provincial, municipal and private effort.

The present emphasis in our public social services upon relief is both misplaced and misleading. The first attack upon unemployment and indigence must be made by reorganizing the economic system so that it can provide work and wages for the great majority of those capable of employment, with social insurance as the first line of defence for those who lack income on account of unemployment, sickness, accident, old age or death of the family breadwinner. Economic security for the mass of the population can only be attained as part of a full programme of economic reconstruction. The need for relief, as we know it to-day in Canada, would decrease as soon as this programme began to take effect. And since many of the social and political problems of which the hard-boiled relief administrators are now beginning to talk are the direct outcome of adverse economic conditions, these should also decline in number. Our capitalistic Canada of to-day is degrading human beings daily and sending them to the scrap-heap, from which those who now administer the social services strive with their limited resources to rescue them, like stretcher-bearers carrying off the wounded from the trenches of war. There would be far less need for "social services" of this type in a socialist Canada.

A Provincial Welfare Administration.

But even in a community where economic security for the bulk of the population is assured there will still be need for certain social services. For there will continue to be some people who are weak or unfortunate, who cannot solve their own problems of existence, and who will require special assistance from the community before they can stand upon their own feet. It is quite safe to prophesy that for years to come social workers will have to deal with casualties of the present depression, no matter how much economic conditions improve.

The different provinces, therefore, should maintain a complete range of social services. These should be designed frankly to do a salvage and repair job for those human beings who cannot attain well-being and adequate citizenship through other means, or to protect the weaker members of society from falling below minimum standards of good citizenship. The principle of social case work should dominate treatment in all these services. Very simply, it means that every person or family requiring assistance should have their case considered on its individual merits, and that a plan of treatment should be worked out to fit their particular needs. The trained social worker is the person who can best apply this principle in practice, and it is essential that men and women with special training of this nature be engaged for the tasks of administration. By virtue of such a policy a real effort could be made to reclaim for social usefulness those who cannot adjust themselves even to the favourable economic and social environment we hope to create in our socialist Canada; and to prevent those near the margin of danger from toppling over. Schools of social work would not be closed in a socialized Canada; they would be accorded adequate State support instead of being left dependent on inadequate and uncertain private funds, and their facilities extended to enable them to supply their needed quota to the social service personnel that the new State will require .

The direct work of social assistance calls for a system of welfare bureaus in large municipalities or local welfare units, where this would be appropriate. As in the case of health, a great many municipalities are too small to have effective welfare services, so that unless there is thorough-going municipal re-organization to reduce the number of municipalities and increase their size, special welfare units, embracing a number of municipalities, must be set up in rural districts. The provincial governments will no doubt find it desirable to continue with the direct administration of certain of the social services, as in the extra-municipal territories of the western provinces. But there should be no need for provincial and municipal welfare officers to work concurrently in the same community. Nevertheless, the provincial governments should exercise control and supervision over municipal effort, in the same manner that has been suggested for health work. Appointments of social workers, in particular, should only be made with the approval of the provincial Department of Welfare; and the provincial department should work to obtain reasonable uniformity in the extent and the quality of the municipal work. Properly administered grants-in-aid from the province to its municipalities for their welfare services would be an effective device to achieve good standards.

There is no reason why some private effort in the welfare field should not continue. Experimental work in the social services will no doubt continue to be done most effectively by private groups in the socialist state. When this work is financed by small contributions from many people, rather than by a few small subscriptions from wealthy donors, it should lose most of the objectionable characteristics which many schemes of private charity have at present. But while legitimate private effort would not be forbidden or hampered by the state, it should not remain entirely free from state control. It should be co-ordinated with the public social services and it should measure up to reasonable standards of competence.

Only a few words need be said about the specific services. Relief must continue for reasons that have already been given. It will be needed not only for those who remain chronically destitute, but also as a guarantee that there will be subsistence for workers and their families, if there should at any time be reasons why they could not properly be provided for through the unemployment insurance scheme. To this extent it will be a second line of defence, which it is to be hoped will not have to be used except on a small scale, but which will be valuable because it is there in case of emergency. Relief should be adequate to sustain life at a reasonable level of subsistence, and it should be administered as humanely as possible. It should be granted in the form most suitable to the individual case (which among other things would make cash allowances the rule rather than the exception).

The care of children would continue to be a most important branch of the social services. What is needed in this field is mainly an extension and strengthening of the work that is now being done by the provincial governments and the children's aid societies, with standards being raised at least to the level of the best that prevail in Ontario, Manitoba, or British Columbia. In the field of delinquency there should be a great improvement in juvenile courts. Some knowledge of child psychology, sociology and economics and modern theories of probation, must be made essential requirements. Judges and magistrates who may know their law but who are completely innocent of any knowledge of the social and economic causes of juvenile law-breaking, all too often sit on juvenile court benches to-day. There is also room for great improvement in our industrial schools and reformatories, which should be made over, from the places of detention which they frequently are at present, into training schools. There should also be a great extension of recreation services conducted by the municipalities, and these should be well integrated with other recreational facilities conducted by private groups.

In the field of the social services, as in the field of health, we do not propose that there should be direct action by the federal government. But the Dominion must assume a general responsibility to see that the standards of services with which people are provided are adequate in all parts of Canada. This could be discharged effectively if the Dominion provided a central research and advice service, supplemented occasionally, perhaps, by modest grants of money to urge backward provinces to improve their services or to encourage the general application of progressive policies.

CHAPTER XVII.

THE REHABILITATION OF AGRICULTURE.

A. THE WIDER CAUSES OF AGRICULTURAL DISTRESS.

AS SOON as we seek to remove the causes of the impoverishment of agriculture, it becomes clear to any intelligent observer that here is a problem to which a host of factors contribute. No simple solution can be adequate to a problem which is in part internal and in part international in character; which is partly a question of faulty organization, and partly a question of inherent conflict and contradiction. Agriculture in Canada exhibits most of the weaknesses which characterize modern capitalism wherever it is found, and some which are peculiar to this country alone. Some arise from the manner in which the balance of political power has been tilted in the direction of the industrial East; others from the fact that a disproportionately large part of the burden of adjustment to the changes caused by shrinking markets has been placed upon the primary producers who, almost alone in the modern world, are subject to unrestricted competition, with wide and uncontrolled price fluctuations. The rehabilitation of agriculture must therefore be sought through simultaneous attack on a number of different fronts.

Most of the proposals widely advocated to-day as panaceas for agriculture fail to appreciate the complexity of the problem. There are some who see trouble in terms of low prices; to others the heavy debts are the most significant factor. (And to those who have eyes for nothing else but these the traps laid by the apostles of "social credit" provide an inevitable doom.) To the doctrinaire Liberal it is purely a fiscal problem, a matter of tariffs and taxes and the re-distribution of the tax burden; to some it is purely a question of price spreads, or of excess marketing profits or some other over-simplification.

All of these, of course, are important, but not one of them can be sufficiently comprehensive. For purposes of prescription, however, the problem must first be broken up into its component parts.

The Slump in World Agriculture.

In the first place, agriculture is impoverished because of the world slump which has fallen with special severity on primary producers the world over. The reason for this is partly because agricultural prices are in an especially exposed position in a world of falling demand, and partly because of the over-expansion of production in the world as a whole.

It would be a mistake to believe that the world slump in agriculture is an altogether recent phenomenon. The coming of the world depression has only intensified the distress of the industry. Agriculture in most countries has had a thin time since the end of the post-war boom in 1920. The explanation is to be found in the fact that the war gave an enormous stimulus to agricultural production in all those countries able to replace the deficiencies of the belligerent countries. Coupled with this situation of over-expansion, judged by peace-time needs, has gone a steady improvement in technique equally effective in increasing output and depressing prices. The result has been that, generally speaking, while industrial production was undergoing boom conditions, agriculture has been relatively depressed.

So far as wheat was concerned, (and the same is true for many other products) the danger of the situation was disguised for some years previous to 1929 because of the operation of public and private price-stabilization schemes, designed to hold up the price by curtailing sales and holding goods off the markets. Perhaps another temporarily favourable factor lay in the manner in which the movement of international capital helped, until the collapse of 1929, to sustain the standards of living and the buying power of Europe in general, so that the demand for agricultural goods was partially maintained. The equilibrium between potential supplies and actual demands for agricultural goods depended therefore on two very unstable elements. The coincidental collapse of stabilization schemes in all countries through the lack of financial strength, and the breakdown of the system of international lending in 1929-1930 destroyed the precarious balance which had been established. Prices fell very steeply for all those products, like wheat, for which the demand is relatively inelastic. And many other agricultural and primary products are in this category.

For manufactured or processed goods the problem of excess supply is different. A fairly small diminution in price may clear the market of a surplus of industrial produce. In addition to this, industrial producers were, and are, in a better position to prevent the appearance of surpluses and to control supply. By restricting supply manufacturers have been able to keep up prices although, of course, at immense social expense in the form of unnecessary unemployment. For industrial products the decline in price was therefore slow and seldom very steep. For wheat and many other agricultural products, however, it requires a very large decline in price to dispose of a fairly small increase in world stock. And agriculturists were in no position to avoid the competition which produced this situation of falling prices. It should also be emphasized that, by virtue of the manner in which farmers in Canada and elsewhere will turn to the production of alternative products when any one farm commodity falls in price, any decline in the price of such an important staple as wheat was bound to result in a fall in the prices of other farm products.

There is another reason why agriculture the world over has been more depressed than industry. As the standards of living of peoples improve with the increase in technical efficiency, the amount of production which is directed towards satisfying their more elementary needs becomes smaller. They consume, relatively speaking, less bread and more meats, less cereals and more fruits and vegetables, less stews and more sirloin steaks. It is of the essence of the doctrine of laissez-faire, under the hypnotism of which so many Canadian leaders labour, that the relative fall in agricultural prices will produce a transference of enterprise from the unprofitable to the more profitable lines. Theoretically it will pay primary producers to turn to the production of special crops, or indeed, to forsake agriculture for industry and commerce. Of course in actual practice it is precisely at this point that the theory has to be qualified, so far as certain regions of Canada are concerned. It is clear that the productive agents engaged in agriculture are sometimes far less mobile than the theory assumes. The alternative employments for the farmer and his land may be very limited. The social and economic adjustments required go too deep. In Western Canada, of all the areas in the world, the natural and economic obstacles to such a re-adjustment are especially numerous. The principal natural obstable is the comparative unsuitability of the soil and climate for other purposes. And the economic problems of adjustment are even more forbidding.

The transportation system of the country, for example, is closely
integrated with the wheat trade, the expansion of which alone
can provide for its heavy overhead costs. Here, clearly, is a
problem requiring intelligent diagnosis and a far-reaching
scheme of controlled adjustment to rectify the evil of a badly
balanced economy and avoid a repetition of it.

We must next observe that a country like Canada, so tightly
integrated with the rest of the world by ties of trade and finance, cannot expect to remain insulated from the effects of falling prices in the world at large. For the grains and cereals
the principal markets are abroad, and the whole domestic output sells at the world price. Even for those numerous agricultural commodities, the market for which is largely in Canada
itself, the price paid for every unit of the whole supply is influenced, amongst other things, by the prices obtained for the
small proportion which is marketed abroad.

For these latter products it might have been possible of
course for producers to have realized a higher price at home
than abroad, providing competition to dispose of the surplus
had been avoided by the establishment of marketing boards with
wide powers to license, establish quotas, and the rest. This type
of solution has obvious limitations, and is referred to later.
The point requiring emphasis here is that the world agricultural
slump has been doubly severe in countries, like Canada, where
agricultural production is large. To the solution of this type of
problem the principles of international planning should be applied. It is indeed probable that the growth of economic nationalism abroad will render this imperative.

Tariffs and Economic Nationalism.

The privileged financial and industrial interests of Canada
would have us regard the tariff as a matter purely of domestic
policy. Actually, the refusal of political leaders in Canada to
admit the mutuality of the interests of trading nations and to
govern in accordance with such a belief has contributed in no
small way to the present impasse in world trade. Responsibility
for the growth of tariffs must be placed mainly on the system of
pursuing profits by the use of privilege. The tariff is a privilege granted to producers absolving them from foreign competition. In addition to this more permanent and persistent
force which will serve to restrict trade as long as competitive
capitalism survives, there has been another contributing factor.

It is roughly described by the term "economic nationalism". Primarily, economic nationalism is the result of the attempt by national governments to find larger markets as an outlet for surplus capacity. The method is to harness the whole apparatus of the state government to the task of beating down the competitive efforts of foreign manufacturers in the interests of domestic manufacturers or producers.

Now the whole complex of problems created by the conditions of four and a half years of war greatly aggravated the initial problems of over-capacity and intense international competition. The war resulted in a duplication of industrial and agricultural equipment in many countries. The peace agreements provided for the creation of new political units in Europe, and forged a chain of inter-governmental debts. To the solution of the problems posed by those new circumstances, the route of economic nationalism offered the least resistance. In order to preserve the whole of the home market for the greatly expanded industrial or agricultural equipment, countries imposed high tariffs. To counteract the frantic attempts of the debtor countries to pay their debts out of the proceeds of an export trade, the creditors imposed special dumping and exchange duties upon such goods. Since the depression this drift towards national self-sufficiency has been naturally strengthened. Governments all over the world, forced to meet the demands of domestic producers for a larger share of a shrinking home market, have used all the old and familiar devices for restricting imports, in addition to the comparatively new invention of currency depreciation. The breakdown of the international gold standard, far from being a cause of international instability, is itself merely symptomatic of the breakdown of the international system of (relatively) free trade. From this situation there is small chance of the world retracing its steps. There are too many permanent elements in national policies directed towards state planning and state intervention to expect that the tide of economic nationalism must soon begin to recede. The collapse of the World Economic Conference in 1933 was due largely to a failure to recognize that fact.

In view of these considerations, it is perhaps futile to denounce Canadian governments for the part they have played in producing this state of affairs by adopting an aggressive tariff policy. In the face of economic nationalism abroad, and the disappearance of internal markets which accompanies the downward swing of the business cycle at home, trade restriction is the inevitable result of the make-shift attempts to mitigate or spread the burden, ineffective as they have been.

Even the Ottawa Agreements, ill-timed as they were, and mischievous as were their discriminatory and therefore aggressive features, can be viewed as merely the forerunner of a series of international trade compacts designed to harmonize the aims of internal planning with the need for maintaining the principles (however attenuated) of international specialization and exchange. Indeed, as we point out later, the beginnings of planning in agriculture for Canada have already been forced upon an unwilling Canadian government as a result of the adoption of a system of import controls in our principal markets abroad.

B. The Marketing Problem.

In marketing his products the farmer labours under two disadvantages. In the first place too great a share of the consumer's dollar is absorbed by the processor and distributor, whose returns are frequently excessive. A succession of parliamentary and other enquiries has brought out the fact that this is largely due to the weak bargaining-power of agricultural producers in the face of semi-monopolistic marketing agencies. In the second place it is only too clear that the costs of marketing or processing are often excessive, due to the duplication of facilities, or inefficiency, or both, or that—and this is particularly true of the export trade—the organization of the marketing is not abreast of developments in other countries.

The consequences of this situation are that the cost of the processed goods are higher than they need be, in which case domestic or foreign consumption is curtailed. Alternatively the farmer himself, occupying the most exposed position in the competitive scheme of things, has to bear the major part of such unnecessary costs in the form of low prices for his raw product.

Costs of Marketing and Processing.

A few illustrations will bring out the nature of these problems.[1] The marketing of milk and its products has almost everywhere created dissatisfaction amongst both producers and consumers in Canada in recent years. Are producers and consumers protected from exploitation by all the safeguards pro-

[1] For a fuller discussion of the distributive system and its defects, see Chapter XVIII.

vided by a genuinely competitive system? Let us look at the facts.

One of the first things discovered by the Select Standing Committee on Agriculture and Colonization (1933), which investigated the industry, was that there is no such thing as a uniform standard price for the milk bought by dairies from farmers. The Committee reported that "Producers are paid a price, called an Association price, for a percentage of milk delivered, and a much lower price for the balance which is designated as surplus milk. So far as the evidence goes, it shows that the determination of what part of a farmer's shipment shall be classed as surplus milk is entirely in the hands of the dairy company". The knowledge of such facts cannot do otherwise than provoke dissatisfaction among the farmers in the Montreal area who have seen the association price per 100 lbs. of milk fall from $2.80 at the beginning of 1930 to $1.35 at the beginning of 1932. The payment for surplus reduces the association price from $1.35 to an actual return of $1.17.

The question of profits made by milk companies engaged the attention of the Committee for a considerable part of the hearings. We may therefore accept the conclusion of the committee that "while returns from most industries have during the past two or three years materially decreased, such cannot be said of those interested in the sale and distribution of whole milk. The salaries and returns to executives and operating officials have, in a large measure, been maintained at the 1927, 1928, and 1929 levels, although business and industry generally have declined very markedly, and milk prices to the producer have been reduced to an extremely low level".

The report of the Saskatchewan Milk Enquiry Commission indicated that much the same conditions prevailed in that province. "Surplus milk, which sometimes reached 50 per cent. of the total milk supply, is a most serious factor in the marketing situation. Surplus of plants and general facilities for milk distribution causes costs of marketing to be high and reduced the price the producer receives".[2] To cope with the problem, the Commission was forced to recommend that the powers of the Local Government Board be extended to include the regulation and control of the production, distribution and marketing of the milk supplies of the cities of the province along lines similar to those authorized in Manitoba and Alberta.

[2] See the Summary of the Report printed in the *Economic Annalist*, issued by the Agricultural Economics Branch of the Department of Agriculture, Ottawa, June, 1934.

Unfortunately the steps taken by some provincial governments to remedy this situation have been, it would seem, lacking in vision. A typical method of approach is to set up a series of regional Milk Boards (as in Ontario) to fix the price paid for whole milk by the distributors and by the public. The price, of course, is arrived at by agreement between the separate associations of producers and distributors. It is held above the price paid for milk used in making cheese, butter and other dairy products only by restricting the amounts of whole milk which the farmer is allowed to deliver under this arrangement. In conformity with this idea, the producers' association allot quotas to their members, and restrict the number of new entrants anxious to be given a quota. The result is to establish certain groups of milk producers as a semi-monopoly, privileged to sell whole milk to the distributors at an "agreed price", leaving all those producers outside the pale to sell their milk at the low "surplus" price paid for milk to be used in other branches of the dairy industry. The effect of this arrangement is to drive the prices of all dairy products (other than whole milk) below their former level, and to give rise to demands for schemes of "output restriction" in these fields. The lesson to be learnt is that economic planning in agriculture cannot afford to be partial in character.

Milk, of course, is only one of a large number of farm products of which the low prices received by the farmer are the result (in part) of inefficient or costly distribution. That a similar situation exists in the milling and baking industries is demonstrated elsewhere in this book[3].

The disadvantages under which live stock producers operate by reason of the activities of the semi-monopolistic packing companies which process and market their output calls for special consideration. It is now recognized that a good deal of the grain production for which Canada is specially suited must ultimately find markets abroad, if they are to be available at all, in the form of animals or animal products,—cattle, hogs, bacon, poultry, cheese, butter, and so on. This being so, it will be increasingly necessary to produce in Canada the kind of animal products which can be sold in overseas markets. In so far as the price paid for such livestock for domestic consumption is set by the world price[4], it is absolutely essential that it

[3]See Chapter XVIII.

[4]A consideration which remains true as long as free competition prevails between domestic and foreign markets.

shall realize the best price possible on such foreign markets. Orderly marketing and adequate provision for the grading of such products is thus essential in this branch of agriculture. At the same time, it is necessary to prevent the relatively few but large packing concerns from levying a toll on the whole live-stock sales, both at home and abroad, in excess of what is necessary for the efficient handling of the product. It is doubtful, however, if any of these requirements are being fulfilled, and the widespread distrust of the packing industry which prevails amongst livestock producers is the natural consequence. There is first the fact that the packing industry is dominated, at most points, by two or three large houses, with inevitable collusion between their buyers on the stock yards. In addition, the technique of the industry is changing with the widespread use of the truck so that increasingly large quantities of live-stock are being trucked in and sold direct to the packers, or are purchased out in the country by the buyers of the packing houses: a system, which, while necessary to efficient and cheap market-ing, tends still further to tilt the bargaining power in favour of the packer.

In packing, as in other branches of industry, we find an unnecessary duplication of plants, despite the succession of mer-gers to which this situation gave rise,[5] the cost of which, in the form of over-capitalization of plants, is ultimately borne by pro-ducers of the product. The system of purchase of hogs by the carload, irrespective of grades, does not lend itself to the im-provement of quality; whilst it operates to enable the packer to pay for best quality hogs the price of a second-grade product.

Speaking generally, we find in this industry another illus-tration of the manner in which problems of modern technique and management are being solved in ways that cannot pro-vide the protection to all interests which the theory of free competition was supposed to guarantee. Clearly the path of wisdom is not to attempt to force a system of competition upon a branch of industry for which it is unsuited, but to consider the whole packing industry as a public utility, and to look for-ward to its ultimate public ownership and operation as part of a rational, planned economic system. Only in this way can the paramount interests of producers and consumers be pro-tected.

---

[5]See the evidence given by J. S. McLean, Canada Packers, Toronto, to the Parliamentary Committee on Price Spreads, March, 1934, p. 256-7.

Co-operative Marketing Problems.

The whole field of marketing has received close attention on the part of farmer co-operatives over the last decade or more. These voluntary organizations have adopted all the expedients of self-help which are possible to remedy the disadvantages of the existing marketing mechanism. Despite the intense opposition of private traders the idea of co-operative control over the storing, transportation and sale of farm products had gained enormous headway throughout Canadian agriculture in the years preceding the slump. This was particularly true of the grain trade in the Western Provinces, and to a lesser extent of the marketing of fruit, vegetables, wool, poultry, and dairy products. It was the common experience that wherever co-operative efforts were effective the mere stimulus of their competition assured the farmers a better deal from the private trade. The onset of the world depression, while it weakened the power of some of the co-operatives, only intensified the search for controlled methods of marketing. The reason is that, now more than ever, disorderly competitive selling between unorganized farmers and quasi-monopolistic processing and distributing firms results in the farmer getting less than a square deal. In more prosperous times a considerable increase in market spreads may pass unnoticed, but when prices are low it becomes all important to see that there are no wastages in the marketing mechanism, and that the price is not unduly depressed by disorderly selling.

The effectiveness of the co-operatives has, however, been continually frustrated by the action of non-co-operating minorities who have remained outside the movement. Thus, for example, wherever the co-operatives were successful in lifting a small but burdensome export surplus off the domestic market, the non-co-operating minority who were unwilling to sell in the export market got the benefit of a higher domestic price. This has been true of poultry, butter, apples, and several other products. Several provincial attempts have been made to overcome this difficulty by the enactment of what amounted to compulsory co-operation. The fruit growers of the Okanagan Valley and the milk producers in the Fraser Valley of British Columbia have for many years sought to improve their economic position by co-operative action. Despite the fact that the fruit and dairy farmers both managed to enlist majority support in their membership, small minorities of non-co-operating producers have remained outside, and have thwarted the efforts of the majority to introduce rational methods of marketing designed to stabilize prices over longer periods, and to retrieve a larger share of the consumer's dollar for the producers. At one time, a few years ago, these producer associations were instrumental in persuading the Government of British Columbia to pass legislation compelling the non-co-operating minorities of producers to fall in line with the policies of the co-operating majorities. This actual legislation was subsequently declared by the courts to be outside the jurisdiction of the province, according to the terms of the British North America Act, since it involved interference with trade and commerce. A later attempt to set up a Stabilization Board was similarly unable to continue since the levying of charges for administrative expenses was treated in the same way. The demand for such control methods, however, became even more insistent, and the recent Marketing Act of the federal government is the result of the pressure of farmer organizations.

So far as the problem of jurisdiction is concerned, it should be observed that whilst the present division of authority under the B.N.A. Act will not permit either a province or the Dominion, acting separately, to do what is necessary to apply the methods of social control to agricultural production and marketing, both authorities may agree on what has to be done, and enact concurrent legislation. Their constitutional powers, in other words, may be pooled. One obstable in the way of agricultural planning has been thereby removed.[6]

C. Agriculture in a Planned State.

The Foundations of Policy.

An intelligent agricultural policy for Canada must be based, first, not upon a belief that free trade will bring an end to our troubles, but upon the recognition that economic nationalism in respect to foreign trade has come to stay, and that it is the part of wisdom for Canada to seek to discover, within this international framework, secure and stable markets for her specialized products.

It is necessary, in other words, to abandon our lamentations over the growth of world trade restrictions, to recognize it as

6Cf. Chapter XXI, section b, on the B.N.A. Act.

an inevitable result of the breakdown of the free competitive capitalist system in all countries, and to make use of those features of planning and stability in it which can be harmonized with the purposes of Canadian social planning. So far as the Canadian tariff is concerned, the farmer as consumer will only get relief when we have wiped out the most costly forms of protection by which politically powerful interests have exploited us all. As an exporter he will benefit by the expansion of international exchange which a socialist plan of import and export control[7] will be able to foster.

As to the more immediate problem, our agricultural policy will have to recognize that in consequence of present international economic dislocations, the agricultural industry has borne too large a share of the social cost involved, and that considerations of equity demand that the burden be more evenly distributed over those classes in the community which have contributed least to the cost of adjustment. Short-term policies of farm "relief" should be recast in recognition of this principle.

If these realities are kept in mind, it is clear that besides the measures necessary to give agriculture its proper weight in a socially planned Canada, the immediate problem—which may recur in the best of all planned worlds—is that of sheltering the farmer from the worst effects of a drastic fall in world prices. Essentially this is a question of spreading the burden over those sections of the community able to share it. Foremost among the various methods will be the partial depreciation of the external value of the Canadian dollar, under Central Bank control. By this device a decline in world demand and world prices will not exercise its full effect on farm incomes. Not that Canada as a whole can avoid a downward adjustment of real incomes in such an emergency; but where this procedure is followed, consumers of imported goods, governments, and private corporation with debts payable abroad, are all compelled to shoulder part of the burden of adjustment by reason of the higher value of all foreign exchanges. This policy has been practised with considerable success by both Australia and New Zealand since 1930, with substantially the same end in view. It should be one of the principal objectives of the Central Bank management to control our monetary policy with a view to introducing a greater measure of stability into the price structure of export products.

[7] See Chapter XIV.

Social Planning of Marketing.

The methods involved in the social control of agricultural marketing, analyzed in section B of this chapter, are capable of being turned to immediate or ultimate purposes. At the moment, the whole weight of governmental effort is being thrust in the direction of immediate gains—anything to raise prices. But within the terms of the Marketing Act there is scope for the most comprehensive type of public control—even to the extent of public operation—of the marketing and processing of farm products. Following the model of the British Agricultural Marketing Act, its Canadian counterpart delegates wide powers of control to the Dominion Marketing Board, and through it to the various local or commodity boards which have been and will be established.

Now it would be vain to imagine that the promoters of the Act intend to apply aggressive methods of social regulation to the marketing and processing of farm products. It is probably true that the authorities will move no faster than they are forced to go by political pressure. It is extremely unlikely that the second part of the Act which provides for "investigations" into the packing, storing and merchandising charges will be successful in preventing the "spread" from becoming "detrimental to the interests of the public in that it is excessive or results in undue enhancement of prices". This type of protection will be as useless, and as ill-suited to its purpose as the Combines Investigation Act was in its sphere. On the other hand, there is no use our hugging the delusion that any one cut-and-dried scheme of public control or operation of the processing or marketing machinery can be applied to most or all farm products. The present Act is so framed as to permit a wide variety of treatment, with a good deal of flexibility of operation. It is also fortunately so constituted as to permit a socialist plan of control to be introduced without greatly enlarging its terms.

As we have indicated elsewhere, it will be essential as a part of a scheme of economic planning to establish a series of Export Boards, subordinate to the Central Board, to control our foreign trade. In no case is this more urgently necessary than in agriculture. Such boards must have power to license exports, to control and improve quality, to arrange adequate shipping, insurance and storage contracts, and to provide for national selling and advertising abroad.[8] This must be the logical step

---

[8] Many of these features are already provided for under the Export Control legislation of New Zealand.

after the inauguration of the projected marketing boards. The experience and technique which will be gained by the persons operating these schemes will prove invaluable when the time comes to extend their activities into the field of socialist economic planning.

The Canadian government has already been forced to take the first steps in this direction as a result of its activities in attempting to stabilize wheat prices. The policy of supporting the price of Canadian wheat by withholding supplies was begun, essentially, as a plan of farm "relief". The metamorphosis of Mr. McFarland's scheme into a federal Wheat Board means, however, the beginning of public control over this important branch of Canadian agriculture. Whatever success this Board enjoys in the future—and no political realist would prophesy much for it so long as the private grain trade is permitted to intrigue against it—at all events it points to the method of control which a socialist government could adopt.

The Internal Market for Farm Products.

If we turn from the international aspect of the problem to consider the domestic market for agricultural produce, it must not be forgotten that, so far as most products except the grains are concerned, there are potential markets at home quite as important as those which exist abroad. The real task is to transform the potential demand of unemployed and underpaid urban workers and their families for more food, more varied food, and better food, into a really effective demand. It has been pointed out by the Minister of Agriculture that Canada consumes at home 97 per cent. of the cattle and beef produced, 99 per cent. of the butter, 97 per cent. of the potatoes, 95 per cent. of the hogs and pork, 99 per cent. of the sheep and lamb, 98 per cent. of the poultry, 100 per cent. of the eggs, 94 per cent. of the oats, 98 per cent. of the barley.

The estimated net agricultural revenue for 1932 (see Table, Chapter V.) was approximately $565 millions. This can be compared with the total value of farm products exported at $224 millions of which a good deal consists of processing and manufacturing costs. In other words, for farm products as a whole, the principal market is the domestic market. It will be seen, therefore, that the size of the market for all these products is capable of considerable increase as soon as the reconstruction of our industrial system has provided for the re-employment of the hundreds of thousands of workers unemployed and for the improvement of the position of the much larger number of poorly paid industrial workers. Those people receiving public relief,—and the figures have run well over a million in recent years,—have only a slight purchasing power over fresh meat, fruit and vegetables. Find jobs for urban workers and the output of Canadian agriculture will not display that appearance of surplus, marked by excessive low prices, which has prevailed in recent years. The characteristic feature of a capitalist economy, particularly in times of business depression, is the plethora of idle labour and unused equipment. Granted the significance of overhead costs, it follows that one of the results of the greater employment of men and resources which a planned, socialist economy would produce would be lower costs in industry. To the farmer it would mean that the articles he uses in production and the goods consumed in the home would be cheaper and more plentiful. The tendency to stress the external factors affecting the money income of farmers should not make us lose sight of the important fact that, under a socially controlled economy, efficient industrial production will redound to the advantage of farmers as well as urban workers.

Reduction of Farm Debts.

The magnitude of the burden of farm debts has already been indicated. It is already apparent that in many parts of Western Canada where the problem is most acute this is gradually reducing the farmer to the status of a European peasant. As a short-run counter move to this drift there is no alternative but to do for agriculture what industrial corporations are able to do for themselves, namely, to write down the debt structure. What is needed is a comprehensive Federal scheme (far more drastic and immediate than the pre-election legislation of the Farmers' Creditors Arrangement Act, 1934) for the scaling down of farm mortgages, both as to principal and interest. Along with this must go an arrangement for the consolidation and liquidation in an orderly manner of other farm debts. The Act referred to is, in effect, a scheme for dealing with individual cases where bankruptcy is imminent. It deals mainly with the more hopeless cases of debt, and its operation, in the nature of things, is a long-drawn-out process. What is proposed here is a reduction in the incidence of all farm debts, (in addition to existing arrangements to prevent foreclosures) by a scheme of re-financing, undertaken under government auspices, so that the cost of servicing the debt might be reduced in proportion to the reduction of farm incomes. As a preliminary to such action the government would have to force down all rates of interest in Canada, either by Central Banking action, or more directly by law, after the manner adopted by the Commonwealth of Australia in 1931. It is idle to imagine that much can be done in this direction so long as the structure of the Canadian economy remains mainly capitalist in character. Anything which threatens the return upon capital destroys that "confidence" which bank presidents rightly insist to be essential to a revival of enterprise and to a restoration of private investment. Not until we have a government in power determined to build the economic system anew upon a socially controlled and planned basis will it be possible to lighten the burden of debt which weighs so heavily on the majority of Canadian farmers.

Permanent Planning for Agriculture.

Most of what has been suggested so far has been concerned with the immediate task, in which the rôle of agricultural "relief" is necessarily emphasized. A permanent program for agriculture must, however, drive down to the roots of the problem. Agriculture, essentially, suffers from the fact that, like the rest of the economy, it has outgrown the competitive and unplanned system within which it formerly operated. The hundreds of thousands of Canadian farmers, each acting separately, with nothing to guide them but an emasculated perversion of a pricing system, are quite incapable of adjusting themselves, without unity of action, to the changing circumstances of to-day.

The situation of the world market has forced upon agriculture the need for export control, and for a re-allocation of resources towards more profitable production (including less for export). This raises questions involving the re-adjustment of tariffs, debts, transportation charges, social services, etc. In this task the place of agriculture in the Canadian economy must be seen as a whole, and not as a series of regional problems. More inter-provincial co-operation is therefore essential. In addition the task of agriculture must be geared to the main objectives of Canadian economic society.

Within the agricultural sector of the economy there must be introduced therefore a series of planning agencies,—in the fields of research, marketing, processing, land utilization and settlement, transportation, exporting, etc.—all co-ordinated under the Agricultural Branch of the Planning Commission. Keeping what is good of the existing administrative machinery, provincial and Federal, and substituting public control for the private control which now exists at the more strategic points, agriculture can be set free from the restraints and defects which keep both it and Canada as a whole impoverished to-day.

It is probable that, for technical and social reasons, the family farm will continue for a long time to remain the typical unit of production in agriculture. That alone makes the task of agricultural reconstruction far more difficult than in industry, where large-scale organization is more evident. For that reason it is inevitable that development in the direction of socialist planning should begin at those points where control is already centralized. This means public ownership of all processing and marketing agencies and establishments. It means public provision, through a socialized banking and investment system, for agricultural credit. It means public ownership and operation of transportation facilities generally. It has been argued elsewhere that these developments are necessary for other reasons—to prevent the exploitation of the many by the few, to foster increased production, and to provide for stability of income. The advantages gained thereby can also, however, be shared by agriculture.

It will be necessary, also, for an agricultural planning body to repair the mistakes of the past, to widen the ambit of soil survey so as to provide a basis for a re-adjustment of farm acreage in accordance with physical possibilities and the demands of changing markets. It will be necessary to eliminate speculations in land values—a potent cause of wasteful land settlement and cultivation. Then there will be the task of revising the whole machinery of public finance in Canada in order to relate taxation to the income of the farmer, and to make better provision for social and community services in rural areas on a scale not permissible under the present unjust system of taxation, which relies so heavily on taxing the things the farmer uses (sales tax, gasoline tax, etc.) or on taxing his property, whether remunerative or not.

The inadequacies of community life and of educational services in many rural areas are well known,—the absence of community centres, the deplorable lack of hospitals, libraries, athletic and adult educational facilities. But there is nothing of a social and educational nature already available, in part, to city-dwellers which should not be equally available to the farm population, if given sufficient individual or collective income. The absence of these facilities causes young people frequently to migrate to urban centres. Moreover, whatever degree of social and recreative development rural people do manage to obtain tends to be patterned after city models. An appropriate and distinctive rural culture will never be attained so long as these economic drawbacks remain.

To avoid misunderstanding, we wish to emphasize again that the public ownership of the agencies of distribution which we propose does not interfere in any way with the full ownership of the land by the farmer. We do not at all recommend the nationalization of land now held by individual owners.

CHAPTER XVIII.

THE DISTRIBUTIVE SERVICES.

A. WHAT THE CONSUMER GETS FROM COMPETITIVE TRADE.

THE ultimate end of all productive activity is the satisfaction of the wants of consumers, or, more succinctly, the goal of production is consumption. The distributive services have been developed to provide the necessary links between producer and consumer which the specialized nature of our economy demands. Upon the efficiency with which the distributive agencies operate depends, in large measure, the stability of production and, viewed from the opposite end, the standard of living of the population. But, however ready the supporters of individualistic enterprise may be to subscribe to the social ends of economic activity, they would be forced to admit that in the present system these can only be sought within the limits set by the profit motive. In our capitalist society the distributive services can be operated under charges no lower than those consistent with the pursuit of gain and no more efficiently than the conditions of competitive business permit. What is the effect of these limitations on the interests of consumers? How far does the present organization of the distributive services adequately supply their wants?

Much has been written of the high costs of distribution and of the wide margins which exist between manufacturing or production costs and final retail prices. No constructive proposals can be advanced to deal with this problem, however, until it is clearly determined how far such margins represent the legitimate costs of rational distribution and how far they represent the costs of monoply or the waste and extravagance of competition. Three matters are of vital interest to the consumer: (a) the costs, (b) the quality and utility of the commodities and services which are supplied, and (c) the extent to which adequate and accurate information is provided for guidance in making purchases. These are the factors which must be considered in a survey of distributive agencies and the marketing methods of the manufacturers engaged in supplying them. The continuance of private enterprise in the field of distribution must depend on the extent to which the interests of consumers can be protected against the losses engendered in a competitive scramble for markets.

425

The organization of the supply of most articles of popular consumption has developed such a complex character that much time would have to be spent in tracing the various channels by which the goods are brought from the factory to the counter before any appraisal could be made of the methods involved. A better approach can probably be made by examining the distribution of some commodities in general demand which are handled by a few relatively specialized agencies.

Milk.

Milk is a commodity which is in daily demand in practically every household. To a considerable extent it is a standard commodity, i.e., sold in recognized grades, for which the demand remains relatively steady from day to day although tending to vary over longer periods. It should be produced within fairly close distance of the community in which it is to be sold and must be furnished to the consumer within a relatively short time after it is produced. Possessing such features, the distribution of milk, if the organization of the trade had developed in the interests of the consumer, should be of a very effective character, but, on the contrary, "gross inefficiency and competitive waste is everywhere the rule".[1] The reasons for this state of affairs are not hard to find. Freedom of enterprise in this field has led to the development of pasteurization plants and delivery services far in excess of the actual needs of the populace. Once the capital investment has been made and the market shared between competing distributors duplication and waste necessarily result. As it is practically impossible for any one distributor to offer better quality of milk or superiority of services at a price which cannot be met by his competitors, the elimination of high-cost firms never proceeds far enough to permit the demand to be met in the most economical manner. Those concerns which make fairly effective use of their equipment can thus secure handsome profits from prices which barely meet the costs of the least efficient operators. That such costs are burdensome is shown by the extent of the margin between the prices paid by consumers and those received by the dairy farmer. In the early part of 1933 the retail price of milk in Halifax was 11 cents per quart and the payment to the producer 5.5 cents; in Montreal the retail price was 9 cents and the dairy farmer received 3.5

[1] W. M. Drummond, "The Functions and Responsibilities of Governments in Agricultural Marketing". *Proceedings of the Canadian Political Science Association,* 1933, Vol. V, p. 143.

cents; in Toronto the rates were 10 cents and 3.7 cents; in Winnipeg, 9 cents and 4.0 cents; and in Vancouver, 8 cents and 3.8 cents.[2]

That the distribution charges for a commodity which undergoes such slight processing as milk should exceed the payment made to the producer is fairly conclusive evidence that the producer or consumer is being unfairly treated. Unfortunately information is not available to show the extent of the unnecessary investment that has been made in the milk trade or the cost of maintaining overlapping delivery services and other forms of wasteful competitive activity. When the rationalization of milk distribution was attempted in the city of Vancouver it was found that eleven out of fourteen pasteurization plants could be closed and that at least 100 dairy wagons could be taken off the streets.[3] In this instance, the attempted reorganization of the milk trade was undertaken by private firms, and as entrance to the trade could not be restricted no permanent benefits accrued either to the public or to dairy farmers. So far as conditions in Vancouver are typical of those prevailing in other cities, this gives some indication of the multiplication of plants and facilities which the economic organization of milk distribution would obviate but for which payment is now being exacted in the form of low prices to dairy farmers and high prices to consumers.

Bread.

The active interest which the public has maintained in the price of bread and the trend toward large-scale bakeries has resulted in the assembling of more detailed statistics for the trade in bread than is the case for milk. The outstanding features of the bread-baking industry in Canada are, firstly, the concentration of the control of the larger baking concerns in the hands of the four leading flour-milling companies, so that the bakeries under mill-control produced in 1929 over 90 per cent. of the bread sold in the localities in which they operated; secondly, the existence of a very large number of small local bakeries; lastly, plant capacity greatly in excess of market requirements and, consequently, extremely costly efforts made by baking companies to increase sales and thus bring their production more in line with plant capacity. In the report of the Registrar of the Combines Investigation Act on the bread-baking industry one reads that

2Select Standing Committee on Agriculture and Colonization of the House of Commons (Canada); Ottawa, 1933, *Minutes of Proceedings and Evidence.*
3*Ibid*, pp. 601 ff .

"all the arts of modern salesmanship have been put to use, extensive and expensive advertising campaigns, special delivery services, credit, feature breads of fancy shapes or fancy ingredients—all designed to secure volume. Sales effort to secure volume has its economic justification when increased volume makes possible lower costs and lower prices. In the bread-baking industry, however, while volume has been secured by a few large baking companies, the selling expenses involved in gaining this volume have been exceedingly heavy and apparently have more than offset whatever may have been effected in the way of economies from large-scale production. Certainly there is no evidence here that increased volume means lower prices"[4]

Indeed, one reads in the same report that in 1930 the total capacity of 72 mill-controlled bakeries was three times their actual output and fifty million pounds in excess of the total bread sales in the Dominion. Is the failure of competition to reduce costs and prices at all surprising? The Registrar found that in the City of Ottawa either one of the two mill-controlled bakeries could produce more bread than was consumed in the entire city; yet there was also 25 other bakeries attempting to secure some share of the market. In some of the larger Eastern cities, delivery and selling costs of bread were more than 30 per cent. of total costs, ranging from $3\frac{1}{2}$ to 5 cents a loaf of 24 ounces.

In addition to the wastes caused by excess plant capacity and duplication of services, there has been added to the consumer's bill the toll exacted by the flour-milling companies through their control of the bakeries. As the latter are forced to make their purchases of flour from the parent companies it has been possible to charge the subsidiaries prices higher than those prevailing in the open market.[5] The benefits of large-scale production have thus been absorbed in the form of higher prices. From whatever angle one views the bread industry there is no escaping the conclusion that as long as the distribution of bread remains under the direction of private enterprise the consumer will have to meet the cost of duplication, waste and quasi-monopolistic control.

Coal.

Coal and gasoline are two commodities which occupy important positions in the budgets of most consumers. They are,

[4]Department of Labour, *Investigation into An Alleged Combine in the Bread-Baking Industry in Canada*, (Ottawa, King's Printer, 1931), p. 34.
[5]*Ibid.*, p. 41.

however, chiefly convenience goods; and the personal tastes of consumers do not enter into their purchase, as is the case with articles of personal consumption or pleasure. Notwithstanding the more favourable conditions for the rational organization of the trade in coal and gasoline, the consumer is as poorly served with these products as he is with milk and bread.

Householders in central Canada are dependent for fuel chiefly upon anthracite coal brought from mines in Pennsylvania or Wales. The production of anthracite coal in the United States has long been controlled by a powerful association which keeps the price as high as is possible without losing its market to competing fuels. As the Canadian distributors of American coal are interested only in securing the customary margin on each ton of coal handled, there are no agencies working in the consumer's interest to see that the prices of American coal are reasonable. Although it was at first thought that the entrance of Welsh coal into the Canadian market would cause a marked reduction in the retail price of coal, the experience of the past few years has demonstrated the futility of the consumer having any faith that his interests would receive any greater consideration when importers were dealing with British rather than American producers. The search for profits is just as strong in one instance as in another; and in the case of Welsh coal the conditions were, in fact, much more favourable for Canadian importers. The recent investigation into the handling of Welsh coal in Canada has revealed one of the most extreme cases of exploitation that can be found in the annals of Canadian business. Through the co-operation of the British exporters, four Canadian firms were given a monopoly of the importation of coal. Their policy was to maintain the price of Welsh coal slightly lower than that of American, and, because of the relative cheapness of the product they were handling, secure a large return on each ton imported. The Ottawa *Citizen* on May 3, 1933, reported that the gross profit secured by the importing companies was between $4 and $5 per ton and that the salaries of three executives of one of the importing companies were $97,000 per annum. Mr. R. W. Lipsett in the *Saturday Night* of May 21, 1933, wrote that a spread of $7.33 per ton was maintained between the f.o.b. price at Montreal and the retail price. This was sufficient, according to Mr. Lipsett, to permit the importing companies to secure profits of 30 per cent. per annum over a four-year period and to mulct the consumers in Ontario and Quebec of millions of dollars on their fuel bills.

The retail distribution of coal is in the hands of the thousands of dealers across the country. In the City of Toronto, for example, there are more than 100 firms specializing in the sale of coal, many of them maintaining branch offices and yards in addition to their central depots. The demand for coal, needless to say, is not affected by the number of dealers, but the price which the consumer must pay is dependent on the efficiency with which the services are operated. When there are more coal yards and delivery equipment than can be fully employed, and when the facilities are not located so that householders in each section of the city can be supplied economically, the costs of distribution become excessive. It is not surprising to find that the spread between the wholesale and retail price of coal ranges from $2.50 per ton in some localities to almost $5 per ton in others.

Gasoline: Monopoly and Competition Both.

The distribution of gasoline in Canada is characterized by semi-monopolistic conditions in refining and in the setting of prices, and by extreme competition in the retail trade. From the public view the consequences are excessive waste, inefficiency, and confusion. The motorist suffers the worst effects of the twin evils of individualistic enterprise.

In 1930, 90 per cent. of the gasoline refined in Canada was produced by the Imperial Oil Company which owned about 60 per cent. of the wholesale outlets in the country. Witnesses before the House of Commons Committee which investigated gasoline prices in 1932 were practically unanimous in declaring that the prices established by the Imperial Oil Company were followed by all distributors. The retail margin on gasoline was established for the first service stations at from 3½ to 4 cents a gallon and this differential remains unaltered whether the station handles 100 or 1,000 gallons a day—a clear indication of uneconomic organization (although by no means confined to the trade in gasoline). The wholesale margin, from which the refineries and bulk distributors derive their profits, varies from time to time, but during the past few years it has tended to be between 20 and 30 per cent. of the retail price for most of Canada. This compares with 13 to 16 per cent. for the retail margin. In practically no other line of trade does the wholesale margin exceed the retail (it would appear that it is cheaper to handle gasoline in bulk than in five or ten gallon lots), and this anomaly of price margins is a second clear indication that the motorist is being subjected to excessive charges. As the prices set by the Imperial Oil Company are followed by all dealers, no bulk distributor can enlarge his sales by under-selling his competitors. There is, therefore, a direct incentive for each refining and importing company to attempt to enlarge the market for its products by conducting expensive sales campaigns and by getting as many service stations and other retailers as possible to act as agents. But the demand for gasoline, as is the case with coal, is not dependent upon the number of dealers, and the competitive efforts of marketers to increase their sales produce no results other than the higher distribution costs which car owners have to meet. Clearly there is something fundamentally wrong with a system which impels competing concerns to employ methods that are detrimental to the interests of consumers.

Modern Marketing Methods.

The wastes of competition and the exploitation of the consumer by monopolistic combinations are not confined to the production and sale of the four commodities dealt with above but prevail in every sphere of distribution. The investigation of the Committee on Price Spreads and Mass Buying have at last made us realize how far-reaching and serious are the losses from such causes. While it is true that the consumer has long suffered from the high costs of competitive distribution he has until recently at least been assured of the personal interest and attention of the merchants with whom he dealt. But the rise to dominance of large-scale retail organizations is removing even this redeeming feature of competitive business, and it is now evident that the consumer is being subjected to merchandizing practices designed, not to provide him with the greatest satisfaction in his purchases, but to yield the highest net profits to the shareholders of the corporate retail enterprises. The pride of the merchant in the confidence of his customers has given way before the demands of capital for protection against losses. Is it surprising then that the interests of consumers are lost sight of in the struggle to widen the spread between cost and selling price by playing upon the ignorance of the public and the weakened bargaining power of producers? Perhaps a protracted discussion of the prevalence of such practices is no longer necessary: it is enough to cite in passing some of the evidence gathered by the Price Spreads Commission.

"Special Sale of Overcoats" will run the page advertisement of some big store, "Values Up To $60 for $30"—and the prospective purchaser will be urged to avail himself of the "Stupendous Bargains". While we may have had some doubts of the real values in such "bargains" these had remained unsolved until the Price Spreads Committee brought the actual details to the light of day. Now we find that while a few relatively high priced articles are thrown in as "bait", the great majority of the garments offered in such sales are secured at low prices from manufacturers and sold at an advance of from thirty to fifty per cent. over the cost price. If you think that very few persons would be misled by such advertising, consider the example of women's coats. These cost the department store $6 a garment, but are sold at both $10 and $15. True, the coats selling at the higher prices, even though they cost the same as the lower-price ones, may have been more attractive in cut or colour. Yet would the purchaser be willing to pay $5 more for such intangible values if she knew the real cost of the garment? We turn the pages of the evidence and note the suites of living-room furniture which cost $46 and yet sell at both $60 and $75. Do real values, or only the ability of the advertiser or salesman to create the illusion of superior qualities, cause the difference in selling prices?

Such tactics are not confined to the distributor but are also engaged in by manufacturers, generally with the co-operation of the retailer. As the case of cheap made-to-measure suits gave rise to considerable discussion in the Parliamentary Committee, the evidence on this subject is open for our inspection. The suits are sold to the big store at a uniform price and are re-sold to the public also at a uniform price about one-third higher. But the records of the manufacturer showed that the cloths from which the suits were made ranged in price from 90c to $2 a yard. The consumer who was an expert in clothing could have secured very good value for his money, but the average individual who could not test the quality of the goods which were offered would probably contribute to the profitableness of such sales. Could a more complete separation of price and value be devised? Or are we to experience even more weird forms of merchandising as large-scale organizations seek to attack public patronage? In fact, the whole trend of modern merchandising seems to be away from any attempt to provide the public with satisfactory goods at reasonable prices, and toward the exaction of the highest possible profits from each class of consumer. Buying thus becomes a gamble, with the odds heavily against the uninformed purchaser. These odds are not lessened by the growing use of advertising by large stores. The evidence before the Commission on Price Spreads showed that in one city alone, two stores spent more than $1,500,000 in a single year for newspaper advertising.

"It Pays to Advertise".

The practices just described and others equally harmful to the buying public are among the ills which have been aggravated by the efforts of large retail companies to avoid losses which might be caused by the decline in the purchasing power of consumers. Turn now to another phase of modern marketing methods, namely the advertising and selling policies of manufacturers. Although the greatest economic losses are caused by the chaotic state of the distributive services, there are serious social losses caused by present-day efforts of manufacturers to make profits out of trade-names, brands, slogans, in fact anything except the real worth of their products. While the competitive methods now pursued tend eventually to defeat themselves by so increasing costs that articles are beyond the reach of a great mass of the public, they result in the stimulation of some wants out of all proportion to others; and by stressing the desire for immediate pleasure rather than lasting satisfactions they have tended to create an unwholesome state of consumer-demand. Advertising and high-pressure salesmanship are held to be the outstanding features of modern marketing methods. No longer does the manufacturer attempt to secure patronage by demonstrating the superior qualities of his products but, instead, he attempts to break down "sales-resistance" by utilizing every possible appeal to popular fears, foibles or fancies; and where these have not existed in a form sufficient to provide the required stimulus to purchase, advertisers have proceeded to develop them.

The high cost of such marketing methods is illustrated in the case of household appliances. According to the census report on chain stores in Canada, the operating expenses for the retail outlets in this field were almost 60 per cent. of the value of sales made in such establishments. In other words, more than half the price which the consumer paid for a washing machine or a vacuum cleaner, was absorbed in the cost of competitive advertising, house-to-house solicitation by salesmen, and the other selling methods of such stores. The Federal Trade Commission of the United States found that the retail margin on vacuum cleaners was almost 50 per cent. of the retail price in independent stores. It is possible that similar margins prevail in Canada for practically all household appliances and equipment. When the manufacturing costs for many modern household appliances are approximately only one-third of their final prices, there is some justification for believing that the standard of living of the Canadian people could be raised very effectively through the economic reorganization of the distributive services and the direction of production to meet an educated consumer demand.

One factor which has contributed in no small measure to the exploitation of consumers through misrepresentation and extravagant claims by manufacturers is the almost complete lack of scientific information available to the public with respect to commodities in popular demand.[6] Not only is the consumer generally unable to apply any standards of quality or performance to the goods which he purchases, but in practically every case he is entirely in the dark as to the real worth of the articles. If the public had been informed of the manufacturing costs of radio tubes, it would have been difficult, if not impossible, for the manufacturers to have maintained a retail price nine hundred per cent. higher! The absence of any authority to establish standards of quality for consumer goods, or to give publicity to manufacturing costs, has made it unnecessary for manufacturers to adhere rigidly to such standards as have been adopted for their products, or to develop tests or measures by which the consumer could readily determine the quality and value of the merchandise on the market. Although advocates of the existing system of business enterprise continue to extol the virtues of competition, the chief purpose of modern marketing methods, and particularly advertising, is to *avoid* tests of comparative

6"Consumer literacy is complicated by the ragged state of development of fundamental scientific work touching the various types of commodities, and by the related uneven acceptance of reliable standards by the industries concerned. . . . Likewise, the reliability of standards and the degree of compliance with them by industry, both relatively high in the case of machinery such as turbines and machine tools for intermediate consumers, and of the services provided by such a public service agency as the Bell Telephone Company and its subsidiaries, drop away in descending order through automobiles, certain foods such as sugar and cereals, medicines used in prescriptions, electrical appliances, certain building materials such as brick and cement and certain kinds of lumber, typewriters, furniture, and other kitchen utensils, with preserves, men's clothing, other building materials such as wall-board and paint, cosmetics, textiles and women's clothing crowding toward the bottom of the list in point of standardized reliability". . . . *Recent Social Trends in the United States*, (McGraw-Hill, N.Y., 1933) p. 881.

superiority, and to secure the uncritical acceptance of goods by brand or trade names, popular slogans, and other devices. While it may be true that when a branded article is first put on the market its qualities may bear some relationship to the claims made for it by its promoters, the public has little opportunity to make a critical comparison of such claims with those put forth on behalf of competing brands. There is also no guarantee that the original quality will be maintained if the manufacturers believe that greater profits can be secured by altering the size of the package, quality of the material, or some other feature without informing the public. The public may even be deprived of the advantages of a cheaper article of equal or better quality, because the reputation established through effective advertising of some popular brand makes it impossible for the new article to replace the old without an expensive sales campaign. A great deal of modern marketing thus resolves itself into a "battle of brands", with consumers (male and female) as the unhappy victims of the warfare. For them the consequences are a lack of protection of their interests, the poor satisfaction of many real wants and the undue stimulation of others, and, finally, the necessity of bearing the costs of the selling campaigns.

B. The Efficiency of Distributing Units.

It is commonly conceded that distribution is the least efficient part of our present industrial structure. A minimum of investigation is enough to indicate that the chief causes of this inefficiency are directly traceable to competitive capitalism and could easily be removed in a socialized society. It is difficult to make an accurate appraisal of the avoidable waste in terms of money, and equally difficult to calculate distributive wastes in terms of capital or man-power employed.[7] For we at once meet the problem of drawing a line between production and distribution. Workers engaged in transportation, communications, finance and other industries serve both the processes of production and distribution; their contributions cannot be allocated definitely to either. Nor, because of the many uses to which any one product may be put, is it possible to measure the consumption of goods in the manufacturing and industrial processes. Coal, for instance, may be used for heating a store, a house, a boiler, or even processed to make coke and by-products.

[7]Valuable material can be obtained from the many detailed reports of the 1931 Census of Merchandising (Dominion Bureau of Statistics).

Personnel Engaged in Distribution.

Even within these limitations, however, there is ample evidence of a tremendous increase in the proportion of the total number of people gainfully employed, who are engaged, not in producing goods, but in moving or selling the products, or directing the process.[8]   In Canada, from 1881 to 1931, the number of persons gainfully employed in agriculture and manufacturing (the two chief branches of production) increased from 823,801 to 1,758,929, an increase of 113 per cent., whereas the number engaged in trade and "service" (including government) increased from 176,928 to 1,153,137, an increase of 552 per cent.   However, such figures are not strictly comparable, as there have been changes in the classifications of occupations from one census to another, and some occupations are included in one total but not in the other.   More definite are the statistics of specific occupations.   In 1921 there were listed 110,266 salesmen and saleswomen; in 1931 there were 145,589.   Insurance agents in 1911 numbered 3,261; in 1931, 17,379.   There were 80,940 retail merchants and dealers in 1911; in 1931 there were 100,874.   The rapid development of corporations in the retail field robs figures of the amount of individual ownership of much significance.

The mere fact that the number of workers engaged in distribution has increased to a greater extent than the number in manufacturing is not sufficient in itself to demonstrate the wastefulness of the present distributive system.   The rapid growth of urban centres, and our desires for increased services and for manufactured rather than home-made articles are, in part, responsible for the enlarged sphere of distribution.   Of course, if the increased costs of distribution were exceeded by the savings obtained from mass production we, as consumers, would benefit; but, unfortunately, it appears that distributive wastes are out-running production economies.

The Efficiency of Large- and Small-Scale Stores.

In 1930 there were 125,002 retail stores in Canada (excluding service establishments), approximately one store to every 80 persons, or one to every twenty families.   The total sales of these stores were $2,753,000,000 or an average annual sale

---

[8] Stuart Chase in *The Tragedy of Waste* (p. 213) quotes the following statistics for the United States as showing the distribution of gainfully employed between "production effort" and "commercial effort" (selling and distribution):

	Production Effort	Commercial Effort
1851	80.2%	19.8%
1921	19.6%	80.4%

volume of $22,000.[9]   Although the average sales per store are $22,000, less than one-quarter of the number of stores actually do that much business.   Almost 40 per cent. of the stores have sales of less than $5,000 per year, while 75 per cent. do less than $20,000.   At the other end of the scale, we find 0.2 per cent. (the largest stores) handling 20 per cent. of the business. These extremes may be illustrated by reference to particular kinds of business.   More than 500 small filling stations sell less gasoline than the 11 largest while the sales of 6,000 small grocery stores scarcely exceed the sales of 44 large ones.   The continued existence of small stores does not represent a direct burden upon the consumer, because the prices in such stores tend to be determined by the competition of larger units, but the indirect burden caused by the misdirection of capital and labour would be serious in a society which was attempting to utilize its resources fully.

The total volume of goods sold at retail in Canada was $2,-753,000,000 in 1930.   It has been estimated that the expenses of the wholesale and retail establishments through which these goods passed from manufacturer to consumer were, roughly, $1,000,000,000.[10]   A reduction of 20 per cent. in the costs of distribution would mean a saving to consumers of no less than $200,000,000 on the basis of the 1930 sales figures.   Yet there is reason to believe that the saving in distribution costs would be much greater than 20 per cent. if the present wasteful methods were superseded by the establishment of municipal, co-operative, and state institutions for the distribution of bulk commodities.   In fact, the current trends in the operating expenses of merchandising concerns may hasten the development of new and improved methods of distribution.   According to the reports which the auditors presented to the Price Spreads Commission, the expenses of department stores in Canada have risen during the past decade.   In 1925 the combined operating expenses for the larger department stores in Canada were 22.1 per cent. of sales.   This percentage rose steadily even in the prosperous years before the depression and advanced sharply to 25.8 per cent. in 1930 and to 30.8 per cent. in 1933.[11]   While part of the increased proportion of expenses to sales in recent years is due to a smaller volume of business, the developments prior to 1930 in merchandising methods and capital investment indicate that department stores in Canada are tending to follow the line of

9*Retail Merchandise Trade in Canada*, 1930.   Dominion Bureau of Statistics Bulletin.
10See *National Income of Canada*, Dominion Bureau of Statistics Bulletin, pp. 12-13.
11*Evidence*, p. 3869.

growth taken by their counterparts in the United States, where operating expenses have been for some time more than 30 per cent. of their sales. If figures were available to show the costs of distribution for other kinds of business over a period of years, they would probably show a general tendency for a greater part of the consumer's dollar to be absorbed by the expenses of distribution and a smaller proportion by the cost of production.

In face of this, what is to be said of the widely alleged inefficiency of the small store, as contrasted with the economies in production and marketing made possible by the development of chain stores and large department stores?

It is clear, first, that what may be true of a single distributive system is not necessarily true of a dozen or more large-scale competing concerns. The inefficiency in retail trade is not confined to the smaller units. Even if all the small dealers were "eliminated" there would still remain an excessive and unnecessary duplication of merchandising facilities. Such economies as result from chain-store technique have been almost wholly confined to the earlier stages of distribution. Competition between different chains and the large independents results in an unknown but undoubtedly enormous amount of duplication of store buildings and fixtures, stocks of commodities, labour, management, delivery and other services. Even the larger establishments do not come within measurable distance of attracting the volume of business which they are equipped to handle. Long before that stage is reached, the promise of profits brings in several firms, all duplicating the machinery of distribution. All our large cities illustrate this.

Secondly, the pressure on manufacturers to find markets has resulted in marked increases in the selling costs of manufacturers and created "our costly system of nation-wide distribution".[12] The attempts of each manufacturer to sell to the nation results in not only excessive sales-cost but also in wasteful transportation. Stoves manufactured in Ottawa are shipped for sale to Toronto, while Toronto stove manufacturers ship their products to Ottawa as their advertising creates a demand in their competitor's territory. This modern "hauling coals to Newcastle" represents a hidden but costly phase of competitive marketing.

On the other hand, not all small shops are uneconomic. Many of them serve a useful function as convenient shopping

12Price Spreads Commission, *Evidence*, Mr. E. S. Sargeant, p. 2170.

points for small purchases, and would be continued even in a more centrally reorganized system. Nor do their operations add greatly to the costs of distribution when they are run as a part-time occupation or in connection with some other line of activity. Moreover, with the decline of the small store there has disappeared a great deal of the personal relationship between employer and employee, and between retailer and customer, which has always characterized retail trade. How much the latter represents a loss to the buying public is perhaps doubtful,[13] but the evidence which has been presented to the Commission on Price Spreads certainly shows that the separation of ownership and management has been detrimental to sales-staffs.

The Place of the Small Business.

Nevertheless, the solution to the problem of maintaining the personal element in retail trade does not lie simply in placing obstacles against the growth of corporate business. What is necessary is to devise methods whereby the small-scale business can be operated as efficiently as the big corporation. That the small business, in many fields, can be operated as efficiently under intelligent management has been proved many times over.[14] What is needed is, first, intelligent guidance and secondly, the removal of all elements of discrimination which now prevail against the survival of the small business. The first must rest with business men themselves; the second will be an obligation of the government, in co-operation with manufacturers and distributors.

The co-operative efforts that independent retailers are now making to maintain themselves against the chain stores have demonstrated that many of the economies in wholesaling which have been made by the corporate chain companies are available to independent merchants if they are willing to act together. The reports of the Federal Trade Commission of the United

13It is probably of less importance to the well-to-do buyer (who is in any case offered a good deal of "service" by the large stores): but it is well known in working class areas, for instance, that small and independent stores have been more accommodating to the unemployed.

14It is interesting to note that merchants themselves are becoming aware of the losses which are entailed in the operation of competitive business. The following quotation is taken from *Retailing and the Public* by L. E. Neal (Allan & Unwin, London, 1932). "It is ~~parent therefore that we have outgrown our average channels of distribution as we have outgrown our average channels of production. Overheads have become topheavy and require challenge, not so much by comparison with past results, or on the basis of present environment, but in the light of potentialities that are waiting to be utilized. Consequently for each group of commodities in turn it would be well worth while to map out a standard performance—not merely that bare level of performance that will support the present methods of handling merchandise, but an optimum that presupposes an organization scaled to the pitch of productive industry". . . . p. 175.

States on chain stores in that country show that when independent merchants set up their own wholesale house and operate it under efficient management, they can reduce the costs of distribution in about the same proportion that chain stores have done. The success of such developments, however, requires careful management on the part of such co-operative enterprises and the wise selection of membership with respect to both location and business standing.

In the smaller communities in Canada the problems of the independent merchant are of a somewhat different character from those facing his counterpart in the city. The major drawback to merchandising in smaller places is the lack of specialization. We find in most places a number of general stores each attempting to carry goods to meet all the requirements of the neighbourhood. The result, of course, is that no one store can provide a sufficient range of goods to satisfy the present day tastes of purchasers who consequently turn to the mail order catalogue or drive to the nearest city. If the merchants in such places could devise a method whereby each one would specialize, as far as possible, in one particular line, a sufficient volume of business would in many cases be available to warrant the maintenance of stores which could provide values and variety of goods to satisfy most consumers. But as long as the present haphazard methods prevail, with each merchant following his inclinations and trying to out-rival his competitors, the future for the independent merchant will be far from bright. The solution of the problem is to a large extent in his own hands. But he will be in a better position to seek it when the trade discriminations to which he is now subject are removed.

The development of standards for consumers' goods (discussed in the following section) will also do much to restore to the independent merchant the position which he has lost through his inability to match the extensive advertising and sharp merchandising practices of the big retail organizations. When goods must be sold by recognized grades of quality and quantity, the greatest advertising points now stressed will no longer be effective in the advertising policies either of the large retail organizations or of the large manufacturers. Such changes should greatly enlarge the opportunities for the small manufacturer or producer who cannot now find a market in the face of the appeal which can be made through mass advertising. The local manufacturer whose products are equal or superior to those of the mass producer would then be able to turn to the neighbourhood retailer as an outlet for his products; for as soon as the public begins to buy *by grade* the advantage in trade names and slogans will largely disappear, and the small merchant will thus be relieved of the necessity of pushing the sales of those products whose price is greatly enhanced by high advertising and marketing costs. That this is not a vain supposition is borne out by the opposition of the big canning interests in the United States to the enforcement of a system of grading, as shown in this quotation from the New York *Times*:[15]

"If government grades are imposed on all labels, the consumer will buy, not on brand, but on government grades, or at least that will be the tendency, it was declared. This would operate to the advantage of private brands and to the disadvantage of the nationally advertised brands, *as the latter would have no greater value than some little-known packers' brands, and price would become a determining factor in retail sales,* it was pointed out." (italics ours).

There is a real need to protect legitimate enterprises against discriminatory policies established because of the superior bargaining power possessed by mass buyers. It is in the general interest of the consumer, however, that no steps shall be taken which will prevent the development of more efficient merchandising outlets, whether under public or private control. But experience tends to show that if merchants are willing to serve the public taste, it is possible to devise methods of operation, which will be favourable both to the public and private interest.

C. REORGANIZATION OF THE DISTRIBUTIVE SERVICES.

A Commission of Internal Trade.

It is inevitable that in the reconstruction of our economy a large measure of control will have to be established over the distributive services. The first step is to place the supply of consumers' goods and their distribution under the general supervision of a Commission of Internal Trade. One of the tasks which will then be undertaken by the Commission will be a complete survey of the markets for consumers' goods, with particular attention to the demands for staple commodities. At the same time, the Commission will make a study of the effectiveness of various types of distributive agencies with a view to the eventual reorganization of merchandise trade. Appropriate

15October 28, 1934.

types of marketing units will be devised on the basis of the commodity to be distributed, and in relation to the size and nature of the demand to be met. While the full benefits of economic planning in the field of distribution will have to await the results of detailed studies of the problems of consumption, the Commission of Internal Trade will, on the basis of its initial surveys, attempt to outline immediate objectives in the reduction of distributive costs. When it is remembered that a reduction of only 10 per cent. in the expense ratios of retail stores, if passed on to the public in the form of lower prices, would add a quarter of a billion dollars to the incomes of consumers, some concept is gained of the possibilities to be derived from a complete reorganization of the structure of distributive services.

It would appear that only for a few commodities could the distribution be directed effectively on a national scale. The actual supervision and control of the greater part of merchandise trade could best be handled by provincial and municipal bodies with the advice and guidance of the Commission of Internal Trade. Such co-operation of Dominion, provincial and local bodies should substitute for the "private chaos" which we have seen to exist, the orderly arrangement of marketing units designed and controlled to meet the merchandising needs of the public. Although it is not possible to outline the manner in which each commodity should be distributed we may illustrate these proposals in the case of the four staple commodities which were dealt with earlier in this chapter.

Milk and Bread.

The conviction that the distribution of *milk* should be brought under municipal control has been steadily gaining ground in Canada. There are two ways in which the interests of consumers and dairy farmers could be adequately protected under municipal control. One of these would be the placing of the milk trade in each city or town in the hands of a municipal corporation or board and the supplanting of existing private distributors by this agency. The other would be the establishment of a monopoly of milk distribution by a strong co-operative association of milk producers. In either case the duplication and waste which now results from the operations of competing firms would be obviated and an efficient organization of the milk trade could be built up under the control or supervision of the municipal body. The production and distribution of *bread* should likewise be placed under municipal control. Where there are a number of adjoining municipalities a commission might be formed to handle the bread trade for the area with representatives from each municipality serving on the board of directors. Outlying municipalities which desired to secure their bread from the metropolitan commission could form their own distributive organizations and contract with the large municipal bakeries for supplies.

Coal and Other Fuels.

As the production and importation of *coal* will be under the supervision of the Power and Fuel Commission,[16] the distribution of coal for domestic consumption will depend to some extent upon the allocation of supplies by the controlling body. The wholesale distribution of imported fuels could be handled by the Power and Fuel Commission, which would eliminate practically all private agencies in this field, as dealers in Canadian fuels could secure supplies directly from the producers. The distribution of coal in larger municipalities should be handled by a municipal corporation or commission which would secure supplies directly from the mines or through the Power and Fuel Commission. The economies which could be secured by municipal control are suggested by the following passage from a report of the Fuel Controller.

"If . . . a municipal organization could be managed on the same basis as a commercial business, with a fixed policy over a period of years, there would be justification for adopting municipal control of the fuel business in larger centres, because in that event the coal yards could be distributed throughout the community at strategic intervals, and all made subservient to a uniform policy".[17]

It is because a public enterprise can be managed in a much more efficient manner than a competitive business, where mediocrity is the rule, that municipal operation is suggested for the coal trade.

The distribution of *gasoline* and other *petroleum products,* whether refining is left to private business or not, should be undertaken by a publicly-owned dominion corporation which would be organized by the Commission of Internal Trade. This corporation would operate as an independent body with a board of directors appointed by the government; and the operating

16See Chapter X, "The Socialization of Industry", section c.
17*Final Report of the Fuel Controller* (Ottawa, March, 1919) p. 58.

records of the corporation would be carefully scrutinized each year by the accounting division of the Commission of Internal Trade. In all other respects the public company would be free to work out the most economical system for the distribution of petroleum products. A monopoly in the bulk distribution of petroleum products would be secured by the national corporation, through the granting of exclusive import privileges for refined products, the control of inter-provincial shipments and, where necessary, authorization from provincial governments. In order that the activities of the national oil corporation should not suffer the disadvantages of too great a degree of centralization, subsidiary companies would be organized in each province or economic area to handle the distribution in their respective territories. It is probable that the greater part of the motorist trade could be best served through outlets owned or operated by the provincial companies, but a system of licensing of private dealers could be followed wherever it appeared advantageous. Distribution through co-operative associations of farmers and fishermen would be followed wherever possible to meet the needs of these classes. Once the public oil companies had commenced operations, the present structure of distribution which is based on competition would disappear. Trade names would be of no value, as products would be sold *by grade*, with full information of the value of each grade as a fuel or lubricant.

An "Efficiency Audit".

In order that the public may be assured of the efficiency with which the distributive services are being conducted, there will be set up in each province an audit board to which will be submitted the operating records of all municipally-owned distributive agencies. The audit boards will be under the supervision of the Commission of Internal Trade and will render disinterested but expert judgment on the manner in which such municipal enterprises are being conducted. These audit boards will also be ready to examine the records of such other distributive services as are brought under municipal or provincial control. On the basis of such audits and the surveys conducted by the Commission of Internal Trade, the further reorganization of the distributive service will proceed.[18]

[18]It is interesting to note that the Webbs suggest an "efficiency audit" as a remedy for many of the shortcomings of the co-operative movement. They propose "an automatic, accurate, and impersonal analysis; made by disinterested experts, having no personal connection with the society reported on, and wielding absolutely no administrative authority; strengthened by comparison with other societies, other periods, and other departments". (*Consumers' Co-operative Movement*, p. 367). This concept of an "efficiency audit" is suggested above as applicable under government authority to the entire field of distribution.

The Place of Consumers' Co-operative Societies.

Such examples as have been given do not exhaust the various forms of organization which may be adopted for the distributive services. They serve merely to illustrate the manner in which the problems will be approached. Nothing has yet been said about the further development of consumers' co-operative associations, whose growth has been of such advantage to the working classes in Great Britain and continental countries. The less rapid growth of consumers' societies on this continent has been attributed to many causes. Perhaps the more important of these are the late development of an industrial class, the relatively small proportion of workers belonging to trade unions, the absence of a large number of workers' associations, and the readiness with which persons were able to change their occupations and places of residence. The higher wage rates prevailing on this continent in comparison with European wage scales, and the stimulation of consumer demand by manufacturers and distributors, have also played their parts in making workers less inclined to build up patiently their own distributive organizations.

The co-operative movement in Great Britain illustrates the possibilities of co-operative trading. It now embraces a large number of different activities, including, among others, banking, insurance, printing and farming, in addition to distribution and production; but the distributive function, which was the first to be undertaken, continues to be the most important. In 1930 there were some 1,250 retail distributive societies, whose aggregate sales amounted to over £217,000,000; on the wholesale, which includes also the productive side, the combined sales of the English and Scottish Co-operative Wholesale Societies were about £103,000,000".[19] The membership in co-operative societies in Great Britain is approximately 6,500,000 and represents between one-third and one-half of the families in the country. Although the co-operative societies sold their goods at or near competitive prices they were able, in 1930, to return to their members in the form of dividends on purchase an average of 1s. 10½d in the £.[20] In view of the facts that such progress has been made with the capital contributed by persons with small incomes and in the face of the competition of private business, considerable weight must be given to the conclusion of the

19L. E. Neal, *Retailing and the Public*, (Allen & Unwin, London, 1932).
20*Ibid.*, p. 40.

Webbs that "We have here, it is plain, a genuine and demonstrably successful alternative to the organization based on the diametrically opposite idea of production and distribution for private profit which we term the capitalist system".[21]

The essential principle of consumers' co-operation, however, is the voluntary association of individuals for mutual advantage. It is clear that no co-operative society can be successfully maintained unless this principle of self-help remains the basis of the movement. Thus the state can encourage and facilitate the growth of the co-operative societies but it cannot, without danger to the movement itself, actually organize the societies. The Commission of Internal Trade, in consultation with existing consumers' co-operative societies and unions, wherever advisable will assist the educational work of co-operative unions, and furnish financial and other aid to the co-operative movement. The sphere of co-operative trading will be carefully outlined in the proposals for the reorganization of the distributive system, and efforts will be made to see that co-operative societies will be ready to fill their positions in the new marketing structure.

Advisory Committees of Consumers.

There is one kind of voluntary associations of consumers which should form an essential part of the control of distribution. These are associations which would be formed to serve as advisory committees on matters affecting the welfare of consumers. Representatives of existing groups, such as co-operative societies, women's institutes, trade and professional associations, etc., would probably be among the first members of such advisory bodies, but, in the course of time, as consumers develop a high degree of consciousness of their own welfare and the ways in which it can best be attained, representatives would be secured from the general public. These associations of consumers would study the adequacy of the distributive services in their communities and make criticisms and recommendations to the municipal bodies and to the Commission of Internal Trade. With the growth of interest on the part of consumers provincial councils might be formed to give greater executive direction, and experience may show the necessity of forming a national body.

[21]*The Consumers' Co-operative Movement,* (Longmans, Green & Co., London, 1921) p. 4.

Standards for Consumers' Goods.

While the rational organization of the distributive services will contribute materially to more effective consumption, it will still be necessary for the Commission of Internal Trade to exercise adequate control over the quality and value of retail commodities. We have already seen that while reliable standards are used in the selection of goods for industrial purposes, there are only a few classes of consumers' goods for which similar protection is offered to the public. It has also been pointed out that the basic principle of modern marketing methods is to secure patronage without enabling the purchaser to test the comparative worth of the articles purchased. The remedy is to set up a national standardization service.

The suggestion that standards should be applied to consumers' goods may give rise to the impression that standardization of consumption is the result sought, with everybody wearing the same kind of clothes, living in the same kind of houses, eating the same foods, and so on. But a little reflection will suffice to show that the adoption of standards for the goods we commonly use will not limit the consumers' range of choice except, perhaps, that we shall no longer be led to purchase shoddy or inferior articles whose possession would only be a cause of dissatisfaction.

A cursory survey of the trade in consumers' goods reveals large groups of commodities for which the provision of adequate standards of quality and worth would be of immeasurable assistance to the buying public. The whole range of processed or packaged foods, kitchen utensils and household supplies, domestic and office appliances, house furnishings, building materials, farm implements and supplies, could be standardized to a considerable degree without limiting their usefulness or restricting the expression of individual taste. To such goods which are purchased primarily for their utility or for which the quality is of prime importance from a health standpoint, can be added the commodities whose usefulness is of chief importance and yet into the purchase of which there enters a large element of personal preference. Such articles as clothing and furnishings, furniture and household decorations, which are purchased largely from the standpoint of style, could have their purchase guided by the adoption of adequate standards. The buyer would know, for the first time in Canada, that such terms as "100 per cent. pure wool", "unshrinkable", "solid oak", etc.

etc., were no longer mere advertising "truths" but statements which would have been attested by reference to standard tests approved by the Commission of Internal Trade. Advertising would thus be brought under the control of the Commission of Internal Trade; by insisting on the scientific accuracy of all claims and the avoidance of half-truths it would restore advertisements to their original purpose—that "of informing or appraising"—instead of the one now pursued, namely, that of taking articles *out of competition* so that they will no longer be compared but just accepted by the buyer. The Commission of Internal Trade will also make available to the public information on the production costs of all articles of popular and stable demand, and on the type of commodities which are best suited for particular uses.

The education of consumers to purchase on the basis of accurate knowledge rather than blindly or as the result of the unsupported claims of manufacturers will not be accomplished in a day, particularly in view of the mis-education which has been pushed so vigorously by competitive business enterprises. Nevertheless signs are not lacking to show that consumers are not unwilling to prepare themselves to be more effective buyers. The growing popularity of Consumers' Research Inc., an organization which "studies and reports on goods and services from the point of view of their selection, purchase and use by the ultimate consumer",[22] demonstrates the effective work which a research organization can perform. There is abundant literature which will indicate the need for such work,[23] but it is perhaps more effective here that a few specifically Canadian examples should be given.

The report on consumers' standards in Canada presented to the Royal Commission on Price Spreads by Dr. H. M. Tory of the National Research Council [24] marks the first realistic attempt in this country to picture the present plight of the consumer. In the investigations conducted by the Research Council it was found that for only a relatively few products could the purchaser place any reliance on the declared grades or the advertised claims. A bundle of shingles was purchased in Ottawa as "Extra

[22]*Introduction to Consumers' Research* (Consumers' Research Inc., Washington, N.J., U.S.A.)

[23]See 100,000,000 *Guinea Pigs*, by Kallet and Schlink (Vanguard Press, N.Y., 1933); *Your Money's Worth*, Stuart Chase and F. J. Schlink (Macmillan, N.Y., 1927); *The Education of the Consumer*, Henry Harap (Macmillan, N.Y., 1929); *The Consumers' Guide*, Consumers Council of the Agricultural Adjustment Administration, Washington, D.O.; *Bulletins* of Consumers' Research, Inc., Washington, N.J.

[24]Royal Commission on Price Spreads, *Evidence*, pp. 5091-5143.

No. 1", but, on examination, proved to consist entirely of "culls" according to western standards. Gasoline which was advertised in the press as a motor fuel with the "highest knock-rating in the world" was found, on being tested, to be well below the premium grade which it was claimed to exceed. In the case of lubricating oils, it was found that the consumer had to be constantly on his guard against poor products. The investigators of the Research Council purchased two samples of oil selling between 45c and 50c a gallon, and found that whereas good quality lubricating oil has a viscosity index of between 60 and 100, these particular oils rated *3*, and *13*. Several cleaning preparations on the market were found to consist mainly of gasoline worth 25c to 40c a gallon but were being sold in small lots under fancy names for $5.70 to $16 a gallon.

The housewife who yields to the blandishments of soap advertisements may be making costly purchases, according to the analyses of soap made by the Research Council. Pure soaps were found to range in price from 13.0c to 27.8c per pound of soap. Dr. Tory informed the Commission that the Research Council was preparing a specification for the Government of a soap of best quality which would probably cost from 6c to 7c a pound. Again, the terms "wool" and "silk" seem to be losing all their literal meanings in the textile field and are now used to describe a variety of products. Goods marked "wool and cotton" often contain negligible proportions of wool, while "silk and wool" fabrics generally contain synthetic fibres rather than natural silk. Even garments which are claimed to be made entirely of wool bear no indication of the qualities from which they may be made. Virgin wool or shoddy may equally claim to be "100 per cent. wool". Of 24 samples of silk goods examined by the Research Council, only 2 were found to be natural silk with no added weighting material. Of the other 22 samples, 17 consisted of natural silk with added inorganic weighting, and the remainder contained no natural silk at all, although all were advertised as "all silk" or "first quality silk".

It is clear from such examples as these that the greater resources of government research laboratories and their ability to command the co-operation of manufacturers would enable the Commission of Internal Trade to proceed much farther than is possible for a private organization. The inspection and grading of food and drug products which is now being done by certain government departments, particularly the Department of Agriculture and the Department of National Health, could also be greatly extended and adequate publicity given to the results of their findings. This publicity alone would be far-reaching in effect.

The Reorganization of Distribution: Summary.

In review, the principal features in the reorganization of distribution which we propose can best be seen through a summary of the functions assigned to the Commission of Internal Trade. These fall naturally into the three divisions which are suggested by the terms *planning, operating,* and *regulation.* The most important fields of work in each division would be as follows:

(*a*) *Planning.*

1. Conducting surveys of the markets and demands for consumers' goods.
2. Drafting schemes for the reorganization of the distributive services.
3. Co-operating with the Planning Commission by providing estimates of the nature and quantity of goods and services that should be supplied, and suggesting the manner in which they should be provided.

(*b*) *Operating.*

1. Organization and supervision of nationally-owned distributive services, e.g., petroleum products.
2. Auditing and analyzing the accounts of all publicly or privately-owned enterprises under public control.
3. Stimulating, encouraging and directing consumers' co-operative societies.

(*c*) *Regulation.*

1. Development of standards for consumers' goods.
2. Inspection and supervision of manufacturing and distribution to secure adherence to standards (including the control of advertising).
3. Research into new uses and kinds of consumers' goods.
4. Education of consumers through publicity, national advertisement, etc., to utilize information obtained.
5. Creation and development of advisory consumers' committees.

Chapter XIX.

A HOUSING PROGRAMME.

A. Making Town Planning a Reality.

When we come to the question of housing, the first essential is
to approach it with imagination and breadth of view—not
as the restricted problem of clearing our worst slum areas or
even of providing cheap "working class houses", but of planning
and building better the urban environment in which so great a
proportion of Canadian citizens are born and live their daily
lives.[1] If capitalism is judged by its ability to provide homes
and cities which will produce free and healthy citizens, it will not
stand high. An unrestrained system of profit-making enterprise
is responsible not only for the arid wastes of city street and slum,
rooming houses and "shack towns", inadequate provision of open
spaces, playgrounds and community centres, but also for the
vulgar ostentation or the mock-antique of many of our "high-
class" residential districts, the crudities of our present civic
architecture, the waste and graft of much of our public works
development. Here too we must start from fundamentals.

Urban Instability.

The first of these is that the urban organism has no natural
maturity. Human communities are alive and growing: the
town is continually getting too big for its boots. Particularly
in our chief commercial cities, no allowance has been made for
this characteristic. From this two important results have
followed:

(1) As the town spreads out into the surrounding country,
land beyond the margin of building development has acquired
a speculative value. Upon the person who holds this land has
rested the great responsibility of planning it for public service.
But much of this land is held not for actual use but in the hope
of re-sale at a profit. These "interim" land-owners have naturally been influenced by the desire to make quick and profitable sales, and for this purpose have subdivided the land in
ways which seemed to be of immediate advantage, regardless

[1] And of course of improving rural amenities also. The bulk of the present section is
concerned with urban areas.

451

of the ultimate needs of the community. The ugly and short-sighted "grid plan" of street lay-out, the multiplication of small properties and unrelated building operations, the heavy financial investment involved in real estate constitute a system which has grown up almost solely for the benefit of the speculator; his operations, it is said, represent a tax on the eventual home-owner and a drain on the householder's resources in excess of all municipal, provincial and federal taxation put together. This speculation in real estate has subjected us to ridiculous land costs and has given us a city plan—or absence of plan—of a most inconvenient, expensive and undignified kind.

(2) As the town grows outwards and its total area increases, the proportions of all its natural parts have had to be continually adjusted to serve the increasing population. The expanding financial centre, for instance, has continually encroached upon the commercial area; the business section is continually de-vouring the older residential streets, while residential develop-ment is for ever encroaching upon the green countryside. This instability and periodic internal decay in the city has been a phenomenon as typical of capitalism as the periodic business depressions.

What are known as "blighted areas" are these districts which have been left behind by the out-growing suburbs; they are areas abandoned by the building industry, which prefers to concentrate on more profitable business amongst the well-to-do in the expanding suburbs. The domestic appointments of these large areas are more often than not out-of-date, but the capi-talist employer who is ready enough to scrap obsolete machinery in his plant is not interested in the domestic equipment of his employees. What is known as a "slum" is really a property which the landlord, thinking that it can be sold soon at a good price to the outgrowing commercial section, does not bother to keep in repair; the landlord is prepared to accept a low rent with few responsibilities and await the harvest. Too often, and par-ticularly during the last few years, the expected commercial expansion fails to materialize and the properties fall into worse and worse disrepair. The low rents attract the poorest and most destitute groups in the community: unable to meet rents elsewhere, they have to crowd into the sub-divided houses under the crumbling roofs of the slums and put up with con-ditions which violate all the principles of lighting, ventilation and sanitation—to say nothing of personal freedom and the proper environment for growing children.

Principles of Town Planning.

Such, very briefly, is the nature of the modern city as we know it. Most of the problems of municipal administration, the heavy urban incidence of crime and disease, traffic congestion, lack of recreation facilities and decent housing accommodation, are directly related to this process of external expansion and internal decay. Organized town planning is the answer to this chaos of irresponsibility and waste. The central principle of town planning is to stabilize each section of the city for its appropriate use by recognizing and anticipating its normal growth. Systematic technical survey, backed by adequate compulsory powers, is obviously necessary to put this into practice. Town planning must be made a specific government responsibility in every large city, co-ordinated and encouraged through the Federal Housing (and Town Planning) Authority which would be set up at Ottawa.

As in designing a dwelling the basic factor in planning is the size of the family for whom accommodation must be provided, so in planning a town it is necessary to form a reasonable judgment of the future population. In Canada we have become so accustomed to a continual multiplication of our numbers that it is difficult to realize that our plans must provide, if not for a stationary condition, at least for only gradually growing populations in our cities.[2] Our aim should be therefore, not to plan for the gigantic cities which the "boosters" of fifteen years ago anticipated, but to perfect the use of our existing urban regions. We should call a halt to the premature sub-division of land. Many municipalities have been put into bankruptcy by overoptimistic capital expenditure on roads and other equipment, thus creating those desolate marginal lands that make the outskirts of our towns so hideous: the ribbon development of "shack towns" is a peculiarly Canadian form of slum which is no less demoralizing to its inhabitants and no less objectionable than the internal urban slum. We must halt the reckless outward expansion of the cities and surround them with green parks and better-equipped suburbs.

Such a revolution in municipal policy requires not only

2See Chapter II, d.

effective planning powers of a preventive nature but also an active stimulation of replanning and rebuilding in the interior of the city. As long as there remained new land to conquer for private profit, capital has been busy and expansive, but the task of remodelling the obsolete and blighted areas over which "enterprise" has already passed will only be begun through public initiative.

In this concept of deliberate control and development according to a comprehensive plan of zones and amenities, there is nothing startlingly new. All we need is the will to do it. We have the technicians, architects, surveyors, draughtsmen— many of the younger ones long graduated from our engineering faculties without having found the jobs for which they are trained. These are projects also which must enlist the good-will as well as the skill of every engineer and architect who has some vision of what his profession could contribute to the community if it were unhampered by considerations of profit in private contracts and patronage or vested interests in public ones. We have an army of manual workers who could readily be marshalled for work on parks, roads, demolitions, grade-crossings, tree-planting and the host of other possible urban improvements, apart altogether from house and building construction itself. A complete regional survey of course takes time, but the need for much of the work of the type mentioned is obvious in so many places that undoubtedly it could be begun rapidly once the requisite authorities had been set up. The modernization of provincial and municipal building and health regulations—and the implementing of those regulations by really effective inspection—are necessary corollaries.

Town planning for *the whole* of a city's residents (instead of for its few wealthy areas) will only become a reality if the principles of land development are interpreted in future strictly in the public interest. Purely speculative enterprise which does not satisfy this test must be heavily taxed or otherwise prevented. Housing programmes have so long a history in Britain alone, that there is abundant and adequate experience to draw on in determining principles of equitable compensation and appropriation where re-allocation of existing land or building space is necessary. A real estate branch of the Court of Appraisal could also be appointed to assist in this task and would be particularly valuable as an arbitral authority.

B. Housing for the Wage Earner.

Housing and slum clearance form one of the largest features of any "emergency programme", and town planning measures themselves are of course only the systematic setting for a new housing policy.

Here again every student of the subject must be struck by the difference between the great potential achievements, raising the standards of living and increasing the happiness of "the lower third" of our population, which could be accomplished in the field of housing, and the little that has actually been done in Canada. To argue the *need* for an active policy to provide better housing for the wage earner should be superfluous, in the face of its long and respectable history in Europe if for no other reason.[3]

European Experience.

In England some of the best experiments in planned housing are associated with the highly respectable names of Cadbury, Lord Leverhulme, Howard, and Chamberlain; while the greater part of the 1,400,000 dwellings erected in Great Britain with state aid since the war were in fact erected under a Conservative government. In Germany the construction of houses by the State has been accepted as an altogether logical expression of civic pride. The great Vienna housing scheme, and some of the less spectacular but even more successful Scandinavian housing developments, are of course more directly socialist enterprises. But a great part of the four and a half-million state-aided houses built in Europe since the war bear the mark of Conservative respectability.

The principle has been thoroughly established: the differences are those of standards, finance, and energy. It is interesting to note the chairman of a recent English Housing Commission observing that the whole enterprise must be regarded "as a kind of crusade", and that even under the most favourable conditions a housing programme requires continual and unremitting toil to outbalance the inherent selfishness and obstructionism of private capital and commercial interests. The Commission stated that it must be regarded as a public service and a national responsibility to provide a million new houses in England at rents of $2.50 per week and under, the building of which should

---

3Cf., however, the sections "Where Canadians Live" and "What Canadians Think of Their Homes" in Chapter I, for a commentary based only on Canadian facts.

be organized on a ten-year programme following upon a national survey of housing needs, a long-term organization of labour and materials, and stimulated technical research. To accomplish this it proposed to finance local authorities and public utilities at trustee rates of interest. In Britain there are plenty of examples of both local authorities and private "limited-profit" housing corporations which have shown a high sense of responsibility in taking advantage of such a policy. But even there it is generally admitted that the success of a housing programme depends on the "drive" which emanates from the central government.

A Federal Housing Authority to Provide Low-Cost Housing.

In Canada it is clear that the problem of providing housing for the lower-paid worker will only be met through a Federal Housing Authority which takes its responsibilities seriously and directly. Our experience after 1921 with subsidized housing on a delegated and ill-supervised basis demonstrated conclusively that any hopes that those of our city workers most in need of better houses (i.e., those with the smallest incomes) will benefit from any similarly-conceived schemes are foredoomed to failure.[4] The Federal Housing Authority which we propose would essentially give detailed attention to building standards, and would authorize federal grants only on the strict condition of these standards being met.

What is even more important, however, if we are to put current housing proposals and building schemes to the test, is their "financial base". If room is still to be left for private profit, or "remunerative investment", or if "the principles of orthodox finance" are to be followed, there will be no houses at really low rents, no attack on the roots of the slum problem through the provision of better alternative housing at the same rents at all. Even at the lowest obtainable rates of interest it is impossible to build houses of an acceptable standard which can be rented at rates within the low-wage worker's capacity to pay. And until they are built, he has to stay in the slum or something approaching it. The recent Toronto Housing Report showed that only one-third of the costs of workers' dwellings could be covered by a 4 per cent. loan and that the remaining two-thirds would have to be met by direct grants from the State, municipal, provincial and federal. This cal-

[4] Cf. Lieutenant Governor's Report (Ontario): *Housing Conditions in Toronto.*

culation was based on a rental of about $20 a month, which would be an appropriate amount for a householder to pay when he is earning 50 cents an hour for a 40 hour week throughout the year. Since the typical slum-dweller under present earning conditions should not pay more than $10 a month in rent, on the above basis the housing equation—on "orthodox" lines—does not admit of a solution.

These facts—the large proportion of our city workers who because of low wages, irregular employment, or unemployment, are unable to pay more than this small rent—and their bearing on the slum problem, are brought out even more forcibly in the Montreal housing report:

"The problem is to secure an adequate supply of housing accommodation at low rentals. It may of course be suggested that the wage earners concerned should devote more of their incomes to the payment of rent. The answer must be, however, that they can do so only at the cost of raising other social problems. To spend more than $120.00 or so of an income of $600.00 on rent, means sooner or later some curtailment or deprivation of food and fuel, and certainly of clothing, minor luxuries, and recreational expenditures. The provision of low rental housing tends to reduce under-nourishment, tuberculosis, hospitalization, destitution, with their attendant social costs, and to release working class purchasing power for the other necessities, comforts, and conveniences of life.

It may be objected that housing at such rents cannot economically speaking be provided—that these minimum rents will not cover the costs. But this again is the essence of the Housing Problem. There is a point at which private enterprise working on ordinary commercial lines cannot provide for certain groups of the community. The figures above suggest clearly that the unskilled and lowest paid wage-earners, and at least some proportion of the intermediate and skilled workers, are within these groups. . . . [5]

". . . It does not help to put forward schemes for slum clearance with replacement of dwellings renting at . . . $20 (a month). Proposals of such character cannot be recommended because they do not relieve government and society of the burden of the slums. They can only bring about a slum elsewhere, or else deprive industry of those lower ranks of labour which should find housing at . . . $10 (a month) within reach of their work".[6]

[5]*Report on Housing and Slum Clearance for Montreal* (Mar 1935), p. 35.
[6]*Ibid.*, p. 8.

This is clear enough—and it means that the recent Housing Bill of the Conservative Government will do nothing for the slums. For the fine-sounding $10,000,000 appropriation which it authorizes is merely a loan fund, providing one-fifth of the capital to be used (whether by individuals or corporations) for building schemes. These individuals or corporations must themselves put up the remaining four-fifths of the capital and pay the government 5 per cent. on their "subsidy". Obviously none of the individuals will be slum-dwellers, and the corporations—unless they are going to be benevolent institutions operating at a loss for the benefit of the public—will be hard put to it on this basis to provide housing at even "white-collar" rentals. Even a less miserly policy which provided for the *expenditure* of $10,000,000 as a direct subsidy, however, could hardly raise high hopes while loan companies or other corporations which "are not in business for their health" are chosen as the media.

A socialist government honestly desiring to get rid of slums and to provide better housing for the wage-earner (and also for the farmer) must expect to spend money for that purpose. In *national* accounting, whether an investment "pays" or not must be judged by its total social benefits. If devoting some part of the budget to subsidized housing "pays" in healthier and happier living conditions for many of the country's workers, in less repressive environments for their children, in reduced burdens of infantile mortality, tuberculosis, juvenile delinquency, contagious diseases, this is "profitable" expenditure in the best sense of the word. One of the first steps to be taken by the government must therefore be a large-scale housing programme frankly intended to provide *wage earners' houses*.

The housing estates created under this policy will not be farmed out to private corporations, but will be owned by the federal, provincial, or municipal government or their agents, the choice depending on what is most effective in the particular local circumstances. Each district or block will also have its estate-manager, an official (often a woman) combining the functions of business manager and social worker of the type whose development has contributed so much to the success of the best managed housing schemes in Britain.

While housing and slum clearance must be begun in the first instance as a frankly subsidized venture (though this is not to mean it will tolerate undue costs from attempts to hold up the government through extortionate land prices or monopolistic prices of materials), reliance does not have to be placed permanently on this policy. The two important factors in the housing equation are rent and cost of construction. As the reconstruction and socialization of industry begins to take effect, one of its results will be a rise in the wage earner's standard of living and consequently in the scale of rent he can afford. Even more can be hoped, however, from reduction in the costs of construction.

Part of the high cost of housing comes of course from elements in the present economic system itself. But in the government's programme the "rake-off" of promoters' profits would be automatically eliminated. The obstacles of the monopolistic production of building supplies or, in some fields, the wastes of monopolistic competition, might be more serious. But with the threat of nationalization of non-co-operative industries at its command, it is reasonable to expect that the government could secure its supplies at terms equitably covering only their true production- and wage-costs. Over and above this, however, it is reasonable to expect that even basic production costs can be reduced—that the technique of mass-production can be turned towards the objective of low cost housing more directly than it is at present.

To achieve this it is necessary to apply to the design and construction of homes the same scientific rationalization that has been applied, for instance, to automobile plants; to reduce the costs of fabrication and assembly so that modern living conditions may become the normal possession of every householder. Standardized units can only be produced at a basic mass production cost provided that the output is sufficiently large, but this is precisely what a national housing policy—both urban and rural—would permit. The standardization of equipment such as metal windows, doors, kitchen cupboards, plumbing and heating would enable them to be installed as prefabricated articles: the standardization of wall-slab units with insulation would enable them to be assembled by unskilled labour; and so forth. One of the tasks of the Federal Housing Authority would be to institute (in co-operation with the Bureau of Standards if necessary) a codification of local building by-laws so as to take advantage of these advances in technique. In short, both by the accumulation of such economics and by the elimination of selling expenses, construction costs would be reduced well below the accepted normal. Labour saving methods in this field would be brought into operation to serve that very part of the community which has been accustomed—often by hard experience—to think of mass production methods as a menace to employment.

Urban Surveys.

A factor of the very greatest importance in economical housing is the stability which results from fitting a housing scheme into a comprehensive town-planning scheme. In the interests of economy a number of municipal politicians have advocated the allotment of city funds for repairing slum dwellings; but although such work may temporarily relieve distress, it is a classic example of misdirected economy and such an allotment represents a total loss to the city. A similar fund, however, used in the development of one unit of a planned housing scheme remains a permanent asset to the community. It is as unwise as ever it was to put new wine into old bottles; a repaired slum still remains a slum.

The plan of campaign of the agencies co-operating with the Federal Housing Authority must be formulated after careful survey of actual conditions in each city. This implies an analysis of the areas given over to industry, commerce, retail business, etc., and these must be considered in relation to existing slums, blighted areas, and the expanding residential sections. In addition there is required a plan of the main traffic system, the park system, the educational and institutional centres and special topographical features such as rivers, ravines and beaches. On a zoning-map made on this basis the defects of the urban composition become apparent, and the town-planner with the co-operation of sociologist and economist is able to decide which are the areas most appropriate for housing schemes.

It is not to be assumed that the areas at present occupied by slums are necessarily the logical sites for housing a large population of low-income families; for the deteriorated property which marks the slum owes its existence to circumstances quite irrelevant to their residential qualifications. Central slum areas in fact have high land-values, because their *commercial* development—rightly or wrongly—is anticipated. The establishment of proper zoning regulations of course goes part of the way to removing these inconsistencies and uncertainties. If an area is scheduled to remain residential land for a specified period its value will automatically drop to residential levels. But the higher value of central areas is bound to remain in some degree; and it must be assumed also that some proportion of the workers resident in slum areas are living there in order to be close to their work and will not therefore wish to move. The replacement of demolished slums by some re-housing must therefore be part of the immediate programme. The land for this purpose must be acquired by the government, and the compensation for it must be based on a reasonable compromise between its (possibly fictitious) commercial value and its actual earning-power as a residential area. On the lines of established British practice, however, no compensation should be allowed for property deteriorated beyond a certain standard.

For a really comprehensive programme the relatively high land costs typical of slum property are not necessarily the drawback they may at first seem. Advantage may be taken of the two facts, that land decreases in value the farther its location from the centre, but that also there is still a wide market for the better housing of the higher paid wage earners and many middle class groups, who are willing and able to pay higher rents and for whom the factors of distance and travel are of less consequence. Hitherto the profits from housing the well-to-do have gone to the particular group of owners and builders catering for this class of tenant, while housing provision for small wage earners has had to stand on its own feet. But governmental housing corporations should be free to build and operate housing in "middle" and "outer" or suburban areas as well as former slum districts where costs are too great for the private capitalist. And with this development there should be definite scope for some balancing of surpluses and deficits on the different types of property operated by the one authority.

It is of significance that the earliest experiments in workers' housing in England such as Bourneville and Welwyn proved so attractive that the homes have come to be occupied by a more well-to-do class than that for which they were intended. Yet these in fact were the practical laboratories in which some of the early experiments in working-class housing were undertaken. Since the reconstruction of our economic system is compelled to pass through a transitional period, this principle may well be adopted for our own use and extended. Housing authorities should be under no obligation to confine their activities to clearing the slums, but should be enabled to explore other fields not hampered by the same rental disabilities. Besides enabling research and experiment to be carried out with greater freedom this would enable governments to build up a valuable equity in well-planned revenue-producing neighbourhoods. This in fact is the normal development of housing in a co-operative economic system.

Housing Types and Standards.

Outside the slum area at least, socialist housing plans could be built up on the principle of what may be called the "Neighbourhood Unit". This is a community or group of dwellings which together with their local services, such as a school, recreation centre, theatre, library and local retail stores, can be considered as a self-contained region. The size of such a community may be conveniently fixed as a neighbourhood large enough to require a school and should be from 100 to 150 acres in extent. Statistics show what are the typical requirements of such a community, the typical proportions of families and single residents, etc.: and with such information the town-planner is able to apportion areas of open space and building sites. The neighbourhood streets should be clearly distinguished from the traffic arteries which pass outside its boundary and which take its inhabitants to work and to the open country, so that children going to school and housewives going to the stores will not have to cross a traffic street.

There are many types of housing each of which can be experimented with to find its appropriate use. At the present time considerable research is being undertaken in both Europe and America, and it is unwise to have preconceived ideas on the subject while we are in a transitional period. In general, apartment houses or "flats" are suited for mid-urban estates and the single dwelling type for suburban and rural use. It is said that there is a prejudice in this country against apartment houses, at least among wage-earners; but this objection is commonly found to be raised by workers who have not lived in a really modern block of flats—and who are often also the victims of a conspiracy between the real estate and speculative building interests to persuade the public that there is some remarkable virtue in home-ownership. If the ultimate ideal really is the single dwelling on its own plot of land a few experiments should determine this. But in the larger city at least there are remarkable advantages in the multi-storey type of housing, a type which is advocated by those who have given the most study to the matter and who have carried out the greatest amount of constructive work. A housing block of several floors permits the highest degree of standardization and economy in the assembly of mass-production materials; it promotes great efficiency and economy in services such as heating, conditioned air, refuse collection, etc.: it makes communal equipment such as laundries and creches much more accessible; it offers scope for the social services of the "estate manager"; it liberates more land for open space and allows the planner to give the greatest number of dwelling units an ideal orientation. Since all these advantages represent real wealth to the householder and his wife, too much attention must not be given to the somewhat sentimental objections which have been raised against life in multiple dwellings.

In the dwelling unit itself, certain standards may be set up for families of various sizes. These should take account of the separation of the sexes for children's bedroom accommodation and of proportionate sizes of living room and kitchen, the whole unit being subjected to the best technical analysis available to provide through-ventilation, light, and correct sanitation, and to reduce the labour of housekeeping. Several types may be evolved as suitable for a Canadian standard of living and these will serve as patterns when plans are made, to conform to the specific conditions of actual sites. Standards of bedroom accommodation will of course vary with size of family: but given proper ventilation, bedrooms may nowadays be reduced to 100 square feet, all additional space permitted by costs being given over to the living room. In multi-storey blocks attention can be given to the design of balcony-porches which are consistent with complete privacy. In general, the mechanization of household equipment and the economy of bedroom space to be cleaned would help to liberate the housewife from the monotonous servitude of domestic chores and allow her to develop family life in more fruitful directions. This liberation, together with the land economies of multi-storey blocks which permit dwellings to be set amidst the space and air of parkland, offers for the ordinary wage earner—who so far has been accorded little indeed of the improvements of which modern housing technique is capable—a veritable renaissance of urban life.

CHAPTER XX.

THE QUESTION OF PARTIES.

A. The Canadian Party System.

A PROGRAMME of far-reaching economic reconstruction such as has been sketched in the preceding pages raises the double issue of how public opinion is to be educated to an understanding and acceptance of the proposals, and how our democratic institutions are to be adjusted to the new socialist state.

That Canadians as yet are far from realizing the need for such social changes as are advocated in this book is obvious. Our country has so recently emerged from the pioneer phase of its history that it is still dominated by the pioneer psychology of individualism and tends to face the problems arising out of the growth of large-scale business organization and of concentration of control by taking emotional refuge in slogans which are fitted to the conditions of two generations ago; and interested politicians and journalists are quite prepared to exploit this tendency.

Politics in Canada has never risen much above the level of being our major national sport. It has been tacitly assumed by everybody that the main responsibility for the development of our natural resources and the building up of a prosperous Canadian nation belonged to private profit-seeking business men and corporations, and that the function of the politician was primarily that of assisting business-men-on-the-make by continual handouts in the shape of tariffs, bounties, railway charters, land grants and such things. The taking over by the public authority of this major responsibility for our national development and the substitution of public servants for private business men as the agents through which this responsibility shall be exercised, involve complex changes in the whole working of our democratic political machinery.

The difficulties which face socialist proposals in a community with the political background of Canada are well illustrated by the reception which has been given by the newspapers to the Co-operative Commonwealth Federation. Here is a movement essentially democratic in its origin and its aspirations, motivated chiefly by the desire to make our democracy more real in this country and to emancipate politics from the domination of plutocratic influences. Yet it has been generally denounced by the orthodox party press as aiming at the setting up of a bureaucratic dictatorship which would endanger our traditional liberties and undermine our parliamentary institutions. Perhaps the Canadian people are not quite so stupid and not quite so ready a prey to ancient shibboleths as our newspaper editors assume. But the fact that journalistic discussion can be carried on at this intellectual level is sufficient proof that, if it be true as we have argued, that fundamental changes are necessary in our economic institutions, then we face a serious problem in educating the public in the political implications of this economic programme. No system of socialism will work without the support of a determined and instructed public behind it, and this work of public education is the more necessary in a democratic movement which does not contemplate a violent or forcible transition to the new order.

The Function of Parties.

In our modern large-scale democratic communities the function of educating the public, organizing the electorate and presenting issues to the voter in a form in which he can make a more or less intelligent decision upon them, is performed chiefly by political parties.

Small units of local government, with no serious inequality of income among the citizens, can conduct their public affairs without the necessity of permanent party divisions. The questions to be decided are within the range of the citizens' own experience, there is general agreement about the functions which the town, the village or the county should perform, and how it should perform them. The main business of local elections is to choose the men who will most honestly and efficiently carry out the agreed policy.

But in the large industrial town or city this is becoming less and less true. With the growth of wide inequalities of income new problems appear: unemployment relief, housing, municipal social services. On these it cannot be taken for granted that rich and poor will think alike. It is no longer simply a question of choosing honest and capable men to carry out an agreed policy.[1]

What is true of the large modern city is even truer of the

[1]The incursions of Labour parties and the C.C.F. into municipal politics is a symptom of this change.

province, truer still of the nation-state with millions of voters. "The really important problems arise out of a complex, unseen environment, which the individual has not the time to study or understand; . . . and differences of opinion are ultimately due to differences of interest".[2] The individual citizen would be helpless in the absence of some kind of organized party system to enable him to join with fellow citizens of like mind and exercise his due influence upon public policy. Democracy, in fact, would be unworkable without a party system.[3]

How incompletely we have emerged, intellectually, from primitive pioneer conditions in Canada, is best shown by the naive political thinking of many of our agrarian reformers, whose main aspirations during the post-war period used to be the abolition of political parties. They appeared to think that we should be on our way to solving our difficulties if only we could get at Ottawa 245 members free from party ties. How the 245 independent members would ever be chosen by a puzzled electorate in the first place, or how they would work out any consistent policy if they were chosen, has never been explained. "The idea that the interests of farmers and manufacturers"— or workers and employers—"can be reconciled simply by their sitting together in the same Cabinet shows a failure to realize how deep are the class cleavages in our society".[4] Much the same comments, as we shall see,[5] are appropriate to some of the propaganda for a "national" government (though there is more evidence that the real backers of this movement are thoroughly "class-conscious").

In reality, it is almost inevitable that party machinery will become more elaborate as the size of the democratic community increases. Party organization developed and expanded steadily through the nineteenth century with the steady extension of the franchise. This process is apt to lead to rigidity of structure and to an oligarchic control of the party machine itself,—so that party, which originates as the expression of democracy, may become one of the chief instruments for the frustration of democracy. But such a result does not prove the inherent evil of a party system; it merely proves the need for more flexibility in the machinery, which in practical terms means the need for a *new* party or parties.

[2]F. H. Underhill. "Mr. Good's Political Philosophy", *Canadian Forum*, August, 1933.
[3]See the discussion of this point in H. J. Laski, *Grammar of Politics*, Chapter VIII, pt. II.
[4]F. H. Underhill, "Mr. Good's Political Philosophy", *Canadian Forum*, August, 1933.
[5]See section c of this chapter.

Students of politics in English-speaking countries are generally agreed that a two-party system works better than the group system which has been usual in continental European countries, because it enables the voter to say yes or no to a given proposal of action. If he is presented with a more complicated task than this he will probably perform it badly or neglect to perform it at all. But a two-party system works well only when the issues about which the parties are divided are real.

In Canada we have suffered from the rigidity of organization which seems an inevitable accompaniment of large-scale democracy, but also during the last generation from the fact that the existing two-party system has offered to the elector no real alternative in choice. Every effort has of course been made to present the parties as different, especially at election times. Not even about the rugged individualism of our economic institutions has there been so much romantic nonsense talked by our public men as about the liberalism of our Liberals and the conservatism of our Conservatives. An understanding of the real nature of our political parties is therefore an essential preliminary to any discussion of the working of democratic political institutions in this country.

The Historical Development of Canadian Parties.

Canada while still in the colonial stage took over the English party names along with the rest of the paraphernalia of the English constitution. With the names went the orthodox interpretation of party divisions, to wit, that human beings are divided by nature into progressives and conservatives and that this psychological difference expresses itself in the alignment of voters into two political camps. But after we had attained Responsible Government these English party names became more and more unreal, because Canadian society did not reproduce the class structure upon which the English party divisions, as everyone now understands, were really based. If Canadian Liberals had ever paused to ask themselves what they were trying to liberate and if Canadian Conservatives had ever paused to ask themselves what they were trying to conserve, we should have achieved before now in this country some degree of realism in our understanding of the economic basis of politics.

Actually, while we have kept the English names, the real parallel to our party politics is to be found in the country which is our neighbour to the south. Canada, like the United States, is a vast, loosely knit continental area. Its political problems have arisen from the task of opening up, settling, and binding together the diverse sections of this half-continent; and its political struggles, while complicated by race and religion, have turned mainly about the methods of developing its natural resources. In the more recent period Canada has followed the United States in her increasing industrialization. Essentially in both countries the division of interest in the past has been between Eastern industry and finance and Western pioneer agriculture. This contest takes new forms with each generation, and the English names for our parties have only helped to give us a literary theory of politics which has had less and less relation to realities as one generation succeeded another.

Our so-called Conservative party arose out of John A. Macdonald's coalition of 1854. Macdonald brought together three groups, the Orange-Loyalist section of Upper Canada, the French-Canadian Catholics of Lower Canada, under the leadership of their Church, and Montreal big business as represented by the Grand Trunk Railway and the Bank of Montreal. His life-long political ally, Cartier, was the avowed spokesman of the French Catholic hierarchy and was also the solicitor of the Grand Trunk Railway. Over against this coalition, which was in office for most of the dozen years before Confederation, stood two other groups who gradually coalesced into the so-called Liberal or Reform party. They were the Rouges of Lower Canada, agrarian and anti-clerical; and (much more important in our history) the Clear Grits of Upper Canada, the spiritual ancestors of all the agrarian protest movements in Canadian politics. Grittism had its main stronghold in the western peninsula of Upper Canada, and it was essentially the political expression of the point of view of the pioneer wheat farmers of that section. Its great organ, the Toronto *Globe* of George Brown, never tired in fighting the cause of "the intelligent yeomanry of Upper Canada"; and while the *Globe* is chiefly remembered now for the violence of its anti-Catholic attacks, a perusal of its columns in those days will show that it devoted much more space to the Grand Trunk Railway than to the French Catholic hierarchy.[6] What this comes to is that Cana-

---

6"With the Grand Trunk and the Bank of Montreal at his back there is no telling how far the reckless financier of the present government may carry his schemes. These institutions are the enemies of the people and of popular rights. They have special interests to advance in Parliament. . . . It is time that we had a government above being the servant of railway or banking institutions. It is time that we had a government which would consider the interest of the whole people and not of a few wily money-makers who can bring influence to bear upon Parliament". This is an extract from an editorial in the

dian party divisions at the time of Confederation did represent a real division in economic interest, although of course economic lines of division were modified—sometimes blurred and sometimes accentuated—by racial and religious forces.

After Confederation the party lines of the old province of Canada were gradually established in the outlying parts of the Dominion.[7] It is now that the similarity with American developments becomes most striking.   Macdonald continued to dominate the scene until his death in 1891.   His work was to build up a united nation out of the scattered particularist provinces who composed the Dominion, (that is, there was nothing that could in the slightest degree be properly called Conservative in his activity) and it is significant that he proceeded in this task of nation-building along pure Hamiltonian lines.   He fought against "provincial rights" and endeavoured to strengthen the national government by tying to it the great interests of business and finance.   The two achievements for which he is best remembered are the building of the C.P.R. and the National Policy of protection.

The Reform party in these early days still continued primarily to represent pioneer agriculture, and as against the centralizing Hamiltonianism of Macdonald it stood for Jeffersonian provincial rights and low tariffs.   Alexander Mackenzie, its leader, was never at ease with contractors and railway promoters.   Goldwin Smith remarked of him that if his strong point consisted in his having been a stone-mason, his weak point consisted in his being one still; and this was only a snobbish Oxford way of saying that Mackenzie was a true democratic representative of the little man in Canadian life.

It was not until the rise of Laurier that the Liberals were able to compete on equal terms with the Conservatives.   Laurier was a more sophisticated man than Mackenzie (he was a University graduate) and he made the Liberals a successful party by finding for them allies in the world of big business.   He propitiated the manufacturers by Fielding's tariffs, and built up a railway and banking interest behind his party to balance the support of the Conservatives by the C.P.R. and the Bank of

---

Globe of August 10, 1867, written in the midst of the first general election campaign of the new Dominion of Canada which had just come into being on July 1.   It shows that George Brown had a sufficiently clear understanding of the economic basis of politics.

7The newer, less settled sections of the Dominion only gradually allowed themselves the luxury of party politics along lines laid down at Ottawa.   The North-West Territories had non-partisan governments until the creation of the new provinces in 1905.   Goldwin Smith reports a conversation with a British Columbian in the 1880's who told him that his politics were "government appropriations".

Montreal. In other words, he made of the Liberal party what
Macdonald had made of the Conservatives,—an essentially Hamiltonian party.[8] The brilliant device of the British Preference
managed to retain for him the support of the low tariff elements;
but nothing could have been more significant than the fact that
when Laurier for the first time committed himself to a policy—
Reciprocity—which favoured agriculture rather than the business interests of Montreal and Toronto, he was deserted by his
most prominent big business followers and defeated by them.

By the opening years of the twentieth century there was
little to choose between the two historic Canadian parties. Each
was dominated by the business interests of the great Eastern
industrial and financial centres, and the essential philosophy
of each was to foster national development by handing over the
resources of the country to be exploited by triumphant business.
That is, each party was Hamiltonian. But, like the two American parties, each party had also taken over all the democratic
professions of Jefferson. While the original sectional and economic differences still survived to some extent in the composition of the parties, each party had become national in the North
American sense, in that it appealed to all sections and succeeded
in collecting votes from all sections. In order to collect votes,
it had made its platform a purely opportunistic assortment of
sectional bribes. In Canada, as in the United States, party
programmes were constructed on the principle of collecting the
largest possible number of carrots to dangle in front of the
noses of the largest possible number of donkeys.

The 1911 Reciprocity election forms a watershed in our political history. Like the 1896 election in the United States, it
marked the first of a series of revolts in national politics by the
western agrarian interests against the steadily tightening grip
of eastern financial and industrial magnates upon the processes
of government. The magnificent energy with which the business interests when challenged rallied their forces, the consum-
mate skill with which they exploited national anti-American
feeling and British imperial loyalty, showed how well entrenched
our governing classes were. Canada relapsed into Hamiltonianism.

---

[8] Sir Clifford Sifton, who was the outstanding man in Laurier's cabinet, next to
Fielding, was, like Fielding, a typical Hamiltonian. In his later years he regretted that
Canada had no provision in her constitution like the "due process" clause in the American
constitution which would prevent legislative attacks upon wealth. He was one of our few
intelligent millionaires.

The Progressive Revolt.

Nevertheless, 1911 is significant in that it initiated a tendency among the prairie farmers to break away from the old party system. After the war, which shook a great many Canadians loose from old moorings, the tendency was accentuated; and in the first post-war election, in 1921, the prairie fire spread into Ontario. The result was that 65 "Progressive" members, mostly farmer representatives, found themselves sitting together in a new party in the Dominion Parliament, though they were unable to agree whether it was a party or not. The vicissitudes of the Progressive movement need not be narrated here since they are a part of recent history. The important point is that, whatever the internal quarrels and desertions from which it suffered, the idea of an independent farmer political movement has remained alive upon the prairie since 1921 and it has made a lasting breach in the solidarity of the old two-party system.

Three or four of the independent members during the 1920's represented another element in the community whose presence in Parliament was also the mark of a new era. These were, of course, the Labour members. Though the growth of industrialism in Canada has produced a permanent wage-earning class, the economic expression of their views in the industrial organization of the workers in trade unions has been weak, as in the United States; and the Gompers tradition of American trade unionism, along with racial and religious divisions among the workers is an obstacle to the emergence of a powerful political Labour movement. Even today the politically minded among the industrial workers are apt to be immigrants from the British Isles or from Europe: presumably there are still many native-born Canadians who cherish the dreams of a more primitive society when every worker could look forward to becoming a master. But Labour in Canada as in older countries has begun to learn that to protect its interests it must organize for action in the political as well as in the industrial sphere.

With the lifting of the post-war depression many of the economic causes which had driven farmers out of the Liberal party had disappeared. In the 1926 election most of the "Progressives" disappeared likewise. There remained a saving remnant of Labour men, United Farmers of Alberta and a few others, who for the next six years worked together in the House of Commons without attempting unified action on a national scale outside. Their co-operation, though loosely organized, was

effective. Capitalist newspapers and politicians have indus-
triously propagated the myth that the group's activity was
wholly negative, that it had nothing "constructive" to offer, and
that it achieved nothing. Actually almost all the important
"reform" measures placed on the statute book in the last ten
years—old age pensions, unemployment insurance, a national
minimum wage and eight-hour day, reform of the Companies
Act, establishment of a central bank and an economic council,
a surtax for large incomes—were advocated first and most persistently by the dozen or so Labour and U.F.A. members. They
have in fact been almost the only constructive element in the
House. The role of the old parties has been first to sneer and
denounce, then to plead that the proposals are unconstitutional,
and finally to adopt them without acknowledgment and in as
weak or anti-social a form as possible.

B. THE BASIS OF THE C.C.F.

Three years of a new depression of unprecedent scope and
severity confirmed the belief of both Farmer and Labour members that a fundamental change in the economic system was
essential. Practical experience of co-operation in the House of
Commons convinced them that the interests of farmers and
workers were basically the same and that the two groups could
work together to achieve their common objective. It was these
convictions which led them to organize, at Calgary in the summer
of 1932, a new national political movement, the Co-operative
Commonwealth Federation.

Farmer and Wage-Earner.

It is worth emphasizing that it was the farmers and workers themselves, not some group of "academic theorists" from
outside, who created the new movement, gave it its name and
form—a federation of autonomous farmer and labour organizations—and its first programme, of which later programmes
are simply detailed expansions. Liberal and Conservative propagandists delight to assert that the C.C.F. is bound to break
up because farmers and workers have dissimilar interests and
so cannot unite in the same party; though of course "there is
room for both" in either of the old parties—each of which, like
the crocodile in *Alice in Wonderland*, "welcomes little fishes in
with gently smiling jaws". In other words, farmers and workers can co-operate politically within the parties of big business,

in the interest of big business which exploits both groups; but they cannot co-operate in their own party in their own interest against the common exploiter. The answer is that the C.C.F. exists precisely because workers' and farmers' organizations have found, through hard practical experience over many years, that their interests are not dissimilar, that they can work together, that, in fact, the only hope of emancipation for either lies in working together.

The Middle Classes.

There is a third group in the community who might naturally be expected to be attracted to a socialist programme, and who in fact have joined the C.C.F. in large numbers. This is composed of the extensive middle class of professional men and women,—teachers, scientists, engineers, physicians, dentists, clergymen, nurses, social workers, etc.,—and of the managers and skilled technicians in the ranks of industry. Most of these have to a considerable extent in their individual lives eliminated the profit motive from their activities. Most of them are painfully conscious of the vulgarization and degradation which are inherent in a society dominated by money-making; and they would welcome the emancipation of creative energies which would come to them if they were active members in a planned and socialized community. For they feel themselves thwarted and perverted now by the necessity of serving mammon as well as following their own professional ideals. There are also a very considerable number of our industrial magnates themselves who are quite capable of appreciating the scope for their capacities of management and organization that would be provided in a socialist state. None of these groups really believes that the chaos and waste, the ignorance and disease and physical suffering of our present society are necessary, or that the machinery of production and distribution will rust and decay unless profit-seeking entrepreneurs are in charge of it.

In our present complex system, as a matter of fact, this great middle class of professional men and technicians are performing more vital functions than the capitalist.[9] They possess the particular kind of training and ability which is indispensable to the successful working of a socialist state. In Canada they have not hitherto been politically minded. The proletarian dogmas and phraseology of orthodox socialism tend to

---

[9]"The technician is the modern Prometheus in chains"—Stuart Chase.

drive them into the arms of the possessing class. But European experience has shown that a socialist strategy which deliberately repels the professional class is headed for disaster. In Canada, on the other hand, one of the most hopeful features of our situation is the success of the C.C.F. in attracting the support of the middle class groups, which elsewhere have too often proved a main strength of rising fascist movements.

Problems of Organization.

In its short history of three years the C.C.F. has achieved a good deal. It has not yet indeed established itself effectively anywhere east of Montreal. The isolation of the Maritime Provinces has prevented any rapid development there, though in eastern Nova Scotia the building up of a co-operative enterprise by St. Francis Xavier University may in time establish an economic basis for political action. In Quebec, the French-Canadian's traditional conservatism and his concern for his church, his language and his civil law (all of which, of course, should be as safe under a C.C.F. government as they are now, or safer) have been unscrupulously exploited by English-speaking capitalists who care nothing for any of them; and certain ecclesiastical dignitaries have thrown their weight on the same reactionary side of the balance. In Ontario, however, the new movement last year polled almost 100,000 votes; it has elected its nominees as Mayors of Toronto and Windsor (the second and eighth largest cities of Canada), and is a powerful force in a number of other municipal governments. In Winnipeg it holds the mayoralty and virtual control of the city council. In Saskatchewan it polled about a quarter of the popular vote and forms the official opposition in the legislature. In Alberta, the United Farmers of Alberta, one of the organizations which founded the C.C.F., have controlled the government since 1920, and had a majority of the Alberta members in the last Dominion Parliament. In British Columbia, one-third of the voters marked their ballots for C.C.F. candidates, and C.C.F. members form the official opposition in the provincial legislature.

Friction between the constituent units has now been almost eliminated, and there is more real unity among the various regions of Canada represented in the C.C.F. than there has ever been in any other Canadian political party. Considering that the C.C.F., alone among Canadian parties, is democratically organized, with annual conventions which choose the leaders and formulate policies, this may seem surprising. But the explanation is not far to seek. The regional groups in the old parties are held together less by any common principles or common economic interest, than by common desire for office and a common source of financial support. The various provincial sections of the C.C.F. can work together with a minimum of friction precisely because they all have a clear, coherent body of common principles, growing out of the recognition of a common exploitation and a common means of emancipation. As recent discussions in the Canadian Political Science Association have made clear, "the economic problems of federalism" are not problems of federalism at all. The Prairies and the Maritimes are "depressed areas". The Nova Scotia fishermen and the Saskatchewan farmers are badly off not because they live in Nova Scotia or Saskatchewan, but because they belong to classes which, all over the world, are exploited. They are the victims not of our political federalism but of our economic capitalism. Only the C.C.F. dare recognize this, and accordingly only the C.C.F. can reconcile the apparent conflict of regional economic interests, and attain nation-wide unity.

All this does not mean, of course, that the new movement has solved all its internal problems. In a federation of farmers, industrial labour, and the middle professional classes the farmers must, if only because of voting power, be for a considerable time the senior partner. They have, in Western Canada at least, the experience of political action in the past and they have formed the backbone of all protest movements in Canadian political history. But an agrarian political movement depends for success upon the organization of the farmers in their economic activities. And even on the prairie, where they have played a dominating rôle, the organized farmer movements have never included more than a comparatively small part of the agricultural community. The wheat pools at their peak handled a little more than half the wheat crop of the prairie, while the educational and political organizations have never approached a membership that would represent this proportion of the farming population. In the East, the inability of the farmers to stick together for any purposes of their own, economic or political, has been proverbial, and is still taken for granted by the business men and the old line politicians who exploit them. So that there is still a great deal of work to be done in the agricultural community itself.

In the urban industrial field, as we have seen, there is no such thing as a mass labour movement. Its development is one of the greatest problems which the C.C.F. must face in its attempt to conquer political power. In consumers' co-operation, too, we find the same backwardness as contrasted with what has been achieved in Great Britain or some continental European countries. The middle class professions are still largely unaware of the social implications of their professional organizations, which are still in the main devoted to purely technical interests. The C.C.F. so far has made its greatest impact upon the teachers, and its state medicine proposals are beginning to attract more doctors and nurses. Here too, however, much still remains to be done.

Democratic Organization and Party Funds.

Everyone knows that Liberal and Conservative policy at any given moment depends very largely on the will of the party leader, who reaches his conclusions as the result of private consultations with a few trusted friends. He must keep his ear to the ground listening for rumblings from the rank and file, but the ordinary party member accepts as a matter of course a role of almost complete passivity in the making of party policy. The occasional national conventions with their elaborate ballyhoo are managed by insiders, as every experienced observer is aware. They are rarely held, and then chiefly to put over a programme decided on beforehand. In contrast with this sham democracy, the United Farmers of Alberta, some local Labour parties, and the C.C.F. itself have continuously endeavoured to work out a method by which leaders and rank and file are kept in contact all the time, and policy is the result of organized discussion and free decision.

But the system is as yet incomplete. Conventions—local, provincial, regional and national—need to be supplemented by a well-staffed education and propaganda office at headquarters, by a local and national party press (as yet only beginning to develop), by summer schools, by further extension of the youth organizations, and above all by a research bureau of economic experts who can study constantly the problems of legislation and administration which would face a socialist government. Such equipment as this is new to our Canadian party organization but most of it is familiar in Britain. This is what gives English parties an intellectual life of their own and saves English party politics from degenerating to the North American level at which so many people scorn to take any active part in it. A lively intellectual activity is especially needed in a new Canadian party which is trying, not merely to get into office, but to carry out a radical programme. Only by such methods can it maintain real unity of doctrine and policy across the whole country, and provide for their continuous adaptation to new circumstances.

All this costs money. The idea that a party member should pay regular dues is quite foreign to Canadian practice, and considerable persistence will be required before the ordinary Canadian can be accustomed to it. But nothing less will save any party from being betrayed into the hand of rich campaign contributors. The C.C.F. must strive strenuously also for the enactment of legislation requiring compulsory publicity for all contributions to party funds, local and central, and imposing effective penalties for breaches of the law.[10] Nothing else that it can do would so clearly show up the hypocrisy of the democratic professions of the two old parties. While no legislation will completely remove the demoralization of politics which results from secret campaign contributions, the laws of Canada on this subject have long been antiquated and we lag far behind the practice of Great Britain and the United States.

Modern society is inevitably committed to a continuous process of expanding the functions and powers of government. But increasing the powers of government in the control of economic processes must result in increasing the powers of the classes which now control government, *unless the other classes also are organized for action.* A mere mass democratic upheaval, deriving its strength from the emotional appeals which are so easy in a period of depression, will sooner or later disintegrate or be captured by the specious cries of "easy money" cranks, superficial reformers, fascist demagogues, and the rest. Only a disciplined socialist political movement, based solidly on the occupational economic organizations of the classes which suffer most from the present chaos of monopoly capitalism, offers any real hope to the Canadian people.

c. A "National" Government?

Many excellent citizens, however, are reluctant to accept this conclusion and are willing to grasp at almost any alterna-

---

[10]On party campaign funds and the deficiencies of the present Canadian law see the article by Prof. R. A. MacKay entitled "After Beauharnois—What?" in *Maclean's Magazine*, October 15, 1931.

tive. They admit the bankruptcy of the Liberal and Conservative parties. They recognize the unreality of the division between the two. They are disgusted by the futile bickerings between "Ins" and "Outs", separated by no ascertainable difference of principle. But at this point their insight fails them. They see, not the logic of a new and unified radical party, but the will-o'-the-wisp of a "national" government.

Almost any student of politics could have predicted the arrival at about the present time of a movement for a "national" government in Canada. The combined circumstances of the prolonged economic crisis, the failure of the old parties to deal effectively with it, and the political immaturity of a large proportion of the electorate made such a movement almost inevitable. And, sure enough, we now have a League for National Government which is conducting vigorous propapanda in Montreal and Toronto with the help of certain newspapers and popular magazines. Its presentation of its case is silly and preposterous. But a dozen years ago the Hitler movement was also considered to be silly and preposterous. We cannot as yet tell whether the drive for a "national" government will finally be carried on through this League or through Mr. Bennett or through Mr. Stevens' Reconstruction party or through some other collection of more skilful and plausible demagogues. But we may be sure that the kind of approach which will be made to the Canadian people will be much the same as that which is at present adopted by the spokesmen of the League. Let us therefore examine its arguments in order that we may be forewarned against the kind of propaganda with which we are certain to be bombarded during the next few years, and also in order that we may uncover, if we can, the real interests and purposes which lie behind the movement.

Whence Does the Movement Come?

What is this magic phrase, "a national government", supposed to mean? Mr. Basil Campbell, one of the organizers of the League for National Government, defines it as "composed of men who will rise above party politics and grapple in a businesslike way with Canadian problems, divested of party bids for power[11]; a "pulling together of all those, in all factions, groups and creeds, from all parts of the country, who are not motivated by selfish interests, and who desire to see a strong

[11]Address No. 1, Toronto, March 14, 1935, p. 22. (Published by the League).

Government at Ottawa for the next five years and one which
will be in a position of deal adequately, fearlessly, fairly, and
without hindrance with the problems confronting it";[12] "drawing its strength from all parties, augmented if necessary by
some not now in political life".[13]   These comprehensive phrases
would seem to invite everybody.   But there are those who stand
beyond the pale even of Mr. Campbell's much-embracing charity.   First, as we have just seen, come those who "are motivated by selfish interests".   Mr. Campbell does not tell us how
he will separate the sheep from the goats.   But the test, if it
could be carried out, might have results which would surprise
him.   Second, he rules out those who do not "believe in our institutions".   This is more definite, but still hardly definite
enough.   Presumably, it means that Mr. Campbell will not
offer a portfolio to Mr. Tim Buck.   But how much more?   The
Prime Minister in recent speeches has implied that relief camps
in which men are denied the right to vote are among "our institutions".   Does the League for a National Government agree?
Third, Mr. Campbell excludes "those who do not want to work—
those who thrive only on illogically conceived agitation—those
whose only idea is to cause confusion and dissatisfaction, at the
expense of orderly and good government".   Elsewhere Mr.
Campbell suggests that there is room for Labour men and "those
for whose benefit social legislation is placed upon our statute
books".   But nowhere does he mention the C.C.F. by name;
the only reference to it, under the ambiguous heading "Socialism Menacing?" is perhaps significant.   National Government
is a great mental haven for those who are still afraid of socialism—or the things they think socialism means.

"National" Policy.

    The next question is, What practical proposals have the
supporters of a "national" government to offer?   The League
in one of its pamphlets lists eight problems which it assures us
a "national" government would solve: railways, revision of the
British North America Act, cost of government, the public debt,
tariffs, unemployment, social legislation, and "Socialism Menacing?".   What does it say on each of these heads?
    1. *Railways*: As we have noted elsewhere, the League speci-
fically states that it does not advocate amalgamation.   But Sir

12*Ibid.*, p. 7.
13Address No. 2, Toronto, May 1, 3, 1935, pp. 3-4 . The quotations from the League
propaganda which follow are taken from one or other of these two addresses.

Edward Beatty has said that "Amalgamation is not a description of my plan",[14] and the League does not mention "unification", so we are not much the wiser on this point. Its second suggestion is that "the C.N.R. should be taken out of politics". This is admirable, but it happens that Mr. Bennett has done it already. Third, Mr. Campbell seems to suggest (his language is not very clear) that the railways should meet motor competition by getting "control of highway motor transport agencies", by "adopting the combined container-car and motor-truck zone service" by "the absorption of the motor-bus for passenger traffic and the adoption of the Diesel engine for tractor units", and by "electrification". Other countries, it seems, are doing all these splendid things, but in some mysterious and unexplained fashion the existence of parties in Canada prevents us from doing the same. Why, if the schemes are practicable, the railways themselves have not adopted them long ago, Mr. Campbell does not explain. But surely five minutes conversation with any experienced railway traffic man would have shown him that electrification at least is completely impracticable on any large scale in this country because traffic density is too low. All the schemes, too, would involve considerable capital outlay, to which Mr. Campbell seems irrevocably opposed, if we may judge from the pages of lamentations over the excessive capital expenditures of both railways. Perhaps it could all be done by amalgamation? But that brings us back to the original disclaimer.

2. *Revision of the B.N.A. Act*: Here the League contents itself with three pages of remarks on the differences in economic interest between the various provinces, and a series of statements like the following: "Quebec is not likely to brook interference in any way". . . . "We hear the low murmur of secession rolling up the St. Lawrence". . . . "Some form of tariff revision might help to sell wheat, lumber and coal abroad, but any such tampering with protection would meet with opposition from Ontario and Quebec. A broad study of the whole question from a non-partisan viewpoint is long overdue". . . . "We are told that this much-needed social legislation is *ultra vires* of the constitution". . . . "The British North America Act requires revision due to the factor of obsolescence". So what? *How is revision to be made?* is surely the real question to be answered.

3. *Cost of government*: Here again the League confines itself to trying to make our flesh creep, prudently refraining from

14Speech to the Toronto Canadian Club, May 20, 1035, p. 7.

offering anything specific. The most spectacular statement, that "we have sufficient government machinery in Canada for a population of a hundred million people" is thrown off without a scintilla of evidence, and is, of course, perfectly meaningless. How much "government machinery" is "sufficient" for a given number of people depends first on the size of the area in which they live, secondly on the functions they expect their government to perform, and thirdly on historically accepted factors, like nationality and language. Ten million people in an area the size of Illinois need less "government machinery", other things being equal, than ten million people scattered across half a continent. Ten million people who expect their governments to do no more than act the policeman will certainly need less government machinery than the same number demanding of their governments modern sanitation, educational facilities, cheap power, good roads, supplies of liquor and a thousand and one other things. Similarly, no French-Canadian would allow all his affairs to be run by a predominantly English-speaking Protestant government at Ottawa.

Mr. Campbell, to be sure, does not suggest that we should have a single government to look after every parish pump from Sydney to Nanaimo; indeed he suggests nothing at all except taking the civil service out of politics (which has already been done to a far greater extent than he seems to realize). But one of his supporters, Mr. C. H. Carlisle, eminent banker, baker and tire manufacturer, is less cautious. In a speech to the Toronto Board of Trade, on November 27, 1934, he declared, according to the Montreal *Star*, that "abolition of the party system at Ottawa and abolition of the nine provincial governments" was necessary to "prevent eventual insolvency". On both the political and fiscal aspects of such proposals we have, however, commented at sufficient length elsewhere.[15]

4. *The public debt*: Again, unrelieved gloom, but absolutely no hint of what we should do about it, appears. "What happened", asks Mr. Campbell sepulchrally, "in Australia?" Answer: Compulsory conversion of debt and exchange depreciation, with certain other measures, as a result of which Australia has recovered a great deal better than we have. Again: "We have almost every conceivable form of tax and more than half of them would not have been necessary if extravagant spending had been curbed". Whatever the truth of this may

---

[15]See Chapter XIII, "Taxation and Fiscal Policy", section b.

be—and it is as easy to check as the statement that if all the postcards sold in Montreal since Confederation were laid end to end, they would stretch to the planet Saturn—it is certainly true that more than half of our Dominion taxation would have been unnecessary but for the War. Is Mr. Campbell suggesting that we should have stayed out of it? If so, he may have a score to settle with his colleague, Colonel Mess. But the War is over, the money is spent, and not all our tears will cancel a brass farthing of it. What the country wants to know—and what it should be the duty of a government to tell it—is, the debt being there, what will a "national" government do with it? Impenetrable silence answers.

5. *Tariffs*: Here we reproduce in full what the League says:

"(British Columbia) chafes under the restraint imposed by the tariff restrictions required in the interests of the manufacturers in the east.

"Premier Pattullo speaks of a regional tariff, but whether he has the power to achieve his desires in this regard is another matter.

"It means that a tariff must be applied which has a particular reference to the trade of that province.

"It means, in certain measure, the removal of duties on certain imports from countries which will take the natural products of British Columbia".

"My friends, there is the tariff problem which must be carefully considered, bearing in mind the best interests of the country as a whole.

"It is essential, however, that those, who evolve the solution, be competent and politically disinterested.

"I do not wish to be the type of alarmist who conjures up imaginary troubles.

What I have said is by no means imaginary.

These conditions are realities.

Partisan government, by its very make-up, cannot solve our troubles.

We are facing trying times.

We want action from our Government at Ottawa.

In face of this I read the following headline on the front page of the Toronto *Globe*, February 28, 1935.

'Old-Line Parties Divide Straight on Vote of Censure'.

There is no attempt to assist in legislation to help conditions.

We are plagued with partisan motives—political manoeuvring—the seeking of every petty advantage.

In the distance we hear the tum-tum-tum of the voodoo drum calling the faithful to the hustings."

"Some form of tariff revision might help to sell wheat, lumber and coal abroad, but any such tampering with protection would meet with opposition from Ontario and Quebec.

A broad study of the whole question from a non-partisan viewpoint is long overdue".

It seems hardly credible that this is all, but it is. How the "national" government is going to square the circle by framing a tariff that will give protection to Ontario and Quebec, free trade to the Maritimes and the West, is left to the imagination.

6. *Unemployment*: Under this head we are treated to a series of commonplaces, to the effect that unemployment is a Bad Thing. The statements end with these two sentences: "Protracted unemployment fills our jails and prisons—one must sometimes sympathize with the offenders. It is an instinct that one must obtain food, even by force, to feed one's offspring". This almost certainly contravenes Section 98 of the Criminal Code; one even begins to wonder whether Mr. Campbell himself "believes in our institutions". His prescription for the evil sets at rest any fears for his personal safety, but can hardly be said to do much more: "Unemployment," he says, "might be largely alleviated if the other matters I have referred to were properly dealt with." This might pass if the "other matters" had been "properly dealt with" by Mr. Campbell himself. But they have not.

7. *Social legislation*: "This subject is fraught with many pitfalls. . . . It is obvious that the Federal and Provincial Governments must admit the necessity for certain social legislation, but it must not be made a political football nor should it be ill-conceived and hurriedly put forward. . . . I am not afraid of fair social legislation". This is reassuring. But almost at once another note begins to sound. "Is Mr. Bennett going to be able to deal with the matter upon equitable lines and without political bias?" The meaning of this innuendo is obscure. Mr. Campbell proceeds:

"Once these problems have become political issues and violent appeals are made to the electorate by scheming politicians, who seek the power and fats of office, partisan considerations enter the picture with all their obnoxious features.

It has been generally true in the past that the assets of Canada have been used to make good the promises which political parties make at elections to class interests and camp followers.

The ability of Canada to implement these promises has been well nigh exhausted.

To-day the taxpayers are weary under the burdens imposed upon them as a result.

How long can the country and the taxpayer continue to satisfy the greed of scheming politicians?"

If these dark sayings mean anything at all, they mean drastic retrenchment on social legislation.

8. *"Socialism Menacing?"* On this question, the League is apparently unable to make up its mind. It quotes, without comment, Mr. W. G. Ernst's prediction that socialism will mean "sweeping bloodshed", Mr. Taschereau's shudders at the possibility of "State control of bread—meat—everything", and a non-existent prophecy, attributed to Mr. Woodsworth by the Toronto *Globe,* that there will be a "C.C.F. administration after the next election". "Perhaps", adds the League, "some measure of state control of the necessities of life would be for the good of the country, but should it be put on our statute books by any group or interest? Should it not be the product of the thought of a Government of National composition". It is surely time to ask Mr. Campbell a question in turn: Would a government composed of representatives—to mention no other groups —of the mass of the farmers and the wage earners of this country be "a government of national composition"?

Anyone who has not read the literature of the League for a National Government may think that we have quoted out of context, or omitted vital passages. A brief perusal of the originals will dispel this idea, and if further proof of the accuracy of our picture is needed, Mr. Campbell himself furnishes it. "It has been said", he confides with engaging candour, "that our plans are nebulous. If our plans are nebulous, it may be that our strength lies therein." The electorate will no doubt also appreciate this further estimate of its intelligence.

What Would a "National" Government Mean?

The leaders of the "national" government movement, observing that there is no significant difference between the Liberal and Conservative parties, have fallen into the error of imagining that there are no real differences of opinion among honest and able men at all, or at least none that will not disappear if those who hold them can only be persuaded to sit down around the same table and exchange their views. The idea that men equally honest, equally able and equally well-informed may differ and continue to differ, deeply and strongly, on major questions of national policy, that such differences arise and persist because of fundamental differences of economic interest, is apparently completely ignored by the National Government advocates.

Taking the official statements of the League for National Government at their face value, it seems that the movement has nothing to offer but a series of platitudes, half-truths, innuendoes, irrelevancies, and incantations. Why, then, has it won the support not only, as it proudly boasts, of "the Simcoe *Reformer,* the Norfolk *Observer,* the Huntsville *Forester,* the Pembroke *Standard-Observer,* the Bowmanville *Statesman,* the Cobourg *World,* and the Huntingdon *Gleaner*", but also the strident advocacy of the Montreal *Star* and the blessing of Mr. C. H. Carlisle, Mr. Arthur Purvis, Mr. A. O. Dawson, and lesser lights of the business firmament too numerous to mention?

The answer is to be found not in what the movement professes but the ends which certain interests would undoubtedly like it to serve. Most of the "national" government editorials of the Montreal *Star* are just as "nebulous" as the literature from which we have quoted. But one thing stands out clearly: the prime purpose of a "national" government is railway unification. Mr. Campbell may disclaim any such intention, but nobody is likely to take this seriously. Whatever else it means, a "national" government means a C.P.R. government.

It means also government by big business even more completely than in the past. "We are not the tools of any interest or group", says Mr. Campbell; and in the next breath, blandly unaware of incongruity, "We are all business men." This last is not quite accurate. On the fringes of the movement hover a number of well-intentioned but unrealistic or misled groups; but unquestionably the great body of its supporters are business men. We have yet to hear of any industrial workers who wear the League's tricolour, and no farmer who keeps his eyes open is likely thus to adorn himself. When Mr. Bennett proposed to nationalize the grain trade, the Winnipeg Grain Exchange and Boards of Trade in various parts of the country protested. The bill went to a special committee, and emerged shorn of the features to which "business" had objected. Whereupon the

Montreal *Star*[16] burst into a jubilant editorial, "The National Government Touch in Wheat". How much the farmer has been "touched" for remains to be seen.

All the supporters of a "national" government agree that it is going to balance the budget. It will also reduce taxation. And of course it will not reduce the interest payments on government bonds, except by voluntary conversion measures. Presumably also it will not cut war pensions. As these "uncontrollable" expenditures amount to fully a third of the total, does this mean that a "national" government would have to make slashing cuts in relief and social services? If so, the implication should be clearly recognized by the Canadian public. It would mean revolt, and revolt means repression, and that means a disagreeable awakening some bright morning to find ourselves in a fascist state. The sponsors of "national" government may be sincere enough in protesting that they do not envisage any such end (though there is, possibly, something ominous in one of Mr. Campbell's *obiter dicta*[17]). But circumstances will force them in that direction whether they will or no.

Economic Realities:the True Issues Before the Electorate.

The great corporations have no party. They never have had.[18] Hitherto, however, they have found it profitable to maintain two dummy parties and to play off one against the other. When the populace grew restive under the Conservatives, big business turned them out and put in the Liberals; when the country murmured against the Liberals, out they went and in came the Conservatives. Through it all, big business went serenely on, working out its manifest destiny of exploiting everything and everybody in sight. But the rise of the C.C.F. shows that the electors are beginning to see through the game. Keeping up two capitalist parties has become very expensive and shows signs of becoming inadequate to the task of preserving to St. James Street and King Street their time-honoured rights. The capitalist mind, partly from force of habit doubtless, leaps

16July 3, 1935.

17"There is fear on the part of some that a National Government, truly representative of the people, might remain a living force. Perhaps there is something in this thought. Who knows?" . . . Address No. 2, p. 15.

18The interesting manoeuvres by which the Bank of Commerce-Canadian Northern interests got their nominee appointed as Minister of Finance in the new Conservative Cabinet of 1911, although he had been a Liberal up to that year, throw a world of light upon the true nature of the two old parties. See W. S. Wallace, *Memoirs of Sir George Foster.*

to the conclusion that what we need is a merger. The old parties are bankrupt. Very well: let us amalgamate them and refloat the combined organization with an imposing list of new directors, plenty of no par value non-voting stock for the ordinary citizen, control vested in a few management preferred shares, and a charter allowing it to do anything under heaven. The cost will be trifling, the dividends on the preferred shares enormous. The remarkable amenability of the "Union" government of 1917 to powerful banking and transportation interests provides a foretaste of what we may expect. Let us then dedicate ourselves anew, that government of the people by big businss and for big business may not perish from the land.

But this conviction has not yet become universal in business circles. On the contrary there are many who think the old game is not yet played out, and who are canny enough to realize that as long as the public can be induced to play it, it would be dangerous for business to try anything else. For a "national" government is, short of outright dictatorship, capitalism's last desperate throw. The function of parties should be to *clarify* issues. The Liberal and Conservative parties exist not to clarify issues but to confuse them. When they fail in that function, capitalism will no doubt entrust it to a "national" government, which at the outset of its career would probably confuse all the issues beyond the wildest dreams of successful party politicians. Unfortunately, however, the enchantment cannot last. As the first effects wear off, it becomes apparent to everyone that in future the electorate will have to choose not between two faithful servants of capitalism, but between a capitalist party and a socialist party. With all the mists raised by Social Credit parties, Reconstruction parties, and the rest, the fundamental issues are at last becoming clarified; and "business" is faced with the horrid prospect that when the electorate tires, as it must, of the rule of the capitalist party, it will have no choice but to put the socialist in power. It will be too late then to conjure up the departed spirits of Liberalism and Conservatism. "Business" will then either have to give way or abolish democracy.

The great economic problems of Canada are not the result of party politics. They are the inevitable results of the working of our economic system. For that reason they cannot be solved piecemeal and within the limitations of that system, nor by allowing ourselves "to be stampeded into doing something,—

anything; going somewhere—anywhere."[19]   They can be solved
only as a whole, only by intelligent leadership and support,
only therefore within the framework of a planned socialized
economy working for the country as a whole.

[19]Hon. R. J. Manion, in a speech on the railway question before the Toronto Canadian
Club, May 1, 1935. (*Financial Post*, May 11, 1935).

CHAPTER XXI.

PARLIAMENT AND THE CONSTITUTION.

A. PARLIAMENTARY INSTITUTIONS.

SINCE the emergence of the C.C.F. it has become a favourite pose with the spokesmen of the old parties to present themselves as defenders of parliamentary liberties and constitutional methods of government against the menace of a socialist revolution. The Liberals especially have been daily dying in the last ditch in defence of parliamentarism and British traditions of government by discussion. Certainly, if attention be concentrated on the machinery of administration which the state direction of our economic life would demand, it is easy to draw terrifying conclusions about the dangers of bureaucratic dictatorship. It is the more easy in Canada because we have not in the past been educated by our publicists into a realistic understanding of how parliamentary government actually works under modern conditions. Most of us have in our minds the picture of the parliamentary system which was supplied to our grandfathers by Walter Bagehot, and we have not adjusted our thinking to the changes in the system which have taken place since Bagehot's day. Hence we are easily horrified by the words "dictatorship" and "bureaucracy", because we do not realize that they are often merely terms of abuse applied to certain tendencies in the operation of government which have been developing before our eyes all our lifetime, and which will continue to develop whether a Liberal or a Conservative or a Socialist cabinet happens to be in office.

The Late Mr. Bagehot.

Bagehot's classic analysis of the English mid-Victorian constitution[1] pictured a Cabinet which had become the real centre of power but which held office only at the pleasure of a House of Commons whose debates decided the coming and going of governments and whose deliberations determined the direction that policy should take. In his picture the electorate stood off at a respectful distance and left the decisive voice to Parliament, although he recognized with some apprehension a tendency

[1] Bagehot's *English Constitution* was published in the year of Confederation, 1867.

489

towards what he called "constituency government". About the Civil Service he had very little to say.

Everyone knows nowadays that this glorification of parliamentarism has been supplanted by a widespread public cynicism and disillusionment about representative institutions. It is a common sport to deride our parliamentary talking-shops and the men who spend their time talking in them. Nevertheless, we still retain in British countries a strong feeling of traditional loyalty to the parliamentary system; and when Liberal stalwarts in Canada such as Messrs. King and Dafoe, who look out upon a twentieth-century world through mid-Victorian spectacles,[2] begin to shudder in public about the menace of a socialist dictatorship which will undermine representative institutions altogether, they do not have much difficulty in making large numbers of Canadians shudder in sympathy with them. The fact is, however, that the shuddering is almost completely about a false issue .

Since Bagehot's time, there have been two main developments in government which have made his picture of the English form of constitutional government largely obsolete. People who follow political discussions in England have been perfectly familiar with these developments since at least the decade before the war, and they are treated at length in all the standard books.[3] One is the growth in the power of the executive at the expense of the power of the Legislature, and the other is the growing tendency to hand over important functions of government to bodies of expert officials of one kind or another who are practically irresponsible in relation to the elected representative legislature.

The Growth of Cabinet Power.

The cabinet has grown in power with the expansion and elaboration of party machinery. The Prime Minister, controlling the machinery of his party, controls the private members of parliament who have been elected through the agency of the party machine for the purpose of supporting him through

---

[2] It may be, however, that we do Mr. King an injustice in referring to him as mid-Victorian. If one were to judge from his famous Magna Carta speech in the 1934 session, his ideas about the British constitution should more properly be classed as Early Gothic.

[3] Sidney Low's *Governance of England*, published in 1904, drew forcible attention to the change in the balance of power between cabinet and legislature. A recent Liberal discussion of these points may be found in Ramsay Muir's *How England is Governed* (1928). The most recent treatment of the subject is by an American, Prof. F. A. Ogg, *English Government and Politics* (1929). See also the discussion in Harold Laski's *Grammar of Politics*, and *Democracy in Crisis*.

thick and thin.[4] The result is, and it is a matter of common observance, that the cabinet has gradually ceased to be in any real sense responsible to parliament. The government is responsible to the electorate who choose it in a general election, and between general elections it does not need to worry much about keeping a majority in parliament. It was Gladstone, the first of the great modern demagogues, who began this process of transferring the centre of gravity from the House of Commons to the constituencies; and the process has been going on ever since—in Canada as well as in Britain. The idea that parliament makes and unmakes governments has ceased to have much relation to actual practice.

We had a vivid illustration in 1926 of how far we have gone since Victorian days. In the 1926 crisis parliament really was called upon to decide which party should be in power; and it was amusing to observe with what unanimity M.P.'s, editors, business men, all agreed that the confusion resulting from this situation was intolerable, and with what a sigh of relief everybody welcomed a general election which took the decision out of the hands of elected representatives. Nothing could have shown more clearly that we no longer really believe, whatever our professions, in entrusting parliament with this particular liberty and responsibility.

More recent events have shown that in times of crisis or emergency the general public in western democratic countries welcomes an executive which takes power into its own hands. The universal acceptance with which President Roosevelt pushed Congress to one side was only a more striking case which was paralleled by the general acquiescence which in Canada greeted Premier Bennett's taking to himself of extraordinary powers, or in England greeted the emergency powers legislation of the "national" government. If the ready abandonment of ancient parliamentary claims and the giving of wide discretionary powers to the executive is undemocratic, then these three particular countries have already become undemocratic and a socialist government will not make them more so.

Perhaps there is something in the fears of old-time Liberals

[4] A striking confession of this occurred in the debate in the House of Commons on the Sweepstakes Bill in 1934. Mr. Fraser, moving second reading, began: "Mr. Speaker, I think under existing conditions I should in the first place express on behalf of the members of the House, as well as those outside who are in favour of this measure, their appreciation of the action of the Prime Minister in allowing this question to be debated and allowing each member to vote on a measure of this kind according to his own best judgment." (*House of Commons Debates*, 1934, p. 3277). Mr. Fraser seems to have been genuinely surprised at the laughter which greeted his tribute.

over these events, for a community which is so willing to abdicate its rights of criticism on the chance that it may thereby find a saviour of society may not have long to wait for the appearance of the man on horseback. But the real reason for this break from nineteenth century parliamentary traditions is the general feeling that in the times in which we live a debating assembly of several hundred men cannot move quickly enough or decisively enough to deal with a rapidly changing situation.

What happens in these times of emergency is only an extreme example of what tends to happen normally. Legislation now is largely the work of the executive and its expert advisers. Private members' bills have little chance of passing, and the executive does not allow its own bills to be held up or amended unduly. The subjects of legislation have become so technical that the criticism of a miscellaneous collection of local representatives is not likely to be very useful anyway. The wide extension of the functions of the state—it was as long ago as the 1890's that an English cabinet minister remarked that "we are all socialists now"—has produced a pressure of legislative measures in every parliament which necessitates a rigid time-table under the control of the executive and prevents thorough parliamentary discussion of most bills. The highly technical nature of most of the administrative functions for which legislation provides in a modern state necessitates also the passing of the legislation in the form of general provisions, leaving the detailed rules to be drawn up and administered by executive officials afterwards.[5]

Most important perhaps of all developments along this line, the control of the legislature over finance, which used to be considered the secret of the power of the House of Commons, has now become largely formal. Anyone who watches parliamentary procedure knows that most of the Estimates are passed with only the most perfunctory criticism from members. In 1918 a Parliamentary Committee, set up in England to investigate this matter, reported that "so far as the direct effective control of proposals for expenditure is concerned, it would be true to say that if the Estimates were never presented and the Committee of Supply never set up, there would be no noticeable difference".

[5]On the recent growth of executive discretion and of administrative law in Canada see the illuminating paper by Prof. A. Corry in the *Proceedings of the Canadian Political Science Association*, 1933.

When we consider all these facts it is brought home to us that those worthies who stand aghast at the dangers of a socialist regime to parliamentary liberties are not talking about a parliament which has any real existence in any twentieth century state.

Government by Experts.

The other main development of the last two generations, the growth in numbers and power of expert administrative bodies, has tended in the same direction of limiting and restricting the effective power of the representative legislature. Every time we set up a new permanent independent Commission to carry on some function of government, we deny in practice the naive theory of democracy in which we still profess to believe —that all power lies with the "Peepul" to be exercised by their elected representatives.

A mere enumeration of some of the most important of these commissions in Canada is enough to show how far we have gone in entrusting the most vital functions to appointed officials, for whose protection from interference by ourselves or our representatives we make very stringent provisions. Railway, telephone, telegraph and express rates are regulated by the Board of Railway Commissioners first set up in 1904. Every step in our most important export trade is under the control of the Board of Grain Commissioners. Boundary waterways between Canada and the United States, which might form a fruitful source of international disputes, have since 1909 been taken out of politics and are under the control of an International Joint Commission. The national railway system is administered by an independent board of trustees. Both Liberal and Conservative administrations have paid at least lip service to the principles of taking the tariff out of politics by setting up a Tariff Advisory Board or Commission. The new function of radio broadcasting, which has unmeasured potentialities for influencing every side of our lives, has been put under the administrative control of an independent commission. And this list could easily be lengthened.

In addition, we have slowly and hesitatingly taken the Civil Service out of politics.[6] It is notorious that, as the independence of the Civil Service has increased and as the expert quality of

---

[6]On the somewhat sorry history of civil service reform in Canada, see Prof. R. M. Dawson, *The Civil Service of Canada.*

its personnel has improved, its influence upon the making of governmental policy has increased. In any given department of government at Ottawa an investigator is likely to find, unless the department is presided over by an exceptionally able and forceful Minister, that its policy is made by the senior permanent officials, imposed by them upon the Minister, and imposed by him upon the House of Commons.

Another development which also tends in the same direction of lessening the importance of the legislature is the habit of referring major questions of policy, which can only be decided after expert objective examination of a complex situation, to Royal Commissions. Radio, railways, banking and retail trade are among the most recent examples. On all these vital matters the main case has been made before the subject reaches parliament at all, public opinion has been enlightened by the discussions of the Commission and the evidence submitted to it, and the discussions in parliament add little to the subject.

We have not yet solved the problem of the best method of appointing all these bodies of experts or of their proper relation to the cabinet and to the legislature. But most people are agreed on the desirability of "taking them out of politics", i.e., of removing them from the liability to be interfered with by the people's representatives. And each succeeding government sets up some new commission of expert administrators or adds some new department to the Civil Service, thereby widening the range of governmental functions which are handed over to men whose chief responsibility is to their own sense of honesty and of professional efficiency. This, again, is a process which goes on continuously in Canada as in all modern countries, and which goes on whether the government in office happens to be Conservative or Liberal or Socialist.

The Conditions of an Effective Parliamentarism.

The proposals for economic reconstruction which have been set forth in this book will certainly, if they are adopted, strengthen both of the tendencies which have just been discussed— the growth in power of the executive at the expense of the power of the legislature, and the extension of the practice of government by independent experts. Is there anything essentially undemocratic in this? Those who affirm that there is, are confusing the general principle of democracy with the particular machinery which was developed in the nineteenth century for giving effect to popular sovereignty. If democracy cannot equip itself with new agencies for fulfilling its purposes, then democratic government will be superseded by some form of government based upon force. In an age when rapid technological changes are daily shifting the whole material basis of our civilization, our political democracy must trust itself more and more to technical experts and must develop a leadership which is experimental in temper and capable of quick decisions.

For the benefit of grandmotherly Liberals, we cannot do better than quote at this point from that major prophet of liberalism, Sir Arthur Salter. In his Massey lecture at McGill University on April 18, 1933, he used these words: "I believe that it will be necessary for Parliaments unspecialized in economic problems to delegate many of their present functions to the Executive, and for the Executive to strengthen themselves for their economic responsibilities by much more regular and better organized advice than at present from outside experts. The failure of representative government in free democratic countries to adapt itself to its modern economic tasks has been the impelling force which has led to its replacement by systems based upon force. If representative government is to preserve the essentials it must probably be prepared to relinquish the unessentials. Among the essentials is the right of an elected Parliament to retain in power or dismiss the Executive and to lay down the main principles of policy and legislation; but the right to draft the detailed clauses of laws or to exercise pressure on the details of administration is among the unessentials, and the insistence upon its exercise may make the whole machine of government unworkable under modern conditions". Sir Arthur exaggerates the power which a modern parliament does actually possess in relation to the executive, but his words may be commended to all the oratorical last-ditchers who have recently become so alarmed about parliamentarily liberties in Canada.

It is not, however, a part of our conception of future changes that parliament shall be retired to a position of decorative insignificance. Policy will still be in the control of the Cabinet who will have their seats in the House and will there defend their actions. The Prime Minister will still be the leader of the House. This is essential, for nothing has so contributed to the degradation of parliament as the frank contempt of a wartime Prime Minister like Mr. Lloyd George who absented himself from the sittings of the House and left its deliberations in the hands of a subordinate. Where the Prime Minister is, there is the focus of all political activity. Great debates will still take place in the House which may have a decisive influence in guiding public opinion. The House will remain the chief forum of the community. And it will continue to perform one indispensable function which it has always performed admirably and which cannot be performed by any other body That is the function of sifting out leaders from the mass of public men, of distinguishing the mere windbags from the men of sound and shrewd counsel, of weighing duly the relative merits of brilliance and originality on the one hand and of cautious common sense on the other.

But it is not necessary for the real usefulness of parliament that the executive should allow itself to be thwarted or hampered by mere filibustering obstruction carried on in the name of freedom of debate. And if a socialist government coming into office in a period of emergency seeks power to proceed by order-in-council without day-to-day reference to the House, it will only be doing what has been already done in both England and Canada by those bulwarks of constitutional traditions, Conservative or "National" governments.

We believe, however, that a great deal can be done to restore the usefulness and efficiency of parliament and thereby to raise its prestige. The favourite prescription of the "co-operating independents" of the 1920's does not appeal to us at all as a desirable step in this direction. They wished to undermine the dominant power which the cabinet now exercises over the House by a constitutional enactment that parliament should not be dissolved without its own consent. The ultimate result of this would be an approximation to the unhealthy domination which the French Chamber of Deputies exercises over the cabinet and the loss of executive morale which follows. It is absolutely necessary that the executive be master of the situation and be in a secure enough position to make decisions that may be momentarily unpopular. Anything which defeats this end defeats the cause of good government. If the executive abuses its discretion the remedy is with the electorate.

Nor are we attracted by most of the fancy schemes for getting a reformed parliament by changing the system of election. The idea that an economic or "functional" parliament, consisting of representatives chosen from the different functional groups in the community instead of from the present geographical con- stituencies, will work with a new efficiency is highly romantic. The problems with which the legislature of a large-scale national state has to deal extend beyond the range of experience of the ordinary voters, however those voters may be grouped. And whatever the system of election, the net result is to assemble at Ottawa some 245 average Canadians.

Undoubtedly the grotesque results of our recent elections under the single-member constituency system present strong arguments for the introduction of proportional representation, at least in urban areas where the size of constituencies would not be too unwieldy. But contrary to much general belief, this type of change is not of major importance.[7] What is most needed in parliament is a change by which 245 average Cana- dians *can work more effectively* when once they get to Ottawa. They are not likely to be experts in anything particular except in the art of getting elected: any tendency which exposes them to the guidance and influence of the experts of the Civil Service and the various government Commissions is to be welcomed. But they do possess one qualification which gives them an ad- vantage over all the administrative experts. That is their knowledge of what ordinary people are thinking about back home. What is needed is to bring them and this knowledge of theirs into more effective and continuous contact with the ad- ministrative experts and their kind of knowledge.

This means chiefly a reform in the present clumsy procedure of Parliament. No sane man can really believe that the inter- minable debates on the Speech from the Throne or the Budget or other temporary matters of interest serve any useful pur- pose after the first few speeches; and no one who has watched the Committee of the House going through the clauses of some bill or passing the votes of some minister's estimates can regard such spending of members' time as being anything but grossly unbusinesslike.

Most of the work now done in the main chamber of the House would be immensely improved by an extension of the committee system. To each of the reorganized departments of the cabinet there should be attached a small standing committee of the House. To it would be referred all legislative proposals

7See again Laski, *Grammar of Politics*, Chapter VIII, section II; and H. Finer, *The Case Against Proportional Representation* (Fabian Society, 1924).

coming within the jurisdiction of that department. It would be the Minister's business to keep in close touch with the committee, and there is no reason why members of the committee should not see many of the confidential papers which cannot be made public on the floor of the House. The details of the departmental estimates could be threshed out here to much better purpose than by the whole House in Committee. The committee would hear evidence from interested parties about any proposed bill, it would be in touch with the Planning Commission or the appropriate branch of it; it would thus have the opportunity of discussing projects while they were still in fluid state. It would especially acquire personal touch with the permanent officials and this would be good both for the parliamentarians and for the bureaucrats. The committee would of course be constructed so as to have a government majority upon it, but its members would consist of those members of the House who were specially interested in or qualified for its work. A body like the present Agricultural Committee functions very much along these lines already. If the whole work of the Commons were so organized, it would acquire a reality which is sadly lacking on most of the days of any present session.

The Senate.

We have so far omitted all mention of the one great change affecting parliament which must be put in the forefront of the demands of the C.C.F. That is, of course, the abolition of the Senate. Almost every economic and political project which has been advocated in this book and which would require legislative action by the Dominion parliament would meet with obsinate and bitter opposition in the Senate. In its composition and in its activity it is one of the most reactionary chambers among all the free governments in the western world.[8]

Political philosophers have devised various ingenious arguments for the creation of a second chamber, but they are all rationalizations of existing fact. In the 14th century it so happened that the English Parliament, owing to certain circumstances in the structure of feudal society, took a bicameral form. Five centuries later, when British parliamentarism had

---

[8]The best and most detailed discussion of the Senate is to be found in *The Unreformed Senate of Canada*, by Prof. R. A. MacKay (1924). He tends to see more good in its activities than we do. On the British House of Lords and the problem of a second chamber in general, see the booklet by A. L. Rowse: *The Question of the House of Lords*, (1934).

become the ideal of all people seeking self-government, it was concluded by the world that the existence of two chambers was part of the secret of British freedom. The unromantic fact, however, was that, as Britain grew steadily more democratic in the nineteenth century, the real function of the House of Lords became that of defending the special privileges of certain propertied classes in the community. In a democratic community the dictum of the famous Frenchman still remains true: a second chamber when it agrees with the lower elected house is unnecessary, and when it disagrees with it, is pernicious.

As for the argument about the need of sober second thought, legislative bodies today, under the domination of a rigid party system, are not likely to be swept off their feet into rash emotional attacks upon property; and the real difficulty under modern conditions is that practically no legislation reaches the statute-book until a period from a year to a generation after an impartial observer would consider that the need for it had been conclusively proved. The evil of badly drafted legislation, which is supposed to justify a revising chamber, could be better corrected by a preliminary drafting commission of technical experts to work over legislative proposals before they reach the Commons.

In federal countries, a second chamber has generally been thought desirable in order to protect weaker sectional interests against the concentrated wealth or population which tends to give the main partners of the federation too much power in the lower house. The United States Senate is the original of all such devices. Our Canadian Senate was modelled upon it, the four sections of Canada—the Maritimes, Quebec, Ontario, and the West—being given equal representation regardless of population or wealth. But, strange to say, the Fathers of Confederation in thus creating a Senate as a bulwark of provincial rights against the central government entrusted the power of making appointments to the Senate to that very central government upon whom it was to operate as a check. Those hardheaded politicians of the Quebec Conference must surely have had their tongues in their cheeks when they presented this particular specimen of their handiwork to a credulous populace.

Actually the Senate has never operated to protect provincial rights, unless accidentally. It has steadily acted on behalf of a party recently defeated at the polls to thwart the government that has just been chosen by the people; and its powers of annoyance in this respect would long ago have compelled some government to undertake reforms were it not for the fortunately high death rate among its aged members. But in recent years, the real function of the Senate has been to act as a bulwark of property interests, i.e., of the interests of large property owners, individual or corporate.[9] The remarkable number of company directorships held by senators is the most significant fact about our upper House. No one who has ever watched its sleepy deliberations will be misled into believing that the old gentlemen are appointed directors because of the services they are expected to render at the board meetings of our big corporations. The real motive is, of course, the services they are expected to render in throwing out bills of which these corporations do not approve. The Senate has, in fact, become one additional line of defence for the real ruling classes in this country, and it can be relied upon to express the opinions of St. James Street as consistently and as persistently as does the Montreal *Gazette*.[10] Under present political conditions big business is surely powerful enough in the influence it exercises directly or indirectly over the House of Commons. It does not need a second line of defence.

The Senate must therefore be abolished. Let it be emphasized that in abolishing it we are not weakening or undermining the security of the provinces in our federal system, and especially the position of the French province of Quebec. It is not the position of Quebec that is being attacked, but only the position of that part of it which is located in the neighbourhood of St. James St., Montreal. The real safeguards for racial and religious minority rights in the Canadian constitution lie in two things: the numerical and hence political strength of the minority (French-Canadians constitute 28 per cent. of our population and Roman Catholics 41 per cent.) ; and certain special sections of the B.N.A. Act which Dominion legislation cannot invade without being declared *ultra vires* by the courts. These safeguards would be just as effective without the Senate as they

[9]The function of a second chamber as a bulwark of the rich against the masses was not, apparently, much discussed by the Fathers of Confederation. But one or two revealing phrases remain from the 1860's. Macdonald remarked in the privacy of the Quebec Conference: "We must protect the interests of minorities, and the rich are always fewer in number than the poor".

[10]Section 98 of the Criminal Code has become a sort of test question of the class sympathies of any Canadian. The Senate has five times thrown out proposals coming from the Commons to delete this section, and these rejections occurred regardless of whether its majority happened to be Liberal or Conservative.

are at present. With the "entrenched clauses" which we propose below, racial and religious minority rights would in fact be safer than at present.

The proposal to abolish the Senate involves an amendment to the British North America Act. On several occasions earlier in this book the question of amendment of our federal constitution has been approached, and we now turn to discuss it at greater length.

B. THE BRITISH NORTH AMERICA ACT.

The Nature of our Constitution.

The Canadian Constitution is a curious blend of custom, imitation and invention. From Great Britain it inherited the monarchic idea and the practice of responsible government; from the United States it borrowed a federal distribution of legislative powers and the principle of judicial review of legislative action; and the Fathers of the Canadian federation balanced the costly error of the Senate by some ingenious ideas of their own, such as the Dominion power to disallow provincial laws and its power to remove certain "works" from provincial jurisdiction by declaring them to be for the general advantage of Canada. The constitution as a whole cannot be found in any one written document, nor in any collection of documents, for some established practices of the utmost importance, like the federal structure of the Cabinet and its responsibility to parliament, are based on unwritten usage alone. Of the written parts of the constitution, by far the most important is the British statute of 1867 and its various amendments, which we call the B.N.A. Act. In it the general scheme of government is provided, and the essential relationships between the federal and the provincial governments are established.

The constitutional question which a socialist government will have to face is simply this: did the Fathers of Confederation rivet a particular economic system upon the backs of the Canadian people in 1867, or did they merely provide a political framework within which Canadian democracy was to work out its own destiny, socialist or capitalist?

The answer is in favour of the view that the B.N.A. Act is a mere political framework, not inextricably tied up with a particular economic system. The American constitution since the Schechter decision, appears to make impossible any effective economic reform in the United States without some fundamental change in the basic law of the land.[11] That is not true of Canada. Constitutional changes of course will come and are here proposed, but they are changes rather in the machinery of government and the distribution of legislative powers —not changes in the essence of the Confederation arrangement. The essence of that arrangement was a political democracy operating through a federal parliamentary system and guaranteeing certain rights to religious minorities. The particular distribution of powers was not essential, save in so far as it touched minority rights. Whether the Dominion or the provinces, for example, control Canadian insurance or trade and commerce is not of the essence of the scheme. The Act itself clearly intended a shift in these powers to take place from time to time, as is shown by the Dominion power to declare provincial works to be for the general advantage of Canada, and by the well-known dictum of the Privy Council in the Liquor Prohibition Appeal[12] that "Their Lordships do not doubt that some matters, in their origin local and provincial, might attain such dimensions as to affect the body politic of the Dominion, and to justify the Canadian Parliament in passing laws for their regulation or abolition in the interest of the Dominion". All the economic changes necessary for the creation of a co-operative commonwealth in Canada could be effected by adjustments in the distribution of powers without involving any change in the essential qualities of the federal scheme such as responsible government, federalism or minority rights.

If it should seem surprising that the difference between the Canadian and the American constitution is so great, it should be emphasized that the Canadian fathers copied the English doctrine of the sovereignty of parliament when framing the B.N.A. Act. In Canada parliament, Dominion or provincial, can do anything. There is no sovereignty reserved to the people. There are no guaranteed rights of property. There is no "due process" clause. There is no protection of contracts, as Mr. Hepburn's action in annulling Ontario Hydro agreements so vividly reminded us. There is no doctrine of separation of powers to prevent the delegation of legislative power to the executive. What laws the people want they can legally get by

11See Prof. H. L. McBain, in *New York Times*, June 22, 1935.
121896 A C., p 361.

the political process of securing a bare majority in the appropriate parliaments. Theoretically any economic change is possible so long as the Dominion and the provinces agree; it is only administrative difficulties that make amendments in the distribution of powers advisable. In eight out of the nine provinces there is no second chamber to capture, Quebec alone having an upper house, appointed for life. In the Dominion Parliament there is, of course, an appointed Senate, which will stand in the way of a socialist government until death or resignation creates sufficient vacancies to allow of the nomination of a majority of governmental supporters. It is thus true that the Senate constitutes at least a temporary protection of a particular economic system by reason of its present personnel, but this creates difficulties different in kind from those of the American constitution, and more easy to remove.

What Powers are Available for Reconstruction?

In facing the constitutional difficulties of the proposed reconstruction of our economic order three lines of approach are possible.[13]

(a) The first is the employment by the Dominion parliament of existing powers which are either imperfectly used or are not used at all. An examination of these powers in relation to the C.C.F. and L.S.R. programmes has been made by Professor F. R. Scott in the pamphlet *Social Reconstruction and the B.N.A. Act.*[14] Without recapitulating the arguments therein, it is sufficient to point out that there are great opportunities in the existing constitution, without any amendment, for Dominion control over economic matters of national importance. A bare enumeration will give some idea of the extent of these powers. The Dominion has already full control over the foreign trade of Canada—and when that has been granted, much follows. It has apparently full control over "inter-provincial" trade as well, though no useful definition of that term has yet been given by the courts. It has full power over banks, banking, currency and interest, thus making possible the nationalization of the banking system with consequent public control of the major sources of credit. It has control over interprovincial

[13]As this book is presenting a plan for the constitutional alteration of our economic system, no time will be spent here discussing the danger of illegal action by fascist and anti-democratic elements. Cf., however, F. R. Scott: *Social Reconstruction and the B.N.A. Act.*
[14]L.S.R. Pamphlet No. 4, 1934.

railways, steamships, telephones, aeronautics and radio. It
creates and controls companies of Dominion incorporation. Its
taxing powers are unlimited and it alone makes criminal law.
Its treaty-making power seems adequate to enable it to provide
Dominion standards on matters of international agreement;
Mr. Bennett is already using this method to support unemployment insurance, the eight hour day, and minimum wages. It
has a great potential power in its ability to remove certain
works from provincial control merely by declaring them to be
for the general advantage of Canada.   Behind all this are
emergency powers of vast if uncertain extent. The present feeling of Canadians that they have a weak central government,
produced by long years of planned inactivity on the part of
Liberal and Conservative governments, would rapidly give way
to a truer appreciation of the wisdom of the Fathers of Confederation if ever a socialist government began to carry out the
wishes of an electorate asking for change.

Obstruction will come from reactionary courts, of course.
Within the next few years test cases will bring out the true
character of our judiciary. The judges will be forced to side
with either the progessive or the reactionary groups. But it is
hardly conceivable that the precise provisions of the B.N.A. Act
can be read out of the constitution. Adverse judgments can be
met by redrafted statutes, and ultimately by amendment to the
constitution. Moreover, the traditional attitude of the Privy
Council, the final court of appeal, viz., favourable to provincial
rights, seems likely to have reached its limit. English judges
are probably more advanced in their social philosophy than
Canadian judges, having had a longer experience with state
control, and it would be reasonable to expect greater liberalism
from them than from our own Supreme Court, particularly as
the latter cannot overcome adverse previous decisions as easily
as can the Privy Council.

(b) The second line of approach to the constitutional problems is by way of concurrent legislation. The term concurrent
legislation is used to denote the passage by the Dominion and
by the provinces of similar statutes relating to some particular
object. It is a process by which all the legislative power of the
Dominion, whatever it may be, is added to all the power of the
province, so that the entire constitutional field must of necessity be covered. It has been used for Old Age Pensions, Market-

ing Boards, Industrial Disputes Acts, Technical Education, Employment Offices, Unemployment Relief, etc. It is obviously a complete answer to the constitutional problem,[15] but is open to the weakness that ten parliaments must become persuaded before any national scheme can be adopted, and an operating scheme could be wrecked by a province which decided to withdraw its support. Quebec, for example, the second largest industrial province, has steadily refused to adopt the Old Age Pensions scheme, thus keeping its standard of living below that of the other provinces. On matters which have a wide popular appeal concurrent legislation is perhaps the easiest solution politically, especially if the Dominion offers to pay a substantial share of the cost.

(c) The third method of dealing with the constitution is to amend it. Fortunately the time has gone by when it was necessary to argue the need for amendment. The parliamentary committee appointed in 1935 on the motion of Mr. Woodsworth has reported that it "recognizes the urgent necessity for prompt consideration of amendments to the B.N.A. Act with reference to a redistribution of legislative power and to clarify the field of taxation".[16] All parties and all save the most rabid reactionaries now admit that the distribution of powers agreed upon by the North American Colonies in 1867 was suitable for agricultural communities living in a *laissez-faire* world, but that it needs modification to meet the necessities of modern economic development. The B.N.A. Act is pre-industrial.

Needed Amendments.

The amendments which are immediately necessary lie chiefly in the field of social legislation. Without uniformity in some degree, laws dealing with wages, hours, insurance benefits, health services, etc., must necessarily fail of their purpose, or at least work under enormous disadvantages and at greatly increased cost. The Dominion has done something to assist uniform standards, but its powers are cramped by the general understanding that social legislation belongs for the most part in the category of the provincial power over property and civil rights. Mr. Bennett's use of the treaty power, though probably sound, is somewhat uncertain; in any case there is no reason

---

[15]Provided the latest invention of the courts is not developed: see *Rex v. Zaslavsky*, 1935, 2 W.W.R. See further on this, Brooke Claxton's, Social Reform and the Constitution, in *Canadian Journal of Economics and Political Science*, August, 1935.

[16]Report, p. 143.

why Canada should be tied in these matters to the snail's pace of the other capitalist powers. An amendment is needed to transfer to the Dominion unquestionable power to establish a national labour code, as suggested in a previous chapter, and to legislate regarding the subject of social legislation generally. This amendment, it has been suggested[17], might well take the form of a grant of concurrent powers to the Dominion, such as exists now for agriculture and immigration, so that the provinces could still legislative for standards above those enforced nationally by the Dominion.

Besides the matter of social legislation, amendments centralizing control over companies and insurance, and clarifying the whole subsidy and taxation basis of confederation, are highly desirable. The financial arrangements of 1867 between Dominion and provinces have resulted in overlapping taxation, haphazard financing and general confusion, and can only be properly resolved by a thorough overhauling of the financial sections of the B.N.A. Act. Further changes will be necessary when the Planning Commission and allied bodies are set up, to enable the national economic plan to be centrally adopted and carried out; at present, although the Dominion controls foreign and interprovincial trade, there is a considerable area of intra-provincial trade and commerce which, the courts have decided, belongs to "property and civil rights". Control of this field should be added to the Dominion's more general power so as to make possible a unified national economic policy. And the abolition of the Senate would also require an amendment.

The Method of Amendment.

The Fathers of Confederation made no provision for the method by which the B.N.A. Act should be amended. The most reasonable interpretation of their silence is that they assumed that the British Parliament, which enacted and alone can change their Act, would make such changes from time to time as were requested by Canada; and further, that the voice of "Canada" would be expressed through the Dominion Parliament, which alone represents the whole country and to which all matters of national importance were entrusted. This interpretation is completely borne out by constitutional usage of over sixty years. There have been seven formal amendments to the B.N.A. Act since 1867; that of 1875, dealing with parliamentary privileges,

17By Carl Goldenberg in 1934 *Canadian Bar Review*, p. 422.

was adopted upon request of the Canadian Cabinet only, without a vote in the Dominion parliament at all; the others were all adopted in response to joint addresses to the Crown by Commons and Senate. The only occasions on which provinces were consulted were in 1907, when provincial subsidies were at issue, and in 1930 when the natural resources of the prairie provinces were being returned: in 1907 the objections of British Columbia were overruled, and in 1930 the six non-prairie provinces were not asked to express any opinion. Consent of the provinces was obtained, in the form of approval of provincial delegates at a Dominion-provincial conference, to the passage of the Statute of Westminster (1931), but this did not amend the B.N.A. Act. In addition to the formal changes, Section 118 of the Act, dealing with provincial subsidies, has been altered on a number of occasions by Dominion action alone without consulting the provinces or obtaining Imperial sanction.

The historical record makes the "compact theory" of confederation, so much beloved of reactionary politicians because it contends that all provinces must consent before any change is made in the Act, utterly untenable.[18] Nor is there force in the argument that previous amendments were matters of no great provincial concern; the amendment of 1871 authorizing parliament to admit new provinces, that of 1886 providing for representation at Ottawa of the territories, that of 1915 in particular enlarging the size of the Senate (thus altering, for example, Quebec's power to block legislation from the Commons), and the various changes in provincial subsidies, were of the greatest importance to the provinces.

It is therefore in keeping with Canadian political tradition that the process of amendment for the future should be as it has been in the past—by action of the Dominion Parliament. Parliament alone represents all provinces, speaks for every Canadian, and should properly be held responsible for a matter of such national importance. It has been due partly to our luck as heirs of British practice, partly to the wisdom of succeeding generations of Canadian statesmen, that we have hitherto avoided in Canada the paralyzing rigidity which renders the American Constitution so unworkable.

18For a more complete demolition of the compact theory, see Rogers, "The Compact Theory of Confederation", in the *Proceedings of the Canadian Political Science Association*, 1931, p. 205; and J. W. Dafoe, "Revising the Constitution", *Queens' Quarterly*, Winter 1930.

Minority Rights.

The dismissal of the extreme form of the doctrine of provincial rights, however, does not dispose of the quite different problem of minority rights. Minority rights involve those matters of race, language, religion and education which, if not legally any more protected than provincial rights, are in a different category from the point of view of moral obligation. These rights have been guaranteed in greater or less degree to various minorities—the French minority generally, the Catholic minority in Ontario and to a lesser degree in the western provinces, and the Protestant minority in Quebec. They should be extended in the B.N.A. Act in such a way that they cannot be touched by the more flexible process of amendment suited to other subjects. Provincial powers over economic matters and social legislation, be it noted, are not in this group. Quebec's right to tolerate sweatshops whose existence holds down living standards in other provinces, is not a minority right.

The list of sections in the Act which require special protection to quiet minority fears would be somewhat as follows: Sections 51 and 51A, dealing with representation in the Dominion Parliament; Section 92, subsection 1, dealing with provincial control over provincial constitutions; Section 92, subsection 12, dealing with the solemnization of matrimony in the provinces; Section 93, dealing with education: Section 135, dealing with the use of the French language; and the amending section itself. It will be quite impossible to concede "property and civil rights in the province" as a minority right unless provision is made for the extension of Dominion control over such portions of that subject as form part of every Dominion law controlling trade and commerce or labour conditions. To entrench an unqualified property and civil rights clause would be to rigidify the entire Act, and to make further social planning dependent on provincial unanimity. The pace of progress would be the pace of Prince Edward Island.

At the same time as minority rights are being thus rendered inviolable, Canadians might well pay equal respect to the individual's right to freedom of speech, of association, of public meeting, and of the press. An entrenched Bill of Rights clause in the B.N.A. Act would do much to check the present drive against civil liberties—a drive which in Canada is promoted by men who pay lip-service to liberty at the very moment they are legislating it out of existence.

Proposals for Amendment: Summary.

Bringing together these ideas in a single proposal, it would seem desirable to provide an amending process for the B.N.A. Act by adding to it, by means of a last request to the Imperial Parliament, a section of the kind suggested by Prof. F. R. Scott in his evidence before the Special Parliamentary Committee on Revision, (1935)[19] the essence of which is as follows:

(1) The power of amendment to rest within Canada.

(2) Ordinary amendments to be by majority vote of the Dominion Parliament, assembled in joint session of the two Houses.

(3) Amendments affecting minority rights to require, in addition to Dominion approval, the assent of all the provincial legislatures.

(4) Any province not dissenting within one year to be presumed to have given its assent.

Some people argue that in any federation the amending process must necessarily involve a vote by provinces or states, as is required by the American, Swiss and Australian constitutions. This is true of ordinary federations, but Canada is not an ordinary federation. Our constitution was carefully drawn so that we should not be ordinary. How else can be explained such unfederal ideas as that the Dominion subsidizes the provinces, appoints and instructs[20] and dismisses[21] provincial lieutenant-governors, appoints provincial judges, appoints provincial representatives in the Senate, may veto provincial laws[22], and may by declaration take over control of provincial works? These centralizing provisions are incompatible with ordinary conceptions of the federal state, and clearly indicate that we were intended to have a particularly unified form of federalism. To hand over now to the provinces, or to a majority of them, a power to veto changes unconnected with minority rights is to retrogress, and means decentralizing our form of government at a time when every development of industry, finance, and international politics calls for greater centralization.

There remains the question of the procedure to be followed

19At p. 86 of *Minutes of Evidence.*

20Note the case of Mr. Tory, Lieutenant-Governor of Nova Scotia, who in 1928 was instructed by the Dominion government to refuse his ministry's request to create additional legislative councillors.

21Note the cases of Mr. Letellier de St. Just in 1879, and Mr. McInnis in 1900.

22It has done so 99 times, the last time in 1923.

in obtaining this amending clause. Must the provinces be previously consulted? Clearly there is no legal necessity for consultation, nor can it be said that constitutional usage requires it. Every member of the federal house comes from some province; to refer the issue back to other provincial representatives is to overweight the possible opposition. Nevertheless political considerations probably make such a course desirable, and suggest, in the words of the *Report* of the Special Committee, that "in the interests of harmony and unity there should be consultation with the provinces with respect to the adoption of a definite mode of amendment". Such consultation however would not imply a veto power, being a matter of grace, not of legal right, and a substantial agreement should be sufficient to justify a Dominion request to London even though one or two provinces fail to concur.

The Senate.

For the abolition of the Senate there are a number of possible methods. The right course of action will depend on the turn of events. If an amending clause is added to the B.N.A. Act before a government pledged to abolition takes office, then presumably the method of amendment provided in the clause will have to be followed. This is a likely eventuality, and it makes the outlook for Senate abolition extremely uncertain, for it may be assumed that the amending process which any Liberal or Conservative government would advocate will be fairly rigid. If there is no amending clause in the B.N.A. Act, then present procedure for amendment should be attempted, that is, a joint resolution of the Dominion Parliament, which should not be introduced until the Senate has blocked some government bill of major importance. If the Senate refuses to sign its own death warrant, as it presumably will, then the government should either call a general election immediately on the single issue "Abolish the Senate", or else proceed direct to London without waiting for further approval. There is no more legal necessity for a joint address now than there was when the 1875 amendment was made at the mere request of the government.

If these methods fail or cannot be attempted, there is always the comforting reflection that vacancies in the Senate occur frequently, and new appointments can be used to change the complexion of the upper House. In any particular deadlock

between the Commons and the Senate there is already a provision that eight new senators may be appointed. Moreover, the
threat of a thorough probing into some of our financial rackets,
or a few exposures of the sort which Mr. Pecora conducted in
the early days of the Roosevelt regime, would undoubtedly influence the issue. In the face of determined public opinion the
second chamber might well hesitate to become the last bulwark
of reaction.

CHAPTER XXII.

FOREIGN POLICY.

THE CANADIAN people as a whole are sincerely devoted to peace. When Europe was drifting into a disastrous war in the years before 1914 we were preparing to celebrate one hundred years of peace with our only neighbour. We still stand aloof from the quarrels which are once more driving the European peoples to spring at one. anothers' throats and from the struggle of rival imperialisms in Asia which threaten some great explosion in the Far East. But it is now slowly dawning upon us that the post-war era is over and that the world has passed into another pre-war era like that before 1914. In such circumstances mere incantations about peace are not enough, although they are all that any of the leaders of the two old parties have given us. It is not sufficient that we all share a genuine abhorrence of war; we must translate our aspirations for peace into a definite policy.

A. THE BACKGROUND OF IMPERIAL RELATIONS.

We may here neglect purely North American questions. It is safe to take for granted that Canada's relations with the United States are on such a basis that any questions arising between the two countries can be dealt with amicably and peacefully. The relations through which we are most liable to be entangled in external wars are those which centre about the British Commonwealth and the League of Nations. Canada is practically secure from all hostile invasion from any source except the United States, and invasion from that quarter worries no one except persons in mental hospitals and military schools. The only wars which can possibly come upon us are those in which we may become involved through our membership in those two eminently peaceful organizations, the British Commonwealth and the League.

The dangers of Canada's position at present arise from the undefined nature of our commitments, moral and material, within these two world-wide organizations. Because our direct connection with world politics is so recent, and because there are so many resemblances between the present world situation and the situation forty years ago when we first became conscious of world contacts, it is worth while to review briefly the manner in which we have faced the issues of foreign policy since we became entangled in the Boer War.

The Laurier Era.

In the generation between Confederation and Laurier's coming into office, Canadian national development had proceeded steadily and quietly without any very fundamental issues of external policy being raised. But in the middle of the 1890's we came to a forking of the roads. Laurier became prime minister at the very time when the flood of British imperialism was rising to its height. With Chamberlain in the Colonial Office there began a drive for the consolidation of the empire which continued without let-up until 1914.

Canada found herself facing two alternative choices. Chamberlain, the Admiralty experts, the crusaders of the *Round Table*, and all the propagandists of the imperialist school invited her to merge national interests in a greater imperial whole, to achieve full self-government by taking a share in the control of the empire's foreign affairs, to become a junior partner in the imperial firm and bring her fresh energies to the assistance of the weary Titan who staggered under the too vast orb of his fate. The invitation was a flattering one and it attracted a good many Canadians who were sick of the petty parochial internal politics of the Dominion. In their eagerness to raise the level of Canadian public affairs and to widen the range of Canadian thinking they were willing to pass over the fact that, when the imperialist proposals were examined in detail, the share which Canada was to have in the control of imperial policy was found to have been worked out much less clearly than the share which she was to pay in men and money for the support of that policy.

But Laurier foresaw another destiny for his country. He aimed at completing the evolution of Canadian autonomy which had begun with Lord Durham's Report by achieving an independent national position, in which, far from merging her individuality in a greater imperial community, Canada would pursue a line of her own based upon the fundamental fact that she was a North American nation living in a peaceful continent and far removed from "the vortex of European militarism". He devoted himself, accordingly, to avoiding the entanglements

in which Chamberlain and his successors tried to involve him.
He put his veto alike upon imaginative aspirations for future
imperial councils and upon practical proposals to make immediate contributions to the imperial navy or to earmark part
of the Canadian militia for imperial service overseas. When
economic imperialism was presented to him as an alternative
for or as a first step towards political and military imperialism,
he manoeuvred warily about the project of mutual imperial
trade preferences and refused to lend himself to Chamberlain's
campaign for the conversion of free trade England. His steady
opposition to all schemes emanating from London kept us in a
critical period from choosing the imperialist path irrevocably
and preserved for us the opportunity to choose the path of national autonomy when the time should be ripe.

Nevertheless Laurier was not able to keep out of imperialist
entanglements altogether. Against his will he was forced to
send troops to the South African War, a war in which Canada
had no interest whatsoever except the sentimental one of giving a demonstration of imperial solidarity. When he guarded
himself by declaring by Order-in-Council that the sending of
the first contingent should not be a precedent, the sufficient
answer was that of Mr. Bourassa:—"The precedent, Mr. Prime
Minister, is the accomplished fact". And it is upon this accomplished fact that all imperial programmes have been built ever
since 1900. When the naval scare of 1909 blew up, Laurier was
compelled to start a separate Canadian naval unit in order to
counter the efforts to force him into making a contribution to
the imperial navy. He acquiesced in Canadian participation in
the Committee of Imperial Defence and thus allowed a web of
intangible commitments to be slowly spun about him.

Laurier, in fact, in his relations with the British government, found himself in the same difficult position in which Sir
Edward Grey at this very same time was finding himself in his
relations with the French government. He was determined to
preserve his freedom of future action and to avoid any automatic commitment. But in the final analysis he had to admit,
just as Grey had to admit in the case of France, that Canada
could not stand aside if Britain were fighting for her life, that
in the world as it was then constituted Canada could not afford
to see Britain eliminated as a first-class power. So he supported our entry into the war of 1914; and as that war progressed
all his dreams of a separate peaceful North American nation
seemed to have been brought to nought.

The Borden Era.

The alternative to Laurier's conception of Canadian nationality was best presented in those pre-war days not by any of the swarm of missionaries from England but by the Canadian Conservative leader, Sir Robert Borden. Sir Robert was, like Laurier, a nationalist; and in his thinking he had gone far beyond the naive and snobbish colonial loyalism which found expression among the "best people" in such centres as Toronto. He had none of Laurier's reluctance about imperial commitments. "Canada cannot be a hermit nation", he said in criticizing Laurier's Naval Bill of 1910. In his mind, Canadian nationalism would attain its full growth only when we played our part in the making of imperial policy. His proposed emergency contribution of three dreadnoughts was accompanied by a demand for admission into the imperial councils on foreign affairs. Before 1914 he could not get the government in Great Britain to listen to this. But by 1917 he was sitting in the Imperial War Cabinet, and the Borden conception of Canada's place in the empire and in the world seemed to have won a complete victory over the Laurier conception.

The Borden conception ruled out any such fantastic schemes as the Imperial Federation of Mr. Lionel Curtis. And it used to be customery to put a great deal of emphasis upon the fact that the Borden-Smuts Resolution of 1917 maintained the separate national identity of the Dominions and their equality of status with the mother-country in the co-operative conduct of foreign policy which was to be the mark of the new Commonwealth. But the essence of the Borden-Smuts conception of the Commonwealth was that there was to be *one* foreign policy for the whole Commonwealth, and this was exactly what Laurier had been trying to avoid before the War. The one foreign policy was no longer to be carried out by an irresponsible benevolent British Foreign Office acting as a trustee for colonies who were still minors: it was to be a policy based upon "continuous consultation", it was to result in "concerted action founded on consultation". But it was still to be one single policy and all the partners in the Commonwealth were to bear a joint and several responsibility for this one policy. The Borden-Smuts conception found its full expression in the Imperial War Cabinet and in the British Empire delegations at Paris in 1919 and at Washington in 1921-22.

What should be specially noted here is the speed and skill

with which British imperialists dropped their own pet schemes and rallied round this Borden-Smuts co-operative Commonwealth. By the beginning of the 1920's they were all agreed, from the *Times* and the *Round Table* down, that this was exactly what they had been aiming at all the time; and they proceeded at once to turn the new Commonwealth into an instrument for the achievement of the same purposes as had been fulfilled by the old Empire. They were tireless in their solicitude for keeping the Dominions informed about the facts of life (i.e. of European life). They never ceased talking about consultation and co-operation. But behind this new facade the old policy of the British Foreign Office went on exactly as before. It was not until the Chanak incident of 1922 that innocent people in the Dominions awakened to the fact that British imperialists were making assumptions about the nature of the co-operative foreign policy which had never been accepted in the Dominions, and were engaged in the old game of presenting us with *faits accomplis*. It was not until the Ottawa Conference of 1932 that we realized fully that they were also making assumptions about the nature of intra-imperial trade which involved Canada's serving permanently as a field for the operations of British industrialism.

The fact is that ever since the ideas of the Manchester School lost their hold upon the English governing classes, i.e. ever since the 1870's and 1880's, the differences between the old parties in Britain on Empire policy have steadily tended to disappear. The fundamental purpose of imperial policy has always remained the same—to use the resources of the empire for British purposes, or rather, to speak more precisely, for the purposes of the British governing classes. From the so-called self-governing Dominions they have always asked one and the same thing—Dominion contributions for the support of British policy. The theorists—the Curtises, the Amerys, the Lothians and the Zimmerns—have endeavoured to stimulate us to an imaginative conception of the lofty ideals of a common Commonwealth policy. The practical statesmen—the Chamberlains, the Greys, the Lloyd Georges and the Curzons—have presented us with accomplished facts. It does not matter whether this continuous drive has had for its professed objective an Imperial Federation, a Zollverein, or a Commonwealth founded on "continuous consultation". *Plus ça change, plus c'est la même chose.*

Essentially it is an effort to get us to help in making the world safe for British capitalism.

The 1920's and 1930's.

Chanak marked a turning point, so far as Canada was concerned. And during the 1920's the Borden-Smuts conception of the Commonwealth slowly disintegrated, in spite of feverish efforts by all schools of imperialists. Its place was taken by what can best be described as the King-Hertzog conception, the essence of which is that it marks a return to the ideas of Laurier.

The single Commonwealth policy did not work out in practice. Canada refused to back Lord Curzon in his Near-Eastern policy and refused to underwrite Sir Austen Chamberlain's commitments at Locarno. She insisted upon complete treaty-making powers for herself and the other Dominions; she began to place her own diplomats abroad in the foreign capitals of most direct concern to her. Finally the Report of the 1926 Conference, followed by the Statute of Westminster, marked the complete triumph of the King-Hertzog school, a triumph which was not substantially lessened by any verbal reservations which the astute Lord Balfour managed to insert into the Report. The British Commonwealth ceased to be a single entity and dissolved into a loose entente of sovereign nation-states, each pursuing its own policy and each co-operating with the others only as it saw fit in those enterprises in which it considered they had a common interest.

This seemed the final defeat of the imperialism which had been gathering force in England ever since Disraeli's Crystal Palace speech. It seemed the final triumph of Laurier. The process of decentralization in the empire had reached the point at which it was admitted that there was no longer any central controlling government, the late Imperial Government being reduced to the status of "His Majesty's Government in the United Kingdom."

But we are now in the 1930's, and the world is once again drifting towards war as it was in the days of Laurier. The Laurierites of the 1930's, if their ideas are not to be frustrated again by the pressure of a war situation as Laurier's were frustrated in the earlier decade, will have to restate their position with much more emphasis and precision. Nationalism by itself is not enough. Canadian nationalism is an achievement of no significance if Canadian policy is in the end always to be determined by the *faits accomplis* of the British Foreign Office. Middle-class pacifist idealism is also not enough. If now, after our experience in the Boer War and in the War of 1914, we are again to be swept off our feet by emotional appeals for some idealist crusade, we may as well give up talking about our national autonomy and our peaceful North American civilization, and settle down to rewrite our history from the point of view of Disraeli and Chamberlain.

Mere national aloofness and mere pacifist spirit of the Laurier type will not be enough to keep us out of the next European war. Laurier was helpless in the end against the sweep of the economic forces of the age of imperialism. An effective policy for keeping us out of war must be based upon an understanding by the Canadian people of what wars are really about. Until we grasp the fact that war is an inherent institution in our present capitalist civilization and that it can only be eliminated by a world-wide reconstruction of our social and economic institutions, we shall always be liable to storms of irrelevant emotion; and we shall be unable to resist when we are invited to fight for democracy or freedom or parliamentary institutions or international law or collective sanctions. If we wish to realize Laurier's dream of a peaceful people living in a peaceful continent, we shall have to concentrate upon this work of reconstruction within our own country.[1]

B.   CANADA AND THE LEAGUE OF NATIONS.

Up to this point in our discussion it has hardly been necessary to mention the League of Nations, save incidentally. Canada's entry into the League was not a sign of any profound international spirit among her people. Membership in it was welcomed because it provided a proof that we were now accepted among the older nations of the world. Our reasons for going into it were essentially as nationalistic as were the reasons of the United States for staying out of it. Nevertheless we did sincerely believe in the experiment of bringing the nations together "around the table" to thresh out their differences in public, and we have played our part in that experiment with reasonably good faith. But against all attempts to turn the Geneva machinery from the purposes of a round-table of the

---

[1]For the best recent discussions of the relationship of capitalism and war, see H. N. Brailsford, *Property or Peace?* and R. D. Charques and A. H. Ewen, *Profits and Politics.*

nations into that of an international war-office, every Canadian government, regardless of party, has set its face. Canada, in fact, took the lead in trying to weaken the sanctions side of the League machinery when she proposed the elimination or amendment of Article 10. And she has steadily refused to ratify all ingenious efforts to make Geneva the centre of a French security system, such as the Draft Treaty of 1923 or the Protocol of 1924.

Why the League Has Failed.

The root criticism of the League is that it is in the main a collection of powers whose governing capitalist classes continue to compete with one another for advantages in markets, raw materials and investments, and to use their national governments as instruments in this competition. A collection of such powers is not likely in the nature of things to do much to remove the underlying causes of international war. But Canadians, whose political thinking is still carried on in an atmosphere, of nineteenth-century bourgeois liberalism have not as a rule made this realistic criticism of the Geneva institution. Observing the failure of the League to deal with the successive crises which have arisen since 1931, they are apt, if they worry about these matters at all, to plunge into fresh outbursts of Wilsonian idealism (like the orthodox right wing of the British Labour Party) and to start crusades for new Pacts, Peace Acts, and other paper Utopias. This is dangerous because a lack of economic realism exposes us to a double pressure in these days; if we do not succumb to the appeals on behalf of British liberty we may fall prey to those on behalf of collective security.

Canadians, however, have always been saved hitherto in their League diplomacy by a shrewd and healthy sense of the essentially European character of the League. They have objected to stiffening up its sanctions procedure for the same reason that they have objected to giving blank cheques to the British Foreign Office. Geneva, like London, is situated in Europe and most cheques drawn in its favour will be cashed for European purposes. No Canadian government has ever been so naive as to fail to perceive behind the imposing façade of internationalism at Geneva the hard reality of European power politics.

The façade is now crumbling, and we are met with demands to "strengthen" the League. All such proposals that have reached us so far are schemes for making the application of sanctions more immediate and more automatic. Since the sanctions will only be applied against dissatisfied powers (the satisfied powers, the victors in the last war, having no motive to upset or threaten the *status quo*) these proposals are in effect, if not in intention, simply expedients for guaranteeing Canadian assistance to maintain the Franco-British domination of Europe which has existed since 1918. This, in fact, is the real purpose which the League has served since the war. By forbidding any violent attack upon the Versailles settlement it has helped to support the victorious powers in their victory without imposing upon them any necessity of making concessions such as would make Europe a more tolerable place for the defeated powers. Peace as an ideal has been indissolubly bound up with the status quo as a fact. In the absence of any effective machinery for modifying the 1919 system or for making such continuous adjustments as are necessary in a dynamic world, all attempts to isolate an "aggressor" are simply methods of building up a preponderance of power against Germany. They will succeed until Germany has manoeuvred herself into a position in which she can count upon sufficient help to make it worth her while to challenge by force the preponderance of power which has been established against her. A League which operates in this way may postpone war, but it has not eliminated it from our civilization. To talk of the kind of diplomacy which has gone on at Geneva during the past decade as a Collective System is to be guilty of unpardonable naiveté or dishonesty.

But even in this uninspiring role as a society of retired burglars defending the principle of property the League is now failing to function. First Japan, then Germany, and now Italy defy its authority. And when the test came the actions of Great Britain and France soon showed that they also had no real loyalty to the principles of a collective system. The British government supported Japan (by thwarting all attempts to use the Geneva machinery as a check upon Japanese aggression) because British imperialism is in too precarious a position in the Far East to risk Japanese hostility. They now oppose Italy, though we do not know what deals may be going on behind the scenes, because Italian ambitions in Abyssinia are potentially dangerous to the British position in the Soudan and in the whole Eastern Mediterranean area. They invoke or refuse to invoke the machinery of collective security in accordance with their self-regarding calculations of British interests. France, in this present crisis, hesitates whether to support Italy, whose support she herself needs against Germany, or to support Britain. If she decides in favour of the latter course we may be sure that it will only be in return for a private guarantee by the British government of more whole-hearted support by Britain against Germany. Or it may be that those elements in both Britain and France who want to make a deal with Germany in Western Europe by giving the Nazis a free hand to attack Russia in the East will succeed in reorientating the policies of the two great Western European powers; clearly they are already very powerful in the councils of the present Conservative government in Britain. All that we can say with certainty is that the Canadian people will not be taken into the confidence of the diplomats who are pulling the strings in this complicated balance-of-power game. But surely not even the most Utopian idealist can now fail to see that the great powers have completely returned to the pre-1914 balance-of-power diplomacy.

A Policy of Neutrality.

The 1920 experiment of a collective system of security is therefore almost bankrupt. It is failing because it is incompatible with the capitalist imperialism of the great powers. What is to be the policy of Canada in this balance-of-power diplomacy? This question can no longer be answered by passionate rhetoric about the need for a collective system. The need is obvious, but it cannot be met in a capitalist world. We must accept the fact that a genuine international collective system is not possible as long as the chief governments of the world are dominated by groups of profit-seeking capitalists in search of markets, raw materials and spheres of influence and inevitably colliding with one another in that search.

Canada has a strong interest in European stability and prosperity. We desire a Europe which enjoys a high and secure standard of living, where we shall find a good market for our products. But we ought to have learnt from everything that has happened since 1914 that sending Canadian troops to fight on one side in a European war is no contribution to European stability or prosperity. Europe will eventually have to reach a healthier balance of power among her states than exists at present, but there is not the slightest reason to believe that we can assist in the process towards this healthier condition by throwing our weight into one side or the other of the balance. This is one of the cases where the patient can only be cured by his own exertions. We should therefore make clear to London and to Geneva that we intend to fertilize no more crops of poppies blooming in Flanders fields.

This is admittedly a somewhat negative policy. By adopting it we frankly proclaim that we are for the moment putting more stress upon keeping out of war than upon preserving world peace. But the plain fact is that a big war is more than likely now, and that a policy of neutrality seems just possible for us, as it does for the United States. In a world at war we should inevitably suffer, but it will certainly cost us less to stay out than to go in. We should serve notice now that we intend to remain neutral, and prepare ourselves for such a position by adopting in advance neutrality legislation of the kind proposed to the United States Senate by the Nye Committee on Armaments. The legislation would prohibit the supply of munitions to all belligerents and loans to all foreign governments or their nationals while they are at war, provide that all trade in contraband with the belligerents would be at the senders' risk subject to claims for compensation at the end of the war, and warn citizens travelling into danger zones that they do so without the protection of their government.[2]

Certainly a policy of neutrality[3] is not easy for a country which sells so much of its produce abroad as Canada has been accustomed to sell. In wartime we should be able to sell only to the belligerent which controlled the sea routes, and this fact would tend to entangle us in that belligerent's cause. It may be that our first determination to stay out of the war would break down under the pressure of those groups who depended for their prosperity upon selling to one belligerent. American writers who have discussed the neutrality of the United States in similar circumstances are not very hopeful that their country would keep out of a European war, whatever its first decision. The price of neutrality comes very close to being a thorough-going

---

[2]Americans have recovered more completely from the idealist debauch of the war to make the world safe for democracy than we have in Canada, and there has been a good deal of discussion in the United States on how to keep out of another European war. See *Foreign Policy Reports*, 3 April, 1935: *American Neutrality in a Future War*, by H. W. Briggs and R. L. Buell; articles in the *New Republic*, beginning 31 July, 1935, by Walter Millis, W. T. Stone, O. W. Riegel, George Soule; and two articles by Charles Warren, *Troubles of a Neutral* (in *Foreign Affairs*, April, 1934), and *Prepare for Neutrality* (in *Yale Review*, Spring, 1935); also C. A. Beard—The Open Door at Home.

[3]On the problems of Canadian neutrality see Escott Reid, "Can Canada Remain Neutral?", in the *Dalhousie Review*, July, 1935.

reorganization of our whole economic system. But if we are not willing to pay this price we shall pay the far greater price of war, which is to be engulfed in the unfathomable social catastrophes toward which Europe appears to be plunging. Are our people capable of making the choice wisely? "If we had given up an unplanned profit system", says Mr. George Soule,[4] discussing the case of the United States, "and were engaged in building a collective order, the chances would be quite different. For then the ultimate ruin of war would have its proper weight in the scales against the immediate gain. . . . Above all, we should have a loyalty that would be an emotional counter to war madness. Peace would be, not merely the absence of war, but the chance to create, undisturbed from abroad, a worthy human society".

Unhappily it is not only in Europe that war threatens. The bankruptcy of both the League and the Kellogg Pact means that nothing can now stop further Japanese aggression in China except the intervention of the United States. It has been a cardinal feature of American policy for the last two generations to maintain an open door in China for American commercial expansion. The big navy policy of the present American government points to a collision sooner or later with Japan in the Pacific, and this would affect us in Canada more directly than troubles in Europe. It is a hopeful sign that many Americans are arguing that the American stake in China is not worth the cost of a great war, but the inherent drive of American capitalism for overseas markets may force a conflict. The Canadian people as a whole have no more interest in this American imperialism than they have in British imperialism, and we must try to keep from being entangled in its operations.

At the same time, while the immediate urgency is to concentrate on keeping out of the wars that threaten, we must work for a world which is genuinely based upon the collective organisation of security. But security is not attainable without an equitable distribution of the opportunities for material well-being among all the peoples of the world. The way to bring this about is to begin to build up at Geneva the institutions of world economic planning. There is little hope of much immediate advance in this direction as long as national policies are in the control of private profit-seeking interests. It can only be a gradual process; and any honest facing of what is involved in it

4*New Republic*, Aug 21, 1935.

would compel us to modify many of our traditional Canadian policies on such matters as tariffs, control of raw materials, and the treatment of Oriental settlers. Canadians who look forward to a League of socialist commonwealths should be doing their best now to educate public opinion in favour of such modifications. But the best contribution we can make in such a direction is to establish a socialist commonwealth within our own borders.

INDEX

This index is intended to suppliment the Table of Contents to which the reader is referred for main topics discussed.